Enlightenment, Legal Education, and Critique

EDINBURGH STUDIES IN LAW

Volumes in the series:

Elspeth Reid and David L Carey Miller (eds), *A Mixed Legal System in Transition: T B Smith and the Progress of Scots Law* (2005)

Hector MacQueen and Reinhard Zimmermann (eds), *European Contract Law: Scots and South African Perspectives* (2006)

John W Cairns and Paul du Plessis (eds), *Beyond Dogmatics: Law and Society in the Roman World* (2007)

William M Gordon, *Roman Law, Scots Law and Legal History* (2007)

Kenneth G C Reid, Marius J de Waal and Reinhard Zimmermann (eds), *Exploring the Law of Succession: Studies National, Historical and Comparative* (2007)

Vernon Valentine Palmer and Elspeth Christie Reid (eds), *Mixed Jurisdictions Compared: Private Law in Louisiana and Scotland* (2009)

John W Cairns and Paul du Plessis (eds), *The Creation of the* Ius Commune*: From* Casus *to* Regula (2010)

James Chalmers, Lindsay Farmer and Fiona Leverick (eds), *Essays in Criminal Law in Honour of Sir Gerald Gordon* (2010)

Elaine E Sutherland, Kay E Goodall, Gavin F M Little and Fraser P Davidson (eds), *Law Making and the Scottish Parliament* (2011)

Neil Walker (ed), *MacCormick's Scotland* (2012)

Eric Descheemaeker (ed), *The Consequences of Possession* (2014)

Remus Valsan (ed), *Trusts and Patrimonies* (2015)

John W Cairns, *Law, Lawyers, and Humanism: Selected Essays on the History of Scots Law, Vol 1* (2015)

John W Cairns, *Enlightenment, Legal Education, and Critique: Selected Essays on the History of Scots Law, Vol 2* (2015)

www.euppublishing.com/series/esil

EDINBURGH STUDIES IN LAW
VOLUME 14

Enlightenment, Legal Education, and Critique

Selected Essays on the History of Scots Law, Vol 2

John W Cairns

EDINBURGH
University Press

For Eibhlís

Edinburgh University Press Ltd
The Tun, Holyrood Road,
12 (2f) Jackson's Entry,
Edinburgh EH8 8PJ
www.euppublishing.com

Typeset in New Caledonia by
Servis Filmsetting Ltd, Stockport, and
printed and bound in Great Britain by
CPI Group (UK) Ltd, Croydon CR0 4YY

A CIP record for this book is available from the British Library

ISBN 978 0 7486 8213 3 (hardback)
ISBN 978 0 7486 8214 0 (webready PDF)
ISBN 978 0 7486 8215 7 (epub)

Contents

Preface

This is the second of two volumes of selected essays on Scottish legal history. It focuses on the eighteenth century and explores themes relating to the Scottish Enlightenment. As with the first volume, what are gathered together are essays, some difficult to access, with others that are easier to obtain, but which are collected together to ensure a thematic coherence to the collection.

I wish here to restate the debts, expressed in the Preface to Volume I, owed to Professors Elspeth Reid, Kenneth Reid and Hector MacQueen for their encouragement to gather these essays together, as well as to the Editorial Board of Edinburgh Studies in Law. Elspeth Reid's support and trust has been admirable. Once more I am grateful to Dr Karen Baston for her assistance. If there is no need to repeat at length what I said in the preface to the first volume, my intellectual debts, particularly to Professor Alan Watson, Hector MacQueen and Dr Paul du Plessis among others, remain; likewise the assistance from the libraries and archives named there should also be acknowledged here.

The period over which I published these essays – 1988 to 2005 – is not as wide as that in the first volume. But, at over a quarter of a century, it is still considerable. Like most legal historians in Scotland I have benefited from attending the British Legal History Conference and the Scottish Legal History Group, where I have learned a lot from the scholarship of others and gained valuable criticism of my own.

Given the focus of this volume, it is necessary, however, to single out the Eighteenth-Century Scottish Studies Society, and the individuals I have met through it. The first conference of the Society I ever attended was in Glasgow in 1990. I presented there a paper which is now the seventh chapter of this volume. It was a memorable conference. Glasgow was that year's European City of Culture, and a highlight was dinner in the wonderful City Chambers, with a recital from members of Scottish Opera. I also remember that a particularly good claret from the City's cellars was drunk with the meal: and, like all Scots who specialise in study of the eighteenth century, I know that the red wine of Bordeaux is our true national drink. But as well as a trip to Burns country and a visit to Auchinleck – not yet restored by the Landmark Trust – the intellectual programme was superb. Glasgow in the eighteenth century was examined from all angles and aspects. For me, this set a high standard. I have not been able to attend all the subsequent conferences of the Society, ably organised by Professor Rick Sher, the indefatigable Executive Secretary, along with local and programme committees; but I have attended many, and have never felt disappointed or that my time has been wasted.

Through the Society I have met many scholars who have helped and enriched my work. It might be thought invidious to single out any individual, but I do need to mention Professors Roger Emerson and Paul Wood, both of whom I met for the first time in Glasgow in 1990. Both helped shape my understanding of the Scottish Enlightenment. Both made me realise the significance of the natural sciences. Paul focuses on the history of science, with which I am not competent to engage; but Roger's decades of outstanding and path-breaking work on patronage, institutions, and societies in eighteenth-century Scotland has profoundly influenced me. This will no doubt be obvious to any who know his work who read these essays. Roger is also one of the most generous scholars I have ever known, happy – indeed delighted – to share his knowledge. Over the years, I have received from him many letters – typically picture postcards – covered with detailed information and references relevant to what I am working on. He once told me he believed in always sharing what he knew, and he had never regretted doing so. I hope I live up to this ideal.

I knew Professor Knud Haakonssen before I ever attended a conference of the Eighteenth-Century Scottish Studies Society. For many years now, my research has had to engage with his work. Knud has encouraged me and engaged me in projects relating to aspects of natural law in the eighteenth century that have helped and challenged me. It has also been fun. Recently he has involved me in the exciting project on natural law in Europe (see *http://www.natural-law.uni-halle.de/*). As some of the chapters below will show, I have learned a lot from Knud with his penetrating intelligence and wide knowledge. As with Roger's work, Knud's scholarship has shaped much of what I have done in studying the eighteenth century.

At least one of these essays was written when I was a Visiting Professor at the University of Miami in Coral Gables, Florida; others were thought about there. As well as the stimulation from students in my classes there on Law and the Enlightenment, I benefited from the support of talented and hospitable colleagues, while enjoying the unique and stunning beauty of South Florida. But other than during the Festival, particularly the Fringe Festival, Edinburgh remains the most delightful and civilised of cities to live in and the School of Law a great place to work.

John W Cairns, Old College, August 2013

Acknowledgements

Full details of the date and place of first publication appear on the first page of each chapter. The author, the publishers, and the Editorial Board of *Edinburgh Studies in Law* would like to thank the various publishers, editors, and presses as follows for kind permission to reproduce material:

Ch 1 *Northern Ireland Legal Quarterly*
Ch 2 *Law and History Review*
Ch 3 Edinburgh University Press
Ch 4 *Fundamina: A Journal of Legal History*
Ch 5 Hambledon Press
Ch 6 *History of Universities*
Ch 7 Tuckwell Press in association with the Eighteenth-Century Scottish Studies Society
Ch 8 *The Philosophical Age*, Almanac 15. St Petersburg Centre for the History of Ideas
Ch 9 *Tijdschrift voor Rechtsgeschiedenis*
Ch 10 *Oxford Journal of Legal Studies*
Ch 11 T & T Clark
Ch 12 *Jahrbuch für Recht und Ethik*
Ch 13 *Grotiana*
Ch 14 *Journal of Legal History*
Ch 15 *Scottish Literary Journal*

Introduction

The essays selected for this volume all deal in some way or another with law and its institutions in eighteenth-century Scotland. The influence of the Enlightenment on Scotland and the impact of the Scottish natural and social or moral sciences on the European and transatlantic Enlightenments are both incontestable. The essays here show how the social – especially historical and philosophical – thought of the eighteenth century affected the essentially Humanist and Dutch-oriented legal culture of early modern Scotland, particularly through formal legal education in the universities.

The Enlightenment, however, was as much about people and institutions as about ideas. Individuals of energy and talent could overcome disadvantages of situation and background if placed properly. Eighteenth-century Scotland was run – often with considerable success – through a system of patronage. Patrons, such as the Earl of Ilay (from 1743 third Duke of Argyll), could promote careers or block them, though themselves subject to ever-changing political and intellectual pressures. Would Adam Smith have achieved what he did without Argyll's initial patronage?[1] It is an interesting reflection. Ideas were promoted not just through publication, but through the possession of positions of influence, such as university chairs or distinguished pulpits.[2] To understand the Scottish Enlightenment properly, it is necessary to think about politics and institutions.

In the later seventeenth century, legal systems and universities with which Scots were familiar had started to innovate, pushing the curriculum in different directions beyond the traditional disciplines of the Civil and Canon Laws. New structures and styles of teaching were also being developed.[3] In France, a *règlement* of 1679 had required the Universities to teach

1 R L Emerson, *Academic Patronage in the Scottish Enlightenment: Glasgow, Edinburgh and St Andrews Universities* (2008) (henceforth Emerson, *Academic Patronage*) 123–124.

2 R Sher, *The Enlightenment and the Book: Scottish Authors & Their Publishers in Eighteenth-Century Britain, Ireland, and America* (2006); R B Sher, *Church and University in the Scottish Enlightenment: The Moderate Literati of Edinburgh* (1985).

3 L Brockliss, "Curricula", in H de Ridder-Symoens (ed), *A History of the University in Europe. Volume II: Universities in Early Modern Europe (1500–1800)* (1996) 563 at 599–608.

"French" law.[4] In the United Provinces of the Netherlands such centralised direction was impossible, each Province being a sovereign republic; but the popular and successful Dutch law schools also started to innovate through the actions of individual professors in response to demand. Thus, professors focused their efforts on their private *collegia*, reflecting student need and economic opportunity.[5] They developed classes on the *ius hodiernum*, on a specialised *ius publicum*, and on *ius naturale* and *ius gentium*. The curriculum opened up in new ways.[6] Further, they started to teach from *compendia*, rather than the actual texts of Roman law; this last was to prove controversial.[7] No Dutch university had a specialised chair in the Law of Nature until 1746;[8] but chairs devoted to the Laws of Nature and Nations were created in a number of German universities.[9] In France, however, according to Notker Hammerstein, the earlier reforming regulations stood in the way of further development during the Enlightenment, so no chairs were created in Public Law or Natural Law in the universities, until a chair of Natural Law was founded at the Collège Royal in Paris in 1771.[10]

These innovations form the backdrop to the introduction of formal law teaching in the Scottish universities. A chapter in the first volume of the *Selected Essays* has already examined the influence of the Dutch law schools and Dutch Humanist thought on the development of legal education in

4 C Chêne, *L'enseignement de droit français en pays de droit écrit* (1982) 12–54; L W B Brockliss, *French Higher Education in the Seventeenth and Eighteenth Centuries: a Cultural History* (1987) 277–330.

5 M Ahsmann, "Teaching in *Collegia*: The Organization of *Disputationes* at Universities in the Netherlands and in Germany in the 16th and 17th Centuries", in A Romano (ed), *Università in Europa: Le istituzioni universitarie dal Medio Evo ai nostri giorni: strutture, organizzazione, funzionamento* (1995) 99 at 106–114.

6 M Ahsmann, "Teaching the *Ius Hodiernum*: Legal Education of Advocates in the Northern Netherlands (1575–1800)" (1997) 65 *Tijdschrift voor Rechtsgeschiedenis* 423; C J H Jansen, "Over de 18E Eeuwse Docenten Natuurrecht aan Nederlandse Universiteiten en de door hen Gebruikte Leerboeken" (1987) 55 *Tijdschrift voor Rechtsgeschiedenis* 103.

7 M Hewett, *Ulric Huber (1636–1694) de ratione juris docendi & discendi diatribe per modum dialogi . . . Academisch Proefschrift* (2010) 75–78.

8 G C J J van den Bergh, *The Life and Work of Gerard Noodt (1647–1725): Dutch Legal Scholarship between Humanism and Enlightenment* (1988) 131 n 29.

9 H Coing, "Die juristische Fakultät und ihr Lehrprogramm", in H Coing (ed), *Handbuch der Quellen und Literatur der neueren Europäischen Privatrechtsgeschichte: Zweiter Band, neuere Zeit (1500–1800). Das Zeitalter des gemeinen Rechts. Erster Teilbad: Wissenschaft* (1977) 3 at 46–47.

10 N Hammerstein, "Relations with Authority", in de Ridder-Symoens (ed), *Universities in Early Modern Europe* (n 3) 113 at 128; Brockliss, *French Higher Education* (n 4) at 279. Brockliss points out that the Universities in France strongly influenced by German culture – Strasbourg and Besançon – reflected developments in Germany.

Scotland.[11] The first section of this volume, "Enlightened Legal Education", after examining the background to the foundation of new chairs in Law, is devoted to the progress of legal education in Scotland under the pressure of differing streams of Enlightenment thought, examining it from a variety of related perspectives.

From the 1680s onwards, the Faculty of Advocates had intermittently campaigned for the establishment of chairs in Law in Scotland.[12] Their primary desire was for a chair in Civil Law, but, when the first chair was created in 1707, an existing and recent privilege granted by Parliament to Alexander Cunningham as "professor of the Civil Law in this Kingdome" meant the new chair was designated as of Public Law and the Law of Nature and Nations – Civil Law was specifically excluded from the sphere of the professor's duties.[13] The apparent success of private teachers in Edinburgh suggests that the market for such classes was sufficiently large to make a chair in Civil Law viable.[14]

The pressure to create chairs in Civil Law raises the question of why the Faculty ignored the fact that in Aberdeen there was in the 1680s and 1690s a functioning chair of Civil Law in King's College, continuously occupied by professors who did in fact teach. In the first volume, it has been noted that, in opposing the proposals to create a chair in Law in Edinburgh in the late sixteenth century, the advocates pointed to the existence of chairs in St Andrews and Aberdeen;[15] if teaching had vanished at St Andrews, at least some of the members of the Faculty of Advocates in the late seventeenth and early eighteenth centuries were aware of the chair at Aberdeen, which presumably was unaffected by Cunningham's privilege since it had long predated it.[16]

11 J W Cairns, *Law, Lawyers, and Humanism: Selected Essays on the History of Scots Law*, vol 1 (2015) (henceforth Cairns, *Law, Lawyers, and Humanism*) ch 8.

12 J W Cairns, "John Spotswood, Professor of Law: A Preliminary Sketch", in W M Gordon, *Miscellany III*, Stair Society vol 39 (1992) 131 (henceforth Cairns, "John Spotswood") at 131–133.

13 J W Cairns, "The origins of the Edinburgh Law School: the Union of 1707 and the Regius Chair" (2007) 11 EdinLR 300 at 313–314. On Cunningham, see J W Cairns, "Alexander Cunningham's proposed edition of the Digest: an episode in the history of the Dutch Elegant School of Roman Law" (2001) 69 *Tijdschrift voor Rechtsgeschiedenis* 81 (Part I) and 307 (Part II); J W Cairns, "Alexander Cunningham, book dealer: scholarship, patronage, and politics" (2010) 5 *Journal of the Edinburgh Bibliographical Society* 11.

14 Cairns, "John Spotswood" (n 12) at 133–134.

15 Cairns, *Law, Lawyers, and Humanism* (n 11) ch 4.

16 J W Cairns, "Academic feud, bloodfeud and William Welwood: legal education in St Andrews, 1560–1611" (1998) 2 EdinLR 158 (Part I) and 255 (Part II).

As is argued in the first chapter, the problem may have been the elementary and perhaps intermittent nature of the teaching. William Forbes described the law classes at Aberdeen as "having dwindled away and resolved into the perfunctory reading of a publick Lesson by one called a Civilist". He then purported to paraphrase Sir George Mackenzie as stating that, "in his Time" the Civilist "had ordinarily as much Law as served those that came to hear him, that is just none at all".[17] Further, after 1690, King's College remained tainted with Jacobitism. This was not a good place for loyal Whigs to send their sons – an institution dominated by a Jacobite family faction that included the Civilist, John Gordon. In 1715, Gordon duly supported the Old Pretender, to be deprived when the two Aberdeen universities were subsequently purged.[18] But there was more to it than this. Even the purged university did not attract law students. Further, between 1720 and 1750, David Verner, a Regent at Marischal College, Aberdeen, also taught elementary Civil Law. This did not lead students from other areas of Scotland to attend his classes for a legal education.

The basic problem for the two Aberdeen universities was locality. The Faculty of Advocates wanted law to be taught close to Edinburgh, preferably in Edinburgh itself. The Advocates wanted classes to prepare students for the Advocates' examinations; they wanted them taught by professors whom they knew and whose appointments and tenure they could influence. Aberdeen was simply too distant and too subject to local pressures. By the 1720s, however, the advocates had achieved their aims. There was a functioning law school with four professors in Edinburgh, and a developing one in Glasgow.[19]

To speak broadly, through much of the first half of the eighteenth century law continued to be taught in a traditional way with the professor dictating notes on a chosen textbook. The second chapter examines how the development of theories of rhetoric affected styles of teaching, leading to the development of the practice of teaching in English rather than in Latin. In most

17 Glasgow University Library, MS Gen 1246 at 83. (This is the first volume of Forbes' "Great Body" – MS Gen 1246–1252. The complexity of the structure of Forbes' manuscript makes it easier to cite by page than in any other way.) Forbes cites G Mackenzie, *Observations Upon the 18. Act. 23. Parl. K. James VI., Against Dispositions Made in Defraud of Creditors*, 2nd edn (1698) at 13. He is clearly relying very closely on the passage from Mackenzie, sometimes word for word, but the passages quoted about the Civilist's ignorance are not found there. I have been unable to trace them elsewhere in Mackenzie's *oeuvre*.

18 R L Emerson, *Professors, Patronage and Politics: The Aberdeen Universities in the Eighteenth Century* (1992) 26, 32.

19 See below, ch 5.

disciplines, the transition was unproblematic; and, in the law schools, Scots law had, in any case, always been taught in English. Where the change was seen to raise difficulties was in the central university legal discipline of Civil Law, which was covered in two courses, one on Justinian's *Institutes*, usually given twice each academic year, and the other on Justinian's *Digest*, both taught using *compendia* in the style of Dutch *collegia*.

The essay discusses the change to teaching in English, the reaction against it by the Faculty of Advocates, and Professor Wilde's resumption of teaching the course on the *Digest* in Latin in the 1790s. Wilde is an interesting and tragic figure already met in the first volume.[20] Also involved are issues arising out of rivalry and competition for students between the professors in the Universities of Edinburgh and Glasgow and between the university professors and private teachers. In a more recent essay, not included here, I have suggested that some of the criticisms I originally thought Wilde to have directed particularly at John Millar in Glasgow were in fact more directly aimed at a private teacher in Edinburgh, John Wright.[21]

The chair of Public Law and the Law of Nature and Nations in Edinburgh may have been the first chair in law created in Scotland in the eighteenth century, but the main focus of legal education remained the classes in Civil Law and Scots law, the former being the sole subject in which intending advocates were examined until an examination in Scots law was added to the advocates' trials in 1750.[22]

The first half of the eighteenth century saw the growing dominance of natural-law thinking in teaching moral philosophy in Scotland.[23] Rejecting certain types of moral rationalism, some Scots philosophers had come to focus on ideas of a moral sense or of moral sentiments that developed through social interaction, recognising a historical development of rights. For law, the crucial figure here was Adam Smith. He gave lectures on jurisprudence in his moral philosophy class in Glasgow.[24] Though he left Glasgow in 1763, his approach was adopted by his pupil, John Millar, the Professor of

20 Cairns, *Law, Lawyers, and Humanism* (n 11) ch 13.

21 J W Cairns, "The face that did not fit: race, appearance, and exclusion from the Bar in eighteenth-century Scotland" (2003) 9 *Fundamina: A Journal of Legal History* 11 (henceforth Cairns, "The face that did not fit") at 18–23.

22 Cairns, *Law, Lawyers, and Humanism* (n 11) chs 11–12.

23 The literature is enormous. See, e.g., K Haakonssen, *Natural Law and Moral Philosophy: From Grotius to the Scottish Enlightenment* (1996) 63–128.

24 See, e.g., D Lieberman, "Adam Smith on Justice, Rights and Law", in K Haakonssen (ed), *The Cambridge Companion to Adam Smith* (2006) 214. The focus is more on the ideas than the institutional context.

Civil Law.[25] Smith, as argued in chapter 3, revitalised the teaching of natural law as a potential discipline for lawyers. He understood law as a dynamic response to social and economic development. From around 1750, the advocates became interested in promoting education focused on more modern, Enlightenment thought, so that, by the 1760s, the Faculty of Advocates were encouraging study of the law of nature and nations in Edinburgh.

Chapter 4 traces the development of teaching from the chair of Public Law and the Law of Nature and Nations in Edinburgh, exploring both the intellectual content of the classes and the politics of appointments. For the first half-century, teaching from the chair was intermittent. But this does not mean that the holder was incapable or unlearned; and Karen Baston's recent thesis has shown the importance of Charles Areskine, the first Regius Professor, as a book collector, and the significance of his collection for our understanding of the intellectual formation of Scots lawyers in this period.[26] When the holder of the chair did teach, the class was based on Grotius' *De iure belli ac pacis*, and a student compend of it was published in Edinburgh in 1760 for the use of the class of the then professor, Robert Bruce.[27]

Bruce was the last holder of the chair to teach Grotius' natural law. The success of his class may have encouraged John Millar in Glasgow to develop his lectures on jurisprudence; but be that as it may, the next successful teacher to occupy the chair was Allan Maconochie, the future Lord Meadowbank. Maconochie's classes were comparable to those of Millar or indeed to Adam Smith's lectures on jurisprudence. He taught the law of nature and nations as a science of legislation founded on the natural history of mankind.[28]

The next section of the volume deals with the "Development of the Glasgow Law School". It traces in detail, in the context of one university, some of the points already developed in the first four chapters. The fifth chapter thus examines the creation of the first chair in law in the University of Glasgow in the early modern period. Probably in emulation of the recent successful creation of a chair of Civil Law in Edinburgh (1710), the University of Glasgow erected a chair in Civil Law in 1713, gaining

25 See below, chs 7–8.

26 K G Baston, "The Library of Charles Areskine (1680–1763): Scottish Lawyers and Book Collecting, 1700–1760", unpublished PhD thesis, University of Edinburgh (2011), available at *http://hdl.handle.net/1842/6417*.

27 *Hugonis Grotii De jure belli ac pacis librorum II. Compendium in usum studiosae juventutis Academiae Edinensis* (1760).

28 Since this chapter was first printed, Edinburgh University Library has acquired some of the surviving papers of Lord Meadowbank, many of which relate to his classes. See Edinburgh University Library, Accession no: E2008.18 Collection no: Coll-1137.

funding through an allocation by the Crown from "King William's Gift". Though the University was allowed to appoint the first professor, the chair was thus a Regius chair, with appointments thereafter made by the Crown. This was to cause problems for the professors when they tried to ensure the appointment of candidates whom they favoured. Managing succession to the chair required the cooperation of politicians in London who could secure the royal signature.[29]

The first professor was William Forbes. He owed much to members of the Dalrymple family; but the support for his appointment to the chair was relatively broad. He had published a number of works, and had embarked on a massive project to restate Scots law. He was keen to gain the post. His new colleagues had defined the scope of his teaching to be Civil, feudal, Canon and Scots Law. This was probably done, not to ensure he had a wide field of competence, but to prevent him from venturing into natural law, which was already taught as an aspect of moral philosophy. He initially offered classes in Civil Law and Scots law (the first time the latter subject was to be taught in a University). The evidence suggests that he never acquired many students; certainly towards the end of his tenure of the chair only Civil Law was being taught. It was later to be made clear that classes in Civil Law were the duty of the occupant of the chair. A manuscript on the Civil Law held in Glasgow University Library has recently been identified as in his hand. This four-volume commentary on Justinian's *Institutes* now awaits further study.[30]

By the 1720s control of the University was disputed by the two main Whig groupings in Scotland, the Squadrone and the Argathelians: the former was basically a family grouping led by the Dukes of Montrose and Roxburgh, along with the Marquess of Tweeddale and a number of significant landed families such as the Dundases of Arniston; the latter consisted of men grouped around the second Duke of Argyll and his brilliant brother, Archibald, Earl of Ilay.[31] From 1714 to 1742 the Duke of Montrose was Chancellor of the University of Glasgow; but the Argathelians were seeking and acquiring influence and power in both the University and the rising commercial city. Though the University was a self-governing corporation, its officers and professors were closely linked to and drawn from the Scottish

29 See below, ch 6.

30 See *http://universityofglasgowlibrary.wordpress.com/2013/07/09/forbess-manuscript-commentary-on-justinians-institutes-rediscovered-in-tercentenary-year/*.

31 On Ilay, see now, R L Emerson, *An Enlightened Duke: The Life of Archibald Campbell (1682–1761), Earl of Ilay, 3rd Duke of Argyll* (2013).

landed and political classes.[32] This inevitably meant that they were players in the Scottish political game, both individually and as a corporation. The changing factional politics of the quarrelsome University, while creating opportunities for politicians to intervene, caused problems for Forbes. At one stage Ilay had considered getting rid of him as a political enemy; in 1728, he simply bought Forbes' shifting loyalty by getting his son made the College's lawyer.[33]

A real problem came for the University on the death of Forbes in October 1745. Contrary to the desires of the masters, William Crosse gained the royal appointment. It was procured for him by Argyll, though Crosse was not his own choice; the circumstances of the time, along with the fall of his ally Walpole, had loosened Argyll's grip on Scottish politics. The story is told in chapter 6. The masters rightly suspected Crosse wished to hold the regius chair of Civil Law as a sinecure. By applying unremitting pressure they quickly forced him out, and got the man whom they had always wanted, Hercules Lindesay. The latter was a well-regarded teacher, who had substituted for both Forbes and Crosse. He taught the traditional course on Justinian's *Institutes* twice each year, and the course on the *Digest* annually. He had to teach if five students presented themselves: the duties had been carefully defined in the course of the masters' quarrels with Crosse. Lindesay started to teach the course on the *Institutes* in English rather than the hitherto normal Latin.[34]

The appointment of Crosse had alerted the masters to the type of problem that could arise from inattention to managing the succession to the Regius Chair of Civil Law. Thus, when Lindesay lay dying they started to organise. He died on 2 June 1761; the next day the masters approved a letter to the Earl of Bute that indicated their unanimous choice of John Millar as Lindesay's successor. On 15 June, Bute secured the king's signature on a warrant appointing Millar.[35]

John Millar's tenure of the chair of Civil Law is the subject of chapter 7. Millar turned Glasgow from a minor law school with very few students to a major centre of legal education. A pupil of Adam Smith, Millar taught Smith's jurisprudence in all his courses at some level or another. He used Smith's theory of rights to understand and to structure his courses in Civil Law. Millar started to develop the curriculum, turning the second course

32 Emerson, *Academic Patronage* (n 1) at 21–149.
33 Ibid at 92.
34 See below, ch 2.
35 See also Emerson, *Academic Patronage* (n 1) at 154–155.

on the *Institutes* into one more focused on Smithian jurisprudence, while progressively adding classes in Scots law, government, and, in the 1790s, English law. Further, he moved away from the traditional reliance on a textbook on which notes were dictated to the class to a much freer form of teaching. He also taught all his classes in English.[36]

In Millar's early years in the chair, he benefited from lack of competition from the University of Edinburgh, where the standards seem to have declined. The successful classes by Robert Bruce, Professor of Public Law and the Law of Nature and Nations at Edinburgh, ended when he resigned the chair in 1764. His successor was unremarkable and probably never taught. John Erskine retired from the chair of Scots Law in 1765 to be replaced by William Wallace, who was not a man of the same distinction. The Professor of Civil Law was Robert Dick, appointed in 1755. By the time he retired, his class, still taught as a commentary on the textbooks of J G Heineccius, must have seemed rather old-fashioned.[37] His successor, John Wilde, appointed in 1792, developed mental health problems and had to be removed from the professorial chair.[38] The most successful teacher in Edinburgh was David Hume, appointed to the chair of Scots Law in 1786. Hume had been Millar's pupil in Glasgow. He developed further Millar's approach to teaching, if not following the Glasgow professor's philosophical approach, so that his class had no connection to a textbook. His lectures were also very elaborate and detailed. Such evidence as there is supports the anecdotal evidence that Millar was acquiring significant numbers of students. It is telling that when Maconochie was appointed to the Regius chair in Edinburgh in 1779 he followed Millar's approach to jurisprudence. Aspects of Millar's teaching in Glasgow were starting to influence practice in Edinburgh.

Millar attracted pupils from all over Great Britain and Ireland. He even had Russian pupils on whom he exerted demonstrable influence, as noted and argued in chapter 8. The Russians' association with Adam Smith has attracted more attention; but they were also – and for a longer time – law students with Millar and took doctoral degrees in law.[39] Since this chapter was written, the doctoral *disputatio juridica* of one of these Russians has become

36 See below, ch 2.
37 H Arnot, *The History of Edinburgh* (1779) 398–399.
38 See Cairns, "The face that did not fit" (n 21) at 19–23.
39 See R L Meek, *Social Science and the Ignoble Savage* (1976) (henceforth Meek, *Social Science*) 5.

more readily accessible.[40] The chapter also further explores the progressive development of his classes. As a teacher Millar moved classes in law from a still traditional focus inherited from the Dutch law schools to instruction informed by the approach and learning of the Scottish Enlightenment. He developed a critical jurisprudence that that explained how law ought to be developed.

Millar died in 1801. His successor, Robert Davidson, was a man of a very different stamp. He lacked Millar's broad, philosophical approach. While, with Millar, the masters at Glasgow had been keen to use the patronage system to gain an active and successful professor who would attract students and promote the values of Enlightened education, Davidson was appointed because he was the Principal's son. He failed to maintain viable classes in Civil Law, and appears to have ceased to teach it after 1819. He did have students for Scots law, seemingly in reasonable numbers. This was because, at a time of significant increase in the size in the legal profession in Scotland, the Royal Faculty of Procurators in Glasgow now required their apprentices to attend a university class in the subject. He thus had a growing captive market. In this way, Davidson, whose lectures on Scots law were based on those of Professor Hume in Edinburgh, can be seen as to some extent a success. But his tenure marks a change in legal education in Glasgow, away from the values of Smith and Millar, and towards a supposedly "practical" rather than theoretical focus. Thereafter, through much of the nineteenth century, legal education in the University of Glasgow was to consist of lectures on Scots law for apprentices.[41] The era of Enlightened legal education in the style of Millar was over.

The third section of this volume explores both the impact of the type of Enlightened education on interpretation and development of the law and, indeed, the limits of such influence. Scholars have explored the general development of interpretation in the Enlightenment, usually perceiving it, to put it simply, as related to a growing "constitutionalism" related to a desire to restrict the authority of judges as interpreters of the law.[42] It has also generally been seen as leading to codification.[43] Intellectual development

40 I A Tret'yakov, *Disputatio juridica ad tit. 4. lib. II. Pand. de in jus vocando* (1766).

41 D Murray, *Memories of the Old College of Glasgow* (1927) 227–234.

42 See, e.g., the essays in Y Morigiwa, M Stolleis and J-L Halpérin (eds), *Interpretation of Law in the Age of Enlightenment: From the Rule of the King to the Rule of Law* (2011).

43 D Klippel, "Legal reforms: changing the law in Germany in the *Ancien Regime* and in the Vormärz" (1999) 100 *Proceedings of the British Academy* 43; F Wieacker, *A History of Private Law in Europe* (1995) 257–275.

in Scotland took a rather different course when it considered authority and interpretation in law.

The first chapter in this section, 10, takes us back once more to the crucial figure of John Millar, and explores his approach to Scots criminal law. His Smithian analysis of law led him to argue that punishment was based on the need to right wrongs done, founded on the resentment of the person wronged supported by the indignation and sympathy of the spectator. The secondary foundation of punishment, if primary in importance and utility, was to discourage crime. The chapter also discusses how others, including earlier law teachers, had classified Scots criminal law. There is no need to go into Millar's arguments here; but his particular approach meant that some crimes could be considered simply as crimes against society and punished purely on the grounds of police or utility, not on that of justice. He comes very close indeed to the modern idea of a victimless crime.[44] In many ways this is a classic example of Enlightened reason and analysis providing a critique of the law, and Millar develops a type of critical criminal jurisprudence.

Hamesucken is the crime of pursuing someone into their home to assault them. Found in medieval Scottish sources, it was generally taken to be a capital offence. Through the eighteenth century its prosecution seems to have become relatively rare, and when it was libelled in an indictment, the prosecutor often restricted the punishment to an "arbitrary" one, that is, one less than death. One of John Millar's last surviving letters is to John Wilde, the Professor of Civil Law in Edinburgh, discussing a recent conviction for the crime, expressing his view that hamesucken had fallen into disuse.[45] Chapter 11 explores prosecutions for hamesucken between 1672 and 1770, the first date being that of the establishment of the refounded Court of Justiciary. It shows how arguments were developed in framing the major premiss in the libel from the law of nature and nations, a practice which also allowed influence from English criminal law.

Chapter 12 explores how the jurisprudence of the Scottish Enlightenment had a potential if indirect impact on reform of the Court of Session and its procedure. The major reforms in the Court and its procedure in the early nineteenth century are well known. The Court was split into two divisions.

44 M Muravyev, "Sex, crime and the law: Russian and European Early Modern legal thought on sex crimes" (2013) 1 *Comparative Legal History* 75 at 91–92 and 95–96 discusses Millar's Russian pupils (though noting only that they had studied with Smith) and Scots commentators, but not mentioning Millar. This is unfortunate as consideration of Millar would have helped her argument.

45 J Millar to J Wilde, 10 June 1800, Edinburgh University Library, MS La.II.475.

A Jury Court was introduced. The Court was transformed into a first instance court – the Outer House – and a primarily second-instance court – the Inner House.[46] Procedure moved away from the developed Romano-Canonical procedure that had been the original foundation of the Court's *stylus curiae*.[47] Much of this has been explored by Nicholas Phillipson, who has identified the reforms with the aspirations and prejudices of the Scottish Whigs.[48] But the chapter shows how Scottish rejection of ethical rationalism and Smith's science of legislation provided what can be described as a sustained critique of the contemporary structure of the Court of Session and of its operation.[49]

The final chapter of the section examines the Scottish legal system's engagement with slavery in the eighteenth century. Extensive involvement of Scots with the Empire in British North America, the Caribbean and India, as immigrants, traders (including slave-traders), and owners of plantations led, as in many European countries, to the presence at home of enslaved men and women of African and Indian descent. This created a number of difficulties and challenges for the legal system. Could such individuals give evidence in a court?[50] How could those who claimed ownership maintain it or successfully emancipate a person claimed as enslaved?[51] Conflict between masters or mistresses and those over whom they asserted ownership inevitably led to claims for freedom before the courts.[52] After a discussion of slavery in Grotius' *De iure belli ac pacis*, chapter 13 explores the legal claims in two of these. It shows how arguments from the *ius naturale* and *ius gentium* as set out by Grotius could be used to justify slavery. To undermine them, counsel had to develop arguments about the historical reality of slavery in the Atlantic world.[53] Debates over the foundation and

46 J W Cairns, "Historical Introduction", in K G C Reid and R Zimmermann (eds), *A History of Private Law in Scotland: Volume 1: Introduction and Property* (2000) 14 at 151–155.

47 J W Cairns, "'The Dearest Birth Right of the People of England': The Civil Jury in Modern Scottish Legal History", in J W Cairns and G McLeod (eds), *"The Dearest Birth Right of the People of England": The Jury in the History of the Common Law* (2002) 1.

48 N T Phillipson, *The Scottish Whigs and the Reform of the Court of Session* (1990).

49 See also Cairns, *Law, Lawyers, and Humanism* (n 11) ch 7.

50 J W Cairns, "Slavery and the Roman Law of Evidence in Eighteenth-Century Scotland", in A Burrows and Lord Rodger of Earlsferry (eds), *Mapping the Law: Essays in Memory of Peter Birks* (2006) 599.

51 J W Cairns, "Slavery without a *Code Noir*: Scotland 1700–78", in F M Larkin and N M Dawson (eds), *Lawyers, the Law and History* (2013) 148; J W Cairns, "Freeing from Slavery in Eighteenth-Century Scotland", in A Burrows, D Johnston and R Zimmermann (eds), *Judge and Jurist: Essays in Memory of Lord Rodger of Earlsferry* (2013) 367.

52 J W Cairns, "After *Somerset*: the Scottish Evidence" (2012) 33 JLH 291.

53 For further discussion of aspects of these arguments, see J W Cairns, "The Definition of Slavery in Eighteenth-Century Thinking: Not the True Roman Slavery", in J Allain (ed), *The Legal Understanding of Slavery: The Historical to the Contemporary* (2012) 61 at 68–83.

validity of slavery were familiar in later eighteenth-century Scotland and the Scottish Enlightenment discussion and critique of slavery fed into developing abolitionist debates.[54]

Towards the end of the seventh chapter of the first volume of these essays, I explored aspects of the transformation of Scots law at the beginning of the nineteenth century, linking them to the development of thinking about law making and interpretation in the later Enlightenment.[55] It is evident that modern Scots law developed on this foundation in the nineteenth century. Here the obscure figure of John Wilde is intriguing. I earlier commented that I now thought that Wilde's criticism of stadial approaches to history as a focus for the teaching of Civil Law was directed at John Wright, rather than Millar; but a criticism of Millar – if left implicit – was probably still intended. In his lectures, Wilde articulated historical views comparable to some of those associated with Gustav Hugo, F C von Savigny, and others of the Romanist wing of the German Historical School. He was, of course, quite unaware of their work; he was also a scholar of no significance.[56] But his thinking reflects the development of historical (or historicist?) thought in this era.

Study of history writing in eighteenth-century Scotland has tended in the relatively recent past to be focused on the type of history varyingly called "stadial" or "natural" or "conjectural" or (sometimes) "philosophical" history.[57] The very identification of this type of history as the significant type of history writing in Enlightenment Scotland can be traced back to Dugald Stewart's biography of Adam Smith in the early 1790s.[58] As Paul Wood has

54 J W Cairns, "John Millar and Slavery", in N Walker (ed), *MacCormick's Scotland* (2012) 73; I Whyte, *Scotland and the Abolition of Black Slavery, 1756–1838* (2006).

55 Cairns, *Law, Lawyers, and Humanism* (n 11) ch 7.

56 J W Cairns, "The influence of the German Historical School in early nineteenth century Edinburgh" (1994) 20 *Syracuse Journal of International Law and Commerce* 191 (henceforth Cairns, "German Historical School") at 193–194. One of the best introductions in English is J Q Whitman, *The Legacy of Roman Law in the German Romantic Era: Historical Vision and Legal Change* (1992).

57 D Forbes, "'Scientific Whiggism': Adam Smith and John Millar" (1954) 8 *Cambridge Journal* 643; C J Berry, "Rude Religion: The Psychology of Polytheism in the Scottish Enlightenment", in P Wood (ed), *The Scottish Enlightenment: Essays in Reinterpretation* (2000) 315 (henceforth Wood, *Scottish Enlightenment*). On the background to such history, see I Hont, "The Language of Sociability and Commerce: Samuel Pufendorf and the Theoretical Foundations of the 'Four Stages Theory'", in A Pagden (ed), *The Languages of Political Theory in Early Modern Europe* (1987) 253; P G Stein, *The Character and Influence of the Roman Civil Law: Historical Essays* (1988) 395–409.

58 See D Stewart, *An Account of the Life and Writings of Adam Smith, LL*, ed I S Ross, in A Smith, *Essays on Philosophical Subjects*, ed W P D Wightman and J C Bryce (1980) 265 at 293. For a general assessment, see M S Philips, *Society and Sentiment: Genres of Historical Writing in Britain, 1740–1820* (2000) 171–189.

pointed out, Stewart has played a significant role in shaping subsequent understanding of what we now call the Scottish Enlightenment in such works.[59] This is the type of historical approach strongly associated with Millar as well as with Smith. In the twentieth century it attracted considerable attention, as scholars traced its links with Marxist thought and debated to what extent Smith and Millar were "materialists" and "determinists" or forerunners of sociology.[60] This debate has now long run its course.

It is still important, however, not to let this tired debate control our understanding of history writing in Scotland during the Enlightenment. Scots wrote many other types of history during the eighteenth century, influenced by other examples and traditions; the power and familiarity of Stewart's analysis should neither distract us from this, nor allow us to think that other histories are somehow "unenlightened".[61] For example, David Dalrymple, Lord Hailes, edited medieval sources and produced detailed analyses and assessments of historical evidence.[62] The cosmopolitan work of famous historians such as William Robertson or David Hume was also less obviously "conjectural" than that of Millar or Smith, though it is commonly considered to be "philosophical". Both attempted to root their historical descriptions and analyses in the type of rich documentary evidence neither so available nor necessary for the stadial-type history of Millar; but underlying their thinking, at some level at least, is a presupposition of a similar analytical framework, with historical development related to manners, morals, and material culture.[63]

It is easy to exaggerate the difference between a Romantic historicism and an eighteenth-century rationalist search for universal truths about historical development. In teaching Civil Law in Edinburgh, John Wilde may have

59 P Wood, "Dugald Stewart and the Invention of 'The Scottish Enlightenment'", in Wood, *Scottish Enlightenment* (n 57) 1. See also M Brown, "Creating a canon: Dugald Stewart's construction of the Scottish Enlightenment" (2001) 16 *History of Universities* 135.

60 R Pascal, "Property and society: the Scottish Historical School of the eighteenth century" (1938) 10 *Modern Quarterly* 167; R L Meek, "The Scottish Contribution to Marxist Sociology", in J Saville (ed), *Democracy and the Labour Movement: Essays in Honour of Dona Torr* (1954) 84; Meek, *Social Science* (n 39) at 99–130; but see N Levine, "The German Historical School of Law and the origins of Dialectical Materialism" (1987) 48 *Journal of the History of Ideas* 431.

61 For an excellent, perceptive short survey, see D Allan, "Scottish Historical Writing of the Enlightenment", in J Rabasa, M Sato, E Tortarolo and D Woolf (eds), *The Oxford History of Historical Writing: Volume 3, 1400–1800* (2012) 497.

62 See P Cadell, "Dalrymple, Sir David, Third Baronet, Lord Hailes (1726–1792)", in L Goldman (ed), *Oxford Dictionary of National Biography* (2004), available at *http://www.oxforddnb.com/view/article/7046*.

63 See, e.g., K O'Brien, *Narratives of Enlightenment: Cosmopolitan History from Voltaire to Gibbon* (1997) 56–166; N Phillipson, "Providence and Progress: An Introduction to the Historical Thought of William Robertson", in S J Brown (ed), *William Robertson and the Expansion of Empire* (1997) 55 at 56–57.

been critical of "conjectural history" and natural law, but his critique emerges out of the writing of history in the eighteenth century: his reading of Gibbon, for example, was clearly crucial.[64] As Catherine Jones has pointed out in a comparable – if different – context, there are "limitations [to] the familiar opposition of neoclassicism and Romanticism".[65] This brings us to the concluding section of the volume, which explores the critique of law that may be found in contemporary literature, and does so by examining two novels by Sir Walter Scott. Scott was born in 1771, as the late Enlightenment in Scotland, with its philosophical interests in history, custom, and tradition, started to blend into early Romanticism. He knew well many of the "philosophical" historians. As a student he had even read an essay to Principal Robertson.[66]

It is impossible to exaggerate the influence of Scott as a novelist.[67] And while scholars sometimes reflect on the decline in his popularity,[68] he has recently rated a publisher's *Companion* – a powerful indication of vitality and continuing intellectual interest.[69] The two chapters in this section both focus on issues of the law on marriage in novels by Scott. Of course, unhappy families with their crises, miseries, and betrayals are the staple diet of novels; but there is more at stake than this in the works discussed.

The first chapter examines *St Ronan's Well*; the second explores the historical background to Scott's remarks about the source material of *The Bride of Lammermoor*, exploring significant contemporary legal resonances. Both novels may, at some level, reflect on issues surrounding the Union between Scotland and England.[70] But what is clear, particularly in *St Ronan's Well*, is the criticism to which Scott subjects the contemporary law on marriage in Scotland.[71] The final chapter examines in detail a court case, with which Scott was perfectly familiar, which illustrated the problems he perceived, and also affected his discussion of *The Bride of Lammermoor*.

64 Cairns, "German Historical School" (n 56) at 193.

65 C Jones, "Scott, Wilkie, and Romantic Art", in D Duff and C Jones (eds), *Scotland, Ireland, and the Romantic Aesthetic* (2007) 208 at 210.

66 P D Garside, "Scott and the 'philosophical' historians" (1975) 36 *Journal of the History of Ideas* 497 at 504. See also D Forbes "The rationalism of Walter Scott" (1953) 7 *Cambridge Journal* 20.

67 See, e.g., M Pittock (ed), *The Reception of Sir Walter Scott in Europe* (2007).

68 A Rigney, *The Afterlives of Walter Scott: Memory on the Move* (2012). The author points out (ibid at 16) that Scott is a "figure of modernity" whose "long-term legacy continues to be felt".

69 F Robertson (ed), *The Edinburgh Companion to Walter Scott* (2012); Scott's novels can be taken as exemplars of and informative about contemporary critical theory: E Gottlieb, *Walter Scott and Contemporary Theory* (2013).

70 P D Garside, "Union and *The Bride of Lammermoor*" (1984) 19 *Studies in Scottish Literature* 72.

71 See also C Jones, *Literary Memory: Scott's Waverley Novels and the Psychology of Narrative* (2003) (henceforth Jones, *Literary Memory*) 133–144.

Scott was a member of the Faculty of Advocates, and he secured patronage from Tory governments that led to his appointment as Sheriff Depute of Selkirkshire and Principal Clerk of Session. He is famously – and rightly – seen as a conservative, who, for example, justified government reactions to the radical agitations in 1819.[72] Legal themes and lawyers are common in his novels, particularly those dealing with the seventeenth and eighteenth centuries.[73] But the critique of the law that one can derive from his novels is far from any complacent celebration of Scots law. James Chandler explores aspects of this sensitively in his study *England in 1819*.[74] He also finds it possible to link *The Heart of Midlothian* with Adam Smith's *Theory of Moral Sentiments*.[75] Rajit Dosanjh has shown that Scott had an essentially Enlightenment distrust of enthusiasm.[76] He had indeed absorbed many lessons from the Scottish Enlightenment.

Some scholars have seen the Enlightenment as a "project" that falls apart under the tensions and struggles between radicalism and tradition in the early nineteenth century;[77] others have seen the "Enlightenment Project" as merely providing an ideological justification and cloak for economic and cultural domination and exploitation.[78] With these views, I do not consider that there is here any need to engage. While there can be neither any doubt of the impact on thinkers of the horrors of the French Revolution followed by Napoleon's quest for universal monarchy, nor of various states' and monarchies' brutal responses to radicalism, I side with those who incline to see a greater continuity, even with significant changes, than others are willing to admit.

I think it is important to recognise Walter Scott here as a figure who nicely

72 See W Scott, *The Visionary*, ed P D Garside (1984); J Sutherland, *The Life of Walter Scott* (1995) 232–233.

73 See, e.g., D Marshall, *Sir Walter Scott and Scots Law* (1932).

74 J Chandler, *England in 1819: The Politics of Literary Culture and the Case of Romantic Historicism* (1998) 303–349.

75 Ibid at 309. See also K Sutherland, "Fictional economies: Adam Smith, Walter Scott and the nineteenth-century novel" (1987) 54 *ELH: English Literary History* 97.

76 R Dosanjh, "Divine Sentences: Philosophical and Literary Responses to Religious 'Enthusiasm'", unpublished PhD thesis, University of Edinburgh (1999) 122–162,

77 D Forbes, "'Scientific Whiggism': Adam Smith and John Millar" (1954) 7 *The Cambridge Journal* 643; M Ignatieff, "John Millar and Individualism", in I Hont and M Ignatieff (eds), *Wealth and Virtue: The Shaping of Political Economy in the Scottish Enlightenment* (1985) 317 at 341–343.

78 A view ultimately deriving from T Adorno and M Horkheimer, *Dialectic of Enlightenment*, trans John Cumming (1972). Originally published in 1944, this work has influenced many, particularly of the left, especially in France. For a good introduction to this type of thinking, see D Brewer, *The Enlightenment Past: Reconstructing Eighteenth-Century French Thought* (2008) 1–23.

represents a continuity from the Scottish Enlightenment. In her study of memory and narrative in Scott's Waverley novels, Jones describes them as "'weaved-up follies' that rework traces of previous stories . . . through the many refractions of Enlightenment memory".[79] It is worth considering here Scott's *Life of Napoleon*. In it he vigorously and at some length attacked one of Napoleon's strategies to impose his universal monarchy on Europe: his *Code civil*.[80] I have briefly noted elsewhere Scott's critique of the *Code Napoléon*. He attacked it in terms derived from thinkers of the Scottish Enlightenment, favouring natural development of the law over imposed legislation:[81] once more a refraction of Enlightenment thought, but this time of its jurisprudence.

The critique of the law provided by many of the *philosophes* of the Scottish Enlightenment did not lead to codification, but to a new type of "common law", a common law different from the old *ius commune*, a common law emerging from tradition and practice in Scotland, a common law favoured by Scott over Napoleonic codification, a common law embodied in the memories of its lawyers and the discussions of its judges, a common law recorded in the decisions of its courts.

But the legacy of the Enlightenment in law, no doubt because of the complexity of the refractions to which Jones points, is rich and multi-coloured. One can identify it in the development of law classes in the style of Professor David Hume, a culmination of a trend away from the lemmatic commentaries on *compendia* inherited from the Dutch. If Davidson as Millar's successor in Glasgow might seem to mark the end of an Enlightenment approach to education in law, he nonetheless adopted the style of teaching that Hume had developed in Edinburgh, one liberated from dictation of notes on a textbook, but also deriving from Millar. The legacy of the Enlightenment can also be traced in Scottish interest in and ready acceptance of many of the tenets of the German Historical School.[82]

The history of Scots law in the first half of the nineteenth century is understudied. There was, for example, probably because the increase in size of the legal profession created a greater market, a significant growth in

79 Jones, *Literary Memory* (n 71) at 178: she is quoting Scott's own quotation of Shakespeare in the preface to his Magnum Opus edition.

80 W Scott, *Life of Napoleon Buonaparte*, 2nd edn (1827) vol vi, 44–65.

81 Cairns, "German Historical School" (n 56) at 201; Cairns, *Law, Lawyers, and Humanism* (n 11) ch 7.

82 Cairns "German Historical School" (n 56).

law publishing.[83] But what is clear is a growing desire for a renewal of the law schools with improved education for lawyers.[84] A Royal Commission appointed in 1826 to look into the state of the Scottish universities emphasised in its report of 1831 that law ought to "be studied as a liberal and enlightened science". Advocates needed to be acquainted with "the general principles of Jurisprudence", so the "science of Law" should be taught to make "an accomplished and enlightened Advocate". Indeed, it would be "in vain to hope that the independence and character of the Bar can be maintained, if the study of Law is not conducted on an enlightened and philosophical plan". The "philosophy and science of Law" ought not to be sacrificed to supposed needs of practice.[85] Though these principles, if implemented, might have meant something different from what they would have meant in 1770, the underlying thinking is connected.

By the 1850s, the development of the Humboldt University in Germany seemed to some Scots to offer an obvious model for emulation.[86] University reform eventually came under the Universities (Scotland) Act of 1858, under which Commissioners were appointed to restructure university education. An executive commission did the actual work. Some of the principles underlying the 1831 Report were now put into operation. The degree of LLB was created to be taken after graduation in arts. Law was to be taught as an academic discipline. To this end, the Regius Chair of Public Law and the Law of Nature and Nations in Edinburgh (which had been vacant for some time) was revived and filled, while the duties of the Professor of Civil Law were expanded. The old chair of Universal History was recreated as the chair of Constitutional Law and History.[87] This again seems like a conscious revival of the principles associated with, say, John Millar or Allan Maconochie. But while the aspirations are comparable, the new setting in Industrial Europe and Imperial Britain gives a different meaning. It is best recaptured by reflecting on the men appointed. After 1858, most of those who occupied

83 J W Cairns, "Law Books 1707–1918", in S Manning (ed), *The Edinburgh History of Scottish Literature. Volume Two: Enlightenment, Britain and Empire (1707–1918)* (2007) 191 at 193–195 only touches on a vast subject.

84 J W Cairns, "A History of the Faculty of Advocates to 1900", in *The Laws of Scotland: Stair Memorial Encyclopaedia* vol xiii (1992) 499 at 530–534.

85 *Report Made to His Majesty by a Royal Commission of Inquiry into the State of the Universities of Scotland*, in 1831 Parliamentary Papers XII 54.

86 See J Lorimer, *Universities of Scotland: Past, Present and Possible; With an Appendix of Documents Relating to the Higher Instruction* (1854).

87 J W Cairns, "English torts and Roman delicts; the correspondence of James Muirhead and Frederick Pollock" (2013) 87 TulaneLR 867 at 871–872; D B Horn, *A Short History of the University of Edinburgh, 1556–1889* (1967) 177–178.

the main chairs in the Faculty of Law in Edinburgh had all passed part of their studies in law in Germany.[88] The number of lawyers who studied in Germany overall was small;[89] but they were an elite group, and those who led reform and sought chairs were well informed about the advances of legal science in Germany.[90]

The first volume of the *Selected Essays* was focused on the influence of the *ius commune* and Civil Law in Scotland, and explored the way in which Dutch Legal Humanism influenced the existing and continuing use of Civil Law, affecting the admission of men as advocates and how they understood their profession. It also demonstrated the need to approach legal history from a comparative perspective. The second volume has traced how a Humanistic legal tradition, developed from experience of the universities of the Northern Low Countries, grew through the Scottish Enlightenment into a particular attitude to the law. Here the events of the early 1800s, also touched on in the first volume, may have generated an initial interest in Scotland in German scholarship, perhaps reflecting both the historical interests of the Scottish Enlightenment, as well as Scottish Romantic interest in Germany.[91] Scots certainly identified the thinking of the German Historical School with that of Millar, Smith, Hume, and Kames. One author argued that the eighteenth-century Scots and the Germans showed the proper scientific – that is, historical – way to investigate the positive law of a people.[92] By the later nineteenth century, initial interest in German scholarship had led to a return to something like the historical and Humanist approach to Civil Law that had been introduced into Scotland through the Dutch law schools. This is a fascinating issue that awaits further research.

88 See, e.g., J W Cairns, *James Muirhead, Teacher, Scholar, Book-Collector*, in *The Muirhead Collection Catalogue. Part One* (1999) 1 (henceforth Cairns, *James Muirhead*) at 4–5.

89 See A Rodger, "Scottish advocates in the nineteenth century: the German connection" (1994) 110 LQR 563 at 563–565.

90 Cairns, *James Muirhead* (n 88) at 23–26.

91 Cairns, *Law, Lawyers, and Humanism* (n 11) ch 7.

92 J Reddie, *Inquiries Elementary and Historical in the Science of Law* (1840) 49–53.

ENLIGHTENED LEGAL EDUCATION

1 Lawyers, Law Professors, and Localities: The Universities of Aberdeen, 1680–1750

The sesquicentenary of a university is an occasion for reflection. If the Queen's University of Belfast is an international and outward-looking university, it is also one with close links to its local community. In this, of course, it is scarcely unusual. Universities live in a symbiotic relationship with the towns and cities in which they are located: and, despite nineteenth-century dreams of academic pastoral, universities in the main are urban institutions. If there have been some recent advances, much scholarship on the history of universities has yet to take this fully into account.[1] It is important to grasp, however, that the location of a university determines much of its institutional character. If the self-conscious "College Gothic", common on so many American campuses, or the style of the Lanyon Building at Queen's says something about the intellectual aspirations of institutions, localities also influence architecture and determine the spaces in which academic life is acted out. Correspondingly, a major university may also have a significant impact on even a large city, as, for example, the major employer or the creator of large, dominating buildings. The complex relationship of towns and universities also affects intellectual life. Thus the development of an academic discipline can be enhanced or retarded by the politics of its locality.[2] The development of knowledge and disciplines in any institution is subject to many contingencies.

One feature of this interdependency of knowledge and locality is the mutual relationship between universities and the local professions they have often served. This interdependency and mutual influence is made more complex by the relationships local universities and professions have with wider constituencies. This paper is the first of two exploring

1 See, e.g., T Bender (ed), *The University and the City: From Medieval Origins to the Present* (1988).

2 See, e.g., J W Cairns, "Academic feud, bloodfeud, and William Welwood: legal education in St Andrews 1560–1611" (1998) 2 *Edinburgh Law Review* 158.

this huge topic through a study of the development of law teaching and professional education in the universities and town of Aberdeen in the era of the Scottish Enlightenment, taking this to run roughly, if somewhat generously, from 1680 to 1830. Roger Emerson has already argued that the size and institutional complexity of a town can determine the nature of its individual enlightenment.[3] Aberdeen is particularly interesting in this context. It had two universities: King's College and University (founded 1495) in the burgh of Old Aberdeen, and Marischal College and University (founded 1593) in the royal burgh of Aberdeen itself. At the beginning of the period here considered, the Poll Tax records show that, of Scottish burghs, Aberdeen had (after Edinburgh) the highest proportion of men following professional occupations.[4] This was presumably due to its position as the most important northern town. As in Edinburgh, the largest professional group was that of the lawyers.[5] Aberdeen possessed a Sheriff Court, a Commissary Court and a Burgh Court, and was a circuit town for the Court of Justiciary.[6] The Society of Advocates was the local group of elite legal practitioners, but Aberdeen had other men practising before the local courts and as writers, notaries, or other law agents.[7] The history of legal practice and legal practitioners in Scotland is still to be written, but these local men would have passed their time drafting the numerous deeds required for land transactions, the bonds required to secure debts, and the

3 R L Emerson, "The Enlightenment and Social Structures", in Fritz and Williams (eds), *City and Society in the 18th Century* (1973) 99.

4 I D Whyte, "The Occupational Structure of Scottish Burghs in the Late Seventeenth Century", in M Lynch (ed), *The Early Modern Town in Scotland* (1987) 219 at 222 (henceforth Whyte, "The Occupational Structure of Scottish Burghs"); H M Dingwall, *Late Seventeenth-Century Edinburgh: A Demographic Study* (1994) (henceforth Dingwall, *Late Seventeenth-Century Edinburgh*) 146.

5 See J Stuart (ed), *List of Pollable Persons within the Shire of Aberdeen. 1696* (1844) (henceforth *List of Pollable Persons within the Shire of Aberdeen. 1696*) vol ii, 595–632. There I counted in Aberdeen: two writers, five notaries, and five procurators (only these last were members of the Society of Advocates, one being in fact listed as Commissioner of Supply) listed, but only seven physicians and apothecary-surgeons. There is also listed the Commissary, and the officials such as the court clerks and messengers necessary to operate the system. One suspects also that the Town-Clerk is a writer. For Old Aberdeen we find, ibid vol ii, 583–595: one advocate and the Commissary Clerk (also an advocate) but no physicians or surgeons other than the mediciner at King's College. On Edinburgh, see Dingwall, *Late Seventeenth-Century Edinburgh* (n 4) 216–217.

6 Aberdeen was one of the few places in Scotland with an active Justice of the Peace Court in the later seventeenth century, but it, like the Kirk Session, was largely engaged with policing morals: G DesBrisay, "'Menacing their Persons and Exacting on their Purses': The Aberdeen Justice Court, 1657–1700", in D Stevenson (ed), *From Lairds to Louns: Country and Burgh Life in Aberdeen 1600–1800* (1986) 70.

7 See n 4 above

inventories and documents required to administer estates, as well as drafting the necessary pleadings and appearing in court to represent clients in litigation.

There have traditionally been two modes of training as a lawyer: apprenticeship to an experienced practitioner for a certain number of years, or academic training in a university – this latter until towards the end of the seventeenth century being solely in Civil (that is Roman) Law and Canon Law. Local faculties and societies of procurators and writers in Scotland, including such leading bodies as the Writers to the Signet in Edinburgh, the Faculty of Procurators in Glasgow, and the Society of Advocates in Aberdeen, required those seeking admission to their ranks to serve an apprenticeship for a number of years. This system had grown up from a mixture of practice, Acts of Parliament, and Acts of Sederunt. In contrast, from at least the later sixteenth century the Faculty of Advocates, the elite organisation of lawyers in Edinburgh who had monopoly rights of pleading in the Court of Session and Court of Justiciary and who by the late seventeenth century were largely recruited from Scottish landed society, had always had a strong preference for the admission as advocates of men trained in law in a university.[8] To secure this they had eventually achieved by the late seventeenth century a system of examination in Latin on Civil Law of virtually all candidates for admission that required them to have a level of knowledge of the discipline that was only readily obtainable in a university.[9] Unfortunately, however, the advocates had prevented the successful creation of the chair in Law proposed for the University of Edinburgh in 1589, while shortly thereafter the teaching of law had been abandoned in St Andrews.[10] The new charters of erection of the universities of Glasgow in 1577 and of King's College, Aberdeen (first proposed in the 1570s, but only ratified in 1597) had not allowed for legal education, while that of Marischal College in 1593 had

8 J W Cairns, "The law, the advocates and the universities in late sixteenth-century Scotland" (1994) 73 *Scottish Historical Review* 171 (henceforth Cairns, "The law, the advocates and the universities"). On the social origins of advocates in this era, see T I Rae, "The Origins of the Advocates' Library", in P Cadell and A Matheson (eds), *For the Encouragement of Learning: Scotland's National Library 1689–1989* (1989) 1 at 3–6.

9 J W Cairns, "The Formation of the Scottish Legal Mind in the Eighteenth Century: Themes of Humanism and Enlightenment in the Admission of Advocates", in N MacCormick and P Birks (eds), *The Legal Mind: Essays for Tony Honoré* (1986) 253 (henceforth Cairns, "Formation of the Scottish Legal Mind") at 255–263.

10 W C Dickinson, "The advocates' protest against the institution of a Chair of Law in the University of Edinburgh" (1926) 23 *Scottish Historical Review* 205; Cairns, "Academic feud, bloodfeud, and William Welwood" (n 2); Cairns, "The law, the advocates and the universities" (n 8).

been modelled on the new Foundation of King's.[11] In the sixteenth century the training thought desirable for advocates was generally obtained abroad, mainly in France.[12] In the seventeenth century the universities of the Dutch republic, especially those of Utrecht and Leiden, attracted Scottish law students, where, by the end of the century, they typically took courses on the *Institutes*, the *Digest*, natural law, and history.[13]

In 1619, on the other hand, the old Foundation of King's College was revived, and with it the offices of Civilist and Canonist.[14] Thus, alone of the universities of Scotland, King's College still preserved two law chairs into the Restoration period: one of Civil Law, the other of Canon Law. By 1690, however, the office of Canonist had been allowed to lapse. Already in 1664 it was noted that there was no Canonist "neither any necessite for that profession".[15] Later, Robert Forbes was appointed Canonist, but some type of special arrangement was made with him, and the office was left vacant, while in 1696 the Principal informed a Visitation that "ther hath nothing bein in this colledge but ane titular Canonist".[16] It was not so for the chair of Civil Law, which was always filled.

This was the era when the Faculty of Advocates started to press seriously for the creation of law chairs in Scotland, especially chairs in Civil Law, yet the existence of these chairs in King's College, Aberdeen was never acknowledged by them in their campaign.[17] The oddity of this omission

11 J Durkan and J Kirk, *The University of Glasgow, 1451–1577* (1977) 328, 330–331; D Stevenson, *King's College, Aberdeen, 1560–1641: From Protestant Reformation to Covenanting Revolution* (1990) (henceforth Stevenson, *King's College, Aberdeen, 1560–1641*) 35–37, 44–51, 149–166; *Acts of the Parliaments of Scotland*, ed T Thomson and C Innes, 12 vols (1814–1875) (henceforth *APS*) vol iv, 153.

12 R K Hannay, *The College of Justice: Essays on the Institution and Development of the Court of Session* (1933) 135–164; J Durkan, "The French Connection in the Sixteenth and Early Seventeenth Centuries", in T Smout (ed), *Scotland and Europe 1200–1850* (1986) 19.

13 P Nève, "Disputations of Scots Students Attending Universities in the Northern Netherlands", in W M Gordon and T D Fergus (eds), *Legal History in the Making: Proceedings of the Ninth British Legal History Conference Glasgow 1989* (1991) 95 at 95–99; K van Strien and M Ahsmann, "Scottish students in Leiden at the end of the seventeenth century: the correspondence of John Clerk, 1694–1697" (1992) 19 *Lias* 271.

14 Stevenson, *King's College, Aberdeen, 1560–1641* (n 11) 67.

15 *Fasti Aberdonenses: Selections from the Records of the University and King's College of Aberdeen, 1494–1854* (1854) (henceforth *Fasti Aberdonenses*) 320.

16 Aberdeen University Library, King's College Minutes 1684–1689, MS K 38 4–5; *Fasti Aberdonenses* (n 15) 377.

17 See, e.g., J W Cairns, "Sir George Mackenzie, the Faculty of Advocates, and the Advocates' Library", in Mackenzie, *Oratio inauguralis in aperienda jurisconsultorum bibliotheca* ed J W Cairns and A M Cain (1989) 18 at 23, 33 n 43; J W Cairns, "John Spotswood, Professor of Law: A Preliminary Sketch", in W M Gordon (ed) *Miscellany III*, Stair Society vol 39 (1992) 131 at 131–134 (henceforth Cairns, "John Spotswood, Professor of Law").

seems not to have attracted the attention of modern scholars, presumably because these chairs are generally believed to have been sinecures by this date. This belief would have been fostered by the familiar comment by Alexander Daunay, the current Civilist, to the Royal Commission on the Universities of Scotland in 1827 that

> I have been now incumbent, as Professor of Civil Law, since the year 1793, and I have never been called upon, nor have I ever given any lectures; nor, as far as I know, has any such thing been attempted to be given by my predecessors for centuries.[18]

The description of King's College published in 1799 in the *Statistical Account of Scotland* is also well known:

> The suppression of the professorship of canon law has already been noticed: that of civil law still subsists; but the study of it not being prosecuted in this part of the country, no lectures have been given for a long time past, in this branch of science.[19]

Already in the 1780s it could be claimed: "In the King's College there has always been a Professorship of laws; but for a century past, none in that office have found the smallest encouragement for opening a class."[20] These published remarks in prominent primary sources much used for the history of the universities of Aberdeen may explain the attitude of modern scholars; they do not account for the way the Faculty of Advocates ignored these endowed chairs in Law, given that, as we shall see, Daunay was wrong: if the chair of Canon Law was ineffective and eventually left vacant, law was taught from the chair of Civil Law at the end of the seventeenth and the beginning of the eighteenth centuries. Moreover, there is evidence of law teaching in Marischal College up to the middle years of the eighteenth century. Given the focus on jurisprudence of much moral thought in the Scottish Enlightenment, the ending of these classes, such as they may have been, is also remarkable.

To solve this conundrum it therefore becomes important to examine the evidence about the teaching of law in the universities of Aberdeen and its relationship, first, to the aspirations of the local legal profession and of the Faculty of Advocates in Edinburgh, and secondly, to local politics (often familial) and

18 *Evidence, Oral and Documentary, Taken and Received by the Commissioners Appointed by His Majesty George IV., July 23rd, 1826; and Re-appointed by His Majesty William IV., October 12th, 1830; For Visiting the Universities of Scotland, Volume IV. University of Aberdeen*, 1837 Parliamentary Papers XXXVIII 45.

19 [W M Gordon,] "University and Kings College of Aberdeen", in J Sinclair (ed), *The Statistical Account of Scotland* (1791–1799) vol xxi, 87.

20 *A Collection of All the Papers Relating to the Proposal for Uniting the King's and the Marischal Colleges of Aberdeen, Which Have Been Published by Authority of the Colleges* (1787) (henceforth *Papers Relating to the Proposal for Uniting the King's and the Marischal Colleges*) 12.

the wider politics of Scotland. The second of these relationships has been the subject of a recent important study by Emerson.[21] Through most of the period with which we are concerned, Scottish politics revolved around rivalry between the great families (and their associates) whose co-operation was necessary for the government of the country. The period from 1715 to 1761 was marked by a struggle for power and control of patronage between two groups of Whig noble families. The first of these was known as the Argathelians. This was an association focused on John, second Duke of Argyll (until he went into opposition in 1739) and his brother Archibald, Earl of Ilay (later third Duke). The second major group was called the Squadrone Volante. This was an association of related families led by the Dukes of Montrose and Roxburghe, containing, notably, the legal dynasty of the Dundases of Arniston. In this period it was mainly animated by opposition to the rise of Ilay and Argyll.

The standard histories of the universities of Aberdeen have in general said little – or little worthwhile – about the study of law.[22] Macfarlane's study of William Elphinstone pays due regard to the significance of law in his foundation of the University and King's College, but for any further discussion of legal education we have to wait for Maclaren's short essay on the relationship between the universities and the professions of medicine, law, the church, and the professoriate in Aberdeen from 1760 to 1860, and Girvin's account of John Dove Wilson who held the chair in Law in the now united University of Aberdeen at the end of the nineteenth century.[23] Nonetheless there has been some relevant scholarship: Stevenson has looked at the suppression and revival of the Law chairs in King's College after the reformation, and Emerson's study of patronage in the Aberdeen universities in the eighteenth century has examined appointments as Civilist, while Wood has also paid

21 R L Emerson, *Professors, Patronage and Politics: The Aberdeen Universities in the Eighteenth Century* (1992) (henceforth Emerson, *Professors, Patronage and Politics*).

22 See, e.g., R S Rait, *The Universities of Aberdeen. A History* (1895) 181–182. N J D Kennedy, "The Faculty of Law", in P J Anderson (ed), *Studies in the History and Development of the University of Aberdeen: A Quatercentenary Tribute Paid by Certain of Her Professors and of Her Devoted Sons* (1906) 235 is distinctly disappointing.

23 L J Macfarlane, *William Elphinstone and the Kingdom of Scotland, 1431–1514: The Struggle for Order* (1985) (henceforth Macfarlane, *William Elphinstone*) 377–382; Maclaren, "Privilege, Patronage and the Professions: Aberdeen and its Universities, 1760–1860", in J J Carter and D J Withrington (eds), *Scottish Universities: Distinctiveness and Diversity* (1992) 96; S Girvin, "Professor John Dove Wilson of Aberdeen" (1992) *Juridical Review* 60. M C Meston, "The Civilists of Aberdeen: 1495–1995" (1995) *Juridical Review* 153 lists the holders of the Chair of Civil Law, while D Hope, "The Universities of Aberdeen and the Court of Session in Edinburgh" (1995) *Juridical Review* 5 has some pertinent remarks though focused on another issue.

some attention to the possibility of law in the curriculum.[24] A new consideration of the evidence is therefore required. This paper will accordingly examine the state of legal education in Aberdeen in order not only to explain why the Faculty of Advocates did not try to use the chairs to found the law school they desired in Scotland, but also to consider the extent and nature of instruction in law in Aberdeen until the middle of the eighteenth century, by the end of which period it had ceased in both the universities.

A. UNIVERSITY CLASSES IN LAW, 1680–1717

In 1741 Principal Chalmers of King's College claimed that under the Foundation the Civilist was required to lecture on the *Institutes* of Justinian.[25] The statutes of 1514 in fact required the students of Civil Law to read the *Institutes*, and provided that the course of their studies should follow that at the University of Orléans, which was of course considerably more extensive than this.[26] Such information as we have for our period, however, tends to suggest that the Principal's interpretation, though put forward to support his protest against an election, was correct.[27]

The most substantial evidence of what the Civilists taught is provided by the manuscript notes of John Gordon's "*Cursus Iuridicus*" of 1701, found among the law books that Gordon, Civilist, 1696–1717, bequeathed to the Library of King's College.[28] This manuscript demonstrates that his classes were lectures on the *Institutes*, although he also prepared "*Positiones Juridicae*" for his students to defend in public.[29] This is supported by the six printed law books he bequeathed to the Library: the 1604 Amsterdam edition of the *Corpus iuris*, an edition of Zasius' *Epitome feudorum*, an edition of the *Institutes* with notes, and three commentaries on the *Institutes*.[30]

24 Stevenson, *King's College, Aberdeen, 1560–1641* (n 11) 28, 48–49, 67; Emerson, *Professors, Patronage and Politics* (n 21) 19–20, 39–40, 63–69, 81–84, 87, 97; P B Wood, *The Aberdeen Enlightenment: The Arts Curriculum in the Eighteenth Century* (1993) 60 (henceforth Wood, *Aberdeen Enlightenment*).

25 See Aberdeen University Library, King's College Minutes 1734–1754, MS K 43 138.

26 Macfarlane, *William Elphinstone* (n 23) 380.

27 See Emerson, *Professors, Patronage and Politics* (n 21) 63–65 for the context of the Principal's claim.

28 Aberdeen University Library, King's College Library Accessions 1710–1750, MS K 112 (list dated 21 July 1736).

29 Aberdeen University Library, MS 132.

30 Aberdeen University Library, King's College Library Accessions 1710–1750, MS K112. Only one of these can now be identified in the Library: *Johannis Borcholten IC. Clarissimi, et in academia Iulia quondam antecessoris, in quattuor institutionum iuris civilis libros, commentarii* (1610).

There is no other direct evidence of what was taught. In October 1684 the Bishop of Aberdeen presented James Scougal, advocate in Aberdeen, to the office of Civilist.[31] The minutes of King's College record that on 19 November 1684 Scougal began his public lessons with an inaugural discourse "*de ratione docendi et discendi juris*". This is a common – indeed, stock – theme, and tells us little of Scougal's actual course, especially since this was evidently a significant public occasion in "the Common Schoole" attended by many individuals other than the students.[32] The next year it is recorded that Scougal began his lessons on 9 December, giving an introductory discourse "*de Justitia et Jure*".[33] This is the rubric of the opening title of both the *Institutes* and the *Digest:* the breadth of the topic and the fact that it was recorded in the minutes suggest, however, that it was again a formal, public lecture, though it could be the opening lecture of a series on either the *Digest* or the *Institutes*. The only other evidence having a bearing on this issue comes from the Visitation of 1680, when it was ordained that "the Civilist shall give attendance and teach his lessone at least once in the weeke, dureing the sitting of the colledge".[34] The small number of lectures possible under such a provision suggests that only the *Institutes* would be taught.

By 1700 the Library had a small collection of books on Civil and Canon Law, those on the former being fairly standard, either medieval or Humanist, works. Although a somewhat old-fashioned selection, it would have supported the teaching of the Civilist.[35] Not enough, however, is known of law libraries in Scotland at this period and how they related to teaching to draw any conclusions from the holdings, especially since the volumes appear to have been acquired in a random fashion.

At the time of the Visitation of 1680, the Civilist was George Nicholson of Cluny and Kemnay, a member of the Faculty of Advocates in Edinburgh, though from the Aberdeen region. He had been elected in 1673, the minute specially noting that this was in part because of all the business the College had pending before the Lords of Council and Session in Edinburgh.[36] Ignoring the issue of the activities of Nicholson's predecessors, this raises the question of the extent to which he ever taught or was even intended

31 Aberdeen University Library, King's College Minutes 1684–1689, MS K 38 1–2, 4–5.

32 Ibid 6.

33 Ibid 14.

34 *Fasti Aberdonenses* (n 15) 356.

35 Aberdeen University Library, *Catalogus Librorum in Bibliotheca Collegij Regij Aberdonensis Contentorum Secundum Ordinem Alphabeticum*, MS K 111 fos 25r–26v.

36 Aberdeen University Library, King's College Minutes 1662–1679, MS K 37 fos 29v–30r.

to teach, given his evident success at the Bar, and his eventual appointment as a Senator of the College of Justice. It is a tempting and likely speculation that the appointment was primarily designed as remuneration for his assistance as an advocate. On the other hand, Nicholson, who had been MP for Aberdeen in 1661–1662, currently held the post of Sheriff-Clerk of Aberdeen (1672–1678).[37] There may have been some hope that he would attend the College. Nonetheless, it is telling that the Visitation, after requiring the Civilist to attend and teach, added that

> if, becaus of the meannes of the salarie due to the civilist, the said Mr. George or any other person refused to give attendance and teache conforme to the foundatione, [the meetting] declaired the place to be vacant and the salarie to be imployed upon annuel rent, for makeing up of ane additional stocke to one who should imbrace that office thereafter.[38]

Nicholson declared that he wished to remain as Civilist but could not attend the current session (1680–1681). He was given leave to stay in Edinburgh for two months, with the Bishop, as Chancellor, given power to extend this for another two.[39] It looks as if Nicholson never taught, as on 24 October 1684 it was noted that the position of Civilist had been vacant for a long time since the removal of Nicholson, now a Senator of the College of Justice (appointed 1682).[40] It was presumably to avoid the problem of an absentee Civilist that Bishop Haliburton of Aberdeen presented to the office in 1684 the local advocate Scougal, who does appear to have tried to teach.[41] If the salary was small, Scougal combined the office with that of Commissary of Aberdeen, a post to which he had been presented in 1680 by his own father, Patrick Scougal, Bishop of Aberdeen 1664–1682.[42] Scougal, however, resigned in 1687, to be succeeded by John Haliburton, son of Bishop Haliburton.[43] Of Haliburton's tenure nothing can be said other than he resigned in 1689.[44] His successor was John Moir, an Edinburgh advocate.[45] Moir held the office

37 F J Grant, *The Faculty of Advocates in Scotland 1532–1943 with Genealogical Notes* (1944) (henceforth Grant, *Faculty of Advocates*) 164.

38 *Fasti Aberdonenses* (n 15) 356.

39 Ibid 357.

40 Aberdeen University Library, King's College Minutes 1684–1689, MS K 38 1–2.

41 Ibid. Civilists were normally elected in a procedure involving the Masters and some individuals elected ad hoc as procurators of the four nations. If a vacancy had not been filled within thirty days by this procedure, the right of presentation devolved on the Bishop as Chancellor ex officio.

42 N Clyne, "The Advocates in Aberdeen. No 3" (1887) 1 *Scottish Notes and Queries* 68 (henceforth Clyne, "The Advocates in Aberdeen. No 3").

43 Aberdeen University Library, King's College Minutes 1684–1689, MS K 38 19–20.

44 Ibid 23–24.

45 Ibid.

until his death early in 1696.[46] Although from an Aberdeenshire family (his father was John Moir of Stoneywood), he appears to have been another absentee who did not teach; his absence prompted Robert Forbes, another local man who was a member of the Faculty of Advocates in Edinburgh, to seek the post in 1694. The Masters opposed this on the grounds, *inter alia*, that he would not be able to attend nor give weekly lessons on Civil Law. Forbes complained to the Visitors currently inspecting the universities.[47] Forbes did not live to gain the office after Moir, as he himself died in March 1696.[48] His complaint, however, may explain why the Visitation of 1696 quizzed the Principal on 21 August on the effectiveness of the chair in Civil Law. The Principal was able to respond that "the present Civilist being but laitly admitted hath had two lessones already".[49] This was John Gordon, who, as we have seen, taught at least some of the time. That he was resident and willing to teach is no doubt part of the explanation of why he was chosen. Gordon was presented to the office by the Principal and Masters on 1 April and admitted by the Commissary on 7 April.[50]

It is possible on the basis of the above discussion to suggest why the Faculty of Advocates did not consider the office of Civilist in King's College, Aberdeen of any significance in their desire to establish chairs in law in Scotland, even though they must have been well aware of its existence, given that some of their members had held it. First, it is plain that the teaching was intermittent. Secondly, the teaching was elementary and probably limited to a course on Justinian's *Institutes*. Moreover, if the course of John Gordon is typical, the level of teaching of *the Institutes* by the Civilists at King's College was considerably more elementary than that of the private teachers in Edinburgh in the early eighteenth century.[51] This course would therefore not satisfy the needs and aspirations of the Faculty of Advocates, who, in any case, would also have wanted a course on the *Digest*. Moreover, Scougal, when he demitted office as Civilist, was admitted as an advocate by the Lords of Session on 8 June 1687 without undergoing the normal examinations in Civil Law, because "he

46 Grant, *Faculty of Advocates* (n 37) 152.

47 Aberdeen University Library, MS K 255/44, Papers Relating to the Visitation Commission . . . 1696. I am indebted to Roger Emerson for this reference and information. Unfortunately, Minute Books are lacking for the period from 1689 to 1700. Forbes was probably the son of Thomas Forbes of Echt who had been admitted to the Faculty of Advocates in 1692.

48 Grant, *Faculty of Advocates* (n 37) 74.

49 *Fasti Aberdonenses* (n 15) 377–378.

50 See Fettercairn MSS, on deposit in the National Library of Scotland, Acc 4796/213, Decreet of Declarator, Sir William Forbes against James Thomson, 13.

51 Compare Aberdeen University Library, MS 132 with National Library of Scotland, Saltoun, MSS 17807–9 (notes on the *Institutes* taken from the lectures of John Cuninghame).

did not suppose himself qualified to undergo the usual trial", though he had pointed out that he had been Commissary of Aberdeen for seven years, in which time he "had applied himself to the study of the municipal and civil laws".[52] This can scarcely have bred confidence among the Faculty in the teaching of the Aberdeen Civilists. Furthermore, if the chair was endowed, the endowment was scarcely generous: towards the end of this initial period the salary was listed as £10 8s 6d, though it seems soon to have risen to £40 14s 11d.[53] Other than as a sinecure the office of Civilist cannot have been at all attractive to members of the Faculty of Advocates, supposing that among their ranks was someone qualified and interested in teaching, since, in Aberdeen, he would be isolated from lucrative practice at the Bar to supplement earnings from the chair. A candidate for the chair in the 1740s, who was a member of the Faculty of Advocates, candidly admitted "that by reason of the more lucrative employment he had during the Session at Edinburgh as an Advocat, and the time necessary during the vacancys to look after and improve his estate in Liddesdale, he could spend little or no time in this place".[54] It is therefore no surprise that when formal instruction in law of the type the Faculty desired started in Scotland, it happened in Edinburgh.[55] As an active chair, that of Civilist was therefore likely only to be attractive to practitioners in Aberdeen, as a supplement to their other activities and sources of income. It is notable that the only definite evidence we have of teaching concerned two advocates in Aberdeen: Scougal and Gordon. The Faculty of Advocates in Edinburgh, however, were unlikely to rely on members of the Society of Advocates in Aberdeen to provide an adequate education for candidates for admission. The Aberdeen practitioners were unlikely to have experienced the modern sophisticated education in law that most members of the Faculty by this date had experienced in the Netherlands and wished to develop in Scotland. Aberdeen, moreover, was too far from Edinburgh, which was where the Faculty of Advocates was based. Edinburgh remained even after 1707 the social hub for the landed class, from which the Faculty were mainly recruited. It is true, however, that the Poll Tax records show that Aberdeen had a proportionally slightly higher group of resident landowners and gentry than Edinburgh, but, as Whyte has pointed out, these "resident heritors were

52 Found quoted in Clyne, "The Advocates in Aberdeen. No 3" (n 42) 68–69.

53 See the separately paginated list of Scottish offices in Chamberlayne, *Magnae Britanniae Notitia: Or, the Present State of Great Britain* (1723) 9; and in ibid (1726) 11.

54 Aberdeen University Library, MS 214, Nineteen Papers Catanach 1743–45, Answers Mr Burnet to the Principals Protest [3].

55 Cairns, "John Spotswood, Professor of Law" (n 17).

mainly small lairds . . . living off rents of under £500 Scots per year".[56] This was not the type of landed society with which members of the Faculty identified themselves. Men preparing for admission to the Faculty had normally passed through their basic university education and could be expected to seek the pleasures of a more sophisticated metropolitan environment than Aberdeen.

This, however, raises the interesting issue of who in fact attended the classes on Justinian's *Institutes* when actually given by the Civilist. There is no direct evidence. If the regular curriculum in arts did not include attendance at the class of the Civilist, some of those following it may nonetheless have taken his course on the *Institutes* when it was offered.[57] The more advanced divinity students may have attended the lectures in Civil Law, as they appear to have been interested in doing in Glasgow a little later.[58] The obvious candidates for attendance at the Civilist's classes, however, are the apprentices of the Society of Advocates. This suggestion might seem to be supported by the tendency to link the chair with the office of Commissary, especially since the Society developed out of the practitioners before the Commissary Court.[59] One can readily infer close linkages between the bishop who appointed the Commissary, and whose Cathedral in Old Aberdeen near King's College was the site of the Court, and the Professor of Civil Law and the Society.[60] By the time with which we are concerned, however, these linkages were becoming uncoupled. The bishops finally disappeared with the restoration of Presbyterianism in 1690. From 1690 the Court sat in Aberdeen rather than in Old Aberdeen.[61] The Sheriff Court and the Burgh Court must now have

56 Whyte, "The Occupational Structure of Scottish Burghs" (n 4) 222–223.

57 See C M Shepherd, "The Arts Curriculum at Aberdeen at the Beginning of the Eighteenth Century", in J J Carter and J H Pittock (eds), *Aberdeen and the Enlightenment: Proceedings of a Conference held at the University of Aberdeen* (1987) 146; Wood, *Aberdeen Enlightenment* (n 24) 1–8, 61–73.

58 See W Forbes to Principal Stirling, 30 January 1717, Glasgow University Library, MS Gen 204/16. See also J W Cairns, "The Origins of the Glasgow Law School: The Professors of Civil Law, 1714–1761", in P Birks (ed), *The Life of the Law: Proceedings of the Tenth British Legal History Conference Oxford 1991* (1993) 151 at 180 (henceforth Cairns, "Origins of the Glasgow Law School").

59 See, e.g., J A Henderson (ed), *History of the Society of Advocates in Aberdeen* (1912) (henceforth Henderson, *History of the Society of Advocates in Aberdeen*) 52–55. The same is true of the Faculty of Procurators in Glasgow: J S Muirhead (ed), *The Old Minute Book of the Faculty of Procurators in Glasgow, 1668–1758* (1948) 35–39.

60 See D Stevenson, "The Commissary Court of Aberdeen in 1650", in D H Sellar (ed), *Miscellany II*, Stair Society vol 35 (1984) 144.

61 Ibid. See Act 1690, c 67 in *APS* (n 11) vol ix, 204; N Clyne, "The Advocates in Aberdeen. No 2" (1887) 1 *Scottish Notes and Queries* 42 at 43; and D Stevenson, "Who was John Spalding?" (1985) *Aberdeen University Review* 102.

loomed large in the practice of the members of the Society. The locus of practice of the advocates had moved definitively to Aberdeen from Old Aberdeen. The Poll Tax records of 1696 thus show only one advocate, George Adam, and the Commissary Clerk, John Gordon, the future Civilist, and an advocate, resident in Old Aberdeen.[62] Attendance of apprentices, now based in Aberdeen, at the lectures of the Civilist, if not impossible, would not have been so easy as it would have been before this development. Furthermore, the low rate of admissions as an advocate suggests that the Society's apprentices could hardly have been the mainstay of the lectures of the Civilist.

Admissions to the Society of Advocates in Aberdeen, 1651–1750, by decade

1651–60	1661–70	1671–80	1681–90	1691–1700
7	10	10	4	7
1701–10	1711–20	1721–30	1731–40	1741–50
8	4	6	7	10

Source: *History of the Society of Advocates in Aberdeen* (1912)

The disappearance of the early records of the Society of Advocates makes it difficult to be certain as to the training of its members. Such evidence as we have, however, suggests that attendance at the lectures of the Civilist would not have been required. Admission was linked to admission to practice as a procurator before the Commissary Court. A regulation of 1685 established a widows' and orphans' fund and provided that if anyone who had been in the service of a member of the Commissary Court – that is of an advocate admitted to practise before it – "for any considerable time" desired to be admitted, he had either to undergo "a tryall" and pay £40 (Scots) or, foregoing a trial, to pay one hundred merks (£66 13s 4d). It was also provided that "no stranger who has not been bred with some member of the forsaid court for some considerable time" was to be admitted as a procurator before it "till they undergoe such examine and tryall as the Commissar and remanent members of the said court shall think fitt". They had also to pay £200 (Scots).[63] Commissaries, if not already members of

62 *List of Pollable Persons within the Shire of Aberdeen. 1696* (n 5) vol ii, 591, 592. Even if other advocates, such as William Baxter (see Henderson, *History of the Society of Advocates in Aberdeen* (n 59) 93) may have lived in Old Aberdeen, but not be listed in the Poll Tax records, the basic point is not affected.

63 Henderson, *History of the Society of Advocates in Aberdeen* (n 59) 52–53.

the Society, were sometimes admitted.[64] Practice before the Sheriff Court required separate admission there, and there seems to have been some cooperation between the Sheriff and the Society of Advocates to regulate this.[65] Such cooperation was easy. The Procurators Fiscal of Aberdeenshire were almost invariably members of the Society,[66] as commonly were the Sheriffs-Substitute.[67] Evidence from the 1740s confirms that admission to the Society of Advocates required apprenticeship to a member and then examination on Scots law and forms of process.[68] Other lawyers in Aberdeen may have been interested in such classes, but we know virtually nothing about them and their training, other than that work as a notary was regulated by an Act of Sederunt of 1595 which required an apprenticeship of five years and a knowledge of Latin.[69] It seems likely, however, that the notaries and lowly writers would have been less concerned with such classes than the more socially aspiring Society of Advocates.

A final point to note is that the Masters of King's College seem to have had a varying level of determination to ensure that the Civilist was an active teacher in these years. If they seem to have been willing to appoint Nicholson because he could be useful to them in Edinburgh, there does seem to have been a preference for someone who would reside and teach. Of course, the politics of appointments were always complicated. John Gordon may have been appointed Civilist in 1696 because he would reside and teach, but he was also closely related to the Gordon family group in King's College,[70] while Haliburton was obviously appointed as son of the Bishop of Aberdeen.

B. UNIVERSITY CLASSES IN LAW, 1717–1750

From 1699 onwards, some advocates taught law privately in Edinburgh in classes modelled on the example provided by legal education in the Dutch universities. Out of these classes grew the chairs in Public Law and the Law of Nature and Nations (1707), Civil Law (1710), Universal History

64 See, e.g., ibid 291 (Robert Paterson).
65 Ibid xi.
66 Ibid 410.
67 Ibid 417.
68 Aberdeen University Library, MS 214, Nineteen Papers Catanach 1743–45, Memoriall ffrom Some of the Members of the Marischall College 5.
69 Act of Sederunt, 31 December 1595, *The Acts of Sederunt of the Lords of Council and Session, from the 15th of January 1553, to the 11th of July 1790* (1790). See also the Act 1587, c 29 *APS* (n 11) vol iii, 448–449.
70 See Emerson, *Professors, Patronage and Politics* (n 21) 19–20.

(1719), and Scots Law (1722) in the University of Edinburgh. The wishes of the Faculty of Advocates were thereby fulfilled. Moreover, a chair of Civil Law was founded in emulation in the University of Glasgow in 1714.[71] Other than that in Universal History, all of these chairs were occupied by members of the Faculty of Advocates. This suggests that whatever may have happened before these developments, thereafter the Faculty of Advocates were unlikely to patronise the Civilists at King's College for their training in law.

The Visitations of the 1690s had been unsuccessful in ridding the Aberdeen universities of Jacobites and episcopalians as the region was a bastion of disaffection, where a Jacobite and episcopalian gentry were able to protect the Masters of the Colleges. The Rebellion of 1715 was now to prove their downfall. A Visitation of 1716–1717 carried out an effective purge.[72] The records of the Visitation noted:

> Mr John Gordon, Professor of Civil law, did not qualify according to Law till the Twenty first of February last: He concurred with the disaffected people of Old Aberdeen in observing a Thanksgiveing for the arrival of the Pretender, by going to Church on that day and hearing the Pretender prayed for by an Episcopal Intruder, Under the name of King James the Eight, and by having Illuminations in the Windows of his House upon that occasion.[73]

He was accordingly deprived of his office on 22 June 1717.[74]

The Government did not trust those Masters of King's College who survived the purge and the procurators of the four nations (individuals elected ad hoc to participate in certain elections, including that of the Civilist) to fill vacant positions with suitable men.[75] A royal Presentation dated 1 October 1717 therefore gave the chair of Civil Law to Alexander Garden, younger of Troup. The Presentation provided that Garden should be admitted to his office by an ad hoc body consisting of the magistrates of Aberdeen, and the ministers of Old and New Aberdeen. He apparently convened these men in a tavern, where, as a jaundiced observer put it, "he was clandestinly admitted over a bottle in order to shun any interruption he might meet with from

71 Cairns, "John Spotswood, Professor at Law" (n 17); Cairns, "Origins of the Glasgow Law School" (n 58).

72 Emerson, *Professors, Patronage and Politics* (n 21) 18–34.

73 P J Anderson, *Records of the Aberdeen Universities Commission 1716–17* (1900) (henceforth Anderson, *Records of the Aberdeen Universities Commission 1716–17*) 9.

74 Ibid 51; Emerson, *Professors, Patronage and Politics* (n 21) 34. Matters had obviously been tense in Aberdeen in the period running up to the Visitation as in May 1716 Gordon and his family had been attacked by students in their home: Aberdeen University Library, King's College Minutes 1716–17, 1717–22, MS K 41 fos 6v–7r.

75 Emerson, *Professors, Patronage and Politics* (n 21) 38–40.

his Predecessor or otherwayes". This was on 4 November 1717.[76] Garden had been admitted a member of the Faculty of Advocates in Edinburgh in 1712.[77] As well as being a local man, he was a supporter of the Squadrone Volante, who had come to power in 1716. This political connection had already secured him appointment as Sheriff-Depute of Aberdeen on 14 August 1716. Emerson plausibly suggests that his appointment as Civilist may also have been due to the position of Sir Francis Grant of Cullen, his father-in-law, on the commission of Visitation.[78]

Garden was to prove an absentee professor. After his admission by the magistrates and ministers, he left for Edinburgh, and he does not feature in the minutes of King's College until 27 March 1719, when he produced his presentation and admission to a meeting of the College and took the Foundation oath and the oath *de fideli administratione*.[79] He returned in March of the next year.[80] At the end of the month he undertook to give a public prelection; he duly delivered one *de Supremi Magistratus officio*, before again departing for Edinburgh.[81] He returned to the College in April of 1721, 1722 and 1723.[82] He evidently only attended when other business brought him to Aberdeen. The Masters started to put pressure on the absentee Civilist, and on 21 October 1723 the minutes record that "the principal and masters considering the great inconveniences to the university by the neglect of the profession and study of the civil Law did judge it their duty to represent the same to Mr Alexander Garden Civilist and to desire his attendance conform to the foundation". The Principal was also authorised to discuss this further with Garden in Edinburgh.[83] The Principal reported on 20 January 1724 that the Civilist had promised to respond in writing.[84] On 3 April Garden had resigned the office. Before filling it, on 6 April the Principal and Masters now declared and enacted:

> [T]hat whosoever shall happen to be nominat and elected shall in the termes of the fundatione be oblidged to actuall residence, and to teach the said Civill law

76 Anderson, *Records of the Universities Commission 1716–17* (n 73) 53–54; Aberdeen University Library, King's College Minutes 1716–17, 1717–22, MS K 41 fos 32v–33r, 34v.

77 J M Pinkerton (ed), *The Minute Book of the Faculty of Advocates Volume 1, 1661–1712*, Stair Society vol 29 (1976) 301; Grant, *Faculty of Advocates* (n 37) 78.

78 Emerson, *Professors, Patronage and Politics* (n 21) 39–40, 137.

79 Aberdeen University Library, King's College Minutes 1716–17, 1717–22, MS K 31 fo 34v.

80 Ibid fos 51v–52r (7, 8, 14 March 1720).

81 Ibid fo 54v (21, 30 March 1720).

82 Ibid fos 64v (17 April 1721), 72v (2 April 1722), 73r (16, 17 April 1722); Aberdeen University Library, King's College Minutes 1722–1733, MS K 42 fo 9r (12 April 1723).

83 Aberdeen University Library, King's College Minutes 1722–1733, MS K 42 fo 12v.

84 Ibid fo 13r.

> during the sessions of the said Colledge in such place as shall be agreed to by the principal and Masters. And In respect that by the fundatione it is appointed that the Civilist should read and teach in his own Manse which of a long tyme hes been (as is reported) by fyre or some accident ruined and quite demolished, Therfor it is enacted and by acceptatione of the presentatione to be now given, Whosoever shall be chosen and accept of the said presentatione shall be oblidged to make no pretext of the want of a Manse for not teaching and giveing prelections publict and private as is above mentioned.[85]

The reference to the Civilist's manse perhaps indicates an argument that Garden had used to support his absence.

The successful pressure on Garden to resign and the resolution to require the new Civilist to reside and teach have two possible and complementary interpretations. First, it could reflect a genuine desire that Civil Law should be taught in King's College. Earlier practice does suggest that there already was a preference for a Civilist who would reside and teach. Moreover, the Principal and Masters would have been well aware of the new Law chairs in Edinburgh and Glasgow which had demonstrated that there was a market in Scotland for legal education in a university. Reinforcing this would have been a recent development in Marischal College in Aberdeen. The issue is much obscured because the evidence for it is found in papers arising out of a law suit in the 1740s, but in the written pleadings of that case there is found the statement:

> Mr. David Verner Professor of Philosophy there [Marischal College], Who had regularly studied the Civill Law Two full years under Professor Craig at Edinburg, and one Year The Civill and Scotch Law under Professor Forbes at Glasgow as by Certificates from these Colleges he can make appear. . . . At the desire of the Lawyers of Aberdeen and by authority of the Rector and faculty of the Marischall College In the Year of 1722 began to profess and to teach that science At which time There was a Civilist in the Old Town who being an Advocate in Edinburgh did not reside and teach.[86]

The question of Verner's classes in law will be discussed a little later, but the evidence shows that he did teach. This innovation at the rival institution would have made the Masters at King's very aware of the absentee Garden's failure to teach. Secondly, as Emerson has shown, Garden was closely linked with the Squadrone. The period when he was ousted was a period when Ilay and the Argathelians were coming to ascendancy in Scotland, including in

85 Ibid fos 15v–16r.

86 Aberdeen University Library, MS K 214, Nineteen Papers Catanach 1743–45, Memoriall ffrom Some of the Members of the Marischall College 4. J Anderson (ed), *Fasti Academiae Mariscallanae Aberdonensis* (1898) vol ii, 40 gives the date as 1724. This may be a mistake. The minute books of Marischal College are silent on the issue.

the universities of Aberdeen, and in 1724 the Squadrone were to lose their control over the Rector's Court of King's College.[87] As Garden was an outsider with no close links with any of the Masters at King's, it may have been easy politically for the Masters to decide to engineer his departure on the grounds that he did not teach and reside in conformity with the terms of the Foundation. It is worth noting in this respect that he was to lose the office of Sheriff Depute in 1728.[88] It was not, however, necessarily especially easy to oust Garden from the Civilist's chair. If the Masters could claim that he was not teaching in conformity with the Foundation, he could in turn point to the requirement in the Foundation that he have a manse in which to teach. Some sort of accommodation had therefore to be reached. It is therefore unsurprising to find William Orem informing us that Garden was bought out for the sum of 4,500 merks, that is, around £250 sterling.[89] This was a fair purchase price, given that at this date the income from the chair was £40 14s 01d per annum.[90]

The purchaser was Alexander Fraser of Powis, the Subprincipal of King's College. Later on the day on which the Masters accepted the demission of Garden and passed their resolutions on the Civilist, Alexander Fraser, son of the Subprincipal, was elected Civilist.[91] Born in 1699, the new professor had been admitted to the Faculty of Advocates in Edinburgh in December 1722.[92] He had also graduated MA from King's College in November of that year.[93] Both Frasers were Argathelians.[94] On 10 April Fraser produced his presentation and admission to the office at a College meeting and duly took his place.[95] The sederunt and minutes of the meetings of the College show that thereafter he resided and participated fully in corporate life, attending virtually every meeting until his death in 1741. He was awarded the degree of LLD on 15 March 1725, and on 29 March was appointed to prepare the

87 Emerson, *Professors, Patronage and Politics* (n 21) 39–40, 43, 45.

88 Grant, *Faculty of Advocates* (n 37) 78.

89 W Orem, "A description of the Chanonry in Old Aberdeen . . . 1728", in Nichols (ed), *Bibliotheca Topographica Britannia* (1782) vol iv, 173. I owe this reference to Roger Emerson.

90 J Chamberlayne, *Magnae Britanniae Notitia* (1727) 13 (separately paginated list of Scottish offices).

91 Aberdeen University Library, King's College Minutes 1722–1733, MS K 42 fo 16r (6 April 1724).

92 Grant, *Faculty of Advocates* (n 37) 76; J M Pinkerton (ed), *The Minute Book of the Faculty of Advocates Volume 2, 1713–1750*, Stair Society vol 32 (1980) 57.

93 Aberdeen University Library, King's College Minutes 1722–1733, MS K 42 5 (7 November 1722).

94 Emerson, *Professors, Patronage and Politics* (n 21) 137.

95 Aberdeen University Library, King's College Minutes 1722–1733, MS K 42 fo 16v.

diploma for the same degree conferred on the College's great benefactor, James Fraser of Chelsea.[96] He was elected as Master of Mortifications on 2 October 1727, serving until 1736.[97] On 27 August 1733 he was elected Dean of the Faculty of Law.[98] He was engaged in other aspects of the College's business, such as attending meetings of the Presbytery to look after the College's interests."[99]

Thus, though Fraser was another advocate in Edinburgh, he was not an absentee professor. His father's position might suggest that Garden was got rid of by a ruse in order to provide an annuity for the son to support him while trying to build up a practice in Edinburgh. This was evidently not the case, and, indeed, it is difficult to accept, especially given his father's position, that the express requirement that the new Civilist reside and teach would have been inserted in the minutes if Fraser was aiming to be a sinecurist. Moreover, as Fraser was very newly admitted as an advocate, he would have had no time to build up any practice in Edinburgh, and may have been willing to return home to Old Aberdeen to reside and teach, instead of waiting for clients in Edinburgh. In this context, it is worth noting that his special graduation as an MA in November 1722 hints that he was more interested in an academic than a forensic career. A further attraction would have been that his father was building up and improving the small estate of Powis which was opposite the College.[100] There was much to draw the new Civilist to his post, and, as we have seen, he resided and had an active career in the College.

The next question is whether he ever taught or was intended to teach. Although we have no details of his studies in law, his admission as an advocate by examination on Civil law suggests he was at least nominally qualified to teach the subject. In 1787 it was alleged that though Fraser "did constantly for near twenty years reside, he never found a class". The source for this is to some extent suspect, however, since the claim was made in the context of an argument against the likely success of a law teacher in a united university.[101]

96 Ibid fo 22v.

97 Ibid fo 45; Aberdeen University Library, King's College Minutes 1733–1754, MS K 43 46 (1 November 1736).

98 Aberdeen University Library, King's College Minutes 1722–1733, MS K 42 fo 88v.

99 Aberdeen University Library, King's College Minutes 1733–1754, MS K 43 50 (31 December 1736).

100 See G G Simpson, "The Medieval Topography of Old Aberdeen", in J S Smith (ed), *Old Aberdeen: Bishops, Burghers and Buildings* (1991) 1 at 10; Burnett (ed), *Powis Papers, 1507–1894* (1951) 53–72.

101 *An Estimate of the Expediency, Justice, and Legality, of the Plan Proposed by the Marischal College of Aberdeen, for an Union of it with the University and King's College of Aberdeen*

There is some further indirect and equivocal evidence concerning the issue of whether or not he ever taught. A major quarrel broke out in the College over the election of Fraser's successor.[102] One candidate was James Thomson of Portlethen, a member of the Society of Advocates in Aberdeen, who had close connections with both the universities of Aberdeen, serving as Dean of Faculty of Marischal College from 1728 to 1745, and as one of the procurators of the four nations at King's in 1743.[103] The other candidate was Sir William Forbes of Pitsligo. Though a local man, he was a member of the Faculty of Advocates in Edinburgh.[104] At the meeting on 24 February to deal with the election of a Civilist, the Principal read the resolutions of the University about the absence of Garden of Troup and the act requiring whoever be appointed Civilist to reside and teach, and emphasised the need to elect someone who would carry out these duties. When the meeting went to a vote, he voted for Thomson, who had promised by letter to reside and teach.[105] The election was disputed and the matter went to the Court of Session, which finally declared on 15 July 1741 that Forbes had been elected.[106] Forbes was duly admitted as Civilist on 27 August 1741; the Principal registered a protest, one of the grounds of which was that Forbes would not reside and teach Justinian's *Institutes* as the Foundation required.[107] The split in the College over this election was evidently related to family interests and the struggles between Ilay's men and the Squadrone (perhaps the adherents of the latter now joined by some who were supporters of Argyll, no longer united with his brother).[108] It is nonetheless tempting to give some value to the Principal's stress that there should be a Civilist who not only would reside (as Fraser had) but would also teach the *Institutes.* Should this evidence be taken as meaning that, as least some of the time, Fraser taught? Or was the Principal mentioning teaching purely because his argument was grounded on the Foundation which required the Civilist to teach as well as to reside? It is impossible to be certain, though the Principal's argument at

(1787), found quoted in Humphries, *William Ogilvie and the Projected Union of the Colleges 1786–1787* (1940) (henceforth Humphries, *William* Ogilvie) 23, and in *Papers Relating to the Proposal for Uniting the King's and Marischal Colleges* 80.

102 See Emerson, *Professors, Patronage and Politics* (n 21) 63–65.

103 *History of the Society of Advocates in Aberdeen* (n 59) 355; Aberdeen University Library, King's College Minutes 1733–1754, MS K 43 186.

104 Grant, *Faculty of Advocates* (n 37) 74.

105 Aberdeen University Library, King's College Minutes 1733–1754, MS K 43 109, 126.

106 See Fettercairn MSS, on deposit in the National Library of Scotland, Acc 4796/213, for papers relating to this litigation, including the extract decree.

107 Aberdeen University Library, King's College Minutes 1733–1754, MS K 43 138.

108 Emerson, *Professors, Patronage and Politics* (n 21) 64–65.

least suggests that to have a Civilist who taught would have been generally regarded as desirable, while the claim in 1787 that Fraser never found a class might suggest that he had sought to have one.

Fraser's immediate successor, Sir William Forbes, did not neglect the College, and is noted sufficiently often in the sederunt of the minutes of the College's meetings as to suggest he resided, at least in 1742–1743.[109] He was twice appointed one of the visitors to inspect the accounts of the Master of Mortifications, and once those of the Procurator.[110] In the litigation over who was rightly appointed his successor, it was alleged in one party's pleadings that "we have never yet had an Instance of a non Resident Member except Mr Garden of Troup". It was further noted that the Act of 24 April 1724 requiring the Civilist to reside and teach was read at Forbes' election, and claimed "that it was the Opinion of the Society yea the unanimous opinion (for there was no opposition to it) that the Article of Residence ought not to be dispensed with".[111] These remarks tend to confirm that Forbes did reside, or spend enough time in Aberdeen for it to be represented that he did. By refusing to dispense only with the requirement of residence the second implies that he did not teach, since residence and teaching had earlier been linked together. Forbes died on 12 May 1743.[112]

After the death of Sir William Forbes, there were two candidates for the Civilist's office in King's College. One was Charles Hamilton Gordon, a member of the Faculty of Advocates in Edinburgh;[113] the other was James Catanach, a member of the Society of Advocates in Aberdeen.[114] Catanach had been awarded the degree of LLD by Marischal College on 31 May 1743, within three weeks of Forbes' death, the minute recording that he was examined by David Verner, and was "found truly well qualifyed in a Strict Examination".[115] At the meeting to elect a successor to Sir William Forbes, there was a dispute over the choice of the procurators of the four

109 Aberdeen University Library, King's College Minutes 1733–1754, MS K 43 142, 160, 167, 168, 169, 177, 178, 179 (15 October 1741, 7 September 1742, 18 September 1742, 14 October 1742, 18 October 1742, 3 November 1742, 16 March 1743, 15 April 1743, 2 May 1743).

110 Ibid 144, 168 (15 October 1741, 18 October 1742).

111 University of Aberdeen, MS K 214, Nineteen Papers Catanach 1743–45, Memoriall from Mr Alexander Rait, 3.

112 Aberdeen University Library, King's College Minutes 1733–1754, MS K 43 180 (1 June 1743); Grant, *Faculty of Advocates* (n 37) 74.

113 Grant, *Faculty of Advocates* (n 37) 83.

114 Henderson, *History of the Society of Advocates in Aberdeen* (n 59) 114.

115 Aberdeen University Library, Marischal College Minutes 1729–1790, MS M 41 fo 110v. For the text of his diploma, see P J Anderson, "The Catanach Case" (1888) 1 *Scottish Notes and Queries* 158.

nations and who was validly elected as such. Depending on who was properly elected, either Catanach or Gordon was in turn elected as Civilist. Both claimed that they had been, and both produced presentations to the office to Robert Paterson, the Commissary, who, as Vice-Chancellor *ex officio*, was empowered to admit the Civilist to his chair.[116] A law suit was necessary to resolve the issue, and Paterson raised an action of multiplepoinding before the Court of Session.[117]

At bottom, the dispute was between two family factions and had political overtones,[118] but once the issue of the procurators of the four nations had dropped away, the focus of the litigation was the meaning of a provision of the Foundation of King's College that required the Civilist to hold a doctorate in Civil Law or, failing that, to have achieved the degree of licentiate in Civil Law *cum rigore examinis* and, within a year of appointment, to be promoted to the doctorate. This provision obviously derived from the medieval practice of awarding the licentiate on the basis of an investigation into the studies of the graduand followed by what was termed a "private" or "rigorous" examination by disputation on a *quaestio*, with the doctorate subsequently awarded after a largely ceremonial "public" examination.[119] Gordon and his supporters claimed that his examinations for admission as an advocate – a private trial in Latin on Civil Law, public defence of printed theses in Latin on Civil Law, and a Latin speech on Civil Law before the Lords of Session – amounted at least to the equivalent of a licentiate in Civil Law awarded *cum rigore examinis*. Catanach argued that he possessed the degree of LLD required by the Foundation and therefore was properly elected Civilist, while Gordon was not. Moreover, should his degree be defective, or should this requirement be in disuse, he had gained the majority of the votes.[120] The obvious argument against Gordon's case was that to be an advocate was not to possess the university degree the Foundation required: no matter how "rigorous" the examination for admission was, it could not create an advocate a licentiate in laws, for only a university degree could give this status. If this point may seem well taken, the advocates in fact had deliberately modelled their examinations on those of a university,[121]

116 Aberdeen University Library, King's College Minutes 1733–1754, MS K 43 181–203.

117 See *Catanach v Gordon* (1745) 1 Pat App 401 at 402.

118 Emerson, *Professors, Patronage and Politics* (n 21) 66.

119 See J Verger, "Teachers", in H de Ridder-Symoens (ed), A *History of the University in Europe. Volume 1: Universities in the Middle Ages* (1992) 144, 145–146.

120 The arguments are neatly summed up in *Catanach v Hamilton-Gordon* (1744) Mor 12253.

121 See Cairns, "Formation of the Scottish Legal Mind" (n 9) at 255–263.

while in 1714 King's College had awarded the degree of LLD to Alexander Cuming (who went on to an even higher rank as Chief of the Cherokees in 1730) on the grounds that he had passed his private trial in Civil Law for admission as an advocate.[122] The substance of the examination of Gordon had undergone was indeed rigorous. The only arguments against Catanach's qualification were either that Marischal College had not the authority to grant degrees in law or that, if it did have such authority, the degree had not been properly conferred on him.

There can be no doubt that the degree of LLD was conferred on Catanach with the purpose of qualifying him for the office of Civilist: this is confirmed by the date, by the phrasing of the minute of Marischal College to echo the terms of the requirement of a "rigorous" examination found in the Foundation of King's, and by the admission by Catanach's supporters of the truth of the accusation to this effect made by the Principal of King's College at the election meeting.[123] Catanach was examined for the degree upon "the principles of Right and wrong (the foundations of all Law) and also on the various kinds of Tutors and Curators the actiones Tutelae directae et contrariae the satsidationes Tutorum etc. De acquisitione Dominii De obligationibus, and many other Questions in the Civill Law". It was claimed that this was substantially the same as the private examinations of advocates and that Catanach had answered the questions satisfactorily in Latin.[124] The award of law degrees in Scotland in the eighteenth century has not been systematically studied. It is often assumed that they were only "honorary", but to view them as such is clearly anachronistic.[125] There are other instances of individuals being examined for the award of the degree of LLD;[126] further study would be necessary to be definitive on the point, but Verner's examination of Catanach is by no means inconsistent with practice in examining for this degree in other Scottish universities. We need not assume the examination was entirely nugatory, although it may not have been so rigorous as that required for admission as an advocate.

122 Aberdeen University Library, King's College Minutes 1709–14, MS K 40 fo 26v (2 January 1714); Grant, *Faculty of Advocates* (n 37) 47.

123 Aberdeen University Library, Minutes of King's College 1733–1754, MS K 43 194; Aberdeen University Library, MS K 214, Nineteen Papers Catanach 1743–45, Memoriall from Mr Alexander Rait 5.

124 Aberdeen University Library, MS K 214, Nineteen Papers Catanach 1743–45, Memoriall ffrom Some of the Members of the Marischall College 5.

125 See D B Johnston, "All Honourable Men? The Award of Irregular Degrees in King's College and Marischal College in the Eighteenth Century", in J J Carter and J H Pittock (eds), *Aberdeen and the Enlightenment: Proceedings of a Conference held at the University of Aberdeen* (1987) 136.

126 See, e.g., Cairns, "Origins of the Glasgow Law School" (n 58) 151 at 176.

Gordon was successful in the Court of Session; the House of Lords reversed this decision and awarded the chair to Catanach.[127] The minutes show that Catanach was certainly useful to the College on a day-to-day basis. Whatever may have been Catanach's skills in law, he most certainly did not teach, as in the law suit that in turn arose in the 1760s over the disputed election of his successor, the position of Civilist could now confidently be claimed to be a "sinecure as to teaching".[128]

It was in the course of the litigation between Gordon and Catanach that, in order to support the alleged right of Marischal College to award degrees in law, the claim was made that David Verner of the College started to teach Civil Law in 1722 at the request of the lawyers in Aberdeen and on the authority of the Rector and Masters of Marischal College. The contrary, however, was also alleged in the same dispute. Thus Principal Chalmers of King's College said in 1743: "[T]here is no profession of Law in [Marischal] College."[129] Later Thomas Gordon wrote:

> To prelect in law might be the pretence, but could not seriously be the intention. Mr Vernor's time was fully occupied alreadie. His attendance on his Philosophy class for three hours a day, rendered it impossible that he could propose with success to take upon himself at the same time the instruction of Law students. Being an obliging worthy man, he gave his assistance in directing some young men of the College, who were designed for the Law, to proper books, in order to pick up the rudiments of the profession; but he never pretended that he was a regular Law Professor or that he ever educated a Law student.[130]

Gordon's purpose was also to deny that Marischal College was a university empowered to award degrees in law. The whole matter obviously requires fresh examination.

Verner studied at the University of Glasgow under the regent Gershom Carmichael, gaining the degree of MA in 1713.[131] Carmichael is noted for having played a prominent role in Scotland in the reorientation of ethics and moral philosophy around theories of natural law derived from Grotius and Pufendorf.[132] The specificity of the claim that Verner had studied Civil Law

127 *Catanach v Hamilton-Gordon* (1744) Mor 12253; *Catanach v Gordon* (1745) 1 Pat App 401.

128 Aberdeen University Library, MS K 216, Memorial for William Thorn Advocate in Aberdeen against Mr David Dalrymple Advocate 2.

129 Aberdeen University Library, King's College Minutes 1733–1754, MS K 43 194.

130 Aberdeen University Library, MS 3107/4/5/1 105.1 am indebted to Roger Emerson for this quotation and reference.

131 C Innes (ed), *Munimenta alme universitatis Glasguensis: Records of the University of Glasgow from its Foundation till 1727* (1854) vol iii, 48, 197.

132 See e.g., J Moore and M Silverthorne, "Gershom Carmichael and the Natural Jurisprudence Tradition in Eighteenth-Century Scotland", in I Hont and M Ignatieff (eds), *Wealth and*

for two years with Craig in Edinburgh and Civil law and Scots law for one year with Forbes in Glasgow – and could prove it with certificates – encourages belief in its truth.[133] It would follow that Thomas Gordon's allegation that Verner had never "passed the threshold of a Law school, nor had opened a law book but as matter of curiosity" is wrong.[134] It is possible to work out the probable sequence of Verner's studies. He would have spent 1713–1715 with Craig in Edinburgh. He presumably studied Justinian's *Institutes* in the first of these years and the *Digest* in the second. He would then have returned to Glasgow. The disruption caused by the Jacobite rebellion meant that Forbes did not open his class in Glasgow in the session 1715–1716 until 3 January 1716. He proposed to teach Scots law and Civil Law. He had three students and Verner presumably was one of them. (In 1716–17, Forbes appears not to have taught.)[135] The next year Verner was one of the men appointed to replace those purged from the Aberdeen universities, becoming one of the regents at Marischal College, an appointment he owed to his Glasgow connections and the Squadrone.[136]

The Commissary Clerk's Office in Aberdeen had been destroyed by fire on 31 October 1721. On 25 January 1722 the Commissary, Commissary Clerk, and various lawyers in Aberdeen met to remedy the destruction of the records both of the court and of the admission of procurators before it. They wrote various styles and forms of process into a book, which they declared to be as valid and sufficient a register as the lost register, and they approved all admissions of procurators before the Commissary Court where admissions were extant in the Sheriff Court books.[137] The coincidence of years means it is tempting to view these events as promoting a consideration of general issues involving the Society which prompted the request "of the Lawyers of Aberdeen" in 1722 that Verner should teach law. In this respect it is worth noting that nineteen men who were either an alumnus or an MA of either Marischal or King's College were admitted as advocates between

Virtue: The Shaping of Political Economy in the Scottish Enlightenment (1983) 73; J Moore and M Silverthorne, "Natural Sociability and Natural Rights in the Moral Philosophy of Gershom Carmichael", in V M Hope (ed), *Philosophers of the Scottish Enlightenment* (1984) 1.

133 Aberdeen University Library, MS K 214, Nineteen Papers Catanach 1743–45, Memoriall ffrom Some of the Members of the Marischall College 4.

134 Aberdeen University Library, MS 3107/4/5/1 104–105.

135 *Scots Courant*, 7/9 December 1715; Forbes to Stirling, 30 January 1717, Glasgow University Library, MS Gen 204/16. See Cairns, "Origins of the Glasgow Law School" (n 58) at 175.

136 Emerson, *Professors, Patronage and Politics* (n 21) 36.

137 Henderson, *History of the Society of Advocates in Aberdeen* (n 59) 54–55. This volume has recently come once more to light: M C Meston and M G Christie, "The jurisdiction of local Commissary Courts. An interim report" (1995) *Juridical Review* 377.

1680 and 1740. Of these, sixteen were alumni or graduates of Marischal College and only four of King's. One of the MAs of King's was an alumnus of Marischal (hence the discrepancy of the figures) who was awarded the degree fifteen years after his admission as an advocate – presumably for reasons other than the successful completion of a course of study.[138] Seven of these alumni of Marischal College were among the men meeting with the Commissary on 25 January 1722. One can well imagine that, in the absence of a Civilist teaching in King's College, these men would turn to their *alma mater* for assistance. It was the university favoured by the advocates, it was conveniently located in Aberdeen rather than Old Aberdeen, and it possessed a Faculty member who had acquired a modern education in law in the universities of Edinburgh and Glasgow.

The first clear evidence we have for Verner's class comes in 1727, in Chamberlayne's reference work *Magnae Britanniae Notitia*, which, in listing office holders in Scotland and describing the universities, noted of Marischal College: "There is also the Institutes of the Civil Law, taught by the said Mr. *David Vernor*, in the said University."[139] From that year onwards, *Magnae Britanniae Notitia* routinely recounts the same until after Verner's death in 1752, when in the 1755 edition it is stated: "There is also the Institutes of the Civil-Law taught by the said Mr. – in the said University."[140] There is an evident tendency for entries in this work to be routinely carried forward from edition to edition without appropriate revision, but these notices of Verner's class nonetheless show that he appears to have started to teach or to offer to teach Justinian's *Institutes*, if perhaps only some of the time, in the 1720s.

Corroborative evidence that he may actually have continued to teach over the next two decades is provided by the *Caledonian Mercury*, an Edinburgh-based newspaper, which carried the following advertisement in 1744: "That Mr *DAVID VERNER* Professor of CIVIL LAW and PHILOSOPHY in the University and Marischall College of Aberdeen, begins his colleges upon the *Imperial Institutes of the Civil Law*, upon Tuesday 13th of this instant

138 See Henderson, *History of the Society of Advocates in Aberdeen* (n 59) 418–427. One of the Marischal graduates appears to be an advocate when he graduates.

139 J Chamberlayne, *Magnae Britanniae Notitia* (1727), separately paginated list of Scottish offices 15. This is mentioned neither in the 1723 edition, where the list of offices dates from 1722, nor in the 1726 edition, where the list of offices is dated 1725. Since the updating of these lists was neither thorough nor comprehensive, it is unsafe to conclude from them that this means that Verner did not teach before 1727.

140 Chamberlayne, *Magnae Britanniae Notitia* (n 139), list of Scottish offices 27.

Month of November."[141] The weight to give to this is unclear, however, since the notice appeared one month before the Court of Session adhered on 4 December to an interlocutor originally given on 20 July 1744 in the law suit in which it was alleged and denied that he taught Civil Law.[142] The advertisement could have been intended to support one side in the litigation and influence the decision of the court. This law suit has been discussed elsewhere;[143] but it is necessary to examine some aspects of it here for the light it throws on the question of Verner's teaching.

This then returns us to the issue of whether Verner was actually teaching in the 1740s. One of the memorials produced in the dispute for the Masters of Marischal College alleged that Verner "has at present students under him". If Thomas Gordon was later to suggest that Verner "gave his assistance in directing some young men in the College, who were designed for the Law, to proper books", this specific allegation, which was a matter of easy proof or disproof, suggests something more, especially since it talked of Verner giving "prelections", that is, formal lectures.[144] Support for this comes from an unexpected source. The mid-1780s saw one of the periodic attempts to unite the two universities. The main opposition came from King's College. One argument raised in favour of the proposal was that it might help to create a successful law school. A memorial from King's College opposing the union remarked that there was already a professorship of law in King's College and added that

> for a century past, none in that office have found the smallest encouragement for opening a class. An attempt at it was made near forty years ago at Aberdeen, by a person unquestionably well qualified, but without a shadow of success.[145]

Putting aside the assessment of Verner's success, this may refer to his attempting to teach in the 1740s.

In sum, the evidence suggests that from 1722 onwards Verner gave an elementary course of lectures on Civil (that is Roman) Law based on Justinian's *Institutes*. There is no evidence of the standard achieved in the course, although it was claimed in 1743 that Verner hoped "to give a good

141 *Caledonian Mercury*, 6 November 1744.

142 *Catanach v Hamilton-Gordon* (1744) Mor 12253.

143 Emerson, *Professors, Patronage and Politics* (n 21) 65–69; P J Anderson, "The advocates in Aberdeen: the Catanach case" (1888) 1 *Scottish Notes and Queries* 129.

144 Aberdeen University Library, MS K 214, Nineteen Papers Catanach 1743–45, Memoriall ffrom Some of the Members of the Marischall College 4; Aberdeen University Library, MS 3107/4/5/1 105.

145 *Papers Relating to the Proposal for Uniting the King's and the Marischal Colleges* (n 20) 12.

account" of his present students, and "before the end of the session to make some of them able to undergo even Mr Gordon's examination, if it be not too rigorous".[146] That is, the students would have achieved the level necessary for success in the examinations for admission as an advocate. Verner's education in Edinburgh and Glasgow made him well able to do this. Whereas we know that in his classes on ethics and moral philosophy Verner taught the works of Shaftesbury and Hutcheson and lectured on natural jurisprudence,[147] there is no indication of what he taught in Civil Law, although it is likely that, as was the general contemporary practice in Scotland, he taught from one of the modern Dutch compends rather than from the actual text of the *Institutes*.[148] He would have used the text as the basis of a commentary and exposition. While the description of his course in the *Caledonian Mercury* is in English, it is fair to assume that he would have taught Civil Law in Latin, as was still the universal practice in Scotland until around 1750.[149] There is no evidence of what materials he used to construct these lectures, though he personally had a large and important private library of books,[150] while at this time Marischal College also had a collection of books on law, mainly on Civil law, but it is difficult, however, to deduce from them anything about Verner's teaching.[151]

The memorial of the Masters of Marischal College admitted that from 1722 Verner continued to teach only "as he has got encouragement".[152] This must mean that he did not teach every year, but only when there was sufficient demand. If the course was not taught every year, it must have been given relatively frequently, should there have been any truth in the claim in 1743 that Verner was spontaneously awarded the degree of LLD around 1739 by the Rector and faculty of Marischal College because of "these Services done the College by these prelections".[153] If correct, this

146 Aberdeen University Library, MS 214, Nineteen Papers Catanach 1743–45, Memoriall ffrom Some of the Members of the Marischall College 4.

147 Wood, *Aberdeen Enlightenment* (n 24) 39–40.

148 See Cairns, "John Spotswood, Professor of Law" (n 17) 145.

149 Cairns, "Rhetoric, language, and Roman law: legal education and improvement in eighteenth-century Scotland" (1991) 9 *Law and History Review* 31 at 39–46.

150 *Aberdeen Journal*, 11 February 1752, calls for the return to Gilbert Gerard, Advocate in Aberdeen, of any books loaned out by Verner; *Aberdeen Journal*, 20 May 1752 advertises the sale of his library. No catalogue has survived, however.

151 Aberdeen University Library, Catalogus Librorum Bibliothecae Academiae Mariscallanae Aberdonensis An: Dom: 1726, MS M 72 [23]–[25]. (There are isolated law books elsewhere in the catalogue.)

152 Aberdeen University Library, MS 214, Nineteen Papers Catanach 1743–45, Memoriall ffrom Some of the Members of the Marischall College 4.

153 Ibid.

suggests that we should not give too much weight to the claim made in the mid-1780s by opponents of proposals to unite the colleges that, although Verner's "class actually opened at Aberdeen" at some time in the period from the mid-1720s onwards, it "had no success".[154]

The next question to consider is that of who actually attended. As with the classes of John Gordon, the Jacobite Civilist, there is no evidence. That Verner started these classes in 1722 on the suggestion of members of the Society of Advocates indicates that some of them thought it useful for their apprentices or those who intended to become apprentices to attend classes on Civil law. How many chose to do so is unknown. The suspicion must be that very few ever did, since it was not a requirement for admission to the Society. In the disputed election of the Civilist in 1743 it appears to have been assumed that advocates in Aberdeen, in contrast with members of the Faculty of Advocates in Edinburgh, would normally have no knowledge of Civil Law.[155] Catanach, for example, had certainly not attended any lectures in Civil Law: his legal training was gained as an apprentice to George Keith.[156] Admissions to the Society of Advocates were, however, still too low to sustain a yearly class in Civil Law. Some other students may have taken Verner's occasional class as part of a polite education. Wood has shown the extent to which several prominent figures in Marischal College believed in grounding the study of natural law, politics, and literature in history. There was an emphasis on the importance of ancient history and the classics.[157] Verner's course on Civil Law would have easily fitted into such a scheme of education. No doubt some men intending to pursue legal study at greater depth, whether in Edinburgh or abroad, prior to examination for admission to the Faculty of Advocates, also might have sought an elementary course of Civil Law as a useful preparation. Furthermore, the course may have been of interest to theological students preparing for the ministry.

We can thus infer that, between 1722 and 1750, when there was sufficient demand, Verner would teach an elementary course on Roman law to a probably small and rather diverse group of students. John Spotswood reckoned to complete an elementary course on the *Institutes* in seventy-five

154 *Estimate of the Expediency, Justice, and Legality, of the Plan Proposed by the Marischal College*, found quoted in Humphries, *William Ogilvie* (n 101) 23, and in *Papers Relating to the Proposal for Uniting the King's and the Marischal Colleges* (n 20) 80.

155 Aberdeen University Library, King's College Minutes 1733–1754, MS K 43198.

156 His education in law is described in Aberdeen University Library, MS 214, Nineteen Papers Catanach 1743–45, Memoriall ffrom Some of the Members of the Marischall College 5.

157 Wood, *Aberdeen Enlightenment* (n 24) 33–60.

days.[158] We do not know how much time Verner devoted to his class on Civil Law but, given his regular teaching commitments, it is difficult to imagine he was willing to teach it for more than three hours a week, but this is pure conjecture.

Verner died late in January 1752.[159] After a gap of several years Marischal College continued to appoint Professors of Law.[160] None of them taught law, however, and their titular appointments were to allow them to serve as promoters for degrees in law. They lacked Verner's qualifications in law.[161] Thus in Marischal College, as already in King's College, all attempts to teach Civil Law came to an end. Verner may have managed to sustain a class, but it is evident that to do so was difficult and that the numbers in Aberdeen interested in attending were few.

C. CONCLUSIONS

In his protest of 1741 over the admission as Civilist of Sir William Forbes, the Principal of King's College commented on the chair of Civil Law:

> That office being appointed also for the instruction of the children and relations of those who live in the towns and adjacent countrie in the knowledge of the laws, without puting them to the trouble and expence of sending them to a greater distance, and it being Nottour that the professor of law at Glasguo doth serve for that good purpose in the countrie thereabout, it may be presumed that if the Civilist in this College should reside and apply himself to serve these ends of that office, it would no less subservient to the good of this corner as well as for the honour of the university.[162]

158 Cairns, "John Spotswood, Professor of Law" (n 17) 145.

159 *Aberdeen Journal*, 28 January 1752.

160 Aberdeen University Library, Marischal College Minutes 1729–1790, MS M 41 fos 67r (Francis Skene, 13 November 1766), 77v (James Beattie, 2 April 1776).

161 After Catanach's death, there was another bitter dispute over the succession to the chair. One candidate was William Thom, advocate in Aberdeen (who had been Catanach's apprentice), who had conferred upon him by Marischal College the degrees of MA and LLB the day before the election of the new Civilist. It is unclear why it should have been the degree of Bachelor rather than Doctor of Laws that was conferred on him. It may be that Marischal College had no one currently appointed Professor of Law and therefore felt unable to award the higher degree: the College had to appoint the Principal as "Decanus" and "Promoter pro *hac vice*" for the conferment of the degree. On the other hand, it may have been because the award was based on the presentation of a certificate testifying to his application "to the study of the Civil and Municipal Laws . . . and of his Progress in them, from Mr George Turner, Advocate in Aberdeen, a Gentleman of acknowledged abilities and Integrity", rather than on any kind of examination, rigorous or otherwise. See *History of the Society of Advocates in Aberdeen* 350–351; Aberdeen University Library, Marischal College Minutes 1729–1790, MS M 41 fo 61r (26 November 1760).

162 Aberdeen University Library, King's College Minutes 1734–1754, MS K 43 138.

It is difficult to be other than somewhat sceptical about this. Before 1761, all the evidence tends to suggest that the classes in law in Glasgow were very small: never greater than five, according to one commentator.[163] Moreover, even if those who took these classes were from the neighbourhood (which is by no means certain), it seems likely that they often were intending members of the Faculty of Advocates in Edinburgh rather than future members of the Faculty of Procurators of Glasgow. In Aberdeen the number of apprentices of members of the Society of Advocates at any given time in this period was minuscule, and the reality seems to have been that, as with the apprentices of procurators in Glasgow, they really had no interest in classes in Civil Law.

Those men who were intending to practise as notaries or simple writers were even less likely to be interested in such classes. Given that those seeking for admission to the Society of Advocates were examined on Scots law and the forms of process, there may have been a market for instruction in Scots law. No one seems to have considered supplying it, however, and, as the statistics for admission to the Society demonstrate, the numbers would still have been extremely low – probably too low to sustain such a class even if members of other groups of lawyers in Aberdeen might also have been interested.

On the other hand, classes on Civil Law could also be viewed as providing polite and useful knowledge for the educated gentleman. If in the Aberdeen universities the science of the human mind was the foundation of the human sciences, including legal theory, and if history was taken to be the foundation of politics and natural law,[164] it was clearly nonetheless difficult to maintain a class in Civil Law. Furthermore, it was only from the 1760s that John Millar in Glasgow was to show how a class on the *Institutes* could be made an introduction to the natural jurisprudence of the Scottish Enlightenment.[165] The market for relatively technical elementary classes on the *Institutes* before this must have been small in Aberdeen. It is difficult to avoid the conclusion that to try to teach Civil Law in Aberdeen between 1680 and 1750 was to try to teach the wrong subject in the wrong place.

Such success as Verner had therefore calls for an explanation, especially given the failure of his contemporary Fraser in King's College to attract any students. The explanation must lie in their respective abilities as teachers

163 Cairns, "Origins of the Glasgow Law School" (n 58) at 189–190.

164 See Wood, *Aberdeen Enlightenment* (n 17) 33–60.

165 K Haakonssen, "John Millar and the Science of a Legislator" (1985) 30 *Juridical Review* 41; J W Cairns, "'As Famous a School for Law as Edinburgh for Medicine': The Glasgow Law School, 1761–1801", in A Hook and R B Sher (eds), *The Glasgow Enlightenment* (1995) 133.

and in the fact that one was in Aberdeen and the other in Old Aberdeen. Verner was a teacher of reputation who could afford to give such classes because his main source of income was from his work as a regent. For even a small group of auditors from time to time it may have been worth preparing and delivering lectures. Aberdeen was where the Society of Advocates was based, and Marischal College was a more dynamic institution than King's College. Verner was the more attractive teacher in the better location. It is also obvious that, in these local circumstances, two classes on the *Institutes* one mile apart were not going to be viable. If Verner was successful, Fraser was almost necessarily compelled not to be. It is also difficult to believe that Fraser's immediate successor, Catanach, despite his "rigorous" examination, was qualified to teach Civil Law. According to one of the memorials in the litigation over his appointment: "He read with Care Domat's Civill Law According to the order of Nature, Wood's Institutions and many other such."[166] Wood's book was an elementary introduction to Civil Law in English, while Domat's was an analytical and rational reworking of Roman law, not of an antiquarian bent. One suspects that the reference was also to the English translation of Domat.[167] This does not encourage confidence in the depth of his knowledge of Civil Law, especially since the same source stressed his knowledge of Scots law, "The Principles of which are the same with, and many of its forms and Statutes borrowed from the Roman Law".[168] After Verner's death, Catanach would therefore be unlikely to capture the market that the former had been able to exploit.

It is therefore no surprise that with the death of Verner such instruction in Civil Law as there had been in Aberdeen came to an end. None of the subsequent professors of law in Marischal College was competent to teach the subject, while the Civilist's chair had definitively degenerated into a sinecure competed for between members of the Faculty of Advocates and local practitioners in complex contests involving difficult issues of patronage arising out of family and political disputes. Members of the Faculty of Advocates

166 Aberdeen University Library, MS K 214, Nineteen Papers Catanach 1743–45, Memoriall from Some of the Members of the Marischall College 5.

167 T Wood, *New Institute of the Imperial or Civil Law* (1704) and Domat, *Les lois civiles dans leur ordre naturel* (1689). See also the translation of Domat's work by W Strahan as *The Civil Law in its Natural Order* (1722; 2nd edn 1737). On Wood, see R B Robinson, "The Two *Institutes* of Thomas Wood: A Study in Eighteenth Century Legal Scholarship" (1991) 35 *AmJLegalHist* 432; on Domat, see, e.g., S Goyard-Fabre, "Montesquieu entre Domat et Portalis" (1990) 35 McGillLJ 715.

168 Aberdeen University Library, MS K 214, Nineteen Papers Catanach 1743–45, Memoriall from Some of the Members of the Marischall College 5.

generally did not want to reside in Aberdeen, while local practitioners could be useful to the College but were usually neither willing nor qualified to teach Civil Law. Even if qualified the latter would want to use their time to pursue their practice rather than devote the effort to writing lectures for an inevitably small audience. It is therefore no surprise that while the Union proposals of 1754–1755 provided that the Professor of Law was to be presented by the United College, they made no mention of classes on law.[169]

Outside Edinburgh success in teaching law was evidently very dependent on the possession of outstanding qualities as a teacher, in order either to attract students who would otherwise have studied in Edinburgh or to cause the local profession to realise that it was desirable for apprentices to take a course in law in a university. Success probably also required the professor to make his classes attractive as part of a general polite education. No one in Aberdeen between 1680 and 1750 could entirely fulfil either of these conditions. Not even such minor success as Verner had could cause the local legal profession to support his classes, even though they had encouraged him to give them. Prospective members of the Faculty of Advocates, who were the only sizable group of individuals interested in university classes in law, were simply not interested in legal study in Aberdeen. Members of the Faculty were also those probably best qualified to teach Civil Law in Scotland, but a chair at Aberdeen was of no interest to men of talent and ability among them except as a sinecure.

The location of Aberdeen therefore doomed it to failure as a potential site of a law school in the period with which we are here concerned. The local lawyers were not interested in formal instruction in law in a university, and certainly not instruction in Civil Law: even if they had been, they were too few to sustain a class. The elite Faculty of Advocates wanted to develop a law school in Edinburgh, and they had succeeded in doing so. Once they had done this, even the possibility of them patronising the Aberdeen chair for the education of their intrants would have vanished completely. After Verner's death, all teaching in law ceased at both universities, until very different circumstances revived it in the next century. The location of the only chair in law to survive in Scotland from the medieval period accordingly reduced it to a sinecure when legal education was fast developing elsewhere. The situation of Aberdeen prevented the discipline of law from succeeding as a subject taught in the university, despite the intense interest of the Scottish Enlightenment in natural jurisprudence.

169 *Papers Relating to the Proposal for Uniting the King's and Marischal Colleges* (n 20) 5, 6.

Fifteen years ago I had the good fortune to start my career as a university teacher in the Faculty of Law of the Queen's University of Belfast. Despite dreadful tragedies that occurred during my time there, notably the murder by terrorists of a respected colleague of ability and promise, I count the years I spent teaching law at Queen's among the happiest of my life. It was therefore with a feeling of honour that I received the invitation to contribute to this special commemorative issue of the journal in which appeared my first scholarly publication. It is some ten years since I left Queen's; it was there that I learned much of my trade, and I am still aware of being marked by my time there. I hope this study of the history of another university (itself in its quincentenary year) is an adequate indicator of my affection, esteem and gratitude. The failure of legal education in the Aberdeen universities between 1680 and 1750 points up the contemporary conspicuous success of Queen's as a law school.[170]

170 This paper is a much-revised part of a longer study presented under the title "Local Lawyers, Elite Lawyers, and Law Professors: The Legal Profession and the Universities in Aberdeen, 1700–1830" at the international conference on "The University in its Urban Setting" co-sponsored by the Aberdeen Quincentenary Project and *History of Universities* at Aberdeen, 2–5 July 1993. I revised this paper while a Visiting Professor at the University of Miami School of Law in the Spring of 1995. I am especially grateful to Ms Nora de la Garza of the Law Library there for her assistance. Given this paper was completed in the quincentenary year of the university of Aberdeen to commemorate the sesquicentenary of the Queen's University of Belfast, it is pleasing to note that the same year is also the sesquicentenary of the admission of Florida as a State of the Union. The Lindsay Bequest Fund of the Faculty of Law of the University of Edinburgh provided a small grant to help me pursue research in Aberdeen, where I had on some earlier occasions enjoyed the hospitality of John A Marr. I am grateful to Aberdeen University Library for permission to quote from the manuscripts and the archival material in its possession. Dr Iain Beavan of that Library's Department of Special Collections was helpful and kind beyond any justified expectation, answering quickly queries from across the Atlantic. Mrs Jo Currie and Mr David Weston of the Departments of Special Collections of the Libraries of the Universities of Edinburgh and Glasgow respectively also promptly dealt with queries from across the Atlantic, as did my colleague Professor Hector MacQueen, who also provided useful criticism. The latter was also supplied by Professors Steve Diamond and Steve Schnably of the University of Miami, Paul Wood of the University of Victoria, and Alan Watson of the University of Georgia. Above all I benefited considerably from the suggestions and criticism of Professor Roger L Emerson of the University of Western Ontario, who helped unstintingly.

2 Rhetoric, Language, and Roman Law: Legal Education and Improvement in Eighteenth-Century Scotland

Education in law in the Scottish universities has a continuous history only from the early eighteenth century. In 1707, the Regius Professorship of Public Law and the Law of Nature and Nations was founded in Edinburgh, to be followed in 1710 and 1722 by Professorships in Civil (Roman) and Scots Law respectively.[1] In the University of Glasgow, the Regius Professorship of Civil Law was established in late 1713 and first filled in 1714.[2] These developments were not entirely novel. Throughout the seventeenth century, there had been regular, if unsuccessful, attempts to create university chairs in Law.[3] While the background to the foundation of the university chairs requires further careful study, we may note that, by at least around 1690, it was thought desirable to introduce the teaching of both Civil and Scots law, though the notion of teaching both does go back at least as far as the *First Book of Discipline* of 1561.[4] After the visitation of the University of Edinburgh that resulted from the political and religious settlements of 1688–1689, it was proposed to establish a single professorship to teach both

1 A Grant, *The Story of the University of Edinburgh during its First Three Hundred Years*, 2 vols (1884) (henceforth Grant, *Story of the University of Edinburgh*) vol i, 232–233, 283–291.

2 J Coutts, *A History of the University of Glasgow from its Foundation in 1451 to 1909* (1909) (henceforth Coutts, *History of the University of* Glasgow) 193–194.

3 See Grant, *Story of the University of Edinburgh* (n 1) vol i, 283–284; J M Pinkerton (ed), *The Minute Book of the Faculty of Advocates, Volume 1, 1661–1712*, Stair Society vol 29 (1976) (henceforth Pinkerton, *Minute Book*) xix; R K Hannay, *The College of Justice: Essays on the Institution and Development of the Court of Session* (1933) 150, 156, 161–162; W C Dickinson, "The advocates' protest against the institution of a chair of law in the University of Edinburgh" (1926) 23 *Scottish Historical Review* 205.

4 J K Cameron (ed), *The First Book of Discipline* (1972) 140, 143, 144; Pinkerton, *Minute Book* (n 3) vol i, 65–66 (12 January 1684), 159–161 (24 December 1695) would suggest the Faculty of Advocates, at least initially, was mainly concerned with promotion of lectures in Civil Law. It is perhaps worth noting that Wyclif proposed the teaching of English law in Oxford and Cambridge: F W Maitland, *English Law and the Renaissance* (1901) 11.

Civil and Scots law.[5] This proposal in the late seventeenth century is in line with general developments throughout Europe.[6] Nothing, however, was done, probably because no person or body was willing to finance a chair.[7]

In the absence of legal education in the universities, members of the Bar started to teach law privately at the end of the seventeenth and the beginning of the eighteenth century. The first three known to have done so were Alexander Drummond in 1699, John Spottiswoode in 1702, and John Cuninghame (or Cunningham) in 1705.[8] They all taught both Civil and Scots law. Nothing is known of Drummond's teaching other than that he offered his services "to all persons who are desirous to be instructed in the knowledge of the Institutions and Pandects of the Civil Law, and the laws of this kingdom, or either of the two, or both", and that he claimed "by reason of a singular method . . . in teaching of the civil law . . . to perfite [sic] and accomplish any of a middle capacity, more in a years time, then [sic] others have been by being abroad and out of the country 3 years".[9] From surviving student notes (and, in Spottiswoode's case, his own records) we can tell that he and Cuninghame taught Scots law by dictating notes to students on

5 A Bower, *The History of the University of Edinburgh; Chiefly Compiled from Original Papers and Records, Never before Published*, 2 vols (1817) (henceforth Bower, *History of the University of Edinburgh*) vol i, 329–334.

6 C Chêne, *L'enseignement du droit français en pays de droit écrit* (1679–1793) (1982) 1–7.

7 But see the curious case of Alexander Cunningham who in 1698 was provided with a salary as Professor of Civil Law by Parliament (renewed in 1704): *Acts of the Parliaments of Scotland, 1124–1707* [with] Supplements, 11 vols in 12 and index (1814–1875), ed T Thomson and C Innes, vol x, 176 (Act 1698, c 37) and Appendix, 27–28; ibid vol xi, 203 (Act 1704, c 9). In 1698, the Town Council of Edinburgh granted Cunningham a licence to teach Civil Law in the city: W A Kelly, "The Library of Lord George Douglas (c 1667/8–1693?)", unpublished MA thesis, University of Strathclyde (1975) 122 (I am grateful to Mr Kelly for allowing me to read and cite his thesis.) On Cunningham, as well as Kelly, see R Feenstra, "Scottish–Dutch Legal Relations in the Seventeenth and Eighteenth Centuries", in T C Smout (ed), *Scotland and Europe 1200–1850* (1986) 128 at 134–136 (henceforth Feenstra, "Scottish–Dutch Legal Relations); and G C J J van den Bergh, *The Life and Work of Gerard Noodt (1647–1725): Dutch Legal Scholarship between Humanism and Enlightenment* (1988) 78–79.

8 For Drummond: D Irving, *Lives of the Scotish* [sic] *Writers*, 2 vols (1839) (henceforth Irving, *Lives of the Scotish Writers*) vol ii, 220–221 n 3; for Spottiswoode (or Spotswood): see National Library of Scotland, MS 2934 fo 129r and J W Cairns, "John Spotswood, Professor of Law: A Preliminary Sketch" (forthcoming) (henceforth Cairns, "John Spotswood"); for Cuninghame (or Cunningham), see *A Discourse by Mr, John Cuninghame Advocate, At the Beginning of his Lessons upon the Scots Law* (1705). In *Joannis Cuninghamii J Cti. oratio inauguralis recitata Edinburgi; cum primumjus civile docere coepit* (n d) 7, Cuninghame states that Drummond was the first, Spottiswoode the second, and himself the third to undertake the teaching of Civil Law in Scotland. There is evidence of other private teachers, though we have no information about them. There is no indication that Alexander Cunningham ever taught, despite the licence and salary, and it is surely significant that Cuninghame excluded him from his list of teachers of Civil Law.

9 See Irving, *Lives of the Scotish Writers* (n 8) vol ii, 220–221 n 3.

Sir George Mackenzie's *Institutions of the Law of Scotland.*[10] (Spottiswoode also gave classes on the style of writs and civil process.)[11] These classes were taught in English. There is no information on Spottiswoode's lectures on Roman law, other than that they were based on Böckelmann's compend of Justinian's *Institutes;*[12] but student notes survive from Cuninghame's classes, and he taught a course on the *Institutes* in Latin.[13]

Throughout the first half of the eighteenth century in Scotland, the practice of teaching Roman law in Latin and Scots law in English seems to have been maintained.[14] After 1750, however, there was a move away from teaching Civil Law in Latin at the University of Glasgow, for on 5 March 1768, the Faculty of Advocates and its Dean deplored Professor John Millar's practice of lecturing in English on Civil Law.[15] Millar, however,

10 See National Library of Scotland, MS 3412; MS 3413; Edinburgh University Library, MS Gen 1735; National Library of Scotland, MS 2934 fo 129r; G Mackenzie, *Institutions of the Law of Scotland*, 2nd edn (1688). On the editions of this work, see F S Ferguson, "A Bibliography of the Works of Sir George Mackenzie Lord Advocate Founder of the Advocates' Library" (1935–1938) 1 *Edinburgh Bibliographical Society Transactions* 1 (henceforth Ferguson, "A Bibliography of the Works of Sir George Mackenzie") at 30–34.

11 See National Library of Scotland, MS 2934 fo 129r–129v; J Spotiswood, *The Form of Process before the Lords of Council and Session . . . Written for the Use of the Students in Spotswood's College of Law* (1711); and *An Introduction to the Knowledge of the Stile of Writs . . . Written for Use of the Students in Spotiswood's Colledge of Law, and now Publish'd for the Common Good* (1708); see also J Spotiswood, *A Discourse Shewing the Necessary Qualifications of a Student of the Laws: And what is Propos'd in the Colleges of Law, History & Philology, Establish'd at Edinburgh. Deliver'd at the Commencement of the College of Law: VI. November MDCCIV* (1704) (henceforth Spotiswood, *Discourse*) 11.

12 See National Library of Scotland, MS 2934, fo 150v; J G Böckelmann, *Compendium Institutionum Justiniani sive elementa juris civilis* (1679 and many other editions).

13 National Library of Scotland, MSS 17807, 17808, 17809 (scattered through these are notes, parts in some confusion, taken by Andrew Fletcher, Lord Milton in 1709–1710); Adv MSS 80.6.11–12 are notes on the first and third books of the *Institutes* which comparison with Lord Milton's notes shows probably to have been from Cuninghame's class, though not catalogued as such, and certainly not identical to Milton's notes.

14 For lectures on Civil Law in Latin, see National Library of Scotland, Adv MSS. 81.8.1–2 and Edinburgh University Library, MSS 1855–1856 [lectures apparently delivered in Edinburgh in 1710–1711 in Latin on J Voet, *Compendium juris juxta seriem Pandectarum* (1682 and many other editions)]; for the lectures on Scots law being in English, see the discussion of lecture notes in Scots law in J W Cairns, "John Millar's lectures on Scots criminal law" (1988) 8 OJLS 364 (henceforth Cairns, "John Millar's lectures") at 383–391. The suggestion in O F Robinson, T D Fergus and W M Gordon, *An Introduction to European Legal History* (1985) 405 n 8 that both Civil Law and Scots law were taught in Latin in Glasgow until 1750 and Edinburgh until 1800 is mistaken.

15 National Library of Scotland, *FR* 2, Minutes of the Faculty of Advocates 1751–1783 255–256 (I am grateful for the permission of the Faculty of Advocates to examine and cite its records); see J W Cairns, "The Formation of the Scottish Legal Mind in the Eighteenth Century: Themes of Humanism and Enlightenment in the Admission of Advocates" in N MacCormick and P Birks (eds), *The Legal Mind: Essays for Tony Honoré* (1986) 253 (henceforth Cairns, "Formation of the Scottish Legal Mind") at 266.

was following and extending an innovation of his predecessor in the chair.[16] Thomas Reid, writing in the 1790s, obviously thought this change to teaching Civil Law in English was natural, and that what needed to be explained was why the practice of teaching it in Latin had lasted so late. His explanation was "want of competition", because there was only one professor teaching law in Glasgow.[17] This seems insufficient, because Scots law was presumably taught in English, and it seems fair to assume that it would have been easier for the professor to teach in English as well as more attractive to the students. Given the dependency, praised by Adam Smith,[18] of Scots professors on fees from students, it is possible, though far from certain, that once the class in Civil Law was taught in English in Glasgow, the Professor of Civil Law in Edinburgh might feel pressure to do likewise. There was, however, more at stake than attracting students. Instead, a new method of teaching, influenced by new emphases in rhetoric in eighteenth-century Scotland, along with a new aim in teaching Civil Law, led some professors to lecture on Civil Law in English, rather than the traditional Latin.

This article will be in four parts. In the first I shall argue that the development of rhetorical theory through the course of the eighteenth century put at issue both methods of instruction and the language most suitable for teaching. The second will be devoted to explaining how the new approach to rhetoric and communication favoured English as the language of instruction. The change from teaching Civil Law in Latin to teaching it in English will be described in the third section, which will also discuss the relationship of language to the content of courses in Civil Law, while the fourth will contain some conclusions.

A. THEORIES OF RHETORIC AND CHOICE OF LANGUAGE

Until the late 1750s, and certainly in the University of Edinburgh, the textbook used to teach Scots law was Sir George Mackenzie's *Institutions of*

16 See text below at nn 74–85.

17 J Sinclair (ed), *The Statistical Account of Scotland. Drawn up from the Communications of the Ministers of the Different Parishes*, 21 vols (1791–1799) (henceforth Sinclair, *Statistical Account*) vol xxi: Appendix, "Statistical Account of the University of Glasgow" (separately paginated) 40; reprinted in T Reid, *The Works of Thomas Reid, D.D. now fully collected with Selections from his unpublished Letters*, ed W Hamilton, 7th edn, 2 vols (continuously paginated) (1872) (henceforth Reid, *Works*) vol ii, 735–736. For the traditional ascription to Reid of this account of the University of Glasgow, see Reid, *Works* vol ii, 721 (note by Hamilton).

18 A Smith, *An Inquiry into the Nature and Causes of the Wealth of Nations*, R H Campbell, A S Skinner and W B Todd (eds), 2 vols (1976) vol ii, 759–761 (V.i.f.4–8).

the Law of Scotland, written in the vernacular.[19] Forbes, the first Regius Professor in Glasgow, wrote in English his own textbook on Scots law after initially using Mackenzie's *Institutions*.[20] Furthermore, there is no hint that Spottiswoode, who seems in so many ways to have established the pattern for legal education in eighteenth-century Scotland, ever considered teaching Scots law in Latin.[21] This might suggest that the decision to teach Scots law in English and Civil Law in Latin was a simple and unexamined one, relating to the materials used as the basis for classes. This would be wrong. At the start of the eighteenth century, Latin was the normal language of instruction in all subjects in the Scottish universities.[22] Scots advocates were familiar, moreover, with the practice in the Netherlands, where the modern law was taught in Latin.[23] In the University of Leiden, for example, Johannes Voet lectured in Latin to his class on *ius practicum* or *hodiernum*, though he used as his textbook Hugo Grotius' *Inleidinge tot de Hollandsche Rechtsgeleerdheid*, written in Dutch.[24] Though it is possible that the choice of the language for teaching may have been related to the languages in which were carried out the trials for admission as an advocate,[25] there were other,

19 See Cairns, "John Millar's lectures" (n 14) 382–388; Cairns, "Mackenzie's Institutions and Law Teaching in Eighteenth-Century Scotland", unpublished paper read to the Scottish Legal History Group, 13 October 1984, abstract in (1986) 7 JLH 86.

20 W Forbes, *The Institutes of The Law of Scotland*, 2 vols (1722, 1730) vol i, iii–iv.

21 Most of the surviving papers relating to his private "Colleges" (in the sense of lecture courses) are in National Library of Scotland, MSS 2934 and 2937; among various memoranda and notes he never discusses the point.

22 See C Shepherd, "University Life in the Seventeenth Century", in G Donaldson, *Four Centuries: Edinburgh University Life 1583–1983* (1983) 1 (henceforth Shepherd, "University Life") at 11.

23 Feenstra, "Scottish–Dutch Legal Relations" (n 7) replaces all previous studies.

24 See R Feenstra, "Die Leydener Juristische Fakultät im 17 und 18 Jahrhundert: Einige neuere Forschungsergebnisse", in L Rothman (ed), *Leipziger Beiträge zur Universitätgeschichte* (1987) vol i, 48; R Feenstra and C J D Waal, *Seventeenth-Century Leyden Law Professors and their Influence on the Development of the Civil Law: A Study of Bronchorst, Vinnius and Voet* (1975) 38.

25 At the start of the eighteenth century it was possible to be admitted to the Faculty of Advocates either by trial on Civil Law alone or by trial on Scots law alone: see Cairns, "Formation of the Scottish Legal Mind" (n 15) at 255–257. Advocates entered, with only a few exceptions, by trial on Civil Law: J S Shaw, *The Management of Scottish Society 1707–1764: Power, Nobles, Lawyers, Edinburgh Agents and English Influences* (1983) 27. While there is no doubt that the trials in Civil Law were conducted in Latin, there is no definite evidence that those on Scots law were conducted in English; but the wording of the Act of Sederunt of 25 June 1692 which governed the procedure would suggest that English was used: *The Acts of Sederunt of the Lords of Council and Session, from the 15th of January 1553, to the 11th of July 1790* (1790) 200; see also Pinkerton, *Minute Book* (n 3) vol i, 117 (23 July 1692). Though the argument is rather circular, it is worth pointing out that Spottiswoode organised his courses in a way reflecting the Act of Sederunt, and taught in English: see Spotiswood, *Discourse* (n 11) 11; and National Library of Scotland, MS 2934, fos 122r and 129r. See Cairns, "John Spotswood" (n 8).

deeper, reasons that underlay all these usages of English in connection with writing, examination, and teaching in Scots law: these were reasons derived from the study of rhetoric and eloquence that led to the use of the two different languages in teaching Scots law and Civil Law.

Sir George Mackenzie was the most erudite of the Restoration lawyers of Scotland. As Dean of the Faculty of Advocates, he pursued policies that emphasised educational matters, and which did much to define the role of an advocate and the character of the Bar.[26] One of his interests was the study of rhetoric. He published two collections of pleadings, one in English, the other in Latin, both of which he prefaced with essays on the eloquence necessary for practice at the Bar.[27] In the English essay of 1672, in his arguments on the benefits to the advocate of the study of rhetoric, he showed himself aware that there were important issues at stake in choice of language. He argued, for example, that Scots was a better language for oral argument in court than English.[28] Furthermore, he wrote that he "love[d] equally ill, to hear civil Law spoke to in the terms of a Stile-book, or accidental Latin, . . . as to hear the genuin words of our Municipal Law, forc'd to expresse the phrases of the Civil Law and Doctors".[29] The choice of language for teaching Scots and Civil Law was accordingly to be related to a sense of what was fit and suitable for communicating the concepts and ideas of the two different systems. It is difficult to know how widespread Mackenzie's ideas on this were, but it is worth noting that this essay appeared in a new edition in 1704 and was included in the first volume of his collected *Works* in 1716.[30]

For Mackenzie, "eloquence [was] that Art, by which the Orator at once convinces, and pleases his hearers".[31] This was a standard, indeed classic,

26 See J W Cairns, "Sir George Mackenzie, the Faculty of Advocates, and the Advocates' Library", in G Mackenzie, *Oratio inauguralis in aperienda jurisconsultorum bibliotheca*, J W Cairns and A Cain (eds) (1989) 18.

27 G Mackenzie, *Pleadings, In some remarkable Cases, Before the Supreme Courts of Scotland, Since the Year, 1661. To which, the Decisions are subjoyn'd* (1672) (henceforth Mackenzie, *Pleadings*); and *Idea eloquentiae forensis hodiernae: una cum actione forensi ex unaquaque juris parte* (1681).

28 Mackenzie, *Pleadings* (n 27) 17.

29 Ibid 16.

30 See *The Works of that Eminent and Learned Lawyer, Sir George Mackenzie of Rosehaugh, Advocate to King Charles II. and King James VII. With Many learned Treatises of His, never before printed*, 2 vols (1716, 1722) (henceforth Mackenzie, *Works*) vol i, 9–102 (Treatises on the Laws of Scotland). Mackenzie's *Pleadings* was also issued with a 1673 title page; but Ferguson, "A Bibliography of the Works of Sir George Mackenzie" (n 10) at 21 points out that this is the same edition as that with the 1672 title page. Mackenzie's *Idea eloquentiae* was published in an English translation by Robert Hepburn (1711), as well as being printed in *Works* (n 30) vol i, 103–138 (Treatises on the Laws of Scotland).

31 Mackenzie, *Pleadings* (n 27) 1.

view. Locke, for example, in 1690, condemned the study of rhetoric, stating that "all the Art of Rhetorick, besides Order and Clearness, all the artificial and figurative application of Words Eloquence hath invented, are for nothing else but to insinuate wrong *Ideas*, move the Passions, and thereby mislead the Judgment. . . . [I]n all Discourses that pretend to inform or instruct, [Oratory is] wholly to be avoided".[32] The aim of rhetoric was to persuade, whether this was viewed with favour, as by Mackenzie, or with hostility, as by Locke.

A major influence on Millar was Adam Smith, who, under the patronage of Lord Kames, had lectured privately on rhetoric in Edinburgh, probably over the years 1748 to 1751.[33] After appointment as Professor, first of Logic, then of Moral Philosophy, in the University of Glasgow, he continued to give lectures on rhetoric and *belles lettres*, from which one set of student notes survives.[34] W S Howell has convincingly argued that in these lectures Smith changed the focus of the study of rhetoric from persuasion to communication.[35] In contrast, for example, with the opinion of Locke, and indeed all other classical definitions of rhetoric, there is the view of another Scot, George Campbell, Principal of Marischall College, Aberdeen, who wrote that "[i]n speaking there is always some end proposed, or some effect which the speaker intends to produce in the hearer. The word *eloquence* in its greatest latitude denotes, 'That art or talent by which the discourse is adapted to its end.'"[36] Hugh Blair, the first Regius Professor of Rhetoric and Belles Lettres at the University of Edinburgh (1762–1784), in his lectures (first printed in 1783), after rejecting the notion that eloquence is a trick of speech, or "[t]he art of varnishing weak arguments plausibly", or pleasing speech, told his class:

32 J Locke, *An Essay Concerning Human Understanding*, ed P H Nidditch (repr with corrections 1979) 508.

33 D Stewart, *Account of the Life and Writings of Adam Smith, LLD*, ed I S Ross, in A Smith, *Essays on Philosophical Subjects*, ed W P D Wightman and J C Bryce (1980) 263 (henceforth Stewart, *Account of the life and writings of Adam Smith*) at 272; A Smith, *Lectures in Rhetoric and Belles Lettres*, ed J C Bryce (1983) (henceforth Smith, *Lectures in Rhetoric*) 7–8 (Bryce's introduction).

34 Smith, *Lectures in Rhetoric* (n 33) 9–23 (Bryce's introduction); R H Campbell and A S Skinner, *Adam Smith* (1982) (henceforth Campbell and Skinner, *Adam Smith*) 66–79.

35 W S Howell, *Eighteenth-Century British Logic and Rhetoric* (1971) 549 (henceforth Howell, *Eighteenth-Century British Logic*); see generally 536–576.

36 G Campbell, *The Philosophy of Rhetoric*, 2 vols, 2nd edn (1801) (henceforth Campbell, *Philosophy of Rhetoric*) vol i, 23; on Campbell, see Howell, *Eighteenth-Century British Logic* (n 35) 577–612; H L Ulman, "Thought and Language in George Campbell's Philosophy of Rhetoric", in J J Carter and J H Pittock (eds), *Aberdeen and the Enlightenment: Proceedings of a conference held at the University of Aberdeen* (1987) 270.

> To be truly eloquent, is to speak to the purpose. For the best definition which, I think, can be given of Eloquence, is, the Art of Speaking in such a manner as to attain the end for which we speak. Whenever a man speaks or writes, he is supposed, as a rational being, to have some end in view; either to inform, or to amuse, or to persuade, or, in some way or other, to act upon his fellow-creatures. He who speaks, or writes, in such a manner as to adapt all his words most effectually to that end, is the most eloquent man. Whatever then the subject be, there is room for Eloquence; in history, or even in philosophy, as well as in orations. The definition which I have given of Eloquence, comprehends all the different kinds of it; whether calculated to instruct, to persuade, or to please.[37]

This redefinition of rhetoric and eloquence greatly broadened its scope. As Howell has argued, all forms of discourse and communication, oral and written, popular and learned, came under the aegis of the new rhetoric.[38] This would include university lectures, which would be comprehended in Blair's category of eloquence calculated to instruct. Though there is no direct evidence, this new approach to rhetoric must have caused thoughtful professors to ponder the question: What is the best way to lecture to a class? A subsidiary question would have been: What is the appropriate language in which to lecture?

B. NEW THEORIES OF RHETORIC AND THE LANGUAGE OF LECTURING

In the second half of the eighteenth century, there are indications of concern about the standard of knowledge of Latin among students. The Faculty of Advocates, who put considerable reliance on examination on Roman law in Latin for admission, expressed worry that there might be a decline in knowledge of Latin.[39] It was suggested that Professor Dick, Professor of Civil Law in the University of Edinburgh from 1755 to 1792, gave up teaching in Latin "because he found many of the students were little acquainted with the

37 H Blair, *Lectures on Rhetoric and Belles Lettres*, 2 vols (1783) (henceforth Blair, *Lectures on* Rhetoric) vol ii, 2 (lecture XXV); on Blair and his milieu, see the outstanding work of R Sher, *Church and University in the Scottish Enlightenment: The Moderate Literati of Edinburgh* (1985); Howell, *Eighteenth-Century British Logic* (n 35) 647–671. Blair had lectured in Edinburgh on rhetoric from 1759, with the title of Professor from 1760. Previously, John Stevenson, the Professor of Logic (1730–1775), had taught rhetoric: Grant, *Story of the University of Edinburgh* (n 1) vol i, 276–277, vol ii, 328–330, vol ii, 357–358; Howell, *Eighteenth-Century British Logic* (n 35) 542–543.

38 Howell, *Eighteenth-Century British Logic* (n 35) 441–442.

39 See *FR* 2, "Minutes" 414 (17 January 1777) and 432–433 (20 December 1777); Cairns, "Formation of the Scottish Legal Mind" (n 15) at 266–267.

Latin language".[40] In 1779, obviously alluding to Professor Millar in Glasgow, Hugo Arnot wrote: "Indeed, nothing appears to us more incongruous than to prelect in English upon the Roman law, a practice which in some places is adopted. Some instances of gross ignorance in the Latin tongue have lately occurred, which make it to be dreaded that this *key* to science is too much neglected."[41] That there was a decline in Latin scholarship in Scotland at this period has often been alleged;[42] improving the standard of Latin and Greek played a large role in debates in the early nineteenth century over the reform of the Scottish universities.[43] This is, however, scarcely conclusive. Ceasing to teach in Latin in the universities in itself would have promoted decline in Latin scholarship. It is necessary to look farther and investigate the methods and aims of teaching as they developed in the century, bearing in mind the development in theories of rhetoric.

At the start of the eighteenth century, the preferred method of teaching was to work through a textbook, summarising individual passages, on which notes were then dictated by the professor. Fortunately, Alexander Bayne, the first Professor of Scots law in the University of Edinburgh, carefully explained his method of teaching:

> The text I chuse is *Sir George Mackenzie's* Institutions. . . . 'Tis wrote very much in the Spirit and Manner of a Text Book, short and concise, and full of Matter. . . .
>
> [M]y first Business will be shortly to give you our Author's Meaning in other Words, and a little more copiously than it was proper for him to do, who meant only to deliver the Elements of our Law for others to comment upon. This being done, I retouch the same Matters in a more formal Discourse, and I add to them such other Matters as are coincident with the Subject of the Paragraph I'm upon, which are to be gathered partly from my Lord *Stair's* Institutions, partly from the later Decisions, and some of the other Authors upon our Law.
>
> These coincident Matters are suppletory to our Text, and I give you References to the most material of them in short Notes which I dictate.
>
> It will be your Care, *Gentlemen*, to take down these Notes as accurately as you can, and to endeavour to make them your own. . . .[44]

40 Found quoted in H Furber, *Henry Dundas First Viscount Melville 1742–1811: Political Manager of Scotland: Statesman, Administrator of British India* (1931) (henceforth Furber, *Henry Dundas*) 3.

41 H Arnot, *The History of Edinburgh* (1779) (henceforth Arnot, *History of Edinburgh*) 399.

42 Grant, *Story of the University of Edinburgh* (n 1) vol i, 268–269, 270–271.

43 G Davie, *The Democratic Intellect: Scotland and her Universities in the Nineteenth Century* (1961) 233–244.

44 A Bayne, "A Discourse on the Rise and Progress of the Law of Scotland, and the Method of Studying it" (1726), in T Hope, *Minor Practicks: or Treatise of the Scottish Law*, ed A Bayne (1726) 151 at 168–169 (henceforth Bayne, "Discourse"). The section on the rise and progress of the law of Scotland (ibid 161–168) is a revised and translated version of his inaugural lecture in Latin: Edinburgh University Library, MS Dc.3.57.

The students were advised to make fair copies of their notes, consulting the cited Acts of Parliament, to help in memorising the contents: memorising the text and notes was emphasised.[45] More advanced students, who were expected to attend the same lectures again, were advised to correct their notes, and consult the authorities to which they were referred.[46] Bayne gave a great deal of further advice on private study, stressing that "it is not enough in the Study [of law] to know and comprehend the Rules and Principles of it; but we must be at pains to fix them on the Memory".[47] These dictated notes were ultimately the basis of Bayne's published *Notes*.[48]

This was the common method of teaching at the start of the century.[49] Spottiswoode said in 1702 that he "begun to teach the Scotch law & dictated to five young gentlemen the forme of Process" and in 1703 he "begun to dictate [his] stylebook".[50] Professors also held "examinations", that is, quizzes for students on material already covered, to test their knowledge.[51] The stress on dictation of notes for memorisation was not unique to legal studies, but derived from the identification of intellectual ability with a retentive memory, and a view of education as the imparting of knowledge.[52]

It is this type of legal education which Lord Kames criticised in the preface to his *Elucidations* of 1777, when he wrote of studies in Roman law: "[N]othing is presented to the young gentlemen but naked facts. Nor are even those facts selected that are more immediately connected with modern law: all are stated indiscriminately . . . They load the weak mind with a heap of uninteresting facts, without giving any exercise to the judgment. Is it surprising, that the Roman law, so taught, is held to be a dry and fatiguing study?"[53] Kames is here especially concerned to argue on utilitarian grounds that only those parts of Roman law should be taught that relate to Scots law, and that the two should be constantly compared to allow the development

45 Bayne, "Discourse" (n 44) at 170–171.
46 Ibid at 172.
47 Ibid at 173. See generally ibid 173–186.
48 A Bayne, *Notes, for the Use of the Students of the Municipal Law in the University of Edinburgh: Being a Supplement to Sir George Mackenzie's Institutions* (1731) ii.
49 See Shepherd, "University Life" (n 22) at 11–12.
50 National Library of Scotland, MS 2934 fo 129r–129v.
51 See Bayne, Professor of Municipal Law, *To the Gentlemen who have attended his college of Prelections*, printed sheet dated 12 April 1725 (National Library of Scotland, pressmark S.302.b.1 no 53); Bayne, "Discourse" (n 44) 172; Arnot, *History of Edinburgh* (n 41) 399, noted that Dick "daily examine[d] his students upon the subject of his former lecture".
52 See Shepherd, "University Life" (n 22) at 13.
53 H Home, Lord Kames, *Elucidations Respecting the Common and Statute Law of Scotland* (1777) (henceforth Kames, *Elucidations*) viii–ix.

of the reasoning faculty; but his point is more general. He wrote elsewhere that "[l]aw. . . . [would become] then only a rational study, when it is traced historically, from its first rudiments among savages, through successive changes, to its highest improvements in a civilized society".[54] He complained that, on the contrary, "law, like geography, is taught as if it were a collection of facts merely: the memory is employed to the full, rarely the judgment".[55] The result is that "[o]ur law-students, trained to rely upon authority, seldom think of questioning what they read: they husband their reasoning faculty, as if it would rust by exercise".[56] The only professor Kames exempted from his criticism was Millar.[57]

Kames' views on specifically legal education should be read in the context of his general opinions on the subject. In 1761, he published *Introduction to the Art of Thinking*, in the preface of which he criticised the current state of education: "Upon the revival of arts and sciences in Europe, the learned languages, being the only inlets to knowledge, occupied almost the whole time that commonly can be spared for education. These languages are and will always be extremely ornamental; but though they have become less essential to education than formerly, yet the same plan continues without much variation."[58] In contrast with the teaching of the ancient languages, the capacity for abstract reasoning in his view was not cultivated sufficiently carefully, and students were introduced too early and too quickly to logic and metaphysics after their preliminary studies and without adequate preparation. His book aimed, through a discussion of human nature, to develop and improve the faculty of abstracting generals from particulars, and hence the ability to reason.[59] The underlying idea obviously was to encourage those working through the book to formulate general principles from rules Kames gave and situations he depicted. In his general attitudes to education, there is an emphasis on developing the reasoning ability and on lessening the significance of ancient languages. Kames' other treatise on education is devoted to the development of sensibility rather than of reasoning; but it is worth noting his view that, for formal, disciplined instruction to be worthwhile, the pupils must be of an age to understand why

54 H Home, Lord Kames, *Historical Law-Tracts*, 2nd edn (1761) [v].

55 Ibid [v]–vi.

56 Kames, *Elucidations* (n 53) vii–viii.

57 Ibid ix n.

58 H Home, Lord Kames, *Introduction to the Art of Thinking. Enlarged with additional Maxims and Illustrations*, 2nd edn (1764) [v].

59 Ibid [v]–vii.

it is necessary, for, "[t]o torment young creatures with Latin before that time, is likely to make them abhor it".[60] In the preface to his *Elucidations*, Kames considered the purpose of legal education. He stated that "[i]n other sciences reason begins to make a figure: Why should it be excluded from the science of law?"[61] In legal studies, however, "the exercise of reasoning [was not] promoted in any degree by public professors".[62] He connected improvement in legal education in this respect with improvement in the laws: "Were law taught as a rational science, its principles unfolded, and its connection with manners and politics, it would prove an enticing study to every person who has an appetite for knowledge. We might hope to see our lawyers soaring above their predecessors; and giving splendor to their country, by purifying and improving its laws."[63] Above all, as David Lieberman has pointed out, the modernisation of Scots law through the activities of lawyers and judges was of central importance to Kames.[64] Legal education that promoted reasoning and judgment rather than authority and memorisation was to bring this about.[65]

In the University of Glasgow, one key figure started to lecture to some of his classes in English, and in a more extemporary fashion. This was Frances Hutcheson, Professor of Moral Philosophy (1729–1746). He was specially noted for his skills in capturing his students' attention by teaching in a lively, interesting way.[66] Alexander Carlyle, for example, who attended Hutcheson's class, stated that Hutcheson "delivered his lectures without notes, walking backwards and forwards in the area of his room. As his elocution was good, and his voice and manner pleasing, he raised the attention of his hearers at

60 H Home, Lord Kames, *Loose Hints upon Education, Chiefly Concerning the Culture of the Heart* (1781) 239. A F Tytler, *Memoirs of the Life and Writings of Henry Home of Kames*, 2 vols (1807) (henceforth Tytler, *Memoirs*) vol i, 4 suggests Kames undervalued the classics.

61 Kames, *Elucidations* (n 53) x.

62 Ibid viii.

63 Ibid xiii.

64 D Lieberman, "The Legal Needs of a Commercial Society: The Jurisprudence of Lord Kames", in I Hont and M Ignatieff (eds), *Wealth and Virtue: The Shaping of Political Economy in the Scottish Enlightenment* (1983) 203; and *The Province of Legislation Determined: Legal Theory in Eighteenth-Century Britain* (1989) 144–175.

65 W R Scott, *Adam Smith as Student and Professor* (1937) 47 suggests that Tytler, *Memoirs* (n 60) vol i, 15–18 sets out a "manifesto" that gives Kames' views on legal education; Campbell and Skinner, *Adam Smith* (n 34) 29 quote part of the same passage as Kames' views. These seem to me to be clearly Tytler's views, though we may speculate that Kames might have endorsed them.

66 See W R Scott, *Francis Hutcheson: His Life, Teaching and Position in the History of Philosophy* (1900) 62–65; letter from James Wodrow to Earl of Buchan, [?] June 1808, Glasgow University Library, MSS 310/26, fos 167, 169, quoted in Campbell and Skinner, *Adam Smith* (n 34) 41.

all times".[67] Adam Smith, a pupil of Hutcheson, lectured in a similar fashion, and of him Millar stated that "[i]n delivering his lectures, he trusted almost entirely to extemporary elocution. His manner, though not graceful, was plain and unaffected; and, as he seemd to be always interested in the subject, he never failed to interest his hearers".[68] There is evidence to suggest that Smith preferred his students not to take verbatim notes in his class, probably expecting them to write them up later, because this involved greater intellectual engagement on their part.[69] A reminiscence of Smith's lectures, probably written in 1808, does suggest, however, that he subsequently gave up extemporary lecturing.[70] However this may be, it is obvious that the more spontaneous method of teaching was thought desirable. This attempt by Hutcheson and Smith to catch more firmly the attention of students was inevitably linked to rejecting Latin as the language of instruction, as it is difficult to imagine that extemporary lecturing would have been possible in Latin.

Millar's biographer Craig later wrote: "By degrees, it was discovered that every man will express his ideas with the greatest clearness and force in that language in which he is accustomed to think; and that an audience must lose much of the substance of a lecture, when part of the attention is necessarily occupied in estimating the exact import of the words."[71] George Jardine, Professor of Logic and Rhetoric, commented that "[n]othing, certainly, can more retard the progress of science, and particularly of elegant literature, than the practice of teaching in a foreign language".[72] While Kames commented succinctly that "[i]t is amusing to observe how well an argument passes in Latin, that would make but a shabby figure in English".[73] Latin might have served when students were expected to memorise dictated notes, but now the emphasis was on developing their reasoning powers, which teaching in Latin would retard.

67 J H Burton (ed), *The Autobiography of the Rev Dr Alexander Carlyle of Inveresk, 1722–1805*, new edn (1910) (henceforth Carlyle, *Autobiography*) 78.

68 Stewart, *Account of the life and writings of Adam Smith* (n 33) 275; letter of Wodrow to Buchan, quoted in Campbell and Skinner, *Adam Smith* (n 34) 41.

69 Smith, *Lectures in Rhetoric* (n 33) 3–4 (Bryce's introduction); Millar noted that Smith gave students permission to take notes in the lectures on Rhetoric: Stewart, *Account of the Life and Writings of Adam Smith* (n 33) 277.

70 Letter of Wodrow to Buchan, quoted in Campbell and Skinner, *Adam Smith* (n 34) 41.

71 J Craig, *Account of the Life and Writings of John Millar, Esq*, prefixed to J Millar, *The Origin of the Distinction of Ranks: Or, An Inquiry into the Circumstances which give rise to Influence and Authority, in the different Members of Society*, 4th edn (1806) (henceforth Craig, *Account of the Life and Writings of John Millar*) xii.

72 G Jardine, *Outlines of Philosophical Education, Illustrated by the Method of Teaching the Logic Class in the University of Glasgow*, 2nd edn (1825) 21.

73 H Home, Lord Kames, *Principles of Equity*, 3rd edn, 2 vols (1778) vol ii, 5n.

Given these views on the desirability of making teaching more spontaneous, and those on the general effectiveness of communicating in the native tongue of the teacher and students, the choice of English rather than Latin cannot simply be explained as reaction to a decline in the standard of Latin: It could be viewed as something desirable in itself.

C. FROM LATIN TO ENGLISH IN ROMAN LAW

In the University of Glasgow, Francis Hutcheson and then Adam Smith used English as the language of instruction in classes in moral philosophy. In the appendix generally attributed to Thomas Reid, published in 1799 in the *Statistical Account of Scotland*, the author wrote of law teaching in Glasgow:

> [T]he custom of lecturing in Latin was longer retained in this, than in other sciences. The predecessor of the present professor was the first who prelected on *Justinian's Institutes* in English; and this example has, for many years, been followed in the prelections upon the Pandects. It may be mentioned, as a strong instance of prepossession in favour of ancient usages, that, upon this last innovation, the Faculty of Advocates made application to the University of Glasgow, requesting "that the old practice of teaching the civil law in Latin, might be restored."[74]

Millar, who was professor until 1801, presumably provided this information, so it is likely to be reliable, especially since the account was probably written in 1794.[75] In the past, however, there has been some confusion over the sequence of events and identity of the original innovator.[76] Millar's

74 Sinclair, *Statistical Account* (n 17) 40.

75 See Reid, *Works* (n 17) vol ii, 721 (note by Hamilton).

76 Coutts, *History of the University of Glasgow* (n 2) 234, states that Hercules Lindesay is said to have started the practice, but that credit is often given to Millar as the initiator. Others state that Lindesay was the innovator, and either imply or state explicitly that the Faculty of Advocates complained about him: L Stephen, "John Millar", in S Lee (ed), *Dictionary of National Biography*, 22 vols and supplements (1908–1909) vol xiii, 401 at 402; D Murray, *Memories of the Old College of Glasgow: Some Chapters in the History of the University* (1927) 220; A D Gibb, "Law", in J BNeilson (ed), *Fortuna Domus: A Series of Lectures Delivered in the University of Glasgow in Commemoration of the Fifth Centenary of its Foundation* (1952) 162; J D Mackie, *The University of Glasgow 1451–1951: A Short History* (1954) 233. Grant, *Story of the University of Edinburgh* (n 1) vol ii, 365, simply states that Millar started lecturing in English in 1768. The confusion seems to stem from Craig's statement, in *Account of the Life and Writings of John Millar* xiii, that "so wedded were the older members of the profession to this practice [of lecturing in Latin], that, when Mr. Lindsay [sic] (Mr. Millar's immediate predecessor) began to deliver lectures on the Institutes of Justinian, in English, the Faculty of Advocates made formal application to the University, requesting that the practice of teaching the Civil Law in Latin might be restored. Mr. Lindsay . . . refused to yield to this interference;

predecessor was Hercules Lindesay, who held the chair from 1750 to 1761.[77] It is to Lindesay that we must impute the original change in Glasgow, though we lack evidence as to why he made it. Millar's innovation that attracted the criticism of the Faculty of Advocates appears to have been to extend this practice to the course on the *Digest*.

According to Hugo Arnot, Dick, the Professor of Civil Law in Edinburgh, still lectured in Latin as late as 1779, the only professor in the university still to do so.[78] In 1826, Professor Irving reported that Dick started to lecture in English around 1786.[79] This is corroborated to some extent by the exclusion of Arnot's remark about Dick from the reissue of his work in 1788.[80] Talking of the 1760s, a student of Dick's reminisced in 1815: "The lectures and examinations of Professor Dick were in Latin and we of course spoke to each other in Latin when conversing on law. This practice our professor shortly after this period gave up."[81] Other than the statement already noted that Dick was influenced in this decision by declining standards of Latin among his students,[82] there is no evidence as to his reasons for making this change: He may simply have been following the trend or been influenced by the views of the period. He may even have been compelled by a desire to attract students, once the professor in Glasgow started to teach in English, in order to maintain his income. Walter Scott's description of Dick as having "never been fit for the situation" might suggest that drawing students had always been for him a problem.[83]

Irving also reported that his own immediate predecessor in the chair of civil law in Edinburgh, John Wilde, who held the chair from 1792 to 1800, lectured in English.[84] This is inaccurate. Wilde taught his class on

and Mr. Millar, from the moment he was appointed to the Chair adopted the English language in all the courses of lectures which he delivered". Relying on, but misrepresenting the statement in Sinclair, *Statistical Account* (n 17) 40, Bower, *History of the University of Edinburgh* (n 5) vol ii, 119, wrote: "Professor Millar's predecessor was the first in the university of Glasgow who prelected in English on the Justinian code; and so tenacious are we of ancient usages, that we are informed, 'the Faculty of Advocates made application to the university, requesting that the old practice of teaching the civil law in Latin might be restored.'"

77 See Coutts, *History of the University of Glasgow* (n 2) 234.

78 Arnot, *History of Edinburgh* (n 41) 399.

79 *Report of the Royal Commission of Inquiry into the Universities of Scotland, Minutes of Evidence vol I. University of Edinburgh*, 1837 Parliamentary Papers 35, 179.

80 H Arnot, *The History of Edinburgh, From the Earliest Accounts to the Present Time* (1788) 398–399.

81 Found quoted in Furber, *Henry Dundas* (n 40) 3.

82 Ibid.

83 J G Lockhart, *Memoirs of the Life of Sir Walter Scott, Bart*, 7 vols (1837–1838) vol i, 58.

84 1837 Parliamentary Papers 35, 179.

the *Institutes* in English and that on the *Digest* in Latin.[85] Latin was thus the medium of instruction in Edinburgh in one class as late as 1800. It is instructive to compare Millar's and Wilde's methods of instruction and attitudes to Civil Law for insights into the reasons underlying their choice of language.

Craig devoted considerable attention to describing Millar's techniques of instruction: "He was not merely desirous to convey to his students just views and accurate information; but he was anxious to convey them in the manner most likely to seize the attention, and to produce habits of original thought and philosophical investigation; thus rendering Lectures, formerly considered as useful only to lawyers, the most important schools of general education."[86] He further stated:

> Mr. Millar never wrote his Lectures; but was accustomed to speak from notes, containing his arrangement, his chief topics, and some of his principal facts and illustrations. For the transitions from one part of his subject to another, the occasional allusions, the smaller embellishments, and the whole of the expression, he trusted to that extemporaneous eloquence, which seldom fails a speaker deeply interested in his subject. In some branches of science, where the utmost precision of language is requisite to avoid obscurity or error, such a mode of lecturing may be attended with much difficulty, and several disadvantages: But in Morals, in Jurisprudence, in Law, and in Politics, if the Professor make himself completely master of the different topics he is to illustrate, if he possess ideas clear and defined, with tolerable facility in expressing them, the little inelegancies into which he may occasionally be betrayed, the slight hesitation which he may not always escape, will be much more than compensated by the fulness of his illustrations, the energy of his manner, and that interest which is excited, both in the hearer and speaker, by extemporaneous eloquence.[87]

The more spontaneous style also permitted the greater and more immediate responsiveness to the reaction of auditors to the lectures for which Millar was especially noted.[88]

Millar delivered lectures in the usual two courses on Civil Law: one on the *Institutes*, the other on the *Digest*.[89] In both, he used the textbooks of

85 See J Wilde, *Preliminary Lecture to the Course of Lectures on the Institutions of Justinian. Together with an Introductory Discourse* (1794) v–vi (henceforth Wilde, *Preliminary Lectures*); National Library of Scotland, Adv MSS 81.8.3–21 are Wilde's own notes for his lectures: MSS 81.8.18–21 are on the *Digest* and are in Latin. Further fragments of Wilde's lectures may be found in Edinburgh University Library, MS La.II.475 (this consists of many bundles of loose papers, which are not foliated, so no precise references are possible).

86 Craig, *Account of the Life and Writings of John Millar* (n 71) xii.

87 Ibid xiv–xv.

88 Ibid xvi; F Jeffrey, "Review of *An Historical View of the English Government in Edinburgh*" (1803) 3 *Edinburgh Review* 155 (henceforth Jeffrey, review of *An Historical View*).

89 Craig, *Account of the Life and Writings of John Millar* (n 71) xix–xx.

Heineccius, standard ones of the day.[90] Millar's lectures on the *Institutes* were divided into two courses, in the first of which he worked carefully through most of Heineccius' relevant volume. The nature of the second course was quite different. One set of student notes of Millar's lectures reports him as describing it thus: "In our Second [course] we Shall Consider it [i.e. the Civil Law], and the Laws of other nations Comparatively, & Endeavour to Investigate the principles on which they jointly Depend, & So Reduce them to General Rules."[91] It could be described as a course of comparative historical jurisprudence. The broad, far-ranging nature of this course can be seen, not only from student notes,[92] but also from Craig's description of it.[93] It was evidently strongly influenced by Adam Smith's lectures on jurisprudence, both in its structure and underlying philosophy.[94] Craig described it as a "course of Lectures in which [Millar] treated of such general principles of Law as pervade the codes of all nations, and have their origin in those

90 See ibid xx for Millar's course on the *Institutes*; for his course on the *Digest*, see Glasgow University Library, MSS Murray 93–95 where study of the paragraph numbers cited shows that the text used is that of Heineccius. The two works are: J G Heineccius, *Elementa juris civilis secundum ordinem Institutionum* (1725) and *Elementa juris civilis secundum ordinem Pandectarum* (1727). There were many subsequent editions of these popular works, which were also used by Dick and Wilde in Edinburgh: Arnot, *History of Edinburgh* (n 41) 398; and the paragraph reference numbers and occasional remarks scattered through Wilde's lectures: Wilde, Preliminary Lecture, see especially the *Institutes* in National Library of Scotland, Adv MS 81.8.7, fos 66–68, and in Wilde's introductory lecture on the *Digest*, Adv MS 81.8.18 fo 8r where he said: "Necesse erit ut elementa juris civilis secundum ordinem Pandectarum a Heineccio conscripta huc cras vobiscum adportetis" ("It will be necessary that you should bring with you to this place tomorrow the Elements of the Civil Law in the Order of the Pandects written by Heineccius"). I hope to discuss elsewhere the significance of the choice of textbooks and the use made of them.

91 National Library of Scotland, MS 2743 fo 8r.

92 The following MSS contain both courses: National Library of Scotland, Adv MS 28.6.8; National Library of Scotland, MS 3930; Glasgow University Library, MSS Murray 78–82; Glasgow University Library, MSS Murray 96–98; Glasgow University Library MSS Gen 812–14; the following contain the second course only: National Library of Scotland, Adv MSS 20.4.7–8; Edinburgh University Library, MSS Dc 2.45–46; Glasgow University Library, MS Murray 332; Glasgow University Library, MS Hamilton 117; the following contain the first course only: Hamilton 117; the following contain the first course only: University Library, MS Murray 77 (note that not all of these are complete).

93 Craig, *Account of the Life and Writings of John Millar* (n 71) xxii–xli.

94 Cf ibid xxvi and xxx; and compare, e.g., National Library of Scotland, MS 3930, 299–301 ("Contents of the Second Course") with A Smith, *Lectures on Jurisprudence*, ed R L Meek, D D Raphael and P G Stein (1978) 399–401, where Smith discusses the basis of justice. It may be noted that the structure of Millar's lectures is closer to that of the later set of student notes of Smith's lectures. On Smith's legal philosophy, see now, above all, K Haakonssen, *The Science of a Legislator: The Natural Jurisprudence of David Hume and Adam Smith* (1981) 83–189. For a discussion of the influence of Smith on Millar, see K Haakonssen, "John Millar and the science of a legislator" (1985) *Juridical Review* 41 (henceforth Haakonssen, "John Millar"); Cairns, "John Millar's lectures" (n 14) passim.

sentiments of justice which are imprinted on the human heart".[95] In one set of student notes dated from 1778, the premises underlying Millar's second course on the *Institutes* are reported:

> It shall now be our cheif [*sic*] employment to enquire into the principles of the Roman Law, and to compare them with those of other countries. The aim of Students of Roman Law at this period, ought to be not merely to know what was the Roman System. That would be of little consequence of itself. . . . It has however a regard paid it as the system of Lawiers and Judges of great experience, and of a country which subsisted for such a long tract of time, and where we may consequently expect to find the rules of Jurisprudence of the most perfect kind. As however in the most perfect of all human Systems, there are numberless imperfections and Blemishes, it will certainly be proper in those who study the Roman Law at this period, to enquire into the justice or propriety of these regulations. This can only be done by comparing it with the Laws of other countries, and with our own natural feelings of right and wrong. This is certainly a very usefull exercise, as it enlarges our experience.[96]

Millar thus viewed detailed knowledge of Roman law in itself as of little significance. His aim in this course was rather to instruct students in the science of legislation. In this, as Haakonssen has admirably demonstrated, he was very much the heir of Smith.[97] Millar derived the rules of justice from the moral sentiments of humankind, whereby actions were approved on the grounds of their utility and propriety. When rules of justice were infringed, the person wronged felt resentment and the spectators felt indignation.[98] Law originated in the interference of spectators in a dispute between individuals to assist the person with whose motives they sympathised – not only disinterestedly to prevent an injustice, but also out of self-interest as they themselves might some day be in a similar situation.[99] Rules of law varied, however, from place to place and time to time, according to the nature, circumstances, and history of different societies. Furthermore, long-established customs were not easily given up, so that, if they were defective, this was not easily perceived.[100] Millar's jurisprudence was thus not only descriptive but provided a means of assessing existing systems of law and, in Craig's phrase, directed "[the enlightened

95 Craig, *Account of the Life and Writings of John Millar* (n 71) xx.

96 National Library of Scotland, Adv MS 20.4.7, fos 1r–2r.

97 Haakonssen, "John Millar" (n 94).

98 Craig, *Account of the Life and Writings of John Millar* (n 71) xxvi–xxxii. In the following account I am drawing on Haakonssen, "John Millar" (n 94) and Cairns, "John Millar's lectures" (n 14) 374–380. (I may correct in the latter footnotes 55 and 56 to read respectively: "Craig, op cit, xxxiv" and "Ibid, xxxiv–xli".)

99 Craig, *Account of the Life and Writings of John Millar* (n 71) xxxii–xxxv.

100 Ibid xxxv–xxxix.

Legislator] in the noble, but arduous, attempt, to purify and improve the laws of his country". The historical and social aspect of Millar's jurisprudence prevented "inconsiderate innovation, and indiscriminate reform" by showing that "no institutions, however just in themselves, can be either expedient or permanent, if inconsistent with established ranks, manners, and opinions".[101] Millar drew on these ideas in his lectures on Scots law, using his philosophy of law to explain, for example, Scots criminal law.[102] Millar's law lectures thus aimed at developing law students' critical and reasoning powers, and it is worth recalling Craig's remark that Millar's style of teaching (as well as content) was calculated to achieve this.[103] It is therefore hardly surprising that Kames exempted Millar from criticism.[104]

John Wilde, who in Edinburgh reverted to teaching the class on the *Digest* in Latin, approached Roman law in a different way. He was strongly conscious, however, of Millar's practice, for he told his students in his first class in 1792 that he would continue Dick's practice of using Heineccius' textbooks, though he was "not certain but a method might be derived better in the arrangement", adding that "[t]here is another method followed by another Gentleman who has long delivered Lectures on the Roman Law in another University and whose example very naturally leads to imitation".[105] Wilde's initial major innovation was to start his class on the *Institutes* with a series of lectures on the history of the Civil Law.[106] He did so in the belief, first, that the best way to understand Civil Law was to approach it historically, and secondly, that students would thereby gain knowledge of the "policy of the Roman people".[107] In explaining this second advantage of the historical approach, Wilde mounted what seems to be an attack on overly conjectural history and abstract theorising about politics:

> The science of law and government can only be studied, by what has taken place among embodied communities of men; whose history affords the lessons and maxims, which a severe and abstract philosophy may then, with safety, examine and search; and may compound into the original principles of government. . . . While if, on the other hand, these principles are taken up and explained, upon the fancied inventions of theorists; who either do not know or disdain historical wisdom; it then requires nothing more than a small portion of acuteness . . . to

101 Ibid xl–xli.
102 See Cairns, "John Millar's lectures" (n 14).
103 Craig, *Account of the Life and Writings of John Millar* (n 71) xii.
104 Kames, *Elucidations* (n 53) ix n.
105 National Library of Scotland, Adv MS 81.8.3, fo 18r.
106 National Library of Scotland, Adv MSS 81.8.4–6; Edinburgh University Library, MS La.II.475 contains a fragment of the concluding lecture of the historical part, dated 24 June 1800.
107 Wilde, *Preliminary Lecture* (n 85) 64–74.

> maintain, and render sufficiently plausible, any set of opinions whatever; and if, by art or by accident, power is given or obtained, to make the weakest, or most frivolous, of these opinions, the engine of overturning or erecting empires.[108]

Rather than a criticism of Millar, these remarks are strongly coloured by experience of the French Revolution (which Wilde had come to abhor).[109] He did carefully distinguish his approach to Civil Law from that of Millar (whom he never specifically names). Wilde stated that he would "not go an inch beyond the territories of the Roman law".[110] Obviously alluding to Millar, he said: "It has frequently been esteemed . . . a necessary part of lectures on the civil law, to give an account of what is called the progress of law; or, in other words, a view of the beginnings and progression of society; or, in other language still, an history of man; or sometimes also an history of government. Such subjects are great and vast and comprehensive indeed; and of as much dignity as can belong to any human study."[111] He complained, however, that "men very little qualified for the task" had undertaken such instruction (though he carefully stated that he did not know this to be the case for those holding university chairs).[112] He added: "But whatever be the dignity and grandeur of the subject, or whatever the abilities of men, it is, without question, a matter which does not belong to the duty of a professor of Civil law."[113] As this could appear to be a direct criticism of Millar, Wilde quickly qualified his comment by adding that such an approach was "not only warranted, but of necessity" when "a law college is employed as a sort of general institution, in science, history, and philosophy; delivered under the general name of LAW. . . . But this is not the case with me. There are other institutions in this university, where that knowledge may be amply acquired. My duty is to instruct you only . . . in the principles of the Roman law."[114] Though he thus gave an institutional reason for not following Millar's example, he nonetheless warned that "this sort of instruction . . . unless when both delivered and heard with great science, and also great sobriety,

108 Ibid 74–76.

109 J Wilde, *An Address to the Lately Formed Society of the Friends of the People* (1793) ix noted his initial approval of the Revolution: the whole work testifies to his abhorrence of it and to the influence of Burke's thought. Wilde, *Preliminary Lecture* (n 85) ix–lxxix, is largely devoted to the state of France and the justice of war against that country. See also Wilde, *Sequel to an Address to the Lately Formed Society of the Friends of the People* (1797).

110 Wilde, *Preliminary Lecture* (n 85) 58.

111 Ibid 59–60.

112 Ibid 60.

113 Ibid.

114 Ibid 61–62.

is very dangerous ground to tread upon."[115] He concluded his remarks on Millar's approach to Civil Law:

> I shall give you no sort of dissertation whatever either about the origin of human society, or of its various establishments; neither of the men in the woods, or of the men in cities and nations. But I certainly should not fulfil my duty . . . if I were not to give you an account of the origin and establishments of the Roman law: of the Roman law, on the great and universal system of private rights; BUT mingling it with no general theories of policy and government; which do not belong to *me* (in the arrangements of study in *this* university) nor to *my* office at all.[116]

It would be interesting to know the tone in which this lecture was read;[117] and though Wilde is careful never to criticise Millar directly, it is difficult not to see these remarks as a strong rejection of the latter's approach. Furthermore, in the preface to his *Elucidations*, Kames had stressed that those parts of Roman law should be taught that had direct relevance for Scots law.[118] Wilde vehemently disagreed, telling his class that to ignore any part of Roman law would cease to make the study a liberal one, would deprive it of the very utility Kames emphasised, and would also prevent the system as a whole from being understood.[119]

With Wilde's stress on Roman law for its own sake, and his rejection of using it to teach the science of legislation, went an emphasis on instruction in Latin. He discussed the choice of language in his first lecture in 1792. He stated that some had recommended him to teach in Latin and others in English. English was recommended, because if he taught in Latin, "considering the little knowledge of the Latin language at present in this Country", there would be a small attendance and those who came would derive little profit from the class. Wilde himself favoured teaching in Latin, considering it "exceedingly preposterous and absurd" to lecture on Roman law in English when all the commentaries were in Latin.[120] He told the class: "I have come to the resolution of Lecturing in lattin [sic] upon the

115 Ibid 62.

116 Ibid 63–64.

117 The printed *Preliminary Lecture* (n 85) is stated by Wilde (at v) to be drawn from the ones delivered to his class. Comparison with the three introductory lectures in Adv MS 81.8.3 confirms this. See this MS at fos 24r–28r for his rejection (in 1792) of Millar's approach and at fos 28r–39r for the advantage of the historical approach. The "Introductory Discourse" was written for the publication and not read to the class; a draft is found in Edinburgh University Library, MS La. II.475.

118 Kames, *Elucidations* (n 53) viii–ix.

119 National Library of Scotland, Adv MS 81.8.7, fos 231r–33r and 236r. For a brief discussion, see J W Cairns, "Book review" (1988) 6 *Law and History Review* 504.

120 National Library of Scotland, Adv MS 81.8.3, fos 19r–21r.

Pandects and of giving the Course of the institutes in English; at least for this season."[121] He maintained this practice in subsequent sessions.[122] He added:

> The Lectures on the Pandects will be altogether taken up with explaining the mere principles of the Roman Law; strictly and without deviating into any sort of collateral enquiry. Constant references will be made to the approved Commentators on that Digest. Of consequence the one half or indeed the greater part of these Lectures must consist of lattin; and in such a course no person can expect to reap any sort of advantage without being tollerably familiar with the Roman tongue. Besides the interlarding (where there is so great a proportion of lattin) of English along with it would only make a sort of distasteful jargon pleasant neither to you nor to me. Accordingly the Lectures on the Pandects are to be in lattin.[123]

In the more elementary course on the *Institutes*, he considered "this employment of English to have been a happy measure indeed if by means of it any zeal shall be kindled for the general study of a law which both as a liberal science and a matter of much professional importance deserves to be very generally studied indeed".[124] But in the course on the *Digest*, because, in contrast to Millar, Wilde intended to focus purely on technical Roman law, "strictly and without deviating into any sort of collateral enquiry", Latin was to be the language of instruction for reasons of convenience and taste.

In the introductory lecture to his course on the *Digest*, Wilde explained further his adoption of Latin. He was aware that there were many, "not wholly ignorant" (*nec prorsus indoctos*), who had decided, and others who had proclaimed, that lectures in Latin were more difficult to understand than in fact was the case. On the contrary, said Wilde, experience daily taught that a sufficiently attentive person could understand lectures in Latin. He alluded to the aesthetic and practical point he raised in the lecture to the class on the *Institutes*, noting that, while sentences read out (in Latin) could be grasped and remembered, this was more difficult than understanding and remembering the meaning of a continuous speech, because when the lecturer mixed languages the words were apt to fall on less attentive ears.[125] He added: "In fact, by virtue of the most acute and attentive intellectual engagement which a continuous discourse demands and, at the same time, produces, it soon comes about that the lecture which is delivered

121 Ibid fo 21r.

122 Ibid fo 82r (third version of introductory lecture, November 1793); and see Wilde, *Preliminary Lecture* (n 85) vi. For the Latin lectures on the *Digest*, see National Library of Scotland, Adv MSS 81.8.18–21.

123 National Library of Scotland, Adv MS 81.8.3, fos 21r–22r.

124 Ibid fo 23r.

125 National Library of Scotland, Adv MS 81.8.18, fos 3r and 4r.

has been adequately perceived by a person scarcely versed in Latin, and unquestionably understood to a large extent."[126] In other words, use of Latin in a continuous discourse promoted understanding and concentration. Even, Wilde continued, were a student not adequately versed in Latin, by being forced to listen he would benefit "by learning not only the Civil law but Latin. Having learned Latin, he will also be even more learned in Civil law".[127] The two would reinforce one another and deepen a student's knowledge of both. The road to knowledge might be difficult, but the labour was worthwhile, and the association of the science of law with letters was delightful.[128]

By thus linking letters and Civil Law, Wilde to some extent associated himself with the school of Humanist jurists for whom Civil Law was not just a practical study but a liberal and elegant science. This in many ways explains his historical approach. Indeed, he identified himself sufficiently with the elegant school to say of one of its leaders, Cujas, "[H]e appears to have taught the way I would wish alone to teach the higher parts", and he recommended Cujas' palingenetic work to his students.[129] Furthermore, in his *Preliminary Lecture*, he called for the restoration of Civil Law "to what it was, long before the compilations of Justinian; when Papinian, Paulus, and Ulpian, were the living oracles of this law; and while it still spoke in the writings of the jurisconsults of old, in the science, and with the vigour, of the republic".[130]

Wilde has completely rejected Millar's approach. Though study of Civil Law did indeed have important practical aims in Scotland, it was nonetheless also to be an elegant and liberal study, joining letters with law, complete in itself. Above all, it was not the means to teach the science of legislation. Profound knowledge required Latin, and this consideration, along with matters of taste, required the advanced course on the *Digest* to be taught in Latin. Millar's use of the course to teach students to reason critically about law made use of Latin unimportant. Furthermore, his conversational,

126 Ibid fo 4r: "In acerrima vero et attentissima cogitatione, quam sermo perpetuus postulat simul gignitque, brevi fit ut literas latinas vel parum callenti, quae habetur oratio satis sit perspecta, maximaque ex parte intelligatur."

127 Ibid: "non jus modo civile verum et ipsas Latinas literas docendo. Latine doctus et juris civilis quoque doctior erit".

128 Ibid fo 3v.

129 National Library of Scotland, Adv MS 81.8.3 fo 114r (this is a displaced folio from a later lecture).

130 Wilde, *Preliminary Lecture* (n 85) 42–43; National Library of Scotland, Adv MS 81.8.3 fo 60r (second introductory lecture, with trivial differences in wording).

extemporary style of lecturing, which was designed to capture the attention of the class, made use of Latin impossible. Wilde, however, considered that the very use of Latin engaged the students intellectually, as they were required to concentrate carefully on the lecture.

D. CONCLUSION

It is obvious that throughout the later eighteenth century there was a general move in Scotland toward teaching in English rather than Latin.[131] This suggests that, although some professors may well have merely followed an existing trend, Millar's adoption, and extension, of Lindesay's innovation of teaching Civil Law in English was not simply related to developments in that discipline. Whereas in the early eighteenth-century lectures had taken the form of traditional dictates on a set textbook, the new theories of rhetoric of the Scottish Enlightenment promoted reflection on the purpose of a lecture and the best mode of fulfilling that purpose. Traditional methods could be tested by these new standards and found wanting. This sheds light both on Millar's continuation and extension of Lindesay's innovation of lecturing in English and on his style of extemporary lecturing from notes rather than a full text. Instruction could be seen arguably to be best carried out in the students' own language in a lively and interesting manner. The utilitarian philosophy (if not in a Benthamite sense) of many thinkers in Scotland in the eighteenth century would reinforce this trend. In strong contrast to the views of Wilde, Millar and some others saw Civil Law as in itself not of particular importance; and the only use Millar made of Latin in instruction was the practical one of examining his students in it, since they would be examined in Latin on Civil Law in the trials for admission to the Faculty of Advocates.[132] It is worth noting in this respect that, whereas the Faculty of Advocates had once emphasised learning in Civil Law almost to the exclusion of anything else, by the time Millar taught, for essentially utilitarian reasons, a greater emphasis was being placed on learning in Scots law.[133]

Millar was remembered as a particularly inspiring teacher.[134] In his obituary in the *Scots Magazine*, the anonymous author discussed Millar's

131 Consider Arnot, *History of Edinburgh* (n 41) 39: "Mr. Dick is now [1779] the only professor in the College who prelects in Latin."

132 Craig, *Account of the Life and Writings of John Millar* (n 71) xiii–xiv.

133 See Cairns, "Formation of the Scottish Legal Mind" (n 15) at 264–274.

134 W C Lehmann, *John Millar of Glasgow 1735–1801: His Life and Thought and his Contributions to Sociological Analysis* (1960) 30–42 (henceforth Lehmann, *John Millar*).

teaching skills: "Few lecturers have possessed, in a more eminent degree, the talents of arresting attention and commanding assent. He never wrote out his lectures, but spoke them from notes which contained his arrangements and facts, trusting for the greater part of his illustrations, and the whole of his language, to his power of speaking; and, though occasionally he might be at a loss for a word, he, by this means, was enabled to give to his manner and expression, an interest, a warmth, an energy, far preferable to the more polished graces of studied composition."[135] In the *Edinburgh Review*, Francis Jeffrey twice made similar remarks about Millar's success in teaching, which he linked to Millar's vivacious conversational style.[136] Neither Smith, nor Campbell, nor Blair appear to have left any opinions on university lecturing from the perspective afforded by their rhetorical theories (the last two focusing on the topics of eloquence at the bar, in political debate, and in sermons),[137] though Professor Ross has argued that Smith followed his rhetorical precepts in his writings.[138] The near-universal praise of Millar's qualities as a teacher, and the close correspondence of his style of teaching with that of his mentor and colleague, Adam Smith, allow us to infer that Millar's style of lecturing was that which was preferred by the proponents of the new rhetoric. It was a style best suited to himself, his subject, and his auditors, even though Smith himself may have given up the extemporary style of lecturing,[139] and, according to Carlyle, Blair was no orator other than in the pulpit.[140] It is worth noting Dugald Stewart's comment that Smith "had sent [his cousin, David Douglas] to study law at Glasgow, under the care of Mr. Millar; – the strongest proof he could give . . . of the esteem in which he held the abilities of that eminent Professor".[141] In discussing sermons, Blair made the following remarks: "No discourse, which is designed to be persuasive, can have the same force when read, as when spoken. . . . What is

135 "Character of the Late Professor Millar" (1801) 63 Scots Magazine 527 (I suspect the obituarist to have been Craig; but I have been unable to verify this).

136 Jeffrey, review of *An Historical View* (n 88) 154–155; F Jeffrey, review of Craig, *Account of the Life and Writings of John Millar* (1806) 9 *Edinburgh Review* 83 at 86–89.

137 Campbell, *Philosophy of Rhetoric* (n 36) vol 1, 207; Blair, *Lectures on Rhetoric* (n 37) vol 2, 47 (Lecture XXVII); cf Smith, *Lectures in Rhetoric* (n 33) 128.

138 I Ross, "Adam Smith as Rhetorician", in R L Emerson, W Kinsley and W Moser (eds), *Man and Nature: Proceedings of the Canadian Society for Eighteenth-Century Studies* 2 (1984) 61 at 69–70.

139 Letter of Wodrow to Buchan, quoted in Campbell and Skinner, *Adam Smith* (n 34) 41.

140 Carlyle, *Autobiography* (n 67) 469.

141 Stewart, *Account of the life and writings of Adam Smith* (n 33) 332; see also J Rae, *Life of Adam Smith* (introduction by J Viner) (1965) 53, who states that Smith sent his cousin to study at Glasgow because of his high opinion of Millar's "unique powers as a stimulating teacher". He cites no source, but the remark is probably derived from Stewart's account.

gained hereby in point of correctness, is not equal, I apprehend, to what is lost in point of persuasion and force. They, whose memories are not able to retain the whole of a discourse, might aid themselves considerably by short notes lying before them, which would allow them to preserve, in a great measure, the freedom and ease of one who speaks."[142] This advice is strongly reminiscent of the description given of Millar's lectures.

Millar taught Civil Law in English because he considered that, where lectures were given in Latin, the language tended to obfuscate the meaning, placing an unnecessary barrier in the way of student understanding. Furthermore, his reliance on a relatively spontaneous style of lecturing led him to favour classes in English. As well as these issues of teaching technique, the substance of his course, with its more broadly defined content, and its utilitarian goal of increasing students' comparative understanding of law and the science of legislation in general, may well have also led him to teach in English rather than Latin to avoid possible restrictions of vocabulary. That this choice of English as the language of instruction was by no means inevitable is demonstrated by Arnot's disapproval and the Faculty of Advocates' attempt to make Millar revert to teaching in Latin. There were respectable views opposite to those of Millar. As late as the 1790s, Wilde was to return to teaching one of his courses in Latin because he rejected Millar's approach to Civil Law. For Wilde, Latin was still the best medium of instruction in Civil Law. Millar, when he decided to adopt and extend Lindesay's innovation, was not simply following an ineluctable trend; his choice of extempore lectures in English reflects his reaction to the new theories in Enlightenment Scotland that had redefined the study of rhetoric as the study of the best means of communicating information. This choice allowed him better to use his class of Civil Law to teach students to reason critically about law and to be aware of the relationship of law to society. This ultimately would further the objective of improvement in the laws. Many of his pupils and followers were indeed to become noted reformers.[143]

NOTES

This article has a long and somewhat complicated genesis and my debts are correspondingly great. Parts of it are derived from a paper, "The Vocation of the Age for Roman Law", read to the British Legal History Conference in

142 Blair, *Lectures on Rhetoric* (n 37) vol ii, 118 (lecture XXIX).
143 See Lehmann, *John Millar* (n 134) 35–42.

Canterbury in July 1985, other parts are derived from two related papers, one entitled "The Language of Law Teaching in Eighteenth-Century Scotland" read to a dining club, "The Other Society", in Edinburgh in 1987, the other entitled "La langue d'enseignement du droit en Ecosse au 18e siècle" read at the Journées Internationales d'Histoire du Droit at Louvain in May 1988. A more final version was delivered as a lecture in the College of Law, Syracuse University in 1989. I am grateful for the comments and criticisms I received on all these occasions. I benefited from the comments of the following individuals: Beverley Brown, David Garland, Michael Hoeflich, Jim Kainen, Neil MacCormick, Hector MacQueen, John Robertson, David Sellar and Alan Watson. I am only too aware that I have not always followed the advice I received.

3 The Influence of Smith's Jurisprudence on Legal Education in Scotland*

A. LEGAL EDUCATION AND NATURAL LAW

On 8 January 1760, it was moved before the Faculty of Advocates that they should recommend those proposing to join their number to attend the lectures given in the University of Edinburgh on the law of nature and nations. The Faculty noted that regular lectures on that topic were now given in the University and expressed satisfaction with "the merit and abilities" of the professor (Robert Bruce), and accordingly recommended all those who intended to become "Candidates for the office of Advocate, to apply to the study of the law of Nature and Nations", because "it concerns the honour of the Faculty that their members should be versant in every part of polite Literature and particularly in the law of Nature and Nations, the fountain of Justice and equity".[1] After noting on 5 January 1762 that

* This chapter was originally read at the Nagoya International Symposium to commemorate the Bicentenary of the Death of Adam Smith and is reprinted here with the kind permission of the Adam Smith Society of Japan. I am grateful to my colleague Professor Neil MacCormick for his comments on this paper, and for many general helpful conversations about Adam Smith.

The abbreviations used in references in the text and footnotes not otherwise explained are all to the Glasgow Edition of the Works and Correspondence of Adam Smith and are as follows:

Corr: *The Correspondence of Adam Smith,* ed E C Mossner and I S Ross (1977).

Stewart: D Stewart, "Account of the Life and Writings of Adam Smith, LL. D.", ed I S Ross, in A Smith, *Essays on Philosophical Subjects*, ed W P D Wightman and J C Bryce (1980).

LJ(A): *Lectures on Jurisprudence* Report of 1762–1763, in A Smith, *Lectures on Jurisprudence*, ed R L Meek, D D Raphael, and P G Stein (1978).

LJ(B): *Lectures on Jurisprudence* Report dated 1766, in A Smith, *Lectures on Jurisprudence*, ed R L Meek, D D Raphael, and P G Stein (1978).

TMS: A Smith, *The Theory of Moral Sentiments*, ed D D Raphael and A L McFie (1976).

LRBL: A Smith, *Lectures on Rhetoric and Belles Lettres,* ed J C Bryce (1983).

WN: A Smith, *An Inquiry into the Nature and Causes of the Wealth of Nations*, ed R R Campbell and A S Skinner, factual editor W B Todd (1976).

1 National Library of Scotland, *FR* 2, Minutes of the Faculty of Advocates, 1751–1783 127. (I am grateful to the Faculty of Advocates for permission to study and cite their records.)

this resolution had not been adhered to, and establishing a committee to consider how to make it effective, the Faculty resolved as follows on 24 November:

> The Dean and Faculty of Advocates considering that they by their Resolution dated the 8th January 1760 recommended it to all young Gentlemen who intended to offer themselves Candidates for the office of Advocate to apply to the study of the Law of Nature and Nations. And considering that it concerns the Honour of the Faculty that their members should be versant in every part of polite literature and more particularly in those parts of Learning which are immediately connected with the Roman Law and the Law of Scotland. They therefore recommend to the private Examinators in both Branches of the Law from and after the twelfth Day of June next to examine Candidates upon the Law of Nature and Nations in so far as it is connected with the Civil Law or the Law of this Country. And they hereby appoint That a Copy of this their Resolution to be sent to all the professors in the University of Edinburgh in order that the same may be intimated to the Students at their respective Colleges.[2]

This requirement was a new departure for the Faculty of Advocates. Until 1750, intrants to the Faculty had been examined on either Scots law or Civil (Roman) law, and, after 1750, on both.[3] These proposals in the 1760s must be seen in the context of the Advocates' attempts after 1750 to respond to the impact of Enlightenment thought in Scotland;[4] and in 1748 Lord President Dundas had already recommended to the Faculty that those intending to come to the Bar should be "careful to learn thoroughly the principles of the Roman Law and the Laws of Nature and Nations", and should not "neglect Academical learning" before studying the laws of their own country.[5]

The chair of Public Law and the Law of Nature and Nations had been founded in 1707, and was the oldest chair in law in the University of Edinburgh.[6] Most of its holders had at least attempted to lecture.[7] The legal

2 Ibid 147, 156–157 (standard abbreviations in MS expanded).

3 J W Cairns, "The Formation of the Scottish Legal Mind in the Eighteenth Century: Themes of Humanism and Enlightenment in the Admission of Advocates", in N MacCormick and P Birks (eds), *The Legal Mind: Essays for Tony Honoré* (1986) 254 (henceforth Cairns, "Formation of the Scottish Legal Mind").

4 Ibid.

5 J M Pinkerton (ed), *The Minute Book of the Faculty of Advocates Volume 2 1713–1750*, Stair Society vol 32 (1980) (henceforth *Minute Book*) 225.

6 A Grant *The Story of the University of Edinburgh during its First Three Hundred Years* vols i and ii (1884) (henceforth Grant, *Story of the University of Edinburgh*) vol i, p 232.

7 Charles Areskine, professor 1707–1734, advertised his lectures in 1711 (see J Lorimer, "The Story of the Chair of Public Law in the University of Edinburgh" (1888) 4 LQR 139 at 144); William Kirkpatrick was professor for one year only; George Abercromby, professor 1735–1759, in 1741 lectured on Grotius' treatise *De jure belli ac pacis* (see (1741) 3 *Scots Magazine* 371

profession does not appear, however, to have been particularly interested in the discipline of Grotian natural law which its holders taught,[8] and Dundas' encouragement of study of the law of nature and nations as preparation for practice at the Bar is the earliest which I have found. In the second half of the seventeenth century, when advocates aimed at the establishment of chairs in Law, what they were concerned with was education in Civil Law.[9] In the 1690s, establishment of a chair of Law in Edinburgh was considered, but the professor would have taught Civil Law and Scots law.[10] The extensive duties of the holder of the chair of Law established in Glasgow in 1714 did not include the law of nature and nations.[11]

By the middle years of the eighteenth century, however, natural law thinking had come to dominate the moral philosophy curriculum in the Universities of Edinburgh and Glasgow.[12] Of primary importance in this development was Gershom Carmichael's adoption of Pufendorf's treatise *De officio hominis et civis* in Glasgow in the 1690s.[13] Following Pufendorf, Carmichael redefined moral philosophy as natural law.[14] Other moral phi-

at 371); Robert Bruce, professor 1759–1764, was the teacher referred to by the Faculty of Advocates. For the next two professors, see below, text at nn 48–52.

8 That it was Grotian natural law is indicated both by the title of the chair which reflects the full title of Grotius' work, and by Abercromby's textbook in 1741: see n 7 above. On the spread of similar chairs in Europe, see G Tarello, *Le ideologie della codificazione nel secolo XVIII: Corso di filosofia del diritto*, 3rd edn (n d) 90–93. On the development of Grotian natural law, see, e.g., K Haakonssen, "Hugo Grotius and the history of political thought" (1985) 13 *Political Theory* 239.

9 J M Pinkerton (ed), *The Minute Book of the Faculty of Advocates Volume I 1661–1712*, Stair Society vol 29 (1976) 65–66 (12 January 1684).

10 A Bower, *The History of the University of Edinburgh; Chiefly Compiled from Original Papers and Records, Never Before Published* (1817) vol i, 329. In the University of Edinburgh, chairs of Civil Law and Scots Law were created in 1710 and 1722 respectively: Grant, *Story of the University of Edinburgh* (n 6) vol i, 284–288.

11 J Coutts, *A History of the University of Glasgow from its Foundation in 1451 to 1909* (1909) 193–194.

12 And probably in Marischall College, Aberdeen: see K A B Mackinnon, "George Turnbull's Common Sense Jurisprudence", in J J Carter and J H Pittock (eds), *Aberdeen and the Enlightenment* (1987) 104.

13 J Moore and M Silverthorne, "Gershom Carmichael and the Natural Jurisprudence Tradition in Eighteenth-Century Scotland", in I Hont and M Ignatieff (eds), *Wealth and Virtue: The Shaping of Political Economy in the Scottish Enlightenment* (1983) 73; and "Natural Sociability and Natural Rights in the Moral Philosophy of Gershom Carmichael", in V Hope (ed), *Philosophers of the Scottish Enlightenment* (1984).

14 See S *Pufendorfii de officio hominis et civis, juxta legem naturalem, libri duo. Supplementis & observationibus in academicae juventutis usum auxit & illustravit Gerschomus Carmichael, philosophiae in academia Glasguensi Professor. Editio secundo priore auctior & emendatior* (1724) vi–vii. Carmichael established a curriculum for moral philosophy in Glasgow of natural theology followed by moral philosophy, using for the latter this work of Pufendorf: see his *Synopsis theologiae naturalis, sive notitiae, de existentia, attributis, & operationibus, summi numinis, ex ipsa rerum natura haustae* (1729) 4.

losophers followed this lead.[15] Scots lawyers were also familiar with natural law. James Dalrymple, Viscount Stair's *Institutions of the Law of Scotland*, published in 1681, was influenced by Grotian natural law.[16] For the first half of the eighteenth century, the text most used to teach Scots law was Sir George Mackenzie's *Institutions of the Law of Scotland*.[17] In the title, "Of Laws in General", Mackenzie briefly alluded in two paragraphs to the law of nature and the law of nations.[18] These two paragraphs inevitably stimulated all the lecturers on Scots law to some comments on natural law and the law of nations; but study of student notes suggests their consideration of the topic was slight.[19]

15 Francis Hutcheson, Carmichael's successor in Glasgow, preserved the same curriculum, and, at least initially, taught Pufendorf's treatise: R Wodrow, *Analecta: or, Materials for a History of Remarkable Providences; Mostly Relating to Scotch Ministers and Christians* (1843) vol iv, 185. W Leechman described Hutcheson's moral philosophy class as covering "Natural Religion, Morals, Jurisprudence, and Government" in "The Preface, Giving some Account of the Life, Writings, and Character of the Author", in F Hutcheson, *A System of Moral Philosophy, in Three Books*, 2 vols (1755) vol i, xxxvi (henceforth Hutcheson, *System of Moral Philosophy*). See also Hutcheson's *Metaphysicae synopsis: ontologiam, et, pneumatologiam, complectens* (1742); and *Philosophiae moralis institutio compendiana, ethices & jurisprudentiae naturalis elementa continens. Lib III* (1742) (henceforth Hutcheson, *Philosophiae moralis institutio compendiana*). On Hutcheson, see, e.g., W R Scott, *Francis Hutcheson: His Life, Teaching and Position in the History of Philosophy* (1900); T D Campbell, "Francis Hutcheson: 'Father' of the Scottish Enlightenment", in R H Campbell and A S Skinner (eds), *The Origins and Nature of the Scottish Enlightenment* (1982) 167. In Edinburgh, W Scott, Regent in Philosophy, then Professor of, in turn, Greek, and Moral Philosophy, published *Hugonis Grotii de jure belli ac pacis librorum III. compendium, annotationibus & commentaris selectis illustratum. In usum studiosae juventutis academiae Edinensis* (1707). Scott's successor in the chair of Moral Philosophy, John Pringle, taught on the basis of Pufendorf's treatise *De officio*: Grant, *Story of the University of Edinburgh* (n 6), vol i, 273–274; vol ii, 336–337.

16 James Dalrymple, Viscount Stair, *The Institutions of the Law of Scotland Deduced from its Originals, and Collated with the Civil, Canon and Feudal Laws, and with the Customs of Neighbouring Nations*, ed D M Walker (first published in 1681, 2nd edn 1693, but circulated in MS for twenty years before). On Stair and Grotius, see N MacCormick, "Obligation and consent: reflections on Stair and Locke" (1979) 65 *Archiv fur Rechts- und Sozialphilosophie* 387; P Stein, "The Theory of Law", in D M Walker (ed), *Stair Tercentenary Studies*, Stair Society vol 33 (1981) 181; and W M Gordon, "Stair, Grotius and the Sources of Stair's Institutions", in J A Ankum, J E Spruit and F B J Wubbe (eds), *Satura Roberto Feenstra sexagesimum quintum annum aetatis complenti ab alumnis collegis amicis oblata* (1985) 571. On Stair's relationship to the Scottish Enlightenment, see, e.g., N MacCormick, "Law and Enlightenment", in R H Campbell and A S Skinner (eds), *The Origins and Nature of the Scottish Enlightenment* (1982) 150.

17 G Mackenzie, *Institutions of the Law of* Scotland, 2nd edn (1688) (henceforth Mackenzie, *Institutions*): on other editions, see F S Ferguson, "A bibliography of the works of Sir George Mackenzie Lord Advocate Founder of the Advocates' Library" (1935–1938) 1 *Edinburgh Bibliographical Society Transactions* 1 at 30–34.

18 Mackenzie, *Institutions* (n 17) 2–3.

19 See, e.g., A Bayne, *Notes, for the Use of the Students of the Municipal Law in the University of Edinburgh: Being a Supplement to Sir George Mackenzie's Institutions* (1731) 2; and Edinburgh University Library, MS Gen 1735 (notes of lectures given by J Cuninghame) 2–4.

Thus, from the second half of the seventeenth century, Scots lawyers and moral philosophers were aware of the natural jurisprudence stemming from the work of Grotius and Pufendorf. In classes in moral philosophy and in the lectures of the Professors of Public Law and the Law of Nature and Nations the natural law approach to the basis of moral and legal obligations had become institutionalised by 1750. In the teaching of Scots law, however, natural law had remained of minimal importance. Furthermore, despite Lord President Dundas' initial endorsement of study of the laws of nature and nations in 1748, it had no necessary place in the training of the profession until the Bar's enthusiastic adoption of the discipline in the 1760s.

Why, then, did the Faculty of Advocates desire in the 1760s that intrants should have studied natural law? In this chapter I shall argue that Adam Smith's *Lectures on Jurisprudence* showed how law could be taught as a dynamic historical process. Though Smith's lectures were given as part of a course on moral philosophy, they had practical significance for lawyers. Until Smith lectured in Glasgow, law professors had used natural law as an organising framework for expounding rules of law for students to memorise;[20] but Smith demonstrated that natural jurisprudence explained how law developed and ought to be further developed. Smith had turned natural law from an abstract ahistorical discipline into a concrete, historical explanation and critique of law. Thus, the lectures given by the Professor of Public Law and the Law of Nature and Nations assumed a greater potential significance for lawyers: no longer were they merely elegant learning, and it is worth noting that in 1762 the Faculty saw them as closely connected with the study of Civil Law and Scots law. This was what made Smith a suitable candidate for that chair in 1758, when his friends David Hume and William Johnstone urged him to seek it (Corr 24–25). Smith's *Lectures on Jurisprudence* thus came at a crucial juncture in the development of legal education in Scotland, and pointed out a new route for it to take. It is perhaps in this respect no coincidence that, in 1762, John Erskine, Professor of Scots Law in Edinburgh, advised his cousin, Lord Cardross, then a student in Glasgow, to take Smith's moral philosophy class (about which Erskine was obviously not too well informed) along with the class in Civil Law.[21] As Dr Phillipson has shown, in the middle years of the eighteenth century the

20 For a discussion of methods of teaching, see J W Cairns, "Rhetoric, language, and Roman law: legal education and improvement in eighteenth-century Scotland" (1991) 9 *Law and History Review* 31.

21 Edinburgh University Library, MS La.II.238 (letter of 24 November 1762).

Faculty of Advocates sought a role as law reformers.[22] Smith's *Lectures on Jurisprudence* showed a method of achieving it.

B. ADAM SMITH'S NATURAL JURISPRUDENCE

On 9 January 1751, Smith was elected Professor of Logic in the University of Glasgow.[23] Before he arrived in October 1751, Thomas Craigie, Professor of Moral Philosophy, had become ill, and Smith agreed to teach natural jurisprudence and politics to the absent professor's class (Corr 4–5).[24] Craigie died in November, and on 22 April 1752 Smith was elected to the vacant chair, the translation taking place on 29 April.[25] Smith's fitness for the post had already been demonstrated by the lectures he had given privately in Edinburgh in 1748–1751 on rhetoric and *belles lettres*, and jurisprudence.[26]

According to John Millar, Smith's moral philosophy course was divided into four parts: natural theology; ethics (which he afterwards published as *The Theory of Moral Sentiments*); justice; and political regulations founded on expediency (which he subsequently published as *The Wealth of Nations*; Stewart 274–275). The last two of these were dealt with in the *Lectures on Jurisprudence* of which we have two sets of student notes dating from the sessions 1762–1763 (LJ(A)) and 1763–1764 (LJ(B)) respectively. It may be noted that Smith finished with a brief account of the laws of nations (LJ(A) 7; LJ(B) 398–399 and 545–554).[27] This four-fold division followed the traditional structure of the Glasgow moral philosophy curriculum.[28] From Dugald Stewart we learn that, after Smith published *The Theory of Moral Sentiments* in 1759, in his remaining four years in Glasgow "the plan

22 N T Phillipson, "Lawyers, landowners, and the civic leadership of post-Union Scotland: an essay on the social role of the Faculty of Advocates 1661–1830 in 18th-century Scottish society" (1976) 21 *Juridical Review* 97 (henceforth Phillipson, "Lawyers, landowners, and civic leadership").

23 W R Scott, *Adam Smith as Student and Professor* (1937) (henceforth Scott, *Adam Smith*) 137–138; see also Corr 4.

24 Before Smith arrived, Hercules Lindesay, Professor of Civil Law, taught his class: Scott, *Adam Smith* (n 23) 139.

25 Ibid 139–140.

26 A F Tytler, *Memoirs of the Life and Writings of the Honourable Henry Home of Kames, One of the Senators of the College of Justice, and one of the Lords Commissioners of Justiciary in Scotland: Containing Sketches of the Progress of Literature and General Improvement in Scotland During the Greater Part of the Eighteenth Century* (1807) vol i, 190–191; Scott, *Adam Smith* (n 23) 46–61; R H Campbell and A S Skinner, *Adam Smith* (1982) 29–39.

27 The relevant section of LJ(A) does not survive.

28 See nn 14 and 15 above. One can trace the resemblance to natural theology followed by a discussion of natural law on the basis of Pufendorf's treatise *De officio*.

of his lectures underwent a considerable change. His ethical doctrines . . . occupied a much smaller portion of the course than formerly: and accordingly, his attention was naturally directed to a more complete illustration of the principles of jurisprudence and of political economy" (Stewart 300). In the lecture course of 1763–1764, Smith altered the structure of his account of jurisprudence, preferring the method of the civilians (LJ(B) 401).

That Smith should have changed the structure of his course in the period of his tenure of the chair is hardly surprising. Furthermore, from the pre-1759 fragment identified by Professor Raphael, and the Anderson notes discussed by the late Professor Meek, we can also see that his own views changed: it was in the course of his professorship that he developed the concept of the impartial spectator and the four-stage theory of social development.[29] Although this development raises interesting questions, there is not the time to deal with it here. Accordingly, the following account of his teaching will be based on the fuller evidence we have of the last five years of his tenure provided by the early editions of *The Theory of Moral Sentiments*[30] and the two student reports of his *Lectures on Jurisprudence* in 1762–1763 and 1763–1764. This will also have the advantage of focusing on his class at the very period when the Faculty of Advocates became seriously interested in natural jurisprudence, when Smith's friends urged him to obtain the Edinburgh chair, and when the University of Glasgow awarded him the degree of LLD because of his reputation in letters and particularly because he had taught jurisprudence "with great applause".[31]

(1) Smith's general approach

Smith is reported as telling his class that "[j]urisprudence is the theory of the rules by which civil governments ought to be directed" (LJ(A) 5; see also LJ(B) 397, and TMS VII.iv.36). His *Lectures on Jurisprudence* therefore attempted to establish "a system of what might properly be called natural

29 D D Raphael, "Adam Smith and 'The infection of David Hume's society': new light on an old controversy, together with the text of a hitherto unpublished manuscript" (1969) 30 *Journal of the History of Ideas* 225 (henceforth Raphael, "Adam Smith"); R L Meek, "New light on Adam Smith's Glasgow lectures on jurisprudence" (1976) 8 *History of Political Economy* 439.

30 What is crucial here are the first two editions of 1759 and 1761 which appeared during Smith's tenure of the Glasgow chair, since I am trying to locate the influence of his theory at a specific time; but the Glasgow Edition may be used as it gives variants. Citations to passages from later editions will be indicated as such for particular purposes.

31 Glasgow University Archives 26645, Minutes of Faculty and Dean of Faculty's Meetings 1732–1768 110 (21 October 1762).

jurisprudence, or a theory of the general principles which ought to run through and be the foundation of the laws of all nations" (TMS VII.iv.37; see also LJ(B) 397). The first aim of governments was to secure justice "to prevent the members of a society from incroaching on one anothers property . . . The end proposed by justice is the maintaining men in what are called their perfect rights" (LJ(A) 5). The second aim was "promoting the opulence of the state. This produces what we call police". This encompassed regulations on trade, commerce, agriculture, and manufacturing. It also covered cleanliness, described as "two [sic] mean and trifling" to be dealt with. Public security also came under this heading in two aspects: first, as security from fires and accidents, also "too trifling" to be discussed; second, as "justice of police" which was devoted to policing in the modern sense, the creation of criminal statutes, and the bringing of criminals to justice. This Smith stated he would deal with under "the former part of jurisprudence", that, is justice, with which it was connected (LJ(A) 5–6). The most important part of police was that relating to commerce and plenty, and this was what he would treat under the heading (LJ(A) 5–6). Government had to cover its expenses, so the third topic to be covered was revenue (LJ(A) 6). Finally, the laws of peace and war would be discussed, as the state had to be protected from external threat (LJ(A) 6–7; see also LJ(B) 398–399).

(2) Justice and rights

Smith told his class that "[j]ustice is violated whenever one is deprived of what he had a right to and could justly demand from others, or rather, when we do him any injury or hurt without a cause" (LJ(A) 7). This concept of rights drew on the theory of justice Smith expounded in *The Theory of Moral Sentiments*. Justice was "upon most occasions, but a negative virtue, and only hinders us from hurting our neighbour" (TMS II.ii.1.9). He erected his moral philosophy on the empirically observable phenomenon of sympathy. Human beings, through their own experience of pleasure and pain, could imaginatively enter into the pleasure and pain of others (TMS I.i.1–4; II.i.5). Thus, when a person saw another assaulted, he could sympathetically appreciate the feelings of both the person attacked and the attacker, and, if fully informed, form a moral judgement of the situation. Should the attacker have no motive or an unworthy one, the assault was unjust (TMS II.ii.1.5–7; II.ii.2.1–3). Of course, human beings are never fully informed about any situation, and real spectators never detached, so Smith proposed the concept of the impartial spectator as providing the test of ideal justice.

Individual human actors judged their own conduct by reference to what they considered would be the reaction of the impartial spectator (TMS II.ii.2.1).[32] If by this test an action was unjust, the other party had a right that it not be carried out.

A first point to note is that for Smith, justice was what made social life possible (TMS II.ii.3.4 and 6; VII.iv.36). Justice, however, was not founded on utility, but arose from humankind's abhorrence of injustice (TMS II.ii.3.9). Second, certain rights were "natural": "Among equals each individual is naturally, and antecedent to the institution of civil government, regarded as having a right both to defend himself from injuries, and to exact a certain degree of punishment for those which have been done to him" (TMS II.ii.1.7). This would include not only physical injury, but injury to reputation (TMS VII.ii.1.10). Third, the greater the injury, the greater was the resentment of the person injured, the greater the sympathetic indignation of the spectator, and, indeed, the sentiments of guilt and shame of the injurer. This led to a variation in the degree of punishment which there was a right to exact (TMS II.ii.2.2). Fourth, that some rights were "natural", being antecedent to civil government, led to the inference that others were not, and brought about through historical development.

Smith enumerated possible injuries in the *Lectures on Jurisprudence*. A man (to use his term) could be injured in three ways: as a man; as a member of a family; and as a citizen or member of a state (LJ(A) 7; LJ(B) 399). As a man, he could be injured in his person, reputation or estate. As a member of a family, he could be injured as a father or son, husband or wife, master or servant, guardian or ward. As a member of a state, he could be injured, if a magistrate, by disobedience, or if a subject, by oppression (LJ(A) 7–8; LJ(B) 399). Injury to a man's person or reputation was injury to a natural right. Injury to his property, or to him as a member of a family or a state was injury to an adventitious right (LJ(A) 8; LJ(B) 399–400). Adventitious rights were those brought into existence by the development of civil government. Smith adopted this terminology of rights from Francis Hutcheson.[33]

32 On Smith's development of this concept, see Raphael, "Adam Smith" (n 29) and "The Impartial Spectator", in A S Skinner and T Wilson (eds), *Essays on Adam Smith* (1975) 83; see generally on the above, A S Skinner, "Adam Smith: Society and Government", in E Attwool (ed), *Perspectives in Jurisprudence* (1977) 195 at 196–202; T D Campbell, *Adam Smith's Science of Morals* (1971) 85–185.

33 Hutcheson, *Philosophiae moralis institutio compendiaria* (n 15) 118 (II. iv. 2); *System of Moral Philosophy* (n 15) vol i, 293 (II. v. 1).

(3) Justice, rights, and history

In the *Lectures on Jurisprudence*, Smith used a four-stage theory to explain historical development.[34] In the first stage, humankind supported themselves by hunting and fishing. When natural increase of population made this impossible, humankind would domesticate animals and support themselves as shepherds. When increase of population again made no longer viable this pastoral, second stage of society, humanity would turn to cultivation of the soil to support themselves. In this agricultural stage, as techniques of cultivation improved, society would develop beyond mere subsistence to produce a surplus, which would lead to the exchange of commodities, eventually inaugurating the final stage of commerce (LJ(A) 14–16; LJ(B) 459–460). Smith expounded this in detail in connection with the adventitious right of property. Hunters and fishers had little need of laws of property: the only injury they could suffer was to be deprived of their game. Pastoral society gave rise to laws of property as shepherds owned their flocks: "[i]n this state many more laws and regulations must take place". In agricultural society, "[t]he laws . . . will be of a far greater number than amongst a nation of shepherds" because "there are many ways added in which property may be interrupted as the subjects of it are considerably extended". Finally, "[i]n the age of commerce, as the subjects of property are greatly increased the laws must be proportionally multiplied" (LJ(A) 16).

The growth of property and of government went together: "among hunters there is no regular government; they live according to the laws of nature" (LJ(B) 404; see also LJ(A) 201–202). That is, they only had natural rights. "The appropriation of herds and flocks, which introduced an inequality of fortune, was that which first gave rise to regular government. Till there be property there can be no government, the very end of which is to secure wealth, and to defend the rich from the poor" (LJ(B) 404–405; see also LJ(A) 202). The existence of property and regular or civil government gave rise to other adventitious rights. Contracts were obviously dependent on the existence of property. Commercial society greatly increased the scope

34 On the use of stadial theories in the eighteenth century, and the development of the four-stage theory, see R L Meek, "Smith, Turgot, and the 'four stages' theory" (1971) 3 *History of Political Economy* 9 and *Social Science and the Ignoble Savage* (1976); and P Stein, *Legal Evolution: The Story of an Idea* (1980) 15–50. In "The Four Stage Theory of the Development of Societies", in *The Character and Influence of the Roman Civil Law: Historical Essays* (1988) 395 Stein points out that we need to be cautious about identifying a four-stage theory when there is really only a three-stage. While I agree with him overall, I am not entirely convinced by his identification of Lord Kames as the originator of the four-stage theory.

of actionable contractual rights (LJ(A) 96–97). That the rights relating to families should be adventitious is not so obvious. The union of man and woman was natural and related to care of offspring. Because human beings took so long to mature, the union of their parents must be of long duration (LJ(A) 141–143; LJ(B) 438). But in early societies, the authority of the husband was very great, since "the government is at first in all nations very weak, and very delicate of intermeddling in the differences of persons of different families; they were still less inclined to intermeddle in the differences that happen'd amongst persons of the same family". So that government might be maintained, the father of the family had absolute authority (LJ(A) 143–144; cf. LJ(B) 439–440). Fathers did not even need to aliment children: to do so was an act of benevolence, not justice (LJ(A) 172; LJ(B) 449). In *The Theory of Moral Sentiments*, Smith had already pointed out that "[t]he laws of all civilized nations oblige parents to maintain their children, and children to maintain their parents". In making this provision, the "civil magistrate" was "promoting the prosperity of the commonwealth, by establishing good discipline, and by discouraging every sort of vice and impropriety". Thus, as an act of police, civil government compelled the performance of a duty originally of beneficence (TMS II.ii.1.8). The authority of a master over his servants in early society was likewise absolute, as was necessary when governments were weak (LJ(A) 175–176; LJ(B) 450–451). In all these relations, as society developed, law affected the relationship more. Thus these more refined legal rights were adventitious rights.

Smith dealt with crimes as injuries to a man's estate. He pointed out, however, that crimes were of two sorts: first, those infringing natural rights; and secondly, those infringing acquired or adventious rights (LJ(A) 105). He started with wilful murder, for which "the only proper punishment is the death of the offender" (LJ(A) 106; see also LJ(B) 476): "injury naturaly [sic] excites the resentment of the spectator, and the punishment of the offender is reasonable as far as the indifferent spectator can go along with it. This is the natural measure of punishment" (LJ(B) 475). Death was the natural punishment for murder, but "amongst barbarous nations the punishment has generally been much slighter", because "the weakness of government in those early periods of society . . . made it very delicate in intermeddling with the affairs of individuals" (LJ(A) 106; see also LJ(B) 476–467). Thus, while dealing with crimes against a person in the discussion of injuries to a person's estate, he was aware that they infringed natural rights. The account is awkwardly placed given Smith's analytical scheme; but this is presumably due to ease of exposition. It is telling that, in early society, infringements of natural rights should not have received their "natural" punishment because of the weakness of government. It was as societies developed strong governments that the natural punishment might be imposed. While the natural jurisprudence of punishment of infringements of natural rights was always the same, what actually was done varied historically for reasons of utility.

In sum, Smith's discussion of rights was complex: some were natural, but their enforcement might vary according to government. Other rights were only brought about by the existence of civil government; but once created, their enforcement became a matter of justice, judged by the standard of the impartial spectator. Furthermore, Smith used his stadial theory in a thorough fashion only in discussing property; but since it was property which gave rise to government, and government affected all rights, the four stages necessarily informed the discussion of the whole.

(4) Government, sovereignty, and positive law

For Smith, sovereignty consisted of three attributes: the power of making laws; the power "of trying causes and passing judgement or of settling other judges"; and "the power of making peace or war". In monarchical governments the monarch possessed all these three powers; in aristocratic, the aristocracy; and in democracy, the "*whole body of the people* conjunctly" (LJ(A) 200–201; see also LJ(B) 404). In societies of hunters, "there can be very little government of any sort, but what there is will be of the democraticall kind". Disputes within families were left to the families to resolve; disputes between others were rare, but if occurring and a threat to the community, the community as a whole resolved them by a process of reconciliation rather than a judicial process. The whole community decided on peace and war. "The legislative power can hardly subsist in such a state; there could be occasion but for very few regulations, and no individuall would think himself bound to submit to such regulations as were made by others, even where the whole community was concerned" (LJ(A) 201–202; see also LJ(B) 404).[35] Pastoral society first gave rise to government by creating property and hence disparity of wealth: the poor became dependent on the rich. Furthermore, with the introduction of property, "many disputes on that head must inevitably occur". Yet far fewer than "in the farther advances of society". Disputes could still be resolved by meetings of the whole community, but the rich

35 But cf LJ(B) 407 which appears contradictory to the whole thrust of Smith's argument, and should probably be explained as relating to community regulation of disputes between families on the grounds of utility.

men, because of their influence over their dependents, would have most influence in deliberation, and indeed, their authority would soon become hereditary. But, "[t]he legislative [power] is never met with amongst people in this state of society. Laws and regulations are the product of more refind [sic] manners and improved government, and are never found till it is considerably advanced" (LJ(A) 202–205). Nonetheless, though there was no legislation, Smith pointed out a little later that "[s]ettled laws . . . or agreements concerning property, will soon be made after the commencement of the age of shepherds" (LJ(A) 209; see also LJ(A) 213).

When arts and manufactures were cultivated, the people as a whole could no longer attend trials. Furthermore, their cultivation multiplied "the causes of dispute". Accordingly, "[a] certain number of men are chosen by the body of the people, whose business it is to attend on the causes and settle all disputes". These judges would always include the leading men, and their authority would accordingly grow. As life became more complex, the executive powers of the state were also delegated to this court. Yet, still "[t]he legislative power makes but a very small figure during all this time" (LJ(A) 205–207).

That in pastoral societies there were laws but initially no legislation indicates that Smith envisaged laws as originating in community practices. He stated that "[t]here must indeed be some sort of law as soon as property in flocks commences, but this would be but very short and have few distinctions in it, so that every man would understand it without any written or regular law. It would be no other than what the necessity of the state required". He again added that written and formal laws were "a very great refinement of government", and only met in its latest periods (LJ(A) 213). Smith appears to have indicated that he would explain the "progress" of the legislative power (LJ(A) 207); but his discussions, as reported, became involved in the politics and history of Greece and Rome, and the rise of allodial and feudal government, and he just assumed legislation was taking place without particularising how this had come about. A little later he returned to the theme of the growth of positive law. He stated: "The thing which has given occasion to the establishment of laws has always been the generall or partiall institution of judges." As soon as property had been established judges would soon be required. "A judge will to such an early nation appear very terrible". This was because to "a rude people" courts of justice "appear . . . to have an authority altogether insufferable". The solution was "to establish laws and rules which may ascertain his [i.e. the judge's] conduct". Smith is reported as telling his class:

> Laws are in this manner posterior to the establishment of judges. At the first establishment of judges there are no laws; every one trusts to the naturall feeling of justice he has in his own breast and expects to find in others. . . . [Laws] do not ascertain or restrain the actions of private persons so much as the power and conduct of the judge over the people. (LJ(A) 313–314)

This explanation raises difficulties. On the one hand, Smith has already stated that property gave rise to a type of law *before* the creation of courts; on the other, he has here apparently identified law with legislation. Furthermore, in a passage in *The Theory of Moral Sentiments* he wrote that "those general rules which the sovereign lays down to direct the conduct of his subjects" are "what are properly called laws" (TMS III.5.6).[36] Professor MacCormick has accordingly concluded that Smith "subscribe[d] to the standard voluntarist notion, later adopted by Benthamite and Austinian 'positivists', that the actual positive law of a state is to be identified with the command of the sovereign".[37]

Part of the answer to this problem must lie in the ambiguity of the terms "law" and "legislation". Smith never completed the "theory and History of Law and Government" which he still optimistically promised in 1790 (TMS (1790), Advertisement; Corr 286–287), and in which he would presumably have dealt with such difficulties. The report of Smith's *Lectures on Rhetoric and Belles Lettres* from 1762 to 1763 suggests, however, that his concept of law making was not simply voluntarist. In a discussion of arguments to prove whether or not anything be a law, he pointed out that law could be discovered "plainly expressed" in a statute, or deduced from a statute, or "supported as Law by former practise and similar adjudged causes or precedents". Given that much of his discussion of law-making and government in the *Lectures on Jurisprudence* was based on evidence from Greece and Rome, it is notable that he pointed out that precedent "was not at all used by the antients" in forensic argument. He explained the origin of judges in the need individuals would feel to submit their disputes "to some impartiall person". Those eminent people who thus became judges would also typically have been generals (and sometimes legislators). They would have found the task of judging irksome and delegated it to others, who, being of less authority, would have felt more constrained in their decisions in contrast to the first judges who would have been "very bold in passing sentence". The newer judges "would [have been] at pains

36 On the original placing of this passage, see the editorial note, TMS 161.

37 N MacCormick, "Adam Smith on law" (1981) 15 *Valparaiso University Law Review* 243 at 248.

even to strengthen their conduct by the authority of their predecessors. . . . Whatever therefore had been practised by other judges would obtain authority with them and be received in time as Law" (LRBL 174–175).[38] Smith, therefore, could conceive of law being created by the practice of the courts.

Smith also expressed a preference for precedent as a mode of law-making. He told his class:

> The Sentences of former Cases [in England] are greatly regarded and form what is called the common law, which is found to be much more equitable than that which is founded on Statute only, for the same reason as what is founded on practise and experience must be better adapted to particular cases than that which is derived from theory only. (LRBL 175)

English law thus had the advantage of "being more formed on the naturall sentiments of mankind", as Smith told the Jurisprudence class (LJ(A) 98), adding later that "[n]ew courts and new laws are . . . great evills. Every court is bound only by its own practise. It takes time and repeated practise to ascertain the precise meaning of a law or to have precedents enough to determine the practise of a court" (LJ(A) 287). These remarks confirm not only that Smith recognised that precedent could be a source of law, but also that the enforcement of statutes through legislation was necessarily mediated through the practice of the courts. On the basis of a somewhat different discussion of these (and other) passages, Dr Haakonssen has commented that Smith approved of case law because "it takes time to find the standpoint of the impartial spectator", which the refinement of law through precedent brought about, especially since "in [case law] the negative, injustice, is inevitably the matter for consideration – that is what a court case is about".[39] Statutes were thought up in the abstract, and it was accordingly more difficult to be precise about the requirement of justice.

(5) The need for law to be developed

Governments had to ensure that law conformed as much as possible to justice. While every system of law was, at a certain level, "a more or less imperfect attempt towards a system of natural jurisprudence", circumstances could

38 Smith made a similar point about the use of precedent in Rome in WN V. i. f 44. Given what he has said about "the antients" not using precedent in LRBL, either he has changed his mind, or more likely, and as I have indicated in my text, was thinking of forensic speeches as the context would imply.

39 K Haakonssen, *The Science of a Legislator: The Natural Jurisprudence of David Hume and Adam Smith* (1981) 152–153.

prevent this from being so (TMS VII.iv.36). There are a number of instances of departure of law from justice noted in Smith's *Lectures on Jurisprudence*. One obvious example is his attack on entails in Scotland (LJ(A) 69–71). Less spectacularly, he also suggested that some treason laws enacted under Queen Anne "might now well be abrogated" (LJ(A) 298; see also LJ(B) 429). If the law did not develop appropriately in line with the state of the country, not only would opulence be retarded, but injustice would give rise to threatening disturbance. If "the public magistrate [did not employ] the power of the commonwealth to enforce the practice of [justice] . . . civil society would become a scene of bloodshed and disorder, every man revenging himself at his own hand whenever he fancied he was injured" (TMS VII.iv.36). A concrete instance of this was the continued practice of duelling: "For when the law do not give satisfaction somewhat adequate to the injury, men will think themselves intitled to take it at their own hand. The small punishment therefore which is incurred by these affronts according to our law is one great cause of duelling, and is to be accounted a deficientia juris." (LJ(A) 124).

C. SMITH AND LEGAL EDUCATION

In his class on moral philosophy, Smith had demonstrated how natural jurisprudence could provide a programme for law reform by treating it as "that science which inquires into the general principles which ought to be the foundation of the laws of all nations" (LJ(B) 397). This was a matter of obvious interest to Scots lawyers, especially when they were contemporaneously involved in projects to abolish entails.[40] Furthermore, there was considerable worry in Hanoverian Britain over the haphazard system of legislation and the disorganised statute book.[41] Legislation was in the hands of politicians, about whom Smith had harsh words to say (LJ(B) 539).[42] In *The Wealth of Nations*, Smith was to draw a sharp distinction between politicians and legislators (WN IV.ii.39).[43] Though legislation would be necessary to

40 See Phillipson, "Lawyers, landowners, and civic leadership" (n 22) at 112–118.

41 D Lieberman, *The Province of Legislation Determined: Legal Theory in Eighteenth-century Britain* (1989) (henceforth Lieberman, *Province of Legislation Determined*) 1–28.

42 See generally D Winch, *Adam Smith's Politics: An Essay in Historiographic Revision* (1978) 158–160.

43 On Smith's "science of legislation", see ibid and D Winch, "Science and the legislator: Adam Smith and after" (1983) 93 *Economic Journal* 501; and J H Burns, "Scottish Philosophy and the Science of Legislation" *Royal Society of Edinburgh Occasional Papers* (1985) 2–6, 11–29. On the science of legislation generally, see J H Burns, "The Fabric of Felicity: The Legislator and the Human Condition", in P King (ed), *The Study of Politics: A Collection of Inaugural Lectures* (1977) 207.

abolish entails (and in this project the Scots Bar lamentably failed because of politicians), Smith's transformation of natural law into historical natural jurisprudence and praise of development through precedent provided lawyers with a plan of action for reform. Not only could they promote legislation "governed by general principles" (WN IV.ii.39; cf WN IV.introd.1 and LJ(B) 397), and act as legislators at one remove, but they could also use precedent dynamically. In 1758, the Scottish judge Lord Kames remarked that "[l]aw in particular becomes then only a rational study, when it is traced historically, from its first rudiments among savages, through successive changes, to its highest improvements in a civilized society".[44] Smith, in this sense, had turned law into a rational study, though admitting he himself was not a profound lawyer (Corr 141). In 1777, Kames applied these remarks specifically to legal education, which he criticised as training students to rely on authority rather than reason. What he wished students to learn was historical reasoning about law, which would lead to fruitful modernisation: "Were law taught as a rational science, its principles unfolded, and its connection with morals and politics, it would prove an enticing study to every person who has an appetite for knowledge. We might hope to see our lawyers soaring above their predecessors; and giving splendor to their country, by purifying and improving its laws."[45] This is obviously a programme derivable from Smith's natural jurisprudence, and, as Professor Lieberman has shown, Kames envisaged reform through the courts rather than legislation.[46] Whether or not Kames derived these ideas on legal education from Smith is unimportant: it is enough that Smith's natural jurisprudence offered an approach to legal education thought desirable.

This returns us to the Faculty of Advocates' desire in 1760 and 1762 that intending advocates should attend the classes of the Professor of Public Law and the Law of Nature and Nations. Just as the Faculty, in Phillipson's words, made "claim to the civic leadership of Scottish society",[47] Smith's natural jurisprudence showed one method of achieving their aims of leadership and improvement in the laws. After 1762, the Faculty did not renew their exhortation to attend the class on the law of nature and nations, possibly

44 [H Home, Lord Kames,] *Historical Law-Tracts,* 2 vols (1758) vol i, v.

45 [H Home, Lord Kames,] *Elucidations respecting the Common and Statute Law of Scotland* (1777) vii–xiii.

46 Lieberman, *Province of Legislation Determined* (n 41) 144–175; and "The Legal Needs of a Commercial Society: the Jurisprudence of Lord Kames", in I Hont and M Ignatieff (eds), *Wealth and Virtue: The Shaping of Political Economy in the Scottish Enlightenment* (1983) 203.

47 Phillipson, "Lawyers, landowners, and civic leadership" (n 22) at 112.

because the successor to the man in whom they placed confidence did not teach.[48] In the University of Glasgow, however, John Millar, as Professor of Civil Law, expounded Smithian jurisprudence to his classes.[49] And he was an outstandingly successful teacher.[50] In 1779, Allan Maconochie was appointed Professor of Public Law and the Law of Nature and Nations in Edinburgh.[51] In 1788 his class was described thus:

> He traces the rise of political institutions from the natural characters and situation of the human species; follows their progress through the rude periods of society; and treats of their history and merits, as exhibited in the principal nations of ancient and modern times, which he examines separately, classing them according to those general causes to which he attributes the principal varieties in the forms, genius, and revolutions of governments. In this manner he endeavours to construct the science of the spirit of laws on a connected view of what may be called the natural history of man as a political agent; and he accordingly concludes his course with treating of the general principles of municipal law. political oeconomy. and the law of nations.[52]

This is the only information about his class; but it indicates that he had adopted an approach at least very similar to Smith's historical natural jurisprudence. Maconochie did not study under Smith. It is, however, intriguing to note that the first known possessor of the second set of notes deriving from Smith's lectures was Maconochie's son. Had his father perhaps obtained them to help prepare his own classes?[53] In Edinburgh as in Glasgow, law students were being equipped with an education to fit them for the task of making the laws of their country a more perfect "attempt towards a system of natural jurisprudence, or towards an enumeration of the particular rules of justice" (TMS VIII.iv.36).

48 H Arnot, *The History of Edinburgh* (1779) 398. It is notable that the Faculty of Advocates at the same period also encouraged intending members to attend classes in Universal History in Edinburgh. They still encouraged this in 1768 (*FR* 2 (n 1) 259). See Cairns, "Formation of the Scottish Legal Mind" (n 3) at 265.

49 See K Haakonssen, "John Millar and the science of a legislator" (1985) *Juridical Review* 41–68; J W Cairns, "John Millar's lectures on Scots criminal law" (1988) 8 OJLS 364; J W Cairns, "Eighteenth century professorial classification of English common law" (1987) 33 McGillLJ 225 at 230 and 233–235.

50 See, e.g., W C Lehmann, *John Millar of Glasgow 1735–1801: His Life and Thought and his Contributions to Sociological Analysis* (1960) 30–42.

51 Grant, *Story of the University of Edinburgh* (n 6) vol II, 315–316.

52 H Arnot, *The History of Edinburgh,* 2nd edn (1788) 398.

53 See the remarks of Cannan in his introduction to A Smith, *Lectures on Justice, Police, Revenue and Arms, Delivered in the University of Glasgow by Adam Smith, Reported by a Student in 1763*, E Cannan (ed) (1896) xv–xvii. I am indebted to Professor MacCormick for bringing this to my attention.

4 The First Edinburgh Chair in Law: Grotius and the Scottish Enlightenment*

A. INTRODUCTION

The influence of natural law in late-seventeenth and early-eighteenth-century Scotland is well known.[1] At a broad political level, the achievements of the modern school of natural law helped the Scots reach varied readings and understandings of contemporary political events such as the Glorious Revolution and the Union of 1707.[2] The work of these secular natural lawyers also provided a new way of approaching moral philosophy that came to dominate the curriculum in the eighteenth-century Scottish universities. A crucial figure here has generally been seen to be Gershom Carmichael in

* The author is grateful for the comments of his colleagues and friends Drs Clare Jackson and Paul du Plessis and Professors Sir Neil MacCormick and Hector MacQueen. He is delighted to acknowledge the permissions of the Keeper of the Records of Scotland, the Keeper of the Advocates Library, the Trustees of the National Library of Scotland, the Librarian of the University of Edinburgh, and the Archivist of the City of Edinburgh to examine, cite and, in some instances, quote from unpublished material in their care.

1 See, e.g., K Haakonssen, *Natural Law and Moral Philosophy: From Grotius to the Scottish Enlightenment* (1996) (henceforth Haakonssen, *Natural Law and Moral Philosophy*). To consider current debates over contested understandings of the Scottish Enlightenment, see now the essays in P Wood (ed), *The Scottish Enlightenment: Essays in Reinterpretation* (2000), especially the chapter by the editor, and A Broadie (ed), *The Cambridge Companion to the Scottish Enlightenment* (2003). Shaw, *The Political History of Eighteenth-Century Scotland* (1999) gives a good introduction to the politics of the period.

2 See, e.g., C Jackson, "Revolution principles, *ius naturae*, and *ius gentium* in early-enlightenment Scotland: The contribution of Sir Francis Grant, Lord Cullen (c 1660–1726)", in T Hochstrasser and P Schröder (eds), *Early Modern Natural Law Theories: Contexts and Strategies in the Early Enlightenment* (2003) (henceforth Hochstrasser and Schröder (eds), *Early Modern Natural Theories*) 107; also *Restoration Scotland, 1660–1690: Royalist Politics, Religion and Ideas* (2003); and "Natural law and the construction of political sovereignty in Scotland, 1660–1690", in I Hunter and D Saunders (eds), *Natural Law and Civil Sovereignty: Moral Right and State Authority in Early Modern Political Thought* (2002) 155; R Von Friedeburg "From collective representation to the right of individual defence: James Steuart's *Ius Populi Vindicatum* and the use of Johannes Althusius' *Politica* in Restoration Scotland" 1998 *History of European Ideas* 19; J W Cairns, "Scottish Law, Scottish Lawyers and the Status of the Union", in J Robertson (ed) *A Union for Empire: Political Thought and the British Union of 1707* (1995) 243.

Glasgow, who adopted Pufendorf's textbook *De officio hominis et civis* as the basis of his classes on moral philosophy, providing editions with important notes founded on his teaching.[3]

It is also evident that natural law was much relied on in the presentation of arguments in court, which were mainly delivered in or reduced to writing in the elaborate written processes that developed in Scottish litigation of any complexity.[4] This meant that Scots viewed their law within a framework drawn from the *ius naturale* and *ius gentium*. The first to articulate this clearly was Thomas Craig around 1600, who identified *ius commune* with *ius naturale* and *ius gentium* rather than *utrumque ius*.[5] The classic account of Scots law understood in this way is that by James Dalrymple, Viscount Stair, first printed in 1681;[6] but such an exposition of Scots law was normal for the following century.[7] Stair depicted Scots law as a coherent and logical whole integrated as a hierarchical series of norms, justified and made obligatory by a higher authority, thereby providing a major synthesis comparable to those of other institutional writers in the era of the *usus modernus*.[8]

It was on the basis of this approach that, in the eighteenth century, judges could clearly debate issues such as copyright and slavery in Scotland using

3 J Moore and M Silverthorne, "Gershom Carmichael and the Natural Jurisprudence Tradition in Eighteenth-Century Scotland", in I Hont and M Ignatieff (eds), *Wealth and Virtue: The Shaping of Political Economy in the Scottish Enlightenment* (1983) 73; and "Natural Sociability and Natural Rights in the Moral Philosophy of Gerschom Carmichael", in V Hope (ed), *Philosophers of the Scottish Enlightenment* (1984) 1. See now J Moore and M Silverthorne (eds), *Natural Rights on the Threshold of the Scottish Enlightenment: The Writings of Gershom Carmichael* (2002).

4 See now D R Parratt, "The Development and Use of Written Pleadings in Scots Civil Procedure", unpublished PhD thesis, University of Edinburgh (2004) 18–83. For an example of use in a particular case, see J W Cairns, "Stoicism, slavery, and law: Grotian jurisprudence and its reception" 2001/2002 *Grotiana* 197 at 216.

5 See J W Cairns, "*Ius civile* in Scotland, *ca* 1600" 2004 *Roman Legal Tradition* 136 (henceforth "*Ius civile* in Scotland") at 150–158; and "The Civil Law Tradition in Scottish Legal Thought", in D L Carey Miller and R Zimmermann (eds), *The Civilian Tradition and Scots Law: Aberdeen Quincentenary Essays* (1997) 191 (henceforth Cairns, "The Civil Law Tradition in Scottish Legal Thought") at 200–203.

6 Stair, *The Institutions of the Law of Scotland: Deduced from its Originals, and Collated with the Civil, Canon and Feudal Laws, and with the Customs of Neighbouring Nations* (1681; 2nd edn 1693; new edn 1981).

7 See, e.g., Cairns, "The Civil Law Tradition in Scottish Legal Thought" (n 5) at 204–220.

8 See K Luig, "The institutes of national law in the seventeenth and eighteenth centuries" 1972 *Juridical Review* 193. On Stair's views of natural law, see, e.g., A H Campbell, *The Structure of Stair's Institutions: Being the Twenty-First Lecture on the David Murray Foundation in the University of Glasgow Delivered on 24th February, 1954* (1954); N MacCormick, "Law, obligation and consent; reflections on Stair and Locke" 1979 *Archiv für Rechts- und Sozial Philosophie* 387; and "Stair's General Concepts. 2. Stair as Analytical Jurist", in D M Walker (ed), *Stair Tercentenary Studies*, Stair Society vol 33 (1981) (henceforth *Stair Tercentenary Studies*) 187;

the language of the *ius naturale* and the *ius gentium*. Thus, in 1773, Lord Kennet gave his opinion that literary property was not found in the law of Scotland. He based this claim partly on the observation that it was "not in *the law of nature*, which is one great fountain of our law". He argued that:

> It is in vain to say, that it is founded on that part of the law of nature, by which we are not to hurt another, or take from him what belongs to him; for that is to apply a *petitio principi*. – It is not in the *law of nations*: there is not the *consensus gentium* . . .

This meant that it was "only such a kind of right as particular states have, in some instances, conferred by a patent, or *privilegium*, for a limited time". He then showed it was not found in Scots law.[9] Five years later, the same judge stressed that the law on slavery in Jamaica was founded not on "equity" but "expediency"; Lord Monboddo noted that slavery was not of the *ius naturale* but of the *ius gentium*, and therefore just.[10]

Given the interest in natural law that existed in Scotland before familiarity with Grotius' and then Pufendorf's works developed (primarily after 1660), it is not possible to state that it was knowledge of *De jure belli ac pacis* that stimulated such concern with the modern movement in natural law.[11] There can be no doubt, however, but that the works and Grotius and Pufendorf and their commentators – Jean Barbeyrac in particular – at least enhanced and developed such interest, and pushed it in a particular direction. Reinforcing this was the Scottish practice of studying law in the Netherlands that reached a peak between 1680 and 1730, though attendance at Dutch universities remained strong until around 1750.[12] While it was in courses on Justinian's

"The rational discipline of law" 1981 *Juridical Review* 146; Stein, "Stair's General Concepts. I. The Theory of Law", in D M Walker (ed), *Stair Tercentenary Studies* 181; J D Ford, "Stair's Title 'Of Liberty and Servitude'", in A D E Lewis and D J Ibbetson (eds), *The Roman Law Tradition* (1994) 135.

9 *The Decision of the Court of Session, Upon the Question of Literary Property; In the Cause John Hinton of London, Bookseller, Pursuer; Against Alexander Donaldson and John Wood, Booksellers in Edinburgh, and James Melrose Bookseller in Kilmarnock, Defenders. Published by James Boswell, Esq; Advocate, One of the Counsel in the Cause* (1774) 1–2.

10 *Knight v Wedderbum* Hailes' Decisions (1826) vol ii, 776 at 777, 779.

11 See Cairns, "*Ius civile in Scotland*" (n 5) at 150–158; and "Scottish Law, Scottish Lawyers and the Status of the Union" (n 2) at 258–259.

12 R Feenstra, "Scottish–Dutch Legal Relations in the Seventeenth and Eighteenth Centuries", in *Legal Scholarship and Doctrines of Private Law, 13th–18th Centuries* (1996) XVI at 33–36 (= H de Ridder-Symoens and J M Fletcher (eds), *Academic Relations Between the Low Countries and the British Isles, 1450–1700. Proceedings of the First Conference of Belgian, British and Dutch Historians of Universities Held in Ghent, September 30–October 2, 1987* (1987) 25); K Van Strien and M Ahsmann, "Scottish law students in Leiden at the end of the seventeenth century. The correspondence of John Clerk, 1694–1697" 1992 *Lias* 271 and 1993 *Lias* 1 (henceforth Van Strien and Ahsmann, "Scottish law students in Leiden").

Institutes and *Digest* that Scottish law students were most interested, they were also keen to attend a class on natural law – a *Collegium Grotianum* as such was commonly described.[13] Such classes were taught by, among others, Ph R Vitriarius and Gerard Noodt in Leiden.[14] If the Scots favoured Utrecht and Leiden among the Dutch universities, some went to Groningen to study natural law with Jean Barbeyrac.[15] It was a matter of disappointment and regret if no classes on natural law were available.[16]

While the significance of both Grotius and Pufendorf in Scotland is generally recognised, there has been a tendency to emphasise the role of Pufendorf's thought, with its focus on the rights and duties of the citizen, largely because of the intellectual significance properly attributed to Carmichael and his edition of the German author.[17] There is no reason to dispute this approach; but the direct and mediated influence of Grotius – especially on the lawyers – should not be forgotten. Before Carmichael produced his edition of Pufendorf's *De officio*, William Scott, one of the regents in philosophy (that is teacher of the general curriculum in arts) in the University of Edinburgh, had published (in Edinburgh in 1707) a compend of Grotius' *De iure* for his students.[18] Indeed, Scott appears to have been offering a private class on Grotius from the 1690s.[19] It is always worth remembering that Adam Smith himself not only wrote in his *Theory of Moral Sentiments* of 1758 that "Grotius seems to have been the first who attempted to give the world any thing like a system of those principles which ought to run through, and be the foundation of the laws of all nations", but also expressed the view that Grotius' "treatise of the laws of war and peace . . . is perhaps at this day the most complete work that has yet been given upon this subject".[20] This reflected what he told his class

13 Van Strien and Ahsmann, "Scottish law students in Leiden" (n 12) at 289–291.

14 Ibid at 290–293, 297; G C J J Van den Bergh, *The Life and Work of Gerard Noodt (1647–1725): Dutch Legal Scholarship Between Humanism and Enlightenment* (1988) (henceforth Van den Bergh, *Gerard Noodt*) 271, 283; C J H Jansen, "Over de 18e eeuwse docenten natuurrecht aan Nederlandse universiteiten en de door hen gebruikte leerboeken" 1987 *Tijdschrift voor Rechtsgeschiedenis* 103 (henceforth Jansen, "18e eeuwse docenten natuurrecht") at 106, 114.

15 See, e.g., Dundas to Mackie, 10 January 1728 in Edinburgh University Library (henceforth EUL) MS La 11.91.B.59.

16 Kenneth Mackenzie to John Mackenzie, 9 March 1719, National Library of Scotland (henceforth NLS) MS 1209 fo 14. Vitriarius was still teaching, but the student considered him a "dotard".

17 J Robertson, "The Scottish Contribution to the Enlightenment", in P Wood (ed), *Scottish Enlightenment* 37 at 46; Haakonssen, *Natural Law and Moral Philosophy* (n 1) 65.

18 *Hugonis Grotii de jure belli ac pacis librorum III. compendium, annotationibus & commentariis selectis illustratum. In usum studiosae juventutis Academiae Edinensis* (1707).

19 See C P Finlayson, "Edinburgh University and the Darien scheme" 1955 *Scottish Historical Review* 97 (henceforth Finlayson, "Edinburgh University and the Darien scheme") at 99–100.

20 A Smith, *Theory of Moral Sentiments*, ed D D Raphael and A L Macfie (1976) 341–342 (VII iv.37).

in his lectures on jurisprudence, which were viewed as complementary to classes on Civil Law.[21]

Smith's natural jurisprudence, however, was founded on an understanding of justice as a personal virtue. It had little place for the universal approach to justice and natural law found in Grotius or Pufendorf; instead justice was a historical and social creation that developed through individuals' dealings with each other and ability to enter into and appreciate each other's sentiments, combined with individuals' desire to conform their behaviour to those practices of which others would approve. Observing when another had been wronged allowed recognition that the other had a right not to be wronged in such a way. The science of legislation was to recognise such rights and to appreciate whether their inscription as laws was best achieved through legislation or by operation of the courts.[22]

B. SCOTTISH UNIVERSITY EDUCATION IN LAW

From the 1690s, there had been considerable interest in Scotland in developing modern university legal education, in particular in Edinburgh. The main focus was on developing classes in Roman law to provide the education necessary to succeed in the private and public examinations for admission as an advocate.[23] From 1699, a few advocates started to teach such classes privately.[24] A chair to teach Roman law could not be erected in the University of Edinburgh until 1710, when the privilege of an exclusive right to be Professor of Civil Law in Scotland, initially granted to Alexander

21 A Smith, *Lectures on Jurisprudence*, ed R L Meek, D D Raphael and P G Stein (1978) 397. See J Erskine to Lord Cardross, 24 November 1762 EUL MS La.II.238.

22 K Haakonssen, *The Science of a Legislator. The Natural Jurisprudence of David Hume and Adam Smith* (1981) (henceforth Haakonssen, *Science of a Legislator*) 154–189; J W Cairns, "Ethics and the science of legislation: legislators, philosophers and courts in eighteenth-century Scotland" 2000 *Jahrbuch für Recht und Ethik* 159; and "Adam Smith and the Role of the Courts in Securing Justice and Liberty", in R P Malloy and J Evensky (eds), *Adam Smith and the Philosophy of Law and Economics* (1994) 31.

23 J W Cairns, "The Formation of the Scottish Legal Mind in the Eighteenth Century: Themes of Humanism and Enlightenment in the Admission of Advocates", in N MacCormick and P Birks (eds), *The Legal Mind: Essays for Tony Honoré* (1986) 253; "Advocates' hats, Roman law and admission to the Scots Bar, 1580–1812" 1999 20, 2 JLH 24.

24 J W Cairns, "John Spotswood, Professor of Law: a Preliminary Sketch", in Gordon (ed), *Miscellany III*, Stair Society vol 39 (1992) 131, 131–134; "'Importing our Lawyers from Holland': Netherlands' Influences on Scots Law and Lawyers in the Eighteenth Century", in G G Simpson (ed), *Scotland and the Low Countries 1124–1994* (1996) 136 (henceforth Cairns, "Netherlands' Influences on Scots Law and Lawyers").

Cunningham of Block by Parliament in 1698, finally expired.[25] This meant that the first chair in law to be erected in the University of Edinburgh was that of Public Law and the Law of Nature and Nations in 1707, a regius chair endowed by conversion of a number of bursaries in divinity.[26]

This article will trace the history of that chair in the eighteenth century, showing how it tracks the development of thinking about justice and law in Scotland. Initially, the professors taught using Grotius' work or a compend of it; but, by the end of the century, the class had been transformed into an exercise in developing an essentially Smithian jurisprudence that inculcated in the students an understanding of justice as an essentially historical phenomenon. By the early 1800s, the chair had failed. If many factors brought this about, changing intellectual life had made the discipline it taught seem irrelevant in a new world in which Smith's jurisprudence had dissolved into a variety of different specialised disciplines. By 1830, it was proposed to suppress the chair.[27]

(1) Charles Areskine, Professor, 1707–1734

The man appointed to the new chair was Charles Areskine, MA (St Andrews) and Regent in Philosophy in the University of Edinburgh, and it has been suggested that the professorship was created solely for his benefit, or that the Regent William Scott also aspired to it.[28] This seems unlikely for a variety of reasons; but the topic is too complex to consider here.[29] It is enough

25 J W Cairns, "Alexander Cunningham's proposed edition of the *Digest*. An episode in the history of the Dutch elegant school of Roman law" (2001) *Tijdschrift voor Rechtsgeschiedenis* 81 (Part I) and 307 (Part II) (henceforth Cairns, "Alexander Cunningham's proposed edition of the *Digest*") at 109–110, 308; "Netherlands' Influences on Scots Law and Lawyers" (n 24) at 146–149.

26 See, e.g., A Grant, *The Story of the University of Edinburgh During its First Three Hundred Years* (1884) (henceforth Grant, *University of Edinburgh*) vol i, 232–233.

27 There is an account of the chair in Lorimer, "The story of the Chair of Public Law in the University of Edinburgh" (1888) 4 LQR 139 (henceforth Lorimer, "Story of the Chair of Public Law"); that given here is somewhat different.

28 A Bower, *The History of the University of Edinburgh; Chiefly Compiled from Original Papers and Records, Never Before Published* (1817–1830) (henceforth Bower, *History of the University of Edinburgh*) vol ii, 65–66; Finlayson, "Edinburgh University and the Darien Scheme" (n 19) at 100. The name is of course normally Erskine, but Areskine invariably spelled his name in the fashion adopted here, as did his brother Robert, MD, who became physician to Peter the Great: R. Paul (ed), "Letters and Documents relating to Robert Erskine, Physician to Peter the Great Czar of Russia", in *Miscellany of the Scottish History Society* (1904) vol ii, 372.

29 See generally my unpublished paper: "Improving our lawyers through the study of natural law: The chair of Public Law and the Law of Nature and Nations in Edinburgh", delivered British Legal History Conference, Cambridge, July 1997.

to remark that Areskine's appointment was largely due to his relative, the Earl of Mar.[30]

Given leave from the chair Areskine went to Leiden to study law, matriculating in February 1708.[31] No information is available about his studies there, but, given the field of his professorship, it is likely that he attended a *Collegium* on *ius naturale*. Such were taught in this period by Noodt and Vitriarius. The former offered a private *Collegium Grotianum;* though he gave a "simple lemmatic explanation" of Grotius' *De jure belli ac pacis*, he addressed the text in a critical fashion.[32] Vitriarius also founded his classes on Grotius, but had written his own textbook *ad methodum Hugonis Grotii*.[33] It may be significant that Areskine owned a copy of this work.[34] An intending advocate, George Mackenzie, a direct contemporary of Areskine at Leiden and a member of the Delvine family, had difficulty in deciding between the two professors' classes on natural law. He considered Vitriarius "lazy" and Noodt "malicious" (because he railed "at Grotius and these he cites").[35] These remarks perhaps reveal more about Mackenzie, a somewhat foolish and immature young man, than about those whom he criticised.[36] Vitriarius also offered a private college on the increasingly popular topic of *ius publicum Romano-Germanicum*.[37] This could well have attracted Areskine.[38]

30 Earl of Mar to D Nairne, 1 February 1707, National Archives of Scotland (henceforth NAS) GD 124/15/487/3; D Nairne to Earl of Mar, 11 February 1707 NAS GD 124/15/487/14.

31 EUL MS Dc 6.108; C Areskine to Earl of Mar, 24 April 1707 NAS GD 124/15/542/1. See *Album studiosorum Academiae Lugduno-Batavae MDLXXV–MDCCCLXXV* (1875) (henceforth *Album Leiden*) col 802.

32 Van den Bergh, *Gerard Noodt* (n 14) 283.

33 Ph R Vitriarius, *Institutiones juris naturae et gentium in usum Christiani Ludovici marchionis Brandenburgici ad methodum Hugonis Grotii conscriptae* (1692) (and many other editions: see M Ahsmann and R Feenstra, *Bibliographie van Hoogleraren in de Rechten aan de Leidse Universiteit tot 1811* (1984) (henceforth Ahsmann and Feenstra, *Bibliographie*) 327–330 (nos 1001–1011)).

34 See his library catalogue: NLS MS 3283 42, 216. The catalogue records the edition of 1704; at some stage, the date 1692 has been added (or substituted) in pencil. Both the import and date of this pencil alteration are unclear. The surviving Alva Collection contains only that of 1692: NLS pressmark Alva 262. The flyleaf records that this was a copy bought in Leiden on 11 December 1693 by John Paterson for 30 stuivers.

35 G Mackenzie to J Mackenzie, 4 March 1708 NLS MS 1118 fo 65.

36 See Cairns, "Alexander Cunningham's proposed edition of the *Digest*" (n 25) at 314–316.

37 Ahsmann and Feenstra, *Bibliographie* (n 33) 320–327.

38 See NLS MS 3283 61 where there is a pencil entry for Vitriarius, *Institutiones juris publici Romano-Germanici selectae* (1714), on which see Ahsmann and Feenstra, *Bibliographie* (n 33) 321 (no 991). The copy survives in the Alva Collection (NLS pressmark Alva 263), but it bears the bookplate of Areskine's son, James Erskine of Alva. Of course, he could have put his plate into one of his father's books.

Areskine followed his studies in Leiden with a version of the Grand Tour, certainly visiting Italy and Germany. He bought large numbers of books in Italy, some, no doubt, are among those Italian works later listed in his Library Catalogue.[39] After spending some time in London, he eventually returned north to be admitted as an advocate on 17 July 1711.[40] Designing himself "her Majesty's Professor of Publick Law, in the University of Edinburgh", he advertised that he would "begin his private Lecture [sic] on the Laws of Nature and Nations" on Friday 16 November 1711 at five pm "at his Lodgings in Frazer's Land".[41] There can be little doubt but that this class was modelled on a private *Collegium Grotianum* that Areskine had attended in Leiden.

Areskine failed to maintain a class; he certainly did not continue to teach.[42] This means it is uncertain from what text he proposed to teach (or actually taught) in 1711. It is, however, a fair assumption that it was from Grotius' *De jure belli ac pacis* or a compend of it. Areskine's education at Leiden, where Grotius was the foundation of the courses of Vitriarius and Noodt, will have demonstrated the possibilities of the work. Further, the collection of books on natural law that may be traced in his extensive library contained eight editions of Grotius' *De jure belli ac pacis* (including a first edition and the translations into French by Barbeyrac and Courtin), two compends or teaching manuals based on it, and four works of commentaries and notes on it.[43] In comparison, he had three editions of Pufendorf's *De jure naturae et gentium* and two of his *De officio* (one of which was that of Carmichael).[44] Other works on natural law may be identified in his collection, but the dominance of that of Grotius is clear. If Areskine's library is any guide to his thinking on natural law, the thought of Grotius was what mattered most, making it likely that he intended to teach from it or a suitable compend. Areskine owned a copy of Scott's *Compendium*;[45] it is possible that he intended it as his textbook, but the copy recorded in his library was probably acquired long after he had given over teaching.[46] A number of the works recorded in his

39 C Areskine to J Erskine, 10 May 1710 NLS MS 5072 fos 8–9. See NLS MS 3283 passim.

40 C Areskine to J Erskine, 7 and 20 April and 12 June 1712 NLS MS 5072 fos 11, 13, and 16; F J Grant (ed), *The Faculty of Advocates in Scotland, 1532–1943, with Genealogical Notes* (1944) 66 (henceforth Grant, *Faculty of Advocates*).

41 *Scots Courant*, 12/14,14/16 November 1711.

42 See W Scott to J Anderson, 7 December 1714 NLS Adv MS 29.1.2 (iv) fos 180–181.

43 NLS MS 3283 23, 24, 31, 32, 42.

44 NLS MS 3283 22, 23, 44.

45 NLS MS 3283 32.

46 The success of Scott's *Compendium* in Edinburgh is questionable, as the unsold sheets turn up, with the title page and preliminary matter cancelled, as the purported London edition of 1718: *Hugonis Grotii de jure belli ac pacis Librorum III. Compendium. Annotationibus & commen-*

manuscript Library Catalogue survive in the Alva Collection in the National Library of Scotland, but they provide no definite guidance on the point. His copy of the 1651 edition of *De iure belli ac pacis* is partially underlined in blue or black as well as red ink, and has minor marginal annotations in the way of cross references, either internal or to other works such as the Bible or the *Digest*.[47] It is not possible to link these to Areskine: the hand is very careful and too unspecific to be identified as his.

If Areskine was unsuccessful in attracting a class, or unwilling to devote the necessary attention, there nonetheless was some interest in such classes, so that, in 1732, John Lookup, advocate, who taught Civil Law privately at his lodgings, also offered weekly "Prelections upon the Law of Nature and Nations".[48] Instead, Areskine had a distinguished legal and political career, entering Parliament in 1722, and serving as Solicitor General (1725–1737) and Lord Advocate (1737–1742), before appointment to the bench as Lord Tinwald in 1742. In 1748 he became Justice Clerk.[49] In many ways he was a typical figure of the early Enlightenment in Scotland, interested in banking and economic development, a member of the Musical Society, and a founder member of that important intellectual club, the Philosophical Society of Edinburgh, the forerunner of the Royal Society of Edinburgh.[50]

(2) William Kirkpatrick, Professor, 1734–1735

Areskine resigned the chair in 1734, to be replaced by William Kirkpatrick, advocate.[51] A close associate of Areskine, Kirkpatrick was a younger son of the noted Dumfriesshire family of Kirkpatrick of Closeburn.[52] Areskine had married Grizel Grierson, heiress of the estate of Barjarg in Dumfriesshire, where he later also acquired the estate of Tinwald. He built up an important political interest in the county, representing it in

tariis selectis illustratum. Londini, Impensis T. Ward in vico dicto Inner-Temple-Lane prope Fleet Street. 1718. I hope to study these *compendia* further elsewhere.

47 H Grotius, *De iure belli ac pacis* (1651): NLS pressmark Alva 190.

48 *Edinburgh Evening Courant*, 12/16 October 1732.

49 See, e.g., R Sedgwick (ed), *The House of Commons 1715–1754* (1970) (henceforth Sedgwick (ed), *House of Commons 1715–1754*) vol i, 420.

50 R L Emerson, "The Philosophical Society of Edinburgh 1737–1747" 1979 *British Journal for the History of Science* 154 at 190.

51 See, e.g., Grant, *University of Edinburgh* (n 26) vol 2, 314–315.

52 For some details, see G E C[okayne], *Compete Baronetage* (1900–1906) vol 4, 329–331. Not all the details in this are accurate. [Kirkpatrick], *Kirkpatrick of Closeburn* (1858) and Kirkpatrick, *Records of the Closeburn Kirkpatricks* [1954] give information about the family, but barely mention William Kirkpatrick.

Parliament from 1722.[53] Kirkpatrick's father had died in 1720 when he and his older brother, Sir Thomas, were under age.[54] Under Areskine's guidance, Sir Thomas, along with Andrew Wauchope, had been educated at Utrecht and Leiden, with George Waddell as tutor to both.[55] It is probable that William Kirkpatrick's education in law at Leiden was also undertaken under Areskine's advice.[56] It may be that, like his elder brother, he there studied natural law with J J Vitriarius, who based his class on Grotius.[57] The closeness of the two men was sealed by Kirkpatrick's marriage to Areskine's daughter Jean in 1746.[58]

Areskine had initially owed his seat in Dumfriesshire to the Duke of Queensberry; but the latter had gone into opposition in 1734, and, by the mid-1730s, Areskine had become close to the "Argathelian" Whigs led by the Earl of Ilay (Duke of Argyll from 1743), whose Scottish manager was the judge Andrew Fletcher, Lord Milton, who became Justice Clerk in 1735.[59] Since the chair was in the patronage of the Crown, political support was necessary for Areskine to be able to resign in favour of Kirkpatrick with certainty that Kirkpatrick would be appointed. Milton and Ilay will have been instrumental in securing the necessary royal warrant. Though Lord Milton's surviving papers throw no light on the matter, he and Areskine were in close touch because of the election in May 1734.[60] Further, he and Ilay were anxious that Areskine should keep the Duke of Queensberry's candidates out of the Dumfries burghs and Dumfriesshire seats.[61] Appointing Kirkpatrick will have helped secure this aim, by keeping both men on side. Suffice it to say that, by 18 April 1734, Kirkpatrick had

53 Sedgwick (ed), *The House of Commons 1715–1754* (n 49) vol i, 384, 420.

54 Commissary Court Records of Dumfries, NAS CC 5/6/8/279.

55 *Album Leiden* (n 31) col 892; see Kirkpatrick to Areskine, 22 October 1723 NLS MS 5072 fos 147–148; Waddell to Areskine, 23 November 1723 and 2 March 1725 NLS MS 5072 fos 154, 164.

56 *Album Leiden* col 905. He is probably to be identified with the Edinburgh student of the same name: EUL (typescript) "Matriculation Roll of the University of Edinburgh. Arts–Law–Divinity" (transcribed by Morgan) (henceforth EUL, "Matriculation Roll of the University of Edinburgh") vol i, 171, 178.

57 G Waddell to C Areskine, 29 February and 28 July 1724 NLS MS 5072 fos 156, 160; T Kirkpatrick to C Areskine, 30 April 1724 NLS MS 5072 fo 158; Jansen, "18e eeuwse docenten natuurrecht" (n 14) at 106, 114.

58 See, e.g., Sedgwick (ed), *House of Commons 1715–1754* (n 49) vol ii, 190.

59 See ibid vol i, 397, 420, vol ii, 190; J S Shaw, *The Management of Scottish Society, 1707–1764: Power, Nobles, Lawyers, Edinburgh Agents and English Influences* (1983) 62–63, 86–113; A Murdoch, *"The People Above": Politics and Administration in Mid-Eighteenth-Century Scotland* (1980) (henceforth Murdoch, *People Above*) 12–14.

60 See C Areskine to Lord Milton, 16 and 28 April 1734 NLS MS 16556 fos 148, 150.

61 See Sedgwick (ed), *House of Commons 1715–1754* (n 49) vol i, 397, 420, vol ii, 190.

obtained a commission under the Privy Seal to be regius Professor.[62] He was duly installed on 2 December.[63]

There is no information on whether or not Kirkpatrick taught, and he held the chair for only a few months. This was because in May 1735 he contested, in Areskine's interest, the Parliamentary by-election for the Dumfries burghs (Areskine had been elected in 1734 for both the Dumfries burghs and Dumfriesshire, opting to sit for the latter, so the former seat became vacant).[64] Kirkpatrick's standing had the support of Ilay.[65] Due to a dispute over the return he did not take up his seat until 1736. He served in Parliament until 1738, when he was appointed Clerk of Session.[66]

(3) George Abercromby, Professor, 1735–1759

Kirkpatrick's successor was George Abercromby, advocate. This again was an appointment managed by Areskine through Milton and Ilay.[67] Areskine was still co-operating closely with both men at this period. Abercromby allegedly paid Kirkpatrick £1,000 for a resignation of the chair in his favour.[68] His father was Alexander Abercromby of Tullibody, advocate; his mother was Mary Duff of the family of Duff of Braco, later Earls of Fife.[69] Abercromby may have had an association with Areskine and his family, arising out of Tullibody's proximity to Alva and Alloa. While much later Milton was to consider Abercromby an enemy in the management of Perthshire elections, it is uncertain whether this was so in 1735.[70] It may well have suited Milton to oblige Abercromby since the estate of Tullibody entitled its holder to a vote in Perthshire. Thus, while it is conceivable that Areskine and Milton managed the appointment simply to oblige Kirkpatrick, it is possible that they also found Abercromby an acceptable candidate at this time. It may further be significant that Abercromby and Kirkpatrick, much of an age, were admitted as advocates within a few days of each other and that Abercromby's

62 Edinburgh City Archives (henceforth ECA) Town Council Minutes vol 55, 277 (27 November 1734).

63 EUL Da.1.35 College [Senatus] Minutes 1733–1790 22 (2 December 1734).

64 Sedgwick (ed), *House of Commons 1715–1754* (n 49) vol i, 397, vol ii, 190.

65 See Campbell to Earl of Ilay, 22 April 1735 NLS MS 16559 fos 198–199.

66 Sedgwick (ed), *House of Commons 1715–1754* (n 49) vol i, 397, vol ii, 190.

67 See C Areskine to Lord Milton, 25 September 1735 NLS MS 16560 fo 253.

68 See D Hume to A Smith, 8 June 1758 in E C Mossner and I S Ross (eds), *The Correspondence of Adam Smith,* rev edn (1987) (henceforth *Correspondence of Adam Smith*) 24–25; Grant, *University of Edinburgh* (n 26) vol ii, 315.

69 Grant, *Faculty of Advocates* (n 40) 1.

70 See D Graeme to R Gardiner, 15 February 1764 NLS MS 16730 fo 206; J Stuart Mackenzie to Lord Milton, 11 February 1764 NLS MS 16731 fo 80.

legal studies at Leiden had partly coincided with those of Kirkpatrick's elder brother.[71]

Born in 1705, Abercromby, after attendance at the University of Edinburgh, had studied in the Netherlands (along with his brother James) in 1724–1725, matriculating at Groningen as well as Leiden.[72] It is fair to assume that the brothers will have matriculated at Groningen in order to study with Barbeyrac, the noted commentator on, and translator and editor of (among others) Grotius and Pufendorf.[73] Barbeyrac taught using Pufendorf as his textbook.[74] In Leyden, colleges on natural law were at this time taught by J J Vitriarius and J O Westenberg, the former, as noted, basing his class on Grotius.[75] Abercromby was admitted as an advocate on 11 November 1728.[76]

Through the second half of the 1730s, Abercromby taught in Edinburgh, on the model of a private Dutch *collegium*, his class being described as "Lectures on *Grotius de Jure Belli ac Pacis*".[77] He was still teaching Grotius in the early 1740s.[78] By the later 1750s, however, Abercromby had ceased to teach.[79] It is impossible to be certain when this happened, since he had given up the practice of advertising his lectures in the newspapers before he stopped teaching.

By the 1750s, however, education in the law of nature and nations was regarded as an important aspect of a legal training. In 1748 the new Lord President of the Court of Session had encouraged intending advocates "to learn thoroughly the principles of the Roman Law and the Laws of Nature and Nations".[80] In 1758, an observer, noting that Abercromby did not teach,

71 Grant, *Faculty of Advocates* (n 40) 1, 119; *Album Leiden* cols 895, 899 (25 October 1724, 3 August 1725) lists Abercromby's matriculations. Sir Thomas Kirkpatrick was still in Leiden in March 1725: G Waddell to C Areskine, 2 March 1725 NLS MS 5072 fo 164.

72 EUL, "Matriculation Roll of the University of Edinburgh" (n 56) vol i, 178; *Album studiosorum Academiae Groninganae* (1915) col 172 (3 November 1724); *Album Leiden* (n 31) cols 895, 899 (25 October 1724, 3 August 1725).

73 See P Meylan, *Jean Barbeyrac (1674–1744) et les débuts de l'enseignement du droit dans l'ancienne académie de Lausanne: Contribution à l'histoire du droit naturel* (1937), although he is disappointing on Barbeyrac in Groningen.

74 See Jansen "18e eeuwse docenten natuurrecht" (n 14) at 107, 114. On Barbeyrac's defence of Pufendorf, see Korkman, "Voluntarism and Moral Obligation: Barbeyrac's Defence of Pufendorf Revisited", in Hochstrasser and Schröder (eds), *Early Modern Natural Law Theories* (n 2) 195.

75 Jansen, "18e eeuwse docenten natuurrecht" (n 14) at 106, 114.

76 Grant, *Faculty of Advocates* (n 40) 1.

77 See, e.g., *Caledonian Mercury*, 27 July 1736, 11 October 1739.

78 See *Scots Magazine* 3 (1741) 371.

79 See D Hume to A Smith, 8 June 1758 in *Correspondence of Adam Smith* (n 68) 24–25.

80 See the remarks of Lord President Dundas reported in J M Pinkerton (ed), *The Minute Book of the Faculty of Advocates. Volume 2, 1713–1750*, Stair Society vol 32 (1980) 225.

commented that "the young gentlemen of the law . . . desire[d] of all things to have the Philosophical elements of their science . . . well taught".[81] Given that, after 1750, it became rare for Scots to study law in the Netherlands, the lack of a class left a serious gap in the education of advocates in particular.[82] (At this time the professor of law at Glasgow taught only Civil Law, although jurisprudence did feature in the class of moral philosophy.)[83]

This background led to two similar projects to replace Abercromby with a more suitable candidate. The first plan was that of David Hume, who informed Adam Smith in 1758 that Lord Milton would be willing to exert pressure on the Town Council, patrons of the University, to require Abercromby "either to attend . . . or dispose of the Office". Hume proposed that Smith should pay Abercromby to resign in his favour, so that Smith could be appointed in his stead.[84] The presumption was that Milton would be willing to secure the royal nomination for Smith in these circumstances. Hume's focus was on acquiring for Smith an income with an appointment in Edinburgh. Though nothing came of this, there can be no doubt of Smith's suitability for this post, given the content of his classes in moral philosophy in Glasgow, in which natural jurisprudence was central.[85] The second project was that of Lord Milton and John Home, author of *Douglas* and secretary to the Earl of Bute, Ilay's nephew. The proposal was that the chair be purchased from Abercromby for Adam Ferguson, then in search of an Edinburgh chair. Home reported to Gilbert Elliot, then an MP, and close to Bute, that Milton was "the great promoter of the scheme" and insisted on "advancing a part of the money".[86] Again this project came to nothing, although it was part of the general scheming of the moderate *literati* to place themselves in posts in the university.[87]

81 J Home to G Elliot (n d but 1758) NLS MS 11017 fo 54.

82 For the decline in studying in the Netherlands, see, e.g., J W Cairns, "Legal Study in Utrecht in the Late 1740s: The Education of Sir David Dalrymple, Lord Hailes" in R Van den Bergh (ed), *Summa Eloquentia: Essays in Honour of Margaret Hewett* (2002) 30–74 [= 2002 *Fundamina]* at 38–39, 69–74.

83 See J W Cairns, "The Origins of the Glasgow Law School: The Professors of Civil Law, 1714–61", in P Birks (ed), *The Life of the Law: Proceedings of the Tenth British Legal History Conference Oxford 1991* (1993) 151 at 185.

84 See D Hume to A Smith, 8 June 1758 in *Correspondence of Adam Smith* (n 68) 24–25.

85 See, e.g., Haakonssen, *Science of a Legislator* (n 22) 99–177; J W Cairns, "The Influence of Smith's Jurisprudence on Legal Education in Scotland", in P Jones and A S Skinner (eds), *Adam Smith Reviewed* (1992) (henceforth Cairns, "The Influence of Smith's Jurisprudence on legal Education in Scotland") 168.

86 J Home to G Elliot (n d but 1758) NLS MS 11017 fo 54 (this is misplaced with letters of the mid-1760s in the Minto Papers).

87 See R B Sher, *Church and University in the Scottish Enlightenment: The Moderate Literati of Edinburgh* (1985) (henceforth Sher, *Church and University*) 93–119.

(4) Robert Bruce, Professor 1759–1764

Though neither plan came to fruition, they probably stimulated some movement on Aberçromby's part, as he must have realised he was going to come under increasing pressure to give up the chair in a way he might not choose. He accordingly resigned it in 1759 in favour of his son-in-law, Robert Bruce of Kennet, who was admitted to it in June.[88] Bruce was the brother-in-law of the "Nabob of the North", Sir Lawrence Dundas of Kerse, the great businessman and landowner, whom Ilay (now Duke of Argyll) considered a political enemy.[89] How Bruce's appointment was worked is as yet unclear, though it may have suited those who advised the now aged Milton and Argyll, since Bruce obviously intended to be an active professor, and an active professor seems to have been desired.[90]

Bruce had attended the University of Edinburgh; where he studied law is unknown, possibly also in Edinburgh.[91]

In October 1759, Bruce advertised that he would begin "his Course of Lectures upon *Grotius de Jure Belli ac Pacis*" on 20 November.[92] Bruce continued to teach every year, eventually attracting large numbers of students to what was evidently a successful and worthwhile class.[93] In 1760, the publishing house of Hamilton and Balfour, as printers to the University of Edinburgh, published *Hugonis Grotii de jure belli ac pacis librorum III compendium in usum studiosae juventutis Açademiae Edinensis*.[94] Presumably aimed at Bruce's class, this textbook was based on, but not identical to, Scott's *Compendium* of 1707, for example, excluding Scott's annotations. Publication of this work indicated confidence in the continuing success of the class.

88 EUL Da.1.35 College [Senatus] Minutes 1733–1790 127 (22 June 1759).

89 See, e.g., L Namier and J Brooke (eds), *The House of Commons 1754–1790* (1964) (henceforth Namier and Brooke (eds), *House of Common 1715–1754*) vol ii, 357–361; Sedgwick (ed), *House of Commons 1715–1754* (n 49) vol i, 627–628.

90 On university patronage at this period, see R L Emerson, "Lord Bute and the Scottish Universities 1760–1792", in K W Schweizer (ed), *Lord Bute: Essays in Re-interpretation* (1988) 147 at 151.

91 EUL, "Matriculation Roll of the University of Edinburgh" (n 56) vol i, 205, 208.

92 See *Caledonian Mercury*, 8 October 1759; *Edinburgh Evening Courant*, 4 October 1759.

93 See, e.g., his adverts in *Caledonian Mercury*, 25 October 1760, 31 October 1761, 25 October 1762, 5 November 1763; *Edinburgh Evening Courant*, 22 October 1760, 28 October 1761, 23 October 1762, 31 October 1763. Numbers are recorded for his classes only for 1762–1763 (five) and 1763–64 (forty). See EUL, "Matriculation Roll of the university of Edinburgh" (n 56) vol i, 256, 262. The latter number meant he had a very large class indeed by the standard of the law classes in the 1760s. The first number is not necessarily the actual number of students: he may have had more.

94 See W McDougall, "A Catalogue of Hamilton, Balfour and Neill Publications", in R Myers and M Harris (eds), *Spreading the Word: The Distribution Networks of Print 1550–1850* (1998) 187 at 225 (no 290).

In 1760, the Faculty of Advocates resolved that, since "regular Colleges upon the law of Nature and Nations [were] now given in the University of Edinburgh" and since it was important that members should be "versant in every part of polite Literature and particularly in the law of Nature and Nations, the fountain of Justice and equity" and since they were "satisfied with the merit and abilities of the present Professor of that College", all candidates for the office of advocate should attend these classes.[95] In 1762, perhaps to ensure that this was effective, the Faculty resolved that the private Examinators in Scots law and Roman law should examine candidates for admission "upon the Law of Nature & Nations in so far as it is connected with the Civil Law or with the Law of this Country".[96]

Despite his success, in February 1764, Bruce agreed to resign the chair in favour of James Balfour of Pilrig, advocate.[97] This was part of an elaborate scheme to remove Balfour from the chair of Moral Philosophy, which he had occupied without distinction – indeed he was regarded as a failure[98] – since 1754, the same year he was rejected as a candidate for admission to the Select Society, one of the intellectual clubs in the vanguard of Enlightenment in Edinburgh.[99] It was proposed that Adam Ferguson (who currently held the chair of Natural Philosophy) would replace Balfour in the chair of Moral Philosophy, Ferguson in turn being succeeded by James Russell.[100] Support for this had been arranged at the highest level. On 21 February 1764 William Robertson, Principal of the University, wrote to the Town Council as Patrons seeking their approval, which was granted on 22 February.[101] By 5 March Milton had secured the necessary governmental support.[102]

While this sequence of events has been discussed before, the reasons why Bruce, who was also Sheriff of Stirling, should have agreed to surrender

95 A Stewart (ed), *The Minute Book of the Faculty of Advocates. Volume 3, 1751–1783*, Stair Society vol 46 (1999) (henceforth *Advocates Minute Book, Volume 3*) 94.

96 Ibid 119.

97 See ECA Town Council Minutes vol 79, 283–285 (22 February 1764).

98 See, e.g., G Lind to Lord Milton, 19 March 1761 NLS MS 16721 fo 108.

99 R L Emerson, "The social composition of enlightened Scotland: The Select Society of Edinburgh, 1754–1764" 1973 (114) *Studies in Voltaire and the Eighteenth Century* 291 at 328.

100 See the letter of Ferguson to Milton, 18 February 1764 NLS MS 16730 fo 139; N Blair to D Hume, 6 April 1764 NLS MS 23153 103–105 (RSE 3/52). See Sher, *Church and University* 119; and "Professors of Virtue: The Social History of the Edinburgh Moral Philosophy Chair in the Eighteenth Century", in M A Stewart (ed), *Studies in the Philosophy of the Scottish Enlightenment* (1990) 87 (henceforth Sher, "Professors of Virtue") at 109–116.

101 ECA Town Council Minutes vol 79, 283–285.

102 Lord Milton to J Stuart Mackenzie, 23 February 1764 (copy) NLS MS 16731 95; J Stuart Mackenzie to Lord Milton, 5 March 1764 NLS MS 16731 105.

this profitable office, in which he was a conspicuous success, have not previously been considered.[103] Balfour will have paid him what was reckoned to be the value of the chair.[104] By this date, Bruce's brother-in-law, Dundas, back in Parliament for an English constituency, supported the ministry, and had given his allegiance to the Duke of Bedford.[105] It is possible that Bruce's resignation in favour of Balfour was facilitated by a promise (or at least a hope) of some further preferment through this route. Certain it is that, shortly after, when a vacancy on the Bench occurred, to which Milton and the Lord Privy Seal, James Stuart Mackenzie, intended that James Ferguson of Pitfour, Dean of Faculty, should be appointed, Bedford made a strong application to the king in favour of Bruce.[106] Two other vacancies on the Bench occurred and Bruce was appointed to one of them.[107] It is clear that there was a certain reluctance to appoint Bruce, but that both he and Dundas were able to make a claim that could not be ignored.[108] On Bruce's part, the way in which he had facilitated the change of chairs may have given him some entitlement.[109] Nonetheless, despite his success in the chair, he was disparaged and John Mackenzie, who favoured the appointment of Sir David Dalrymple to the Bench, described Bruce ("the Dreaded Rivall") as "an inoffensive Lad, without experience for a Decreeing head[,] Little Genius and Less Dignity".[110] Rather than a fair estimate of Bruce's talents, however, Mackenzie's comments may reflect the heat of all these rivalries for promotion. Bruce was after all to become a founder member of the Royal Society of Edinburgh in 1783 as a member of the Physical Class.[111] Later in 1764, he duly took his place on the Court of Session Bench as Lord Kennet.[112]

103 See Sher, *Church and University* (n 87) 117–119; and "Professors of Virtue" (n 100) at 109–116.
104 There is no direct evidence, but it is certain.
105 See, e.g., Murdoch *"People Above"* (n 59) 113.
106 See A Gray to Lord Milton, 13 April 1764 NLS MS 16730 fo 272; J Stuart Mackenzie to Lord Milton, 5 May 1764 NLS MS 16731 fo 142.
107 See Lord Milton to R Bruce (copy) June 1764, R Bruce to Lord Milton 6 June 1764 NLS MS 16730 fos 58, 59.
108 See Murdoch *"People Above"* (n 59) 113–114; Namier and Brooke (eds), *House of Commons 1754–1790* (n 89) 359.
109 It is worth noting that the ministry was anxious about an election in Perthshire in the Spring of 1764 and an approach had been made to Abercromby, Bruce's father-in-law, to try to secure his vote for the ministry's candidate. This was happening about the time that the change in the chairs was proposed. This may also have led to some promises about Bruce. Abercromby, however, did not support the ministry's candidate: see D Graeme to R Gardiner, 15 February 1764 NLS MS 16730 fo 206; J Stuart Mackenzie to Lord Milton 11 February 1764 NLS MS 16731 fo 80.
110 J Mackenzie to G Elliot, 5 May 1764 NLS MS 11017 fo 14.
111 "History of the Society" (1788) 1 *Transactions of the Royal Society of Edinburgh* 3 at 83.
112 *Caledonian Mercury*, 4 July 1764.

(5) James Balfour, Professor, 1764–1779

Balfour had received his commission as Regius Professor by May 1764, and was admitted to the office by the University on 22 June.[113] He is generally regarded as holding this chair as a sinecure. Given Bruce's evident success as a professor, and the aspirations of the Faculty of Advocates, it is possible that this was not the original intention behind the elaborate scheme of appointments that resulted in his securing this chair; rather, it may have been thought that this was a chair more suited to Balfour's talents, given his education in law at Leiden, after his preliminary studies in Edinburgh.[114] However this may be, Balfour does not appear initially to have taught. In 1777 and 1778, however, classes to be taught by him from this chair were advertised in the general advertisements for the university entered in the Edinburgh newspapers.[115] In 1779, Hugo Arnot nonetheless described Balfour as teaching "no class".[116] It is possible that the advertisements were intended to put pressure on the aged Balfour to encourage him to resign, so that someone more effective could be appointed. His resignation was now obviously in the air, as, in 1777, the first year in which Balfour's classes were advertised, Gilbert Stuart believed himself, allegedly through the influence of Henry Dundas, to have secured a promise of the reversion of the chair. He must have believed that, if Balfour resigned in his favour, Dundas would ensure that he obtained the royal presentation.[117] Principal Robertson blocked this proposal.[118] Balfour was in difficulty elsewhere. Treasurer of the Faculty of Advocates since 1739, problems and incompetence had latterly marked his stewardship of the Faculty's funds, and two reports of Faculty dated 22 December 1777 and 12 January 1778 precipitated his tender of his resignation as Treasurer on 19 December 1778; this took effect on 18

113 J Balfour to Lord Provost, 14 May 1764, ECA McLeod's Collection Bundle 11 Shelf 36 Bay C; EUL Da 1.35 College [Senatus] Minutes 1733–1790 153 (22 June 1764). See also ECA Town Council Minutes vol 80, 3–4 (16 May 1764) 12–13 (23 May 1764).

114 *Album Leiden* (n 31) col 919; EUL, "Matriculation Roll of the University of Edinburgh" (n 56) vol i, 174, 178, 180, 193. Some details of his time in Leiden are preserved in his correspondence with his father; they do not cover his legal studies, but we know he attended the classes of the classicist and antiquarian Burman that were popular with Scots law students: see J Balfour to J Balfour, 27 May 1729 NAS GD 69/296/5.

115 See, e.g., *Edinburgh Advertiser*, 12 September 1777, 4 September 1778.

116 H Arnot, *The History of Edinburgh* (1779) 398.

117 See W Zachs, *Without Regard to Good Manners: A Biography of Gilbert Stuart 1743–1786 (1992)* (henceforth Zachs, *Without Regard to Good Manners*) 105–107. On the role of Henry Dundas, his rise to power, and his control of Scottish patronage, see M Fry, *The Dundas Despotism* (1992).

118 Zachs, *Without Regard to Good Manners* (n 117) 105–107; Sher, *Church and University* (n 87) 140 n 200.

December 1779.[119] These troubles must have weakened Balfour's position more generally, rendering him susceptible to pressure to resign the chair. By the summer of 1779, he had resigned in favour of Allan Maconochie, in return for two promissory notes, each to the value of £500 and dated 6 July 1779, payable by 20 November 1779 and 6 March 1780 respectively. Another bill of 19 January 1780 ordered payment from Maconochie of £412.18.2 on the order of Barfour.[120] Maconochie was a relative of Principal Robertson; and he had recently supported the latter and Henry Dundas' liberal policy of Catholic relief in the Church Courts.[121] The chair was his reward. Robertson, however, must have intended that Maconochie should be active. At this period, the law school at Edinburgh was facing very stiff competition from Glasgow under John Millar, a pupil of Adam Smith, and enrolments had been falling during the 1770s.[122] Maconochie's appointment was to help revive the school.

(6) Allan Maconochie, Professor, 1779–1796

Between 1762 and 1769, Maconochie was educated at the University of Edinburgh, following the usual undergraduate curriculum, before devoting three years to the study of Civil Law.[123] He was a founder member of the Speculative Society in 1764.[124] A man of wide-ranging interests, including the natural as well as the moral sciences, all his life he maintained a serious, practical interest in chemistry.[125] Around 1778 he became a member of the Philosophical Society, and he was a member of the Royal Society of

119 *Advocates' Minute Book, Volume* 3 (note 95) xxxviii–xxxix; 292–297 (22 July 1778), 298 (19 December 1778), 307 (18 December 1779).

120 See the documents in EUL Mic M 1070 (Meadowbank Papers); EUL Da 1.35 College [Senatus] Minutes 1733–1790 289 (16 July 1779). See Grant, *University of Edinburgh* (n 26) vol ii, 315–316.

121 Sher, *Church and University* (n 87) 140; [Maconochie,] *Memoir of the Late Hon Allan Maconochie of Meadowbank: One of the Senators of the College of Justice in Scotland* (1845) 6–7.

122 See J W Cairns, "'Famous as a School for Law, as Edinburgh . . . for Medicine'; Legal Education in Glasgow, 1761–1801", in A Hook and R B Sher (eds), *The Glasgow Enlightenment* (1995) 133 (henceforth Cairns, "Legal Education in Glasgow") at 149–150; and "The face that did not fit: Race, appearance, and exclusion from the bar in eighteenth-century Scotland" (2003) 11 *Fundamina* 11 at 18–19.

123 "Matriculation Roll of the University of Edinburgh" (n 56) vol i, 251, 260, 266, 273, 275, 283, 290, 297.

124 *The History of the Speculative Society 1764–1904* (1905) (henceforth *History of the Speculative Society*) 59.

125 See A Ferguson to A Maconochie, 12 October 1779 in EUL Mic M 1070; Lord Meadowbank, *Directions for Making Compost Dunghills from Peat-Moss* (1802); and *Directions for Preparing Manure from Peat. Instructions for Foresters* (1815).

Edinburgh from its foundation in 1783.[126] It is no surprise that, though normally active in the Literary Class of the Royal Society, he was also active in the Physical Class, which he sometimes chaired.[127]

Maconochie continued a successful career at the Bar, allegedly earning £1,400 a year from his practice and the office of Sheriff of Renfrew (to which he was appointed at the end of 1787), not counting his income from the chair.[128] He was nonetheless determined to be an active professor, and his classes were advertised from 1779 until he resigned the chair in 1796.[129] This ambition led him and his close friend Alexander Tytler, appointed Professor of Universal History and Greek and Roman Antiquities in 1780, to petition the Town Council in 1781 requesting that, as Patrons of the University, they should provide a proper classroom in which both could teach. The difficulty was that, having no allocated room, they had to teach in other professors' classrooms "on which account they are obliged to confine themselves to hours of lecturing very disadvantageous both to themselves and their students".[130]

Maconochie's general class was described thus by a contemporary:

> He traces the rise of political institutions from the natural characters and situation of the human species; follows their progress through the rude periods of society; and treats of their history and merits, as exhibited in the principal nations of ancient and modern times, which he examines separately, classing them according to those general causes to which he attributes the principal varieties in the forms, genius, and revolutions of governments. In this manner he endeavours to construct the science of the spirit of laws on a connected view of what may be called the natural history of man as a political agent; and he accordingly concludes his course with treating of the general principles of municipal law, political economy, and the law of nations.[131]

126 R L Emerson, "The Philosophical Society of Edinburgh 1768–1783" (1985) 18 *British Journal for the History of Science* 255 at 300; "History of the Society" (1788) 1 *Transactions of the Royal Society of Edinburgh* 3 at 86.

127 N Campbell and M S Smellie, *The Royal Society of Edinburgh (1783–1983): The First Two Hundred Years* (1983) 22.

128 A Maconochie to Lord Advocate (Charles) Hope [n d but 1804] in EUL Mic M 1070.

129 See, e.g., *Edinburgh Evening Courant*, 1 September 1779, 28 October 1780, 20 October 1781, 31 August 1782, 6 September 1783, 2 October 1784, 1 October 1785, 9 September 1786, 20 September 1787, 20 September 1788, 7 September 1789, 13 September 1789, 17 September 1791, 15 September 1792, 14 September 1793, 13 September, 1794, 3 October 1795. Oddly enough, he still is advertised in *Edinburgh Evening Courant*, 15 September 1796: This is probably a mistake and his successor Hamilton's name should have been inserted. *Caledonian Mercury*, 17 September 1796 advertises Hamilton as professor.

130 Petition of Mr Allan Maconochie . . . and of Mr Alex Tytler with Tytler to Lord Provost, 13 February 1781, both in ECA McLeod's Collection Bundle 11 Shelf 36 Bay C.

131 H Arnot, *History of Edinburgh*, 2nd edn (1788) 398. *The Summary Catalogue of the Advocates' Manuscripts* (1971) 72 (no 902) states that Adv MS 25.6.4 is a set of lectures on actions possibly by Allan Maconochie. These two, continuously paginated, volumes contain the dates

Henry Brougham gave a full description of Maconochie's lectures, based on some level of examination of the manuscript:

> They are arranged under two great divisions – the State of Nature and the Political State. Under the first, by which is meant the earlier state, are treated, the savage state; the origin of the political union; the first structure of government; language, and the origin of its grammatical structure; the agricultural and pastoral state; the rise of religion and mythology; women and their domestic relations in uncultivated society. The other and principal branch begins with the gradual changes and transitions from the rude to the polished state. . . . We are thus [after a comprehensive account of history and government], by slow degrees, but from a most comprehensive view of the world and its history led to the origin, predominancy, and decline of the feudal institution; and then comes the present state of the European governments.[132]

This course gave rise to the first paper to be delivered to the Literary Class after the foundation of the Royal Society of Edinburgh in 1783, when, on 15 December in that year, Maconochie read the first part of his "Essay on the Origin and Structure of the European Legislatures". The second part was delivered on 19 July 1784.[133]

It is evident that by now the nature of what was taught from the chair had changed from the rational type of natural law associated with Grotius and his immediate successors. Instead, Maconochie started with examination of human nature, a natural history of man:

> In the line of Study, to which my profession in the university carried me, I had occasion to examine into the Origin of Government and therefore to consider the circumstances in human nature, which rendered our species alone of all the races of animals susceptible of that progress which in its course gave birth to political society.[134]

He also saw morals generally, and the virtue of justice in particular, arising from the strongly social nature of man. In this he followed Adam Smith,

10 October 1783 (at 1) and 15 November 1783 (at 559) which must indicate dates of copying rather than of lecturing. It is unclear why the *Catalogue* considers these to be lectures, as they much more resemble a treatise on actions, and why it attributes them to Maconochie. They are certainly not in his hand.

132 [W Brougham,] *Memoir of the Late Hon Allan Maconochie of Meadowbank, One of the Senators of the College of Justice . . . in Scotland* (1845) 10–12; see appendix for Brougham's full account of Maconochie's lectures.

133 A Maconochie, "Essay on the Origin and Structure of the European Legislatures" (1788) 1 *Transactions of the Royal Society of Edinburgh*: II: *Papers of the Literary Class* 3 and 133.

134 (MS) Treatise on what distinguishes Man from Brutes [1], in EUL Mic M 1070. It is likely that this work was written for delivery to the Royal Society of Edinburgh; the ideas developed in his lectures can be traced in it. The MS appears to be a fair copy not in Maconochie's hand and is generally unpaginated.

explicitly rejecting Rousseau's view of man in a state of nature. Thus, he argued that human beings observe the actions of others, which arouse in them "a variety of agreeable or disagreeable sentiments". Acts of injustice and cruelty "outrage" and acts of ingratitude and intemperance are "disagreeable to the cool or impartial spectator". He pointed out that human beings seek the approval of others and when about to act consider third parties' views of their conduct. In sum, he explicitly approved Smith's opinions on how from this origin, principles of duty and propriety formed the basis of "Codes of Laws and Systems of Morality".[135] His aim was to give a course on jurisprudence developed on the same basis as that of Adam Smith.[136] Brougham noted Maconochie's lectures on women. Among the latter's papers can be recognised a fragment of these lectures, in which he discussed the changing position of women in a way reminiscent of John Millar's account in the *Origin of Distinction of Ranks*. Indeed, he cited Millar approvingly to his class.[137]

Maconochie's aim seems to have been to develop a modern course on the science of legislation. Despite his adoption of Smith's theory of morals, his natural jurisprudence seems to have been comparative, historical and explanatory rather than critical, in this resembling that of John Millar, rather than that of the author of *The Wealth of Nations*. It was this comparative, conjectural history that required his use of maps in his class.[138] We can assume that the paper he read to the Royal Society in 1788 – "Observations respecting the country, religion, political institutions, and sciences of the Hindoos" – reflected his interests in his class.[139] Nonetheless, it cannot be doubted that his aim was to inculcate in his pupils an understanding of the

135 Ibid.

136 It is worth noting that the first known possessor of the second set of notes from Smith's student class in jurisprudence was Maconochie's son: see the remarks of Canaan in his introduction to *Lectures on Justice, Police, Revenue and Arms, Delivered in the University of Glasgow by Adam Smith, Reported by a Student in 1763* (1896) xv–xvii. On Smith in this respect, see, e.g., Cairns, "The Influence of Smith's Jurisprudence on Legal Education in Scotland" (n 85).

137 These notes (in Maconochie's hand) are scattered towards the end of the Treatise on what distinguishes Humanity from Brutes, where the papers are clearly disorganised: EUL Mic M 1070. See J Millar, *Observations Concerning the Distinction of Ranks in Society* (1771). On Millar's teaching, see Cairns, "Legal Education in Glasgow" (n 122); and "John Millar, Ivan Andreyevich Tret'yakov, and Semyon Efimovich Desnitsky: A Legal Education in Scotland, 1761–1767", in T V Arternieva, P H Jones and M I Mikeshin (eds), *Scotland and Russia in the Enlightenment: Proceedings of the International Conference 1–3 September 2000, Edinburgh* [= *The Philosophical Age*, Almanac 15] (2001) 20 (henceforth Cairns, "John Millar, Ivan Andreyevich Tret'yakov and Semyon Efimovich Desnitsky").

138 Petition of Mr Allan Maconochie . . . and of Mr Alex Tytler with Tytler to Lord Provost, 13 February 1781, both in ECA McLeod's Collection Bundle 11 Shelf 36 Bay C.

139 "History of the Society" (1790) 2 *Transactions of the Royal Society of Edinburgh* 3 at 25.

historical relationships between society, law and government, so that they could see how laws could be developed and improved through legislation and the work of the courts.

Bower alleged in 1830 that Maconochie only lectured for two sessions, as his success at the bar prevented him from having time to teach.[140] Bower's claim is questionable. First, lectures by Maconochie from his chair were continuously advertised for nearly two decades until his demission of the office. In principle, this would seem an odd practice on the part of the University if Maconochie had given up teaching around 1781 or so. It is worth noting, however, that there is some variation in the advertisements. In academic years 1779–1780, 1780–1781, 1781–1782, 1782–1783, the general advertisements for the whole university just advertised that the law classes were beginning at a specific date.[141] In 1780 and 1781, Maconochie also inserted in the *Caledonian Mercury* a specific advertisement for his classes, the second of which gave a different date for the start of his course from that in the general advertisement for the law classes.[142] From 1783–1784 until academic year 1790–1791, the general advertisement for the University gave either a specific time or, from 1785, date and time or, from 1786, date for Maconochie's class.[143] On 25 March 1786, Maconochie specially advertised a class after the end of his usual winter course, on the "Origin of Government", in which he stated he would deal with "the Rise and Characters of the different Forms it has assumed – and, particularly, of the Modern European Governments, the Revolutions which they have undergone, and the various causes to which they owe their present Form".[144] This is presumably just an abbreviated description of his usual course, and the general advertisements show that from then on he started his course on a specific date in March, rather than November.[145] It may be that more such advertisements in February await discovery. From 1791 until his resignation

140 Bower, *History of the University of Edinburgh* (n 28) vol iii, 215.

141 *Caledonian Mercury*, 4 September 1779 (17 November), 30 September 1780 (22 November), 5 September 1781 (22 November), *Edinburgh Evening Courant*, 31 August 1782 (18 November).

142 *Caledonian Mercury*, 28 October 1780, 20 October 1781 (15 November).

143 *Edinburgh Evening Courant*, 6 September 1783 (2 pm), 15 September 1784 (2 pm), 1 October 1785 (23 November 1 pm), 9 September 1786 (12 March 1787), 20 September 1787 (11 March 1788), 20 September 1788 (9 March 1789), 7 September 1789 (8 March 1790), 13 September 1790 (9 March 1791).

144 *Caledonian Mercury*, 25 February 1786.

145 *Edinburgh Evening Courant*, 9 September 1786 (12 March 1787), 20 September 1787 (11 March 1788), 20 September 1788 (9 March 1789), 7 September 1789 (8 March 1790), 13 September 1790 (9 March 1791).

of the chair, the general advertisements placed by the University leave blank the space for time and date for the commencement of his class.[146] If the specific times and dates inserted in the advertisements mean anything, it must be that, in those years at least, Maconochie aimed to teach and continued to have sufficient encouragement to plan a date on which his classes should commence. It is also worth noting that, from 1786 onwards, he taught his class in the Spring, rather than Winter term. This may have been a reflection either of his own growing practice at the bar, or to enhance the attractiveness of his course to students. If Maconochie gave up teaching, it would seem to have been in or around 1791, when he was probably already thinking of resigning the chair.

(7) Robert Hamilton, Professor, 1796–1831

By the session from 1795–1796, Maconochie had resolved to give up the chair and had agreed to resign in favour of Robert Hamilton, a close relative of Lord Braxfield the Justice Clerk, in return for the same payment he had made to purchase the chair from Balfour. The agreement of Henry Dundas, then Secretary of State for War and in control of Scottish patronage, and Robert Dundas, the Lord Advocate, was secured.[147] Meanwhile, Maconochie was offered a position on the Bench of the Court of Session, which he accepted, though anxious to ensure that his arrangement with Hamilton would still be upheld; his appointment, taking his seat on the Bench as Lord Meadowbank, dated from 11 March.[148] This preferment perhaps came because of his energetic activity in being one of the leaders of the campaign to ensure that Henry Erskine was not re-elected as Dean of the Faculty of Advocates in 1796.[149]

146 *Edinburgh Evening Courant*, 17 September 1791, 15 September 1792, 14 September 1793, 13 September 1794, 3 October 1795.

147 A Maconochie to H Dundas, 27 February 1796 EUL Mic M 1070.

148 Grant, *Faculty of Advocates* (n 40) 141; Maconochie to Dundas, 27 February 1796 EUL Mic M 1070.

149 This event can be traced in *Caledonian Mercury*, 3 and 10 December 1795, 14 January 1796. For a discussion see, e.g., G W T Omond, *Lord Advocates of Scotland From the Close of the Fifteenth Century to the Passing of the Reform Bill* (1883) vol ii, 167–169. Maconochie later considered that he did not get further promotion that he deserved. In 1799, he thought he should have been made a Lord of Justiciary (he eventually became one in 1804); in 1811, he considered that he had an entitlement to the office of Justice Clerk. His papers contain some bitter correspondence about this and he threatened to resign from the Bench in 1799: see, e.g., A Maconochie to R Dundas, 25 May 1799; J Bruce to R Dundas, 20 June 1799; A Maconochie to Viscount Melville, 15 October 1811; Viscount Melville to A Maconochie, 19 October 1811; R Dundas to A Maconochie, 28 October 1811 EUL Mic M 1070.

In April 1796, Robert Hamilton was duly appointed to the chair.[150] Hamilton had followed the usual undergraduate curriculum at Edinburgh between 1780 and 1784, before matriculating at the University of Glasgow in 1785, almost certainly to study law with Smith's pupil Millar.[151] This suggests that, initially at least, he was well qualified to continue the approach to teaching that Maconochie had initiated from the chair.[152] His membership of the Speculative Society and election to the Royal Society of Edinburgh in 1795 both suggest intellectual liveliness and interests.[153] It also perhaps worth noting that he was one of thirty-eight members of the Faculty of Advocates who voted to re-elect Henry Erskine as their Dean.[154]

It is not certain, however, that Hamilton ever taught. His classes certainly were continually advertised through to the end of the century and well beyond; but, as with the last classes advertised for Maconochie, and in contrast to the other classes in law, a specific time and date for the class to start was never mentioned.[155]

He apparently informed the Royal Commission of inquiry into the Universities of Scotland in 1826 that:

> [H]e had fully determined to teach his class, and even previously to his appointment had directed his attention and studies to prepare himself for doing so; but from bad health after his induction, and afterwards from the arduous official duties which in another capacity he was called to perform, he abandoned his design . . .[156]

Given that this purports to be based on information from Hamilton himself, without further research, it must at the moment be accepted that he never taught, despite the continued advertisements for his class. It may be relevant to note that, in 1802, augmentation of the stipend of the minister of St Cuthberts, from the lands of which parish the salary of the chair had been

150 EUL Da.1.35 College [Senatus] Minutes 1790–1811 121 (2 April 1796).

151 EUL, "Matriculation Roll of the University of Edinburgh" (n 56) vol ii, 388, 389, 396, 398, 408, 412. 423, 424.

152 W Addison (ed), *Matriculation Albums of the University of Glasgow from 1728 to 1858* (1913) 144 (no 4546).

153 *History of the Speculative Society* (n 124) 82; "History of the Society" (1798) 5 *Transactions of the Royal Society of Edinburgh* 1 at 33.

154 *Caledonian Mercury*, 14 January 1796.

155 See, e.g., *Caledonian Mercury*, 17 September 1796, 16 September 1797, 15 September 1798, 16 September 1799, 25 September 1800, 19 September 1801, 18 September 1809, 20 September 1810. I have not traced this through continuously.

156 *Report Made to His Majesty by a Royal Commission of Inquiry into the State of the Universities of Scotland* 1831 Parliamentary Papers XII (henceforth *Report . . . by a Royal Commission of Inquiry into the State of the Universities in Scotland*) 141. He became a Principal Clerk of Session.

allocated, reduced Hamilton's salary to around a quarter of what it had been. Although the Treasury in lieu allocated an annual sum of £200 from Crown revenues in 1806 for so long as Hamilton held the office, it is plausible that the dramatic reduction of salary for four years may have removed whatever motivation to teach Hamilton ever had.[157]

C. CONCLUSIONS

The Report (1830) of the Royal Commissions of inquiry into the Scottish Universities of 1826 and 1830 roundly condemned the chair of Public Law and the Law of Nature and Nations:

> [A]s far as we have been able to learn, it never was successful; and it is certain that in the last fifty years it has been found impracticable, even by Professors of high genius and attainments, to render it a class of general attraction, or even to obtain for it a moderate attendance of Students. It has not been taught at all during the time that the office has been held by the present Professor, and had not been taught for many years before he entered on it.[158]

Two pieces of evidence led the Commissioners to this conclusion. The first was that of Francis Jeffrey, who stated of the class:

> It was taught by a succession of able persons in this University, – among others by the late Lord Meadowbank, than whom no man was more full of discursive knowledge and originality; yet in his hands, as well as those of his successors, it proved in practice a complete failure, so that they could hardly get through the course with a larger attendance than is now round the table of the Commissioners.[159]

The second was a written return by the *Senatus Academicus* to a query about whether any chairs were held as sinecures:

> The present incumbent [of the chair of Public Law and the Law of Nature and Nations] has not delivered any lectures on public law. His predecessor gave a course of lectures in the year 1780 or 1781: but the study of that branch of the law having fallen into neglect, he gave it up; and though in 1795 he resumed the subject, yet the result being the same, he after giving a few lectures, desisted so that there has been no regular course for about forty-six years.[160]

Papers relating to the funding of the chair supported this general view. Thus, in 1806, in recommending an annual sum of £200 from Crown revenues to

157 Ibid 109, 159.

158 Ibid 55.

159 *Report of the Royal Commission of Inquiry into the Universities of Scotland. Minutes of Evidence vol 1. University of Edinburgh* 1837 Parliamentary Papers XXXV (henceforth *Minutes of Evidence vol 1*) 398.

160 Ibid appendix 121.

replace the diminution of Hamilton's salary in 1802, the Barons of Exchequer stated that "arising from the neglect of the study of that branch of law in this country . . . no lectures have been read by [Professor Hamilton] or by his predecessors in that Chair for a considerable number of years".[161]

If we accept the evidence that Hamilton never taught, it is still clear that – at the very least – some of the assertions made about Maconochie's classes in the Report of 1830 and in the evidence before the Commissioners were simply wrong. While it is just conceivable that his classes were continuously advertised in general advertisements for the University without his teaching, close study of the changing nature of those advertisements, as well as of his own specific advertisements, in particular of that in 1786, suggests that he did in fact continue to teach well past the date of 1781. Further supporting this is his letter to the Lord Advocate, Charles Hope, in 1804, in which he stated that the latter attended his class.[162] Hope first matriculated at the University of Edinburgh in 1777, progressing through a fairly regular arts curriculum until 1781.[163] In 1782–1784 Hope matriculated in Civil Law and Scots law.[164] It seems likely that it was in this period that he studied with Maconochie and we should note that Maconochie still specially advertised in 1786.[165] All of this suggests that individuals in the later 1820s, discussing a period of over forty years earlier, projected Hamilton's lack of teaching back to the period of his predecessor. The evidence as it currently stands suggests that Maconochie either taught or made a serious attempt to teach from 1779 to 1790 or 1791.

It is also possible that there was a desire among the Commissioners to suppress the chair, especially since the fund originally allocated to support it was no longer available, and the special allocation made by the Crown to Hamilton would expire with his death. The Commissioners commented on what they considered to be the remit of the chair:

> At one period, it was thought the most important perhaps of all branches of liberal instruction, and for a century after the time of Grotius, it attracted more attention than any other part of Philosophy; and yet for many years, although entrusted to men whose talents would have qualified them to do it ample justice, it has been regarded with complete and with hopeless indifference.[166]

161 Grant, *University of Edinburgh* (n 26) vol ii, 317; *Report . . . by a Royal Commission of Inquiry into the State of the Universities of Scotland* (n 156) 109, 159.

162 Maconochie to Hope [n d but 1804] EUL Mic M 1070.

163 EUL, "Matriculation Roll of the University of Edinburgh" (n 56) vol ii, 360, 371, 382, 383, 385, 392, 393.

164 Ibid vol 2, 412, 421.

165 *Caledonian Mercury*, 25 February 1786.

166 *Report . . . by a Royal Commission of Inquiry into the State of the Universities of Scotland* (n 156) 141.

In this, they were greatly guided by Francis Jeffrey, of whose evidence to them in 1826 the above is a very close paraphrase.[167] He had been dismissive of the class, and the Commissioners had copied his tone. Implicit in all of this was the notion that time had moved on and somehow left behind the discipline of public law and the law of nature and nations. The obvious inference from the wording of the report implies was that, about 1750 or so, public law and the law of nature and nations had become redundant as a university subject. It is also notable how much Jeffrey and the Commissioners identified the topic with the work of Grotius. This understanding of the work of the chair and its lack of success is particularly interesting, since Charles Hope, the former pupil of Maconochie in the early 1780s, and now Lord President, was appointed to the Royal Commission in both 1826 and 1830.[168]

The work of Grotius had indeed provided the foundation for the teaching of the professors up to the appointment of Balfour in 1764, whether they taught from the actual work or from a compend. Its impact on legal thinking and legal practice had thus been profound. There may have been problems in sustaining teaching from the chair in its first half century, but it nonetheless had played an important role in disseminating the thought of the school of modern natural law to lawyers. Bruce's resignation in 1764, however, marked the end of the direct teaching of Grotius' work as the foundation of legal philosophy in Scotland. This said, by defining and developing the field of the law of nature and nations, it was Bruce's success as a teacher that probably indicated to Millar in Glasgow that a similar class might be worthwhile.[169]

Millar did not teach from Grotius' work or a compend of it, but unfolded his own Smithian account of the nature of law and its progress in a course that followed the structure of Justinian's *Institutes*.[170] The evidence of Maconochie's teaching shows that what was taught in his day from the chair of Public Law and the Law of Nature and Nations was comparable to what Millar taught in Glasgow. The class had moved on from expositions of a

167 *Minutes of Evidence vol 1. University of Edinburgh* (n 159) 398: "Public Law was at one time thought the most important, perhaps, of all branches of liberal instruction; and everybody knows, that for a century after the time of Grotius, it attracted more notice than any other part of philosophy."

168 Ibid 1, 3. It is worth noting that he did not attend as frequently as some of the other Commissioners, and was not present when Jeffrey was questioned: ibid 7, 69 and 13. He nonetheless signed the General Report: Report . . . *by a Royal Commission of Inquiry into the State of the Universities of Scotland* (n 156) 89.

169 Cairns, "John Millar, Ivan Andreyevich Tret'yakov, and Semyon Efimovich Desnitsky" (n 137) at 30.

170 Cairns, "Legal Education in Glasgow" (n 122) at 139–141.

Grotian natural law to classes that had assimilated the lessons – and reflected the concerns – of the Scottish Enlightenment. Legal theory was now, as in Glasgow, concerned with a science of legislation founded on the natural history of humankind.

The proposal in 1830 that the chair should be suppressed (it was in fact left vacant on the death of Hamilton in 1831) does seem to have proceeded on a misunderstanding of the effectiveness of Maconochie. The focus, however, on the claim that the discipline was in a way outmoded was perhaps a fair one. By the 1820s, the type of unified Enlightenment social project that Maconochie expounded was no longer accepted. The Scottish school of "common sense" philosophy, developed by Thomas Reid and his important disciple, Dugald Stewart, was now dominant. In their hands the science of legislation had become a more restricted, narrower discipline. The strongly historical Smithian approach, which unified economics, politics, history, government and law, was rejected, and was certainly incompatible with Reid's and Stewart's realist approach to morals. Disciplines were separating and specialising.[171]

The chair of Public Law and the Law of Nature and Nations was only to revive when reforms in legal education, as part of the general reforms of the Scottish universities, gave it a new role;[172] meanwhile the changing intellectual project which it had supported in the eighteenth century was over.

171 See on this Haakonssen, *Natural Law and Moral Philosophy* (n 1) 179–181, 226–260.

172 Scottish Universities Commission, *General Report of the Commissioners under the Universities (Scotland) Act, 1858. With an Appendix, containing Ordinances, Minutes, Reports on Special Subjects, and Other Documents* (1863) xxxv–xxxvi, Ordinance No 23 XVII (Appendix 47). The professor was to deliver lectures on international law. In fact, the chair became one from which classes were given on legal philosophy and international law: see Lorimer, "Story of the Chair of Public Law" (n 27) at 152–158.

THE DEVELOPMENT OF THE GLASGOW LAW SCHOOL

5 The Origins of the Glasgow Law School: The Professors of Civil Law, 1714–1761*

The exact role of lawyers in Scotland – especially that of the Faculty of Advocates in Edinburgh – after the Union of 1707 is a matter of debate; no one doubts, however, that they were important in the administration of Scotland in the system of government through patronage operated by men such as the Earl of Ilay and the Earl of Bute. They also were important social figures in Edinburgh society, even if not to the extent that Lockhart's *Peter's Letters to his Kinsfolk* suggests for the era just prior to the Reform Bill.[1] Members of the Faculty of Advocates can be found as improving landlords; a number of them were well-known *literati* of the Scottish Enlightenment. There has been some study of the Scottish legal profession in the eighteenth century; much, however, remains to be done.[2]

* I am grateful for the comments on this paper of Roger L Emerson, Hector L MacQueen and Alan Watson. I am much indebted to Michael Moss and Lesley Richmond of Glasgow University Archives, David Weston of Glasgow University Library, Robert Smart of St Andrews University and John A Marr.

1 J G Lockhart, *Peter's Letters to his Kinsfolk*, W Ruddick (ed) (1977) 65–67 and passim; for a useful discussion of some of these issues, see N Phillipson, *The Scottish Whigs and the Reform of the Court of Session, 1785–1830*, Stair Society vol 37 (1990) 1–41, 175–183.

2 A C Chitnis, *The Scottish Enlightenment: A Social History* (1976) 75–90; N T Phillipson, "Lawyers, landowners, and the civic leadership of post-Union Scotland: an essay on the social role of the Faculty of Advocates 1661–1830 in 18th century Scottish society" (1976) *Juridical Review* 97 (henceforth Phillipson, "Lawyers, landowners, and the civic leadership of post-Union Scotland"); and "The Social Structure of the Faculty of Advocates in Scotland 1661–1840", in A Harding (ed), *Law-Making and Law-Makers in British History: Papers Presented to the Edinburgh Legal History Conference, 1977*, Royal Historical Society, xxxii (1980) 146–156; A Murdoch, *"The People Above": Politics and Administration in Mid-Eighteenth-Century Scotland* (1980) 53–62 (henceforth Murdoch, *"The People Above"*); and "The Advocates, the Law and the Nation in Early Modern Scotland", in W Prest (ed), *Lawyers in Early Modern Europe and America* (1981) 147 (henceforth Murdoch, "The Advocates, the Law and the Nation"); J S Shaw, *The Management of Scottish Society, 1707–1764: Power, Nobles, Lawyers, Edinburgh Agents and English Influences* (1983) 18–40 (henceforth Shaw, *Management of Scottish Society*); J W Cairns, "The Formation of the Scottish Legal Mind in the Eighteenth Century: Themes of Humanism and Enlightenment in the Admission of Advocates", in N MacCormick and P Birks (eds),

This essay is part of a much larger project devoted to an examination of legal education in eighteenth-century Scotland. The topic is of particular importance. The *literati* of the various European Enlightenments were very concerned with education generally. Study of legal education reveals much not only about the values and aspirations of perhaps the most powerful profession in Early Modern societies, but also about the complex linkage of knowledge and politics that characterised societies that worked on the basis of patronage.[3] It also provides a necessary background for an exploration of how the thought of the Enlightenment started to influence legal practice and the development of rules of law.[4]

This essay will examine the establishment of legal education in the University of Glasgow in 1714 and its development over the next fifty years. It is closely related to three others published elsewhere.[5] Read together, all four present a picture of legal education in one institution from shortly after the Union with England until the Reform Act of 1832. Here we shall address the following issues: why the university founded a chair in Law; how the first professor came to be appointed and why he desired the position; his tenure of the chair; and the appointment and tenure of his two immediate successors. Discussion of these topics will allow an approach to an understanding of how issues of politics and personality affected the growth of teaching in law, and impeded or furthered its development. If this is a study of one chair in one university in which there was considerable external influence, there is no need to believe that the types of issues that affected instruction in law in Glasgow were unique to that institution.

The Legal Mind: Essays for Tony Honoré (1986) 253 (henceforth Cairns, "Formation of the Scottish Legal Mind").

3 M Ultee, "The politics of professorial appointment at Leiden, 1709" (1990) 9 *History of Universities* 167; J W Cairns, "William Crosse, Regius Professor of Civil Law in the University of Glasgow, 1746–1749: a failure of enlightened patronage" (1993) 12 *History of Universities* (forthcoming) (henceforth Cairns, "William Crosse").

4 C Chêne, *L'enseignement du droit français en pays de droit écrit (1679–1793)* (1982); J W Cairns, "Hamesucken and the Major Premiss in the Libel, 1672–1770: Criminal Law in the Age of Enlightenment", in R F Hunter (ed), *Justice and Crime: Essays in Honour of the Right Honourable the Lord Emslie* (1992) 138.

5 Cairns, 'William Crosse" (n 3); and "'Famous as a School for Law, as Edinburgh . . . for Medicine': Legal Education in Glasgow, 1761–1801", in A Hook and R B Sher (eds), *Glasgow and the Enlightenment* (forthcoming) (henceforth Cairns, "'Famous as a School for Law, as Edinburgh . . . for Medicine'": and "From 'Speculative' to 'Practical' Legal Education: The Decline of the Glasgow Law School, 1801–1830" (forthcoming).

A. THE FOUNDATION OF THE CHAIR

From the 1680s, the Faculty of Advocates had campaigned for the creation of chairs in Law in the Scottish universities in order to save the expense of study abroad.[6] Such foreign study was deemed necessary because the faculty examined virtually all their intrants exclusively on Civil (Roman) Law to assess their suitability for admission.[7] The type of education this was considered to require was not available in Scotland. A chair of Civil Law had survived in King's College, Aberdeen, and its holder taught at least occasionally; this does not seem to have entered into the Faculty's calculations, perhaps because of the type of men who held the chair and because the teaching was irregular or not of the required standard.[8] It was possible to be admitted as an advocate by examination in Scots law; this was heavily discouraged, however, by being penalised with doubled entry fees and the stigma of being less honourable.[9] The Faculty's initial lack of success in their campaign for chairs of Civil Law led a number of advocates to start teaching privately. These advocates' labours demonstrated that there was indeed a demand for courses in law, especially Roman law.[10] This led to the appointment of James Craig as Professor of Civil Law in the University of Edinburgh in 1710.[11]

The University of Edinburgh and its patrons, the Town Council, were evidently engaged in an attempt to develop a school of law. A Regius Chair of Public Law and the Law of Nature and Nations had been erected in the university in 1707, while Chairs of Universal History and Scots Law were

6 J W Cairns, "Sir George Mackenzie, the Faculty of Advocates, and the Advocates' Library", in Sir George Mackenzie, *Oratio inauguralis in aperienda jurisconsultorum bibliotheca*, J W Cairns and A M Cain (eds) (1989) 18 at 23, 33 n 43; and "John Spotswood, Professor of Law: A Preliminary Sketch", in W M Gordon (ed), *Miscellany III*, Stair Society vol 39 (1992) 131 (henceforth Cairns, "John Spotswood").

7 Cairns, "Formation of the Scottish Legal Mind" (n 2) at 255–263.

8 By the end of seventeenth century, the only university chairs surviving in law were at King's College, Aberdeen; see, e.g., R. G Cant, "Origins of the Enlightenment in Scotland: The Universities", in R H Campbell and A S Skinner (eds), *The Origins and Nature of the Scottish Enlightenment* (1982) 42 (henceforth Cant, "Origins of the Enlightenment in Scotland") at 49; for evidence of Civil Law teaching, see "Cursus iuridicus quatuor libros Iustiniani Institutionum iuris civilis comprehendens a magistro Johanno Gordon ejusdem in collegio regio Aberdonensi Professore, in usum academiae studiosorum praesens – compilatus et ab eo [blank] die Ianuary inchoatus, Anno Domini 1701", A[berdeen] U[niversity] L[ibrary], MS 132. There is scattered evidence of law teaching in both King's and Marischall Colleges in the eighteenth century that deserves further study.

9 Cairns, "Formation of the Scottish Legal Mind" (n 2) at 255–263; Shaw, *Management of Scottish Society* (n 2) 27.

10 Cairns, "John Spotswood" (n 6).

11 Sir A Grant, *The Story of the University of Edinburgh during its First Three Hundred Years*, 2 vols (1884) (henceforth Grant, *Story of the University of* Edinburgh) vol i, 284–285.

soon to follow in 1719 and 1722.[12] The creation of the Chair of Civil Law in 1710 seems to have spurred the University of Glasgow into development in emulation, just as the "emulous rivalry" between Glasgow and Edinburgh at this time stimulated the growth of medical education in the universities.[13] John Stirling, the Principal, accordingly proposed to the faculty of the University of Glasgow on 3 August 1713 that they should consider how, after the payment of debts, the yearly deficiency of the college's revenue might be supplied out of King William's gift, with the remainder of the gift secured to support professorships of law and medicine.[14] The faculty considered Stirling's proposal the next day, stating that the long neglect of these disciplines had been "to the great prejudice" of the university. The Royal Visitation of 1664 had suggested that "the said Professions ought to be revived", and the faculty considered that to do so "would tend much to the advantage and honour of the society". A letter from the Rector, Sir John Maxwell of Pollok, a Lord of Session, in support of the establishment of the chairs was read to the meeting, while "severall persons of quality" were noted as having also desired the "revival" of these disciplines. The faculty accordingly enacted:

> That the said two professions of Law and Medicine by Revived, and Law and Medicine taught as soon as possible by professors fitted for that purpose, and Ordains that application be made to the Soveraign for obtaining the Remaining part of King William's Gift being one Hundred and Thirty pounds for the support of the said two professions.

The Principal was authorised to apply to the sovereign and to do whatever was necessary to secure these ambitions, including going to London.[15]

12 Ibid vol i, 232–233, 286–288; vol ii, 313–317, 364–376; some of what Grant writes requires extensive revision in the light of current research.

13 R L Emerson, "Medical Men, Politicians and the Medical Schools at Glasgow and Edinburgh, 1685–1803" (I am grateful to Professor Emerson for allowing me to read and cite this unpublished paper).

14 Minutes of Meetings of Faculty, 1701–1717, G[lasgow] U[niversity] A[rchives] 26632 110.

15 Ibid 110–111. In *Munimenta alme universitatis Glasguensis: Records of the University of Glasgow from its Foundation till 1727*, ed C Innes, 3 vols and index, Maitland Club vol 70 (1854) (henceforth *Munimenta*), vol ii, 408 this meeting is dated to 6 November 1712 being added to the end of a minute correctly attributed to that date. The reason is hard to explain; Minutes of Meetings of Faculty, 1702–1720, GUA 26631 166 (3 August 1713) 166–168 (4 August 1713) (of which GUA 26632 is the fair copy) confirm the date I have given in the text. The wrong dating in the *Munimenta* has misled scholars into thinking that the faculty decided to "revive" the chair in 1712: see J Coutts, *A History of the University of Glasgow from its Foundation in 1451 to 1909* (1909) (henceforth Coutts, *History of the University of Glasgow*) 193; D Murray, *Memories of the Old College of Glasgow: Some Chapters in the History of the University* (1927) 214 (henceforth Murray, *Memories of the Old College of Glasgow*); J D Mackie, *The University of Glasgow, 1451–1951: A Short History* (1954) 165 (henceforth

The Principal and Charles Morthland, the Professor of Oriental Languages, left for London the next month in pursuance of the faculty's aims.[16] Queen Anne assigned £90 *per annum* to support a chair in Law on 16 December 1713.[17] Stirling and Morthland reported their success to the faculty on 15 January 1714. The queen had left the nomination of the professors to the university.[18] Stirling had already taken soundings as to who should be appointed and had been given the name of William Forbes.[19] Stirling obviously mentioned Forbes at the meeting, but the faculty refused simply to endorse his appointment, perhaps suspicious that this was a put-up job engineered by the Principal and the Rector; they certainly expressed the worry that Forbes did not have a reputation to match that of Craig in Edinburgh. The Rector wrote to Stirling in exasperation that he knew "not how these gentlemen may be satisfied that this person is of equall reputatione with Mr. C[rai]ge . . . he hath been ane older lawier and hath writt more on the law then the other did".[20] The faculty, often in conflict with the autocratic and high-handed Stirling, pursued their own course, and at a meeting on 21 January 1714 appointed Alexander Dunlop, the Professor of Greek, to go to Edinburgh "where the Civilians do most reside" so that he could "inform himself who is esteemed the fittest to undertake the said profession of Law". He was to consult not only the Rector but also "the Lawyers that may be most Capable to inform and advise him" and to report back.[21] Dunlop reported on 28 January 1714 that "Mr. William Forbes Advocat . . . is Esteem'd a man very well skill'd in the Civil Law and Capable to teach the same, and (Considering the present Circumstances) thought the fittest for that post". The faculty accordingly elected Forbes to the chair, noting in their act that the Rector had written to the Principal expressing his approval of Forbes, who was described as "of known Integrity and good affection to our present happy Constitution in Church and State". Before this election was intimated to Forbes, however, the faculty decided that regulations should be made governing the scope and exercise of his professorship.[22]

Mackie, *University of Glasgow*); D M Walker, *A History of the School of Law: The University of Glasgow* (1990) (henceforth Walker, *History of the School of Law*) 20.

16 GUA 26632 111 (9 September 1713).

17 *Munimenta* (n 15) vol i, 467–468.

18 GUA 26632 111–112.

19 R Alexander to J Stirling, 12 January 1714, G[lasgow] U[niversity] L[ibrary], MS Gen 205/134.

20 J Maxwell of Pollok to J Stirling, 16 January 1714, GUL MS Gen 205/133.

21 GUA 26632 112–113.

22 Ibid 113.

The faculty met on 29 January 1714 to draw up the necessary regulations. These are important in understanding the aims of the professors and require to be considered in some detail. Students of law were to matriculate should they not formerly have been students in the university. The professor had to assess all students for a contribution to funds to build up a collection of the books necessary to study law. The Professor of Law was limited to teaching Civil, feudal, Canon and Scots law to prevent his encroaching on the provinces of any of the other professors. The faculty noted that some law students might require to take classes from other professors, and resolved to take into account how to make this possible. In the meantime the new professor was "to be carefull his students be all of them duely prepared for the study of Law by having a Competency of the Languages and philosophy necessary for that study". The faculty considered that these regulations might "be better adjusted" when the new professor was present, and adjourned further consideration of them to then. The problem of the precedency to be given to the Professor of Civil Law was also raised but left undetermined; we shall return to this below. Forbes' election was to be notified to the Rector, and an extract of the act electing him sent to Edinburgh.[23]

These regulations demonstrate that the faculty were concerned to introduce into Glasgow legal education conforming to the best contemporary ideals. For example, in 1701 John Spotswood had contrasted the present state of legal education in Scotland with the past when lawyers had been at pains "to attain the Knowledge of the Laws, Civil, Feudal, Canon, and Municipal" (a list interestingly identical to the teaching prescribed for Forbes) but also were concerned to attain "the full Knowledge of History, Politics, Philosophy and Classical learning".[24] Spotswood had been educated in law at the University of Leiden and, by 1714, as an influential private teacher he had done much to map out in Scotland a curriculum of legal studies developed on the continental Humanist model and building on the regulations for admission to the Faculty of Advocates. As regards the purely legal component, this had come to mean separate courses of lectures on the *Institutes* of Justinian, the *Digest* of Justinian, and Scots law.[25] The primary focus was on Civil Law, the object of university legal study *par excellence.* Legal education was, of course, broader than this, as the quotation from Spotswood in 1701 indeed indicates; the Faculty of Advocates, for example, had stated in 1695, in the

23 Ibid 114.

24 *A Collection of Decisions of the Lords of Council and Session, in Two Parts,* [J Spotswood (ed)] (1701) 7 (first sequence of pagination).

25 Cairns, "John Spotswood" (n 6).

course of one of their attempts to secure the foundation of a chair in law, that "[t]he professione of the laws carys necessarly with it all the belles Letres and the knowledge of ancient and moderne history".[26] Spotswood expected his students to come to him already proficient in languages and "skillfull in *Grammar, Rhetorick*, and *Logick*".[27] At one time, he provided teachers of history and philology for his students, because lawyers required a knowledge of history and "to be made Partakers of the *Grecian* and *Roman* Wit and Prudence".[28] Studying classics and history was generally taken as a necessary supplement to studying law: thus, in 1710 John McDowall advertised private classes on "several of the classick Authors" for "those who Study the Civil Law" where he would "take occasion to give the rise and Progress of the Civil Law as it's to be gathered from the Classicks".[29]

The above discussion allows us to see that the faculty envisaged Forbes as teaching Civil Law and Scots law, and as ensuring that his students had already achieved suitable standards in classics, history, logic and ethics; or, if after his first year of teaching men were admitted without these attainments, then they would be required to take the necessary classes with other professors in Glasgow. Forbes was not himself to teach the students these courses. This explains the restriction of his teaching, which was most obviously aimed at preventing him from teaching the law of nature and nations. Gershom Carmichael had reoriented the course in moral philosophy in Glasgow around Pufendorf's theories of natural law.[30] At this period Scots lawyers were becoming increasingly concerned with natural law, and the Regius Professor of Public Law and the Law of Nature and Nations in the University of Edinburgh had already advertised classes "on the Laws of Nature and Nations" in 1711.[31] Had Forbes taught this subject he would

26 J M Pinkerton (ed), *The Minute Book of the Faculty of Advocates, Volume 1, 1661–1712*, Stair Society vol 29 (1976) 160 (24 December 1695) (henceforth *Advocates' Minutes* vol i).

27 J Spotiswood, *A Discourse Shewing the Necessary Qualifications of a Student of the Laws: And what is Propos'd in the Colleges of Law, History and Philology, Establish'd at Edinburgh. Deliver'd at the Commencement of the College of Law. VI. November MDCCIV* (1704) 10.

28 Ibid.

29 See, e.g., *The Evening-Post, or, the New Edinburgh Gazette*, 26/28 December 1710.

30 See J Moore and M Silverthorne, "Gershom Carmichael and the Natural Jurisprudence Tradition in Eighteenth-Century Scotland", in I Hont and M Ignatieff (eds), *Wealth and Virtue: The Shaping of Political Economy in the Scottish Enlightenment* (1983) 73 (henceforth Moore and Silverthorne, "Gershom Carmichael and the Natural Jurisprudence Tradition in Eighteenth-Century Scotland"); and "Natural Sociability and Natural Rights in the Moral Philosophy of Gershom Carmichael", in V Hope (ed), *Philosophers of the Scottish Enlightenment* (1984) 1.

31 *Scots Courant*, 12/14 and 14/16 November 1711; he never advertised thereafter and whether he continued to teach seems uncertain.

have been directly competing with other professors' courses. That Forbes might have been tempted to teach natural law appears from his view that the law of nature and nations was part of the Civil Law, and that it was distinct from philosophy as was evidenced by there being a separate chair devoted to it in Edinburgh.[32] His contemporary Spotswood also viewed natural law as an aspect of Civil Law.[33] Despite this restriction on the scope of the chair in Law, the Faculty at Glasgow were evidently determined to introduce the best modern practice in legal education of the type familiar from the Netherlands.

The faculty had failed to resolve on 29 January 1714 the vexed issue of Forbes' precedency as Professor of Civil Law.[34] The Rector expressed the hope on 30 January that "these gentle-men need not be so punctilious about their Ranking" and would accept what was done at other Scottish and foreign universities.[35] The matter was postponed several times until the Rector was present at a meeting.[36] The problem was that the regents in philosophy (or some of them) wished to claim precedency over Forbes. The latter entered vigorously into the debate using his legal skills (precedency being a legal question). He argued that the invariable practice was to rank professors of law after those of divinity but before those of medicine and philosophy. Stirling had told Forbes that one of the reasons urged for postponing his precedency to that of the regents in philosophy had been that Pufendorf as Professor of the Law of Nature at Heidelberg took precedency over the Professor of Civil Law and the Glasgow regents taught natural law. While not conceding the factual claim, Forbes pointed out in a letter the special status of Pufendorf and argued, as noted already, that the law of nature and nations was part of the Civil Law and distinct from philosophy.[37] He later wrote that, in any case, Pufendorf had not had precedency over the professors of law in Heidelberg.[38] At a meeting on 10 August 1714 the matter was finally settled. The faculty considered first a paper given in by Carmichael, which the Principal also signed, and secondly the practice and custom of other universities (no doubt to some extent from the material furnished by Forbes) before deciding to rank the Professorship of Civil

32 W Forbes to J Stirling, 25 March 1714, GUL MS Gen 205/143.

33 Cairns, "John Spotswood" (n 6) at 150–151.

34 GUA 26632 114. (It is not stated in this minute that precedency was the problem; but subsequent minutes and correspondence show that it was.)

35 J Maxwell of Pollok to J Stirling, 30 January 1714, GUL MS Gen 205/137.

36 GUA 26632 115 (1 February 1714) 116 (15 February 1714)120 (26 May 1714).

37 W Forbes to J Stirling, 25 March 1714, GUL MS Gen 205/143.

38 W Forbes to J Stirling, 6 April 1714, GUL MS Gen 205/144.

Law after that of Divinity and before that of Medicine. It is notable that none of those concerned, other than Carmichael, attended this meeting. There the matter rested until the Visitation of 1727 altered precedency by making professors rank according to date of election: a decision which Forbes understandably protested.[39]

B. THE APPOINTMENT OF FORBES

To understand how Forbes came to be appointed as the first Professor of Civil Law in the University of Glasgow it is important to examine his life to the time of his election to the chair. Although much of his biography is obscure, such details as emerge suggest why such an office was attractive to him and how he had come to the attention of the men who secured it for him.

William Forbes' father was Thomas Forbes, who was the son of William Forbes of Colton (perhaps to be identified with the place of that name in Forfarshire).[40] William Forbes of Colton's brother was Alexander Forbes, minister of Campsie, whose son, another William Forbes, was minister at Cadder. Both these parishes are in the Presbytery of Glasgow.[41] These two Forbes ministers were educated in Aberdeen at King's College and Marischall College respectively.[42] Like his cousin William, Thomas Forbes may have studied at Marischall College before he matriculated, aged twenty, in the Faculty of Law in Leiden in 1649. He then progressed to Italy, where he was inscribed at Padua in 1650, taking the degree of MD in 1652.[43] Sometime thereafter he must have come home to Scotland, as he

39 Minutes of Meetings of Faculty, 1727–1730, GUA 26635 16–17 (26 December 1727); for Forbes' placing after 1727 see Order of University Members, 1735, GUA 10149). I am indebted to Roger Emerson for the point that the change in 1727 had the effect of giving Ilay's men precedency.

40 R W Innes Smith, *English-Speaking Students of Medicine at the University of Leyden* (1932) (henceforth Innes Smith, *English-Speaking* Students) 87.

41 See Thomas Forbes' renunciation of his right to enter heir to his cousin, William Forbes, in 1671, S[cottish] R[ecord] O[ffice], RD. 2/32 267; H Scott (ed), *Fasti ecclesiae Scoticanae: The Succession of Ministers in the Church of Scotland from the Reformation*, new edn, 7 vols (1915–1929) (henceforth *Fasti ecclesiae Scoticanae*) vol iii, 373, 375.

42 P J Anderson (ed), *Fasti Academiae Mariscallanae Aberdonensis*: Selections from the Records of the Marischal College and University, MDXCIII–MDCCCLX, 3 vols, New Spalding Club (1889–1898) (henceforth *Fasti Academiae Mariscallanae Aberdonensis*) vol ii, 225; P J Anderson (ed), *Roll of Alumni in Arts of the University and King's College of Aberdeen 1596–1860* (1900) 5.

43 *Fasti Academiae Mariscallanae Aberdonensis* (n 42) vol ii, 213; *Album studiosorum Academiae Lugduno-Batavae, MDLXXV–MDCCCXXV* (1875) (henceforth *Album studiosorum Academiae Lugduno-Batavae*) col 397; Innes Smith, *English-Speaking Students* (n 40) 87.

was associated with a group of men interested in founding a College of Physicians in Edinburgh in 1656.[44] Forbes went back to Italy – perhaps the Commonwealth regime was inimical to him – and was appointed Professor of Philosophy in Pisa in 1658, being translated to a chair of Medicine in 1659. He resigned in 1662 and returned to Scotland.[45] It is worth noting that in arguments about the precedence of professors in the University of Glasgow his son drew on two annual printed lists detailing the subject and hours that each professor at Pisa was to teach.[46] Where Thomas Forbes initially settled in Scotland is uncertain, but it may have been in Edinburgh, as a bond was there executed in his favour in January 1666, and he married Isobel Edgar in the parish of Edinburgh in 1666.[47] However this may be, Forbes evidently maintained links with Forfarshire and the north east, as this bond was granted by a merchant burgess of Aberdeen and Dundee, and his bride's family came from the parish of Brechin. After his marriage Forbes moved to Dundee, as in January 1684 he was designated in a deed as Doctor of Medicine in that burgh.[48] Shortly after this date he moved to St Andrews, where he was living by May 1685, and where he died in 1687.[49]

The maternal background of the future professor at Glasgow is also of great importance in understanding his career. Isobel Edgar was the daughter of David Edgar of Keithhock in Forfarshire.[50] The lands of Keithock were held of the Bishop of Brechin.[51] The Edgars of Keithock, though landowners, were evidently relatively impoverished. Under the marriage contract between her parents, Isobel Edgar became entitled to 4,000 merks Scots on her father's death. She sued her brother, David Edgar, for this sum in 1665. Two years of litigation resulted between them, until she and her now husband, Thomas Forbes, had Keithock adjudged to them for the debt, and gained sasine of it in January 1667.[52] Prior to this, she had not been entirely

44 J D *Comrie, History of Scottish Medicine*, 2nd edn, 2 vols (London, 1932) vol i, 267; see also J S G Blair, *History of Medicine in the University of St Andrews* (1987) 4.

45 Innes Smith, *English-Speaking Students* (n 40) 87.

46 W Forbes to J Stirling, 25 March 1714, GUL MS Gen 205/143.

47 SRO RD. 4/28 364–365; H Paton (ed), *The Register of Marriages for the Parish of Edinburgh, 1595–1700*, Scottish Record Society vol 27 (1905) (henceforth *Register of Edinburgh Marriages*) 213.

48 SRO RD. 2/63 265.

49 SRO RD. 4/78 871–872; Register of St Andrews Testaments, SRO CC 20/4/15 fo 192v.

50 Committee of the Grampian Club (eds), *Genealogical Collections Concerning the Scottish House of Edgar: With a Memoir of James Edgar, Private Secretary to the Chevalier St George* (1873) (henceforth *House of Edgar*) 17–23.

51 See, e.g., SRO RS. 3/16 fos 167v–169v.

52 SRO RS. 3/16 fos 167v–169v; SRO RD. 2/58 816–830.

resourceless, as she had the capital to lend £149 6s 8d (Scots) to James Farquharson, younger of Whitehouse, in 1663, and her mother, Anna Blair, as liferentrix of Keithock, had disponed some of the victual from Keithock to her which she had assigned to Farquharson also in 1663 in return for certain income.[53] It was probably Anna Blair's death that prompted Isobel Edgar to sue her brother in 1665 for her entitlement under the provisions of her parents' marriage contract. Keithock was later sold to another David Edgar, a writer in Edinburgh, who was probably a relative.[54] Certainly James Edgar of this family, who was to flee Scotland after the Rebellion of 1715 and to serve as the Old Pretender's secretary, dying in Rome in the 1760s, considered himself and William Forbes to be kin, sending his greetings to the latter in 1738, via Father Thomas Innes and the Foulis brothers, stressing he was "the same as to [his] principles, in relation to religion and government, as when [he] parted with him".[55]

Isobel Edgar was a widow aged thirty-one years at the time of her marriage to Thomas Forbes.[56] Her first husband had been James Pitcairn of Cordoun, one of the Pitcairns of Pitlour in Perthshire. Under the contract of marriage between them, she had become infeft in income from the lands of Haltoun and the fishings of Cordoun in January 1661, the income to become due after her husband's death. He died in October 1662.[57] James Pitcairn and his father Andrew, who survived him, had severe financial problems.[58] The heritage from which Isobel Edgar was to derive her income had come into the possession of William Oliphant of Provostmains, by virtue of an apprising against Andrew and James Pitcairn. Isobel Edgar sued Andrew Pitcairn and Oliphant and obtained a decree of poinding and apprising for her income under her marriage contract in accordance with her infeftment. Oliphant accordingly granted a series of heritable bonds in her favour undertaking to pay her.[59] His spouse executed a further disposition in favour of Isobel

53 SRO RD. 3/8 310–311; SRO RD. 3/11 524–525. Forbes later also loaned money to Farquharson: SRO RD. 3/13 615. James Farquharson of Whitehouse granted a lot of bonds in this period and should be distinguished from the James Farquharson, son of Anna Blair and Archibald Farquharson, her second husband, who was Isobel Edgar's half-brother (see SRO RS. 35/7 fos 105–107v).

54 SRO RD. 2/58 816–830; SRO RS. 35/7 fos 105–107v.

55 T Innes to J Edgar, 27 October 1738, *Edinburgh Magazine and Literary Miscellany*, 10 (1822) 336.

56 She died, aged eighty, in 1715: *House of Edgar* (n 50) 35.

57 For details, see SRO RD. 4/12 869–877.

58 C Pitcairn, *The History of the Fife Pitcairns with Transcripts of Old Charters* (1905) 338.

59 SRO RD. 4/12 869–877; SRO RD. 3/23 94–96.

Edgar and Thomas Forbes in 1670.[60] The problem clearly was that the heritage did not produce enough income to satisfy all those entitled to it, and considerable arrears were owed at the time of Thomas Forbes' death.[61] By the 1690s, Isobel Edgar had acquired direct control of Haltoun and the fishings of Cordoun and was setting them in tack herself.[62]

Forbes' parental background was thus among the Scottish professional classes and minor landowners: the comfortable middle ranks from which advocates were so frequently drawn. His father's absences from Scotland may suggest a certain ambivalence towards the Commonwealth, and a corresponding support for the House of Stuart. In this respect it is worth noting that the Edgars who acquired Keithock and were related to Isobel Edgar were an Episcopalian, Jacobite family, much patronised by the Earls of Panmure who regularly acted as godparents to their children. Forbes was thus related not only to the Old Pretender's secretary but also to the latter's brother John Edgar, who died in Stirling Castle after the Rebellion of 1715.[63] Thomas Forbes' support in 1656 for the establishment of a College of Physicians in Edinburgh looks forward to significant developments in Restoration Scotland, when the intellectual interests of the *virtuosi* combined with favourable politics to create institutions such as the College of Physicians and the Advocates Library in Edinburgh.[64] William Forbes' background thus was also one committed to intellectual endeavour.

Forbes was almost certainly born before 1670, probably in 1668.[65] He was presumably named for his grandfather, but it may be that the death of William Forbes, his father's cousin, in August 1668 also influenced the choice of Christian name.[66] He studied in the University of St Andrews from 1684 to 1688, if he may be identified with the William Forbes who matriculated in St Salvator's College under the Regent, John Menzies, in 1685 and graduated on 14 July 1688.[67] His father's move to St Andrews at some time between

60 SRO RD. 3/27 300–302. Forbes obviously became involved in the parish of Abernethy, to whose minister he was to lend 100 merks on 4 July 1677: SRO RD. 4/43 574.

61 Register of St Andrews Testaments, SRO CC. 20/4/15 fo 192v.

62 SRO RD. 4/74 801–804.

63 *House of Edgar* (n 50) 17–23, 25–26.

64 H Ouston, "York in Edinburgh: James VII and the Patronage of Learning in Scotland, 1679–1688", in J Dwyer, R A Mason and A Murdoch (eds), *New Perspectives on the Politics and Culture of Early Modern Scotland* (1982) 133–155 (henceforth Ouston, "York in Edinburgh").

65 This latter date depends on his being the student who matriculated at Leiden, aged twenty, in 1688: *Album studiosorum Academiae Lugduno-Batavae* (n 43) col 701.

66 *Fasti ecclesiae Scoticanae* (n 41) vol iii, 373.

67 I am grateful to Mr Robert N Smart, Keeper of the Muniments at St Andrews, for this information and for supplying me with copies of the relevant pages. The signatures could not easily be

January 1684 and May 1685 supports this identification; the move may have been intended to facilitate Forbes' education. Furthermore, a manuscript in Aberdeen University Library gives some intriguing circumstantial evidence supporting the identification of this student as the future professor.[68] This manuscript contains a great deal of miscellaneous material with a strong focus on religious and legal matters. The first seventy-eight folios contain a manuscript of William Forbes' collections of the decisions of the Lords of Session between 1713 and 1715 (they are not in his hand).[69] A later folio contains some theses that a hand, different from that in which they are written, has annotated as being by William Forbes the future Professor of Law. The theses are not in Forbes' handwriting.[70] Another single folio contains a copy of a glowing testimonial to William Forbes, student in St Andrews, given by his Regent, John Menzies, when Forbes was to be examined at the end of his bachelor year. This is written out in the same hand that noted that the theses were by William Forbes, the future professor.[71] All this is enigmatic. Who wrote these notes? Is the attribution of the theses to Forbes correct? Why was all this material gathered together, and when and by whom? But with the residence of Forbes' father it does tend to support the suggestion that Forbes the future professor was the same man as the student at St Andrews.[72] All the universities were dominated by Episcopalians until purged after 1689; Forbes' own regent, along with virtually all the teachers at St Andrews, was purged in 1690 after the Faculty had put up an admirably spirited defiance and defence to the Commissioners of Visitation.[73] This raises the interesting issue of Forbes' early religious formation.

It is worth pointing out that a William Forbes matriculated in Marischall College in 1681; while this is another possible candidate for the professor, whose own father may have studied there before going to Leiden, it seems less likely, given the date and the signature's considerable variation from that

identified with those of the maturer Forbes, but they are not such as to make it impossible for them to have been his.

68 AUL MS 671; *Aberdeen University Library Bulletin*, 4 (1918–1922) 291–293.

69 Forbes' role as a collector of decisions will be discussed below.

70 AUL MS 671 fo 169a.

71 Ibid fo 168.

72 Ibid fo 272v contains a pencil note stating that this book (one of the other parts of this enigmatic collection) was "given me by my maternal grandmother Elizabeth Carmichael". Although Forbes' daughter married a Carmichael, this probably has no significance, since we do not know when all these MS tracts were drawn together. Like so many such MSS, it remains enigmatic.

73 R K Hannay, "The visitation of St Andrews University in 1690" (1915) 13 *Scottish Historical Review* 1.

of the adult Forbes.[74] The signature is also quite different from that of the student at St Andrews: they were not the same man.

A few months after William Forbes graduated from St Andrews, the matriculation records of Leiden record a William Forbes, a Scot, aged twenty, matriculating as a student in philosophy on 28 October 1688.[75] Twenty was a very late age for a Scot to embark on studies in a university for the first time. This tends to suggest that the St Andrews' student had moved on to further study in the Netherlands. Unfortunately, since the Leiden matriculation albums do not contain signatures, it is impossible to be certain.[76] Given that the professor's father studied at Leiden, he may well have done likewise: perhaps his father's recent death made this financially possible or easier.

The annotator of the folio in the Aberdeen manuscript that contains *Theses philosophicae de natura possibilitatis* stated that Forbes prepared them to defend in the competition for the position of Regent in Philosophy in the University of Edinburgh which was won by William Law. The future law professor had ultimately been unable to compete because of illness.[77] This competition took place in 1690.[78] This is compatible with attendance at Leiden over 1688 to 1689. The annotator's claim that Forbes wished to be regent fits with what we know of his future career and with his family background.

The confusion and uncertainty of the evidence has required a somewhat complex discussion; it therefore may be helpful to set out the suggested career of Forbes. He attended the University of St Andrews from 1684 to 1688. He then studied in Leiden before offering himself as a candidate for the office of Regent in Philosophy in Edinburgh. Disappointed in this ambition because of illness, Forbes may have decided to devote himself to legal study preparatory for admission to the Faculty of Advocates. Perhaps he spent some time in the office of a Writer to the Signet as was not unusual for future advocates and studied civil law on his own. He may even have studied law in the Netherlands without matriculating.[79] He appears to have been living in Edinburgh in 1694 when he made a return for the poll tax on behalf

74 AUL MS M2 (I am grateful to Mr Iain Beavan of Aberdeen University Library for supplying me with a copy of the signature); *Fasti Academiae Mariscallanae Aberdonensis* (n 42) vol ii, 251.

75 *Album studiosorum Academiae Lugduno-Batavae* (n 43) col 701.

76 Ibid VI.

77 AUL MS 671 fo 169a.

78 Edinburgh University Library, MS Dc. 5.5 60.

79 Consider the career of Spotswood: see Cairns, "John Spotswood" (n 6) at 135–138.

of his mother.[80] All becomes certain, however, when Forbes was publicly examined by the Faculty of Advocates on 8 February 1696, defending theses on D 28.1,[81] and was admitted as an advocate by the Lords of Session on 15 February.[82]

Forbes' early years in the faculty are obscure. He first appears in the Faculty's minutes in 1700 as one of the proposed examiners in a projected reform of the public examination.[83] He served as Clerk of Faculty from 6 January 1702 to 5 January 1703, and again as joint-Clerk from 24 November 1705 to the end of 1714. He was also joint-Keeper of the Advocates Library in the second of these periods.[84] He presumably demitted these offices when he took up his teaching duties in Glasgow. Forbes had proved to be a regular user of the Advocates Library;[85] Brian Hillyard has noted, however, that "Forbes seems hardly to have counted as a Keeper at all".[86] On the other hand, he seems to have been an active Clerk.[87]

What practice at the Bar Forbes may have had is unknown. It is, however, highly suggestive that he took to writing, which strongly indicates that he may have been underemployed as an advocate. Within a short period he published works on bills of exchange (1703), church lands and tithes (1705), justices of the peace (1707) (adding a second part to this work in 1708), and elections (1710). From 1705 he had collected the decisions of the Session, and, when elected to the chair in Glasgow, was putting his *Journal of the*

80 M Wood (ed), *Edinburgh Poll Tax Returns for 1694*, Scottish Record Society vol 82 (1951) (henceforth *Poll Tax Returns for* 1694) 44.

81 *Advocates' Minutes* (n 26) vol i, 166; W Forbes, *Disputatio juridica, ad titulum ff. in testamenta facere possunt, et quemadmodum testamenta fiant* (1696) (henceforth Forbes, *Disputatio juridica*).

82 Books of Sederunt of the Lords of Council and Session, SRO CS. 1/9 fo 121r.

83 *Advocates' Minutes* (n 26) vol i, 208 (1 February 1700).

84 Ibid vol i, 229, 241, 261; J M Pinkerton (ed), *The Minute Book of the Faculty of Advocates, Volume 2, 1713–1750*, Stair Society vol 32 (1980) (henceforth *Advocates' Minutes* vol ii) 1 (20 January 1713) 4 (19 January 1714), note his continuance as joint-Clerk, but at 8 (21 January 1715) only Adam Coult was continued as Clerk.

85 P Wellburn, "The Living Library", in P Cadell and A Matheson (eds) *For the Encouragement of Learning: Scotland's National Library, 1689–1989* (1989) (henceforth Cadell and Matheson, *For the Encouragement of Learning*) 186 at 192.

86 B Hillyard, "The Formation of the Library, 1682–1728", in Cadell and Matheson, *For the Encouragement of Learning* (n 85) 23 at 46.

87 For mention of his activity, *see Advocates' Minutes* (n 84) vol ii, 4 (12 December 1713). That he was an active clerk can be deduced from the allowances made to his servitor, John Russell: *Advocates' Minutes* (n 26) vol i, 273 (24 January 1708) 278 (18 February 1709) 285 (4 February 1710) 296 (12 January 1712); *Advocates' Minutes* (n 84) vol ii, 2 (14 February 1713) 5 (20 February 1714) 8 (19 February 1715). The mention of an allowance to the clerk's servant in *Advocates' Minutes* (n 26) vol i, 6 (6 January 1711) is probably also a reference to Russell. Russell was much involved in Forbes' affairs and, as a writer, was his agent in his private legal business: see SRO CC 20/4/17 485 (as a cautioner in the executry) and SRO RS. 3/11 fo 354 (agent in registering a sasine).

Session (1714) through the press.[88] He also completed the notes to the 1706 edition of Mackenzie's *Institutions*.[89] From 1708 onwards he had also been writing a voluminous and ultimately unpublished, probably unpublishable, treatise on Scots law.[90] The reasons for all this activity become obvious when his proposal to collect the decisions of the Lords is considered. He was made joint-Clerk and joint-Keeper in order to furnish him with a salary as recompense for the labour: from 1705 until 1714 he was gaining a salary from collecting the decisions and furnishing the Advocates Library with two manuscript copies of them.[91]

These literary endeavours suggest Forbes needed money. His total resources at this period are unknown. The matriculant at St Andrews was described as *potens*, indicating that he could pay for his education.[92] His father's net moveable estate, however, was less than £300.[93] Yet the family – Forbes, his mother, and his younger brother, David – were obviously comfortable. Isobel Edgar could lend out relatively significant sums on bond in 1688 and 1689 to individuals in St Andrews.[94] She moved to Edinburgh in the 1690s, presumably to be with her elder son, and there lived genteelly, if modestly, with a single maid servant.[95] David Forbes seems to have died by the early 1690s, which must have relieved financial pressure. Certainly in 1694, Isobel Edgar felt sufficiently financially secure to assign her rights in the lands of Haltoun and fishings of Cordoun to her son, perhaps to help

88 *A Methodical Treatise, Concerning Bills of Exchange . . . according to the Analogy of the Scots Law* (1703) (henceforth Forbes, *Bills of Exchange*); *A Treatise of Church-lands and Tithes: In two Parts* (1705) (henceforth Forbes, *Church-lands and Tithes*); *The Duty and Powers of Justices of the Peace, in this Part of Great-Britain called Scotland. With an Appendix concerning Weights and Measures* (1707); *The Duty and Powers of Justices of Peace, In this Part of Great-Britain, called Scotland, Part II* (1708) (henceforth Forbes, *Justices of Peace*); *A Letter from William Forbes Advocate, to his Friend in England a Member of the House of Commons, Concerning the Law of Election of Members of Parliament* (1710); *A Journal of the Session* (1714) (henceforth Forbes, *Journal of the Session*). *A Legal Bibliography of the British Commonwealth of Nations, 5, Scottish Law to 1956*, ed L F Maxwell and W H Maxwell and comp, 2nd edn (1957) 42 lists: "Forbes (W) On Elections. 12mo 1700; 8vo 1710." The 1700 edition does not exist: it cannot be traced in Aldis or elsewhere. The entry is mistaken as Forbes in the preface to his work on tithes described it as his second publication. The *Bibliography* has other inaccuracies and omissions in the entry on Forbes. For the date of putting the *Journal of the Session* through the press, see *Advocates' Minutes* (n 26) vol i, 298 (11 June 1712).

89 Sir George Mackenzie, *Institutions of the Law of Scotland* (1706) sig A4r.

90 GUL MSS Gen 1246–1252; *Advocates' Minutes* (n 26) vol i, 276–277 (16 November 1708).

91 *Advocates' Minutes* (n 26) vol i, 257–258 (23 June 1705) 261 (24 November 1705).

92 I am indebted to Mr Robert N Smart for this information and explanation.

93 Register of St Andrews Testaments, SRO CC 20/4/15 fo 192v.

94 SRO RD. 4/78 997–999; SRO RD. 4/66 738.

95 *Poll Tax Returns for 1694* (n 80) 44.

support him in his preparation for admission as an advocate.[96] Mother and son were prosperous enough in 1699 to purchase together a substantial second-floor flat (having six rooms with fireplaces) that opened at the front onto the Royal Mile in the splendid and newly built Mylne's Court.[97]

What must have dramatically affected Forbes' financial position was his marriage to Margaret Lindsay in 1700.[98] And it is notable that his writing starts shortly thereafter. She was one of the four children of Alexander Lindsay, a merchant burgess, and the deceased Catherine Abercromby, and her father had recently remarried to one Janet Knox.[99] Though the poll tax returns show her father to have been relatively prosperous, the number of her siblings and her father's remarriage suggest that she may not have brought much wealth to Forbes. Alexander Lindsay died in 1712, and on 4 August 1713 his widow by a deed of cognition at her instance against his children before the Commissaries of Edinburgh claimed from his estate his funeral expenses, her mournings, and the aliment she had provided for his children. Some of these claims and her appointment as executrix resulted in bills of advocation to the Session, as other debtors disputed them. Forbes participated in this litigation as administrator in law of his daughter, Janet, to whom Alexander Lindsay had granted a bond of 1,000 merks to take effect on his death. These matters were still unresolved at the date of the death of Janet Knox in 1714. Such litigation, although Lindsay allegedly left heritage sufficient to satisfy all his creditors, tends to confirm that Forbes' wife may have had relatively slender provision.[100]

Forbes may have had prospects in the early 1700s, but they were contingent on his mother's death and the recovery of debts still owing on her provision under her marriage contract with James Pitcairn. This suggests that, with a family, his professional earnings would have become very important. At this time, there were 200 advocates, of whom 170 were regularly in practice;[101] a contemporary observer was of the view that fewer than

96 SRO RD. 4/78 880–883.

97 SRO B. 22/2/14 fos 67v–68v. They bought it from Laurence Gellatly, on whom see R M Pinkerton and W J Windram, *Mylne's Court: Three Hundred Years of Lawnmarket Heritage* (1985) 32.

98 *Register of Edinburgh Marriages* (n 47) 239.

99 *Poll Tax Returns for 1694* (n 80) 20; H Paton (ed), *Register of Internments in the Greyfriars Burying-Ground, Edinburgh, 1658–1700*, Scottish Record Society vol 26 (1902) 1; *Register of Edinburgh Marriages* (n 47) 410.

100 Register of Edinburgh Testaments, SRO CC 8/8/86 fo 41r; *Forbes v Knox*, 23 February 1714, 25 June 1714, and *Forbes v Lindsay's Creditors*, 25 June 1714, to be found in AUL MS 671 fos 24r–25r, 50v–51v.

101 Forbes, *Journal of the Session* (n 88) vii.

one-third of the advocates could make a living from their practice.[102] Forbes seems likely to have been one of the other two-thirds. While Forbes did not totally lack connections with Scottish landed society, they were slight, hardly intimate, and with very minor families. They were not such as were likely to prove as important a source of business as such links were for other advocates.[103] It is perhaps significant that an adversary of Forbes sneered at him as appearing "to be an Advocate of the *first Rate*, or a Star of the first Magnitude for being so ill acquaint with many other Modes of Defalcation or Diminution . . . before the Commission, for the greatest pleaders at the Bar, usually think it below them to wait on that Court".[104] The sarcasm has obvious bite.

What Forbes evidently needed was a patron able to procure for him an office that would provide him with a regular and secure income. The books were important in achieving this end. That on justices of the peace dealt at considerable length (about two-thirds of the first part of 1707) with the duties of justices of the peace in connection with customs and excise.[105] These were currently controversial and important topics with the establishment of the new Scottish Customs Board and Excise Commission. The English Excise commissioners pointed out the need for justices of the peace to enforce the law on the English model. The responsibility was given to the Scottish justices, but they lacked the authority to enforce the law.[106] Forbes called in the preface of his work for the Scots justices to be given more power. Forbes gained the Privy Council privilege for this work on 3 October 1707.[107] In December 1707 the Squadrone, in committee in the House of Commons, proposed the abolition of the Scottish Privy Council and the permanent strengthening of the authority of Scottish justices of the peace. This was done. This necessarily raised the issue of the relationship between the powers of the justices of peace and those of the holders of

102 Sir James Agnew to Earl of Stair, 31 January 1718, in J M Graham, *Annals and Correspondence of the Viscount and the First and Second Earls of Stair*, 2 vols (1875) vol ii, 379.

103 For a consideration of the importance of this, see Phillipson, "Lawyers, landowners, and the civic leadership of post-Union Scotland" (n 2).

104 [J Gordon,] *Some Charitable Observations on a late Treatise of Church Lands and Tithes; by Mr Forbes Advocat; And tendered to the Publick by a Moderat Son of the Church of England* (1706) (henceforth [Gordon,] *Some Charitable* Observations) 102–103.

105 Forbes, *Justices of Peace* (n 88) contains sixty-eight pages of main text, of which pp 23–68 concern customs and excise.

106 P W J Riley, *The English Ministers and Scotland 1707–1727* (1964) (henceforth Riley, *English Ministers and Scotland*) 61, 67–68, 68 n 1.

107 Forbes, *Justices of Peace* (n 88), on verso of leaf after index of 1st part.

heritable jurisdictions.[108] This explains the second part added to Forbes' work in 1708, on which he commented:

> I was Induced to Lengthen out my Book, by adding a Second Part to it. Wherein my Business is, to show what Justices of Peace, and their Constables may, and should do by the Laws of *England*, without taking notice of private Statutes that give some Power to them in relation to particular Counties or Cities; And to clear up the Relative Duties and Powers of Sheriffs, Stewarts, and Judges of Regality, and Royalty: Running the Parallel all along, and Explaining the Differences betwixt the *Scots* and *English* Laws, in so far as concerns the Subject in Hand.[109]

Forbes was keen to write on a subject that would inevitably draw attention to himself. It may even be that he was prompted by a patron to write on this particular topic as part of the political pressure to increase the authority of the Scots justices of the peace.

Forbes' books would not only generate useful income if successful, they would also, and perhaps, in the long run more importantly, demonstrate that he was a person worthy of patronage and preferment and would allow him to dedicate them fulsomely to potential and actual patrons. The dedications of Forbes' books indicate the men from whom he hoped to gain assistance, to whom he felt the need to make some acknowledgement, and with whom he wished publicly to associate himself. They raise some difficult issues, and suggest that Forbes was not especially politically astute and was either politically eclectic or transferred political allegiance. His behaviour as a professor at Glasgow certainly shows a certain political naivety and vacillation that was to make him powerful enemies who were to try to deprive him of his office.

Forbes dedicated his theses for admission as an advocate to the fourth Earl of Panmure, describing himself as the Earl's "*cliens*". Panmure was, as noted above, a patron of Forbes' mother's family, and this may well explain the dedication; he was, however, a Jacobite and non-jurant who rejected the Revolution Settlement, and who was to be attainted after the Rebellion of 1715.[110] This dedication signalled to Forbes' new colleagues his willing association with those who rejected the Revolution Settlement and the Presbyterian Church. Panmure may have been important because of his great land-holdings, but he could do nothing politically for Forbes at this time. Forbes' background suggests that he may have shared Panmure's political and religious views; on the other hand, his intention to participate in a

108 Riley, *English Ministers and Scotland* (n 106) 90, 92–93.

109 Forbes, *Justices of Peace . . . Part II* (n 88) sig a[l]r.

110 Forbes, *Disputatio juridica* (n 81) 3–4; on Panmure, see Shaw, *Management of Scottish Society* (n 2) 199; Sir J Balfour Paul (ed), *The Scots Peerage*, 9 vols (1904–1914) vol vii, 24–26.

competition for a regent's position in 1690 shows that he was acceptable to a Kirk purged of Episcopalians, although the illness preventing him from competing may have been a politic one. Forbes also was willing to take the oaths of loyalty necessary for admission as an advocate. He may simply have been either naive or pulled in two ways as many Scots were. Had Forbes sympathised with Panmure's views, it is likely that his marriage to the daughter of an Edinburgh burgess altered them; his wife's family was undoubtedly Presbyterian. It is certainly notable that Forbes started to find effective patrons and jobs in the Faculty of Advocates after 1700. It is possible that he had had his vision on the road to Damascus, deciding to become a Whig and Presbyterian to enable him to support a wife and family, but it seems more likely that, as an adult, he had always been of strict Presbyterian views.

Forbes dedicated his next work, that on bills of exchange, to Lord Forbes in 1703: "I cou'd not chuse but Address my Chief as my Patron."[111] Lord Forbes, although a Scottish Privy Councillor before the Union, thereafter became obscure, dying in London in 1716.[112] The next book, which concerned teinds, was dedicated to Sir Hew Dalrymple of North Berwick, the Lord President;[113] the following one on justices of the peace was dedicated in 1707 to Sir David Dalrymple of Hailes, then Solicitor General.[114] The star of the Dalrymple family was still in the ascendant: these two men were a more likely source of effective patronage.[115] We accordingly find Hailes approaching James Erskine, Lord Grange, a Lord of Session, in 1708 seeking an appointment for Forbes as auditor in the new post-Union Court of Exchequer: a position that would have had to be specially created.[116] That his book on justices of the peace devoted so much attention to their duties as regards excise and customs may have been intended to indicate his fitness for such an office. Hailes later was to use his position when Dean of Faculty (having been elected after losing the office of, by then, Lord Advocate),[117] to help Forbes. The original act of faculty endorsing Forbes' resolution to collect the decisions of the Session had provided that they should be published when convenient and printed at the Faculty's expense,

111 Forbes, *Bills of Exchange* (n 88) sig A2v.
112 Shaw, *Management of Scottish Society* (n 2) 11.
113 Forbes, *Church lands and Tithes* (n 88) sig q.2.
114 Forbes, *Justices of Peace* (n 88) sig [a2].
115 On the rise of the Dalrymples, see P W J Riley, *King William and the Scottish Politicians* (1979) 16–18.
116 Lord Grange to Earl of Mar, 4 October 1708, SRO Mar and Kellie Muniments, GD. 124/15/768/19.
117 *Advocates' Minutes* (n 26) vol i, 295 (1 January 1712).

the benefit to go to their fund for the poor.[118] Forbes now proposed that he would undertake the printing of the decisions at his own expense and gain any profit that accrued. Under Hailes' leadership the faculty now agreed.[119] Forbes fulsomely praised the ancestor of these Dalrymples, Viscount Stair, in the preface to his *Journal of the Session*: indeed so keen was he on praising Stair that he used the viscount's very own words.[120] He there also thanked three members of the family for their assistance.[121] He praised Stair in other works too; although the work on bills of exchange was dedicated to Lord Forbes, it contains the following passage:

> Nothing of this nature hath come Abroad in *Scotland* to this day; except that little which as it were by parenthesis, the Learned and Judicious Viscount of *Stair* hath left us in his Institutions. The bulk of matter and Learning couch'd in that admirable and useful Book, wou'd suffer no more room to be spar'd for handling Bills of Exchange. No, the performance being so vast, as never a one was capable to have complimented the publick with; But a person of his Lordship's capacity and parts, Learning and Experience; Who seems (as *Straccha* said of *Baldus*) to have known all things; and whose Memory will ever flourish while Law and good sense are in request.[122]

In the treatise on teinds, dedicated to the Lord President, Sir James Dalrymple of Killoch is thanked and described as "that Great Antiquary" and Stair's *Institutions* is again praised: "To which Book for its Universal Use, I may Justly apply the ancient Proverb concerning Azo's Summ: He who wants it, should sell his Cloke and buy it."[123] Forbes was very successful in becoming close to the Dalrymple family; he was intimate enough with the Lord President, Sir Hew, to spend part of the summer of 1714 as his guest at North Berwick.[124]

Forbes sought patronage further afield. Lord Grange and the Earl of Mar were obviously keen to do something for him in 1708, the first writing to the latter: "I hardly know any of our Lawyers who deserves better to be encouraged than he does, and you was pleas'd to say that you would do for him when occasion offer'd."[125] Grange also was impressed by Forbes' proposal for his "Great Body", approved by the Faculty on 16 November

118 Ibid vol i, 257–258, 261 (23 June, 24 November 1705).

119 Ibid vol i, 298–299 (11 June 1712).

120 H L MacQueen, "Stair's Later Reputation as a Jurist: The Contribution of William Forbes", in W M Gordon (ed), *Miscellany* (1992) *III* 173–194 (henceforth MacQueen, "Stair's Later Reputation").

121 Forbes, *Journal of the Session* (n 88) xlviii.

122 Forbes, *Bills of Exchange* (n 88) sig [A5] v.

123 Forbes, *Church-lands and Tithes* (n 88) sig [qq4] r.

124 W Forbes to J Stirling, 25 March 1714, GUL MS Gen 205/143.

125 Lord Grange to Earl of Mar, 4 October 1708, SRO Mar and Kellie Muniments, GD 124/15/768/19.

1708, sending it to Mar on 25 November, stressing again that it was worth doing something for him.[126] Had Mar been minded to act on Forbes' behalf he could have achieved much as, until the abolition of the Scottish Privy Council in 1708, as secretary, he acted as a link between it and the Queen; his compensatory office as Keeper of the Signet also allowed him to act as a channel for patronage.[127] At this time, Forbes could also count on Gilbert Burnet, Bishop of Salisbury and William Nicolson, Bishop of Carlisle as "friends".[128] Nicolson was an associate of the Dalrymples, and it was probably through them that he became acquainted with Forbes.[129] Forbes felt sufficiently close to Nicolson to rely on his authority in a dispute in 1706 with Scottish Episcopalians.[130] Nothing was done for Forbes, however, at this time.

The vagaries of the swiftly changing politics of Early Modern Scotland meant that none of the above were the men directly influential in gaining Forbes the chair in Glasgow in 1714. Indeed, those who championed Forbes for the office at the beginning of 1714 feared that Lord President Dalrymple and Erskine of Grange, currently Lord Justice-Clerk, might use their influence with him to dissuade him from taking the chair at Glasgow, as he was useful in collecting the decisions of the Session.[131] The election of 1710 had brought in an essentially Tory administration. Though Sir David Dalrymple remained Lord Advocate until 1711, the Dalrymples lost influence and would have become less able to do anything significant for Forbes.[132] Mar remained influential until the death of Anne;[133] he had

126 Lord Grange to Earl of Mar, 25 November 1708, SRO Mar and Kellie Muniments, GD. 124/15/768/24; *Advocates' Minutes* (n 26) vol i, 276–277 (16 November 1708).

127 Riley, *English Ministers and Scotland* (n 106) 29, 100–102; W Ferguson, *Scotland 1689 to the Present* (1968) (henceforth Ferguson, *Scotland*) 53.

128 Lord Grange to Earl of Mar, 25 November 1708, SRO Mar and Kellie Muniments, GD 12/15/768/24.

129 C Jones and G Holmes (eds), *The London Diaries of William Nicolson Bishop of Carlisle 1702–1718* (1985) (henceforth *London Diaries of William* Nicolson) 10.

130 *A Few Remarks by William Forbes Advocat, On a Scurrilous, Erroneous, and Pedantick Pamphlet, Entituled, Some Charitable Observations on his late Treatise of Church-lands and Tithes, By the Author of the Reformed Bishop, under the Vizard of a Moderat Son of the Church of England* (1706) (henceforth *A Few Remarks by William Forbes Advocat*) 3; *A Letter from William Forbes Advocat, To a Gentleman in the Country, Concerning the Parson of Banchory, and his late Pamphlet, entituled, Some Just Reflections on a Pasquil against him, &c* (1706) 23.

131 R Alexander to J Stirling, 12 January 1714, GUL MS Gen 205/134.

132 Ferguson, *Scotland* (n 127) 58–59; Riley, *English Ministers and Scotland* (n 106) 149–157; G W T Omond, *The Lord Advocates of Scotland from the Close of the Fifteenth Century to the Passing of the Reform Bill*, 2 vols (1883) (henceforth Omond, *Lord Advocates of* Scotland) vol i, 291–295.

133 Riley, *English Ministers and Scotland* (n 106) 254–255; E Gregg, "The Jacobite Career of John, Earl of Mar", in E Cruickshanks (ed), *Ideology and Conspiracy: Aspects of Jacobitism, 1689–1759* (1982) 179 (henceforth E Cruickshanks (ed), *Ideology and Conspiracy*) at 180–181.

shown no inclination, however, to accede to his brother's wishes to find a post for Forbes. Moreover, Queen Anne had authorised the university to elect the first professor; this meant that the connections and interests of the university's officers and professors were likely to be most influential. While one should never underestimate the interest great men took in the filling of even insignificant posts, the looming crisis of the approaching death of Queen Anne may have given the professors more scope for manoeuvre, especially since the Squadrone Duke of Montrose, who was later to try to exert considerable influence in the university, was not elected Chancellor until later in 1714. And they certainly felt free to question the advice of the Rector.

If the professors seem to have tried to act independently, and to draw on the advice of their own friends, there were certain individuals whose views obviously could not easily be ignored. One such was Maxwell, the Rector, and, close to the Principal, he seems to have been the prime mover in placing Forbes in the Regius chair. He was certainly regarded slightly later by an obviously well-informed observer as Forbes' patron.[134] Maxwell heartily endorsed Forbes, and both his office in the university and his position as a Lord of Session ensured his opinion carried weight. Maxwell was the one man whom Dunlop was specifically requested to consult on his visit to Edinburgh. Among the first who originally identified Forbes for the professorship were Robert Alexander of Blackhouse, advocate, and Robert Alexander, Principal Clerk of Session. A prominent advocate and future Lord of Session, Sir Walter Pringle of Newhall, also supported Forbes, as did Walter Steuart of Steuarthall, advocate, and (probably) Sir William Calderwood of Polton, Lord of Session.[135] These were the men, along with Maxwell, who had suggested Forbes to those whom the Principal consulted; whom Dunlop consulted, other than the Rector, on his trip to Edinburgh is unknown, but it is very likely that the Dalrymple brothers were among them, as well as his uncle, William Carstares, the influential Principal of the University of Edinburgh, and Grange, as Justice-Clerk.[136] If so, it was hardly surprising that Forbes was named to the post. He himself was very keen to

134 Unknown to R Wodrow, 27 September 1718, N[ational] L[ibrary of] S[cotland], MS Wodrow Corr. XIII fo 86 (I am indebted to Roger Emerson for bringing this letter to my attention).

135 R Alexander to J Stirling, 12 January 1714, GUL MS Gen 205/134; J Maxwell to J Stirling, 16 January 1714, GUL MS Gen 205/133.

136 R L Emerson, *Professors, Patronage and Politics: The Aberdeen Universities in the Eighteenth Century* (1992) (henceforth Emerson, *Professors, Patronage and Politics*) 4–5 discussing the influence of Carstares.

gain it.[137] This group included noted strict Presbyterians and some men with leanings towards the Squadrone.

If the opinion of men trusted by the Principal and faculty at Glasgow predominated in making this appointment, it is easy to see why Forbes was a prime candidate. It may not be entirely coincidental that his great uncle and second cousin had been ministers in the Glasgow presbytery. His writings had given him prominence as a deserving and able man (Maxwell and Alexander of Blackhouse specifically mentioned them in letters to Stirling).[138] The collecting of the Lords' decisions would also have helped him considerably; this was a task that the advocates and the Bench were very anxious to have carried out,[139] and the work would have brought Forbes into very close association with the Lords, such as Maxwell and Calderwood, and principal clerks, such as Alexander. His book on teinds shows him to have been a firm Presbyterian and upholder of the Church of Scotland as established in 1690 – at least now, if he had not been before. This work in fact involved him in a minor pamphlet war with some Scottish Episcopalians because of some remarks he made on patronage as "popish" and on the legal foundation of tithes (he doubted they were *jure divino*).[140] It certainly showed his views were very different from those of Episcopalians and Jacobites who could describe the book as "peevish".[141] But his general acceptability to the Presbyterian religious establishment is probably demonstrated by his considering candidacy for the position of Regent in Edinburgh in 1690 after the purge. Indeed, Erskine of Grange may have patronised Forbes because both men favoured a strict, evangelical Presbyterianism and were interested in witchcraft and demonology.[142] It is likewise worth noting that in copying

137 R Alexander to J Stirling, 12 January 1714, GUL MS Gen 205/134.

138 R Alexander to J Stirling, 12 January 1714, GUL MS Gen 205/134; J Maxwell to J Stirling, 16 January 1714, GUL MS Gen 205/133.

139 *Advocates' Minutes* (n 26) vol i, 109 (16 January 1692) 257–258 (23 June 1705).

140 Forbes, *Church-lands and* Tithes (n 88) 39–70 (esp 51) 275–284; see [Gordon,] *Some Charitable Observations on a late Treatise of Church Lands & Tithes; A Few Remarks by William Forbes Advocat, on a Scurrilous, Erroneous and Pedantick Pamphlet; Some Just Reflexions on a Nonsensical and Scurril Pasquill, against the Parson of Banchory, Penned by a Brainsick Bigott, named William Forbes Advocat* (1706); *A Letter from William Forbes Advocat, to a Gentleman in the Country; A Letter from Mr. Andrew Symson to Mr. William Forbes Advocat* (1706). It is all good, vicious knock-about stuff.

141 T Innes to J Edgar, 29 September 1738 (1822) 10 *The Edinburgh Magazine and Literary Miscellany* 135. For the mental world of the Scottish Episcopalians, see B Lenman, "The Scottish Episcopal Clergy and the Ideology of Jacobitism", in E Cruickshanks (ed), *Ideology and Conspiracy* (n 133) 36.

142 For Grange's views, see A Carlyle, *Anecdotes and Characters of the Times*, J Kinsley (ed) (1973) (henceforth Carlyle, *Anecdotes and Characters*) 7–9; on Forbes' views, see below.

from Lord Stair's apology for the introduction to the *Journal of the Session*, Forbes changed the former's description of himself as supporting "Prelacy reformed from Popery" to one as "a true son of the Presbyterian Church of Scotland".[143] Though perhaps done to please the Dalrymples and to reflect Stair's own change after 1690, this does suggest something of Forbes' own views. On the other hand, Forbes' friendship with two Anglican bishops and his family background would have indicated that his Presbyteriansim was suitably of not too fanatical character. He evidently was also well affected to the Protestant Succession to the throne as established: a very important consideration in 1714 as Anne's death was awaited. The affair of the Jacobite medal in 1711 had caused problems for a number of advocates.[144] But the Rector could happily consider Forbes' appointment to the chair on 30 January, a day, being the anniversary of Charles I's execution, when there were fears of riots in Edinburgh.[145] Furthermore, Forbes was one of the first to take seriously the future legal implications of the Union of 1707. His huge manuscript work on Scots law was intended from the beginning to compare it with that of England.[146] The second part of his treatise on justices of the peace sets out both the English and the Scots law.[147] The second edition of his work on bills of exchange took account of English law.[148] He was a firm supporter of the Union. He was also willing to push for preferment and not afraid of controversy as the dispute over his work on teinds shows. Thus, his pamphlet on elections published in 1710 was intended to

143 For this, see MacQueen, "Stair's Later Reputation" (n 120) 182. Stair's apology was presumably published before May 1690 (when he became a Viscount), and before the re-establishment of Presbyterianism.

144 Omond, *Lord Advocates of* Scotland (n 132) vol i, 291–295; I G Brown, "'This Old Magazine of Antiquities': The Advocates' Library as National Museum", in Cadell and Matheson, *For the Encouragement of Learning* (n 85) 149 at 162; Murdoch, "The Advocates, the Law and the Nation" (n 2) at 156.

145 J Maxwell to J Stirling, 30 January 1714, GUL MS Gen 205/137: the fear presumably was that the rabble might attack the Episcopalian meeting houses.

146 *Advocates' Minutes* (n 26) vol i, 276–277 (16 November 1708).

147 W Forbes, *The Duty and Powers of Justices of Peace, in this Part of Great-Britain, called Scotland. Part II and an Explanation of the Conformity and Difference betwixt the Scots Law, and that of England, in so far as concerns the Subject Treated of* (1708). The work is more restrainedly comparative than this title suggests; see ibid sig a [l]r: "I was Induced to Lengthen out my Book, by adding a Second Part to it. Wherein my Business is, to show what Justices of peace, and their Constables may, and should do by the Laws of *England*, without taking notice of private Statutes that give some power to them in relation to particular Counties or Cities . . ." See also sig [a3]r–v.

148 W Forbes, *A Methodical Treatise Concerning Bills· of Exchange . . . according to the Analogy of the Law of Scotland: With incident comparative Views of the Laws and Customs of England, and other Countries* (1718).

counter that on the same topic published earlier in the same year by John Spotswood.[149] Both pamphlets were obviously prompted by the election of that year.[150] Spotswood was a rival of Forbes, being a man of similar interests also seeking patronage.[151] Deserving, needy and ambitious, with powerful patrons influential in Glasgow, it is easy to see why Forbes was appointed. He had worked hard to gain preferment.

C. FORBES' TENURE AS PROFESSOR

Forbes was informed of his appointment early in February 1714. He wrote to the Principal acknowledging the notification of his election and expressing his sense of the respect and confidence thus given to him by the university. He said that he hoped to thank them personally in Glasgow very soon.[152] By 15 February he was accordingly in Glasgow, and the faculty resolved to admit him "before he go East" were he ready to give his inaugural lecture, and fixed the date of 18 February for this (declaring this was not to prejudice the settling of the issue of precedence).[153] On that date, Forbes duly signed the Confession of Faith before the presbytery of Glasgow, took the oath of loyalty before a justice of the peace, had the oath *de fideli administratione* administered to him by the Principal, and delivered his inaugural lecture *De natura, fortuna, dignitate, utilitate, atque auctoritate juris civilis* in the public hall of the university.[154] He then left Glasgow, not returning until October, passing part of the period between involved in litigation over his father-in-law's estate on behalf of his daughter and part with the Lord President at North Berwick.[155]

149 See W Forbes to unknown correspondent, December 1710, holograph letter pasted into *A Letter from William Forbes . . . Concerning the Law of Election,* NLS pressmark 5.757(13); J Spotswood, *The Law Concerning Election of Members for Scotland, to Sit and Vote in the Parliament of Great-Britain* (1710).

150 See Ferguson, *Scotland* (n 127) 58–59; consider also John Walter and William Forbes, *Lymington Case* [1710] a single sheet on the Lymington election of 1710 (not seen: British Library, pressmark B.P. 33 (15)).

151 Cairns, "John Spotswood" (n 6).

152 W Forbes to J Stirling, 6 February 1714, GUL MS Gen 205/138.

153 GUA 26632 116.

154 Ibid: *Oratio inauguralis, de natura, fortuna, dignitate, utilitate, atque auctoritate juris civilis: habita XII Kal. Mart, anno Aerae Christianae MDCCXIV, in auditorio publico Academiae Glascuensis; a D. Gulielmo Forbesio Advocato, cum juris civilis professionem illic auspicaretur* (1714) (henceforth Forbes, *Oratio inauguralis*).

155 GUA 26632 127 (1 October 1714) records Forbes' first attendance at a Faculty Meeting; see AUL MS 671. ff 24r–25r, 50v–51v and Forbes to Stirling, 25 March 1714, GUL MS Gen 205/143.

Forbes scheduled his first session of classes to begin on 10 October 1714. He advertised them as to be on "the Civil and Scottish Laws", stating that he would "explain in his Colleges the Harmony, Analogy, and Differences betwixt the Roman law, and the Law of Scotland; and also how far either of these Laws do agree with, and differ from the Law of England".[156] It is unclear from this whether he proposed to give one set of lectures covering both Scots and Civil Law or one set of lectures on each. The comparison with English law is notable and reflects the obvious interest Forbes had in this issue after the Union; he similarly described his manuscript "Great Body of the Law of Scotland" as "containing the harmony [of the law of Scotland] with, and differences from the civil and feudal laws; and shewing how far the Scots and English law do agree and differ".[157] While some of the advocates who lectured privately in Edinburgh had taught Scots law, these seem to have been the first courses on the discipline to be taught in a university. Whatever Forbes may exactly have taught, this first year does not seem to have been outstandingly successful, as he attracted only a single student.[158] In the next session Forbes started his classes later because of problems caused by the Jacobite Rebellion. The University of Glasgow advertised in November 1715 that, contrary to rumour, the university was open and classes were being taught.[159] Forbes, however, had remained in Edinburgh, where his aged mother had just died early in November, and presumably troop movements and general disturbance hampered communications and his return to Glasgow.[160] He may even have believed the university to be closed. He inserted a notice in the *Scots Courant* in December that "by Reason of the Troubles in the Country, [he had] been hindered from attending his Post". He proposed "to open his College there, and commence his Lessons upon the Civil and Scots Laws" on 3 January 1716.[161] He taught three students this session.[162] Forbes intended to open his classes in the next session on 20 November 1716. He proposed to teach only Civil Law.[163] The low numbers of students he had hitherto attracted perhaps made it prudent to teach only the one course; it is conceivable that students had shown an interest only in

156 *Scots Courant*, 8/10 September 1714.
157 *Advocates' Minutes* (n 26) vol i, 277 (16 November 1708).
158 W Forbes to J Stirling, 30 January 1717, GUL MS Gen 204/16.
159 *Scots Courant*, 18/21 November 1715.
160 Forbes' mother was buried in Greyfriars Kirkyard on 8 November 1715: *House of Edgar* (n 50) 35.
161 *Scots Courant*, 7/9 December 1715.
162 W Forbes to J Stirling, 30 January 1717, GUL MS Gen 204/16.
163 *Scots Courant*, 12/15 October 1716.

Roman law. This year, however, he had no students.[164] Thereafter there is no information about Forbes' teaching schedule, as he ceased to advertise his classes in newspapers; nor is there any certain information about the size of his classes.

No notes taken by students who attended Forbes' lectures have been identified as surviving.[165] In interpreting his duties as to teach Scots law and Civil Law, he was following the practice already well established by the advocates who taught privately in Edinburgh.[166] If not initially, then certainly later Forbes taught Civil Law in two different classes: one on the *Institutes* and one on the *Digest*. This had become the practice by the time of his death.[167] How he taught them, and what was encompassed in them, can only be a matter of speculation. The Visitation of 1664 had envisaged a chair teaching both Civil and Canon Law;[168] the latter was certainly within the subjects open to Forbes under the faculty's regulations of 1714 and was commonly regarded as closely connected with the former. Thus, James Craig in Edinburgh sometimes described himself as Professor of Civil and Canon Law;[169] one advocate who lectured privately offered classes on "some particular Parts of the Cannonical Law, as founded on material Justice" as well as the usual two classes on the Civil Law because "in which Points, both Laws hath a Reciprocal Dependence on each other".[170] There is no evidence of Forbes' practice in this respect, although he is sometimes referred to in the sederunt of meetings as JUP rather than JCP;[171] when Dean of Faculty he usually signed the minutes designating himself as the former.[172] It may be significant that, when he presented a candidate for the degree of LLD in 1735, the candidate was examined on both Civil and Canon Law.[173] Forbes was certainly alive to the importance of Canon Law, noting that it "hath since

164 Inferred from W Forbes to J Stirling, 30 January 1717, GUL MS Gen 204/16.

165 Murray, *Memories of the Old College of Glasgow* (n 15) 216 (followed by Walker, *History of the School of Law* (n 15) 24) states that in GUL there is a MS commentary on Justinian's *Institutes* that has been attributed to Forbes. This seems mistaken: at least there is no such identifiable, possible MS. I am grateful to Mr David Weston for assisting me with this point.

166 Cairns, "John Spotswood" (n 6) at 133–134, 153–155.

167 See below.

168 *Munimenta* (n 15), ii, 480.

169 See, e.g., *Scots Courant*, 25/28 March 1715, 25/57 March 1717, 17/19 February 1720; *Caledonian Mercury*, 11 October 1720 and 13 October 1729.

170 *Scots Courant*, 14/16 June 1710.

171 As *iuris utriusque professor* rather than *iuris civilis professor*: see, e.g., Minutes of Meetings of Faculty, 1720–1727, GUA 26634 28 (31 October 1721) 72 (11 October 1722), 130 (as LLP, 4 May 1724) 147 (23 March 1725) 210 (29 March 1727).

172 Minutes of Meetings of Faculty and Dean of Faculty's Meetings, 1732–1768, GUA 26645 4–5.

173 GUA 26645 7–8 (8 and 13 May 1735).

the *Suppression* of *Popery* been little studied in *Scotland*"[174] It had a bearing on practice before the Commissary Courts. Forbes' inaugural lecture gives no indication of how he was going to teach Civil Law; for its period, it is a relatively conventional account focused on the external history of Roman law from the XII Tables to Justinian and from Irnerius to the modern period, Cujas gaining predictable praise.[175] It is most probable that Forbes taught the courses on the *Institutes* and *Digest* using a compend rather than the actual Justinianic texts as the basis of his lemmatic commentary and exposition. This was the regular practice in Scotland at this time, and corresponds with how he taught Scots law.[176] He may even have used Voet's *Compendium juris juxta seriem pandectarum* as his compend to teach a course on Justinian's *Digest*, since it was to this work that he compared the elementary book that he published as the text from which to teach Scots law.[177]

More information is available about Forbes' classes on Scots law. He seems initially to have taught Scots law by expounding and commenting on Sir George Mackenzie's *Institutions*, to the 1706 edition of which he had provided some of the annotations.[178] Mackenzie's *Institutions* was the standard work for students of Scots law until the 1750s. But as Forbes worked on his "Great Body", he became dissatisfied with Mackenzie's account of Scots law. He developed his own analysis of Scots law on the basis of which he produced a different classificatory scheme. This he used to write his own textbook.[179] It has a more rigorous and elaborate analytical framework than was possible in Mackenzie's simple Justinianic exposition. In this it reflects contemporary development in legal philosophy in works such as those of Grotius and Pufendorf or those deriving from them. For example, Forbes made a strict division between private law and public law, including criminal law in the latter. This means that his view of crimes

174 Forbes, *Church-land and Tithes* (n 88) sig [q.3]r.

175 Forbes, *Oratio inauguralis* (n 154)

176 See Cairns, "John Spotswood" (n 6) 145; I hope to discuss elsewhere and more fully the whole issue of the use of compends by Scots teachers.

177 J Voet, *Compendium juris juxia seriem pandectarum, adjectis differentiis juris civilis et canonici* (1682 and many others); see W Forbes, *The Institutes of the Law of Scotland Volume First Comprehending the Private Law: To which is subjoin'd, The Constitution of the Session, etc. And of the Commission for the Plantation of Churches, Valuation of Tithes, etc. With a Scheme of the form of process obsderv'd in these Courts* (1722) iii (henceforth Forbes, *Institutes*).

178 Forbes, *Institutes* (n 177) i, iii (this is one possible interpretation of what was written).

179 Ibid i, i–iv.

differs from that of a number of other Scottish theorists.[180] His strict division between public and private law could have been derived from a number of works, such as those of Domat, with which he was certainly familiar, although it should be stressed that Domat's jurisprudence and legal classification have not recognisably influenced those of Forbes.[181] Had Forbes been the student who went to Leiden, he would there have found separate treatment of *ius publicum.*[182] If the first volume of his textbook is devoted to private law, the second from the field of public law deals only with criminal law: to have ventured further into the topic as understood in early eighteenth-century Scotland would have taken Forbes into the areas taught by other professors in courses on the law of nature and nations, thereby going outwith the limitations put on his teaching. At least from the publication of the volumes of his *Institutes*, he presumably taught Scots law in this way, working through the volumes commenting on the passages in the traditional lemmatic fashion. Though these works are apparently very modern, derived from the contemporary schools of legal philosophy, they reveal some oddities, such as, most notably, Forbes' very strong belief in witchcraft.[183] There is none the less no reason to suppose they would have done other than have served their purpose perfectly well. Though Forbes would have taught Roman law in Latin, he presumably taught Scots law

180 W Forbes, *The Institutes of the Law of Scotland Volume Second Comprehending the Criminal Law. In Two Parts. I. Concerning Crimes and Offences. II Of Criminal Jurisdiction* (1730); on Forbes' treatment of criminal law, see J W Cairns, "John Millar's lectures on Scots criminal law" (1988) 8 OJLS 364 at 386–387. On the influence of Grotius and Pufendorf in Scotland, see Moore and Silverthorne, "Gershom Carmichael and the Natural Jurisprudence Tradition in Eighteenth-Century Scotland" (n 30); K Haakonssen, "Hugo Grotius and the history of political thought" (1985) 13 *Political Theory* 239; "Natural law and the Scottish Enlightenment" (1985) 4 *Man and Nature: Proceedings of the Canadian Society for Eighteenth-Century Studies* 47; "Moral philosophy and natural law: from the Cambridge Platonists to the Scottish Enlightenment" (1988) 40 *Political Science* 97; and "Natural Jurisprudence in the Scottish Enlightenment: Summary of an Interpretation", in N MacCormick and Z Bankowski (eds), *Enlightenment, Rights and Revolution: Essays in Legal and Social Philosophy* (1989) 36.

181 J Domat, *Les loix civiles dans leur ordre naturel, le droit public, et legum delectus*, new edn, 2 vols (1723) (first publication dating from 1689); see Forbes, *Bills of Exchange* (n 88) 11 n 6.

182 G C J J van den Bergh, *The Life and Work of Gerard Noodt (1647–1725): Dutch Legal Scholarship between Humanism and Enlightenment* (1988) 269–274 (henceforth van den Bergh, *The Life and Work of Gerard Noodt*); R Feenstra and C J D Waal, *Seventeenth-Century Leyden Law Professors and their Influence on the Development of the Civil Law: A Study of Bronchorst, Vinnius and Voet* (1975) 17; on the development of the distinction between *ius privatum* and *ius publicum*, see G Chevrier, "Remarques sur l'introduction et les vicissitudes de la distinction du 'jus privatum' et du 'jus publicum' dans les oeuvres des anciens juristes français" (1952) 1 *Archives de philosophie du droit (NS)* 5.

183 Forbes, *Institutes* (n 177) ii, 32–41, 371–373 (this latter passage has curious ambiguities); see also Forbes, *Justices of Peace* (n 88) 155–159 discussing witchcraft, sorcery and necromancy.

in English: this would probably have made him the first professor in the University of Glasgow to teach a class in English.[184]

Forbes himself eulogistically wrote of Stair as having "studied hard the *Greek* and *Latin* languages, with the History and Antiquities of *Greece* and *Rome*, in order to the study of the Civil Law".[185] This suggests Forbes' own view of the desiderata for legal study; it was the common opinion of the ideal. Forbes had to ensure that his students had the necessary Greek and Latin; as regards the history and antiquities of the ancient world, he was debarred by the faculty's regulations from teaching these necessary adjuncts to the class in Roman law. There had been a lecturer in civil history from 1692, but it seems unlikely that he taught the type of history and courses on Roman antiquities desired by law students.[186] William Anderson, Professor of Ecclesiastical History, offered classes in universal history in 1722, however;[187] the Professor of Humanity offered a course on Roman books for, among others, law students in 1723.[188] Whether this type of teaching was sustained is unknown, but it is obvious that there was some attempt to provide it at least some of the time. Gershom Carmichael and his successor Francis Hutcheson continued to provide instruction in natural law in the class on moral philosophy.[189] That law students might well be expected to attend these classes is shown by their inclusion among the categories of "students without gowns" that might attend "the praelecting hours" of the philosophy classes.[190]

The publication of Forbes' textbook suggests that he at least hoped for some students in Scots law in the 1720s. It seems likely, however, that he gave up teaching Scots law in the 1730s, if not earlier: his substitute

184 Contrary to what is sometimes alleged, Scots law was always taught in English by both the private teachers and the university professors in Edinburgh. Forbes presumably followed this. Until much later in the century Civil Law was always taught in Latin: see J W Cairns, "Rhetoric, language, and Roman law: legal education and improvement in eighteenth-century Scotland" (1991) 9 *Law and History Review* 31 (henceforth Cairns, "Rhetoric, language, and Roman law").

185 Forbes, *Journal of the Session* (n 88) xxx.

186 Coutts, *History of the University of Glasgow* (n 15) 170.

187 *Edinburgh Evening Courant*, 11/15 October 1722.

188 Ibid 10/14, 17/21, and 21/22 October 1723; see also Coutts, *History of the University of Glasgow* (n 150) 188.

189 Hutcheson initially preserved Carmichael's curriculum: R Wodrow, *Analecta: Or Materials for a History of Remarkable Providences; mostly relating to Scottish Ministers and Christians*, ed M Leisman, 4 vols, Maitland Club vol 60 (1842–1843) (henceforth Wodrow, *Analecta*) vol iv, 185. For his more developed teaching, see F Hutcheson, *Philosophiae moralis institutio compendiaria, ethices & jurisprudentiae naturalis elementa continens. Lib III* (1742); and *A System of Moral Philosophy, in Three Books*, 2 vols (1755).

190 GUA 26634 199; 1837 PP XXXVI 277.

and his two immediate successors certainly did not teach it.[191] We have seen that he offered only Civil Law in 1716. Wodrow, dealing with 1726, alleged that Forbes (along with two other professors) did not teach. He attributed this to Forbes' requirement of "exorbitant fees".[192] To what extent one should rely on this is uncertain, while Wodrow's comment about fees probably derived from his knowledge of an earlier quarrel between Forbes and the Principal.[193] There is some support, however, from the famous reforming "Act Regulating the University of Glasgow" issued on 19 September 1727 after the Visitation of that year. The Professor of Law was specifically required to teach "whenever five or more scholars shall apply", giving not under four lessons a week. Should fewer apply, he was still to praelect publicly once a week.[194] This tends to support Wodrow's allegation, because another professor whose teaching was specifically regulated this way, that of medicine, was also one of the three identified by him as generally not teaching or teaching little, while the third had a separate regulation to govern his conduct.[195] Forbes met Brisbane and Johnstone, the two other professors named by Wodrow, on 28 January 1728 in order to set times when each would give their weekly praelection, with that on law being fixed for 2.30 pm on a Tuesday.[196] That the three professors had to do so suggests that none was teaching in the session 1727–1728 (or at least had fewer than five students). It is conceivable that it was the regulation of 1727 that caused Forbes to give up teaching Scots law. The overall impression is that Forbes failed to attract significant numbers of students of law to Glasgow.

Forbes' tenure of the chair was also troubled by the complex politics of the university which involved him in an early breach with Principal Stirling. The background to this seems to have been the latter's view that Forbes shirked his duties. On 18 October 1716, when the session had begun and Forbes was still absent and not preparing to teach until 20 November, it was moved at a meeting of faculty that rules should be made on the time of attendance and teaching of the "new erected and Revived professions". The Faculty resolved that rules regulating the "several Professors" should

191 See below.
192 Wodrow, *Analecta* (n 189) vol iii, 333.
193 See below.
194 1837 PP XXXVI 277.
195 Ibid.
196 GUA 26635 21.

be made.[197] On 31 December a committee was appointed consisting of John Simson, Gershom Carmichael, Alexander Dunlop and Charles Morthland, all long-established professors, and the two new professors, Forbes and John Johnstone. This committee's remit was broader than originally envisaged, encompassing "the way of teaching and the necessary qualifications of the Schollars'"[198] Its deliberations and report (if any) cannot be traced. Conceivably it never met because of the major quarrel that was about to break out. If one can see the Principal's hand in the original motion, and the faculty's response in the gradual broadening of the committee's remit, by January 1717 Forbes and the Principal had quarrelled bitterly over the former's reluctance to teach law to divinity students either gratis or for a reduced fee. Stirling hinted that Forbes wished to be a sinecurist and obviously had called him "an useless professor": Forbes vehemently denied the charge and strong words passed between them.[199] Stirling was irascible, autocratic and authoritarian. This dispute drew Forbes into the group of discontented teachers who opposed Stirling, and on 1 March 1717 he took part in the election of a new Rector in defiance of Stirling. This caused Forbes a particular problem since this meant opposing Sir John Maxwell of Pollok, his patron, who had been influential in gaining him the chair, and to whom he was anxious to explain his actions in terms of Stirling's autocratic behaviour.[200] He also tried to justify himself to the new Chancellor, the Duke of Montrose.[201] That Forbes was willing to oppose Pollok indicates his depth of feeling. Forbes was disciplined for this in 1718 by the Commissioners for Visitation.[202] Forbes next successfully opposed Stirling's desire over 1717 to 1720 to have James Dick appointed Professor of Ecclesiastical History.[203] Forbes also maintained a lengthy struggle over how much of the salary of £90 he was entitled to for his first year. This disagreement was not finally settled until 1725.[204] This presumably fuelled Forbes' bitterness, for he indicated

197 Ibid 154 (18 October 1716).
198 Ibid 156(31 December 1716).
199 W Forbes to J Stirling, 30 January 1717, GUL MS Gen 204/16.
200 W Forbes to J Maxwell of Pollok, 4 March 1717, GUL MS Gen 204/17; unknown to R Wodrow, 27 September 1718, NLS MS Wodrow Corr XIII f 86; Mackie, *University of Glasgow* (n 15) 174–176.
201 W Forbes to Duke of Montrose, 11 March 1717, SRO Montrose Muniments, GD 220/5/1936/3.
202 GUA 26631 272 (22 October 1718).
203 Mackie, *University of Glasgow* (n 15) 173–164.
204 See GUA 26631 286 (23 April 1710) 288 (27 April 1719) 292 (3 June 1719) 307 (27 October 1719) 309 (5 November 1719) 309–310 (25 November 1719); GUA 26634 81 (6 December 1722) 82 (13 December 1722) 159 (25 November 1725) 160 (30 November 1725) 160 (6 December 1725).

in 1722 that he would not be involved in (presumably) legal business by the Principal unless he were to be paid for it.[205]

These quarrels had greater than merely local significance and implications. Forbes found himself drawn into a political grouping within the faculty opposed to the Squadrone Chancellor of the university, the Duke of Montrose, who was a strong supporter of Principal Stirling. This grouping sided with the Argathelians under the leadership of Archibald, Earl of Ilay. Forbes was now playing a difficult game, as the wider political quarrels of these two great men were also acted out within the university which each sought to control. Early in 1722 the Barons of Exchequer raised a question over the validity of the election and admission, without appointment by a Crown warrant, in 1714 of Forbes and the Professor of Medicine.[206] Montrose hoped this would provide the possibility of replacing Forbes with a law professor more sympathetic to his interest.[207] To emphasise his allegiance to the Argathelians, Forbes fulsomely dedicated the first volume of his *Institutes* to Ilay in 1722, recalling Ilay's early education in the University of Glasgow and his continued interest in that seminary of learning.[208] This could scarcely have pleased the Squadrone, especially when the Argathelians routed them in the election of that year – a success that may have confirmed Forbes' support for Ilay.[209] It is worth noting that at this time at least three of the Barons of Exchequer were Argathelians.[210] Forbes was not unseated because of the permission given by Queen Anne to the professors to elect the two new professors, but the Crown reserved its right to appoint for the future.[211]

Sometime after this, however, Forbes seems to have gone over to the Squadrone interest in the faculty. Why is unknown. It may have been related to the successful (and generous) compromise in 1725 on the matter of his first year's salary. It is worth noting that the original compromise to which Forbes

205 W Millar to J Stirling, 9 June 1722, GUA 272000. Whether for payment or not, Forbes did become involved in advising: see Millar to Stirling, 8 February 1722, GUA 27197; Millar to Stirling, 26 January 1723, GUA 27210.

206 GUA 26634 36 (5 February 1722); GUA 47638 (I am grateful to Roger Emerson for bringing this memorandum of the barons of Exchequer to my notice after I had searched the Exchequer records fruitlessly for some time).

207 Duke of Montrose to M Graeme of Gorthie, 6 February 1722, SRO Montrose Muniments, GD 220/5/838/15.

208 Forbes, *Institutes* (n 177) i, sig a2–a3v.

209 R Sedgwick, *The House of Commons, 1715–1754*, 2 vols (1970) vol i, 34 (henceforth Sedgwick, *Commons*) at 159.

210 Riley, *English Ministers and Scotland* (n 106) 271.

211 See GUA 47638.

had objected was based on the advice of Dundas, then the Squadrone solicitor general.[212] This was a foolish time to shift allegiance, however, as from 1720 the Squadrone were losing power, and in 1725 the Squadrone Duke of Roxburghe lost the office of Scottish Secretary. Ilay, who now embarked on his long ascendancy in Scottish affairs, took a particular interest in his *alma mater*.[213] He described himself at the end of 1727 as "preparing some measures to make uneasie some of the foe at Glasgow Colledge". It was now his turn to raise the question of the validity of Forbes' election, and he sought the names of possible alternative professors of law in case he "should happen to molest knave Forbes".[214] This potential conspiracy soon came to Forbes' own ears, and was communicated secretly to other supporters of the Squadrone who were anxious to enlist Montrose to fight the attack, because Forbes was "at present very usefull to us and very stout and bold in our cause".[215] Nothing came of this possible attempt to remove Forbes. It was perhaps Ilay's success in placing Neil Campbell as new Principal in December 1727 that had made him think of the possibility of removing Forbes.[216] Campbell and his supporters now tried to woo Forbes over to Ilay's interest by securing the post of college lawyer for Thomas Forbes, his son, also an advocate.[217] Charles Morthland was convinced in a few days that this had succeeded.[218] This says something of Forbes' colleagues' perception of his character. If this ruse had succeeded, which is not certain, Forbes changed sides once more, as in 1732 Principal Campbell and professors opposed to Montrose's interest minuted their opposition to the election of Forbes as Dean of Faculty.[219]

Forbes' political trimming may be related to that of one of his patrons, James Erskine, Lord Grange. Grange moved over to supporting Ilay at much the same time as did Forbes.[220] Forbes and Grange – who had many interests in common – certainly maintained their links over the years, and the former lent large sums of money to Grange and some of his associates (mainly

212 GUA 26631 288 (27 April 1719) 309–310 (25 November 1719).
213 Murdoch, "*The People Above*" (n 2) 30–33; see, e.g. Cairns, "William Crosse" (n 3).
214 Earl of Ilay to Lord Milton, 2 December 1727, NLS Saltoun MS, 16535 fos 133–134.
215 C Morthland to M Graeme of Gorthie, 26 January 1728, SRO Montrose Muniments, GD 220/5/1081/2.
216 Coutts, *History of the University of Glasgow* (n 15) 214.
217 GUA 26635 62 (14 October 1728); C Morthland to M Graeme of Gorthie, 14 October 1728, SRO Montrose Muniments, GD 220/5/1081/29.
218 C Morthland to M Graeme of Gorthie, SRO Montrose Muniments, GD.220/5/1081/30.
219 Minutes of University Meetings, 1720–1747, GUA 26639 21 (26 June 1732); see also W Forbes to J Simson, 29 June 1732, GUA 34693.
220 Sedgwick, *Commons* (n 209) vol ii, 15; Shaw, *Management of Scottish Society* (n 2) 61.

connected with Stirlingshire and Clackmannanshire) in 1723 and 1726.[221] It may even be that Forbes' large loan on bond to Sir James Cunynghame of Milncraig, an Argathelian, in 1725 reflected the change of allegiance that he was soon to change once more. But given that Cunynghame was also closely related to Forbes' other patrons, the Dalrymples, and given that in 1739 Forbes lent money to Sir John Baird of Newbyth, described at one point as a "creature" of the Dalrymples, this may simply reflect Forbes' connection with that family.[222] Whatever may have been the continuing relationship between Forbes and Grange, the latter certainly deserted Ilay for the Squadrone a few years after the former.[223]

Forbes was in his forty-sixth year when appointed to the chair in Glasgow; by the middle of the 1730s he was becoming quite elderly. His effectiveness as a teacher seems to have been affected, as Hercules Lindesay taught in his stead from around 1739.[224] (Lindesay does not appear to have been a relative of Forbes' wife.) He continued to attend university and faculty meetings virtually up to his death.[225] He never stopped working on his "Great Body", which he left incomplete,[226] and he appears to have carried out preparatory work for new editions of his *Institutes* and *Treatise Concerning Bills of Exchange*.[227] He also continued to reflect on the issues raised by his book on teinds.[228] He died on 27 October 1745.[229]

221 Register of Glasgow Testaments, SRO CC 9/7/59 207. A bond of corroboration was granted in 1739 by Sir Hugh Paterson of Bannockburn, a Jacobite and Grange's brother-in-law, and his son.

222 Register of Glasgow Testaments, SRO CC 9/7/59 207–208; Sedgwick, *Commons* (n 209) vol i, 428, 598.

223 Emerson, *Professors, Patronage and Politics* (n 136) 54, 60–61.

224 W Anderson to Marquess of Tweeddale, 2 November 1745, NLS Yester MS 14422 fo 81.

225 See, e.g., Minutes of Meetings of Faculty, 1745–1753, GUA 26649 5 (14 October 1745); he did not attend a University meeting on 18 October 1745, Minutes of University Meetings, 1730–1749, GUA 26639 194, presumably because he had now been struck by his final illness.

226 In GUL MS Gen 1249 472 he added in a reference to a trial in 1742; GUL MS Gen 1250 is clearly incomplete. The entire work has clearly been worked over several times.

227 See Forbes, *Institutes* (n 177) i and ii, GUL Sp Coll 2183 and 2184 containing MS notes by Forbes amending, correcting and supplementing the text; Forbes, *Bill of Exchange* (n 88) 2nd edn. GUL pressmark B110–1.10 has seventeen pages of MS notes at end and occasional interlineations working towards a new edition.

228 See the supplementary MS (post-1734) bound in with *A Few Remarks by William Forbes, Advocat* and *A Letter from William Forbes Advocat, to a Gentleman in the Country*, GUL pressmark BE6–e.23.

229 See, e.g., Register of Glasgow Testaments, SRO CC 9/7/59 209. For the reasons for preferring this date to that of 23 October 1745 given in, e.g., F J Grant (ed), *The Faculty of Advocates in Scotland 1532–1943, with Genealogical Notes*, Scottish Record Society (OS), vol 76 (1944) (henceforth Grant, *Faculty of Advocates*) 74, see Cairns, "William Crosse" (n 3) n 24.

D. WILLIAM CROSSE AND HERCULES LINDESAY

Forbes' substitute, Hercules Lindesay, had hoped to succeed him; he was also the choice of the faculty and, initially, of Ilay, now third Duke of Argyll. The special political circumstances of late 1745, however, led Argyll, on the solicitation, most notably of Duncan Forbes of Culloden, to secure the appointment of William Crosse. Crosse was an advocate who had studied law at Leiden and, on the face of it, was not unsuitable; the faculty feared in 1745, however, that he would treat the chair as a sinecure if appointed, while Lindesay had already shown himself to be both diligent and competent. The faculty's fears were realised, Crosse succeeding in avoiding teaching, despite the faculty's best endeavours to compel him to carry out his duties. During Crosse's tenure of the chair, Lindesay continued to teach Civil Law in Glasgow either privately or as Crosse's substitute. The faculty at Glasgow maintained an unremitting, hostile pressure on Crosse, however, to which he eventually succumbed, resigning in October 1749. It is possible that influence was brought on him from above to urge him to go.[230]

The faculty now achieved their aim of securing Lindesay's appointment. His presentation as professor was read at a university meeting on 19 January 1750, and he was admitted in due form on 7 February.[231] As well as substituting for Crosse, he had remained actively interested in the affairs of the university during the latter's tenure.[232]

Lindesay had been born around 1708, the son of an Episcopalian minister, whom the Episcopalian David Lindsay of Edzell had twice intruded into the parish of Edzell: he had likewise been twice deprived of it.[233] Early in the 1720s, Lindesay studied in the University of Edinburgh.[234] Some time thereafter he studied law, perhaps in Edinburgh (no class lists survive from this period for law), since he was able to tutor Sir James Steuart for his trials

230 Cairns, "William Crosse" (n 3).

231 Minutes of University Meetings, 1749–1759, GUA 26640 22, 23.

232 H Lindesay to J Erskine, 9 May 1746, NLS MS 7075 f 196 (written to a former pupil about an election of a rector).

233 For Lindesay's date of birth, see *Album studiosorum Academiae Lugduno-Batavae* (n 43) col 969. On his father, see Grant, *Faculty of Advocates* (n 229) 124; *Fasti ecclesiae Scoticanae* (n 41) v, 390; *Lord Lindsay, Lives of the Lindsays: Or, a Memoir of the Houses of Crawford and Bacarres*, 3 vols (1849) vol ii, 261.

234 "Matriculation Roll of the University of Edinburgh, Arts–Law–Divinity, Transcribed by Dr Alexander Morgan, 1933–34. Vol 1 1623–1774", Edinburgh University Library, Department of Special Collections ff 177, 184.

for admission as an advocate in February 1735.[235] Lindesay accompanied Alexander Stewart, the son of Lord Garlies (the future Earl of Galloway) to the University of Leiden in 1737, where both matriculated as law students on 24 September.[236] Even when Forbes' substitute, he continued to eke out what must have been a meagre living by tutoring young men for the advocates' examinations: thus, he spent the summer of 1744 tutoring John Grant, the son of Lord Elchies, to prepare him for his trials.[237]

Lindesay's links with Steuart and Garlies are interesting; Steuart was a Jacobite and Garlies had at one time had Tory and Jacobite connections, though in the 1740s he was obviously trying to rehabilitate himself with his relative, the Marquess of Tweeddale, Squadrone Secretary for Scotland from 1742 to 1746. Though Lindesay was clearly acceptable to members of both the Squadrone and the Argathelians in the university, he was unremittingly opposed by Robert Dundas, the Squadrone Solicitor General. He had no one to push his cause in 1745 in a way to make Argyll ignore Duncan Forbes' claims on Crosse's behalf.[238]

Little is known about Lindesay's teaching. He only taught courses on the *Institutes* and *the Digest*.[239] He gave that on the former twice each year, as was standard practice.[240] At some time, however, he started to teach the course on the *Institutes* in English rather than Latin. This was an innovation of major importance, as he was the first in Scotland to teach any course on Roman Law in English.[241] Alexander Carlyle described him as "of some Note", while according to James Wodrow he was "reputed an able teacher" who "educated . . . some noted scholars".[242] His education and abilities were such that he could substitute for Adam Smith in the logic class until the latter

235 J Steuart (ed), *The Works, Political, Metaphisical, and Chronological, of the late Sir James Steuart of Coltness, Bart*, 6 vols (1805) vol v, 363 (there is no reason to accept Lindesay tutored Steuart in Glasgow); R Dundas to Marquess of Tweeddale, 4 October 1744, NLS Yester MS 14423 fos 23–24.

236 *Album studiosorum Academiae Lugduno-Batavae* (n 43) col 969; see R Dundas to Marquess of Tweeddale, 4 October 1744, NLS Yester MS 14423 fos 23–24.

237 R Dundas to Marquess of Tweeddale, 4 October 1744, NLS Yester MS 14423 fos 23–24.

238 For a full discussion of these issues, see Cairns, "William Crosse" (n 3).

239 *Glasgow Journal*, 11/18 October 1756: "Dr Hercules Lindesay, advocate, begins his colleges on the institutions and Pandects at the college of Glasgow, on Monday the first day of November next." See also ibid 27 October/3 November 1755: "Colleges of Law".

240 See L Gordon and D Ross to the Rector, 17 November 1748, GUA 30222, stating they had taken Lindesay's course on the *Institutes* twice the previous year; on the same practice in Edinburgh, see, e.g., H Arnot, *The History of Edinburgh* (1779) 399.

241 See Cairns, "Rhetoric, language, and Roman law" (n 184) at 39–40, 54–55 n 76.

242 Carlyle, *Anecdotes and Characters* (n 142) 37; J Wodrow to Earl of Buchan, 9 May 1808, typed transcript of original, GUL Murray MS 506/23.

arrived to take up his post.[243] Lindesay's views and outlook may be gauged both from his support of David Hume as the successor to Adam Smith in the chair of Logic when the latter was translated to that of Moral Philosophy,[244] and from the fact that he was a founder member of the Glasgow Literary Society.[245] His colleagues evidently respected him, referring to his period as Forbes' substitute as one when law had been taught "sufficiently . . . for several years past".[246] They also awarded him the degree of LLD, though that was evidently in part a calculated insult to Crosse.[247]

Lindesay died on 2 June 1761 after "a lingring illness".[248] Previously assiduous in attending university business, he had not attended a university meeting since 4 November 1760.[249] No mention can be found of a substitute in the university records; one may have been appointed in 1760–1761 or classes in law may simply have been suspended. It is worth noting that Lindesay died having taught law in Glasgow for over twenty years as substitute for Forbes and Crosse and finally as Regius Professor of Civil Law.

Robert Wodrow attributed the expansion of the University of Glasgow to the energy and activity of Principal Stirling; with some reservations this may be accepted as undoubtedly correct.[250] The reservations, however, are important. Glasgow was not the only university to be expanding, and law was not the only discipline in which there had been moves to create chairs from the 1680s onwards, partly as a response to professional pressure, and partly as a result of the notable cultural and intellectual development in late-Restoration Scotland.[251] In legal education this meant the development of a curriculum on the model familiar from the Netherlands where many Scots had studied law.[252] Polite, Humanistic education in law focused on

243 GUA 26640 51 (16 January 1751).

244 A Smith to W Cullen, November 1751, *The Correspondence of Adam Smith*, E C Mossner and I S Ross (eds) (1977) (henceforth *Correspondence of Adam Smith*) 5–6 (no 10). See the discussion in E C Mossner, *The Life of David Hume*, 2nd edn (1980) 247–248.

245 *Notes and Documents Illustrative of the Literary History of Glasgow, During the Greater Part of the Last Century*, Maitland Club vol 14 (1831) 132.

246 GUA 26639 218 (15 October 1746).

247 GUA 26645 49 (27 June 1746); see Cairns, "William Crosse" (n 3).

248 *Glasgow Journal*, 28 May/4 June 1761; see also Lord Cardross to A Smith, 6 June 1761, *Correspondence of Adam Smith* (n 244) 75–76 (no 55).

249 Minutes of University Meetings, 1760–1763, GUA 26642 26.

250 Wodrow, *Analecta* (n 189) vol iii, 445; see also Mackie, *University of Glasgow* (n 15) 153–177.

251 Cant, "Origins of the Enlightenment in Scotland" (n 8); Ouston, "York in Edinburgh" (n 64), and "Cultural Life from the Restoration to the Union", in A Hook (ed), *The History of Scottish Literature, 1660–1800* (1987) 11; R L Emerson, "Scottish universities in the eighteenth century, 1690–1800" (1977) 167 *Studies on Voltaire and the Eighteenth Century* 453.

252 P Nève, "Disputations of Scots Students Attending Universities in the Northern Netherlands", in W M Gordon and T D Fergus (eds), *Legal History in the Making* (1991) 95 (henceforth

Roman law and related historical studies along with a study of the law of nature and nations and municipal law. It was legal studies in this mode that the faculty in Glasgow wished to introduce in the early eighteenth century. The choice of the right type of professor was of paramount importance in order to achieve these aims. A good and successful professor of law would attract students some of whom would undoubtedly take classes with other professors. All would benefit financially and the university's reputation would grow. To what extent were these hopes fulfilled in Glasgow?

The professors found in Forbes a man of inevitably mixed qualities and achievements. There are signs that in religion he was an evangelical Presbyterian with a strong belief in the operation of providence.[253] His apparent conviction of the reality of witchcraft might suggest a certain lack of a sceptical, scientific mind, even if he was somewhat apologetic and ambiguous on the point; but he would not have been the only "scientific" contemporary to hold such views. Nonetheless he obviously shared certain of the characteristics of the patriotic *virtuosi* of early eighteenth-century Scotland. He claimed to be no antiquary;[254] yet his treatise on teinds is strongly historical in its approach, marshalling historical and literary evidence to argue, for example, that tithes were not *jure divino*.[255] Robert Wodrow evidently considered him worth consulting in his antiquarian researches.[256] He and Wodrow were on sufficiently intimate terms to borrow one another's books.[257] Forbes' connection with Bishop Nicolson is particularly suggestive. Nicolson was an undoubted *virtuoso*,[258] who associated with such a significant Scottish figure as Sir Robert Sibbald.[259] Was Forbes an associate of those patriots grouped around Sibbald in Edinburgh who pursued interests in history and science and who were concerned with the improvement of their country? That he

Nève, "Disputations of Scots Students"); R Feenstra, "Scottish–Dutch Legal Relations in the Seventeenth and Eighteenth Centuries", in T C Smout (ed), *Scotland and Europe, 1200–1850* (1986) 128.

253 W Forbes to J Stirling, 17 January 1717, GUL MS Gen 204/16: "to begin as I would end, act openly and becomingly in any station, that God in his providence calls me to".

254 *A Few Remarks by William Forbes Advocat* (n 130) 19.

255 Forbes, *Church-Lands and Tithes* (n 88) 275–284.

256 R Wodrow to W Forbes, 11 October 1714, *The Correspondence of the Rev Robert Wodrow, Minister of Eastwood*, T McCrie (ed), 3 vols, Wodrow Society vol 5 (1842–1843) vol i, 587.

257 W Forbes to R Wodrow, 24 August 1727, NLS MS Wodrow Corr XVII f 330.

258 *London Diaries of William Nicolson* (n 129) 11–17.

259 Ibid 10. On Sibbald, see R L Emerson, "Science and Moral Philosophy in the Scottish Enlightenment", in M A Stewart (ed), *Studies in the History of the Scottish Enlightenment*, (1990), 11 at 20–21; and "Sir Robert Sibbald, KT, the Royal Society of Scotland and the origins of the Scottish Enlightenment" (1988) 45 *Annals of Science* 41 (henceforth Emerson, "Sir Robert Sibbald").

could also claim as a friend a Whig latitudinarian and historian such as Burnet likewise suggests his range of interests and influences.

In line with this is Forbes' acceptance of natural law, and his very analytical approach to the exposition of Scots law. His definition of law as a command of a supreme power obliging subjects to act or forbear to act under a penalty, of natural law as the dictate of right reason, and of positive law as divine or human, and so on, is scarcely unique or original[260] – though I have not sought to identify his sources or the influences on the basis of which he produced this account – but it does show that his approach to law was thoroughly modern. Moreover, his legal philosophy affected his account of law: for example, the discussion of persons was divided into persons in their natural capacity and in their civil capacity. In all this he was at one with the most advanced legal thinking in Scotland.

Forbes also shared the Scottish *virtuosi*'s concern with the development of trade and the economic improvement of Scotland. It was perhaps not surprising in this respect for the son-in-law of an Edinburgh burgess to be interested in such an important economic device as bills of exchange. He sounded an optimistic note in his discussion:

> *Scotland* being for the present, what with the growing credit of a Bank, and the thriving of Manufactures, as it were on the rising hand; and standing so fair for a share in all the Privileges of a Rich and well founded Trade: I thought fit in my weak capacity, to offer at a Discourse upon those short circular Letters, commonly called *Bills of Exchange*; that are the very Sinews of Commerce. To which I was the rather inclin'd, having never met with any thing done upon the Subject, to good purpose, and of much great use to us.[261]

These are especially intriguing comments given that they were written in 1703 (the privilege for the work is dated 3 November 1703), when Parliament passed a series of acts, notably the Act of Security, to put pressure on the English Parliament to open up English colonial trade to the Scots.[262] Forbes returned to the need for the enforcement of the laws intended to develop trade and manufacturing in his treatise on justices of the peace.[263] He presumably viewed the Union of 1707 as one way of promoting these aims. And he developed close links with Glasgow's mercantile elite, participating in

260 Forbes, *Institutes* (n 177) i, 1–2.
261 Forbes, *Bills of Exchange* (n 88) sig [A3] r–v.
262 *Acts of Parliaments of Scotland*, ed T Thomson and C Innes, 12 vols (1814–1875) vol xi, 136, c 3; see Riley, *English Ministers and Scotland* (n 106) 6–7; T C Smout, *Scottish Trade on the Eve of Union* (1963).
263 Forbes, *Justices of Peace* (n 88), preface.

the growing Glasgow capital market by lending large sums to the prominent merchants involved in developing the Silvercraigs Weaving Factory and the Port Glasgow Ropeworks.[264]

If Forbes had the right type of credentials – to some extent at least – in these respects, likely to recommend him to Edinburgh *virtuosi*, the question remains of how suited he was to his position as professor. He was evidently learned in Civilian legal literature: his works on bills of exchange and tithes indicate this well enough. He obviously was interested in the intellectual problems associated with sovereign and political authority and the union, and with the relationship between Scots and English law. He may not have been a great antiquarian in all respects as regards the ancient world;[265] but, if not an elegant scholar in the manner of Gerard Noodt, he had a good grasp of the sources of Roman law.[266] Furthermore, he had a huge library – large enough for its auction by Robert Foulis to be worth advertising in the newspaper and for a room in his house to require to be extensively altered to accommodate his "book presses".[267] At his death his library was valued at the enormous sum of £800 sterling, which was presumably a conservative estimate.[268] It is unfortunate that little is known about the contents of his collection.[269] The few choice works singled out in the newspaper advertisement are mainly on history, law and religion, but include, interestingly enough, the works of Hippocrates and Galen and a collection of the sermons delivered at the Boyle Lectures – lectures that popularised latitudinarian views and in which some lecturers used Newtonian natural philosophy, although Forbes may have been more interested in the sermons' attacks on Jews, Atheists, Deists, pagans, Turks and heretics.[270] But it may be that his scientific interests were not as

264 Register of Glasgow Testaments, SRO CC 9/7/59 208–209. See T M Devine, *The Tobacco Lords: A Study of the Tobacco Merchants of Glasgow and their Trading Activities, c 1740–1790* (1975; repr 1990) (henceforth Devine, *Tobacco Lords*) 37–39, 177–184. Devine's list of merchants includes most of those merchants to whom Forbes lent money.

265 See [Gordon,] *Charitable Observations* (n 104) 35–36.

266 *A Few Remarks by William Forbes Advocat* (n 130) 20; Forbes, *Oratio inauguralis* (n 154); see van den Bergh, *The Life and Work of Gerard Noodt* (n 182).

267 *Glasgow Courant*, 13/20 and 20/27 October 1746; Minutes of Meetings of Faculty, 1745–1753, GUA 26649 38 (26 June 1747).

268 Register of Glasgow Testaments, SRO CC 9/7/59 206–207.

269 P Gaskell, *A Bibliography of the Foulis Press*, 2nd edn (1986) 75–76 conjectures that a sale catalogue would have been printed; no copy is known to survive.

270 *Glasgow Courant*, 13/20 October 1746. On the significance of the Boyle Lectures, see J Gascoigne, *Cambridge in the Age of Enlightenment: Science, Religion and Politics from the Restoration to the French Revolution* (1989) 81–82. (I have not sought to identify the collection of sermons.) This would suggest an intellectual approach to science similar to that of Sibbald: see Emerson, "Sir Robert Sibbald" (n 259) 43–44. I am grateful to Roger Emerson for some further remarks and explanations about the sermons and lectures.

negligible as might otherwise appear. Forbes' classifications and divisions of Scots law drawing on natural law philosophy and, ultimately, if indirectly, probably Ramus, make it clear and comprehensible – indeed, scientific. His representation of Scots law as scientific knowledge rather than as a technical art is undoubtedly at one with the contemporary attempts to assert law as polite knowledge, as is his focus on organising criminal law, for example, in its natural order according to its objects.[271]

Although Forbes' scientific method and writing skills show him to have had a gift of clear exposition,[272] there is no way to gauge his abilities as a teacher. No contemporary accounts of his qualities in the class room survive. It seems likely that he never drew many students to Glasgow, but the need for a substitute in his old age suggests there was a steady, if small, trickle of students in the university who wished to take courses in Roman law. Problems in attracting large numbers of students probably stemmed from difficulties other than Forbes' abilities as a teacher; they do indicate, however, that he had no exceptional gifts as a teacher such that students wished to attend his classes and specially went to Glasgow to do so. It is surely important, however, in this respect that, despite his trimming and shifting in faculty politics, sufficient of his colleagues thought well enough of him that he could command the votes to be elected Dean of Faculty and Quaestor.[273] Stirling's description of him as "an useless professor" was presumably hasty, made in the context of an obviously heated quarrel.

Lindesay likewise seems to have been a competent man, and is vouched for as a teacher of ability. It is impossible to assess how good a scholar he was because no lecture notes survive from his courses, and he published nothing after his theses for admission as an advocate. His support for David Hume suggests an essentially secular, philosophic outlook, and his membership of the Glasgow Literary Society suggests a commitment to the ideals and concerns of the Scottish Enlightenment. His move to teaching Justinian's *Institutes* in English indicates that he was not someone hide-bound by tradition. Much of the difference from Forbes, of course, no doubt reflects their different generations. The Faculty of Glasgow evidently valued him highly, awarding him, as we have seen, the degree of LLD and electing him Dean

271 For a contemporary lawyer's attempts to assert the practice of law as a science rather than a mechanical act, see Cairns, "John Spotswood" (n 6) at 151–52; see also Forbes, *Institutes* (n 177) ii, 28.

272 It is instructive in this respect to compare his pamphlet on elections with that of Spotswood.

273 GUA 26639 21 (26 June 1732); GUA 26645 11 (26 June 1736).

and Quaestor.[274] Despite these qualities, if John Craig's evidence is reliable, Lindesay rarely succeeded in attracting more than four or five students each year; often there were fewer.[275]

This suggests that there were problems with the development of legal education in Glasgow: problems that the appointment of William Crosse threw into sharp relief. The salary was ninety pounds per annum; while by no means low by the standards of the Scottish universities in 1714, it probably was insufficient to attract very able men – who might have prospects at the Bar – unless they were guaranteed the large classes that would boost their income through fees. Furthermore, under the Acts 7 Geo I, St I, c 27, s19 (1720) and 12 Geo I, c 2, s 1 (1725), the salary became less as the government clawed back 6d in the pound on all salaries of over £50 derived from Crown revenues.[276] The acquisition of the education necessary for admission to the Faculty of Advocates was expensive; most advocates of any ambition who had suitable connections to exert influence on their behalf would aspire to offices that carried greater income than this. Such offices were available to the right men.[277] Ninety pounds, as subject to the 6d in the pound reduction, and around fifteen pounds in fees would not be competitive for the able and well connected, especially when the professor would be cut off from the centre of legal patronage in Edinburgh, unable to undertake some practice in the Court of Session.[278] "From the absence of the higher Courts of Justice, Glasgow lies under many obvious disadvantages, as a school of law", wrote Craig.[279] Forbes was plainly disappointed in his initial earnings.[280] Although the figures are uncertain, it is a fair assumption that the professors in Edinburgh attracted considerably greater numbers of students, without the disadvantages of being in Glasgow: John Spotswood, for example, teaching Scots law privately had nineteen students in 1710 – and this at a time when there was considerable competition (in 1703 he had

274 GUA 26645 76 (26 June 1753) 92 (26 June 1758).

275 J Craig, *Account of the Life and Writings of John Millar, Esq* (henceforth Craig, *Life and Writings of John Millar*) prefixed to J Millar, *The Origin of the Distinction of Ranks: Or, an Inquiry into the Circumstances which Give Rise to Influence and Authority, in the different Members of Society*, 4th edn (1806) xi.

276 For details of how this worked in the time of Lindesay, see the accounts of the Bishops Rents in Glasgow over 1749 to 1754 in SRO E. 221/9/1.

277 See Shaw, *Management of Scottish Society* (n 2) 18–40.

278 Spotswood charged three guineas for a course; my rough, suggested fee income is based on the assumption of a similar charge.

279 Craig, *Life and Writings of John Millar* (n 275) xi.

280 W Forbes to J Stirling, 17 January 1717, GUL MS Gen 204/16.

had thirty-seven students).[281] It is important to note that Forbes eventually acquired a modest fortune that gave him a considerable measure of independence. He left a moveable estate valued at just under £5,400 stg. Nearly £2,000 of this consisted of gold, silver and banknotes, while slightly over £2,400 was lent on bonds (the remainder was made up of furniture and the like valued at £200 and his books at £800).[282] A few years later another bond for 2,000 merks Scots (£111 2s 2d stg) was discovered by his executors.[283] This last was probably not currently paying interest,[284] but on the other bonds interest had been paid virtually to date or was at most two years in arrears. Should Forbes have regularly lent around £2,500 on bond he could probably have expected £125 annually in interest, as 5 per cent was the normal rate of interest on such bonds in the west of Scotland at this time.[285] It may well have been Forbes' practice to lend more on bond, and thus increase his income further, as £2,000 is a surprisingly large liquid sum to have by him at his death. Penalties of just over £200 were also payable on these bonds. Forbes could thus expect to earn more as a *rentier* than as a law professor. Forbes could not have accumulated so much capital from the profits of his chair; the basis of his stock must have been his inheritance judiciously managed, and the oldest bond at his death was granted in May 1716, just a few months after his mother's death. At the same time he had also made effective his mother's and father's claims to the rent from the lands of Haltoun granted to Isobel Edgar by her first husband, James Pitcairn of Cordoun: thus, in June 1716 he gained a confirmation of his right, as his father's executor, to the income from these lands over 1672 to 1687, as having belonged to his father *jure mariti*,[286] and he next had the lands of Haltoun and Cordoun in Abernethy adjudged to him for debt, gaining sasine of them in 1717.[287] There is no point here in tracing Forbes' financial dealings, but the possession of this capital may well have reconciled him to his position in Glasgow. The low earnings from the chair became unimportant. He was willing to stay in an honourable and congenial, if not especially remunerative, office.

281 Cairns, "John Spotswood" (n 6) at 148 n 141. Competition in the 1710s, however, whittled away his classes.

282 Register of Glasgow Testaments, SRO CC 9/7/59 206–210.

283 Register of Glasgow Testaments, SRO CC. 9/7/61 234–235.

284 The bond was missed at Forbes' death, though he had acquired no less than two bonds of corroboration. All three were registered in the Books of Council and Session which suggests the debt was a problem one.

285 Devine, *Tobacco Lords* (n 264) 97–98.

286 Register of St Andrews Testaments, SRO CC 20/4/17 485.

287 General Register of Sasines, SRO RS. 3/111 ff 345–348.

In these circumstances, it is understandable that Crosse, a relatively young man with important patrons and a fortune to make, wished to treat the chair as a sinecure. It was not worth possessing on any other condition. For example, when he was appointed sheriff-depute of Lanarkshire he acquired a salary of £200 *per annum* – and this was not a full-time post.[288] Viewed in this perspective, the university was very lucky to get Forbes and Lindesay; it is also easy to see why they took the position. Forbes may have hoped that the chair would prove to be more lucrative than actually transpired; he was, however, forty-five years old with a family to support. Any office with a regular salary was better than none. He may have had patrons, but they evidently had not the desire, or perhaps influence, to secure him anything better, and although he was a Whig he had a potentially suspect background and family connections, which he may have lacked the brilliance to overcome. Furthermore, he and his connections were probably simply not important enough to gratify with a significant position. Later, he must have been happy to stay as his need for money became less pressing and he acquired financial security and independence after his mother's death. Much the same could be said for Lindesay, who also had a somewhat difficult family background and problematic social connections. He clearly was desperate for some sort of office to support him, and had fixed his ambitions on succeeding to the chair at Glasgow after Forbes' death. His anxiety to gain it is demonstrated by his undergoing the expense and effort of admission to the Faculty of Advocates in 1745 when, at the age of thirty-seven, he had no intention of practise, or hopes of gaining any business. This was a move calculated to make him more acceptable to those likely to influence the appointment.[289] Although he had important supporters, neither he nor his relations and friends were important enough to override the contrary wishes of Duncan Forbes of Culloden. Yet it was the fact that Lindesay was able to exert such little influence, but was able enough, that made him rather well suited to the chair.

For professors and students, the University of Edinburgh would always tend to be more attractive as a law school: the former could hope for considerably better earnings from the chairs and some practice at the Bar; the latter, if ambitious, would be closer to the centre of the legal world focused on the Court of Session and the Faculty of Advocates. Presumably lack of students discouraged Forbes from teaching Scots law and from 1722 he was

288 Cairns, "William Crosse" (n 3).

289 Books of Sederunt of the Lords of Council and Session, SRO CS.1/13 fo 33v (9 July 1745); *Advocates' Minutes* (n 84) ii, 202 (7 July 1745); see Cairns, "William Crosse" (n 3).

competing for students in Scots law against the evidently able Alexander Bayne, who was succeeded by the even more distinguished John Erskine.[290] His ceasing to teach it was unlikely, however, to encourage students to come to Glasgow. Furthermore, from 1719, Charles Mackie in Edinburgh always taught courses on history and Roman antiquities aimed at law students.[291] It is uncertain that these were always available at Glasgow. On the other hand, it was possible to follow a full curriculum in law in Edinburgh. During Lindesay's tenure of the chair the lack of a course on Scots law must have been a greater gap in the provision at Glasgow, as the Faculty of Advocates decided in 1750 to examine all intrants on the subject.[292] One set of individuals who might well have taken a course on Scots law given in Glasgow were the apprentices of the local Faculty of Procurators, which decided on 27 January 1736 that all joining should undergo a private and public examination.[293] By not offering a course, this potentially lucrative market was ignored. The one positive thing for legal studies in Glasgow was the teaching of natural law by an outstanding succession of distinguished professors of moral philosophy, culminating, in the period under consideration, in the appointment of Adam Smith, who so emphasised natural jurisprudence in his classes that it was one of the grounds given for the award to him of the degree of LLD in 1762.[294]

One thing that the tenures of Forbes, Crosse and Lindesay showed beyond doubt was that, to make legal education in the University of Glasgow a success, it was necessary to ensure the appointment of a man of quite exceptional abilities, who, by his energy and natural talents, was able to draw students away from the professors at Edinburgh, and who could thus counteract the naturally superior attractions of the University of Edinburgh. This suggested that a young man of promise was the ideal person to appoint: someone who could not yet have hopes of a better office, who required a job, but whose gaining a more attractive place would be dependent on being a success in teaching law in the University of Glasgow. In John Millar the faculty were to find the right man, who was to develop legal education in Glasgow as a polite discipline oriented around natural jurisprudence and the science of legislation, disseminating enlightened values of legal,

290 Grant, *Story of the University of Edinburgh* (n 11) vol ii, 371–372; W Menzies, "Alexander Bayne of Rires, Advocate" (1924) 36 *Juridical Review* 60.

291 L W Sharp, "Charles Mackie, the first Professor of History at Edinburgh University" (1962) 41 *Scottish Historical Review* 23.

292 Cairns, "Formation of the Scottish Legal Mind" (n 2) at 264–265.

293 J S Muirhead (ed), *The Old Minute Book of the Faculty of Procurators in Glasgow, 1668–1758* (1948) 159.

294 GUA 26645 110 (21 October 1762).

social, and political improvement.[295] Alexander Carlyle commented of the 1760s that it was the period when "[t]he Lawyers had Contented themselves with Studying Law at Home".[296] Matriculation statistics in the Netherlands bear this out.[297] But it is not to this alteration in social habits that Millar's success should be attributed; there was no need for students to go to his classes, as they could all have gone to Edinburgh. Rather, as this essay has tried to demonstrate, finding an individual with suitable personal qualities and abilities was all important to the success of a chair, especially one, as was that in Civil Law in Glasgow, that was perceived to have a number of disadvantages when it came to attracting students. The polite education in law that the faculty at Glasgow wished in 1713 to initiate, and that Forbes and Lindesay, drawing on the concerns of the *virtuosi* and of the *literati* of the Enlightenment, had tried to develop, was eventually secured from 1761 on the basis both of the lessons learned from what had gone before and of the earlier professors' achievements. The University of Glasgow was set to become the outstanding law school in the British Isles for as long as Millar held the chair.

295 Cairns, "'Famous as a School for Law, as Edinburgh . . . for Medicine'" (n 5); and, "Language, rhetoric, and Roman law" (n 184).
296 Carlyle, *Anecdotes and Characters* (n 142) 234.
297 See Nève, "Disputations of Scots Students" (n 252) at 96–99.

6 William Crosse, Regius Professor of Civil Law in the University of Glasgow, 1746–1749: A Failure of Enlightened Patronage*

Maarten Ultee has recently written in this journal that "[t]here were close links between knowledge and power in the early modern period, and historians of universities are in an excellent position to explore them".[1] An important way of examining such links is by studies of how individual professors came to be appointed. To see who was able to influence professorial appointments is to acquire an insight not only into who exercised power at any given time in the shifting politics that characterised Early Modern societies, but also into how they exercised it. Controlling elections to university chairs was a means of controlling dissemination of knowledge, as the choice of a particular professor affected how and with what success a discipline was taught. The formal methods of election to professorships in Early Modern Europe varied considerably from country to country, and, indeed, from institution to institution within one country.[2] Neither the study of the formal regulations on

* A version of this paper was read on 13 March 1991 to the Legal History Discussion Group of the Faculty of Law of the University of Edinburgh. I am grateful to the participants for their comments. My greatest debt is to Roger Emerson for his kind and helpful criticism and for directing me to some relevant sources that I had missed. His influence on this paper will be evident to those who know his work. He also made me see the importance of this type of study for a proper understanding of the development of legal education in eighteenth-century Scotland. I am also delighted here to acknowledge that I owe much to the staff of Glasgow University Archives. I have kept to the original spelling in MSS, but have expanded common abbreviations. I have retained the traditional rather than the modern spellings of the names of Crosse and Lindesay; other individuals' names are given in the form most familiar to modern scholars.

1 M Ultee, "The politics of professorial appointment at Leiden, 1709" (1990) 9 *History of Universities* 167 (henceforth Ultee, The politics of professorial appointment") at 188.

2 See, e.g., L W B Brockliss, *French Higher Education in the Seventeenth and Eighteenth Centuries: A Cultural History* (1987) 37–51; R L Emerson, "Lord Bute and the Scottish

appointing professors found in university statutes, nor the knowledge that chairs were in the gift of the Crown or other patrons exhausts the explanation of how particular appointments came about. What is required is detailed investigation of how individual professors gained their positions. While little of such work has been carried out, that that has been done demonstrates how important it is to undertake it.[3] Exploring professors' social and political connections provides insight into their intellectual concerns. Such studies will allow us to develop a more nuanced understanding of the professoriate and universities of Early Modern Europe.

The University of Glasgow in the middle of the eighteenth century was an institution in which there was considerable outside influence on appointments.[4] This paper examines the nomination of one professor. It demonstrates how issues of politics and personality could interact in a complex process to bring about an election. It also shows that, though the election to a chair could be brokered by powerful men, the relationships of patronage involved were ambiguous: it was certainly not the case that those at the supposed centre of political power had a free hand in such appointments. Furthermore, it suggests that professors had strategies open to them for ridding themselves of colleagues whom they did not want or found in some way insufficient. The adoption of such a strategy had disciplinary effects both on those brokering chairs and on those considering seeking them. Knowledge and power may indeed have been closely linked, but the links had a complex articulation: they did not form a simple chain of command and control.

A. PATRONAGE AND LEGAL EDUCATION

William Mure of Caldwell wrote to James Stuart Mackenzie: "I did not know you were to take such a charge of the College of Glasgow as your uncle did." The context was the election of a successor to Adam Smith in 1764.[5]

Universities 1760–1792", in K W Schweizer (ed), *Lord Bute: Essays in Re-interpretation* (1988) 147 (henceforth Emerson, "Lord Bute and the Scottish Universities") at 147–150.

3 See R L Emerson, *Professors, Patronage and Politics: The Aberdeen Universities in the Eighteenth Century* (1992); and "Lord Bute and the Scottish Universities" (n 2); Ultee, "The politics of professorial appointment" (n 1). It is worth pointing out that most studies of the operation of government in eighteenth-century Scotland necessarily discuss patronage and touch on the politics of appointment to university chairs; Emerson's work, however, is the most sustained account of patronage and the universities.

4 Emerson, "Lord Bute and the Scottish Universities" (n 2) at 147–150.

5 J Stuart Mackenzie to W Mure of Caldwell, 2 February 1764, in *Selections from the Family Papers preserved at Caldwell,* 2 parts in 3; Maitland Club vol 71 (1854) (henceforth *Caldwell Papers*) vol II, i, 232.

The uncle alluded to was Archibald Campbell, first Earl of Ilay and third Duke of Argyll, who had recently died, passing on his political machine to Stuart Mackenzie and his brother, the Earl of Bute.[6] Though Stuart Mackenzie was Lord Privy Seal, an office given to him to allow him to take charge of Scottish appointments, he disclaimed any intention to interfere in the appointment. He wished only to be informed of vacancies in Regius chairs.[7] But Mure's comment indicates the significant role Argyll was recognised to have played in appointments to the University of Glasgow. Argyll is rightly remembered as the substantial political manager of Scotland from the 1720s until his death in 1761. For a considerable part of this time he tried to control Scotland in the interest of Sir Robert Walpole (until the latter's fall from power in 1742), relying much on his Edinburgh agent, Andrew Fletcher of Saltoun, Lord Milton, the Lord Justice-Clerk from 1735 to 1748. At the centre of this role was the dispensing of patronage.[8] Argyll's career and personality have inevitably given rise to controversy: detractors quote the uncharitable remarks of Horace Walpole and Lord Hervey;[9] those disposed to favour Argyll repeat the flattering assessment made by John Ramsay of Ochtertyre.[10] But a proper appreciation of Argyll requires that we go beyond the spiteful gossip of his contemporaries and consider how and to what effect he used his influence.

6 See A Murdoch, "Lord Bute, James Stuart Mackenzie, and the Government of Scotland", in Schweizer, *Lord Bute* (n 2) 117 (henceforth Murdoch, "Lord Bute, James Stuart Mackenzie, and the Government of Scotland"); a family tree is found on 118.

7 J Stuart Mackenzie to W Mure, 2 February 1764, *Caldwell Papers* (n 5) 232–233.

8 For a general account of the politics of this period (now somewhat in need of revision) see W Ferguson, *Scotland 1689 to the Present* (1968) 133–165. On Argyll and patronage, see J M Simpson, "Who Steered the Gravy Train, 1707–1766?", in N T Phillipson and R Mitchison (eds), *Scotland in the Age of Improvement: Essays in Scottish History in the Eighteenth Century* (1970) 47 (henceforth Simpson, "Who Steered the Gravy Train?", and Phillipson and Mitchison, *Scotland in the Age of Improvement*); A Murdoch, *"The People Above": Politics and Administration in Mid-Eighteenth-Century Scotland* (1980) (henceforth Murdoch, *"The People Above"*); and J S Shaw, *The Management of Scottish Society 1707–1764: Power, Nobles, Lawyers, Edinburgh Agents and English Influences* (1983) 41–57 and 147–191 (henceforth Shaw, *Management of Scottish Society*). As Lord Justice-Clerk, Milton headed the Court of Justiciary, the Scottish supreme criminal court (the nominal head was the Lord Justice-General, at this time always a nobleman, and contemporaneously Ilay/Argyll). He is usually known as Lord Milton which was the judicial title he bore as a Lord of Session, a judge on the Court of Session, the Scottish supreme civil court.

9 H Walpole, *Memoirs of the Reign of King George II*, ed Lord Holland, 3 vols (1846) vol i, 275–278; John, Lord Hervey, *Some Material Towards Memoirs of the Reign of King George II*, ed R Sedgwick, 3 vols (1931) (henceforth Hervey, *Memoirs*) vol i, 296.

10 J Ramsay, *Scotland and Scotsmen in the Eighteenth Century*, ed A Allardyce, 2 vols (1888) vol i, 87.

Richard Sher has argued that the Church and the universities were significant cultural bearers of Enlightenment in Scotland.[11] This is undoubtedly correct, though one should not be tempted to slight the importance of figures who held legal and other civil offices. It nonetheless follows that patrons (whether intentionally or not) did much to promote enlightened values in Scotland through the exercise of influence over appointments to pulpits and chairs. Roger Emerson has argued this most persuasively in an important study of the third Duke of Argyll. He has shown that Argyll was a learned and cultivated man, a noted amateur scientist, and an agricultural improver, who used his influence to further the careers of men who held similar values and aspirations. The appointments that he secured helped institutionalise in the universities the values of the Scottish Enlightenment.[12]

Argyll's own taste may have been for science (in the modern sense), but, though schooled at Eton, he had had a Scottish university education at Glasgow, and had studied Civil (i.e. Roman) Law in the Netherlands – a higher education similar, in fact, to that typical for many members of the Faculty of Advocates at this period.[13] We cannot tell how interested Argyll may have been in Civil Law, but it is worth noting Hervey's scathing characterisation of him: "A pedantic, dirty, shrewd, unbred fellow of a college, with a mean aspect, bred to the sophistry of the civil law, and made a peer, would have been just such a man."[14] The evil of Civil Law was a stock Whig theme in eighteenth-century England, and for Hervey's description to have had any point, some of Argyll's legal training must have marked him. And it cannot but be significant that he ensured that his nephews Lord Bute and Stuart Mackenzie also had an education in the Netherlands in Civil Law

11 R B Sher, *Church and University in the Scottish Enlightenment: the Moderate Literati of Edinburgh* (1985).

12 R L Emerson, "The Scottish Scientific and Medical Patronage of Archibald Campbell, 3rd Duke of Argyll 1723–1761" (I am grateful to Professor Emerson for allowing me to read and cite this unpublished paper); see also the assessment of Argyll in Murdoch, *"The People Above"* (n 8) 33–34.

13 For a sketch of one advocate's education and views on legal education, see J W Cairns, "John Spotswood, Professor of Law: a Preliminary Sketch", in W M Gordon (ed), *Miscellany* III, Stair Society vol 39 (1992) 131 (henceforth Cairns, "John Spotswood); see also J M Gray (ed), *Memoirs of the Life of Sir John Clerk of Penicuik, Baronet . . . 1675–1755*, Scottish History Society, First Series, vol 13 (1892) 12–18 for an account of the type of studies likely pursued by Argyll in the Netherlands. The Faculty of Advocates is the corporation to which belong all members of the Scottish Bar, known as advocates. It is located in Edinburgh.

14 Hervey, *Memoirs* (n 9) vol i, 296.

and related disciplines.[15] Argyll must have considered it a useful part of a polite education fitting a man for public affairs both foreign and domestic.

That Argyll valued education in Civil Law makes particularly interesting his securing the appointment of William Crosse as Regius Professor of Civil Law in Glasgow in 1746. By the time Crosse was appointed, successful education in law had continuously existed for less than fifty years in the Scottish universities. Many of the earliest teachers, both private teachers and university professors, had been educated in law in the Netherlands, and it is obvious that they attempted to introduce into Scotland legal education on the model provided by the Dutch universities, linking studies of Civil Law and Scots Law to the study of natural jurisprudence, Roman antiquities, history, and philology. While much of the teaching was evidently aimed at the "trials" for admission as an advocate, such a broad ideal of legal study, even if not always fulfilled, made it an eminently polite and important discipline, closely linked to the general university enterprise and curriculum as it had come to be conceived in Scotland in Argyll's lifetime.[16] For legal education to be successful, and to take firm root in the Scottish universities, it was necessary that able, enthusiastic, and energetic men be appointed to university chairs. Crosse was not such a man. His unfortunate tenure of the Glasgow chair has already been briefly told in standard histories of the University;[17] to understand properly the significance of the period of his professorship, however, it is necessary to examine both how the politics of Scotland in late 1745 brought Argyll to recommend him (though he was not Argyll's choice), and how he misused his office, but was eventually ousted from it by the unremitting pressure maintained on him by the faculty at Glasgow, who were unwilling to tolerate a colleague who did not teach and do it passably well. Since professors relied to a large extent on fees from students for their incomes, a professor who was a sinecurist had to be got rid of, as in the long run he would only hurt everyone's income by discouraging student enrolments. Crosse's appointment thus demonstrates some of the problems faced

15 Murdoch, "Lord Bute, James Stuart Mackenzie and the Government of Scotland", (n 6) 120; Emerson, "Scottish Scientific and Medical Patronage of Archibald Campbell, 3rd Duke of Argyll" (n 12).

16 See Cairns, "John Spotswood" (n 13).

17 J D Mackie, *The University of Glasgow 1451–1951: A Short History* (1954) 190–192 (henceforth Mackie, *University of Glasgow*); D Murray, *Memories of the Old College of Glasgow: Some Chapters in the History of the University* (1927) (henceforth Murray, *Memories of the Old College of Glasgow*) 219–220; J Coutts, *A History of the University of Glasgow from its Foundation in 1451 to 1909* (1909) 232–234; see also D M Walker, *A History of the School of Law. The University of Glasgow* (1990) 24–25.

in establishing modern education in law in the Scottish universities in the eighteenth century, while pointing up some aspects of what was necessary to make such education successful.

B. THE APPOINTMENT OF CROSSE

Appointments to chairs in the University of Glasgow were highly politicised in the eighteenth century, as indeed they were in all the Scottish universities. Since the chair of Civil Law was a Crown appointment, influence in London was of paramount importance. Other chairs in Glasgow were basically filled by election by the professors.[18] This mode of appointment was also open to interest and patronage, as professors would canvass supporters for preferred candidates, and support candidates favoured by those to whom they were linked or obligated, or from whom they might expect further patronage.[19] And the faculty at Glasgow was notably divided in political allegiance.[20]

To understand how Crosse came to be appointed, it is necessary to sketch in briefly the politics of the period as it had affected Argyll. Grouped around Argyll (or Ilay as he then was) and, until the late 1730s, his brother John, second Duke of Argyll, was a political faction or interest aptly known as Argathelian. The Argathelians were opposed by the Squadrone. This latter faction had roots going back beyond 1707, but by the middle years of the eighteenth century it essentially consisted of those opposed to Ilay. There was no obvious ideological divide between the two factions, both of which were groupings of Whigs; they battled in Scotland for control of power and its concomitant, the dispensing of patronage. Shaw has pointed out that the Squadrone was essentially a family interest: prominent members included the Marquesses of Tweeddale, the Dukes of Montrose (who in

18 The constitution of the University of Glasgow in the eighteenth century, and the respective authority of Rector, Principal, University Professors, College Professors, and the various meetings of differently constituted bodies is a matter of some complexity which was even to result in litigation later in the century. The statement in the text about election is broadly correct. In the mid-eighteenth century, such professors were elected at meetings known as University Meetings. For a brief discussion of some of these problems, see Mackie, *University of Glasgow* (n 17) 197–209. I use the term "Faculty" in a relatively loose way to refer to the professors collectively; the distinction between the "Faculty" and the "University" is here immaterial.

19 See Emerson, "Lord Bute and the Scottish Universities" (n 2) 147–150.

20 I have benefited from R L Emerson, "Medical Men, Politicians and the Medical Schools at Glasgow and Edinburgh 1685–1803", in A Doig, J P S Ferguson, I A Milne and R Passmore (eds), *William Cullen and the Eighteenth Century Medical World* (1993) 186, for an understanding of the volatile politics of the Glasgow faculty and their relationship to patronage and of the political affiliation of individual professors.

the eighteenth century were successive Chancellors of the University of Glasgow), and the Dundases of Arniston.[21]

The alliance of the second Duke of Argyll with Ilay and Walpole was always an uneasy one. The second Duke went into opposition in 1739, and in the election of 1741 succeeded in swinging many Scottish seats against the ministry. Walpole fell from power in 1742.[22] The change of ministry brought in a Squadrone administration for Scotland. The Marquess of Tweeddale was appointed Scottish Secretary of State. Robert Craigie of Glendoick became Lord Advocate, and Robert Dundas, younger of Arniston, Solicitor General. (These latter two offices were those of the law officers of the Crown in Scotland.) Ilay was left isolated, and, in Shaw's term, eclipsed. He was to ally himself with Henry Pelham and his brother, the Duke of Newcastle. The second Duke of Argyll died in 1743. Ilay's succession to the Dukedom and to the chieftainship of Clan Campbell inevitably helped restore his position somewhat. And it is worth noting that the Squadrone was never secure. Tweeddale's abilities were limited, and his incompetence not only did much to enable the Rebellion of 1745 to take place in the Highlands, but also prevented him from making any adequate response. He was to resign on 4 January 1746; he had already lost most of his influence.[23]

William Forbes, the first Professor of Civil Law in Glasgow, died on 27 October 1745.[24] Three months earlier, the Young Pretender had landed in the Western Isles. By the time Forbes died, Edinburgh had been occupied

21 Shaw, *Management of Scottish Society* (n 8) 48–55.

22 R Sedgwick, *The House of Commons 1715–1754*, 2 vols (1970) (henceforth Sedgwick, *House of Commons*) vol i, 44–50.

23 Shaw, *Management of Scottish* Society (n 8) 43–48; Murdoch, *"The People Above"* (n 8) 28–51. R Mitchison, "The Government and the Highlands, 1707–1745", in Phillipson and Mitchison (eds), *Scotland in the Age of Improvement* (n 8) 24 (henceforth Mitchison, "The Government and the Highlands"), convincingly argues that the outbreak of the Rebellion owed much to Tweeddale.

24 There are conflicts over the date of Forbes' death. I have preferred that given in W Anderson to Marquess of Tweeddale, 2 November 1745, N[ational] L[ibrary of] S[cotland] Yester MS 14422 fo 81 which is confirmed in S[cottish] R[ecord] O[ffice] Register of Glasgow Testaments CC 9/7/59 209, in Minutes of Meetings of Faculty 1745–1753 G[lasgow] U[niversity] A[rchives] 26649 167 (26 June 1752), and by Charles Mackie in his "Index funereus 29 annorum", Edinburgh University Library, MS Dc 1.47 72. The date of 23 October 1745 is given in F J Grant (ed), *The Faculty of Advocates in Scotland, 1532–1943, with Genealogical Notes*, Scottish Record Society (OS) vol 76 (1944) (henceforth Grant, *Faculty of Advocates*) 74, and is also found in the draft answer written on R Mackintosh to Principal Neil Campbell, 30 March 1747, GUA 30312 and has been (later) added in the margin in connection with the admission of Forbes' successor in Minutes of University Meetings 1730–1749, GUA 26639 202 (4 April 1746). Anderson's evidence is the most contemporary and likely to be correct; but nothing here hinges particularly on it. On Forbes, see J W Cairns "The Origins of the Glasgow Law School: The Professors of Civil Law 1714–61" in P Birks (ed), *The Life of the Law: Select Proceedings*

by the Jacobites on 17 September, Cope defeated at Prestonpans on 19 September, and the commanders of the rebel army were considering whether or not to march south to England: a decision they were soon to make and act on.[25] The Jacobite Rebellion was to complicate the politics of the appointment of a new professor to replace Forbes in a university divided between Argathelians and Squadrone men. By the end of October, it was known that there were at least two candidates, Hercules Lindesay and William Crosse.[26]

The majority of the professors favoured the appointment of Lindesay, and feared that Crosse, if appointed, intended to treat the chair as a sinecure. They were also concerned about who had the right to elect Forbes' successor. They accordingly approached a former Rector, John Graham of Dougalston, a supporter of the Squadrone connected to Montrose, and asked him to write to the Chancellor, Montrose, letting him know that they favoured Lindesay.[27] Eight of the professors also wrote separately to Montrose on 2 November 1745 seeking the appointment of Lindesay.[28] At this time the complement of the university was twelve professors (including that of Civil Law) and the Principal, and since one of the professors was absent when the letter was written, Lindesay obviously enjoyed overwhelming and broad support among the Faculty.[29] The professors first considered officially the question of the successor to Forbes at a University Meeting held on 4 November. The Meeting appointed a committee to search the charter chest for papers relating to the establishment of the chair in Civil Law, and any such were to be given to Thomas Miller, advocate, who was to draw up a memorial to be given to two other advocates, James Graham and George Sinclair, for their opinion as to whether the University had any

of the Tenth British Legal History Conference (1993) 151 (henceforth Cairns, "Origins of the Glasgow Law School").

25 The most recent account focusing chronologically on these movements of the Jacobite army is J Black, *Culloden and the '45* (1990) 66–103; a more convincing political and social analysis is found in the incisively written and mordantly witty B Lenman, *The Jacobite Risings in Britain 1689–1746* (1980).

26 J Graham of Dougalston to M Graeme of Gorthie, 3 November 1745, SRO Montrose Muniments *GD* 220/5/1606/21.

27 Ibid.

28 Ibid; W Anderson to Marquess of Tweeddale, 2 November 1745, NLS Yester MS 14422 fo 81.

29 As well as the Principal, there were the following professors: Anatomy, Divinity, Ecclesiastical History, Greek, Humanity, Law, Logic, Mathematics, Medicine, Moral Philosophy, Natural Philosophy, and Oriental Languages. Since one professor was absent (see W Anderson to Marquess of Tweeddale, 2 November 1745, NLS Yester MS 14422 fo 81) and the Law chair vacant, only two professors and possibly the Principal could have been unwilling to sign the letter.

right to elect the Professor of Law.[30] Queen Anne had allowed the University to elect the first professor, and the professors were obviously concerned whether they had a right to elect his successors, though suspecting they did not.[31] The committee reported on 16 December that they had given the papers to Miller who had laid the case before a Mr Ferguson as Graham and Sinclair were unavailable. Ferguson and Miller's opinion was read, but consideration of it was postponed to a later Meeting.[32] The opinion must have been that the University did not have the right to elect the Professor of Civil Law, for a Meeting held on 17 March 1746 resolved by a majority to send a memorial to the Duke of Argyll asking him to recommend Lindesay who had "taught the Civil Law here with success for several years". The University had delayed for far too long, however, since the Principal had already received a letter from Argyll stating that the government had decided to give the office to another. The memorial nonetheless was sent, two professors – both Squadrone men – requesting it to be minuted that they opposed approaching Argyll, since the choice of another candidate had already been made.[33]

While one might normally expect that delays in such a matter reflected differences of opinion within the faculty, it is clear that the greater part of the professors, of whatever faction, wished Lindesay to be appointed. The troubled times may possibly explain the University's tardiness. Rumours of a French invasion were common in December, when the University Meeting considered the lawyers' report on who could elect a professor. Furthermore, the shifting politics in London may well have made it uncertain as to who should be approached to secure the royal nomination. Since Tweeddale was Scottish Secretary, the appointment should have come through him; but he had lost control of such matters by this time, while it was not until 1746 that Argyll, in alliance with the Pelhams, was to become the obvious person to

30 GUA 26639 196. James Graham was probably the advocate (admitted 1723) who was the younger brother of Dougalston, and may well have been chosen for that reason: see J Graham of Dougalston to M Graeme of Gorthie, 3 November 1745, SRO Montrose Muniments GD 220/5/1606/21. The other possibility was James Graham of Buchlyvie. George Sinclair was the son of Sir John Sinclair of Stevenson. Miller was the future Lord Justice-Clerk and Lord President. Forbes' pew in the College Church had already been allocated to William Anderson, the Professor of Ecclesiastical History, GUA 26649 5 (1 November 1745).

31 W Anderson to Marquess of Tweeddale, 2 November 1745, NLS Yester MS 14422 fo 81; on the appointment of Forbes, see Cairns, "Origins of the Glasgow Law School" (n 24) at 144–145 and 158–174.

32 GUA 26639 200. Ferguson could have been either James Fergusson of Pitfour or James Fergusson of Craigdarroch.

33 GUA 26639 201. The two professors were Robert Dick, Professor of Natural Philosophy, and Anderson.

solicit.[34] The rebel army was in Northern England by 16 December on its retreat from Derby, and in three days it was to reach Carlisle. The natural route for it to take north was through Glasgow: an alarming prospect for such a staunchly Hanoverian city and University, and Glasgow was described on 1 December as being in a panic.[35] The Jacobites in fact occupied the city on 26 December 1745, and exacted money and supplies before leaving on 3 January 1746 for Stirling.[36] But whatever may have been the reasons for the University's lack of expedition, the professors had easily been outmanoeuvred by others who were not so slow or uncertain; and the appointment of Crosse seems to have been decided by the end of November.

Hercules Lindesay, the University's choice, had taught law privately for six years in Glasgow in place of Forbes.[37] He was the son of an Episcopalian minister who twice had been intruded into and twice deprived of the charge of Edzell, and he had studied in the University of Edinburgh in the early 1720s, perhaps going on also to study law there.[38] The death of the elderly Forbes had been expected.[39] Lindesay obviously considered himself the natural successor to Forbes, and he was described in 1744 by Anderson, the Squadrone Professor of Ecclesiastical History, as having "been about us gaping for Forbes['s] death these four years past".[40] He and his supporters claimed in 1744 that Argyll had promised to secure the chair for him, and by the summer of that year his friends had certainly approached both Argyll and Montrose on his behalf.[41] And there can be no doubt that Lindesay was the

34 Simpson, "Who Steered the Gravy Train?" (n 8) at 59; Murdoch, "*The People Above*" (n 8) 6.

35 J Lockhart to R Dundas, 1 December 1745, SRO microfilm of Dundas of Arniston MSS vol 4 RH 4/15/4.

36 On the movements of the Jacobite army, see Black, *Culloden and the '45* (n 25) 127–138.

37 W Anderson to Marquess of Tweeddale, 2 November 1745, NLS Yester MS 14422 fo 81; see Cairns, "Origins of the Glasgow Law School" (n 24) at 183–185.

38 On Lindesay's father, see Grant, *Faculty of Advocates* (n 24) 124; *Fasti ecclesiae Scoticanae: the Succession of Ministers in the Church of Scotland from the Reformation*, new edn, 7 vols (1915–1928) vol v, 390; Lord Lindsay, *Lives of the Lindsays; Or, a Memoir of the Houses of Crawford and Balcarres*, 3 vols (1849) vol ii, 261. For his education, see Edinburgh University Library, "Matriculation Roll of the University of Edinburgh. Arts–Law–Divinity, Transcribed by Dr Alexander Morgan 1933–1934", 3 vols in MS, vol i, fos 177 and 184.

39 W Anderson to Marquess of Tweeddale, 23 October 1745, NLS Yester MS 14422, fos 73–74, commenting that Forbes could not live two days. Grant, *Faculty of Advocates* (n 24) 74 gives no date of birth for Forbes, but I believe him to have been born no later than 1670. He was admitted as an advocate on 15 February 1696: Books of Sederunt of the Lords of Council and Session, SRO CS 1/9 fo 121r. The issues of Forbes' age and education are fully explored in Cairns, "Origins of the Glasgow Law School" (n 24) at 161–164.

40 W Anderson to Marquess of Tweeddale, 26 September 1744, NLS Yester MS 7063 fos 135–136.

41 Lord Garlies to Marquess of Tweeddale, 22 August 1744, NLS Yester MS 7063 fos 104–105; W Anderson to Marquess of Tweeddale, 26 September 1744, NLS Yester MS 7063 fos 135–136.

candidate initially favoured by Argyll.[42] But Lindesay also could draw on support from members of the Squadrone, and obviously cultivated their interest among the professors at Glasgow. As part of his campaign for the succession, Lindesay sent to Tweeddale, some time in late summer or early autumn 1744, a memorial seeking the nomination to the chair.[43] Probably in response to a query from Tweeddale prompted by Lindesay's memorial, Anderson wrote to Tweeddale on 26 September 1744, noting Lindesay's claim of Argyll's support, but also commenting that he had never doubted that Lindesay would also have Tweeddale's support, "considering his patron". He added that "they who wish for a better may wish on", as he presumably believed there was enough interest in Lindesay's favour to secure him the post.[44] A later letter of Anderson shows Lindesay's patron to have been the sixth Earl of Galloway, a man at one time of Tory and Jacobite connections.[45] As Lord Garlies, before inheriting the Earldom, he had recommended Lindesay to Tweeddale in August 1744, and Lindesay had accompanied the eldest son of Garlies to the University of Leiden where both had matriculated in law in 1737.[46] Anderson assumed that Galloway's recommendation and wishes would influence Tweeddale, as the two men were related through Galloway's wife whose grandmother was also Tweeddale's mother. To what extent it would have done so is uncertain, because, although Galloway claimed to support Tweeddale, their relationship was obviously uneasy, and during the latter's period as Scottish Secretary, the former regularly importuned him in an often petulant manner for offices for himself and his friends. Tweeddale sent Lindesay's memorial to Dundas, the Solicitor General, on 13 September 1744, noting Garlies' recommendation, and asking for Dundas' opinion of

42 See Duke of Argyll to D Forbes of Culloden, 15 February 1746, in *Culloden Papers: Comprising an Extensive and Interesting Correspondence from the Year 1625 to 1748* (1815) (henceforth *Culloden Papers*) 469. Argyll can only be referring to Lindesay, the only other candidate.

43 R Dundas to Marquess of Tweeddale, 4 October 1744, NLS Yester MS 14423 fos 23–24; the memorial was sent sometime after late August: Lord Garlies to Marquess of Tweeddale, 22 August 1744, NLS Yester MS 7063 fos 104–105.

44 W Anderson to Marquess of Tweeddale, 26 September 1744, NLS Yester MS 7063 fos 135–136.

45 W Anderson to Marquess of Tweeddale, 2 November 1745, NLS Yester MS 14422 fo 81, where Anderson wrote: "I doubt not but his friends, particularly my Lord Galloway will have wrote to your Lordship". On Galloway's politics, see Sedgwick, *House of Commons* (n 22) vol i, 395.

46 Lord Garlies to Marquess of Tweeddale, 22 August 1744, NLS Yester 7063 fos 104–105; R Dundas to Marquess of Tweeddale, 4 October 1744, NLS Yester MS 14423 fos 23–24; in *Album studiosorum Academiae Lugduno-Batavae MDLXXV–MDCCCLXXV* (1875) (henceforth *Album studiosorum Academiae Lugduno-Batavae*) col 968, Lindesay's matriculation on 24 September 1737 immediately follows that of "Alexander Stuart", presumably Garlies' son, Alexander Stewart. Garlies inherited the title Earl of Galloway on his father's death in February 1745.

Lindesay.[47] Dundas replied early in October. He was vehemently opposed to appointing Lindesay, whose qualifications for the post and learning in law he disparaged. The motivation of Dundas' attack seems to have been a personal objection the Dundases of Arniston had to Lindesay because of his association with Sir James Steuart of Coltness. Early 1744 had been marked by fears of French invasion, and Dundas wrote that Steuart's "principles are now unknown to none" (although Steuart was not yet openly Jacobite). Dundas described Lindesay as "no better in his political principles than he ought to be". Dundas noted that Lindesay had tutored Steuart for his examinations for admission as an advocate, and argued that he was entirely managed by Steuart.[48] While Lindesay was not mentioned in 1748 in a list of "advocates universally known to be well affected", there is no evidence of his having Jacobite sympathies, which Dundas must have deduced, perhaps from the career of Lindesay's father, but most likely from his associations with Garlies and Steuart. Dundas indeed later admitted to Tweeddale that he knew "no more" about Lindesay than that he had been a private teacher in Glasgow.[49] The animus of the objection of Dundas and his father Arniston to Lindesay derived from the Midlothian election earlier in 1744. Steuart was a freeholder in Midlothian and entitled to vote. Arniston had been preses of the election meeting, and in calling over the roll of voters had omitted Steuart's name. (The candidates were Sir John Baird, a relative of Steuart, and Sir Charles Gilmour, Arniston's nominee.) Steuart sued Arniston for malpractice before the Court of Session (on which Arniston was a judge). This humiliation meant that Dundas and his father could not countenance the appointment of a friend of Steuart to the Glasgow chair. Dundas further argued, rather unconvincingly, that Lindesay's appointment would hurt Tweeddale's interest in Edinburgh. He urged Tweeddale to recommend someone who would be grateful and serviceable to him and his friends, since the professors at Glasgow were divided into factions.[50]

47 Marquess of Tweeddale to R Dundas, 13 September 1744, SRO microfilm of Dundas of Arniston MSS vol 3 RH 4/15/3.

48 R Dundas to Marquess of Tweeddale, 4 October 1744, NLS Yester MS 14423 fos 23–34.

49 List of advocates universally known to be well affected, SRO photostats of State Papers (Scotland) RH 2/4/368/359; R Dundas to Marquess of Tweeddale, n d [early Nov. 1745?], NLS Yester MS 14423 fo 105.

50 R Dundas to Marquess of Tweeddale, 4 October 1744, NLS Yester MS 14423 fos 23–24. Tweeddale already knew Argyll supported Lindesay: W Anderson to Marquess of Tweeddale, 26 September 1744, NLS Yester MS 7063 fos 135–136. On the Midlothian election, see also the remarks by Andrew Skinner in J Steuart, *An Inquiry into the Principles of Political Oeconomy*, ed A S Skinner, 2 vols (1966) vol i, xxviii–xxix. (Skinner errs in stating Arniston was Lord President; he was not to be appointed to this post until 1748.) On Lindesay's tutoring of Steuart,

Lindesay continued his campaign for the chair in the next year. He was admitted as an advocate in July 1745, at the relatively advanced age of thirty-seven.[51] It may have been because Lindesay was not an advocate that Dundas had felt so free to doubt his qualifications in 1744. Members of the Faculty of Advocates had hitherto monopolised all appointments to chairs in law in Edinburgh and Glasgow, and it was always likely that members of the Faculty and Senators of the College of Justice would be consulted about, and possibly able to influence, the nomination or election of a law professor.[52]

After Forbes' death, matters became more pressing. Lindesay had continued to cultivate the Squadrone interest associated with Montrose in the University, especially Professor Anderson, and its members supported his candidature. He had visited Mungo Graeme, the Duke's agent, at Buchanan, and John Graham of Dougalston was persuaded that Lindesay was attached to Montrose's interest, and, shortly after Forbes' death, Graham of Dougalston sought to further Lindesay's search for the appointment.[53] Anderson obviously thought on 23 October 1745 that Lindesay's nomination would be automatic and supported by Tweeddale.[54] He reported to Tweeddale on 2 November that eight of the professors, including himself, had written to Montrose' supporting Lindesay, who "has taught Law privately amongst us . . . with applause And we think him the best qualified for this post of any who have yet been in the list of Candidates". Anderson also expected Galloway had already solicited Tweeddale on Lindesay's behalf: whether he had again done so is unknown.[55] By this time Crosse had emerged as a rival for the post, and the faculty feared he would be a sinecurist. The professors continued to campaign for Lindesay. On hearing of Forbes' death, Dundas wrote to Tweeddale. He acknowledged that many would solicit the office for Lindesay. He obviously did not want Lindesay to be nominated, and hinted that Tweeddale should delay, pointing out that it would be important

see also *The Works, Political, Metaphisical, and Chronological, of the late Sir James Steuart of Coltness, Bart*, coll and ed J Steuart, 6 vols (1805) vol vi, 363 (this last suggests Lindesay tutored Steuart in Glasgow, which is unlikely).

51 Books of Sederunt of the Lords of Council and Session, SRO CS.1/13 fo 33v (9 July 1745). Grant, *Faculty of Advocates* (n 24) does not give a date of birth; *Album studiosorum Academiae Lugduno-Batavae* (n 46) col 968 shows Lindesay gave his age as twenty-nine when he matriculated in law in Leiden on 24 September 1737.

52 Senators of the College of Justice is an alternative name for the Lords of Council and Session, the judges of the Court of Session.

53 J Graham of Dougalston to M Graeme of Gorthie, 3 November 1745, SRO Montrose Muniments GD 220/5/1606/21.

54 W Anderson to Marquess of Tweeddale, 23 October 1745, NLS Yester 14422 fos 73–74.

55 W Anderson to Marquess of Tweeddale, 2 November 1745, NLS Yester MS 14422 fo 81.

to ensure a friend had the position. He enclosed a letter from an unnamed candidate whom he favoured should Tweeddale have immediately to nominate someone.[56] Pressure on Tweeddale also came from Montrose, who, presumably prompted by the professors' letter of 2 November 1745, pointed out that the University would be displeased if Crosse was appointed as it was thought "he would not attend". Tweeddale wrote to Dundas on 17 December that the professors still favoured Lindesay.[57] By this time, however, events had overtaken Tweeddale, Dundas, and the professors. A promise of Crosse's appointment had been secured by Argyll.

Crosse probably decided to seek the nomination after Forbes' death, since Anderson had been unaware of his interest in the post on 23 October 1745; soon after it had occurred, he approached the Principal, Neil Campbell, a friend of Argyll, seeking the chair, and by the end of October was an acknowledged candidate.[58] Crosse feared the opposition of the Squadrone, specifically of the Dundases, whom he suspected would favour Charles Gordon, an advocate who was "their fast freind and allyed to Lord Arniston", and who had been a disappointed candidate for the chair of Civil Law in Edinburgh in February 1745.[59] (It is unknown, but it seems unlikely that this was the man whom Dundas was later to suggest to Tweeddale.)[60] Crosse had two influential supporters who exerted pressure on Argyll on his behalf: Andrew Cochrane, the Provost of Glasgow, and Duncan Forbes of Culloden, the Lord President of the Court of Session. Cochrane started to campaign for Crosse around the end of October or beginning of November, most probably

56 R Dundas to Marquess of Tweeddale, n d [early November?], NLS Yester MS 14423 fo 105. The date is suggested because the letter was written from Berwick, which Dundas probably left about 12 November, and in the letter he stated he was just about to leave for Edinburgh: see G W T Omond, *The Arniston Memoirs: Three Centuries of a Scottish House 1571–1838* (1887) 136.

57 Marquess of Tweeddale to R Dundas, 17 December 1745 (draft), NLS Yester MS 7078 fos 194–195; (final copy in clerk's hand) SRO microfilm of Dundas of Arniston MSS vol 4 RH 4/15/4.

58 John Graham of Dougalston to M Graeme of Gorthie, 3 November 1745, SRO Montrose Muniments GD 220/5/1606/21.

59 W Crosse to Provost Andrew Cochrane, 13 November 1745, in J Dennistoun (ed), *The Cochrane Correspondence Regarding the Affairs of Glasgow M. DCC.XLV–VI*, Maitland Club vol 37 (1836) (henceforth *Cochrane Correspondence*) 33–34; on the appointment to the chair, see J M Pinkerton (ed), *The Minute Book of the Faculty of Advocates Volume 2 1713–1750*, Stair Society vol 32 (1980) 202 (19 February 1745). Gordon is not mentioned; but this must be the election to which Crosse alluded.

60 R Dundas to Marquess of Tweeddale, n d [early November?], NLS Yester MS 14423 fo 105. It seems unlikely since the unnamed candidate's father had been useful to Dundas in the "West country" and was a "very able man to assist in these Boroughs". Gordon's father had political interests in the north: Sedgwick, *House of Commons* (n 22) vol ii, 69–70.

by soliciting Argyll.[61] Forbes also wrote to Argyll in November seeking the chair for Crosse;[62] and he wrote on 13 November to Tweeddale to the same effect, asking him to recommend Crosse if he had not undertaken to support someone else.[63] On receipt of Forbes' letter, Argyll solicited Pelham, who had received the king's assurance in the closet that Crosse would get the chair, although Tweeddale had tried to oppose Argyll and had advised the king to delay. The matter seems to have been settled by 1 December 1745, although the warrant for the presentation was not to be issued until well into the new year.[64]

Tweeddale and Dundas had been outmanoeuvred by Argyll. Though Tweeddale had advised the king to delay, he appears to have been unaware for the best part of December that the king had already undertaken to nominate Crosse. He wrote to Dundas on 30 November, reporting that Forbes had recommended Crosse to him for the professorship, but saying that he would do nothing until he had heard from Dundas.[65] Dundas responded on 10 December, agreeing that Crosse deserved the chair, and accepting the weight of Forbes' recommendation.[66] Tweeddale was still unaware on 17 December that the matter was concluded, and it is ironic that he then wrote that "the settling of this small office still occasions some difficulty".[67] He was

61 W Crosse to A Cochrane, 13 November 1745, *Cochrane Correspondence* (n 59) 33. I suspect it was Argyll whom Cochrane solicited because Argyll wrote to him about the appointment, and he wrote to Argyll to thank him: see below.

62 Forbes' letter is unlocated; but see Duke of Argyll to D Forbes, 10 January 1746, *Culloden Papers* (n 42) 469. Forbes may well have written to Argyll on 13 November, the date he wrote to Tweeddale: see n 63 below. As Lord President, Forbes was the head of the Court of Session.

63 D Forbes to Marquess of Tweeddale, 13 November 1745, NLS Yester MS 7073 fo 22.

64 The chronology is difficult. Duke of Argyll to D Forbes, 10 January 1746. *Culloden Papers* (n 42) 469 states that Argyll recommended Crosse on receipt of Forbes' letter, that Tweeddale advised delay (perhaps on Dundas' advice given in his letter of November? 1745, n 56 above), but that Pelham had received the king's assurances in the closet. Argyll obviously wrote to Cochrane to this effect (see W Crosse to D Forbes, 15 February 1746, *Culloden Papers* (n 42) 269). Cochrane wrote to Argyll thanking him for procuring the chair for Crosse on 1 December 1745: *Cochrane Correspondence* (n 59) 46. This would suggest that Pelham had secured the king's agreement in middle to late November. The problem is that this last letter may be wrongly dated. It states that Crosse has left for Stirling with the Glasgow Volunteers: W Crosse to Lord Milton, 6 December 1745, NLS Saltoun MS 16606 fo 207 suggests that they have not yet left. Even if Cochrane's letter to Argyll ought to be dated later, it cannot have been written much later, so Argyll had secured the promise of Crosse's nomination in late November or early December, especially if Forbes wrote to Argyll at the same date as that on which he wrote to Tweeddale (13 November) and Argyll acted instantly on receipt of the letter.

65 Marquess of Tweeddale to R Dundas, 30 November 1745, SRO microfilm of Dundas of Arniston MSS vol 4 RH 4/15/4; (draft), NLS Yester MS 7078 fo 188.

66 R Dundas to Marquess of Tweeddale, 10 December 1745, NLS Yester MS 14423 fo 130.

67 Marquess of Tweeddale to R Dundas, 17 December 1745 (draft), NLS Yester MS 7078 fos 194–195; (final copy in clerk's hand), SRO microfilm of Dundas of Arniston MSS vol 4 RH 4/15/4.

already a spent political force, unable to control appointments that should have come through him as Scottish Secretary. For much of November he had been ill, and by the middle of December he recognised that the government of Scotland was being conducted without his knowledge and without his being consulted. By the end of December he had decided to resign.[68] From the tenor of Dundas' and Tweeddale's correspondence, it nonetheless seems quite possible that Tweeddale might also have supported Crosse on Forbes' solicitation, although his irresolution seems to have been such that he was possibly still open to influence from Montrose and the professors.[69]

Argyll told Forbes that he had secured Crosse's nomination "in prejudice of a friend of my own".[70] What had caused Argyll to switch his support from Lindesay in 1744 to Crosse in late 1745? Crosse was not an Argathelian (no more was he a supporter of the Squadrone), and he was later to represent himself as politically neutral.[71] It was obvious that the indecisive Tweeddale's days as Secretary of State were drawing to a close: he had become irrelevant. Argyll could easily circumvent him by going to Pelham. Pelham and Newcastle were soon, by the tactic of resigning in February 1746, to come back to reinforced power, but Argyll's alliance with them was always uncertain.[72] The power vacuum caused in Scotland by Tweeddale's weakness and the government's consequent unpreparedness in the face of the Rebellion had been filled by Milton and Forbes, especially the former, who acted energetically in the government's interest. Argyll's position was delicate. He had been in Inverary when the Rebellion started, and had immediately left for London.[73] Placed in London where Tweeddale was powerless and the Pelham brothers manoeuvring, in a time when communications were difficult and rumours common, he was very dependent on Scottish supporters

68 On Tweeddale's illness, see, e.g., A Mitchell to R Dundas, 12 and 19 November 1745, and Marquess of Tweeddale to R Dundas, 23 November and 12 December 1745; on Tweeddale's recognition of his loss of power, see Marquess of Tweeddale to R Dundas, 17 December 1745 (private letter in Tweeddale's hand); on his decision to resign, A Mitchell to R Dundas, 31 December 1745; all in SRO microfilm of Dundas of Arniston MSS vol 4 RH 4/15/3 and 4. Tweeddale resigned on 4 January 1746, A Mitchell to R Dundas, 4 January 1746, SRO microfilm of Dundas of Arniston MSS vol 5 RH 4/15/4.

69 Marquess of Tweeddale to R Dundas, 17 December 1745 (in clerk's hand), SRO microfilm of Dundas of Arniston MSS vol 4 RH 4/15/4; (draft) NLS Yester MS 7078 fos 194–195.

70 Duke of Argyll to D Forbes, 10 January 1746, *Culloden Papers* (n 42) 469.

71 Shaw, *Management of Scottish Society* (n 8) 46.

72 See, e.g., Simpson, "Who Steered the Gravy Train?" (n 8) at 58; Sedgwick, *House of Commons* (n 22) vol i, 56; M S Bricke, "The Pelhams vs Argyll: a struggle for mastery of Scotland, 1747–1748" (1982) 61 *Scottish Historical Review* 157.

73 Murdoch, *"The People Above"* (n 8) 34–35; Shaw, *Management of Scottish Society* (n 8) 165–167; Mitchison, "The Government and the Highlands" (n 23) at 37–45.

and correspondents such as Milton and Forbes, especially since he had not regained the authority he had lost on the fall of Walpole. His men in Scotland were in a strong position to put pressure on him. Furthermore, Steuart had now openly come out for the Pretender; even though there is no indication that Lindesay shared his political views, his commonly known association with Steuart would have made his appointment difficult to work towards the end of 1745. It is particularly telling that Argyll was so strongly influenced in this appointment by Forbes' recommendation, since Forbes was independent-minded and not Argyll's man in the way Milton was.

It is easy to see why Cochrane, Forbes, and (possibly) Milton favoured Crosse over Lindesay. Crosse was the son of a merchant who had been Dean of Guild of Glasgow.[74] He was on familiar terms with the Provost; the two men worked sufficiently closely at this period that Crosse could write letters for Cochrane to sign.[75] Crosse took a very active part on the government's side as soon as the Rebellion started. Shortly before the Jacobites occupied Edinburgh, he had dissuaded some Glaswegian citizens from treating with the rebels.[76] Through October to December he corresponded regularly with Cochrane about what was happening, and was active on the city's behalf:[77] he even published (anonymously) a patriotic address to Glasgow's citizens.[78] He evidently made himself invaluable to the Provost. Crosse also kept Milton informed about events at the same time.[79] Though I have no evidence of Milton exerting influence over the appointment, it is difficult to accept that he would have found Crosse unsuitable. Although he was to try very hard to prevent Crosse from being appointed Sheriff Depute of Lanark in 1748, this was simply to secure the desirable post for his favoured candidate, George Sinclair, rather than because of opposition to Crosse himself, whom he was also recommending for the less lucrative office of Sheriff Depute of

74 Grant, *Faculty of Advocates* (n 24) 46; Mackie, *University of Glasgow* (n 17) 190.

75 A Cochrane to Lord Milton, 15 September 1745, NLS Saltoun MS 16606 fo 94 is in Crosse's handwriting.

76 A Cochrane to R Craigie, Lord Advocate, 15 September 1745, *Cochrane Correspondence* (n 59) 15; A Cochrane to Lord Milton, 15 September 1745, NLS Saltoun MS 16606 fo 94; Marquess of Tweeddale to R Dundas, 30 November 1745, SRO microfilm of Dundas of Arniston MSS vol 4 RH 4/15/4; (draft), NLS Yester MS 7078 fo 188.

77 W Crosse to A Cochrane, 13 November 1745, 14 November 1745, 16 November 1745, November 1745, December 1745, 16 December 1745, December 1745, 21 December 1745, 22 December 1745, December 1745, *Cochrane Correspondence* (n 59) 33–34, 34–35, 38–40, 40–43, 48–49, 50, 57–58, 58, 59, 59–60.

78 [W Crosse,] *A Loyal Address to the Citizens of Glasgow, Occasioned by the Present Rebellion* (1745).

79 W Crosse to Lord Milton, 27 November 1745, 2 December 1745, 6 December 1745, [24 December 1745], NLS Saltoun MS 16606 fos 203–209.

Renfrew.[80] Crosse volunteered with the regiment raised in Glasgow, and marched with them to Stirling in December.[81] He was already known as "a favourite of the Presidents [i.e. of Forbes]",[82] who described Crosse to Tweeddale as "a Companion and Friend of Mine".[83] Since Forbes played such an important role in organising against the Rebellion, he could only have approved of Crosse's activities on the government's behalf. In short, Crosse was a man whose claims on Cochrane and Forbes simply could not easily be denied. He was to thank them in 1748 by writing that Argyll was a great man not only by reason of his estate and employments, "but great also by his personal abilitys, which last have enabled him to make choice of the men of the best Judgments and greatest parts in the Country to serve under him".[84] Nor was Crosse obviously unsuitable. Like his rival Lindesay, he had studied law at Leiden, and he had been admitted to the Faculty of Advocates in 1735.[85] Forbes wrote to Tweeddale that he would answer for Crosse being

80 Lord Milton to Duke of Newcastle, 24 and 30 March 1748, SRO photostats of State Papers (Scotland) RH 2/4/368/264 and 279; see also H Bland to Duke of Newcastle, 24 March 1748, SRO photostats of State Papers (Scotland) RH 2/4/368/267. On Milton's recommending Crosse to be Sheriff Depute of Renfrew, see SRO photostats of State Papers (Scotland) RH 2/4/368/208. Scotland is divided into sheriffdoms, the judge heading each being known in 1748 as the sheriff depute. Sheriffs depute also had important administrative duties. The appointment of sheriffs depute in 1748 was particularly important, following on from the abolition of heritable jurisdictions in 1747 after the 1745 rebellion.

81 A Cochrane to Duke Argyll, 1 December 1745, *Cochrane Correspondence* (n 59) 46; W Crosse to Lord Milton, 6 December 1745, NLS Saltoun MS 16606 fo 207.

82 J Graham of Dougalston to M Graeme of Gorthie, 3 November 1745, SRO Montrose Muniments, GD 220/5/1606/21.

83 W Forbes to Marquess of Tweeddale, 13 November 1745, NLS Yester MS 7073 fo 22.

84 W Crosse, "Some Considerations by way of Essay, upon The means of civilizing the Highlands and extinguishing Jacobitism in Scotland", NLS MS 5201 fo 58v. He also disparaged the Squadrone who opposed him by stating, ibid: "There are few, or rather none among them That have a true Judgement of Men and things . . ." On Crosse's views of the Argathelians and the Squadrone, see Shaw, *Management of Scottish Society* (n 8) 46 and 52–53. Shaw dates this MS to 1746. I accept the date (admittedly added by a later hand) of 1748; given that at fo 7r it refers to the sums necessary to purchase the heritable jurisdictions and at fo 8r to changing tenure from ward to feu. It is dedicated (fo 4r), however, to Bland as Commander in Chief in Scotland; but this designation of Bland has obviously been added later and it was at one time dedicated to him as Humphrey Bland, Esquire. This may suggest that it should be dated earlier than 1748 and was later revised. On the other hand, Crosse perhaps dedicated or rededicated it to Bland as the latter secured him the post of Sheriff Depute of Lanarkshire in 1748 (SRO photostats of State Papers (Scotland) RH 2/4/368/194 and 212) at much the same time as Bland became Commander in Chief.

85 Crosse matriculated in Leiden on 13 October 1735, *Album studiosorum Academiae Lugduno-Batavae* (n 46) col 953. He had already been admitted as an advocate on 29 July 1735: Books of Sederunt of the Lords of Council and Session, SRO CS.1/12 fo 38v. Studying at Leiden after admission was unusual, though by no means unknown, but the name is sufficiently uncommon for the identification to be certain. Presumably Crosse had already studied law in Scotland, though I have been unable to trace this.

"a very Good scholar";[86] he presumably wrote similarly to Argyll. The suspicion that he would be sinecurist, however, was obviously widely shared. It was certainly known to Montrose who told Tweeddale, which might suggest that Argyll also may have known it; Montrose's information came from the professors, however, and since we do not know if he or they had approached Argyll at this time, it must remain uncertain whether Argyll knew of this fear when he solicited Pelham to gain Crosse's nomination, and even if he did, the Squadrone source might have made him dismiss the information as prejudiced (even if favouring his preferred candidate) in the face of Forbes' warranty of Crosse's suitability.

Crosse was thus able to write to Forbes in February, thanking him for the successful recommendation.[87] He laid his royal presentation to the chair of 26 March before a University Meeting on 4 April and was duly admitted.[88] He enjoyed the salary from the date of Forbes' death, although in 1752 the University sought the return from him of an overpayment.[89] When Cochrane wrote to Argyll thanking him for procuring Crosse's appointment, he stated that he had "to make the acknowledgements of the Magistrates and most of our principal inhabitants".[90] The acknowledgements of the professors are notably missing. Though Cochrane, of course, could not claim to speak for them, their sentiments seem to be well indicated by the unanimous award to Lindesay of the degree of LLD on 27 June 1746, because he had "taught the Civil Law in this place with great success and approbation for several years, and [had] thereby been of considerable use to the university, and that his skill in the Laws [was] well known".[91] Crosse was joining a University whose professors were hostile to him, whether Argathelians or supporters of the Squadrone.

C. CROSSE'S TENURE OF THE CHAIR

The patriotic Hanoverian professors of Glasgow unanimously decided on 27 June 1746 to award the degree of LLD to the Duke of Cumberland. Cumberland was still in Scotland enthusiastically pursuing the government's

86 D Forbes to Marquess of Tweeddale, 13 November 1745, NLS Yester MS 7073 fo 22.

87 W Crosse to D Forbes, 15 February 1746, *Culloden Papers* (n 42) 269.

88 GUA 26639 202–204.

89 J Stewart to Principal Campbell, 17 October 1747, GUA 30315; R Mackintosh to N Campbell, 30 March 1747, GUA 30312; GUA 26649 167 (26 June 1752). He had been accidentally paid for a period preceding Forbes' death.

90 W Cochrane to Duke of Argyll, 1 December 1745, *Cochrane Correspondence* (n 59) 46.

91 Minutes of Meetings of Faculty and Dean of Faculty's Meetings 1732–1768, GUA 26645 49.

policy of harsh repression after Culloden, and it was intended that the Rector, Principal, Professor of Divinity, and Professor of Law should present his diploma to him when he travelled south.[92] Principal Campbell accordingly travelled to Edinburgh only to discover that Cumberland, having stayed there only a short time, had already left. Campbell and Crosse consequently waited on Cumberland's secretary, Sir Everard Fawkener, at Holyrood on 24 July, intending to present Cumberland's diploma. Before Fawkener arrived, however, the two men discovered that St Andrews and other places had given Cumberland a gold box, which they did not have. They decided they could not present the diploma, but instead gave Fawkener the university's compliments to Cumberland, and stated that the diploma was being got ready to send to London.[93] It is no surprise that a University Meeting decided on 30 July to procure a gold box for the diploma for Cumberland's LLD. The same Meeting appears to have decided (somewhat irregularly) to award the same degree to Fawkener. A silver box was to be prepared for him.[94] Crosse supervised the making of the boxes in Edinburgh; they do not seem to have been finished until late August, at the earliest.[95]

Crosse meanwhile was assisting the town of Glasgow in its attempts to gain compensation from the government for the exactions of the Jacobites. He had already drafted a memorial on the town's conduct during the rebellion,[96] and was involved in negotiations with Milton and Lord President Forbes on the city's behalf.[97] He accordingly was leaving for London in September to support Glasgow's claims for compensation, bearing letters of introduction from Provost Cochrane to Argyll and Fawkener and burgess tickets for Cumberland and Fawkener in gold and silver boxes.[98] This trip was carried

92 Ibid 48–49.

93 N Campbell to R Simson, 24 July 1746, GUA 58445.

94 GUA 26639 216. I can find no trace of the awarding of the degree to Fawkener in the minutes of the Dean of Faculty's Meetings 1732–1768 which were the meetings that awarded degrees at this time.

95 W Crosse to G Ross, 5 August 1746, GUA 58445; Principal Campbell to unnamed, 15 August 1746, GUA 27007; on the account for the gold box, see GUA 26649 25 (10 February 1747).

96 "Memorial stating the Facts relative to the Conduct of the Town of Glasgow during the present Rebellion" (original in Crosse's hand), *Cochrane Correspondence* (n 59) 80–85; see also "Reasons for Compensation of the Losses sustained by Glasgow during the Rebellion", ibid 78–80.

97 W Cochrane to D Forbes, 31 May 1746, W Cochrane to Lord Milton, 1 June 1746, ibid 87–88 and 90–91; W Cochrane to D Forbes, 2 June 1746, D Warrand (ed), *More Culloden Papers*, 5 vols (1923–1930) vol v, 95.

98 W Cochrane to Duke of Argyll, September 1746, W Cochrane to E Fawkener, September 1746, *Cochrane Correspondence* (n 59) 98–99. See also the extract from Glasgow Town Council Minutes, 8 September 1746, ibid 122–125.

out at Crosse's own expense, as he presumably saw it as a good opportunity to further his acquaintance with men who could advance his career, and it enabled him to thank Argyll in person for securing him the professorship.[99] (A year later the city compensated him for his expenses.)[100] Crosse's trip must have seemed to his colleagues an excellent chance for the delivery to Cumberland and Fawkener of the diplomas with their gold and silver boxes. It was therefore decided to entrust the task to him. His sojourn in London was to prove protracted.

Crosse wrote from London to the Principal on 2 October 1746, reporting the delivery of the diplomas to their recipients that morning. He also stated that he would be detained "much against [his] will" for some further weeks in London. He explained that "[t]he Troubles in which the country was involved, put all thoughts of application to business out of everybody's head as well as [his]", so that he could not be ready to teach law this winter, "the First forming of prelections being as everybody knows a work of very great labour, especially in Law". He accordingly asked to be excused from teaching.[101] A University Meeting held on 15 October considered this letter. The minutes record the Meeting's view of 'the importance of having Law taught here sufficiently, and the advantage of having had it taught so here for several years past, and the loss the University will certainly sustain if it be not taught this year". A committee was appointed to write to Crosse by "this post" expressing this opinion, insisting that law be taught this session, and desiring him to reply speedily "in regard the time of Teaching Law is so near at hand".[102] The University went on to insert in the newspapers notices that "the College of Civil Law" would open at the beginning of November.[103] Crosse wrote from London on 25 October submitting his judgement to that of the faculty that law should be taught this year, and undertaking to "give the proper directions for satisfying the faculty". He supposed that "the Gentleman who taught during [his] predecessors time [would] not be disagreeable".[104] This letter was considered at a Meeting on 19 November, to which it was also reported that Crosse had agreed with Lindesay that the latter should teach if this was agreeable to the University.

99 W Cochrane to Duke of Argyll, September 1746, ibid 98–99.

100 Extract, Glasgow Town Council Minutes, 7 May 1747, ibid 125–126.

101 W Crosse to N Campbell, 2 October 1746, GUA 58445.

102 GUA 26639 218.

103 *Glasgow Courant*, 13–20 and 20–27 October 1746.

104 W Crosse to R Simson (Clerk of the University Meeting), 25 October 1746, GUA 30281.

The Meeting consented.[105] Lindesay thus taught in Crosse's place, although the two disputed over how much of the salary should go to the former.[106] This episode must have confirmed the faculty in their prejudice against Crosse; their firm opposition to his request (not on the face of it unreasonable in the circumstances) and their subsequent actions seem to have been calculated to make Crosse's life difficult in an attempt to hound him from the chair.

Crosse examined a candidate for the degree of LLD in the summer of 1747, for which he received a fee.[107] But he wanted leave of absence for another year. The University noted at its Meeting on 14 October 1747 at the opening of the next academic year that Crosse "at his earnest desire" had been allowed an approved substitute to teach for him the previous year, and appointed the Clerk Robert Simson, to send an extract of a resolution requiring him to come to Glasgow "to reside and teach at the Statute time the first of November Next", because it was "prejudicial to the Interest of this societie" to allow him to continue using a substitute.[108] Crosse wrote back to the Clerk on 15 October acknowledging receipt of the extract of the resolution which he thought "a little hard"; he promised a definitive answer "in a post or two", though noting that the leave he requested was for one year only, "and the inconvenience of residing very great", which he hoped would cause his colleagues to change their minds.[109] This they refused to do, and Crosse wrote again on 29 October promising to be at Glasgow in the next week, and undertaking to begin teaching on 10 November.[110] He sent another letter to the Clerk on 7 November, stating that business continued to detain him in Edinburgh for a week longer, promising to be at Glasgow the week after next.[111] Seven days later Crosse wrote again to the Clerk, indicating that his business in Edinburgh would not so soon be finished, and that it would be inconvenient to move his family at this time of year upon such short notice. He added that Lindesay was willing to teach Civil Law, and he asked his colleagues to excuse his attendance this year, but declared his resolution either to reside the next year or "dispose of the Office".[112] This last promise must have been attractive, as the Clerk wrote on 16 November stating the

105 GUA 26639 221–222.

106 W Crosse to R Simson, 15 October 1747, GUA 30282 mentioning Lindesay's refusal of the share of the salary offered him by Crosse, which must refer to academic year 1746–1747.

107 GUA 26645 51–52, 55 (26 June 1747, 27 June 1748). He received £7/10/–.

108 GUA 26639 236–237.

109 W Crosse to R Simson, 15 October 1747, GUA 30282.

110 W Crosse to R Simson, 29 October 1747, GUA 30283.

111 W Crosse to R Simson, 7 November 1747, GUA 30284.

112 W Crosse to R Simson, 14 November 1747, GUA 30285.

masters' view that Crosse should declare by the end of May next whether he would teach or resign his post. Crosse undertook to do so in a letter dated 17 November.[113]

A University Meeting held on 23 November considered Crosse's letters of 29 October and 7 and 14 November. The Meeting granted Crosse leave on "the Express condition That he shall before the beginning of May next send to the University meeting a plain and final Declaration whether he is to reside here, or quit his office in such time, that the University may be provided with a Professor of Law against the beginning of Next sessions of the College". The Meeting went on to authorise Lindesay to teach but resolved that in future no permission would be given for the teaching of law by a depute, and that the Professor of Law should reside and teach himself. The Clerk was instructed to send an extract of the permission granted and of the resolutions requiring Crosse to answer.[114] He replied from Edinburgh the next day promising to conform to his colleagues' resolutions.[115]

Whether or not Crosse gave the necessary undertaking by the end of May is unknown, but he was in residence for the next academic year, and advertised classes in the *Glasgow Journal*.[116] It is tempting, if perhaps unjust, to suppose this residence was not unconnected with his recent appointment as Sheriff Depute of Lanarkshire.[117] Three students applied to him in November for the course on the *Digest*. Crosse refused their request, telling them that he was unprepared for such a college. Two of these students, Lockhart Gordon and David Ross, then wrote to the Rector, George Bogle of Daldowie, on 17 November complaining of Crosse's refusal, narrating that they had already studied the *Institutes* with Lindesay the previous year, now wished to progress to the *Digest*, and had only returned to Glasgow this session on assurances that Crosse would teach.[118] This must have confirmed the Faculty's fears that a sinecurist as Professor of Law would discourage enrolments. The same day the Rector wrote to Crosse telling him of the complaint. Crosse replied on 21 November. He explained that in his view the best method

113 W Crosse to R Simson, 17 November 1747, GUA 30286 (the letter of R Simson to W Crosse, 16 November 1747, not located).

114 GUA 26639 238–239.

115 W Crosse to R Simson, 24 November 1747, GUA 30287.

116 See L Gordon and D Ross to G Bogle of Daldowie, Rector, 17 November 1748, GUA 30222. (A relevant copy of the newspaper has not survived.)

117 For his warrant as Sheriff Depute, see SRO photostat of Warrant Books (Scotland) RH 2/4/411/198; W Crosse to Lord Milton, 4 April 1748, NLS Saltoun MS 16657 fo 182 (accepting office as Sheriff Depute). This may explain why he was in Glasgow on 24 June 1748, GUA 26639 246.

118 L Gordon and D Ross to G Bogle, 17 November 1748, GUA 30222.

of teaching Civil Law and the practice of other professors was to begin the first year's teaching with the *Institutes* and the next year to go on in a second course to the *Digest*, "the more difficult and abstruse parts of the Law". He had accordingly declined to begin a course on the *Digest* because young students were not capable of being taught it, and because students who had been taught the *Institutes* "upon a Plan and System different" from his could not profit from it but would become confused. He further pointed out that the two students who had complained were taking a course on the *Digest* with Lindesay, "a private teacher here", and a second course on the same topic from a different teacher would only confuse them. Crosse concluded his letter by observing that he was the proper judge of how he would teach Civil Law "when a competent number of Scholars shall offer", and what part of it he would teach, but that he desired his colleagues' advice.[119] The same day was held a University Meeting that Crosse attended. The students' and Crosse's letters were considered. The Meeting decided that "it was very Necessary for the advantage of the Society, that the Pandects as well as the Institutes should be taught to such students as applied to the Professor of Law for them". Crosse undertook to teach a course on the *Digest* and asked the Rector to inform the students of this decision.[120]

The two students accordingly twice waited on Crosse and were told by him on 29 November that he would not teach the *Digest* unless he had five students for the course. The two wrote to the Rector the next day informing him of this and asking for redress.[121] The same day three other students, George Maxwell, John Damer and Alexander Wedderburn, wrote to the Rector stating that, following an advertisement in the *Glasgow Journal*, they had applied to Crosse for a course on the *Institutes*, and had been told by him that he would not teach the *Institutes* unless he had five students for the course. They also asked for redress.[122] The Rector wrote on 30 November to Crosse informing him of the students' complaints, and received a reply the next day. Crosse relied for his position on an interpretation of the Act of 1727 that had arisen from the Royal Visitation in 1726–1727. This stated:

> That the professors of Divinity, Law, Medicine, Oriental Languages, Mathematics, and History, shall yearly teach the business of their respective professions whenever five or more scholars shall apply to them, and that they give not under four lessons every week.

119 W Crosse to G Bogle, 21 November 1748, GUA 34674 (typed transcript of original).

120 GUA 26639 256.

121 L Gordon and D Ross to G Bogle, 30 November 1748, GUA 34676 (typed transcript of original).

122 G Maxwell, J Damer, and A Wedderburn to G Bogle, 30 November 1748, GUA 34675 (typed transcript of original).

> That in case the said number of five scholars do not apply to the said professors betwixt the sitting down of the College and the first day of December thereafter, that such professors shall, after the first day of December aforesaid, prelect publicly once every week at such hour and upon such day of the week as the Faculty shall appoint.
>
> That the professors above specified shall either continue their Colleges from the first day of November to the last of May yearly, or if their classes be sooner finished, that they shall weekly thereafter give public prelections to the last day of May, as in the case of scholars not applying for teaching.[123]

Crosse argued that this Act required him to teach only if five students applied for one course, not three for one and two for the other. He added that if the Faculty put another construction on the Act, then he would teach "as well as [his] present low state of Health [would] allow".[124] The Rector produced these three letters to a University Meeting held on 1 December 1748. Crosse was not present. The Meeting ruled:

> [T]hat the Statute of Visitation obliged any Professor to teach whenever five or more scholars applied to him; whether all for one part of his Profession or some of the five for one and the rest for another, and particularly that the Professor of Law was obliged to teach if five students, tho some for the Institutes and others for the Pandects applied to him. . . . And that in all time coming he shall be obliged to teach whenever five students shall apply to him whether all for the Institutes, or all for the Pandects, or some of these five for one and the rest for the other.

Crosse thus had to teach the five students, and was allocated the Divinity Hall as his class room, where he was to begin on Monday 5 December at a time convenient to the students who had other classes to attend. The Meeting postponed further consideration of Crosse's conduct until he was present.[125]

Crosse and the students next disagreed over fees. They applied to the University for regulations on the fees that they should pay him. A Meeting on 7 December delayed consideration of this proposal until Crosse was present.[126] The fees he should charge were considered on 27 December. Crosse gave his view, and left the Meeting "by reason of Indisposition". The Meeting accordingly postponed further consideration until he could again be present.[127] Such consideration did not take place.

The Rector intimated to a University Meeting on 30 January 1749 that he had received a letter from Crosse on 17 January, stating that the professor

123 Royal Visitation 1727, in 1837 Parliamentary Papers XXXVI 274–278 at 277.
124 W Crosse to G Bogle, 1 December 1748, GUA 30288.
125 GUA 26639 257–258.
126 Ibid 259.
127 Ibid 261.

had been advised by his physicians to go to the country for some weeks, and had resolved to do so for three weeks or a fortnight, and return to carry out the duties of his office as soon as his health permitted. Crosse had enclosed the "Consultation" of his physicians with his letter, and had already left town. Consideration of this was deferred until the next University Meeting.[128] This took place on 1 February. The University declared that it was "blameable in any Master to leave the Town in time of session" without its permission, but added that Crosse was excused by virtue of his physician's advice to leave as soon as he could. The Clerk was appointed to write to Crosse to ask him when he thought he would be able to return, or if it would be necessary to appoint a substitute.[129]

The Clerk wrote to Crosse on 4 February. The latter replied from North Berwick on 10 February, stating his health was rather better, but that he was recuperating slowly, so he could not yet decide whether he could return this season or at what time; he undertook, however, to send a positive reply in ten days or a fortnight, after he had spoken with his physicians in Edinburgh.[130] The Clerk reported this letter to a University Meeting on 27 February, informing it that Crosse had not sent the promised positive answer. The Meeting appointed the Clerk to write back, asking Crosse again whether he would be able to return in time to resume his lessons, or, if not, would immediately appoint a substitute with the approval of the University.[131] Crosse wrote on 2 March to the Rector, stating that he could not return soon enough to finish the course on the *Digest* by the end of the session, and would not be able to tell until the end of the month if he could return to finish the course on the *Institutes*. He had not replied to the Clerk's letter.[132] A University Meeting on 20 March asked the Clerk to write again to Crosse by this post, since he had not given an explicit answer to the former's letter, and had not mentioned a substitute in his letter to the Rector. The Clerk was to tell Crosse that the University Meeting thought that he had "not treated them in the manner he ought", and required him either to return forthwith to finish his lessons, or immediately nominate an approved substitute. Failing either of these, "they [would] take what methods they think proper to do the University justice".[133]

128 Ibid 263.
129 Ibid 264.
130 W Crosse to R Simson, 10 February 1749, GUA 30289.
131 Minutes of University Meetings 1749–1759, GUA 26640 1.
132 (Not surviving) reported in ibid 4 (20 March 1749).
133 Ibid 4.

Crosse next wrote to the Rector on 21 March from North Berwick, stating that he had had no answer to his last letter, that he had been taking medicines and exercise to recover his health, but that his physicians did not think him well enough to teach even one class. He asked the Rector to inform his colleagues that he could not teach the *Institutes* as he had proposed, and suggested that the students attend the class being taught by a private teacher (obviously Lindesay).[134] The Rector sent this letter on to the Clerk.[135] Crosse next wrote to the Clerk from Edinburgh on 28 March, acknowledging receipt of the latter's letter of 20 March, and claiming not to have received the earlier letter. He stated that he had not thought it necessary to name a substitute, since "there was a private Teacher, who formerly had been approven by the University actually teaching the same Colledges [he] had taught". Crosse left it to his colleagues to name that teacher or any other they thought fit. Crosse presumably had not wished to name a substitute as it would have meant sharing the salary; he now promised to "take care" that the substitute would be "satisfied", if in his power.[136] A University Meeting considered this letter on 31 March 1749, and duly appointed Lindesay as Crosse's substitute.[137]

D. CONCLUSION

Crosse resigned the chair with effect from 10 October 1749, shortly before the next year's classes in law were due to start.[138] The Faculty's fears in 1745 that he would treat the chair as a sinecure had been proved right.[139] The immediate resistance to Crosse's application for leave in October 1746 was probably prompted by this worry, and the Faculty's continuing attempts to compel Crosse to teach, or, if he would not, to appoint a substitute must also reflect this and their chagrin at failing to have Lindesay as Forbes' successor. The four years of Crosse's professorship can only have confirmed the Faculty in the view expressed in 1745 to John Graham of Dougalston that

134 W Crosse to G Bogle, 21 March 1749, GUA 30290.

135 G Bogle to R Simson, 22 March 1749, GUA 30290.

136 W Crosse to R Simson, 28 March 1749, GUA 30291.

137 GUA 26640 5.

138 R Mackintosh to N Campbell, 11 February 1751, GUA 30322. Mackie, *University of Glasgow* (n 17) 191, suggests that at the beginning of this session (1749–1750) the same problems occurred; but this presumably was a plausible guess based on Lindesay's appointment in January 1750. Murray, *Memories of the Old College of Glasgow* (n 17) 219, and Walker, *History of the School of Law* (n 17) 25 also err in stating that Crosse resigned at the beginning of 1750.

139 J Graham of Dougalston to M Graeme of Gorthie, 3 November 1745, SRO Montrose Muniments GD 220/5/1606/21.

Lindesay ought to be appointed "Because, they had sufficient Experience of his qualifications for teaching the Law, and were Convinced, that he would give very closs application in attending the students".[140] It was known by early January 1750 that Lindesay had been appointed in Crosse's stead.[141] It is probable that this was an appointment managed by Argyll.

Sinecurists were rare in Glasgow: the only other professor in the middle years of the century who treated his chair as a sinecure was William Rouet, the Professor of Ecclesiastical History, whom the professors succeeded in having deprived of the position because of his absenteeism.[142] But the appointment of a law professor was particularly likely to cause difficulty, since the danger would always exist of the appointee being reluctant to forgo the possibility of lucrative practice in Edinburgh and to leave the centre of patronage in the legal profession. Given the small number of law students that seems to have been attracted to the University of Glasgow at this time,[143] the fees earned by the professor would probably not be such as to counterbalance the temptation to remain in Edinburgh, unless the professor were sufficiently energetic and talented to draw students. The minutes of the University Meetings, however, show that the professors were very anxious that law teaching should continue. It attracted students who would probably enrol in other classes, and who might well go on to hold influential positions from which they could assist their *alma mater*. The University Meetings stressed how important it was "to have Law taught in the best manner in this University".[144] A minimum requirement was that the professor not treat the chair as a sinecure.

One may wonder if Crosse's appointment as Sheriff Depute early in 1748 had not been made in the hope either that he would resign the chair so Lindesay could succeed, or that he would pay greater attention to his duties at the University because he would necessarily be more frequently present in the area. That the appointment was made on the recommendation of General Bland rather than of Argyll or Milton does not necessarily contradict this, especially as Milton wished to have Crosse appointed Sheriff Depute of Renfrew. Bland, of course, may simply have favoured him because of his activities in the Rebellion and because he was neither an Argathelian nor a supporter of the Squadrone. The office of Sheriff Depute of Lanark was

140 Ibid.
141 See *Caledonian Mercury*, 16 January 1750. Lindesay's presentation was read to a University Meeting on 19 January 1750 and he was admitted on 7 February 1750, GUA 26640 22 and 23.
142 Mackie, *University of* Glasgow (n 17) 192–193.
143 See Cairns, "Origins of the Glasgow Law School" (n 24) at 175–176, 179–180 and 190–194.
144 GUA 26639 258 (1 December 1748); see also ibid 219 (15 October 1746).

lucrative, with a salary of £200 per annum. Fees and perquisites would have made the office worth more.[145] One may likewise speculate whether pressure from above was exerted on Crosse to resign, given that he did so just shortly before the new session of classes on Civil Law was due to start. On the other hand, it seems most likely that he may simply have been unable any more to face the continuing war of attrition with the Faculty, who had deprived him of much of the benefit of treating the chair as a sinecure by compelling him each year to appoint a substitute with whom he had to share the salary. The pressure from his colleagues may even have promoted his breakdown in health in 1748–1749. The way Crosse was driven from the chair would have warned those controlling appointments only to choose those who were serious candidates and those who sought appointments that they would have to teach.

The choice of Lindesay as Forbes' successor made by the faculty and, initially, until other influences came to bear, by Argyll had been shown by events to have been correct. It is obvious that Crosse's appointment came about in very special circumstances. Men with considerable influence on Argyll had solicited it in a time of emergency. Crosse had been very useful to them. The chair may have seemed a fitting reward. The choice of Crosse also shows that a politician based in London, as was Argyll, was open to pressure from his Scottish agents, on whom he had to rely, to secure appointments he himself did not favour, especially in times of general political crisis. If Montrose and the professors knew in November 1745 that Crosse wished the chair as a sinecure, so may well have Argyll; were this the case, he must have been aware that the appointment of a sinecurist whom the University did not want might well lessen his influence with the Faculty. This must have been particularly galling. William Forbes had at one time been regarded by Argyll as a political enemy;[146] now his successor would be a man on whom he could place little reliance and from whom he could expect little support. This would only underline the difficulties faced by Argyll in the difficult months of October to December 1745, especially since Crosse's patron, Duncan Forbes, was scarcely Argyll's loyal adherent. Whatever may have been Argyll's authority at other times, this episode shows his control over appointments to have been very weak indeed at this period. His dependency on his Scottish agents had deprived him of any real choice in the matter. This raises the tantalising question – which cannot be answered

145 On the recommendation and the salary, see SRO photostats of State Papers (Scotland) RH 2/4/368/194 and 212; on Milton's recommendation of him for Renfrew, see SRO photostats of State Papers (Scotland) RH 2/4/368/208 and 213.

146 Earl of Ilay to Lord Milton, 2 December 1727, NLS Saltoun MS 16535 fos 133–134.

here – of whether at other times Argyll's power may have been shakier than is commonly supposed. Indeed, what is most notable is how little control over this appointment was exercised by any of the "great men" in London – Argyll, Montrose, Tweeddale – who were interested in it.

The secure system of management of appointment to offices had broken down with the political collapse of Tweeddale and the Squadrone and the eclipse of Argyll, allowing the University, both Argathelians and Squadrone men, to support Lindesay who had been dealing with both and whom they knew to be suitable, but also allowing Argyll to be manœuvred into securing the nomination of Crosse. Roger Emerson has written of Argyll that "[h]e seems to have wanted to appoint polite, accomplished and meritorious gentlemen to university chairs; generally he did so".[147] Crosse was one of his failures: an absentee professor could do nothing to further the type of polite, enlightened education in Civil Law that Argyll seems to have valued and had experienced in the Netherlands.

The professors of the University of Glasgow seem to have learned the lesson that speed was important to ensure the appointment of a suitable person to a chair in the gift of the Crown. What happened after Lindesay's death on 2 June 1761 demonstrates this clearly. His death had obviously been expected.[148] The day after it occurred, a University Meeting convened to consider the vacancy, and it was considered as "of the highest importance to the University to have it properly supplied". The Meeting resolved to recommend to the Earl of Bute that John Millar was "a proper person for the office that no time may be lost in making application". A letter to this effect had already been written, and it was produced and read to the Meeting. It was approved and signed at the meeting by Leechman, the Vice-Rector. The minute recorded that the letter was "to be sent by this nights post".[149] Bute replied from London on 10 June stating that he hoped to transmit the royal nomination in a few days.[150] This letter was read to a University Meeting on 16 June, and Leechman was appointed to write thanking Bute in the name of the University.[151] On the same day Bute had written to Leechman informing him that he had laid the University's request for Millar's appointment before

147 Emerson, "Lord Bute and the Scottish Universities" (n 2) at 150.

148 *Glasgow Journal*, 28 May–4 June 1761 noted that Lindesay's death on 2 June was "of a lingring illness".

149 Minutes of University Meetings 1760–1763, GUA 26642 55 (3 June 1761).

150 Earl of Bute to W Leechman 10 June, 1761, GUA 31999. The original letter seems missing from the archives; but it was copied into the minutes of the University Meeting, GUA 26642 56 (16 June 1761).

151 GUA 26642 56.

the king who had acceded to it, and had already signed a warrant for the presentation in favour of Millar.[152] Millar's presentation was read on 26 July 1761 before a University Meeting that decided he would be admitted after signing the Confession of Faith, giving a discourse *De testamentis ordinandis* "by way of trial", and taking the oath *de fideli*.[153] He was duly admitted in this way on 15 July.[154] This was remarkably speedy.

In an important study of Bute's exercise of patronage over the Scottish universities, Roger Emerson has argued that Bute and the political machine he had inherited from Argyll were "even more insistent than Argyll had been that merit and known achievements be the criteria for university appointments".[155] This no doubt made him ready to support the choice of Millar, who was a protégé of both Adam Smith and Lord Kames, and who was to have a brilliant career in the Regius chair.[156] The absentee Rouet expressed the hope that Millar had been recommended by the university,[157] and the professors' apparent unanimity must also have influenced Bute who presumably had already been solicited for Millar's appointment before Lindesay's death; Bute was high in the king's confidence, which, as Emerson has pointed out, "made quick work of this business".[158] But what is notable is just how organised and quick off the mark was the University, even though this was not unusual when Regius chairs were concerned.[159] The appointment of Crosse against the professors' wishes had taught them that to secure the appointment of the man they considered most suitable for the Regius Professorship of Civil Law it was necessary to act both decisively and rapidly. This they did in the summer of 1761 with outstanding success, ensuring the nomination of a man who was to raise the University of Glasgow to an unrivalled position of eminence and prestige in legal education in late eighteenth-century Britain.

152 Earl of Bute to W Leechman, 16 June 1761, GUA 32001. The warrant had been issued on 15 June 1761: J Redington (ed), *Calendar of Home Office Papers of the Reign of George HI. 1760–65* (1878) 141.

153 GUA 26642 61. His appointment was reported in the *Glasgow Journal*, 25 June–2 July 1761.

154 GUA 26642 65. Leechman had questioned the authority of this meeting, and Millar was admitted only after several hours' wait: a meeting on 26 August 1761, ibid 66–67, which the Rector, the Earl of Errol, attended, approved the proceedings.

155 Emerson, "Lord Bute and the Scottish Universities" (n 2) at 151.

156 John W Cairns, "'Famous as a School for Law, as Edinburgh . . . for Medicine': Legal Education in Glasgow, 1761–1801" (forthcoming).

157 W Rouet to Simson, 10 July 1761, GUL MS Murray 660.

158 Emerson, "Lord Bute and the Scottish Universities" (n 2) at 153–154.

159 I am indebted to Roger Emerson for the information that expedition was not unusual as regards the succession to Regius chairs, but that it tended to be greatest when death was unexpected and the succession unplanned (private communication).

7 "Famous as a School for Law, as Edinburgh . . . for Medicine": Legal Education in Glasgow, 1761–1801*

On 9 January 1827 a special sub-commission of the Royal Commission for Visiting the Universities and Colleges in Scotland questioned the current Regius Professor of Civil Law at Glasgow University, Robert Davidson. Davidson described his professorship as being in Civil or Roman law, adding that he lectured on Scots law in a course lasting one year. He revealed, however, that the course on Roman law was not always taught, because often fewer than five students appeared to take it, and he was no longer willing to lecture to such a small number. He had not taught it now for four or five years. When the commissioners asked him if, before that, it had been regularly taught, Davidson replied: "Mr. Millar, my predecessor, was a man of great eminence; he was quite a speculative man; I consider myself rather a practical man. This was a very famous school of Roman Law in Mr. Millar's time."[1]

Davidson explained that the bulk of his pupils were writers' clerks and apprentices in Glasgow, who afterwards regularly went to writers' offices in Edinburgh and often took a course of lectures from the Edinburgh Professor of Scots Law before returning to practice in Glasgow. Very few joined the Faculty of Advocates. Statistics provided to the commissioners also showed that enrolments in law were relatively low. Davidson only attracted students to his lectures in Scots law, which the Faculty of Procurators in Glasgow,

* I have benefited much from the enthusiastic help of Michael Moss and his staff in Glasgow University Archives (henceforth referred to in the text and footnotes of this essay as GUA) and David Weston in Glasgow University Library. To my advantage, earlier drafts were read by Roger Emerson, Andrew Hook, Hector MacQueen, Richard Sher and Alan Watson.

1 *Evidence, Oral and Documentary, taken and received by the Commissioners appointed by his Majesty George IV, July 23^d^, 1826; and re-appointed by his Majesty William IV, October 12th, 1830; for visiting the Universities of Scotland. Volume II. University of Glasgow*, 1837 Parliamentary Papers XXXVI, 146 (henceforth *Evidence*).

the local society of lawyers, required future members to attend (*Evidence* (n 1) vol ii, 145–146). Almost all of his students were from Glasgow and its immediate neighbourhood (University Register of Law Students 1818–1843, GUA 26,798).

The location of the University of Glasgow is one possible reason for Davidson's failure to attract students. "Glasgow lies under many obvious disadvantages, as a school of law", wrote John Craig in 1806.[2] Proximity to the courts was recognised as a major asset in attracting students and eminent professors to the University of Edinburgh.[3] Nor was Davidson alone among Glasgow professors of law in having difficulty attracting significant numbers of students. John Craig reported that law students "seldom exceeded four or five, and sometimes fell short even of that number" before the appointment of John Millar in 1761, although this has proved impossible to verify (Craig (n 2) xi). Yet Millar's extraordinary success during a tenure of forty years shows that Glasgow's distance from the courts is not an entirely adequate explanation for Davidson's problems.

That John Millar was outstandingly successful is clear from all accounts. Arthur Browne, Professor of Civil Law in Dublin, wrote in 1797 that "above all, the learned Professor of Glasgow . . . has acquired most deserved celebrity, and has attracted many of the youth of the country, as well as of England within the sphere of his instruction".[4] Thomas Newte remarked in 1791 that the income from "the Professorship of Law, owing to the reputation of the present incumbent, Dr. Millar, is generally about 900l. per annum". He expressed surprise that Millar had "not been removed to Edinburgh"![5] Robert Heron stated in 1793 that "although Glasgow be the seat of no Supreme Court of Justice; yet has it become famous, above almost every other place in Britain as a school for Law". To hear Millar's lectures, "students resort hither from all quarters of Britain. Glasgow is, in

2 J Craig, "Account of the Life and Writings of John Millar, Esq", prefixed to J Millar, *The Origin of the Distinction of Ranks: or, an Inquiry into the Circumstances which give rise to Influence and Authority, in the different Members of Society*, 4th edn (1806) i at xi (henceforth referred to in the text and footnotes as Craig).

3 *The Edinburgh University Journal, and Critical Review* (1 January 1823) 8–13, excerpted in J T D Hall, *The Tounis College: An Anthology of Edinburgh University Student Journals 1823–1923* (1985) 13.

4 A Browne, *A Compendious View of the Civil Law, being the Substance of a Course of Lectures read in the University of Dublin*, 2 vols (1797) vol i, 17.

5 T Newte, *Prospects and Observations; on a Tour in England and Scotland: Natural, Oeconomical, and Literary* (1791) 65.

short, famous as a school for Law, as Edinburgh as a school for medicine".[6] It is another kind of testimony to Millar's influence that so many of the royal commissioners who visited Glasgow University in 1827 were former students who had risen to positions of eminence in law and government, including the Earl of Lauderdale, Sir William Rae, Lord Justice-Clerk Boyle, George Cranstoun (Lord Corehouse) and James Moncrieff.[7]

The reasons for Millar's success were complex, but they seem to lie in his expansion of the Glasgow law curriculum, in the content of his courses and in his abilities as a teacher, as well as in the weakness of legal education in contemporary Edinburgh during crucial periods of his tenure. Millar taught law as a polite, enlightened discipline; Davidson did not, and so lost what Millar had gained.

A. MILLAR AND THE CURRICULUM

The Regius Professorship of Civil Law at Glasgow University was founded late in 1713 and first filled in 1714.[8] There had been three professors prior to Millar: William Forbes, William Crosse and Hercules Lindesay. Forbes taught courses on Roman law and Scots law, but at some point he seems to have given up teaching the latter. Born around 1670, he stopped teaching in the later 1730s, possibly in 1739, because of increasing age, leaving Lindesay to teach classes on Justinian's *Institutes* and *Digest*. Lindesay had hoped to succeed Forbes, but after the latter's death in 1745 the chair was given to Crosse, who attempted to treat it as a sinecure. Lindesay taught in his stead, either privately or as his substitute. Crosse resigned in October 1749 and was replaced early in 1750 by Lindesay, who continued to teach only courses on the *Institutes* and *Digest*, at some time starting to teach the former in English rather than the customary Latin.

6 R Heron, *Observations Made in a Journey through the Western Counties of Scotland; in the Autumn of 1792*, 2 vols (1793) (henceforth Heron, *Observations*) vol ii, 418.

7 On these men as Millar's pupils, see W C Lehmann, *John Millar of Glasgow, 1735–1801: His Life and Thought and his Contributions to Sociological Analysis* (1960) 36–37n (henceforth Lehmann, *John Millar of Glasgow*); for their membership of the sub-commission, see *Evidence* (n 1) vol ii, 1.

8 The following discussion of the early years of the Glasgow chair is drawn from J W Cairns, "The Origins of the Glasgow Law School: The Professors of Civil Law, 1714–61", in P Birks (ed), *The Life of the Law: Proceedings of the Tenth British Legal History Conference* (1993) 151, and "William Crosse, Regius Professor of Civil Law in the University of Glasgow, 1746–1749: a failure of enlightened patronage" (1993) 12 *History of Universities* 159 (henceforth Cairns, "William Crosse").

The creation of the chair in Civil Law was part of the general expansion of the Scottish universities during the early eighteenth century. The faculty at Glasgow were probably influenced in their decision to establish it by the success of the private teachers of law in Edinburgh, and almost certainly by the creation of a chair of Civil Law in the University of Edinburgh in 1710. They wished to develop legal education in Glasgow on the model provided by the faculties of law in the Netherlands, which had built on the work of Humanist scholars in sixteenth-century France. The focus was primarily on Civil Law, though collateral studies in universal history, Roman antiquities and philology were also emphasised. By the time of the creation of the Regius chair, natural law had come into prominence as an integral part of legal education, and municipal law was also increasingly seen as a desirable university discipline.

Legal education did not live up to this ideal under the first three professors in Glasgow. After Forbes stopped lecturing on Scots law, the practice was not resumed – a serious deficiency after 1750, when the Faculty of Advocates started to examine all candidates in that subject. Collateral studies in history and classics had been available at one time; whether they remained so is unknown. On the other hand, natural law was always taught by successive professors of moral philosophy. The main problem faced by legal education in Glasgow, however, was the difficulty of attracting significant numbers of students. This difficulty would have made the chair unattractive to men of ambition, who would have been unable to supplement their low earnings from student fees by practising at the Bar. Nevertheless, the faculty at Glasgow were determined that legal education should succeed, and for that reason they drove the sinecurist Crosse from the chair. They learned from their experience of the first three professors that what was needed was a young, energetic man of ability as a teacher, who would be committed to building up the law classes in competition with those offered by the professors in Edinburgh.

Believing that John Millar was such a man, the faculty moved remarkably quickly to secure his appointment by the Crown. Lindesay died on 2 June 1761; the king signed a warrant for Millar's presentation to the chair on 15 June, and he was duly admitted on 15 July.[9] Just twenty-six years of age, Millar was younger on appointment than any of his predecessors. Unlike

9 See Cairns, "William Crosse" (n 8) at 182–183; R L Emerson, "Lord Bute and the Scottish Universities 1760–1792", in K W Schweizer (ed), *Lord Bute: Essays in Re-interpretation* (1988) 147, esp at 153–154.

Crosse, who at thirty-two had also been relatively young, Millar had not had time to build up connections at the Bar, and the faculty must have hoped he would devote his youthful energies and full attention to developing law classes in Glasgow. As a highly regarded protégé of Adam Smith and Lord Kames, and the first occupant of the Civil Law chair to have been educated entirely in Scotland rather than at least partly in the Netherlands, Millar would have been expected to introduce the polite education in law that the faculty desired.[10]

On the basis of a ruling that the university gave to Crosse, Craig described the classes on the *Institutes* and *Digest* that Millar taught five days each week as "the proper business of the Professorship".[11] Craig suggested that Millar found he still had some leisure, and consequently taught a class on government three days a week and, in alternate years, a class on Scots law on the other two days.[12] He added that "a few years before his death, Mr Millar was led . . . to prepare and deliver a course of Lectures on English Law" (Craig (n 2) xxi), though there is some uncertainty about just when he began to give that class.[13] However this may be, in years when Millar taught either English or Scots law, he would usually have lectured for three hours each day, five days per week.[14] But Craig's remarks raise the general question of whether Millar taught all the other courses from his first appointment to

10 Lehmann, *John Millar of Glasgow* (n 7) 16–18; I S Ross, *Lord Kames and the Scotland of his Day* (1972) 95–97; A F Tytler, *Memoirs of the Life and Writings of the Honourable Henry Home of Kames*, 2 vols (1807) vol i, 198–201.

11 Craig, "John Millar" (n 2) at xix; Cairns, "William Crosse" (n 8) at 177–178. NLS MS 3930 (Lectures on the Institutes, 1779–80) shows that he lectured daily, giving in total 123 lectures; GUL MSS Murray 93–95 (Lectures on the Digest, 1790–91) shows that he gave 116 lectures and also indicates daily lecturing.

12 NLS MS 3931 (Lectures on Government, 1780–81) shows that Millar taught government on Mondays, Wednesdays and Fridays.

13 Heron's *Observations* of 1793 (n 6) vol ii, 418, mentions lectures on English law along with those on jurisprudence, government, Civil Law and Scots law that attracted students to Millar's classes "from all quarters of Britain", but Heron may have attributed to John Millar the lecture course on English law that his son James, then Assistant Professor of Mathematics, was given permission to teach by the faculty on 7 December 1792 (GUA 26694 269). W C Lehmann, "Some observations on the law lectures of Professor Millar at the University of Glasgow (1761–1801)" (1970) *Juridical Review* 74 (henceforth Lehmann, "Observations on the law lectures") points to a letter that John Millar wrote to William Adam on 4 August 1798, which suggests that the lectures on English law were first given by him in 1798–1799 (see also GUL MS Gen 243).

14 "Statistical Account of the University of Glasgow" (1794), in T Reid, *Philosophical Works*, 2 vols (1895; repr 1967) (henceforth Reid, *Works*) vol ii, 734, states that "in his public department" Millar lectured daily for two hours: that is, two hours daily on Roman law, which was what the Act of 1727 was interpreted as requiring him to teach, one hour on the *Institutes*, one on the *Digest*. The third hour of lectures was devoted to government, Scots law, or English law. See *Evidence* (n 1) vol ii, 277.

the chair or introduced them gradually, as Craig implied. The rest of this section will be devoted to teasing out the sequence of Millar's development of the law curriculum, and to considering what may have been his reasons for acting as he did.

We can assume that Millar taught both his statutory, "public" classes on the *Institutes* and *Digest* in every academic session from his appointment until his death in 1801, with the possible exception that in 1761–1762 he taught only that on the *Institutes*, as was common for professors first undertaking their duties. Lehmann claimed that "in his first years, Millar tells us, he tried also to cover, or at least deal with, the Pandects in his basic year-course on civil law".[15] It is implausible that Millar would have taught only one of the two traditional courses on Roman law for more than his first year, or have had a novel, "combined" course, and Lehmann's remark is unsupported by any evidence and probably rests on a misunderstanding of a remark reported in a set of student notes of lectures on the *Institutes*.[16] Craig commented that Millar considered "the employment of a whole winter in tracing . . . the exact line of Roman Law . . . a mere waste of time and study. Whatever it was useful to know of the Institutes, he thought might be sufficiently taught in the half of the session, or term; and he wished to devote the rest of it to a course of Lectures on Jurisprudence". Millar accordingly divided his course on the *Institutes* into two parts, covering, first, the *Institutes* itself and, secondly, jurisprudence (Craig (n 2) xx). Craig implied that before Millar's appointment the whole of one academic year was taken to teach the *Institutes* in Glasgow. The traditional practice in Scotland, however, had been to teach the same course on the *Institutes* twice in one year, as Lindesay did.[17] It is therefore likely that Millar replaced a second, identical class on the *Institutes* with the lectures on jurisprudence.[18]

If, as Craig implied, these lectures on jurisprudence were added some years after Millar's occupancy of the chair in 1761, there is some circumstantial evidence pointing to when and why Millar carried out this innovation.

15 Lehmann, "Observations on the law lectures" (n 13) 67.

16 NLS Adv MS 28.6.8 165–166, first pagination sequence. In so far as newspaper advertisements survive for Millar's lectures, they confirm the teaching of both courses from 1765 onward.

17 See L Gordon and D Ross to G Bogle, Rector, 17 November 1748, GUA 30222. For Professor Dick's similar practice in Edinburgh, see H Arnot, *The History of Edinburgh* (1779) 398.

18 John Erskine's letter to Lord Cardross, 24 November 1762, EUL MS La.II.238, confirms that Millar gave two courses on the *Institutes* in 1762–1763. It also implies that they were identical or nearly identical, but Erskine was probably not well informed about Millar's practice in this respect.

First, it is most unlikely that he would have introduced his lectures on jurisprudence before Smith's resignation as Professor of Moral Philosophy at Glasgow in 1764, as otherwise he would to some extent have duplicated what his teacher taught from that chair.[19] Secondly, it is possible that Millar developed the jurisprudence lectures to counteract the influence of Thomas Reid, who replaced Adam Smith as Professor of Moral Philosophy at Glasgow in 1764.[20] Millar had actively opposed Reid's appointment in a letter of 2 February 1764 that urged Smith to do the same,[21] and Reid and Millar were to become noted for their philosophical disagreements at meetings of the Glasgow Literary Society (Craig (n 2) lxi–lxii). Since Reid, like Smith, included jurisprudence in his moral philosophy classes, which were commonly attended by law students because of the complementary nature of the subject matter,[22] Millar may have wished to teach jurisprudence in a manner more like that of his teacher Smith than Reid could be expected to do. Thirdly, there was by this time a definite demand for classes in jurisprudence. Robert Bruce, the Edinburgh Professor of Public Law and the law of nature and nations, had forty students in session 1763–1764, the last that he taught.[23] Bruce's resignation from this chair in 1764, to be replaced by the sinecurist James Balfour, might mean that Millar started teaching jurisprudence in order to fill a gap in the market. This market demand was created in part by the Faculty of Advocates' exhortations, in 1760 and 1762, that young men proposing to become advocates attend the

19 The strong Smithian foundation of Millar's legal teaching is discussed below. If there is any truth to the speculation I am putting forward here, Millar's lectures on government may also have been started as a Smithian response to Reid's very different way of teaching that subject.

20 This speculation was suggested to me by Nicholas Phillipson.

21 E C Mossner and I S Ross (eds), *The Correspondence of Adam Smith*, 2nd edn (1987) 99–100. Millar wished Thomas Young to succeed Smith. It is unknown what Smith's views were on his potential successors, and there is no reason to believe he agreed with Millar. See *Selections from the Family Papers preserved at Caldwell*, 2 vols in 3 (1854) vol ii, part I, 232–233.

22 On the natural jurisprudence component of Reid's moral philosophy course, see T Reid, *Practical Ethics: Being Lectures and Papers on Natural Religion, Self-Government, Natural Jurisprudence, and the Law of Nations*, ed K Haakonssen (1990). (Reid's assistant and successor, Archibald Arthur, also taught natural jurisprudence; see "Notes, Taken by James Neilson, from Mr Arthur's Lectures on Natural Jurisprudence, given in the University of Glasgow. Glasgow. From 10 March 1788 to [blank] 1788", GUL MS Gen 832.) On Millar's students attending Reid's classes, see T Reid to A Skene, 14 November 1764, in Reid, *Works* (n 14) vol i, 40. On the general relationship of law and moral philosophy, see J Erskine to Lord Cardross, 24 November 1762, EUL MS La.II.238, where Erskine, obviously anxious that Cardross know Pufendorf, agrees that Cardross should take Smith's class on moral philosophy along with Millar's on the *Institutes*.

23 See "Matriculation Roll of the University of Edinburgh. Arts–Law–Divinity", transcribed by A Morgan, EUL, 3 vols (henceforth "Matriculation Roll of the University of Edinburgh") vol i, 262.

classes of the Professor of Public Law and the law of nature and nations in Edinburgh, as well as by the advocates' proposals that intrants be asked questions on the law of nature and nations in their examinations.[24] These factors, then, point to Millar beginning to lecture on jurisprudence as his second course on the *Institutes* some time after 1764.

Much can be learned about the range of Millar's teaching from an examination of newspaper advertisements for his classes. Millar does not appear to have started specially advertising his individual classes until the *Glasgow Journal* for 3/10 October 1765 advertised that he would begin prelections on the *Institutes* and *Digest* on 4 November, and lectures on the law of Scotland on 11 November. An advertisement to the same effect appeared in the same paper on 2/9 October 1766. An advertisement on 15/22 January 1767, however, stated that Millar's lectures on "the Private Law of Scotland" would begin on 3 February. Either Millar was giving the same course of lectures on Scots law twice in 1766–1767, or else his lectures in the first half of the session were on Scots *public* law. Since there was no January advertisement in the session 1765–1766, we do not know which, if either, of these two possibilities applied then. In the *Glasgow Journal* for 15/22 October 1767 Millar advertised prelections on Justinian's *Institutes* and *Digest* and lectures on the public law of Scotland that would begin in November. The same three classes were advertised in October 1768 and 1769, whereas in November 1770 he only advertised lectures on the public law of Scotland. In none of these academic years were there advertisements in January for a class on Scots private law.[25]

On 10/17 October 1771 Millar advertised in the *Glasgow Journal* prelections on Justinian's *Institutes* and *Digest* and "Lectures on Government" (the first time that term is used). In January 1772 he advertised "Lectures on the Law of Scotland" as beginning on the twenty-first of the month (*GJ* 26 December 1771/2 January 1772, 9/16 January 1772). The following

24 Minutes of the Faculty of Advocates, 1751–1783, NLS FR 2 127 (8 January 1760) and 147 (5 January 1762). I am grateful to the Faculty of Advocates for permission to examine and cite their records. For a discussion of this development, see J W Cairns, "The Influence of Smith's Jurisprudence on Legal Education in Scotland", in P Jones and A Skinner (eds), *Adam Smith Reviewed* (1992) 168, and "The Formation of the Scottish Legal Mind in the Eighteenth Century: Themes of Humanism and Enlightenment in the Admission of Advocates", in N MacCormick and P Birks (eds), *The Legal Mind: Essays for Tony Honoré* (1986) 253, esp 265–266.

25 *Glasgow Journal* (henceforth GJ), 20/27 October 1768, 26 October/2 November 1769, 1/8 November 1770. The last of these advertisements does not mention the classes on the *Digest* and the *Institutes*, probably because they had already begun on 4 November; those on public law were due to begin on 11 November and, at this period, normally started a week later.

academic year, for session 1772–1773, Millar advertised prelections on the *Institutes* and *Digest* and lectures on government (*GJ* 8/15 October 1772). There was no advertisement in January 1773 for lectures on Scots law. On 7/14 October 1773, however, the *Glasgow Journal* advertised that Millar would begin in November lectures on government and Scots law, as well as his prelections on the *Institutes and Digest*. Thereafter, with occasional insignificant gaps, due to either missing issues of newspapers or a failure to advertise, the newspaper advertisements reveal the pattern described by Craig of annual prelections on the *Institutes* and *Digest* and lectures on government (sometimes described as public law), and lectures every second year on Scots law (once described, in the *Glasgow Chronicle* for 12/19 October 1775, as Scots private law).[26] This pattern breaks down in the 1790s, apparently because of a change in Millar's practice of advertising rather than a change in his teaching: in 1791, 1793 and 1795 he advertised only lectures on Scots law (these are years when he would have taught this class according to his regular pattern), and in 1799 he once again advertised classes on the *Institutes, Digest*, government and Scots law, thus conforming to his earlier established practice.[27]

The start of Millar's almost continuous practice of special advertising in 1765 suggests that the session 1765–1766 marked a change in his teaching, and this change must have been the introduction of classes on Scots law. Before this date it had been sufficient to advertise generally, so that the *Glasgow Journal* of 21/28 October 1762 merely stated that "the Professors of Medicine and Law will begin their Lectures upon Monday the first of November". This wording implies that Millar then gave only his statutory, "public" classes on Civil Law, and that interpretation is supported by the allocation to Millar by a university meeting on 11 May 1762 of a classroom for

26 GJ, 27 October/3 November 1774 (*Institutes*, *Digest*, government); *Glasgow Chronicle: or, Weekly Intelligencer*, 12/19 October 1775 (*Institutes*, *Digest*, government, private law of Scotland); no advertisements traced in 1776, 1777, 1778 (probably due to missing issues in surviving runs of newspapers); *Glasgow Mercury* (henceforth GM), 21/28 October 1779 (*Institutes*, *Digest*, public law, law of Scotland); GM, 5/12 October 1780 (*Institutes*, *Digest*, public law); GM, 4/11 October 1781 (*Institutes*, *Digest*, public law, law of Scotland) (see also GJ, 4/11 October 1781); GM, 10/17 October 1782 (*Institutes*, *Digest*, public law); GM, 16/23 October 1783 (*Institutes*, *Digest*, public law, law of Scotland); GM, 14/21 October 1784 (*Institutes*, *Digest*, government); GM, 20/27 October 1785 (*Institutes*, *Digest*, public law, law of Scotland); no advertisements traced in 1786 and 1787; GM, 7/14 October 1788 (*Institutes*, *Digest*, public law); GM, 13/20 October 1789, and *Glasgow Advertiser and Evening Intelligencer*, 16/19 October 1789 (*Institutes*, *Digest*, law of Scotland, public law); GM, 21/28 September 1790 (*Institutes*, *Digest*, public law).

27 GM, 18/25 October 1791; *Glasgow Courier* (henceforth GC), 20 October 1791, 24 October 1795 and 15 October 1799; *Glasgow Advertiser*, 21/25 October 1793.

lectures on civil law, making no mention of other classes (GUA 26642 147). This dating of the introduction of Millar's Scots law lectures is further supported by the fact that his account of criminal law is strongly influenced by that in the third edition of John Erskine's *Principles of the Law of Scotland*, which appeared in 1764.[28] Since Millar appears to have done little in the way of radical re-thinking of any of his lectures in later years, this suggests that he introduced those on Scots law after 1764, that is, in academic year 1765–1766. The lectures on government or public law seem to have grown out of his classes on Scots law which, at least from 1767, if not earlier, he divided into the public law of Scotland and the private law of Scotland, possibly not teaching the latter every year, and teaching it from January to May. From 1771 to 1772 he described the former course as being on government or public law generally, and from 1773 he described the latter class, which he now taught every second year beginning in November, as being on Scots law (only once described as Scots private law). Finally, Millar added a class on English law in the 1790s, probably in the sessions 1798–1799 and 1800–1801, in academic years when he would not normally have taught Scots law.

B. MILLAR'S TEACHING

Whatever the exact stages of development, it is clear that by around 1770 Millar had greatly expanded the curriculum of legal studies in the University of Glasgow. Although this achievement in itself is insufficient to explain his success, it clearly suggests that he was attracting enough students to make it worthwhile to develop new courses. Millar's curriculum might seem to reflect a traditional, Humanist ideal in legal studies of history and natural law, combined with study of Civil and municipal law, but he had transformed it into something new and exciting. This section will suggest that the content of his courses and his methods of teaching did much to make him such an outstanding success, especially when legal education was weak in Edinburgh between 1765 and 1786.[29]

28 See J W Cairns, "John Millar's lectures on Scots criminal law" (1988) 8 OJLS 364 (henceforth Cairns, "John Millar's lectures"), esp 388–391.

29 See J W Cairns, "Rhetoric, language, and Roman law: legal education and improvement in eighteenth-century Scotland" (1991) 9 *Law and History Review* 31 (henceforth Cairns, "Rhetoric, language, and Roman law"), and "John Millar's lectures" (n 28). Lehmann, "Observations on the law lectures" (n 13) gives a very useful survey of Millar's classes; see also Lehmann, "John Millar, Professor of Civil Law at Glasgow (1761–1801)" (1961) *Juridical Review* 218.

Millar grounded all his courses on law in a philosophy derived from Adam Smith's *Theory of Moral Sentiments*. Millar strongly identified himself as Smith's pupil, even using Smith's image as his seal (see GUL MS Gen 1035/178). It is unnecessary to discuss Millar's legal theory at length, as it has recently been the subject of an important article by Knud Haakonssen,[30] but some general remarks will be useful. Millar's starting point in discussing law is his notion of rights. Laws are based on "the various rights acknowledged and protected by society" (Craig (n 2) xxxii). These rights are derived from the moral sentiments, according to which actions are approved on the basis of their utility and propriety. When individuals are wronged, they feel resentment, and spectators feel indignation. Rules of justice arise in this way, spontaneously, from concrete situations. Individuals, then, have a right not to be wronged. Spectators interfere in disputes in order to assist individuals with whose motives they sympathise. They do so not only disinterestedly, in order to prevent an injustice, but also out of self-interest, since they realise that they themselves might someday be in a similar predicament (Craig (n 2) xxvi–xxxv). Rights so established vary from place to place and time to time, according to the character, history and manners of different societies, though Millar also stresses that long-established customs are not readily abandoned and can continue to exist even if defective for a changed society (Craig (n 2) xxxv–xxxix).

The historical elaboration of rights is of great importance in Millar's theory, because once societies have developed beyond a primitive stage, governments provide the means of enforcing rights in the courts and possess the authority to legislate them into law. In his first course on the *Institutes*, Craig says, Millar expounded Johann Gottlieb Heineccius's *Elementa juris civilis secundum ordinem institutionum* (1725) (Craig (n 2) xx).[31] This was the most popular textbook of the day.[32] He started, however, with some

30 K Haakonnssen, "John Millar and the science of a legislator" (1985) *Juridical Review* 41. For a fuller account of what follows, see also Cairns, "Rhetoric, language, and Roman law" (n 29) at 41–43, and "John Millar's lectures" (n 28) 374–380.

31 Craig's claim is readily verified from surviving student notes, e.g., NLS MS 2743 fo 18v. As well as this (incomplete) manuscript of the first course on the *Institutes*, so far the following notes have been discovered as surviving: NLS Adv MS 28.6.8 (first and second course on the *Institutes*, 1777–1778); NLS Adv MSS 20.4.7–8 (second course, 1778); NLS MS 3930 (first and second course, 1779–1780); GUL MSS Murray 78–82 (first and second course, 1788–1789); GUL MSS Murray 96–98 (first and second course, 1789–1790); GUL MSS Gen 812–814 (first and second course, ascribed to 1789); GUL MS Murray 77 (first course incomplete, copied from GUL MSS Murray 96–98 in 1794); GUL MS Murray 332 (second course, incomplete, 1793); EUL MSS Dc.2.45–46 (second course, 1794); GUL MS Hamilton 117 (second course, 1798).

32 An edition of this work aimed at Scottish law students was published at Edinburgh in 1780.

lectures discussing vice and virtue and distinguishing law from ethics.[33] He then raised the question of whether or not legal studies should start with the law of one's own country. He pointed out that in most European countries other than England the practice was to begin with the laws of other nations before concluding with the national law. If this practice were adopted, he commented, then "the Roman law must attract particular notice. The Romans were a great people, possessed extensive territories and therefore must have had much experience as of necessity many private quarrels and disputes would come to be decided in their wide empire" (Adv MS 28.6.8 12). There followed a survey of the history of Roman law and its reception in Europe (Adv MS 28.6.8 12–19).

Then Millar moved on to the text of Heineccius, going through it paragraph by paragraph, though not lecturing on each, and occasionally departing from the sequence for reasons of clarity and ease of exposition (Adv MS 28.6.8 98). He finished with obligations arising *quasi ex delicto*, leaving aside the account of actions. It appears that at one time he had continued to follow Heineccius to the end of the *Institutes*, but gave that up because the account of actions was so cursory that students could not readily follow it. He explained that in the second class, however, he would pay more attention to the courts and forms of procedure of the Romans (Adv MS 28.6.8 165–166). This first course was at a relatively elementary level, though Millar did allude to the social and political causes underlying the law on, for example, *patria potestas* (Adv MS 28.6.8 31–32); it seems normally to have run to around seventy lectures, delivered between early November and early to mid-February (e.g Adv MS 28.6.8 163–166, lecture 73).[34]

The second course on the *Institutes*, that dealing with jurisprudence, opened with advice on reading and then presented a discussion of moral theory, leading to an account of rights and the progress of law (e.g. NLS Adv MS 20.4.7 fos 2–23). Millar analysed law as concerning rights and actions, with rights, in turn, concerning either persons or things. The rights of persons arose from the relationships of husband and wife, parent and child, master and servant, guardian and ward. The rights of things were divided into real and personal. Real rights concerned property, servitude, pledge and

33 E.g., NLS Adv MS 28.6.8 1–11, first pagination sequence; lects 1–3. Parenthetical references in the discussion that follows refer to Adv MS 28.6.8, using (unless otherwise noted) the first pagination sequence.

34 See also, e.g., NLS MS 3930 155–56 (lecture 72, 15 February 1780); GUL MS Murray 96, fo 111v (lecture 65, 8 February 1790).

exclusive privilege. Personal rights arose by contract, delinquency or crime. Actions were the means of asserting these rights.[35]

This analysis is familiar from Smith's *Lectures on Jurisprudence*.[36] In fact, Millar's lectures strongly resemble Smith's, except for Millar's sharper focus on Roman law.[37] The division of law in this way was fundamental for Millar. Thus, in discussing persons in the first course, he told his class that "the method used by our Author is a little faulty beginning with Master and Servant It would have been more natural to begin with the Rights of Husband and wife than of Parent and child, Master and Servant Guardian and Pupil" (Adv MS 28.6.8 25). He thus ignored or failed to appreciate the historical and legal significance of the divisions of the law of persons in the *Institutes*.

A student reported Millar as characterising the second course thus:

> In the first course I endeavoured to explain the fact of the Roman law which seems to have been the chief thing intended in the publication of the Institutes – In doing this I have avoided reasoning on the principles whereon their decisions are founded. In going over the subject a second time I think these principles ought to be the chief consideration and in the course of this Investigation we shall be led to compare the Roman law with that of other Nations. (Adv MS 28.6.8 1; second pagination sequence)

In another set of notes, he is recorded as stating:

> It shall now be our cheif employment to enquire into the principles of the Roman Law, and to compare them with those of other countries. The aim of Students of Roman Law at this period, ought to be not merely to know what was the Roman System. That would be of little consequence of itself. It has properly no authority by the Law of this country, or of most of the other modern nations in Europe. It has however a regard paid to it as the system of Lawiers and Judges of great experience, and of a country which subsisted for such a long tract of time, and where we may consequently expect to find the rules of Jurisprudence of the most perfect kind. As however in the most perfect of all human Systems, there are numberless imperfections and Blemishes, it will certainly be proper in those who study the Roman Law at this period, to enquire into the justice or propriety of these regulations. This can only be done by comparing it with the Laws of other countries, and with our own natural feelings of right and wrong. This is certainly a very usefull exercise, as it enlarges our experience. (NLS MS 20.4.7 fos 1r–2r)

Craig aptly characterised this second class as one "in which [Millar] treated of such general principles of Law as pervade the codes of all nations, and

35 For a useful analytical breakdown of the second course, see NLS MS 3930 299–301. All surviving manuscripts of the second course follow this structure.

36 On Smith's analytical jurisprudence, see above all K Haakonssen, *The Science of a Legislator: The Natural Jurisprudence of David Hume and Adam Smith* (1981) 99–134.

37 A Smith, *Lectures on Jurisprudence*, ed R L Meek, D D Raphael and P G Stein (1978) 397–554.

have their origin in those sentiments of justice which are imprinted on the human heart" (Craig (n 2) xx). This course usually consisted of forty-six lectures, given between mid-February and the start of May (e.g. 1 and 399; second pagination sequence: 46 lectures, 21 February–1 May 1778).

Millar's course of approximately 116 lectures on the *Digest* started at the beginning of November and ran to around the beginning of May.[38] The notes that survive seem to be schematic outlines rather than full reports of what was said.[39] Paragraph references in these notes demonstrate that Millar used as his textbook Heineccius' compend of the *Digest, Elementa juris secundum ordinem pandectarum* (1727), which was, like his compend of the *Institutes*, the popular student textbook of the day. Craig commented on this course:

> The multifarious doctrines to be explained in the Pandects prevented him from shortening the time alloted for that branch of legal study; but, aware that the ordinary arrangement is confused, and almost unintelligible, he soon published a new syllabus, following very nearly the order of the Institutes, according to which he discussed the various and sometimes discordant laws of Rome, and the still more discordant opinions of Roman lawyers. (Craig (n 2) xx)

Although printed syllabuses survive for other courses, none has yet been discovered for Millar's lectures on the *Digest*. One set of student notes states: "The order observed in the Institutes has been formerly explained – But no regard is had to this order, either in the Pandects or Codex and it is difficult to say what has been the view of arrangement in these compilations." Millar accordingly discussed the deficiency of the structure of the *Digest*, and he seems to have referred to his published outline for the order to be observed in the course (GUL MSS Murray 93 fos [1]r–[3]r). Study of the notes shows that, as in the second course on the *Institutes*, he expounded the *Digest* according to the Smithian analysis of law into rights and actions, an approach that involved a complete rearrangement of the sequence of the *Digest* (see Cairns, "John Millar's lectures" (n 28) 378 n 70). Given that the surviving manuscripts contain only a detailed scheme, rather than a full report of what Millar actually said in his class, it is difficult to give a full assessment of this course. As Lehmann notes ("Observations on the law lectures"

38 E.g., GJ, 3/10 October 1765, starting 4 November; GM, 13/20 October 1789, starting 3 November; GC, 15 October 1799, starting 5 November GUL MS Murray 92, fo 55V shows he finished on 29 April 1791, which fits with having started that year on 1 November 1790 (GM, 21/28 September 1790), generally lecturing five days per week and delivering 116 lectures in all.

39 GUL MSS Murray 91–92; GUL MSS Murray 93–95. The first of these consists of two volumes from an originally four-volume set of notes. The second is possibly a copy of the complete version of the first; if so, both date from 1790–1791.

(n 13) 68–70), he obviously dealt with the *Digest* in considerable detail and raised the type of historical issues that interested him. He seems also to have made at least occasional references to modern Scots law (e.g. GUL MS Murray 94 fo [60]r, lect 59). The lectures assumed that students had already attended the course on the *Institutes* (GUL MSS Murray 93 fo [1]r, and 94 fo 48v, lect 54).

From 1773 onward, Millar usually started his lectures on Scots law a week after those on the *Institutes* and *Digest* (e.g. *GJ*, 7/14 October 1773; *Glasgow Chronicle*, 12/19 October 1775; *GJ* 4/11 October 1781), though in the late 1780s and 1790s he tended to start them in the same week (e.g. *GM*, 20/27 October 1785; *GM*, 13/20 October 1789; *GC*, 15 October 1799). The syllabus that Millar published for this course under the title *Heads of the Lectures on the Law of Scotland, in the University of Glasgow* (1777 and 1789) indicates that he aimed to deliver fifty lectures, and surviving class notes confirm this pattern.[40] He finished the course about the beginning of May (e.g. GUL MS 347 477 has the date 4 May 1776 at the end of lect 52). One set of student notes reports Millar as describing this course in these words:

> The Law of any Country comprehends a Set of Rules which the Inhabitants are bound to obey and wherever there is a Rule for performing an obligation there must be a corresponding right to inforce the performance – To every Rule therefore there is a corresponding Right – The enumeration of these Rights will be the same thing as the enumeration of the Rules. – To enumerate the Rights then is the first object of Law
>
> But as it is necessary that every Rule of conduct be promulgated to the people that they may know how to observe them, So it is necessary that some provision be made for enforcing these Rules and compelling the people to observe them – For this purpose Courts of Justice are established – The knowledge of the different Courts – The Causes to which they are competent – and the legal methods of obtaining redress of grievances before these Courts, constitute the second great object of Law – But as the different Courts of Justice and the Jurisdiction of Judges fall properly to be considered in a political point of view though no doubt connected with the Law of a Country – We have therefore reserved these for part of a Course of Lectures on Government
>
> The Lectures therefore proposed to be given on the Law of Scotland naturally divide themselves into the consideration of
>
> 1st Rights and 2d Actions.

40 GUL MS Gen 347, 52 lectures from 1775 to 1776; MS Gen 178, 51 lectures (MS dating from 1783); MSS Murray 83–87, 50 lectures from 1789 to 1790; MS Gen 1078, 50 lectures (MS dated 1792); and (incomplete) MSS Gen 181/1–3 (originally) 50 lectures dating from 1789 to 1790. Special circumstances apply to the last three sets, since they are schematic outlines rather than student transcripts of what Millar actually said in class. An incomplete set of lectures on Scots law dating from 1778 to 1779 is still in the possession of Meyer Boswell Books of San Francisco: J H Baker, "Migrations of manuscripts" (1985) 6 JLH 236.

> Rights may be divided into two Grand divisions, vizt. such as arise from the distinctions of persons and their Ranks in society – and such as are independent of this distinction which is understood to comprehend every other Right – These Rights are therefore distinguished into
> 1st. Rights of Persons.
> 2nd. Rights of Things.

Millar next described the various rights of persons and things, before concluding his analysis of his course with this comment: "Actions depend upon the Nature of the Right they are intended to vindicate, for as every Right may be violated, so there must of course be an action corresponding to every Right" (GUL MS Gen 178 2–5, second pagination sequence).

Thus, the starting point for Millar's account of Scots law was once more his version of Smithian analytical jurisprudence. Millar did not explain here the philosophy underlying it, but rather used it as a scheme of exposition and classification. But just as he referred students to the lectures on government for an account of the Scottish courts,[41] so he probably assumed that students had already taken the lectures on the *Institutes* or were taking them concurrently. Although presented as an assumed classification, it was nonetheless so central to his account of Scots law that it determined his attitude to it (see Cairns, "John Millar's Lectures" (n 28)). Millar himself described the course as following, with a few exceptions, the structure of Justinian's *Institutes*, "chiefly because the order observed therein is best in itself" and "because students of the Law of Scotland are generally supposed to be acquainted with the Civil Law of which the Institutes of Justinian make a part" (GUL MS Gen 178 1–2).

Given that the lectures on English law were slotted, in alternate years, into the time occupied by those on Scots law, they had to be roughly the same length, and this is confirmed by the one set of surviving notes, consisting of forty-eight lectures from session 1800–1801 (GUL MS Gen 243). Whereas the lectures on Scots law, after a short historical survey of sources and some introductory remarks on literature, started with an analysis of the law into rights and actions before dealing straight away with the substantive law in terms of that analysis, those on English law commenced with a relatively lengthy history of the law, a discussion of its peculiarities, and an account of its sources, before explaining the "method" to be followed (GUL MS Gen 243 1–27). Millar told his class:

41 In GUL MS Gen 347, the student who wrote up the fair copy of the notes on Scots law added after them the lectures on the Scottish courts from Millar's course on government.

> To find out a sort of method corresponding with the divisions observed by the English Lawyers, and at [the] same time to enable us to form a distinct idea of the whole system, is one of the most difficult parts of the English Law; and this arises from the want of method in the writings of the English Lawyers. All systems of law ancient as well as modern are subject to this defect, but the English, in a particular manner, from the circumstances already taken notice of, and which it is needless for us here to repeat [suffer from it particularly]. (GUL MS Gen 243 27)[42]

He went on to explain:

> In the first place then, the method followed by the Roman Civilians, and in imitation of them, by the later writers upon Roman jurisprudence, is the radical method we wish to follow. In the next place, we shall with a small degree of accommodation, give the outlines of the English method, reduced to that of the Roman. According to the method adopted by the Roman Civilians, law is divided into two great classes, the doctrine of rights and the doctrine of actions. (GUL MS Gen 243 27)

Millar in fact treated English law according to his Smithian analysis, influenced slightly by the structure of Blackstone's *Commentaries* (GUL MS Gen 243 31–32). For one following a Smithian theory of justice, English law was of particular interest, as Haakonssen explains (*Science of a Legislator* (n 36) 151–53). Millar stated:

> Though considered as a practical system of laws, the English is perhaps as compleat as any system can be; yet it has in it this peculiarity, that it has not like all other systems, been introduced by the speculations of philosophers and legislators; but has arisen to its present state of perfection, slowly and gradually, assisted in its progess by certain accidents, and completed by long experience and observation. (GUL MS Gen 243 1)[43]

Millar's lectures on government or public law attracted the most attention among his contemporaries, and allegedly the most students. The topic was inevitably controversial, and Millar felt obliged, in a letter of 16 August 1784 to Edmund Burke, then Rector of the university, to defend himself from the charge of using the lectures on government to inculcate republican principles (GUL MS Gen 502/36).[44] A comparison of the 1778 and 1783 editions of Millar's published syllabus, *A Course of Lectures on Government; Given*

42 The bracketed words are a conjectural reconstruction, as the manuscript ends at "repeat".

43 For further discussion of Millar's lectures on English law, see J W Cairns, "Eighteenth-century professorial classification of English common law" (1987) 33 McGill LJ 225, esp 233–235, and Lehmann, "Observations on the law lectures" (n 13) 73–76.

44 This letter shows that the allegations of Millar's supposed republicanism (discussed in Lehmann, *John Millar of Glasgow* (n 7) 67–71) predated the era of the French Revolution, when attention was drawn to them by hostile contemporaries.

Annually in the University (the first is bound into NLS MS 3931), reveals that Millar originally intended to devote forty-four lectures to the subject, but sometime between 1781 and 1783 he increased the planned lectures to forty-eight by introducing a new preliminary lecture and another four on the government of Ireland, the national debt, the constitution of Parliament with regard to its division into three branches and the period of its duration, and the state of the royal prerogative, while at the same time reducing three lectures on the English courts to two.[45] This expanded version was thereafter substantially maintained, although Millar did add new matter, such as on the French Revolution, without altering the overall structure of the course.[46]

As actually delivered, the number of lectures could greatly exceed that mentioned in the published syllabus. Thus, in 1780–1781, when following the earlier syllabus of forty-four lectures, Millar in fact delivered fifty-eight (NLS MS 3931 299). Newspaper advertisements reveal that sometimes he started the lectures on government during the same week as those on the *Institutes* and *Digest*, sometimes the week after, but always on the same week as that in which he started to lecture on Scots law, should it be a year in which he was doing so.[47] In 1781 the course finished on 6 April (NLS MS 3931 299), whereas subsequently it ran a few weeks longer (e.g. GUL MS Gen 180/3 fo 665, ending on 29 April 1789; GUL MS Hamilton 116[530], 1 May 1798). This change in timing most probably reflects the expansion of the course.

In 1798 Millar is reported telling his students:

> In studying the Science of Government, the most important object is that of our own Country – but the Governments of other Countries must also be taken into consideration –
>
> The Governments of all Countries discover a great analogy and resemblance from the great uniformity in the faculties, the desires, the wants, the circumstances of mankind –
>
> There must also be, in the government of different nations, a great diversity of regulations –
>
> Thus by comparing the Systems in different Countries we may judge concerning the expediency of different institutions and enlarge our views concerning the principles of Government.

45 That this change occurred after 1780–1781 is clear from the fact that lectures from that date (NLS MS 3931) conform to the 1778 edition of the Course of Lectures on Government. AUL MS 133 is dated 1782 and conforms to the earlier syllabus; since it is a fair copy, however, it is impossible to be certain of the date of the lectures it contains.

46 See *A Course of Lectures on Government; Given Annually in the University of Glasgow* (1787) (bound into GUL MS Gen 180/1); GUL MS Hamilton 116 (1798); GUL MS Gen 290 34–44.

47 E.g., GJ 10/17 October 1771, 8/15 October 1772, 7/14 October 1773, 27 October/3 November 1774; GM 4/11 October 1781, 10/17 October 1782, 16/23 October 1783; GC 15 October 1799.

> For similar reasons we ought to examine each particular system historically, tracing each regulation from the origins through all the subsequent changes. (GUL MS Hamilton 116 1–2)

These considerations led Millar to cover three broad topics in the lectures on government: the origin and progress of government in society; illustrations of this topic from particular governments, namely Athens, Sparta, Rome, France, Germany, England, Scotland, Ireland (after 1781) and ecclesiastical jurisdiction; and the present state of government in Great Britain, including discussions of Parliament, the royal prerogative and English and Scottish courts.[48] The lectures again show Millar's indebtedness to basic tenets of Smith's thought and demonstrate his historical and comparative approach. He thus based the origins of authority either on personal qualities or superior wealth, strengthened by custom which created a habit of obedience (e.g. Mitchell Library MS 99 fo i; GUL MS 289 15–29; GUL MS Gen 180/1 fos 7–16). The progress of government was explained according to Smith's stadial analysis (e.g. GUL MS Gen 289 31–33). Whereas the other four courses all concerned the rights of individuals and the method of their enforcement, that on government dealt with legislative power, national defence and securing public tranquillity by the appointment of magistrates and the establishment of courts of justice (GUL MS Gen 289 1). It thus dealt with the framework within which private rights arose, were recognised and could be enforced.

Millar's five classes were all interrelated and to some extent built on one another. The courses on the *Digest*, Scots law and English law presupposed that students had taken the course on the *Institutes*. The course on government dealt with Roman government at some length, while also dealing with the courts of Scotland and England; the lectures on Scots law referred to those on government in this respect. Within Millar's curriculum, the accounts of legal theory and government were of particular importance, and they obviously indicated where his main intellectual interests lay. His lectures were calculated to promote critical reflection on law by placing it within a historical and political context. His stress on law as recognising the rights of individuals was an aspect of this perspective: government ought to be aimed at preserving and enforcing these rights and inscribing them in law.

48 For a good account of these lectures, see Craig, "John Millar" (n 2) xli–lvii. Among the surviving sets of notes on these lectures are the following: Mitchell Library MS 99; GUL MS Gen 203; NLS MS 3931; AUL MS 133; GUL MS Gen 179; GUL MSS Gen 289–291; GUL MSS Gen 180/1–3; GUL MSS Murray 88–90; GUL MS Hamilton 116. Other sets are privately owned. These sets are listed in chronological order, although the first two are undated. Not all are complete.

Craig rightly summed up Millar's course in jurisprudence in these terms:

> By proving that no institutions, however just in themselves, can be either expedient or permanent, if inconsistent with established ranks, manners, and opinions, a system of Jurisprudence checks inconsiderate innovation, and indiscriminate reform; while, on the other hand, it points out, to the enlightened Legislator, such parts of the municipal code, as, introduced during ruder times, have remained in force, long after the circumstances from which they arose have ceased to exist, and directs him in the noble, but arduous, attempt, to purify and improve the laws of his country. (Craig (n 2) xl–xli)

The course in government instructed the "young Lawyer . . . in the spirit and real intention of the Laws" and opened up "to the future statesman . . . views of human society, of the nature and ends of Government, and of the influence of Public Institutions on the prosperity, morals, and happiness of states" (Craig (n 2) lvii). The type of questions Millar wished his students to consider is indicated by the prizes offered to the law class for essays in 1786 and 1787, on such topics as "Is it expedient that the National Representatives in Parliament should be obliged to follow the instruction of their constituents?" and "Whether is a popular Government favourable or unfavourable to the Fine Arts?" (*GM*, 27 April/4 May 1786 and 25 April/2 May 1787).[49]

The traditional way of teaching law had been for the professor to adopt a particular textbook on which to dictate notes, section by section.[50] Professors would also quiz or "examine" students on the topics of previous lectures. The focus was on students' memorisation of what had been dictated to them. Whereas Scots law was always taught in English, dictates and examinations in Civil Law were traditionally given in Latin (see Cairns, "Rhetoric, language, and Roman law" (n 29) 35–37). Though he followed examples established elsewhere, Millar was very much an innovator as a teacher of law. He extended to the course on the *Digest* Lindesay's innovation of teaching the *Institutes* in English – thus earning the disapproval of the Faculty of Advocates in 1768 (NLS FR 2 (n 24) 255; Cairns, "Rhetoric, language, and Roman law" (n 29) 39–40, 54–55 n 76). In his classes on Civil Law, he examined his students daily on the topics of previous lectures, using Latin because that language was used in the trials in Civil Law for admission as an

49 No other law prizes are ever mentioned in the prize lists published every year at the beginning of May.

50 The method is explained by Alexander Bayne, the first Professor of Scots Law at Edinburgh University, in "A Discourse on the Rise and Progress of the Law of Scotland, and the Method of Studying it", in Sir Thomas Hope, *Minor Practicks: or Treatise of the Scottish Law*, ed A Bayne (1726).

advocate (Craig (n 2) xiii–xiv).[51] Only his first course on the *Institutes* and his course on the *Digest* were closely connected with textbooks, and these were the standard ones of the day.

Millar nonetheless routinely recommended various works to his students. In the second course on the *Institutes*, he continued to examine the class on Heineccius' textbook (Adv MS 28.6.8 1, second pagination sequence), but he also recommended Vinnius' commentary on the *Institutes*, though "both large and often dry", and he generally preferred Vinnius' view to that of Heineccius (Adv MS 28.6.8 2, second pagination sequence; NLS Adv MS 20.4.7 fo 2r). Whereas students with little time were advised to stick to Heineccius, Millar also suggested that they should read "some good author on general Jurisprudence". In words reminiscent of the opening of one set of Smith's *Lectures on Jurisprudence*, Millar recommended Grotius, "the first who wrote on this subject and . . . still one of the best" (Adv MS 28.6.8 2, second pagination sequence; cf Smith, *Lectures on Jurisprudence* (n 37) 397–398). Of commentaries on Grotius, he recommended as by far the best that of Cocceius the younger, presumably *Samuelis de Coccеii introductio ad Henrici de Coceii Grotium illustratum* (1748). The advice to read Grotius was intended for all students, not just those short of time; but he added that "upon disputed points [he] wou[l]d advise [the class] to turn up the Corpus and exercise [their] own Judgment on it" (Adv MS 28.6.8 2, second pagination sequence; NLS Adv MS 20.4.7 fo 2r).

In Scots law, Millar recommended John Erskine's *Principles of the Law of Scotland* (1754) both as the "most distinct book on this Subject", and because "his method is much the same with that we intend to follow". He undertook to refer students to parts relevant to his lectures. He also referred them to Erskine's *Institute of the Law of Scotland* (1773). These two works were the ones he chiefly recommended to students. After Erskine, he recommended *The Institutions of the Law of Scotland* by Lord Stair because "he makes many Comparisons with the Roman law, and reasons much upon the principles". Students were warned, however, that Stair's account of the law was obsolete, and that the work was "ill arranged" (presumably because it did not follow the Smithian division of the law into rights and actions). Millar next described Lord Bankton's *Institute of the Laws of Scotland in Civil Rights* (1751–1753) as gathering together "a most laborious Collection of Facts" and containing many things not found in Erskine or Stair, but "Collected

51 See further G Jardine, *Outlines of Philosophical Education, Illustrated by the Method of Teaching the Logic Class in the University of Glasgow*, 2nd edn (1825) 463–464.

with little Judgement". He also recommended that the class read a complete collection of decisions, and pointed out that Sir George Mackenzie's *Laws and Customes of Scotland, In Matters Criminal* (1678) was inaccurate and obsolete on criminal law (GUL MS Gen 347 6–8). The collection of decisions that Millar wished his students to read would have been an alphabetical one such as Lord Kames' two compilations, *Remarkable Decisions in the Court of Session, 1716–52* (1728, 1766) and *Decisions of the Court of Session; Abridged in Form of a Dictionary* (1741).

Besides not using a textbook as the basis of instruction in most classes, Millar also departed from the tradition of dictating set notes to students. He preferred to speak extemporaneously from headings. The notes surviving from his lectures seem to be of two types: notes taken by students in class, even if written into a fair copy, and schematic but relatively full and detailed outlines of the lectures. Since two of the latter type (GUL MS Gen 1078 and MSS Gen 289–291) are in the hand of Millar's son James, the mathematician, they probably indicate what the professor had in front of him when he spoke.[52] Other sets of outlines may be copies of the notes from which Millar was accustomed to lecture extemporarily.[53] Millar's aim in adopting a freer, more extemporaneous style of lecturing was to engage the students intellectually by making the presentation livelier. In this he is said to have succeeded. He was reputed to be a compelling teacher, who could kindle his pupils' enthusiasm for whatever he taught, and to whom they felt able to turn for advice about their examinations for admission to the Faculty of Advocates.[54]

It is unfortunate that no precise information is available about the size of Millar's classes. On 11 May 1762 a chamber within the college was assigned as a classroom for civil law (GUA 26642 147), possibly because Millar's classes had grown too large for their old quarters. It is certain that Millar attracted increasing numbers of students, for on 10 and 18 October 1775 the faculty authorised alterations in the law classroom in order to increase the number of seats (GUA 26690 324; see also the faculty minutes for 24 January 1777, GUA 26691 90). Anecdotal evidence is unanimous about the large size of his

52 For the argument about the connection with Millar of GUL MS Gen 1078 and MSS Gen 289–291, see Cairns, "John Millar's lectures" (n 28) at 369–371 n 33.

53 In GUL MSS 88–90, on what was originally the title page of each of the first two volumes (now pasted to the end boards), is written: "These Notes contain nothing additional to what are used in the class, unless some very few particulars marked on the left hand page." See also GUL MS Murray 91 fo [i]r: "Copy of the Notes used by Mr. Millar upon the Pandects in the University of Glasgow".

54 See J Millar to A Campbell, Scottish Record Office, GD 170/1990. For a fuller account of Millar's style of teaching, see Cairns, "Rhetoric, language, and Roman law" (n 29) at 39–43, 47–49.

classes. Craig stated that "he had, frequently, about "forty students of Civil Law; while those who attended his Lectures on Government, often amounted to a greater number" (Craig (n 2) xi). Craig's claim gains some collateral support from a pamphlet published early in 1785, in connection with one of Professor John Anderson's many disputes with his colleagues. Hostile to most of the faculty, including Millar, it claims that, as a result of the disputes among the faculty, "the students in the first Law Class are 12 or 14, in the second 4, and in the Government Class about 15; which numbers do not make the half of what were in these classes a few years ago".[55] In the academic session 1784–1785 Scots law was not taught, so it is easy to identify the first class as that on the *Institutes* and the second as that on the *Digest*. Thus, the pamphlet leads to the conclusion that Millar could normally have expected about thirty to forty students in Civil Law and over thirty in government. In the next academic year, in fact, Millar claimed in a letter to Burke dated 13 November 1785 that his enrolments were the highest they had been in some years, despite the continuing dispute in the university (GUL MS Gen 502/40).

Matriculations in law at Edinburgh University provide indirect evidence that throughout the 1770s and 1780s Millar's classes grew significantly in size.[56] Between 1763 and 1770 Robert Dick, the Professor of Civil Law, had between twenty and twenty-eight students each year. During the next twenty years, Dick's students numbered between two and nineteen a year, and matriculations showed a generally downward trend, with no students listed in some years. Between 1763 and 1765 John Erskine, the Professor of Scots Law, had class sizes ranging from thirty-one to forty-six. His successor, William Wallace, had a peak of fifty-two students in 1766–1767, but thereafter his largest class was forty and his smallest ten, with a generally downward trend from around 1770. These figures probably underestimate the total size of the classes, but they suggest that enrolments in law at Edinburgh were dropping over these years. Since it was becoming much less common for Scots to study Civil Law in the Netherlands during this period,[57] the students must have been going to Glasgow.

55 *A Letter by Students of Divinity, Law, Medicine, and Philosophy, in Glasgow College, to the Reverend William Taylor, DD* (1785), sig Cr. For the background, see J D Mackie, *The University of Glasgow 1451–1951: A Short History* (1954) 206–209.

56 What follows is based on data in "Matriculation Roll of the University of Edinburgh" (n 23) vols i and ii.

57 R Feenstra, "Scottish–Dutch Legal Relations in the Seventeenth and Eighteenth Centuries", in T C Smout (ed), *Scotland and Europe 1200–1850* (1986) 128; P Nève, "Disputations of Scots Students Attending Universities in the Northern Netherlands", in W M Gordon and T D Fergus (eds), *Legal History in the Making* (1991) 95.

Millar attracted students not only because he was a skilful teacher but also because Dick and Wallace were not especially distinguished professors. When Millar's pupil David Hume was appointed to the Edinburgh chair of Scots Law late in 1786, enrolments there virtually doubled; and when John Wilde replaced Dick in 1792, the listed students of Civil Law jumped in number from five to twenty-four, though they dropped dramatically in the later 1790s, as Wilde became mentally ill. Millar may well have exploited the weakness in Edinburgh legal education between 1765 and 1786 in order to build up his own classes. He probably started to teach Scots law in the year Erskine resigned, just as he may have started teaching jurisprudence in his second class on the *Institutes* when the Edinburgh chair of Public Law passed to a sinecurist in 1764. The fortunes of Edinburgh as a centre of legal education revived with the appointment of Allan Maconochie to the Public Law chair in 1779, and especially with the appointments of Hume and Wilde in 1786 and 1792, respectively. By then, however, Millar's reputation was well established. The relatively poor state of legal education at Oxford, Cambridge and Trinity College, Dublin no doubt increased Millar's attractiveness among English and Irish students;[58] but his main rivals for students must always have been the professors in Edinburgh, and the statistics drawn from Edinburgh classes suggest that he was very successful in building up his own classes at their expense. Nor do we need to assume that increases in matriculations in law at Edinburgh after the appointments of Hume and Wilde necessarily caused a decrease, or, at any rate, a significant decrease, in the size of Millar's classes because, since students not uncommonly moved between Glasgow and Edinburgh, some who enrolled in law at Edinburgh could also have attended Millar's lectures, while, from the 1780s, the total number of law students in Scotland was increasing.[59]

58 See J L Barton, "Legal Studies", in L S Sutherland and L G Mitchell (eds), *The History of the University of Oxford. Volume 5. The Eighteenth Century* (1986) 593; D A Winstanley, *Unreformed Cambridge: A Study of Certain Aspects of the University in the Eighteenth Century* (1935) 57–60, 122–126; and R B McDowell and D A Webb, *Trinity College Dublin 1592–1952: An Academic History* (1982) 65–66, 81, 138–139.

59 For the increase in the total number of law students, see the statistics on admission to the Faculty of Advocates in the following works by N Phillipson: *The Scottish Whigs and the Reform of the Court of Session 1785–1830* (1990) 189; "Lawyers, Landowners, and the Civic Leadership of Post-Union Scotland", in D N MacCormick (ed), *Lawyers in their Social Setting* (1976) 171, esp at 175; "The Social Structure of the Faculty of Advocates in Scotland 1661–1840", in A Harding (ed), *Law Making and Law Makers in British History* (1980) 146, esp at 148–150. If the Faculty of Advocates was increasing in size, so probably were all bodies of lawyers.

C. CONCLUSION

In 1777 Millar's mentor, Lord Kames, said of current legal education in Scotland:

> Our law-students, trained to rely upon authority, seldom think of questioning what they read: they husband their reasoning faculty, as if it would rust by exercise.
>
> Nor is the exercise of reasoning promoted in any degree by public professors . . . [N]othing is presented to the young gentlemen but naked facts.[60]

The only professor exempted from these criticisms was Millar. "Were law taught as a rational science", Kames added, "its principles unfolded, and its connection with manners and politics, it would prove an enticing study to every person who has an appetite for knowledge. We might hope to see our lawyers soaring above their predecessors; and giving splendor to their country, by purifying and improving its laws" (Kames, *Elucidations* (n 60) xiii).

The success enjoyed by Millar in his forty years in the Glasgow chair of Civil Law was due in large measure to his offering students a full and interesting curriculum intended to foster the type of critical thinking about law that Kames recommended. A key factor in this process was the comprehensive, integrated character of Millar's courses. Millar provided a complete legal education of the polite and philosophical type deemed desirable in the age of the Scottish Enlightenment, covering government and politics, jurisprudence, Civil Law and municipal law. Although some scholars have perceived a tension or contradiction in Millar's thought between his politics and his "scientific" natural jurisprudence,[61] the exposition of politics in his lectures on government was apparently developed from his lectures on the public law of Scotland and was clearly considered by Millar himself to be part of his general curriculum. Rights might emerge historically, but in polite societies, or societies advancing in civilisation, it is the task of government, through the political process, to inscribe rights in legislation and to provide courts to recognise and enforce them. Millar's personal qualities as an energetic and stimulating teacher enhanced the presentation of this new legal curriculum. Although Glasgow's situation may not have been advantageous for a school of law, Millar's ability and energy

60 Henry Home, Lord Kames, *Elucidations Respecting the Common and Statute Law of Scotland* (1777) viii–ix (henceforth Kames, *Elucidations*). For a discussion of Kames' views on legal education, see Cairns, "Rhetoric, language, and Roman Law" (n 29) at 37–38.

61 On this point, see M Ignatieff, "John Millar and Individualism", in I Hont and M Ignatieff (eds), *Wealth and Virtue: The Shaping of Political Economy in the Scottish Enlightenment* (1983) 317. Cf Haakonssen, "John Millar", which I find convincing.

overcame this limitation. This was especially true during the crucial period from the mid-1760s to the mid-1780s, when Millar was making his reputation and had little serious rivalry as a law teacher. The type of complete education in law envisaged by the Glasgow University faculty in 1714 was thus finally achieved by Millar, who succeeded in turning Glasgow into the pre-eminent university for legal study in Britain during the second half of the eighteenth century.

The Glasgow faculty made a brilliant decision in 1761 when they resolved to secure the appointment of Millar; he more than justified their expectations. By teaching law as "a liberal and enlightened science", Millar attracted future statesmen and leaders of the bar to classes that were designed to educate "an accomplished liberal and enlightened Advocate".[62] By contrast, under his successor Robert Davidson, the son of Principal Archibald Davidson, the Glasgow University law school was reduced to providing courses for the apprentices and clerks of provincial lawyers. Davidson made no attempt to perpetuate the broad, intellectually innovative curriculum that had enabled Millar to overcome the problems Glasgow faced as a law school. He had neither the ability nor the will to offer the range of legal education that Millar had developed. It is true that Davidson was competing, very unequally, for students of Scots law against David Hume in Edinburgh, but so, at times, had Millar; and Davidson in his first, years offered only courses in Civil Law, where he did not face such strong rivalry. It is difficult to escape the conclusion that, had not the Faculty of Procurators in Glasgow from July 1796 required apprentices being examined for admission to produce evidence of attendance at a class on Scots law,[63] Davidson would have had virtually no students at all.

Six days after Millar's death on 30 May 1801, Henry Brougham wrote to his friend James Loch, complaining that "they mean to give poor J. Millar's class to that stupidest of all brutes Robt. Davidson".[64] Whatever the justice of Brougham's characterisation, which no doubt owes much to political differences, it is plain that Davidson's personal limitations contributed to the decline of the Glasgow law school from the enlightened eminence to which it

62 These words are drawn from *Report Made to His Majesty by a Royal Commission of Inquiry into the State of the Universities of Scotland*, in 1831 Parliamentary Papers XII, 54.

63 This regulation was introduced by the royal charter granted to the Faculty of Procurators on 1 July 1796. See the Sederunt Books of the Faculty of Procurators, 1761–1796 (esp 4 March 1796) and 1796–1832 (esp 15 July 1796, pp 1, 8, 15, 47), Library of the Royal Faculty of Procurators, Glasgow. I am grateful for permission to examine and cite these records.

64 In R H M Buddle Atkinson and G A Jackson (eds), *Brougham and his Early Friends: Letters to James Loch, 1798–1809*, 3 vols (1908) vol i, 275.

had risen under Millar. In the summer of 1827, a few months after his interview with the royal commissioners, Davidson was rather coolly described in the pages of the *Caledonian Mercury* as "fully adequate" in his academic position, whereas the same article in marked contrast waxed enthusiastic when discussing his more illustrious predecessor: "Celebrated as an author at a time when our country was singularly fertile in great writers, this eminent person acquired a still more enviable reputation as a teacher of law, and by the united force of genius, talents and indefatigable perseverance, raised himself to the very highest place amongst modern *Antecessores*."[65] Small wonder that the royal commission's general report of October 1830, without mentioning names, by implication severely criticised the narrowly "practical" and "technical" programme of the Glasgow law school under Davidson and voiced approval for the broadly "speculative" approach to the training of lawyers that Millar had done so much to develop. "It will be in vain to hope that the independence and character of the Bar can be maintained, if the study of Law is not conducted on an enlightened and philosophical plan", the report asserted.[66] Millar's educational programme was thus endorsed and vindicated.

65 J Browne, *Remarks on the Study of the Civil Law; occasioned by Mr Brougham's Late Attack on the Scottish Bar* (1828) 34–35 (containing Browne's articles from the *Caledonian Mercury*).
66 *Report Made to His Majesty*, in 1831 Parliamentary Papers XII, 53–54.

8 John Millar, Ivan Andreyevich Tret'yakov, and Semyon Efimovich Desnitsky: A Legal Education in Scotland, 1761–1767*

On 15 July 1761, after delivering a discourse "de testamentis ordinandis", John Millar was admitted as Regius Professor of Civil Law in the University of Glasgow.[1] His appointment was to bring a sea-change to the law school at Glasgow, which had languished somewhat in the past few years.[2] The professors of Glasgow, having successfully vanquished the sinecurist William Crosse just a few years before, wished for an active and successful teacher of law and they were determined to have one;[3] in Millar they gained just what they sought and he turned Glasgow into the premier school of law in the United Kingdom.[4] The year of Millar's arrival in Glasgow is significant. It is also the year that two young Russian students, Semyon Efimovich Desnitsky

* I am grateful to the Librarians of Glasgow University Library, Edinburgh University Library, and the Mitchell Library, Glasgow, the Archivist of Glasgow University, and the Trustees of the National Library of Scotland for permission to cite and quote from the unpublished MSS in their care, and to Mr Angus Stewart, QC, Keeper of the Advocates Library, for a similar permission with respect to the Advocates' MSS.

1 Glasgow University Archives (henceforth GUA) 26642, Minutes of University Meetings 1760–1763 65.

2 The following discussion of the early years of the Glasgow chair is drawn from J W Cairns, "The Origins of the Glasgow Law School: The Professors of Civil Law, 1714–61", in P Birks (ed), *The Life of the Law: Proceedings of the Tenth British Legal History Conference* (1993) 151 (henceforth Cairns, "Origins of the Glasgow Law School"), and "William Crosse, Regius Professor of Civil Law in the University of Glasgow, 1746–1749: A Failure of Enlightened Patronage" (1993) 12 *History of Universities* 159 (henceforth Cairns, "William Crosse").

3 Cairns, "William Crosse" (n 2) passim.

4 J W Cairns, "'Famous as a School for Law, as Edinburgh . . . for Medicine': Legal Education in Glasgow, 1761–1801", in A Hook and R B Sher (eds), *The Glasgow Enlightenment* (1995) 133 (henceforth Cairns, "Famous as a School for Law, as Edinburgh ... for Medicine").

and Ivan Andreyevich Tret'yakov, arrived to study in that university, where they were to stay until 1767.[5]

A. SEMYON EFIMOVICH DESNITSKY AND IVAN ANDREYEVICH TRET'YAKOV

While Desnitsky and Tret'yakov attended the lectures of other professors, we know for certain that they attended "Dr Smith's class of Ethicks and Jurisprudence" and "Mr Millar's classes of civil law"; indeed they had attended the last for three years by December 1765.[6] Millar's teaching had thus been of great importance for the two Russians. On 31 December 1765, the two petitioned to be allowed to offer themselves as candidates for the degree of "Doctor in Laws" and Millar was appointed to examine them privately.[7] On 9 January 1766, Millar was able to report that he had examined them privately and found them "qualified to undergo a publick examination".[8] This took place on 16 January, when the professors "approved the specimen they had given of their knowledge in Law" and allocated to Tret'yakov the title *de in ius vocando* of Justinian's *Digest* (D 4.2) and to Desnitsky that *de testamentis ordinandis* (D 28.1).[9] On 8 February, the two students read their theses to the Faculty at Glasgow and left them to be examined: a duty devolved to Millar and George Muirhead, then Dean of Faculty.[10] On 8 April, on Muirhead and Millar's favourable report upon the theses, the two Russians were given permission to print them.[11]

There was no further progress in the examination process for a year; the reasons for this are unclear but, as Brown points out, they cannot exclusively be because of the quarrel of Desnitsky with the famously irascible and difficult – if talented – John Anderson. Desnitsky had pulled off Anderson's wig in the quadrangle of the College, after he had considered himself insulted by the Professor.[12] Desnitsky's delicate position was considered and

5 See A H Brown, "Adam Smith's First Russian Followers", in *Essays on Adam Smith*, ed A S Skinner and Thomas Wilson (1975) 247 (henceforth Brown, "Adam Smith's First Russian Followers") at 247; A G Cross, *"By The Banks of the Thames": Russians in Eighteenth Century Britain* (1980) 122–128 (henceforth Cross, "By the Banks of the Thames").

6 Brown, "Adam Smith's First Russian Followers" (n 5) at 252.

7 GUA 26645, Minutes of Meetings of Faculty and Dean of Faculty's Meetings 1732–1768, 141.

8 Ibid 143.

9 Ibid 144.

10 Ibid 145.

11 Ibid 148.

12 GUA 26643, Minutes of University Meetings 1763–1768, 176 (9 December 1766). For further details, see Brown, "Adam Smith's First Russian Followers" (n 5) at 256–258. On Anderson,

he was given the light punishment of making appropriate public apologies, rather than being expelled.[13] Why this cannot explain the long delay is that the quarrel took place on 8 December 1766. Whatever the explanation, the public defence of the theses was dispensed with on 20 April 1767, because Tret'yakov and Desnitsky had "received orders to go home with all convenient speed", and the Faculty "being satisfied with the specimens given of their knowledge in the Civil Law, appoint[ed] the Degree of Doctor to be conferred upon them by the Vice Chancellor".[14]

The two men returned to Russia to face problems at Moscow University, where there was a reluctance to recognise their qualifications. They had to undertake oral examinations; Tret'yakov failed an examination in mathematics (which they had studied at Glasgow) that Desnitsky, sensibly, had refused to take. It is good to note, however, that these two possessors of a doctoral degree in law from the University of Glasgow "distinguished themselves" in the oral examination in law.[15] In 1768, they were both appointed as Professors of Law in Moscow University. Tret'yakov resigned his chair in 1773 and the two men's experiences as professors in Moscow were not entirely happy.[16]

This said, it is worth considering briefly the work of these two pupils of John Millar. Any scholar interested in Millar will note Desnitsky's *A Legal Discourse on the Beginning and Origin of Matrimony among the Earliest Peoples and on the Perfection to which it would appear to have been brought by Subsequent Enlightened Peoples* of 1775. The correspondence with a large part of the Glasgow professor's *Observations Concerning the Distinction of Ranks in Society* of 1771 is evident.[17] By 1783, Desnitsky was teaching a course on the History of Russian Law; one on Justinian's *Digest*, using the compend of Johann Gottlieb Heineccius; and a comparison of Roman and Russian Law. Moreover, among the problems they faced were disagreements with their (mainly German colleagues) over their teaching in Russian rather than in Latin.[18] The influence of Smith on these two men has often been noted and indeed some attention has been paid to Millar's influence on them; yet, these remarks drawn from Brown's research make it

see, above all, P Wood, "Jolly Jack Phosphorous in the Venice of the North; or, Who was John Anderson?", in A Hook and R B Sher (eds), *The Glasgow Enlightenment* (1995) 111.

13 GUA 26643 (n 12) 193 (6 January 1767).

14 GUA 26645 (n 7) 163.

15 All of this is from Brown, "Adam Smith's First Russian Followers" (n 5) at 259; Cross, *"By The Banks of the Thames"* (n 5) 126.

16 Brown, "Adam Smith's First Russian Followers" (n 5) at 249–250, 259–260.

17 Ibid at 269.

18 Ibid at 250, 259.

worth considering the nature of the legal education these men acquired in Glasgow and its likely effect on them. Brown has pointed out that the two Russians only mentioned studying Civil (that is Roman) Law with Millar, but suggests, on the basis of their published works, that they also attended his classes on Scots Law and Government.[19] All of this opens up the issue of Millar's first years in occupation of the chair in Glasgow.

B. DESNITSKY, TRET'YAKOV, AND MILLAR'S EARLY YEARS AS PROFESSOR OF LAW

The first holder of the Regius chair of Civil Law in Glasgow had at one time taught some Scots law; but, by the time of Millar's immediate predecessor, Hercules Lindesay, the duties of the chair had come to be defined as offering courses on Justinian's *Digest* and courses on Justinian's *Institutes*.[20] By the middle years of the century these were considered "the proper business of Professorship".[21] The course on the *Institutes* was much shorter and was given twice each year.[22] Lindesay had at some stage started to teach the course on the *Institutes* in English, reflecting the general trend away from teaching in Latin in the Scottish universities.[23]

One of the evident features of Millar's occupancy of the chair is his expansion of this curriculum.[24] Millar's biographer John Craig suggested that Millar found he still had some leisure after teaching each of these courses five days a week, and added a class on government three days a week and, in alternate years, a class on Scots law on the other two days, adding that "a few years before his death, Mr Millar was led . . . to prepare and deliver a course of Lectures on English Law".[25] Can Brown's speculation that Tret'yakov and Desnitsky attended Millar's classes, not only in Civil Law, which is certain, but also in Government and Scots Law be supported by any evidence? Was it possible for the Russians to have attended Millar's classes in Scots Law and Government?

19 Ibid at 253.

20 Cairns, "Origins of the Glasgow Law School" (n 2) at 174–183, 185.

21 J Craig, "Account of the Life and Writings of John Millar, Esq", prefixed to J Millar, *The Origin of the Distinction of Ranks: or, an Inquiry into the Circumstances which give rise to Influence and Authority, in the different Members of Society*, 4th edn (1806) xix (henceforth Craig, "Account of the Life and Writings of John Millar").

22 See L Gordon and D Ross to the Rector, 17 November 1748, GUA 30222.

23 J W Cairns, "Rhetoric, language, and Roman law: legal education and improvement in eighteenth-century Scotland" (1991) 9 *Law and History Review* 31 at 35–46.

24 See Cairns, "'Famous as a School for Law, as Edinburgh . . . for Medicine'" (n 4) at 136–139 has a full discussion of this.

25 Craig, "Account of the Life and Writings of John Millar" (n 21) xxi.

When the students petitioned for examination for the degree of LLD in December 1765, they stated that they had given "attendance for three years on Mr Millar's classes of civil law".[26] Given that the degree was awarded by examination in Civil Law, it is conceivable that they did not mention attendance at other law classes simply as irrelevant; they might have attended classes in Scots law, but considered it unnecessary to mention them. This is not entirely plausible, however, since they mention attendance at "Dr Smith's class of Ethicks and Jurisprudence" as qualifying them for examination.[27] One might have expected them to mention attendance at any law classes as relevant.

Newspaper advertisements give some assistance. Millar first inserted notices about his classes in the Edinburgh newspapers in 1763, when he advertised lectures on the *Institutes* and *Digest*, beginning on 1 November.[28] In 1764, he again advertised that his lectures on the *Institutes* and *Digest* would begin on 1 November.[29] In 1765, he advertised (in both Glasgow and Edinburgh newspapers) that his prelections on the *Institutes* and *Digest* would begin on 4 November and his lectures on the law of Scotland on 11 November.[30] This means that it was certainly feasible for Tret'yakov and Desnitsky to attend the classes on Scots Law over the academic year from 1765 to 1766 when they were undergoing the rather drawn-out process of examination for the degree of LLD. Indeed, they could also have attended them in part over 1766–1767, as Millar advertised in October 1766 prelections on the *Institutes* and *Digest* beginning on 4 November and lectures on Scots law on 10 November.[31]

Millar did not advertise lectures on Government (as such) until 1771.[32] This does not mean, however, that Tret'yakov and Desnitsky could not have attended classes on this topic from Millar. We have noted that in October 1766 Millar advertised lectures on Scots law beginning on 10 November.[33] In January 1767, however, he advertised that lectures on "the Private Law of Scotland" would begin on 3 February.[34] Was Millar giving the same course of lectures on Scots law twice in academic year 1766–1767, or was his first

26 Found quoted in Brown, "Adam Smith's First Russian Followers" (n 5) at 252.
27 Ibid.
28 *Edinburgh Evening Courant*, 12 October 1763.
29 *Caledonian Mercury*, 6 October 1764.
30 *Glasgow Journal*, 3/10 October 1765; *Caledonian Mercury*, 12 October 1765.
31 *Glasgow Journal*, 2/9 October 1766; *Caledonian Mercury*, 8 October 1766.
32 *Glasgow Journal*, 10/17 October 1771.
33 *Glasgow Journal*, 2/9 October 1766.
34 *Glasgow Journal*, 15/22 January 1767.

set of lectures something different? Here we can look at his advertisement in October 1767, after the two Russians had returned home. This stated that he would begin his prelections on the *Institutions* and *Digest* on 2 November and "his Lectures on the Public Law of Scotland" on 8 November.[35] This strongly suggests that the lectures on Scots Law he started on 10 November 1766 were also on the *public law* of Scotland, to be followed by those on the *private law* of Scotland on 3 February 1767. Indeed, it may even be that his class on Scots Law in 1765 also started with an account of public law. When in 1771 Millar first offered a course described as on Government, this was in fact carrying on his lectures on the Public Law of Scotland (which he advertised in 1768, 1769, and 1770), under another name.[36] One may speculate that, as his popularity as a teacher grew, he realised that a course called Government or Public Law was more marketable to students than one called the Public Law of Scotland.

This means that it was clearly possible for Tret'yakov and Desnitsky to have attended Millar's class on Scots Law and probably also his class on Government, in its earlier guise as a class on Scots public law. Brown's speculation based on the works of the two Russians seems likely to be correct. It may also be possible to work out the probable sequence of the two men's studies. It was normal to take a course on the *Institutes* before a course on the *Digest*. It is always possible that they attended Millar's two courses on the *Institutes* over 1761–1762; but this seems unlikely, as they had extremely weak English on arrival and Millar taught this course in English. If this be correct, then the next year, 1762–1763, would have been when they attended Millar's two courses on the *Institutes*. One can then suppose that they took the course on the *Digest* twice in 1763–1764, and 1764–1765, making in all the three years of study of Civil Law mentioned in the petition of December 1765.[37] In 1765–1766, they could then have attended the course on Scots law, starting off perhaps with a series of lectures on Scots Public Law (or Government), although they could have attended the course on the Public Law of Scotland almost certainly given over the winter of 1766–1767 immediately prior to their departure. A measure of support for this comes from a Russian source

35 *Glasgow Journal*, 15/22 October 1767.

36 *Glasgow Journal* 20/27 October 1768; 26 October/2 November 1769; 1/8 November 1770 (in none of these academic years is there a special advertisement for the lectures in Scots private law, suggesting either that the course continued on without notice to deal with it or that he did not teach it).

37 Found quoted in Brown, "Adam Smith's First Russian Followers" (n 5) at 252. Their weak English is noted in ibid at 261 n 261.

that reveals Desnitsky and Tret'yakov in 1766 following Millar's classes in Roman Law as well as studying "British" Law.[38]

If Desnitsky and Tret'yakov did attend Millar's classes on Scots Law and Government, it must have been in 1765–1767, because there is no evidence that he gave them before that date. If absence of evidence is not conclusive, there is a great deal of supporting circumstantial evidence to suggest these classes were a new departure in 1765. Thus, a university meeting of 11 May 1762 allocated to Millar a classroom for lectures on Civil Law, making no provision for any other classes.[39] Furthermore, in October 1762, the *Glasgow Journal* stated that "the professors of Medicine and Law will begin their Lectures upon the first of November".[40] The lack of detail suggests that Millar was simply going to give the "prelections" on the *Institutes* and *Digest* that were the well-recognised, statutory, "public" duties of his chair.[41] If so, the earliest he could have started to teach Scots law and government would have been academic year 1763–1764. This, however, seems very unlikely. First, the evidence of his advertisements in 1763 and 1764 suggests that he only taught the courses in the *Institutes* and *Digest* in those years. Secondly the content of his lectures on Scots Law also strongly suggests that they dated from after 1764. This is because in them Millar's Smithian analysis and account of Scots criminal law is strongly influenced by the tripartite division of crimes found for the first time in the third edition of John Erskine's *Principles of the Law of Scotland* of 1764.[42] This work, first published in 1754, was the textbook he recommended to his students.[43] Given that Millar, so far as we can tell, never recast his lectures drastically, this suggests that his account of Scots Law dates from after the publication of the third edition of Erskine's *Principles*.[44] This means that the earliest he could have lectured on Scots Law would have been 1764–1765. While possible, his earlier practice in advertising strongly suggests that the innovation of advertising classes on Scots Law in 1765 probably also marks an innovation in the classes offered.

38 Cross, *"By The Banks of the Thames"* (n 5) 125.
39 *Glasgow Journal*, 21/28 October 1762.
40 GUA 26642, Minutes of University meetings 1760–1763, 147.
41 "Statistical Account of the University of Glasgow" (1794), in T Reid, *Philosophical Works*, 2 vols (1895; repr 1967) vol ii, 734 (henceforth Reid, *Works*), states that "in his public department" Millar lectured daily for two hours; that is, two hours daily on Roman law, one hour on the *Institute*, one on the *Digest*. See also Cairns, "William Crosse" (n 2) at 177–178.
42 For the detailed demonstration of this, see J W Cairns, "John Millar's lectures on Scots criminal law" (1988) 8 OJLS 364 at 388–391.
43 Glasgow University Library (henceforth GUL) MS Gen 347, 6–8; John Erskine, *The Principles of the Law of Scotland: In the Order of Sir George Mackenzie's Institutions of that Law* (1754).
44 See further below.

C. WHAT DESNITSKY AND TRET'YAKOV LEARN FROM MILLAR?

The earliest surviving sets of student notes of lectures given by Millar date from the 1770s.[45] Thus, a set of lectures on Government is known from the class of 1771–1772.[46] An early set of lectures on the *Institutes* dates from around the same period.[47] A set of lectures on Scots Law dates from the session of 1775–1776.[48] There are no notes from classes on the *Digest* until 1790.[49] This raises the question of whether we can have any sense of what Millar taught his Russian pupils.

It seems likely, however, that we can be fairly certain that Millar's classes were – perhaps with one exception – much as they were in the 1770s and that we have reasonably good evidence of what he might have taught Desnitsky and Tret'yakov. This is because, as pointed out above, he seems rarely to have changed the content of his classes in a radical fashion. This means that, though it is obvious his classes did develop through the years, there was a considerable measure of continuity, even if new matter might be added in and old deleted. The lectures on Government provide a good example. Study of student lecture notes and published syllabuses shows that the only major change made to his lectures on Government came between 1781 and 1783, when he increased the number of lectures by introducing a new preliminary lecture and another four on the government of Ireland, the national debt, the constitution of Parliament with regard to its division into three branches and its period of duration, and the royal prerogative, while reducing three lectures on the English courts to two.[50] He later added new matter, without altering the course overall, such as a lecture on the French Revolution.[51] The

45 For details of surviving notes (other than in private hands), see Cairns, '"Famous as a School for Law, as Edinburgh . . . for medicine"' (n 4) at 155–156 (n 31), 156 (nn 39–40), 157 (n 48). The one set of notes surviving from the class on English law is GUL MS Gen 243.

46 Glasgow, Mitchell Library, MS 99. There is also an outline syllabus: *A Course of Lectures on Government; Given Annually in the University* (1771) (National Library of Scotland (henceforth NLS), pressmark RB.s.402).

47 NLS MS 2743.

48 GUL MS Gen 347.

49 GUL MSS Murray 91–92 and 93–94.

50 NLS MS 3931 consists of lectures on Government dating from 1780 to 1781, conforming to the earlier syllabus set out in *A Course of Lectures on Government; Given Annually in the University* (1778), while the new syllabus is found in *A Course of Lectures on Government; Given Annually in the University* (1783).

51 See *A Course of Lectures on government; given Annually in the University of Glasgow* (Glasgow, 1787) (bound into GUL MS Gen 180/1); GUL MS Hamilton 116 (1798); GUL MS Gen 290, 34–44.

basic nature of the lectures and the bulk of their content did not change, however, between 1771 and the late 1790s. It seems a fair supposition that the core content of the later lectures on Government was found in the earlier lectures on Scots Public Law. Indeed, given the strong dependence of Millar's thinking on that of Adam Smith, his basic thinking is unlikely to have changed, even if the details, illustrations and examples in the lectures were altered and perhaps even greatly elaborated. One question which cannot be answered is the length of these classes on Scots Public Law and Scots Private Law: we do not know if each was as long as the successor courses in the 1770s, or if each was half the length of one of the successor courses.

It is as well to deal here with that one exception to general continuity. Millar's first biographer, Craig, remarked that Millar considered "the employment of a whole winter in tracing . . . the exact line of Roman Law . . . a mere waste of time and study. Whatever it was useful to know of the Institutes, he thought might be sufficiently taught in the half of the session, or term; and he wished to devote the rest of it to a course of Lectures on Jurisprudence." Millar accordingly divided his course on the *Institutes* into two parts, covering, first, the *Institutes* itself and, secondly, Jurisprudence.[52] If Craig is implying that, before Millar's appointment, the whole of one academic year was taken to teach the *Institutes* in Glasgow, this is wrong. Millar had replaced a second, identical class on *Institutes* with the Lectures on Jurisprudence.[53] When did he do this? Craig suggests that this development took place some time after Millar first occupied the chair. A first point to make is that the content of Millar's class on Jurisprudence (still usually referred to in student notes as the second course on the *Institutes*) is very similar to that of Smith's *Lectures on Jurisprudence*. If, for example, Desnitsky and Tret'yakov, after attending Smith's class on Ethics and Jurisprudence, attended Millar's, they would have found much duplication, although Millar's class would have had a greater focus on Roman Law.[54] It is easy to demonstrate this.

Millar's second course on the *Institutes* opened with advice on reading and then presented a discussion of moral theory, leading to an account of rights and the progress of law.[55] Millar analysed law as concerning rights and

52 Craig, "Account of the Life and Writings of John Millar" (n 21) xx.

53 J Erskine to Lord Cardross, 24 November 1762, Edinburgh University Library (henceforth EUL), MS La.II.238, confirms that Millar gave two courses on the *Institutes* in 1762–1763. It also implies that they were identical or nearly identical, but Erskine was probably not well informed about Millar's practice in this respect.

54 Adam Smith, *Lectures on Jurisprudence*, ed R L Meek, D D Raphael and P G Stein (1978) 397–554.

55 See, e.g., Advocates' (henceforth Adv) MS 20.4.7 fos 2r–23r.

actions, with rights, in turn, concerning either persons or things. The rights of persons arose from the relationships of husband and wife, parent and child, master and servant, guardian and ward. The rights of things were divided into real and personal. Real rights concerned property, servitude, pledge and exclusive privilege. Personal rights arose by contract, delinquency or crime. Actions were the means of asserting these rights.[56] This analysis is very familiar from Smith's *Lectures on Jurisprudence*.[57] The aim was:

> It shall now be our chief employment to enquire into the principles of the Roman law, and to compare them with those of other countries. The aim of Students of Roman Law at this period, ought to be not merely to know what was the Roman System. That would be of little consequence of itself. It has properly no authority by the Law of this country, or of most of the other modern nations in Europe. It has however a regard paid to it as the system of Lawiers and Judges of great experience, and of a country which subsisted for such a long tract of time, and where we may consequently expect to find the rules of Jurisprudence of the most perfect kind. As however in the most perfect of all human Systems, there are numberless imperfections and Blemishes, it will certainly be proper in those who study Roman Law at this period, to enquire into the justice or propriety of these regulations. This can only be done by comparing it with the Laws of other countries, and with our own natural feelings of right and wrong. This is certainly a very useful exercise, as it enlarges our experience.[58]

Craig aptly characterised this second class as one "in which [Millar] treated of such general principles of Law as pervade the codes of all nations, and have their origin in those sentiments of justice which are imprinted on the human heart".[59]

This content, analytical approach, and philosophical foundation in the theory of moral sentiments all suggest that it was unlikely that Millar taught a course in rivalry to that of Adam Smith (whom he revered sufficiently, after all, to use his image on his seal).[60] A plausible – but no more than plausible – explanation is that it was after Smith's resignation from the chair of Moral Philosophy in 1764 that Millar introduced his own Lectures on Jurisprudence. Secondly, Smith's successor was Thomas Reid. Millar had strongly opposed

56 For a useful analytical breakdown of the second course, see NLS MS 3930, 299–301. All surviving manuscripts of the second course follow this structure.

57 On Smith's analytical jurisprudence, see above all K Haakonssen, *The Science of a Legislator: The Natural Jurisprudence of David Hume and Adam Smith* (1981) 99–134.

58 Adv MS 20.4.7 fos 1r–2r.

59 Craig, "Account of the Life and Writings of John Millar" (n 21) xx. On Millar's jurisprudence, see K Haakonssen, *Natural Law and Moral Philosophy: From Grotius to the Scottish Englisghtenment* (1996) 154–181.

60 It survives very clearly on Millar's letter to David Douglas, 10 August 1790, GUL MS Gen 1035/178.

Reid's appointment and in a letter of 2 February 1764 urged Smith to do the same.[61] Reid and Millar were noted for their philosophical disagreements at meetings of the Glasgow Literary Society.[62] Reid included jurisprudence in his moral philosophy classes, which were commonly attended by law students because of the complementary nature of the subject matter.[63] It is thus possible that Millar developed the jurisprudence lectures to counteract Reid's influence, wishing to teach a Smithian jurisprudence to his students, which could hardly be expected of Reid.[64] At the same time, Millar was probably conscious of a need to ensure his students had an adequate grounding in jurisprudence, since the Faculty of Advocates had exhorted, in 1760 and 1762, young men proposing to join their body to attend the classes of the Professor of Public Law and the Law of Nature and Nations in Edinburgh, while also proposing that intrants be asked questions on the law of nature and nations in their examinations.[65] Thirdly, there was by this time a definite demand for classes in jurisprudence. Robert Bruce, the Edinburgh Professor of Public Law and the Law of Nature and Nations, had forty students in session 1763–1764, the last that he taught.[66]

If these arguments are correct, they suggest that Millar introduced

61 E C Mossner and I S Ross (eds), *The Correspondence of Adam Smith*, 2nd edn (1987) 99–100. Millar wished Thomas Young to succeed Smith. It is unknown what Smith's views were on his potential successors, and there is no reason to believe he agreed with Millar. See *Selections from the Family Papers preserved at Caldwell*, 2 vols in 3 (1854), vol ii, part I, 232–233.

62 Craig, "Account of the Life and Writings of John Millar" (n 21) lxi–lxii.

63 On the natural jurisprudence component of Reid's moral philosophy course, see T Reid, *Practical Ethics: Being Lectures and Papers on Natural Religion, Self-Government, Natural Jurisprudence, and the Law of Nations*, K Haakonssen (ed) (1990). (Reid's assistant and successor, Archibald Arthur, also taught natural jurisprudence; see "Notes, Taken by James Neilson, from Mr Arthur's Lectures on Natural Jurisprudence, given in the University of Glasgow. Glasgow. From 19 March 1788 to [blank] 1788", GUL MS Gen 832.) On Millar's students attending Reid's classes, see T Reid to A Skene, 14 November 1764, in Reid, *Works* (n 41) vol i, 40. On the general relationship of law and moral philosophy, see John Erskine to Lord Cardross, 24 November 1762, EUL MS La.II.238, where Erskine, obviously anxious that Cardross know Pufendorf, agrees that Cardross should take Smith's class on moral philosophy along with Millar's on the *Institutes*.

64 The speculation was first suggested to me by Nicholas Phillipson.

65 A Stewart (ed), *The Minute Book of the Faculty of Advocates. Volume 3, 1751–1783*, Stair Society vol 46 (1999) 94 (8 January 1760), 112 (5 January 1762) (henceforth *Minute Book of the Faculty of Advocates. Volume 3*, 1751–1783. For discussion of this development, see J W Cairns, "The Influence of Smith's Jurisprudence on Legal Education in Scotland", in P Jones and A Skinner (eds), *Adam Smith Reviewed* (1992) 168, and "The Formation of the Scottish Legal Mind in the Eighteenth Century: Themes of Humanisation and Enlightenment in the Admission of Advocates", in N MacCormick and P Birks (eds), *The Legal Mind: Essays for Tony Honoré* (1968) 253, esp 265–266.

66 See "Matriculation Roll of the University of Edinburgh. Arts–Law–Divinity" (transcribed by A Morgan), EUL, 3 vols, vol i, 262.

his class on Jurisprudence only after 1764; this means that if Desnitsky and Tret'yakov studied the *Institutes* with him in 1762–1763, as argued above, they will not have attended his second course when it dealt with jurisprudence. Of course, they could always have attended it later: it may even have been the course of Roman law they took with him in 1766.[67] In any case, the influence of Smith would have meant that their philosophical outlook would have suited Millar's classes.

Turning to classes that the two Russians certainly took, Millar's class on Justinian's *Institute* was based on the textbook of Heineccius, according to Craig.[68] This was the most popular textbook of the day.[69] Millar started, however, with some lectures discussing vice and virtue and distinguishing law from ethics.[70] He then raised the question of whether or not legal studies should start with the law of one's own country. He pointed out that in most European countries other than England the practice was to begin with the laws of other nations before concluding with the national law. If this practice were adopted, he commented, then "the Roman law must attract particular notice. The Romans were a great people, possessed extensive territories and therefore must have had much experience as of necessity many private quarrels and disputes would come to be decided in their wide empire". There followed a survey of the history of Roman law and its reception in Europe.[71] Thereafter Millar went through the text of Heineccius, paragraph by paragraph. In later years, the first course did not reach the end of Heineccius' compend; but it presumably did when taken by Desnitsky and Tret'yakov. In all, this class amounted to around seventy lectures.[72]

Paragraph references in the surviving notes of lectures on the *Digest* show that Millar used Heineccius' compend as his textbook, the popular student work of the day.[73] Craig commented that the "multifarious doctrines to be explained in the Pandects" meant that Millar could not shorten the length of

67 Cross, *"By The Banks of the Thames"* (n 5) 125.

68 Craig, "Account of the Life and Writings of John Millar" (n 21) xx. His claim is readily verified from surviving student notes, e.g., NLS MS 2743 fo 18r.

69 J G Heineccius, *Elementa juris civilis secundum ordinem institutionum* (1725 and numerous other editions). An edition of this work aimed at Scottish law students was published at Edinburgh in 1780.

70 E.g., Adv MS 28.6.8, 1–11, first pagination sequence (lects 1–3).

71 Ibid 12–19.

72 See Cairns, "'Famous as a School for Law, as Edinburgh . . . for Medicine'" (n 4) at 140–141.

73 J G Heineccius, *Elementa juris secundum ordinem pandectarum* (1727 and many subsequent editions). See GUL MSS Murray 91–92; GUL MSS Murray 93–95. The first of these consists of two volumes from an originally four-volume set of notes. The second is possibly a copy of the complete version of the first; if so, both date from 1790–91.

this course and indeed he gave 116 lectures on the *Digest*, from the beginning of November and ending about the beginning of May.[74] He added, however, that "aware that the ordinary arrangement is confused, and almost unintelligible, he soon published a new syllabus, following very nearly the order of the Institutes, according to which he discussed the various and sometimes discordant laws of Rome, and the still more discordant opinions of Roman lawyers".[75] No printed syllabus has yet been discovered for Millar's lectures on the *Digest*. Study of the surviving notes shows, however, that, as in the second course on the *Institutes*, he expounded the *Digest*, not according to the order of the *Institutes*, but according to the Smithian analysis of law into rights and actions, an approach that involved a complete rearrangement of the sequence of the *Digest*.[76] Since the surviving manuscripts contain only a detailed scheme, rather than a full report of what Millar actually said in his class, it is difficult to assess this course. The lectures assumed that students had already attended the course on the *Institutes* and obviously dealt with the *Digest* in considerable detail, raising the type of historical issues that interested Millar.[77] He also seems to have made – at least – occasional references to modern Scots law.[78]

The lectures on Scots law also started from Millar's version of Smithian analytical jurisprudence, using it as a scheme for exposition and classification. Smith's thinking in fact determined Millar's account of and entire approach to Scots law.[79] He told his class:

> The Law of any Country comprehends a Set of Rules which the Inhabitants are bound to obey and wherever there is a Rule for performing an obligation there must be a corresponding right to inforce the performance – To every Rule therefore there is a corresponding Right – The enumeration of these Rights will be the same thing as the enumeration of the Rules. – To enumerate the Rights then is the first object of Law.

74 Craig, "Account of the Life and Writings of John Millar" (n 21) xx. See, e.g., *Glasgow Journal*, 3/10 October 1765, starting 4 November; *Glasgow Mercury*, 13/20 October 1789, starting 3 November; *Glasgow Courier*, 15 October 1799, starting 5 Nov. GUL MS Murray 92, fo 55v shows he finished on 29 April 1791, which fits with having started that year on 1 November 1790 (*Glasgow Mercury*, 21/28 September 1790), generally lecturing five days per week and delivering 116 lectures in all.

75 Craig, "Account of the Life and Writings of John Millar" (n 21) xx.

76 Cairns, "John Millar's Lectures" (n 42) at 378 n 70.

77 W C Lehmann, "Some observations on the law lectures of Professor Millar at the University of Glasgow (1761–1801)" (1970) 15 *Juridical Review* 56 at 68–70. See GUL MSS Murray 93 fo [1]r, and 94 fo 48v, lect 54 for the assumption that the students had taken the course on the *Institutes*.

78 GUL MS Murray 94 fo [60]r, lect 59.

79 Cairns, "John Millar's Lectures" (n 42) at 374–395.

When it came to exposition of these rights, he stated:

> The Lectures therefore proposed to be given on the Law of Scotland naturally divide themselves into the consideration of
>
> 1st Rights and 2nd Actions.
>
> Rights may be divided into two Grand divisions, vizt. Such as arise from the distinctions of persons and their Ranks in society – and such as are independent of this distinction which is understood to comprehend every other Right – These Rights are therefore distinguished into
>
> 1st Rights of Persons.
>
> 2nd Rights of Things.[80]

He followed this scheme rigorously in his account.

The close link with the lectures on government can easily be seen from Millar's remark in the class on Scots law that:

> But as it is necessary that every Rule of conduct be promulgated to the people that they may know how to observe them, So it is necessary that some provision be made for enforcing these Rules and compelling the people to observe them – For this purpose Courts of Justice are established – The knowledge of the different Courts – The Causes to which they are competent – and the legal methods of obtaining redress of grievances before these Courts, constitute the second great object of Law – But as the different Courts of Justice and the Jurisdiction of Judges fall properly to be considered in a political point of view though no doubt connected with the Law of a Country – We have therefore reserved these for part of a Course of Lectures on Government.[81]

Millar covered three broad topics in his lectures on government: first, the origin and progress of government in society; secondly, illustrations of this from particular governments, namely Athens, Sparta, Rome, France, Germany, England, Scotland, Ireland (after 1781), and ecclesiastical jurisdiction; and thirdly, the present state of the government in Great Britain, including discussions of parliament, the royal prerogative, and English and Scottish courts.[82] The lectures again not only show Millar's indebtedness to basic tenets of Smith's thought, but also his historical and comparative approach.[83] The advantages of such an approach were that "by comparing the Systems [of Government] in different Countries we may judge concerning the expediency of different institutions and enlarge our views concerning the principles of Government", while this also meant that "we ought to examine each particular system historically, tracing each regulation from the

80 GUL MS Gen 178, 2–5, second pagination sequence.

81 Ibid.

82 For a good account, see Craig, "Account of the Life and Writings of John Millar" (n 21) xli–lvii.

83 See Cairns, "'Famous as a School for Law, as Edinburgh . . . for Medicine'" (n 4) at 145–146.

origins through all the subsequent changes".[84] The authority that was one of the ultimate foundations of government was based on personal wealth or qualities strengthened by the custom that created a habit of obedience, while the progress of government was explained utilising Smith's stadial analysis.[85]

The content of the courses that Desnitsky and Tret'yakov took with Millar will have taught them that laws were based on "the various rights acknowledged and protected by society". These rights were derived from the moral sentiments, according to which actions were approved on the grounds of their propriety and utility. When individuals were wronged, they felt resentment and spectators felt indignation. Rules of justice thus rose spontaneously this way from individual concrete situations. Individuals thus had rights not to be wronged. Spectators would interfere in disputes in order to assist individuals with whose motives they sympathised – not only disinterestedly in order to prevent an injustice, but also out of self-interest, as they themselves might some day be in a similar predicament. Rights so established might vary from place to place and time to time according to the character, history and manners of different societies, though long-established customs were not readily abandoned and could continue to exist even if defective for a changed society.[86]

The courses on Civil Law, Scots Law, and Government followed by Desnitsky and Tret'yakov were all interrelated and put forward a coherent view demonstrating how such rights were elaborated historically. The class on Government showed how the legislative power, national defence and the securing of public tranquillity by the appointment of magistrates and the establishment of courts of justice created the framework within which private rights arose, were recognised and could be enforced. The classes on Scots Law and Civil Law showed how this worked out in particular historical contexts. This was a rich and detailed theory of legislation.

So far the focus has been on the content of Millar's classes. A further important lesson learned by the two Russians would also have been that the manner of teaching can dramatically affect the success of the learning of the students. Here there are two linked points. It had been traditional in teaching for the professor to dictate notes on a set text to his students; in law, traditionally this had been done using the *Corpus iuris civilis*, though

84 GUL MS Hamilton 116, 1–2.
85 See, e.g., GUL MS Gen 289, 15–29, 31–33.
86 See Craig, "Account of the Life and Writings of John Millar" (n 21) xxxii–xxxix.

from the later seventeenth century it had become increasingly common for teachers to lecture on the basis of a compend, such as that of Heineccius, rather than on the original texts. Moreover, lectures had traditionally been delivered in Latin. (It is worth pointing out that Scots law was always taught in English in the Scottish universities.)

Taking the language of instruction first, we have noted above that Millar's predecessor in the chair, Hercules Lindesay, had started to teach the *Institutes* in English. At some stage, Millar extended this innovation to the course on the *Digest*.[87] When he did so is unclear. What is certain is that, after the departure of Desnitsky and Tret'yakov, the Dean of the Faculty of Advocates in Edinburgh (the Scottish Bar) reported to the advocates in 1768 that "he understood that the Professor of Civil Law in Glasgow lectured to his students in the English Language". He thought that it was "incumbent upon the Faculty" to find a way to put "an effectual Stop" to this "unprecedented way of teaching the Civil Law". The Faculty recommended the Dean to communicate their worries to the Rector of the University of Glasgow and request him to "use his authority in ordering that the Lectures on the Civil Law be, for the future, in Latin and not in English".[88] This complaint was ineffective, though it stimulated a small pamphlet debate, which does not seem to have been studied, but to which a return will be made below.[89] There is no evidence to suggest that Millar's innovation had just taken place in 1768; indeed it may well be that Millar always lectured in English on the *Digest*. If so, then his two Russian students will have been taught the *Digest* by him in English.[90]

87 "Statistical Account of the University of Glasgow" (n 41) at 734. For a fuller discussion of this issue, see Cairns, "Rhetoric, language, and Roman law" (n 23).

88 *Minute Book of the Faculty of Advocates. Volume 3, 1751–1783* (n 65), 184 (5 March 1768).

89 See, strongly in favour of Millar's approach, *Considerations on the Practice of Teaching the Civil Law in English* (1768). A wider examination was given in *Essays. Viz. I. On the Origin of Colleges, Or Universities. II. On the Origin of the Custom of Lecturing in Latin. III. On the Impropriety of this Custom, at Present* (1769) countered in *An Inquiry Whether the Study of the Ancient Languages be a Necessary Branch of Modern Education? Wherein, by the way, some observations are made on a late Performance, intitled, Essays on the Origin of Colleges, of the custom of Lecturing in Latin, &c.* (1769) (although accepting the fact of lecturing in English).

90 The *Caledonian Mercury*, 16 December 1767 carried an advertisement for all "who studied Law under Mr. Millar at Glasgow" to meet at Fortune's tavern on Saturday 19 December. It is possible that this reflects knowledge of the forthcoming complaint; on the other hand, it seems more likely that it may be to do with the Faculty of Advocates' recent return to the issue of entails, a matter of earlier controversy and in which Millar was deeply interested and that we discussed in his classes: see *Minute Book of the Faculty of Advocates. Volume 3, 1751–1783* (n 65), 177 (12 December 1767); N T Phillipson, "Lawyers, landowners, and the civic leadership of post-Union Scotland: an essay on the social role of the Faculty of Advocates 1661–1830 in 18th century Scottish society" (1976) 21 *Juridical Review* 97.

Why this seems likely is that Millar did not read his lectures, but always lectured extempore from detailed headings. His biographer commented that Millar "was not merely desirous to convey to his students just views and accurate information", but also "to convey them in the manner most likely to seize the attention, and to promote habits of original thought and philosophical investigation". This meant that Millar "never wrote his Lectures"; any disadvantages encountered by not reading a full text were "much more than compensated by the fullness of his illustrations, the energy of his manner, and that interest which is excited, both in the hearer and speaker, by extemporaneous eloquence". Millar was indeed noted for his powerful lecturing and his ability to respond to the reactions of his auditors.[91] No doubt Millar's skills in teaching developed over his tenure of the chair; but such a belief in how to communicate effectively with his audience must have been held from the beginning. Lecturing in Latin would have made any kind of extempore and responsive teaching impossible. The professor would have had to read full notes slowly to the class.[92] All of this suggests that Millar always taught the class on the *Digest* in English and that, as his classes became increasingly popular, his innovation came to the attention of the Faculty of Advocates.

D. SOME CONCLUDING POINTS

Desnitsky and Tret'yakov will have returned to Moscow with a view of law that was rooted in a historical theory of society, in which government (necessary for the protection of property that was the foundation of society) was based on authority and utility, and which saw political obedience as based on habit, custom, fear, and utility. Law was not derived from higher norms of divine law; there was indeed a philosophical underpinning in the Smithian theory of the moral sentiments, but rules of justice emerged from social life.

Others can discuss more fully the extent to which this teaching influenced the two new doctors of law of Glasgow University on their return to Moscow; a few remarks will suffice here. Brown has certainly claimed that Desnitsky's socio-political and legal views can be traced to Smith and Millar and that "a

91 Craig, "Account of the Life and Writings of John Millar" (n 21) xii, xiv–xvi; F Jeffrey, review of *Historical View of the English Government* (1803) 3 *Edinburgh Review* 155.

92 A point recognised in *Considerations on the Practice of Teaching the Civil Law in English* (n 89) 10, where it was also suggested that teaching in Latin encouraged professors to be content "with reading over the same written lecture from year to year", ibid 11.

great many of the ideas of a theoretical nature in the lectures of Desnitsky and Tret'yakov, as well as numerous points of detail, can be traced back to the Glasgow lectures of Smith and Millar".[93] While Brown fully recognised the importance of Millar's teaching for the two men, he understandably does tend to focus on Smith, undoubtedly the greater thinker. Yet, more courses were taken with Millar than with Smith, so it is possible that many Smithian ideas in the work of the two Russians came second-hand, so to speak, through Millar. Desnitsky has been described as "the founder of Russian jurisprudence"; the jurisprudence he developed was based on that learned in Glasgow in the classes of John Millar. For example, he utilised Millar's clearly developed version of Smith's theory of the four stages as his major analytical tool in his comparative historical approach to law and society.[94] Even a cursory examination of Desnitsky's *Proposal for the Establishment of Legislative, Judicial and Executive Power in the Russian Empire* reveals the influence on him of his experiences in Scotland.[95] Thus, his proposal for a jury of fifteen to assist judges and his suggestion as to how such a jury should operate in criminal cases was distinctly reminiscent of eighteenth-century Scottish criminal practice.[96] The aim to make judges accountable through publishing their decisions reflected a strong theme in the thinking of Smith.[97] The general curriculum for the studies to be undertaken by judges also derived from legal education in Glasgow, with its emphasis on moral philosophy, natural law, Roman law and then Russian law.[98] More could be said on this.

Both Desnitsky and Tret'yakov were in favour of the change to lecturing in Russian rather than in Latin in the University of Moscow; a change understandably strongly resisted by the Germans who composed the majority of the professors.[99] It is fair to assume that the two Russians' experience of education in the University of Glasgow and, in particular, of Millar's lectures

93 Brown, "Adam Smith's First Russian Followers" (n 5) at 260.

94 Ibid at 269–272.

95 S E Desnitskii, *Proposal for the Establishment of Legislative, Judicial and Executive Power in the Russian Empire* (1768), in *Russia under Catherine the Great*, ed and trans P Dukes (1978) vol i, 44–65 (henceforth Desnitskii, *Proposal*).

96 Ibid 53; see J W Cairns, "Hamesucken and the Major Premiss in the Libel, 1672–1770: Criminal Law in the Age of Enlightenment", in R F Hunter (ed), *Justice and Crime: Essays in Honour of the Right Honourable The Lord Emslie* (1993) 138 at 142–145.

97 Desnitskii, *Proposal* (n 95) 53; see J W Cairns, "Adam Smith and the Role of the Courts in Securing Justice and Liberty", in R P Malloy and J Evensky (eds), *Adam Smith and the Philosophy of Law and Economics* (1994) 31.

98 Desnitskii, *Proposal* (n 95) 54.

99 Brown, "Adam Smith's First Russian Followers" (n 5) at 250.

on law, predisposed them to this reform, directly contrary to current practice in the German universities. It is therefore interesting to note that, in the debate started in 1768 over Millar's teaching of Civil Law in English, one pamphlet noted that "the law is, at present, taught in the Russian language, in the university of Moscow".[100] The practice of Desnitsky and Tret'yakov in Moscow, reported to their *alma mater* by the Clyde, could be prayed in aid of the general prevalence and good sense of the methods of their former professor.

100 *Essays. Viz. I. On the Origin of Colleges, Or Universities, etc* (n 89) vi.

9 From "Speculative" to "Practical" Legal Education: The Decline of the Glasgow Law School, 1801–1830*

A Royal Commission for Visiting the Universities and Colleges in Scotland was appointed on 23 July 1826. Its members were: the Duke of Gordon; the Duke of Montrose; the Marquis of Huntly; the Earl of Aberdeen; the Earl of Rosebery; the Earl of Mansfield; Viscount Melville; Lord Binning; Lord President Hope; Sir William Rae, Lord Advocate; Lord Justice-Clerk Boyle; Chief Baron Sir Samuel Shepherd; William Adam, Chief Commissioner of the Jury Court; John Hope, Solicitor General; George Cranstoun, Dean of the Faculty of Advocates; Dr Taylor, Moderator of the General Assembly; and Dr Cook, former Moderator.[1] A supplementary commission of 28 September added to this list the Earl of Lauderdale, Sir Walter Scott, the Rev Dr Lee, Henry Home Drummond, advocate, and James Moncrieff, advocate.[2] This was a distinguished body of the great and the good of early-nineteenth-century Scotland. Of these, Lauderdale, Rae, Boyle, Adam, Cranstoun and Moncrieff had studied at Glasgow under

* I am grateful to Michael Moss and Lesley Richmond of Glasgow University Archives and David Weston of Glasgow University Library for their assistance. I am indebted to the Faculty of Advocates in Edinburgh and the Royal Faculty of Procurators in Glasgow for permission to consult and cite their private records. To my great advantage, Roger Emerson kindly brought the correspondence of Professor Jardine to my attention as containing material relevant to my concerns. He also offered much useful criticism. The staff of the Special Collections in Edinburgh University Library were helpful in innumerable ways. I benefited from the criticism of the editorial board of the *Tijdschrift voor Rechtsgeschiedenis* and of Raymond Cocks, Hector MacQueen, David Sellar, and Alan Watson, though not all – if any – of these individuals would entirely agree with what I have written here.

1 Commission for Visiting the Universities and Colleges in Scotland 23[d] July 1826, in *Evidence, Oral and Documentary, taken and received by the Commissioners appointed by his Majesty George IV. July 23[d], 1826; and reappointed by his Majesty William IV, October 12th, 1830; for visiting the Universities of Scotland. Volume I: University of Edinburgh* (henceforth *Evidence . . . Volume I: University of Edinburgh*), 1837 Parliamentary Papers XXXV, 1–2.

2 Commission for Visiting the Universities and Colleges of Scotland, in ibid 3–5.

John Millar, who there had held the Regius chair of Civil Law from 1761 to 1801.[3]

A special sub-commission that included five of Millar's pupils visited the University of Glasgow, and on 9 January 1827 took evidence from Robert Davidson, Millar's successor.[4] What these Commissioners discovered at their *alma mater* cannot have pleased them.[5] When the report of the Royal Commission was published in 1831 it resolutely stated: "It is perhaps scarcely necessary to observe, that it is only in the University of Edinburgh that a full course of instruction in the Science of Law can with propriety be established; at least in the present circumstances of the country."[6] The report stressed that law ought to "be studied as a liberal and enlightened science", so that students did not "enter on practice at the Bar without any acquaintance with the general principles of Jurisprudence, and with limited and contracted views of the subject of their profession". The "science of Law" had to be taught in a way suitable "for making an accomplished and enlightened Advocate". The Commissioners emphasised:

> The real interests of the community may be most materially sacrificed, if the Course of Study of Law shall be adapted wholly to the supposed convenience of a portion of the Students. The country is deeply interested in the character, the independence and influence of the Advocates to whom the defence of their property and liberties may be entrusted; and it will be in vain to hope that the independence and character of the Bar can be maintained, if the study of Law is not conducted on an enlightened and philosophical plan.
>
> The great extension of the subject only renders it the more important to provide that the instruction of the Students shall not be limited to the details of a technical art, and the philosophy and science of Law sacrificed, in order to furnish materials for the Manual of a Practitioner.[7]

3 On these men as Millar's pupils, see W C Lehmann, *John Millar of Glasgow, 1735–1801: His Life and Thought and his Contributions to Sociological Analysis* (1960) (henceforth Lehmann, *John Millar of Glasgow*) 36–37.

4 *Evidence, Oral and Documentary, taken and received by the Commissioners appointed by his Majesty George IV. July 23^{d}, 1826; and re-appointed by his Majesty William IV, October 12th, 1830; for visiting the Universities of Scotland. Volume II: University of Glasgow* (henceforth *Evidence . . . Volume II: University of Glasgow*), 1837 Parliamentary Papers XXXVI, 1, 17, 145–148.

5 Lauderdale, Rae, Boyle, Cranstoun (now Lord Corehouse), and Moncrieff (now Dean of Faculty) were on the Glasgow sub-commission; none was present at the questioning of Davidson, however, but they would have had access to his oral testimony and to the documentary evidence.

6 *Report Made to His Majesty by a Royal Commission of Inquiry into the State of the Universities of Scotland*, in 1831 Parliamentary Papers VII, 53.

7 Ibid 54.

This was a firm endorsement of broad, liberal legal education: the study of law was not to be narrowly "practical" – indeed focusing on the "practical" to the exclusion of the "philosophical" was viewed as a self-defeating delusion. These were ideals of the education of lawyers that reached back to the seventeenth century in Scotland, and ultimately back to the Legal Humanists of sixteenth-century France.

It is tempting to see in these remarks the influence of John Millar's pupils. Millar had been an outstandingly successful teacher, turning the University of Glasgow into the leading law school in the British Isles, both through his sheer ability as a teacher, and through his offering a broad, polite, and liberal curriculum of Roman law, jurisprudence, government, Scots law and English law. He emphasised the dynamic aspect of law and its links to history, philosophy and society in classes that attracted future statesmen and leaders of the Bar.[8] Millar's exceptional qualities were recognised by his colleagues, one of whom wrote to a friend on the professor's death: "[O]ur society has sustained an irreparable loss: as a Professor we shall never see the like of him – a most indefatigable, able and successful Teacher – and taught Branches of General Education scarcely taught any where or at least no where so well."[9]

The story of legal education in Glasgow under Davidson was sad. When questioned by the sub-commission he described his chair as devoted to Civil or Roman law, but stated that he had not taught Roman law for four or five years because he was no longer willing to lecture to fewer than five students. He did, however, lecture upon Scots law in a course lasting one year. The bulk of his pupils were writers' clerks and apprentices in Glasgow, who afterwards often went to a writer's office in Edinburgh, frequently attending the lectures of the Professor of Scots Law in that city's university. It was rare for one of his students to become an advocate. He only attracted students to his lectures in Scots law because the Faculty of Procurators required future members to attend such a course. He wished they were also required to attend one in Civil Law. Almost without exception, his students came from Glasgow and its immediate neighbourhood.[10]

8 See J W Cairns, "Rhetoric, language, and Roman law: legal education and improvement in eighteenth-century Scotland" (1991) 9 *Law and History Review* 31; and "'Famous as a School for Law, as Edinburgh . . . for Medicine': Legal Education in Glasgow, 1761–1801", in A Hook and R B Sher (eds), *The Glasgow Enlightenment* (1994) 133 (henceforth Cairns, "'Famous as a School for Law, as Edinburgh . . . for Medicine'").

9 G Jardine to R Hunter, 16 July 1801, Glasgow University Library (henceforth GUL) MS Gen 507/118.

10 *Evidence . . . Volume II: University of Glasgow* (n 4) 145–146; University Register of Law Students, 1818–1843, Glasgow University Archives (henceforth GUA) 26798.

The members of the sub-commission asked Davidson if Roman law had once been regularly taught in Glasgow. He replied: "Mr. Millar, my predecessor, was a man of great eminence; he was quite a speculative man; I consider myself rather a practical man. This was a very famous school of Roman Law in Mr. Millar's time."[11] It is obvious that in the view of the Commission it was Davidson's rejection of the "speculative" in favour of the "practical" that had made a large contribution to the decline of the University of Glasgow from the United Kingdom's leading school of law to an institution teaching the clerks and apprentices of local, provincial lawyers.

This paper – the last of four dealing with the history of legal education in the University of Glasgow between 1714 and 1830[12] – will address that decline. In so far as Davidson made no contributions of significance to legal science, he is now deservedly forgotten. Yet it is important to understand his tenure of the Regius chair in Glasgow. First, it indicates the types of pressures and influences that shaped the history of legal education in Scotland and elsewhere. We must not approach that history as the inevitable onward march of the intellect. We must accept its contingency. It is necessary to explore the impact of politics and biography on *Universitätsgeschichte*. Secondly, his tenure of the Regius chair not only marked the end of one aspect of the Scottish Enlightenment (the scientific Whiggism we associate with Adam Smith and John Millar and their development of a science of legislation) but also brought forth condemnation of his narrow, limited approach to legal education. When the degree of LLB was created in Scotland in 1862, and when the Faculty of Advocates reformed its requirements for admission at the same period, it was the broad, liberal tradition of legal education deriving from Millar in Scotland, and now experienced by some Scots in Germany, that ensured that Roman law and jurisprudence were seen as vital in a legal education that was viewed as essentially academic and properly centred in the universities.[13]

11 *Evidence . . . Volume II: University of Glasgow* (n 4) 146.

12 J W Cairns, "The Origins of the Glasgow Law School: The Professors of Civil Law, 1714–1761", in P Birks (ed.), *The Life of the Law*, Proceedings of the Tenth British Legal History Conference, Oxford 1991 (1993) 151; and "William Crosse, Regius Professor of Civil Law in the University of Glasgow, 1746–1749: a failure of enlightened patronage" (1993) 12 *History of Universities* 159 (henceforth Cairns, "William Crosse"); and "'Famous as a School for Law, as Edinburgh . . . for Medicine'" (n 8).

13 J W Cairns, "A History of the Faculty of Advocates to 1900", in *The Laws of Scotland: Stair Memorial Encyclopaedia* vol 13 (1992) 499 (paras 1239–1288) at 527–534 (paras 1278–1283).

A. STUDENT NUMBERS

The first issue to consider is that of the numbers of students of law in Glasgow. J D Mackie suggests that John Millar "may have gone on too long, for his successor Robert Davidson found few students in Civil Law when he took over".[14] He offers no evidence for this statement and opinion, which he presumably based on the known statistics for students during Davidson's tenure of the chair. There is no precise, direct evidence for the size of Millar's classes.[15]

Mackie's suggestion presupposes that Millar, by the time of his death, was a man of failing powers. There is no evidence of this. Born in 1735, Millar was only in his middle sixties when he died on 30 May 1801 after completing his courses for the academic year 1800–1801.[16] We do have the evidence of William Lamb, however, who attended the University of Glasgow and stayed with Millar in the latter's last two years. Lamb found Millar an energetic, vigorous man.[17] Though ill at the end of 1799, Millar had fully recovered, and his death was the result of a sudden illness and quite unexpected.[18] He attended Faculty and Senate meetings right up to his death.[19] Furthermore, in his final session he taught both of his two courses on the *Institutes* of Justinian, and those on the *Digest*, government, and English law.[20] Indeed, the introduction of this last course, probably in 1798, was not the action of a man of diminishing energy and ability who was finding it difficult to attract students.[21] Mackie's suggestion must therefore be rejected as unfounded.

14 J D Mackie, *The University of Glasgow 1451–1951: A Short History* (1954) (henceforth Mackie, *University of Glasgow*) 234. See also ibid 166 n 3 and 187 for similar comments.

15 For a discussion of this, see Cairns, "'Famous as a School for Law, as Edinburgh . . . for Medicine'" (n 8) at 148–150. Law students of Millar can be found in the "Book of Attested Students 1766 to 1843", GUA 26680, but the names provide no guide to the size of the class.

16 See, e.g., *Glasgow Courier*, 2 June 1801.

17 P Ziegler, *Melbourne: A Biography of William Lamb 2nd Viscount Melbourne* (1976) 29–31.

18 G Jardine to R Hunter, 16 July 1801, GUL MS Gen 507/118; J Craig, *Account of the Life and Writings of John Millar, Esq* (henceforth Craig, *Life and Writings of John Millar*), prefixed to J Millar, *The Origin of the Distinction of Ranks: Or, an Inquiry into the Circumstances which give rise to Influence and Authority, in the different Members of Society*, 4th edn (1806) cxxviii–cxxix.

19 Minutes of Meetings of Faculty, 1800–1806, GUA 26696 44 (21 May 1801); Minutes of Meetings of Senate, 1787–1802, GUA 26687 329 (4 May 1801).

20 See GUL MS Gen 243, for lectures on English law dating from 1800 to 1801. He taught the other courses every year. See Cairns, "'Famous as a School for Law, as Edinburgh . . . for Medicine'" (n 8) at 136–139.

21 See W C Lehmann, "Some observations on the law lectures of Professor Millar at the University of Glasgow (1761–1801)" (1970) *Juridical Review* 56 (henceforth Lehmann, "John Millar of Glasgow") at 73–74; Cairns, "'Famous as a School for Law, as Edinburgh . . . for Medicine'" (n 8) at 136, 139, 153 n 13.

Unmentioned by Mackie are two other possible causes of a reduction in the number of Millar's students. The first was the opprobrium he attracted in the 1790s because of his political views as a Whig believed to have republican leanings.[22] Francis Jeffrey, for example, was alleged to have been forbidden by his father to attend Millar's classes.[23] The second was the reviving success of legal education in Edinburgh from the late 1780s.[24] Neither of these necessarily requires us to suppose that the size of Millar's class was diminished significantly or, indeed, at all. Not all parents shared the attitude of Jeffrey's father. For example, George Jardine, the Professor of Logic, expected one father to find unacceptable the prospect of his son, a law student in Glasgow, boarding with Millar because of the latter's politics, but, after Millar's death, suspected the father might withdraw his son and send him to Edinburgh to study law.[25] Millar's fame as a teacher could thus overcome Tory prejudices against his Whig views. Furthermore, at this time the overall number of law students in Scotland was probably starting to increase in a significant way, suggesting that Edinburgh's revival may not necessarily have been at Glasgow's expense.[26] However this may be, the only definite evidence we have – if anecdotal and indirect – suggests that Millar continued to be successful in attracting students through the 1790s. Not only did John Craig, Millar's biographer, fail to qualify for the 1790s his comment in 1806 that Millar "had, frequently, about forty students of Civil Law; while those who attended his Lectures on Government, often amounted to a much greater number", but more neutral observers such as Thomas Newte, Robert Heron, and Arthur Browne also continued throughout the 1790s to stress Millar's phenomenal success in drawing students to Glasgow.[27] The correspondence of Professor Jardine suggests that there may have been some reduction in the size of the law classes in the 1790s, but for reasons other than Millar's qualities and politics, and

22 Lehmann, "John Millar of Glasgow" (n 21) at 67–71.

23 Lord Cockburn, *Life of Lord Jeffrey with a Selection from his Correspondence*, 2nd edn, 2 vols (1852) vol i, 10–12.

24 See Cairns, "'Famous as a school for Law, as Edinburgh . . . for medicine'" (n 8) at 149–150.

25 G Jardine to R Hunter, 6 May 1801, GUL MS Gen 507/117; and 16 July 1801, GUL MS Gen 507/118.

26 Cairns, "'Famous as a School for Law, as Edinburgh . . . for Medicine'" (n 8) at 150, 158 n 59.

27 Craig, *Life and Writings of John Millar* (n 18) xi; T Newte, *Prospects and Observations; on a Tour in England and Scotland: Natural, Oeconomical, and Literary* (1791) 65; R Heron, *Observations Made in a Journey through the Western Countries of Scotland; in the Autumn of M,DCC,XCII*, 2 vols (1793) vol ii, 418 (remarks repeated, 2nd edn, 2 vols (1799) vol ii, 418); A Browne, *A Compendious View of the Civil Law, being the Substance of a Course of Lectures read in the University of Dublin*, 2 vols (1797) vol i, 17.

which would have been equally applicable to contemporary Edinburgh. Thus he commented in 1797 that, in contrast to other classes, "[t]he Law Classes always suffer in time of War".[28] This suggests some reduction in size. If so, how significant it was is unknown. Jardine stated in 1801 that the *Institutes* class "had greatly diminished of late years" which he attributed to the fact that "the knowledge of the Civil Law is not cried up so much at present as formerly".[29] If correct, this does not necessarily mean that the overall number of Millar's students had been significantly (if at all) reduced. Despite these two instances, the general tenor of Jardine's correspondence was overwhelmingly to stress Millar's tremendous success right up to his death in comparison with the professors in Edinburgh.[30] Taken with the other anecdotal evidence, this tends to show that Millar remained a successful and popular teacher.

Davidson's appointment therefore brings a very obvious change in the fortunes of the chair of Civil Law. Whereas Millar in his final year had taught courses on the *Institutes*, the *Digest*, government, and English law, Davidson in his first in 1801–1802 taught only one, on the *Institutes*, and only on three days a week instead of Millar's five.[31] Davidson attracted six students.[32] Jardine wrote: "Our new Professor of Law has a small Class as was expected – as that Class here depended wholly upon the Great abilities and reputation of the former Professor". He expected Davidson, however, to "raise a very considerable Scotch Law Class".[33] The next academic year, 1802–1803, Davidson again offered only a course on Justinian's *Institutes* which he taught to eleven students.[34]

Faculty minutes reveal why in his second year Davidson still taught only the course on the *Institutes*, although the normal duties of the chair had been taken to be to teach both a course on the *Institutes* and one on the *Digest* (at least if a total of five students appeared).[35] On 8 June 1802, Davidson represented to the Faculty that many writers in Glasgow had mentioned to him that young men training for that profession would be inconvenienced if

28 G Jardine to R Hunter, 3 April 1797, GUL MS Gen 507/104.
29 G Jardine to R Hunter, 8 December 1801, GUL MS Gen 507/119.
30 G Jardine to R Hunter, 16 July 1801, GUL MS Gen 507/118.
31 *Glasgow Courier*, 17 October 1801; on Millar's classes, see Cairns, "'Famous as a School for Law, as Edinburgh . . . for Medicine'" (n 8) at 136–139.
32 *Evidence . . . Volume II: University of Glasgow* (n 4) 527.
33 G Jardine to R Hunter, 8 December 1801, GUL MS Gen 507/119.
34 *Glasgow Courier*, 5 October 1802; *Evidence . . . Volume II: University of Glasgow* (n 4) 527.
35 Craig, *Life and Writings of John Millar* (n 18) xix. This was based on an interpretation of the famous Act of 1727 given to William Crosse: Cairns, "William Crosse" (n 12) 177; *Evidence . . . Volume II: University of Glasgow* (n 4) 277.

he did not lecture on Scots law "the Winter after next" (that is, 1803–1804) at the latest. He proposed "to give a daily practical course", but claimed that he would not be able to do this even in 1803–1804 if he had to lecture on the *Digest* in 1802–1803. He further argued that the numbers in the class on the *Institutes* in 1801–1802 made it doubtful if any students would offer themselves for the course on the *Digest* in the coming session, and, if any were to do so, they could not number more than one or two. He accordingly requested the Faculty's permission to postpone giving classes on the *Digest* until 1804–1805 on his undertaking to lecture daily on Scots law in 1803–1804, and also to read and explain the *Digest* in that session to any students who offered themselves. He requested that the Faculty not be influenced in their decision by considering the increase in his earnings that would result from the adoption of his proposal. Since students paid a fee to attend his course, this last remark indicates that he expected (no doubt with justice) a class on Scots law to be more popular with students than one on Civil Law. The Faculty acceded to his request.[36]

Scots law had last been lectured on in Glasgow – by Millar – in 1799–1800.[37] From 1796, the Faculty of Procurators in Glasgow had required those seeking admission to provide proof of attendance at a course of lectures on Scots law. Apprenticeships for those intending to join the Faculty lasted five years.[38] It is therefore obvious that, by 1802, the absence of a class in Scots law must have started to become a serious worry for lawyers in Glasgow.

In 1803–1804, despite the undertaking to teach Scots law, Davidson once more only advertised classes on the *Institutes* and *Digest*. He attracted a single student.[39] Jardine wrote his friend that "Our Law Class has altogether failed. Indeed that depended so much upon the personal abilities of our late friend – that nothing else was to be expected."[40] Offering the same two courses in 1804–1805, Davidson had no students at all.[41] Jardine now

36 GUA 26696 112–113.

37 *Glasgow Courier*, 15 October 1799.

38 This was introduced by the Royal Charter granted to the Faculty of Procurators on 1 July 1796. See Library of the Royal Faculty of Procurators, *Sederunt Book 1761–1796*, 4 March 1796 (no page or folio number), and *Sederunt Book of the Faculty of Procurators 1796–1832* 1, 8, and 15 (15 July 1796). For the regulations putting the requirement of the charter into effect, see *Sederunt Book 1796–1832* 40–49 at 47. Apprentices would have to produce evidence of attendance at the lectures at their examinations for admission.

39 *Glasgow Herald and Advertiser*, 7 October 1803; *Evidence . . . Volume II: University of Glasgow* (n 4) 527.

40 G Jardine to R Hunter, 9 June 1804, GUL MS Gen 507/126.

41 *Glasgow Herald and Advertiser*, 24 September 1804; *Evidence . . . Volume II: University of Glasgow* (n 4) 527.

described the "Law-Class" as "quite annihilated – no Civil Law Lectures these two years". Perhaps his comment that "it is said that the Scotch Law Lecture is only to begin next session" should be read as betraying some impatience with Davidson's inactivity.[42] The course on Scots law was finally added in 1805–1806, but no students offered themselves for any of the three courses.[43] In this session, James Millar, Professor of Mathematics, the son of Davidson's predecessor, was authorised by the Faculty on 25 November 1805 to give lectures on English law.[44] Millar had previously been granted such a permission during his father's lifetime, and, of no great distinction as a mathematician, had at one time considered a career at the English Bar, and had studied law with his father.[45] This must have appeared threatening to Davidson, given that Millar obviously had some knowledge of and experience and interest in law.[46] Millar accordingly wrote to Davidson on 27 January 1806 that the Faculty should minute that the proposed lectures would not prejudice Davidson's right to lecture on the same subject in the future. This was done by inscribing the letter in the Faculty's minute book on 7 March 1806.[47] Perhaps Davidson was particularly sensitive on this subject in an academic year when the Professor of Medicine had been authorised to teach in the unused law class room.[48]

Davidson's luck started to turn the next year, and he had one student in Civil Law and twenty-nine in Scots law.[49] Thereafter until 1825, he never had fewer than twenty-one students in Scots law and never more than forty-nine.[50] Numbers remained low in Civil Law, however, and after

42 G Jardine to R Hunter, 15 August 1805, GUL MS Gen 507/128.

43 *Glasgow Herald*, 7 October 1805; *Evidence . . . Volume II: University of Glasgow* (n 4) 527.

44 GUA 26696 373.

45 Minutes of Meetings of Faculty, 1789–1794, GUA 26694 269 (7 December 1792); J Leslie to J Brown, 20 January 1796, Edinburgh University Library (henceforth EUL) MS Dc 2.57, fos 207–208; Mackie, *University of Glasgow* (n 14) 217; GUA 26680 49.

46 He had copied out his father's lecture notes on government and Scots law: see J W Cairns, "John Millar's lectures on Scots criminal law" (1988) 8 OJLS 364 (henceforth Cairns, "Millar's lectures") at 370–371 n 33. In that footnote, I suggested that it was unlikely that James Millar had attended his father's lectures as a student. This was wrong, as GUA 26680 49 shows. I stand by the other comments, however, in that note, and I remain convinced that GUL MSS Gen 289–291 and MS Gen 1078 are not student notes but copies by James Millar of the notes from which his father lectured.

47 GUA 26696 388.

48 Ibid 376 (29 November 1805).

49 *Evidence . . . Volume II: University of Glasgow* (n 4) 527. Curiously enough, he only advertised classes on the *Institutes* and the *Digest* in the *Glasgow Herald*, 29 September 1806.

50 *Evidence . . . Volume II: University of Glasgow* (n 4) 527. For his advertisements, see *Glasgow Herald*, 2 October 1807, 26 September 1808, 22 September 1809, 24 September 1810, 16 September 1811, 25 September 1812, 20 September 1813, 30 September 1814, 29 September

1819 he seems to have decided not to teach it unless he had at least five students.[51] Whereas Davidson's maximum of forty-nine students might seem a good number in comparison with the size of classes in the middle of the eighteenth century, when, for instance, John Erskine in Edinburgh, the leading Professor of Scots Law in his day, had classes varying in size from thirty-one to forty-six between 1763 and 1765,[52] in the first quarter of the nineteenth century this was no longer so. Thus, between 1801 and 1825 there were never less than twenty-one students and never more than fifty-two in Civil Law in the University of Edinburgh, and numbers in Scots law varied between ninety and 257.[53] The contrast with Davidson's classes in Glasgow is striking.

Given that the bulk of the students whom Davidson attracted probably took his class because of the Faculty of Procurators' requirement that apprentices attend a course of lectures on Scots law, it is small wonder that he expressed the wish that they should also require attendance in Civil Law. His class numbers should also be placed in the context of a doubling of admissions to the Bar in this period – between 1802 and 1806 thirty-seven men were admitted to the Faculty of Advocates, while between 1822 and 1826 eighty-nine men were admitted. The numbers had been progressively increasing in the intervening years.[54] This growth in the number of advocates must have been part of an increase in recruitment to the legal profession as a whole. In Glasgow in particular, as the town grew in this period into a major commercial and industrial centre, the number of writers and procurators must have been expanding. Davidson was thus failing to capture a significant share of a growing demand in Scotland for legal education.

1815. His particular courses are not thereafter noted. In all these years he advertised courses on the *Institutes*, the *Digest*, and (except for 1808 when he none the less taught it) Scots law.

51 The statistics in Roman law were, 1807–1808: 5; 1808–1809: 4; 1809–1810: 3; 1810–1811: 1; 1811–1812: 0; 1812–1813: 6; 1813–1814: 1; 1814–1815: 0; 1815–1816: 6; 1816–1817: 12; 1817–1818: 0; 1818–1819: 4; 1819–1820: 0; 1820–1821: 0; 1821–1822: 11; 1822–1823: 0; 1823–1824: 0; 1824–1825: 0; 1825–1826: 0. *See Evidence . . . Volume II: University of Glasgow* (n 4) 527, and, for his change of policy, ibid 146.

52 EUL (MS) Matriculation Roll of the University of Edinburgh, Arts–Law–Divinity, transcribed by Dr Alexander Morgan 1933–1934, 3 vols (henceforth Edinburgh Matriculations) vol i, fos 256–257, 262, 268–269.

53 *Evidence . . . Volume II: University of Edinburgh* (n 4) appendix, 130–131 (this gives no students for 1811–1812 for either Civil or Scots law, but the matriculations listed in ibid 128 show that there were plenty of students, so I have discounted this year in giving student figures).

54 N Phillipson, *The Scottish Whigs and the Reform of the Court of Session 1785–1830* (1990) (henceforth Phillipson, *The Scottish Whigs*) 189.

B. THE APPOINTMENT OF DAVIDSON

If the initial disappearance of students of law from Glasgow in the first years of the nineteenth century did not follow a significant decline in numbers under Millar, it is necessary to explain why Davidson was so spectacularly unsuccessful, and why he ultimately attracted only local apprentices. To do so requires, first, examination of how he came to gain the chair and why he wished to have it, before, secondly, consideration of the evidence of his teaching.

There can be little doubt that Davidson gained the chair because he was the son of the Principal, Archibald Davidson. This in itself is no indication that he was likely to be unsuited for the office. Such family connections were commonplace in the Scottish universities.[55] It is interesting to note, however, that Professor Jardine was approached by some of his colleagues about the possible candidature of his own son when the post became vacant on Millar's death. As well as indicating the significance of kinship in appointments, this is important because of Jardine's response. He did not wish his son to seek the chair: "None who like the Bar and have any prospect of rising there could be tempted by it."[56] This suggests that Davidson sought the chair because he was a man with no prospects at the Bar, for whom a small academic salary and sparse student fees would be attractive. Davidson's life to the time of his presentation to the chair is instructive in this respect.

Born in 1768, Davidson studied Scots law in Edinburgh with William Wallace in 1785.[57] He matriculated in Glasgow in 1788, most likely to help prepare for his private examination in Civil Law for admission to the Faculty of Advocates. This examination probably took place in the summer of 1789.[58] This choice of university would have been dictated by his father's appointment as Principal in 1785. Dr Paton states that Davidson studied

55 See, e.g., D Murray, *Memories of the Old College of Glasgow: Some Chapters in the History of the University* (1927) (henceforth Murray, *Memories of the Old College of Glasgow*) 247 n 1.

56 G Jardine to R Hunter, 16 July 1801, GUL MS Gen 507/118.

57 Edinburgh Matriculations (n 52) vol ii, fo 446. Comparison of the actual signature in the original register in Edinburgh with that of Davidson in the relevant album at Glasgow (GUA 26678 229) confirms that this is the future professor at Glasgow. For his date of birth, see W Innes Addison, *A Roll of the Graduates of the University of Glasgow from 31st December 1727 to 31st December 1897 with short biographical notes* (1898) 144.

58 *The Matriculation Albums of the University of Glasgow from 1727 to 1858*, ed W Innes Addison (1913) 154; GUA 26678 229; National Library of Scotland, Minute Book of the Faculty of Advocates, 1783–1798, FR 3 100–101.

with Hume in Edinburgh in 1789–1790 and 1790–1791.[59] Since Davidson was admitted as an advocate on 6 July 1790, it is unlikely – though possible – that he studied with Hume in the second of these two academic sessions.[60] The year between the private trial in Civil Law and admission was normally devoted to the study of Scots law in preparation for the trial in that subject.[61] It is always possible that Davidson attended Hume's class in 1789–1790 to assist his study, without his name appearing in the records of Hume's classes; on the other hand he may have remained in Glasgow, as 1789–1790 was one of the years in which John Millar taught Scots law.[62] Supporting this latter view is the fact that another Davidson can be traced as studying with Hume in these two academic sessions. Paton's comment (for which unfortunately he gives no reference) seems likely to be based on a misidentification of this Davidson as Robert Davidson.[63] Lehmann certainly described Robert Davidson as Millar's pupil.[64] Davidson married in 1794:[65] if he was unsuccessful at the Bar, it is easy to see that, approaching his mid-thirties with a family to support, the position at Glasgow, even with its slim pickings, would have been attractive, especially since he could presumably be easily shoehorned into it.

Jardine may not have wished his son to be a candidate for the chair, but he took the view that in any case his son would not have obtained it because of the opposition of the Chancellor, the Duke of Montrose.[66] Davidson was appointed during the last years of Henry Dundas' long ascendancy in Scottish politics. Dundas indeed had served as Rector of the University of Glasgow in 1781–1782. Given that the chair was under royal patronage, Dundas or his supporters will have exerted influence in the appointment. In contrast

59 G C H Paton, "Biography of Baron Hume", in G C H Paton (ed), *Baron Hume's Lectures 1786–1822*, 6 vols (1939–1959) (henceforth *Hume's Lectures*) vol vi, 327 at 411.

60 F J Grant (ed), *The Faculty of Advocates in Scotland, 1532–1943, with Genealogical Notes* (1944) (henceforth *Faculty of* Advocates) 52. John Jardine attended Hume's lectures after admission as an advocate: G Jardine to R Hunter, 13 March 1801, GUL MS Gen 507/116. Grant gives Davidson's date of birth as 1763 rather than 1768; this is probably a printing error.

61 J W Cairns, "The Formation of the Scottish Legal Mind in the Eighteenth Century: Themes of Humanism and Enlightenment in the Admission of Advocates", in N MacCormick and P Birks (eds), *The Legal Mind, Essays for Tony Honoré* (1986) 253 at 264–265.

62 *Glasgow Mercury*, 13/20 October 1789; *Glasgow Advertiser and Evening Intelligencer*, 16/19 October 1789.

63 See EUL MS Da 1.42 fo 150v: "Gul Davidson" (1789) and fo 178v: "Gul Davidson" (1790). This is a register of payments for the Library. Neither William Davidson nor any other Davidson appears in the Matriculation albums for these years as a student of Hume.

64 Lehmann, *John Millar of Glasgow* (n 3) 37.

65 *Faculty of Advocates* (n 60) 52.

66 G Jardine to R Hunter, 16 July 1801, GUL MS Gen 507/118.

to some earlier dispensers of patronage such as the Earl of Ilay or the Earl of Bute, Dundas seems to have been less concerned with the promotion of merit: political allegiance was what was of paramount importance.[67] Thus, the appointment of Davidson's father as Principal was attributed to the interest of the Lord Advocate, Ilay Campbell, a Dundas supporter, "the great conductor of such Jobs", who was the local MP.[68] When William Taylor was appointed Principal in 1802, Professor Jardine remarked: "This nomination like some others of late have heed of persons Loyalty rather than Literary merit or Character."[69] This presumably applied to Davidson and explains largely why he gained the chair. It is difficult to believe that anyone would have been able to write of a man supported by Lord Ilay as Henry Brougham did thus six days after Millar's death in a letter to James Loch: "[T]hey mean to give poor J. Millar's class to that stupidest of all brutes Robt. Davidson."[70] That Brougham was a remarkably unpleasant and arrogant man does not deny this comment all force. Clearly Davidson did not sparkle intellectually.

The date of Brougham's letter was also the date of the first official notification of Millar's death to the Faculty. This shows that Davidson's father and supporters planned and managed his appointment efficiently and swiftly, with the dispatch typical for Regius chairs, even if the position seemed unattractive to others.[71] As well as forestalling rivals, swift action was no doubt necessary in order to ensure that someone was presented to the chair in time for the coming academic year. Davidson's presentation was accordingly delivered to the Faculty on 30 July who appointed for his trial the reading on 6 August of a Latin dissertation *De lege Julia majestatis*. On that date, he read his dissertation, took the necessary oaths, and was admitted to the office.[72]

67 R L Emerson, *Professors, Patronage and Politics: The Aberdeen Universities in the Eighteenth Century* (1992) 100. M Fry, *The Dundas Despotism* (1992) defends Dundas from many of the criticisms made of him; he does not directly address the issue of university patronage, however, and nothing written there suggests a need to revise Emerson's views on this point.

68 G Jardine to R Hunter, 1 December 1785, GUL MS Gen 507/82; L Namier and J Brooke, *The House of Commons 1754–1787*, 3 vols (1964) vol i, 505–506, vol ii, 184.

69 G Jardine to R Hunter, 22 September 1803, GUL MS Gen 507/125.

70 H Brougham to J Loch, 5 June 1801, R H M Buddle Atkinson and G A Jackson (eds), *Brougham and his Early Friends: Letters to James Loch, 1798–1809*, 3 vols (1908) (henceforth *Brougham and his Early Friends*) vol i, 275. This is not to deny that Ilay had some failures: see, e.g., Cairns, "William Crosse" (n 12). These took place, however, in special circumstances.

71 GUA 26696 47 (5 June 1801).

72 Ibid 54–56, 56–57.

C. DAVIDSON'S CLASSES

Turning to the issue of Davidson's teaching, we find that a number of sets of notes taken by students survive from his lectures on Scots law, giving a picture of his classes in that subject over the period with which we are concerned.[73] A first point to consider is that Davidson's course was very heavily influenced by that of David Hume in Edinburgh. While it is always possible that he may have studied with Hume, it is more likely that he simply procured a copy of Hume's lectures, notes of which circulated widely in Scotland at this time. However this may be, Davidson adopted Hume's variation on the structure of Millar's lectures (reversing Millar's treatment of personal and real rights).[74] He told his class: "This method is now followed by Mr. Hume Professor of Law in the University of Edinburgh to whom I lye under very great obligations."[75] And the structure of Davidson's lectures followed very closely, though not identically, that of those of Hume and Millar.[76] For example, he included a brief account of criminal law as had done the latter but not the former, who treated it in a separate summer course.[77] Davidson's course is three times the length of that of Millar on Scots law, if not quite reaching the extent of that of Hume.[78] It should be stressed, however, that despite the strong influence of Hume, Davidson's course is not a simple copy of his, although the same topics are covered in much the same order and much the same cases are cited.[79]

Qualitative assessment of Davidson's classes on Scots law is difficult. Reading of the student notes suggests his course of lectures was somewhat plodding. Later David Murray fairly assessed the classes as "commonplace and dull".[80] There is none of Millar's interest in theoretical issues and penetrating philosophical and historical insight. Instead there is a routine and unexciting journey through the relevant cases and statutes. In this, of course, Davidson's classes rather resemble those of Hume in Edinburgh.

73 GUL MSS Gen 1045/1–3 (1807–1808); GUL MSS Murray 340–341 (1817–1818); GUL MS Gen 472; GUL MSS Gen 323–324 (1821–1822); GUL MSS Murray 275–276 (1827–1828) (not all of these are complete).

74 Cairns, "Millar's lectures" (n 46) at 396–397.

75 GUL MS Murray 340 7.

76 See Appendix A for a comparative outline of Millar's, Hume's and Davidson's lectures on Scots law.

77 Cairns, "Millar's lectures" (n 46) at 395–400.

78 In 1817–1818 Davidson gave 141 lectures. Millar generally aimed at fifty. See Cairns, "'Famous as a School for Law, as Edinburgh . . . for Medicine'" (n 8) at 142–143.

79 Compare, e.g., GUL MS Gen 1045/1 fos 1r–10r with *Hume's Lectures* (n 59) vol ii, 125–142.

80 Murray, *Memories of the Old College of Glasgow* (n 55) 228.

James Brougham could comment to a friend in 1802: "The excellency of Hume's course is acknowledged by everybody, but this excellency consists chiefly, I may say only, in his arrangement of the decisions."[81] More disparagingly, Thomas Carlyle and others could find Hume's lectures tedious and frustrating.[82] It is difficult to believe, however, that anyone could have written of Davidson's lectures as Walter Scott did of Hume's, describing the Edinburgh professor with enthusiastic warmness and some justice as having been "an architect ... to the Law of Scotland".[83] Hume's genius makes Davidson's similar lectures appear a distinctly pedestrian affair; given that they were heavily influenced by those of Hume – a lesser, derivative version so to speak – it is perfectly understandable that students preferred to go to the greater originals in Edinburgh, unless there were pressing reasons – such as apprenticeship – tying them to Glasgow. Hume resigned the chair in Scots Law in 1822, but his successor George Joseph Bell was also a man of considerable distinction with whom Davidson obviously found that he could not really compete.[84] That Bell was so successful is particularly telling against Davidson, as, no matter how distinguished a scholar, Bell was reputed a poor teacher whose students were inattentive.[85] Moreover, as a younger man he had suffered from troubles due to his Whig political views.[86] Even so, his classes ranged in size between 240 and 128 over 1823 to 1830.[87] This was very respectable, especially since from 1825 Bell faced competition from Macvey Napier, in the newly erected Professorship of Conveyancing, who attracted 110 students in 1825–1826 and 152 in 1827–1828, and who was known as a clear and attractive lecturer.[88]

Alexander Irving held the chair of Civil Law in Edinburgh from 1800 to 1826. Though presumably a competent teacher and an able enough man (he was made a judge in 1826), there is nothing to suggest that he was the

81 J Brougham to J Loch, 25 April 1802, in *Brougham and his Early Friends* (n 70) vol i, 328.
82 Paton, "Biography of Baron Hume" (n 59) at 405–406.
83 D Hewitt (ed), *Scott on Himself: A Selection of the Autobiographical Writings of Sir Walter Scott* (1981) 42.
84 A Grant, *The Story of the University of Edinburgh during its First Three Hundred Years*, 2 vols (1884) (henceforth Grant, *University of Edinburgh*) vol ii, 373–375.
85 T St J N Bates, "Mr M'Connachie's Notes and Mr Fraser's Confessional" (1980) *Juridical Review* 166 (henceforth Bates, "M'Connachie's Notes") at 175–176.
86 Phillipson, *The Scottish Whigs* (n 54) 144, 152–156.
87 *Evidence . . . Volume I: University of Edinburgh* (n 1) appendix, 131.
88 Grant, *University of Edinburgh* (n 84) vol ii, 376–377; *Evidence . . . Volume I: University of Edinburgh* (n 1) appendix, 131; Bates, "M'Connachie's Notes" (n 85) at 175–176.

type of striking, innovative teacher that Millar had been.[89] His lectures on the *Institutes*, for example, were competent, but somewhat dry, expositions of Heineccius' *Elementa juris civilis secundum ordinem institutionum.*[90] Davidson, however, was unable to exploit this situation to build up a class by capitalising on the fame Millar had brought to the study of Roman law in the University of Glasgow, and thus failed to take advantage of the fact that the Edinburgh Professor of Civil Law was not a Civilian equivalent of Hume or Bell.

No notes taken by students in Davidson's classes on Roman law survive. There are, however, indications of what his teaching must have been like. Glasgow University Library possesses a copy of the eight-volume Geneva edition of Heineccius' *Opera omnia.*[91] This particular copy was in the Library by 1791.[92] The fifth volume, which includes Heineccius' compendium of the *Institutes*, contains pencil notes in two hands which suggest that lectures were being delivered from it on the *Institutes* in 1815–1816 and 1816–1817, to the six students in Civil Law in the first of these sessions and to the twelve in the next.[93] There are some annotations to the section of the volume containing Heineccius' compendium of the *Digest*; it is impossible, however, to confirm that they are for teaching, and they are far fewer than those relating to the *Institutes*.[94] One of the two hands is possibly that of Davidson, the other is probably that of a William Davidson whose signature appears on several pages.[95] This latter may be Davidson's son who certainly

89 Grant, *University of Edinburgh* (n 84) vol ii, 366.

90 See EUL MSS Gen 1389–1390.

91 J G Heineccius, *Operum ad universam iuris prudentiam, philosophiam et literas humaniores pertinentium [tomi octo]* (1744–1748) GUL pressmark B19-f 10–17.

92 A Arthur, *Catalogus impressorum librorum in bibliotheca universitatis Glasguensis, secundum literarum ordinem dispositus* (1791) 207 col a.

93 J G Heineccius, *Operum . . . tomus quintus, in quo elementa iuris civilis secundum ordinem Institutionum et Pandectarum, commoda auditoribus methodo adornata*, GUL pressmark B19-f.14; see ibid 262 for the dates of the sessions.

94 The only suggestion that the notes may relate to classes on the *Digest* is on Heineccius, *Elementa iuris civilis secundum ordinem . . . Pandectarum*, in *Operum . . . tomus quintus* 275: "Begin on Monday". On its own this merely confirms that someone was making his way through the text for some purpose; given the frequency with which the name William Davidson is found in this section of the volume (see n 95), once with a date in February 1817 (ibid 315), it was probably he. There are other curious notes, such as the aide-memoire in ibid 201: "I neglected to give the Gaslight Bill to [illeg] the Day before yesterday 28 April 1817"; "Ha Ha Civil Law" in ibid 108; and the Lord's prayer on ibid 291 (also found in part in *Elementa iuris civilis Institutionum*, in ibid 331 (deleted)).

95 There are ink notes on the *Elementa iuris civilis secundum ordinem . . . Pandectarum* which are fairly certainly in the hand of Robert Davidson. Comparison of the signatures in the volume with that of William Davidson in the Matriculation Album (GUA 26679 fo 19r) tends to confirm that it was he who signed his name over and over again in the volume. In the *Elementa*

was later to read his father's lectures to his class.[96] Perhaps he helped his father in some way in 1816–1817, although he would have been quite young. However all this may exactly be, the annotations show that Davidson and perhaps an assistant or substitute were teaching Roman law to the Glasgow students in these two academic years from Heineccius' compendium. The notes themselves have little juridical content, but consist, first, of trivialities tracing the class's progress through the text. A few examples will suffice to give their flavour: "Begun on Monday 25th Novr. 1816 my second session"; "Mr Shaw not present"; "Begin on Monday Decr Ist"; "Begin on Friday 13th Decr"; "no examin[atio]n"; "There being no examination on the sections read this day the examin[atio]n which begins at Sect, [blank]".[97] Secondly, there are annotations which indicate that part of the text was omitted, often because it dealt with the *usus hodiernus*: "Omitted Modern German Law"; "omitted".[98] Thirdly, there are marginal comments which simply indicate the content of a section, often being merely a translation of the printed marginal note from Latin: "2 ways of acquiring paternal power"; "In this section the real contracts known in the Roman law are ment[ione]d"; "This section mentions those who can constitute mutuum", "requisites of the hire"; "The power which the Emphyteuta had over the subject".[99] Finally, a number of the notes make some substantive point about the law, usually of a most banal nature.[100] Some of the annotations may relate to examinations (that is, the quizzing of students on past lectures) rather than to the actual lectures; but it is evident that many of them are for use in lectures.[101] These annotations

. . . *secundum ordinem . . . Pandectarum* in ibid, we find on 163 the name "Robert Davidson 1788" and on 334 the same name three times, twice with the date 1788. This is the date the future Professor matriculated in Glasgow. The name on its own occurs in ibid 645, while "Robert" on its own is found a number of times. The signature is not his, however, either of that date or later. In fact it looks to be written by William Davidson, who among other versions of his name wrote on ibid 315: "W. Davidson College Glasgow 21st February 1817"; and such was his obsession that on D 38.10 *De gradibus et adfinibus et nominibus eorum* (ibid 561), he wrote: "Et ego vero Gul. David.".

96 J Coutts, *A History of the University of Glasgow from its Foundation in 1451 to 1909* (1909) 390.

97 Heineccius, *Elementa iuris civilis secundum ordinem Institutionum*, in *Operum . . . tomus quintus*, GUL pressmark B19-f.14 19, 23, 49, 193, 215.

98 Ibid 61, 87.

99 Ibid 36, 208, 209, 239, 242.

100 See Appendix B.

101 Thus, there are notes on *emphyteusis* in Heineccius, *Elementa iuris civilis secundum ordinem Institutionum*, in *Operum . . . tomus quintus*, GUL pressmark B19-f.14 241–243 but at 241 is noted "No examination on this title"; likewise at 77 is written "No examination on this title as it is not of much importance no person in England or Scotland being compelled to accept of the office of a tutor or Curator".

none the less are important, despite their vacuity, because they demonstrate that whoever was teaching was doing so directly from this volume and apparently without further notes. He could only have been reading and glossing the text. Such simple exposition of an elementary text was far removed from Millar's intellectually innovative and advanced teaching. While Millar related his account of the law to issues of philosophy and history, these notes show that the lecturer omitted the first two titles of the *Institutes*, those *De iustitia et iure* and *De iure naturae, gentium et civili*, and simply plunged into an exposition of the substantive law ignoring all theoretical issues. If this indicates a lack of concern with legal theory, the entire fourth book seems not to have been the subject of classes, for reasons less easy to explain, because, although the lecturer elsewhere seems to have preferred to emphasise titles having a bearing on modern law, this would not account for omitting book four.[102] The notes generally suggest a laziness about preparing for the classes on Civil Law. The standard cannot have been high. It is easy to see that students would not have found such an approach attractive.

D. DAVIDSON'S TENURE OF THE CHAIR

Craig wrote in 1806 that "[f]rom the absence of the higher Courts of Justice, Glasgow lies under many obvious disadvantages, as a school of law".[103] This inherent unattractiveness, certainly to Scots, of studying law in Glasgow, correspondingly meant, given the reliance on student fees for a significant part of a professor's income, that the chair of Civil Law in Glasgow was not necessarily a desirable office. To overcome student reluctance to study law in Glasgow, and hence make the chair more remunerative, it was necessary for the professor to be particularly able and energetic as a teacher. Davidson evidently was not. That there was only one chair in law was a further problem. Only if a professor were able and willing to make Millar's efforts could anything approaching the type of curriculum desired by law students be offered. Yet, the fact remains that Millar showed legal education to be viable at Glasgow given the right professor. The comparative failure of the Glasgow law school after 1801 must thus be largely attributed to Davidson; at the very least, it should be acknowledged that he contributed significantly to its decline. Despite the delay in introducing the promised course in Scots law and in teaching the course on the *Digest*, it is, however, difficult simply

102 Heineccius, *Elementa iuris civilus secundum ordinem Institutionum* in ibid 19, 17, 262.
103 Craig, *Life and Writings of John Millar* (n 18) xi.

to dismiss Davidson as lazy and unwilling to put effort into his teaching. Even if prejudiced, Brougham's remark on Davidson's quality is impossible to ignore, indicating that Davidson's lack of success may have been due to lack of ability rather than straightforward idleness. Furthermore, Jardine's remark about the unattractiveness of the chair suggests Davidson sought it because he lacked the ability and stamina to succeed at the Bar, where, in contrast to Jardine's son, he was politically very acceptable. In this respect it is important to examine Davidson's activities as Professor of Civil Law.

All the previous Professors of Civil Law – except for Crosse the sinecurist – had participated in the general administration of the University, and Millar had certainly been much involved in the University's legal business.[104] All this was standard practice in the University, which was a largely self-governing corporation with a small number of professors. With Davidson, however, there is a qualitative change. In 1804 the Faculty delegated to him "a general superintendence of their business in so far as relates to their Revenue; and in an especial manner to valuations of Teinds".[105] This work evidently occupied a great deal of Davidson's time.[106] He was suitably recompensed for it each year at sums of from thirty to sixty guineas.[107] Once, he was allowed to use £30 of the money he had recovered from discovering unpaid teinds to purchase books on English law for the Library.[108]

Davidson was obviously a useful and competent administrator. As he had only one student in 1803–1804, and none in 1804–1805, delegating to him

104 Forbes acted as Dean of Faculty, Minutes of University Meetings, 1730–1749, GUA 26639 21 (26 June 1732), and Quaestor, Minutes of Meetings of Faculty and Dean of Faculty's Meetings, 1732–1768, GUA 26645 11 (26 June 1736). Lindesay served in the same two offices: GUA 26634 76, (26 June 1753) and 92 (26 June 1758). Millar served as Quaestor, Minutes of Meetings of Senate, 1771–1787, GUA 26686 68 (10 June 1773), Clerk of Faculty, Minutes of Meetings of Faculty, 1771–1776, GUA 26690 76 (10 June 1772), Clerk of the Comitia, Minutes of Meetings of Senate, 1771–1787, GUA 26686 55 (15 November 1772) and was appointed by Andrew Stewart as his vice-rector, GUA 26686 171 (9 June 1778). Millar was much involved in the University's legal affairs and other general business. Many traces can be found of his work in Glasgow University Archives. See, e.g., GUA 10025 (on a conveyancing problem), GUA 5154 (consulted on litigation initiated by Professor Anderson against his colleagues), GUA 11553 (draft letter concerning the building of the Hunterian Museum). He was also involved in consultations with Balliol College about the Snell Exhibition: GUA 26690 263 (12 November 1774), GUA 26694 228 (18 April 1792) 229–230 (27 April 1792), and 266 (6 November 1792).

105 Davidson to J Balfour, 22 March 1804, in Letter Book of Professor Davidson, Professor of Law, 22 March 1804–22 May 1808, GUA 234731.

106 See, e.g., ibid, passim, and Professor Davidson's Letter Book No 2 relative to the affairs of the College from 22 May 1808 to 30 April 1810, GUA 17038.

107 Minutes of Meetings of Faculty 1806–1813, GUA 26697 1–2 (9 June 1806): "professional fee"; 36 (17 March 1807); 57 (3 June 1807): 30 guineas; 222 (20 July 1808): £47.5.0d; 343 (4 March 1811): 60 guineas. (See also GUA 58353: detached minute authorising payment to Davidson.)

108 GUA 26697 379 (10 March 1812).

the collection of the University's revenue was obviously a sensible use of his time, allowing him to contribute to the general running of the institution, if in an uptypical way for a professor.[109] It used the skills that he had. He also appears to have given up collecting the teinds sometime after 1811, when the numbers of his students in Scots law started to increase significantly.

Yet, Davidson and his colleagues evidently felt his position to be unfortunate. In 1803–1804, for example, he was anxious to be appointed Town Clerk of Glasgow.[110] Moreover, that Davidson spent so much time as a collector of the University's revenue because he had few or no students must have made a painfully obvious contrast with Millar's position as a successful and famous professor who attracted students from throughout the British Isles and even from abroad. In a Faculty deeply divided by politics, Davidson's position would accordingly have often been unpleasant. In this respect, it is worth noting that in one of the years in which Davidson had no students a dispute arose within the Faculty over the appointment of an agent in Edinburgh. Two men were considered. One was Archibald Millar, WS, "son to our late Colleague Mr Millar Professor of Laws in this University", and the other was James Davidson, WS, who was Robert Davidson's cousin. James Davidson was elected on 18 November 1805 on the casting vote of the Principal, William Taylor.[111] Four members of the Faculty protested over this use of the Principal's casting vote. Prominent among the reasons for their dissent was that Davidson's appointment was "a departure from that old and Kindly practise, which, so far as is known to the Dissentients, has been constantly observed by this Society" to give preference for this type of office to the son of a professor. The dissent eulogised John Millar:

> [W]ho, during the long period of forty years, discharged the duties of that profession with uncommon ability and industry, and by his strenuous exertions, raised the law department of Education in this College to a degree of celebrity unknown in any former time: and whose zeal for the interests of this Society

109 Some of the tedium involved in this administration can be grasped from, e.g., C Stirling to J Dundas, 11 June 1808 inclosing copy letter of J Davidson WS (on whom see below) to R Davidson, 3 June 1808, EUL MS Dk 7.47/51.

110 "James Reddie, LLD" (1853) 17 *Law Review, and Quarterly Journal of British and Foreign Jurisprudence* 63 at 65–66.

111 GUA 26696 370–371; on James Davidson being Davidson's cousin, see *Historical Sketch of the Glasgow Society of the Sons of Ministers of the Church of Scotland*, 5th edn (1910) 31–32, showing that the Rev Robert Davidson of Crawfordjohn was the father of Principal Archibald Davidson and of Rev John Davidson of Old Kilpatrick, the latter being the father of James Davidson, WS.

> disposed him at all times to give such professional advice and assistance as its business from time to time required.[112]

For a successor who currently had no students, and who was being specially paid to collect the University's teinds, this minuted dissent to the appointment of his cousin as University agent cannot have been pleasant reading. It must have seemed an implicit criticism, as it indeed may well have been intended. Davidson's colleagues were willing to attribute the failure of legal education in Glasgow to his lack-lustre performance and apparent intellectual mediocrity.

It was certainly very much Davidson's fate and misfortune to be regarded as the undistinguished successor to a great and famous man. Thus, in an account of the University in 1825, he was simply noticed as having "succeeded that accomplished scholar, and excellent man, John Millar".[113] There was obviously some sensitivity on this issue, since at least one reader and correspondent construed this as slighting Davidson, though his defence of him was notably silent on Davidson's merits as a scholar and teacher.[114] Likewise, Millar was described as follows in the *Caledonian Mercury* in the summer of 1827:

> Celebrated as an author at a time when our country was singularly fertile in great writers, this eminent person acquired a still more enviable reputation as a teacher of law, and by the united force of genius, talents, and indefatigable perseverance, raised himself to the very highest place amongst modern *Antecessores*.

The comment on Davidson was that "[t]he present Professor may not be, in all respects, equal to any of these distinguished men [Millar, Lindesay, Hutcheson, and Carmichael]", though it was conceded that he was "fully adequate to the duties of his office" which were believed to be "very faithfully discharged".[115] Such faint praise was especially damning.

If the opinion of Davidson's contemporaries was that he was intellectually mediocre, his own work does little to dispel that view. As we have seen, his courses were not impressive. His one published contribution to his discipline is *A Short Exhibition of the Poor Laws of Scotland*. Including the title page, it is a tiny pamphlet of twelve pages, eight of which merely contain

112 GUA 26696 374–375 (25 November 1805). Note that "Kindly" in this context relates to "kinship".

113 "Notice of the University of Glasgow – Its Professors and Students" (May 1825) 16 *The Edinburgh Magazine, and Literary Miscellany; a New Series of the Scots Magazine* 513 at 515.

114 Ibid 16 (June 1825) 647 at 648.

115 J Browne, *Remarks on the Study of the Civil Law; occasioned by Mr. Brougham's Late Attack on the Scottish Bar* (1828) 34–35 (containing Browne's articles from the *Caledonian Mercury*).

extracts from other works and relevant legislation. Davidson's contribution is a preface, two pages of queries and answers, and a paragraph setting out the steps for applying for poor relief. All that the work really testifies to is Davidson's humanity.[116] It is a very tiny achievement indeed when set beside David Hume's *Commentaries on the Law of Scotland, Respecting Crimes*, or Millar's *Origin of the Distinction of Ranks* and *Historical View of the English Government*. In contrast with the "speculative" Millar, the "practical" Davidson had had even less to say to the world than he had to his students. His was an infertile mind. And it was the comparable reduction of teaching to the "practical" from the "speculative" that his intellectual insufficiency engendered that did much to destroy the reputation of the University of Glasgow as a school of law.

E. FROM "SPECULATIVE" TO "PRACTICAL"

Davidson's poor performance ended an astonishing development begun in 1714 with the appointment of William Forbes as the first Professor of Civil Law in the University of Glasgow.[117] From that date we can see the growth of legal education in Glasgow in a way that made it for a brief forty years the outstanding exemplar of enlightened excellence in studies in law in the British Isles. It was undoubtedly correct that the law school of Edinburgh was the most advantageously situated in Scotland. Moreover, it had the inestimable benefit for the institutional maintenance of legal education of possessing separate chairs of Civil Law and Scots Law, and additional chairs, first, of Public Law and the Law of Nature and Nations, and, secondly, of Universal History and Greek and Roman Antiquities (even if these latter two were not always successfully in operation). It was thus easier not only to offer a broad curriculum in Edinburgh, but also to sustain a viable school when one of the professors was mediocre or poor. Yet, Millar's tenure of the Glasgow chair showed what could be done there when the correct man was chosen. Forbes seems only to have been successful in a small way, as does Hercules Lindesay, the third professor to hold the chair; if they did not attract many students (they certainly never had Davidson's numbers in Scots Law, but in the context of their time they were probably doing not too badly), they

116 *A Short Exhibition of the Poor Laws of Scotland, And the Method of Applying for Relief from the Parish, Drawn from Authentic Documents. To which is added, the Answers to Five Queries, relative to the Rights of the Poor, by Mr Robert Davidson, Professor of Law, College of Glasgow*, 3rd edn (1816). I have failed to discover a copy of any earlier edition.

117 The remarks in this paragraph derive from the articles cited in n 12 above.

at least showed what could be done, if the right man were appointed, and they managed to establish Glasgow as a centre for liberal education in law through their teaching of Roman law, even if they were never successful in the way that their contemporaries at Edinburgh were. But the appointment of the right man was always going to be the crucial issue given the University of Glasgow's situation and its institutional disadvantage of possessing only a single chair in law. Given that appointments at Glasgow were very open to outside political influence, patronage was always important in assuring a suitable man was presented by the Crown to the chair. The Faculty themselves played no small part in securing the appointment of Forbes, Lindesay, and Millar (indeed they were allowed by the Crown to elect Forbes themselves) through deft consultation with and solicitation of patrons such as Ilay and Bute who were themselves men of education and marked scholarly and scientific interests, and who evidently favoured intellectual merit, promise, and achievement in brokering appointments to chairs. It is notable that William Crosse, who turned out to be a sinecurist and a disaster, was foisted on the University in the face of the concerted opposition of the Faculty – deeply divided though they were by politics – by a reluctant Ilay, against his better judgement, in a time of political crisis when he could not resist a pressing demand for favours. Such success as Forbes and Lindesay had and Millar's phenomenal success were related to their intellectual concerns and achievements. Forbes and Millar established reputations as authors. All three had marked interests in virtuoso and scientific and polite knowledge generally; for them, law was just one part of an encyclopaedia of knowledge. Millar certainly taught it as such. In contrast, Davidson was appointed by a regime less concerned with merit; he had a restricted view of his function and was mediocre as a teacher. From being a centre of elite and "speculative" education in law, the University of Glasgow thereby became the dispenser of a narrow, technical, and "practical" education that was of interest only to the apprentices of local practitioners. Davidson did not even succeed in attracting in significant numbers the apprentices of provincial lawyers from other areas, who generally preferred to go to Edinburgh, when they could as easily have gone to Glasgow. There was nothing in Glasgow to attract other than local apprentices. The great days thereby came to an end. Jardine's prophecy in July 1801 that "[t]he Study of the law will for the future be transferred to Edinburgh", proved all too accurate.[118]

118 G Jardine to R Hunter, 16 July 1801, GUL MS Gen 507/118.

F. CONCLUSION

A year after Davidson had been questioned by the Royal Commission, the Senate of the University of Glasgow unanimously resolved to confer on him the degree of LLB.[119]. Some months later, the Senate received the Commission's provisional resolutions. They were first considered on 16 December 1828.[120] The Commission proposed a curriculum for law extending over three sessions. In the first year, Civil Law would be taught two hours every day – one employed in lecturing, the other in examinations, exercises and the like. Lectures on Scots law would extend over the remaining two sessions, the professor lecturing daily for one hour to each class with a separate hour on two days of the week for each class for examinations.[121] These proposals were obviously aimed at the practice and conditions in Edinburgh. Further consideration of these provisional resolutions was postponed several times,[122] until the Senate agreed the following response on 22 April 1829:

> In regard to the Law chair in this University the Commissioners have been already furnished by the Professor with the plan on which his lectures are conducted. His Students consist chiefly of young men attending writers offices and the Senate are unanimously of opinion that if any material change were made either in the plan or the hours of teaching it is at least very doubtful whether a class could be commanded.[123]

This is a clear acknowledgement of Davidson's failure. Glasgow could now only hope to attract provincial apprentices to its "practical" legal curriculum.

The Royal Commission endorsed "speculative" legal education:

> In this, as in other professions, it is necessary to provide a regular Course of instruction, so that Law may be studied as a liberal and enlightened science. It may be true that many Students desire only to acquire the Rudiments of Law, and the materials for immediate practice, perhaps in the inferior Courts. From this cause, if the Course shall not be recast, many important subjects may be entirely omitted. International Law, and other important branches of the science, may not engage the attention of the Professor: and thus Students are gradually accustomed to enter on practice at the Bar without any acquaintance with the general principles of Jurisprudence, and with limited and contracted views of the subject of their profession. We apprehend that it is essentially necessary to prevent the natural operation of this external cause from lowering the Course

119 Minutes of Meetings of Senate, 1819–1829, GUA 26689 312 (22 April 1828).

120 Ibid 337.

121 *Evidence . . . Volume II: University of Glasgow* (n 4) 557.

122 GUA 26689 337 (22 December 1828), 338 (15 January 1829), 342 (7 April 1829).

123 Ibid 345–346; *Evidence . . . Volume II: University of Glasgow* (n 4) 510.

> of Study, and that the Professor, as part of his regular duty, should have time for teaching the science of Law in the manner in which it should be taught for making an accomplished and enlightened Advocate.[124]

By reducing legal education in Glasgow to the supposedly "practical", Davidson destroyed all that Millar had built up.

The modern establishment of the Scottish universities dates from the Universities (Scotland) Act 1858, under which a body of University Commissioners was established to draft ordinances to regulate detailed matters. One such ordinance created the degree of LLB in 1862. The degree was founded on the traditions of Scottish legal education developed in the eighteenth century. It was open only to graduates in arts. Students had to attend courses, and be examined, in Civil (Roman) Law, Scots law, conveyancing, public law, constitutional law and history, and medical jurisprudence. The degree was to be a mark of "academical" rather than "professional" distinction, and examiners accordingly were to pay close attention to attainments in "public law" and "constitutional history". "Public law" in this context meant jurisprudence and international law. These were the subjects taught from the revived Regius chair of Public Law and the Law of Nature and Nations in Edinburgh, and the regulations and the terms they used were in general heavily dependent on practice in that University.[125]

It is true that the new degree – for a long time only available in the University of Edinburgh and at first taken by very few – reflected the interests of men such as James Lorimer who were strongly influenced by the impressive development of the law schools of Germany in the nineteenth century;[126] none the less, in its focus on the "academic", on jurisprudence, on history, and on Roman law, it reflected the type of legal education developed by Millar and endorsed by the Royal Commission of 1826.[127] Aeneas Mackay commented in 1880:

124 *Report Made to His Majesty* (n 6) 54.

125 See D B Horn, *A Short History of the University of Edinburgh, 1556–1889* (1967) 177–178.

126 See J Lorimer, *The Universities of Scotland Past, Present, and Possible* (1854). For the numbers taking the degree, see, e.g., Lorimer, "Professional graduation" (1880) 24 *Journal of Jurisprudence* 617 (henceforth Lorimer, "Professional graduation") at 622. For a discussion, see R D Anderson, *Education and Opportunity in Victorian Scotland: Schools and Universities* (repr 1989) 57–68. Anderson's is a more persuasive account of Lorimer than that found in G E Davie, *The Democratic Intellect: Scotland and her Universities in the Nineteenth Century* (1961) 41–75. Indeed, much of what has been written in this paper implicitly disagrees with Davie's view of the Royal Commission of 1826.

127 On the central role of legal theory in legal education, see J Lorimer, *Reasons for the Study of Jurisprudence as a Science* (1868); and *The Institutes of Law: A Treatise of the Principles of Jurisprudence as determined by Nature*, 2nd edn (1880).

> In doing what they have done the legal profession in Scotland has done all, or almost all, it could have done for the furtherance of legal education upon a liberal basis. It has, after deliberate consideration, associated that education with the Universities, which are permanent national institutions for the promotion of liberal culture, and has gradually organized it on a model which, though not so complete as the Continental model, is of a similar kind.[128]

The importance of "scientific jurisprudence" was recognised.[129] The reality was, of course, more complex. The provision to support legal education was still small, and the reality hardly reached the ideal.[130] All this, however, is outwith the scope of this essay. But, despite the inevitable doubters,[131] the ideal was one in which the value of Millar's "speculative" over Davidson's "practical" legal education was authoritatively recognised. If reformed and altered by the experience of the nineteenth century, the tradition of education in law developed in eighteenth-century Scotland on humanistic models and transformed by the Enlightenment was asserted as the appropriate model for legal education. Well educated lawyers were ideally to have a broad, liberal education in a university in arts and law.

APPENDIX A

Comparative Outline of Millar's, Hume's and Davidson's Lectures on Scots Law[132]

Millar	*Hume*	*Davidson*
Order of Lectures and Sources	Nature of Subject and Plan of Treatment	General Introduction Sources and Treatises

128 Ae[neas] M[ackay], "Legal education and the Scottish universities" (1880) 24 *Journal of Jurisprudence* 626 at 636.

129 Lorimer, "Professional graduation" (n 126) at 624.

130 See, e.g., F, "Legal training in Glasgow and Heidelberg" (1891) 7 *Scottish Law Review* 104.

131 "Legal education" (1899) 5 *Scottish Law Review* 125. At 127, however, the anonymous author remarked: "As to the Roman law, its study is invaluable, – delivering the practitioner from the intangible abstractions of the mere philosopher, and saving him, at the same time, from the misleading analogies and confusions of the uneducated case-lawyer."

132 For this outline I have used [J Millar,] *Heads of the Lectures on the Law of Scotland, in the University of Glasgow, M DCC LXXVII* (1777); *Baron Hume's Lectures* (n 59); GUL MSS Murray 340–341. I have taken the description of the lectures from the headings of the lecturer in Millar's case, from the chapter headings in the published version of Hume's lectures, and from the divisions and contents of Davidson's lectures as given by the student. I have, however, silently abbreviated, explained or expanded these from time to time for comparative purposes. Occasionally, different titles have been given to the same topics, but this is usually obvious and easily understood. The divisions in the Appendix are not equivalent to individual lectures.

Millar	*Hume*	*Davidson*
Husband and Wife	Husband and Wife	Husband and Wife
Parent and Child	Parent and Child	Parent and Child
Master and Servant	Guardian and Ward	Guardian and Ward
Guardian and Pupil or Minor	Voluntary Servants	Master and Servant
Things–Real Rights	Distinctions of Things– Rights – Personal Rights – Contract	Things – Obligations
Nature of Property–Feudal	Sale	Sale
Military Tenure– Frankalmoigne – Soccage – Burgage – Blench	Location – Tack	Location – Leases (Tacks)
Casualties of Superior	Charter Party	Charter Party Carriers
Present State of Tenures in Scotland	Loan – Interest – Usury Depositation[133]	Mandate
Acquisition of Property by Occupancy Depositation	Mandate	Loan, Interest, Usury, *Commodatum*
By Accession	Society (Partnership)	Cautionry
Delivery	Cautionry	Joint Obligation and Copartnership
	Bills of Exchange	Bills of Exchange of Crimes[134]
		Obligations Resulting from Equity
		Quasi-delict
	Assignation of Personal Claims	Assignations
Conveyance of land – Charter – Sasine – Resignation – Confirmation	Extinction of Obligations by Payment	Discharges
Servitude	Compensation and Retention	Compensation and Retention

133 Hume dealt with depositation here in notes from 1796 to 1797.
134 Hume gave a separate set of lectures on crimes: Cairns, *Millar's Lectures* 396.

Millar	*Hume*	*Davidson*
Tithes	Novation	Novation, Delegation
Pledge – Wadset	Prescription	Prescription
Exclusive Privilege	Obligations *ex delicto*[135]	
	Obligations *quasi ex contractu*	
	Obligations *quasi ex delicto*	
Personal Rights and – Obligations – Contract – Crime – Delinquency – Equity and Utility	Right of Property	Real Rights – Property (including a discussion of modes of acquisition)
Contracts	Servitudes	Servitudes
Sale, Loan	Pledge and Hypothec	Pledge and Hypothec
	Tithes	
Deposit – Pledge – Commission (Bills of Exchange)	Exclusive Privilege	Exclusive Privilege
Copartnership – Suretyship (Cautionry)	Tacks	Leases (Tacks)
Rights Proceeding from a Crime or Delinquency	Feudal Investiture	Charters, Sasines
Crimes against Religion – Crimes against Civil Government	Superior's Estate	Ward, Feu, Blench, and Burgage Holding, Casualties of Superiority etc.
High Treason – Crimes against Police	Vassal's Estate	Parts and Pertinents, Regalia, Rivers, Salmon Fishing, Dovecotes, Hunting
Crimes against Individuals – Homicide	Transmission of Feudal Rights	Rights and Disposal and Modes of Transmission – Resignations – Confirmations –Base Holdings
Rape – Mutilation and Demembration	Infeftments in Conjunct Fee	Conjunct Fees

135 Hume sometimes delivered his lectures covering from obligations *ex delicto* to those *quasi ex delicto* inclusive before his lecture on assignation and after that on bills of exchange. Davidson is following that alternative scheme of Hume's lectures in this section of his course.

Millar	*Hume*	*Davidson*
Crimes against Property – Theft, Robbery – Falsehood	Liferent	Liferent – Terce – Courtesy
Crimes against Individuals' Character	Wadset	Wadset
Delinquencies against Person, Property, Character and Reputation	Heritable Bonds	Heritable Bonds
Rights and Obligations arising from Equity and Utility – Restitution	Real Liens	Reserved Faculty
Recompense Obligations founded on utility		Tithes
Extinction of Personal Rights (performance, compensation, acquittance, novation, confusion)	Adjudication	Adjudications
Transmission of Personal Rights 1) Voluntary; 2) By law	Judicial Sale	Judicial Sales
Prescription	Prescription	Positive Prescription
Heritable Succession	Heritable and Moveable	Succession
Moveable Succession	Heritable Succession	Succession
Testamentary Succession	Settlements and Tailzies	Entails and Contracts of Marriage
Entails	Privileges of Apparency	Heirs Privileges Arising from Apparency
Heirs	Service of Heirs	Services
Executors	Moveable Succession	Succession in Moveables Bankruptcy
Actions[136]	Jurisdiction	Actions – Jurisdictions

136 Millar dealt with the Scottish courts and their jurisdiction in his Lectures on Government: see, e.g., [J Millar,] *A Course of Lectures on Government; Given Annually in the University* (1778) 7–8 found bound in NLS MS 3931, and NLS MS 3931 278–305.

Millar	*Hume*	*Davidson*
	Jurisdiction of Supreme Courts (Session, Commissary, Admiralty, Exchequer)	Court of Session – Admiralty – Commissary Court
	Jurisdiction of Inferior Courts	Inferior Judges
Commencement of Actions (Civil and Criminal)	Summons and Execution	Proofs[137]
Procedure – proof in Civil Causes	Proof of Oath of Party	
Procedure in Criminal Causes	Proof by Witness	
	Probation by Writing	
	Decrees	
	Process of Review in Court of Session	
Execution of Sentences in Criminal and Civil Causes	Inhibitions	Diligence
Poinding – Arrestment	Poinding	
Adjudication – Inhibition	Arrestment	
	Confirmation qua Creditor	
Personal Execution	Personal Diligence	
	Meditatio fugae: Liberation	
	Cessio bonorum	

APPENDIX B

The following manuscript notes are published, with permission, from Heineccius, *Operum . . . tomus quintus, in quo elementa iuris civilis secundum ordinem Institutionem et Pandectarum, commoda auditoribus methodo adornata*, GUL pressmark B19-f 14. They are all from the *Elementa iuris civilis secundum ordinem Institutionum*, and the paragraph of the work as well as the relevant page is noted for convenience.[138]

137 Davidson gave several lectures under this heading.

138 The notes are not carefully keyed to paragraphs; I have usually judged the appropriate paragraph by position and topic. It should be noted that some of the notes here tend towards the

Paragraph	*Page*	*Note*
100	25	This was the most formal of any of the modes of manumission. This mode of manumission is an example of the *actio legis*.
101	25	Sect 101 & the 3 following contains merely the less formal methods of manumission.
137	34	A slave being once sold, could not be recalled.
140	35	The father punished his children in the quality of a domestic judge but this was not the case as if he judged them in the way there might have been reference made to other courts which never was the case.
148–150	37–38	It was necessary that when a marriage took place both parties should be Roman citizens as it was not thought proper that a Roman Citizen should unite himself to a person of another Country. There were cases in which a child could marry without the leave of his father such as when the father was insane 2 where the father was a prisoner-of-war & 3 where the father appeared to be unreasonable.
151	39	The marriage of relatives within certain distance was not allowed.
182	47	Relations connected by males were called *agnati* & those connected by female were called *cognati*.
204	53	Tutory was a *munus publicum* which the tutor was bound to undertake & pupils were bound to receive.
224	59	*[capitis deminutio]* from which we derive our term for capital punishment.
243	65	Nomination of Tutor could not be performed by deputation.
279	75	The security for any thing of importance was personal.
376	102	*accessio nullum hab[et] locum in fr[uctuum] perc[eptione] est mod[us] acq[uirendi] tantum.*[139]
638	171	Those legacies called *Captatoria* arose from the profligacy of Roman manners.
876	227	no part of the doctrine cont[aine]d in this Section is applicable to the Laws of Scotland.
948	245	*sors* means the Capital or stock of a Company.

category of mere restatements of the paragraphs. In Heineccius, *Elementa iuris civilis secundum ordinem Institutionum*, in *Operum . . . tomus quintus* 121, the MS note corrects a citation to the *Novels* in para 450.

139 In Heineccius, *Elementa iuris civilis secundum ordinem Institutionem*, in ibid 102, the annotator has deleted "species accessionis" from the clause "*Fructuum perceptio est species accessionis*" and substituted "*modus acquirendi possessionem*"

ENLIGHTENED CRITIQUE: CRIME, COURTS, AND SLAVERY

10 John Millar's Lectures on Scots Criminal Law*

A. INTRODUCTION

John Millar occupied the Regius Chair of Civil Law in the University of Glasgow from 1761 to 1801.[1] He was the pupil, then friend and colleague of Adam Smith.[2] Before being called to the Bar in 1760, Millar had served as tutor to George Home Drummond, the son of Lord Kames.[3] Kames had a high regard for his protégé, whose lectures on law were the only contemporary ones to escape the judge's censure.[4] Yet in 1952, W C Lehmann could justly describe Millar as "to-day almost completely forgotten".[5] Apart from accounts in histories of the University of Glasgow,[6] in the previous fifty years Millar had been discussed, and then briefly, only three times: twice as a type of materialist sociologist, somehow anticipating Marx, and once as a constitutional historian of the "conjectural" school.[7]

* I am grateful to Tony Carty, Neil MacCormick, John MacLean, Hector MacQueen, David Sellar, Alan Watson and Peter Young for commenting on an earlier draft of this paper. I received exceptional, and enthusiastic, help from Mr David Weston of Glasgow University Library.

1 See W C Lehmann, *John Millar of Glasgow 1735–1801: His Life and Thought and his Contributions to Sociological Analysis* (1960) (henceforth Lehmann, *John Millar of Glasgow*); "John Millar, Professor of Civil Law at Glasgow (1761–1801)" (1961) *Juridical Review* 218 (henceforth Lehmann, "John Millar, Professor of Civil Law"; and "Some observations on the law lectures of Professor Millar at the University of Glasgow (1761–1801)" (1970) *Juridical Review* 56 (henceforth Lehmann, "Some observations on the law lectures of Professor Millar").

2 Lehmann, *John Millar of Glasgow* (n 1) 16–17; cf D Stewart, "Account of the Life and Writings of Adam Smith, LLD", in W Hamilton (ed), *The Collected Works of Dugald Stewart, Esq, FRSS* (1858) vol x, 5 at 10–11, 80.

3 Lehmann, *John Millar of Glasgow* (n 1) 17–18; I S Ross, *Lord Kames and the Scotland of his Day* (1972) 40.

4 H Home, Lord Kames, *Elucidations Respecting the Common and Statute Law of Scotland*, new edn (1800) ix.

5 W C Lehmann, "John Millar, historical sociologist: some remarkable anticipations of modern sociology" (1952) 3 *British Journal of Sociology* 30.

6 See J Coutts, *A History of the University of Glasgow* (1909) (henceforth Coutts, *A History of the University of Glasgow*) 234–235 and passim; D Murray, *Memories of the Old College of Glasgow* (1927) 221–227 (henceforth Murray, *Memories of the Old College of Glasgow*).

7 W Sombart, "Die Anfänge der Soziologie", in M Palyi (ed), *Hauptprobleme der Soziologie:*

Since that date, discussion of Millar, if not quite burgeoning, has developed considerably, in line with the ever-growing interest in the Scottish Enlightenment. This literature has tended to focus on Millar's role as a social theorist and historian, concentrating on his published works, *The Origin of the Distinction of Ranks* and *An Historical View of the English Government*.[8] He has been viewed as a precursor of Marx,[9] or, more generally, of sociology.[10] In a more sophisticated approach, Duncan Forbes has argued in an important essay that Millar was a "scientific Whig" who forms the link between Adam Smith and the English Utilitarians.[11] Peter Stein has viewed Millar as a legal evolutionist, anticipating, if not directly influencing, Henry Maine, though R J Smith has argued that Millar was a "Whig" historian (in both the political and pejorative sense) of the English constitution.[12]

Errinerungsgabe für Max Weber (1923; repr 1975) vol i, 3 at 5, 11, 13–14; T P Peardon, *The Transition in English Historical Writing 1760–1830* (1933) 17–18, 82–84; R Pascal, "Property and society: the Scottish Historical School of the eighteenth century" (1938) 1 *Modern Quarterly* 167 at 175–176.

8 J Millar, *The Origin of the Distinction of Ranks: Or, An Inquiry into the Circumstances which give rise to Influence and Authority, in the Different Members of Society*, 4th edn (1806); and *An Historical View of the English Government: From the Settlement of the Saxons in Britain to the Revolution in 1688; to which are Subjoined some Dissertations Connected with the History of the Government from the Revolution to the Present Time,* 4 vols, 3rd edn (1803). For a bibliography of his works, including some pamphlets his authorship of which is contentious, see Lehmann, *John Millar of Glasgow* (n 1) 417–418, to which may be added the translation of *The Origin of the Distinction of Ranks* as *Vom Ursprung des Unterschieds in den Rangordnungen und Ständen der Gesellschaft*, ed W C Lehmann (1967).

9 J Kuczynski, *Zur Geschichte der Wirtschaftsgeschichtsschreibung* (1978) 93–106 at 93 writes "Millar actually connected the evolution of the superstructure with the way men gained their livelihood", and at 103: "[Millar, Home and Smith] are the immediate predecessors of Marx and Engels . . ." See also R L Meek, "The Scottish Contribution to Marxist Sociology" in his *Economics and Ideology and Other Essays: Studies in the Development of Economic Thought* (1967) 34–50. Both are following the general approach of Sombart and Pascal: see n 7. See also Meek's *Social Science and the Ignoble Savage* (1976) (henceforth Meek, *Ignoble Savage*) 160–176 for an account of Millar's use of a materialist conception of history. Cf A O Hirschman, *The Passions and the Interests: Political Arguments for Capitalism before Its Triumph* (1977) 87–93; A Skinner, "Economics and history – the Scottish Enlightenment" (1965) 12 *Scottish Journal of Political Economy* 1.

10 See Lehmann, "John Millar, Historical Sociologist", in *John Millar of Glasgow* (n 1); and "Comment on Louis Schneider, 'Tension in the Thought of John Millar'" (1971–1972) 13 *Studies in Burke and his Time* 2099; L Schneider, "Tension in the Thought of John Millar" (1971–1972) 13 *Studies in Burke and his Time* 2083.

11 D Forbes, "'Scientific Whiggism': Adam Smith and John Millar" (1953–1954) 7 *Cambridge Journal* 643; cf his "Sceptical Whiggism, Commerce, and Liberty", in A S Skinner and T Wilson (eds), *Essays on Adam Smith* (1975) 179. A L Macfie, "John Millar: A Bridge between Adam Smith and Nineteenth Century Social Thinkers?", in his *The Individual in Society: Papers on Adam Smith* (1967) 141 also argues for Millar's influence on the utilitarians.

12 P Stein, *Legal Evolution: The Story of an Idea* (1980) 46–50; R J Smith, *The Gothic Bequest: Medieval Institutions in British Thought, 1688–1863* (1987) 103–105.

Caroline Robbins and J G A Pocock have interpreted Millar as a republican commonwealthman following in the tradition of Harringtonian Civic Humanism,[13] while Hans Medick and Annette Lepert-Fögen have considered him the ideologist of the petty bourgeoisie.[14] Michael Ignatieff partly explains the variety of approaches by arguing that Millar was "caught between two languages which bifurcate in his own lifetime – civic humanist moralism and political economy", whose "work palpably did not hold together", and who showed how the synthesis in Smith of morality and economics could be sundered.[15] Knud Haakonssen has disagreed, arguing on the contrary that "Millar was the heir to Smith's whole science of a legislator, which revolved around a new concept of natural jurisprudence. . . . [but who] shifted the focus from jurisprudence in a philosophical sense to the history and sociology of law".[16]

Whether or not we should ultimately interpret Millar as Civic Humanist or sceptical or scientific Whig, it is important to realise that he also stands firmly within another tradition, that constituted by the law professors of eighteenth-century Scotland. Only David Murray and Lehmann have paid much attention to this aspect of Millar's work,[17] though Medick, Meek,

13 C Robbins, *The Eighteenth Century Commonwealthman* (1959) 214–217; J G A Pocock, *The Machiavellian Moment: Florentine Political Thought and the Atlantic Republican Tradition* (1975) 502–503.

14 H Medick and A Leppert-Fögen, "Frühe Sozialwissenschaft als Ideologie des kleinen Bürgertums: John Millar of Glasgow, 1735–1801", in H-U Wehler, *Sozialgeschichte Heute: Festschrift fur Hans Rosenberg zum 70. Geburstag* (1974) 22; cf H Medick, *Naturzustand und Naturgeschichte der bürgerlichen Gesellschaft: Die Ursprünge der bürgerlichen Sozialtheorie als Geschichtsphilosophie und Sozialwissenschaft bei Samuel Pufendorf, John Locke und Adam Smith* (1973) (henceforth Medick, *Naturzustand und Naturgeschichte*) 186–189.

15 M Ignatieff, "John Millar and Individualism", in I Hont and M Ignatieff (eds), *Wealth and Virtue: The Shaping of Political Economy in the Scottish Enlightenment* (1983) 317 (henceforth Ignatieff, "John Millar and Individualism"), esp 341–342.

16 K Haakonssen, "John Millar and the science of a legislator" (1985) *Juridical Review* 41 at 67 (henceforth Haakonssen, "John Millar and the science of a legislator"). Both this paper and that of Ignatieff contain useful discussions of the literature. See also Haakonssen, "Natural Justice. The Development of a Critical Philosophy of Law from David Hume and Adam Smith to John Millar and John Craig", PhD thesis, University of Edinburgh (1978) 215–285 (on Millar and Craig) and 299–312; and *The Science of a Legislator: The Natural Jurisprudence of David Hume and Adam Smith* (1981) (henceforth Haakonssen, *Science of a Legislator*).

17 Murray, *Memories of the Old College of Glasgow* (n 6) 222–224; Lehmann, "John Millar, Professor of Civil Law" (n 1); and 'Some observations on the law lectures of Professor Millar) (n 1). D M Walker, *The Scottish Jurists* (1985) (henceforth Walker, *Scottish Jurists*) 248–266 discusses Millar's lectures in an account substantially derived from Murray and Lehmann's work: it adds nothing to our knowledge and could mislead. See Cairns, Book Review, (1987) 66 *Scottish Historical Review* 98. Though I have not been able to take M Clancy, "John Millar and

Ignatieff and Haakonssen have examined some of the sets of student notes surviving from Millar's lectures to help in more general interpretations of his thought.[18] It is, however, worth looking at the copies of the lecture notes in a different way, as evidence of the manner in which Millar taught his courses, and approached the problems facing a university professor of law in the eighteenth century, especially since he was the most renowned law teacher of his day in either Scotland or England, to whose lectures, according to one contemporary observer, "students resorted . . . from all quarters of Britain".[19]

B. AIMS OF THE STUDY

When the Regius Chair of Civil Law was established in Glasgow, its duties were broadly defined to include not only Civil Law, but also Canon Law, Feudal law and Scots law, and the first incumbent, William Forbes, appointed in 1714,[20] certainly taught Scots law.[21] John Craig, nephew and literary executor of Millar, has left a brief description of the courses Millar taught: "The proper business of the Professorship to which Mr Millar was appointed, is to deliver Lectures on the Institutions and Pandects of Justinian."[22] Craig explained that Millar "[i]n these two courses . . . gave every information that could be desired on Civil Law . . .".[23] He added:

> These Lectures, which most men would have found sufficient to engross all their time, and occupy all their attention, still left Mr Millar some leisure, which he thought he could not employ more usefully, than in giving a course of Lectures on Government. As this class occupied an hour only three times a week, he was afterwards induced to appropriate the same hour, on two other days, to the teaching of Scotch Law, a branch of study useful to every Scotchman, and particularly necessary to a number of young men, who had no other opportunity

the School of Law at Glasgow" (1987) 21 *Chukya Hogaku* 68 into account, it does not affect any of my arguments.

18 See Medick, *Naturzustand und Naturgeschichte* (n 14) 186 n 41; Meek, *Ignoble Savage* (n 9) 165 n 143; Ignatieff, "John Millar and Individualism" (n 15) at 323; Haakonssen, "John Millar and the science of a legislator" (n 16) at 43–44.

19 R Heron, *Journey through Western Scotland in 1792* (1793) vol ii, 418; found quoted in Lehmann, "John Millar, Professor of Civil Law" (n 1) at 219; see also Lehmann, *John Millar of Glasgow* (n 1) 30–42.

20 Coutts, *A History of the University of Glasgow* (n 6) 193–194.

21 See W Forbes, *The Institutes of the Law of Scotland,* 2 vols (1722 and 1730) vol i, ii–iv.

22 J Craig, *An Account of the Life and Writings of John Millar, Esq*, prefixed to Millar, *The Origin of the Distinction of Ranks* (1806) (henceforth Craig, *Life and Writings of John Millar*) xix.

23 Ibid xx.

of becoming acquainted with the principles of that profession, which they were afterwards to exercise. The class of Scotch Law he thought it sufficient to teach every second year.

A few years before his death, Mr Millar was led, by the attention he always paid to the advantage of his pupils, to prepare and deliver a course of Lectures on English Law. In this course it could not be expected that he should convey more information than is contained in the best authors; but he greatly simplified and improved the arrangement, and accounted for the various rules and even fictions of English Law, in a manner more satisfactory, than by vague analogies, or that last resource of ignorance, an unmeaning reference to the pretended wisdom of our ancestors.[24]

Craig's reference to Millar's simplification and improvement of the arrangement of English law alludes to a problem common to all professors of national laws in the eighteenth century – that of providing a rational structure within which to expound the law.

In this paper, I shall focus on Millar's lectures on Scots law, and specifically on his account of criminal law. There are three good reasons for doing so.

First, apart from brief discussion by Lehmann,[25] this aspect of Millar's work has been universally ignored, though we have good evidence for Millar's treatment of Scots law in five sets of notes, ranging in date from 1775 to 1792, in the Special Collections Department of the Library of the University of Glasgow.[26] Millar published outlines of his lectures, and two of the sets of notes have printed outlines of the lectures on Scots law bound in

24 Ibid xxi–xxii.

25 Lehmann, "John Millar, Professor of Civil Law" (n 1) at 227–228; and "Some observations on the law lectures of Professor Millar" (n 1) at 71–73.

26 Glasgow University Library (henceforth GUL), MS Gen 347, "Notes taken From a Course of Lectures On the Private Law of Scotland Given Annually in the University of Glasgow" (written by John Robinson as a fair copy and dated 1777, but taken from session 1775–1776); GUL MS Gen 178, "Lectures on the Law of Scotland Delivered in the University of Glasgow by IOHN MILLAR ESQR: and written from Notes of said Lectures 1783" (no marks of ownership or indication of notetaker, but GUL MS Gen 179, "Lectures on Government Delivered in the University of Glasgow by John Millar Esq and Written from Notes of said Lecture [sic] 1783" is in the same hand, and bears on the flyleaf the name "Alexr Campbell": as the titles indicate both are fair copies); GUL MS Murray 83–87 (no title page, and no marks of ownership, but comparison with MS Murray 78–82 show the notetaker was Robt Ferguson, 1789–1790); GUL MS Gen 181 (1–3), "Lectures on the Law of Scotland . . . Glasgow. 1790" (taken by W Rae (Sir William Rae of St Catherines) 1789–1790); GUL MS Gen 1078, "Lectures on Scotch Law MDCCXCII" (on title page, name "James Millar"). J H Baker, "Migrations of manuscripts" (1985) 6 JLH 236 notes (at no 103) a set of notes on Scots law from Millar's course of 1778–1779. I have been unable to obtain any further information about it.

at the front of their first volume.[27] It may be noted here that, though from the surviving notes we can detect development in Millar's treatment of Scots law, so that, for example, while the earliest set of lecture notes does not discuss bottomry and insurance, later ones do,[28] there are no traces of any significant alteration in Millar's approach to criminal law.

Some sets of the Scots law notes seem to be schematic outlines rather than student transcripts of what Millar actually said.[29] Other sets are more obviously student notes written up into a fair copy.[30] Craig stated that:

> Mr Millar never wrote his Lectures; but was accustomed to speak from notes, containing his arrangement, his chief topics, and some of his principal facts and illustrations. For the transitions from one part of his subject to another, the occasional allusions, the smaller embellishments, and the whole of the expression, he trusted to that extemporaneous eloquence, which seldom fails a speaker deeply interested in his subject . . . [I]n Morals, in Jurisprudence, in Law, and in Politics, if the Professor make himself completely master of the different topics he is to illustrate, if he possess ideas clear and defined, with tolerable facility in expressing them, the little inelegancies into which he may occasionally be betrayed, the slight hesitation which he may not always escape, will be much more than compensated by the fulness of his illustrations, the energy of his

27 GUL MS Gen 83 and GUL MS Gen 181(1): *Heads of the Lectures on the Law of Scotland, in the University of Glasgow, M.DCC.LXXXIX* (henceforth *Heads of the Lectures on the Law of Scotland*).

28 Compare GUL MS Gen 347 (1775–1776) with the others, but note that GUL MS Gen 178 (1783) sets out the structure of the lectures, separately paginated 2–16, in which neither bottomry nor insurance are mentioned; but insurance is in fact mentioned in the actual lecture notes after co-partnery at 273. In the later lectures, insurance and bottomry were discussed in lecture 28: see [Millar,] *Heads of the Lectures on the Law of Scotland* (n 27) 14. Note that Blackstone's original lectures also did not discuss bottomry and marine insurance: I G Doolittle, "Sir William Blackstone and his *Commentaries on the Laws of England* (1765–9): A Biographical Approach" (1983) 3 OJLS 99 at 111–112 and n 71.

29 GUL MS Murray 83–87; GUL MS Gen 181(1–3); and GUL MS Gen 1078 come into this category.

30 GUL MS Gen 347 and GUL MS Gen 178 are of this kind. The same type of division of the surviving MSS notes into two types can be traced in other courses taught by Millar. For example, GUL MS Murray 91–92 (notes (incomplete) on the *Pandects* taken by D Boyle), and GUL MS Murray 93–95 (on the *Pandects,* possibly a copy of the notes taken by Boyle) are both probably schematic outlines. MS Murray 92 at fo [i] states: "Copy of the notes used by Mr Millar upon the Pandects in University of Glasgow 1790. Any addition to the original notes, is stated on the left hand page – with this mark. [–]." National Library of Scotland (henceforth NLS), Advocates MS (henceforth Adv MS) 20.4.7–8 (1778, second course on the *Institutes,* not recognised in the catalogue as a set of notes from Millar's lectures) and NLS MS 3930 (1779–1780, first and second course on the *Institutes*) are undoubtedly actual student notes. This is clear both from their fullness and certain other touches, such as in MS 3930, 39 where under lectures 19 to 22, on 30 November to 3 December 1779, the note-taker wrote: *"Abfui frigore male affectus"*. On all of this further study is necessary.

manner, and that interest which is excited, both in the hearer and speaker, by extemporaneous eloquence.[31]

The notes more in the form of schematic outlines may be copies of the notes used by Millar for his lectures,[32] while one set has a direct connection with the professor himself.[33] Along with the general similarity of treatment

31 Craig, *Life and Writings of John Millar* (n 22) xiv–xv. It may be noted that Millar's dynamic style of lecturing is comparable to the style of preaching advocated by Hugh Blair and practised by the moderate ministers, and to the style of lecturing of Adam Ferguson: R B Sher, *Church and University in the Scottish Enlightenment: The Moderate Literati of Edinburgh* (1985) 170–174.

32 Cf Medick, *Naturzustand und Naturgeschichte* (n 14) 186 n 41 who comments that the notes of the lectures on government are "of extremely variable quality", but that one set "represents a transcript of Millar's personal lecture notes in their 1787–88 version". He is presumably thinking of GUL MS Gen 289–291, "Lectures on Government. 1787–88". See further n 33 below. It is possible that there was a trade in Millar's notes, whether of student transcripts of the professor's notes or of student notes from auditing lectures: certainly copies of notes of other professors were bought and sold. Brougham wrote to James Loch on 25 April 1802 of Hume's lectures on Scots law: "I attended his course three years ago and shall take out a ticket next winter and attend as long as I am here, and in that way I shall have no scruple in taking assistance from the Copies of his lectures which are in circulation." R H M Buddie Atkinson and G A Jackson (eds), *Brougham and his Early Friends. Letters to James Loch, 1795–1809*, 3 vols (1908) vol i, 328. Earlier, Thomas Dundas wrote to Charles Mackie asking him to ask Robert Duncan to give him a copy of the notes he took at Barbeyrac's class on Civil Law: Edinburgh University Library, MS La II 91, letter of 10 January 1728. Alexander Bayne explained that he published his notes on Mackenzie because of the increasing number of incorrect MS copies in circulation: *Notes, for the Use of Students of the Municipal Law in the University of Edinburgh* (1731) ii.

33 See GUL MS Gen 1078, "Lectures on Scotch Law. MDCCXCII" which is written in the same hand as GUL MS Gen 289–291, "Lectures on Government 1787–88". Both have on the flyleaf the signature of James Millar, son of John Millar, and Professor of Mathematics in the University of Glasgow from 1796 to 1831 (he was assistant and successor to the previous Professor from 1789). Comparison of these MSS with examples of James Millar's handwriting in the Archives of Glasgow University (see GUA 9086 and GUA 9132) shows him to have been the copyist. The third volume of the set of notes on government (MS Gen 291) has, bound in before the title page, a letter dated 1833 from James Millar to R Brown presenting the notes on government to the Duke of Hamilton. The Duke has made some notes on the volumes, and on the title page of MS Gen 289 is written: "NB Given to me by Professor Millar to be taken care of – " and "The original lectures of James [sic] Millar given to me by his son. Highly valuable & to be taken great care of; in three volumes". Both notes are signed "H & B" (Hamilton and Brandon) and dated "Hamilton Palace 1833". Lehmann, "Some observations on the law lectures of Professor Millar" (n 1) 57 considers the notes on government to have been *taken* by John Millar's son James; but, as a mathematician, he is unlikely to have attended as a student these two courses given by his father, especially since he matriculated in Glasgow in 1775 (see *The Matriculation Albums of the University of Glasgow from 1728 to 1858,* transcribed and annoted by W Innes Anderson (1913) 111 (no 3536); see also Coutts, *A History of the University of Glasgow* (n 6) 318–319). The five-year gap between the dates on the notes also makes James Millar's attendance as an auditor most unlikely. (To take one student, W Rae probably attended the lectures on government in 1788–1789 and those on Scots law in 1789–1790 (if not in the same year) – see GUL MS Gen 180(1–3) and MS Gen 181(1–3). What seems much more likely is that James Millar transcribed his father's notes on government and Scots law, perhaps acting as his father's

of criminal law in the notes, all this suggests that it is fair to rely on the notes as a reasonably accurate account of what Millar taught, even though they continue in some respects to be puzzling.

The second reason for here concentrating on the lectures on Scots law is that, while there was a traditional method of expounding Civil Law according to the schemes of the *Institutes* and the *Digest*,[34] in lecture courses on municipal law there was more scope for the professor to develop a structure which suited his own approach. In fact, in the eighteenth century, when organised university instruction in national law was relatively novel throughout Europe,[35] the solution typically adopted to the problem of methodical

amanuensis, as an act of filial piety. This makes it possible that these MSS are in fact the sets of notes from which John Millar lectured towards the end of his tenure of the chair, as the Duke of Hamilton appears to have thought. Millar's own notes came into the hands of his literary executors, one of whom was his son James, and Craig, *Life and Writings of John Millar* (n 22) xviii described them thus:

> [I]n Mr Millar's notes, now before me, I find some pages effaced, many references, and many leaves inserted; and, from a distinct recollection of particular conversations, I can decidedly assert, that, although he delivered the same courses of Lectures for forty years, many improvements were made, many important disquisitions were introduced, within a very short period of his death.

Does this, for example, describe GUL MS Gen 289–291, in the second volume of which (MS Gen 290) on pp 34, 36, 38, 40, 42, 44, are inserted new notes on France? Also, the lectures at some time have been renumbered, while on, for example, MS Gen 290, 105–111, 114, 119 and others it is recorded that parts of the text were "omitted" in 1788. On the other hand, Craig's description is not one from which one could identify Millar's MSS with any certainty; but it is worth noting that Craig, *Life and Writings of John Millar* (n 22) xi stated that Millar gained his chair "through the interest of the guardians of the Duke of Hamilton" which could explain why the notes came into the Hamilton Palace collection. It is obvious that GUL MS Gen 1078 and MS Gen 289–291 have a very close connection with John Millar. Whether James Millar transcribed them for his father, or for some other purpose of his own, we can be certain that the substance of these MSS is genuinely John Millar's. The strong similarity to this MS of the other notes – GUL MS Murray 83–87 and MS Gen 181(1–3) indeed being virtually identical – suggests we have excellent evidence of what Millar said. (Meek, *Ignoble Savage* (n 9) 165 n 143, is doubtful if MS Gen 289–291 was used by Millar: he did not, however, consider it alongside MS Gen 1078. Cf Haakonssen, "John Millar and the science of a legislator" (n 16) 43: "Millar's own lecture notes have not been preserved". He also has not considered MS Gen 1078 which must affect our understanding of MS Gen 289–291, whatever be our conclusion.)

34 Though by the eighteenth century often following a manual derived from these works rather than the originals, apparently an innovation of the Leyden professor Johannes Böckelmann: see R Feenstra and C J D Waal, *Seventeenth-Century Leyden Law Professors and their Influence on the Development of the Civil Law. A Study of Bronchorst, Vinnius and Voet* (1975) 36. On Millar's practice, see below.

35 See C Chêne, *L'enseignement du droit français en pays de droit écrit (1679–1793)* (1982) 1–7 (henceforth Chêne, *L'enseignement du droit français*); J W Cairns, "Institutional Writings in Scotland Reconsidered", in A Kiralfy and H L MacQueen (eds), *New Perspectives in Scottish Legal History* (1984) 76 at 81–88, 94–98 (henceforth Cairns, "Institutional Writings in Scotland Reconsidered") ((1983) 4 JLH 76, 81–88, 94–98).

exposition was to follow the Gaian scheme of Justinian's *Institutes*, and divide the law into the topics of persons, things and actions, and discuss it accordingly, though the institutional structure could sometimes be treated with considerable freedom.[36] This was Millar's avowed way of dealing with Scots law. He stated that the structure of his course was derived "with a few Exceptions" from that of Justinian's *Institutes*, which he followed because Scottish law students could be expected to be familiar with it, and "chiefly because the order observed therein is best in itself".[37]

The final reason for looking at these lectures of Millar is that the *Institutes*' inclusion of criminal law at the end of the account of actions was manifestly awkward, and the account unsatisfactorily slight – a mere list of crimes and punishments.[38] A number of authors – including Millar – preferred to relocate the treatment of crime to beside their accounts of obligations arising from delicts at the end of their discussions of "things".[39] Though conceptually satisfactory to some extent, this could be seen as breaching the distinction between public and private law; but it was nonetheless tempting because in Roman law delictual liability enforced by private suits included wrongs which in modern systems were classed as public crimes. As well as its intrinsic interest, examination of Millar's account of Scots criminal law is worthwhile because his mentor, Lord Kames, wrote a notable essay on the history of crimes,[40] and because his own outstanding pupil, Professor David Hume, the nephew of the phi-

36 See Chêne, *L'enseignement du droit français* (n 35) 289–307; J W Cairns, "Blackstone, an English institutist: legal literature and the rise of the nation state" (1984) 4 OJLS 318 at 321–326, 340–352. See Inst 1.2.12 and D 1.5.1; cf D R Kelley, "Gaius Noster: substructures in Western social thought" (1979) 84 *American Historical Review* 619.

37 GUL MS Gen 178, 1–2. Cf GUL MS Gen 347, 1: "We intend to Follow the method of Justinian, which is much the same with Mr. Erskine's method." The other notes on Scots law all state identically:

> We propose to follow the method observed in the Inst. of Justinian or at least by the commentators on that work, & by the bulk of writers on Jurisprudence – 1. This appears the best method that has been suggested – 2. It is farther convenient because the study of civil law, in this country, precedes that of our own municipal law.

See GUL MS Murray 83, fo [19r] (including in numbering title page, but excluding printed Heads); GUL MS Gen 181(1), 17; GUL MS Gen 1078 fo 4r.

38 J Inst 4.18; cf books 47 and 48 of the *Digest* to which Inst 4.18.12 alluded, telling the young men desirous of law that: "In general, if God is favourable, knowledge of them [i.e. *publica iudicia*] will have been acquired by you from the more extensive books of the *Digest* or *Pandects*."

39 See Cairns, "Blackstone, an English institutist" (n 36) at 325.

40 H Home, Lord Kames, *Historical Law-Tracts*, 4th edn (1792) (henceforth Kames, *Historical Law-Tracts*) 1–65.

losopher, is best known as the author of an authoritative account of Scots criminal law.[41]

On the basis both of Craig's description of his uncle's lectures and of an examination of student lecture notes,[42] David Murray commented as follows on Millar's lectures:

> The fuller treatment of Criminal law and procedure was a new departure and one of great importance. Sir George Mackenzie's book was out of date, there were no reports of Criminal trials such as there were of civil cases. Professor Erskine no doubt treats of criminal law in his *Institute*, but this work was not published until 1773, and his observations are principally founded on the Civil law and the commentaries of foreign writers, and he does not deal with procedure. In this matter Professor Millar was followed by his pupil Professor Hume of Edinburgh,

41 D Hume, *Commentaries on the Law of Scotland, Respecting the Description and Punishment of Crimes* (1797) 2 vols (on substantive law); *Commentaries on the Law of Scotland, Respecting Trial for Crimes* (1800) 2 vols (on criminal courts and procedure). Later was issued [D Hume], *Supplemental Notes to Mr Hume's Commentaries on the Law of Scotland Respecting Crimes* (1814) and both the 1797 and 1800 works were combined and updated as *Commentaries on the Law of Scotland, Respecting Crimes*, 2nd edn (1819) 2 vols, 3rd edn (1829). In 1844 was published B R Bell, *A Supplement to Hume's Commentaries on the Law of Scotland Respecting Crimes* (1844) which as well as separately is also found bound with the *Commentaries* (1844) 2 vols. This last has been reprinted (1986) in 2 vols, with a foreword by Lord Cameron and an introduction by D M Walker. In this paper, I shall cite the 1797 first edition, abbreviating it as *Commentaries*. Later editions will be cited as *Commentaries* with their date in brackets. The variations between 1797 and 1829 were essentially updating and incorporation of new material: for example, in the *Supplement* (1814) 135–141, Hume added an account of combinations of workmen which appeared in *Commentaries* (1819) vol i, 488 inserted into ch XXIV. There are trivial changes and some additions to the author's introduction; but overall the pattern of the 1797 edition is followed. I prefer to cite this edition as closest in time to Hume's attendance at Millar's classes and as appearing in Millar's lifetime. On the high authority of the *Commentaries*, see, e.g., *The Laws of Scotland: Stair Memorial Encyclopaedia* vol 22 (1987) 219 para 441; T B Smith, *A Short Commentary on the Law of Scotland* (1962) 119–121. On the description of the *Commentaries* as an "institutional" work found in, e.g., D M Walker, *The Scottish Legal System*, 5th edn (1981) 401–402, 426–427, see Cairns, "Institutional Writings in Scotland Reconsidered" (n 35) at 98–104. On a recent use see "Baron Hume's law clinches case of a 'free' brothel", *The Scotsman*, 2 March 1976. (I am indebted to Mr W Windram for bringing this report to my attention.)

42 Murray, *Memories of the Old College of Glasgow* (n 6) 222. The notes he possessed when he wrote were: Glasgow University Library, MS Murray 78–82 (notes on the *Institutes* and on Jurisprudence taken by R Ferguson); Glasgow University Library, MS Murray 83–87 (notes on Scots law taken by R Ferguson); Glasgow University Library, MS Murray 88–90 (notes on Government taken by D Boyle); Glasgow University Library, MS Murray 91–92 (notes (incomplete) on the *Pandects* taken by D Boyle); Glasgow University Library, MS Murray 77 (copy by A Boswell of notes on the *Institution* taken by D Boyle); and Glasgow University Library, MS Murray 96–98 (notes on *Institutes* and Jurisprudence, at least one volume a copy by A Boswell of notes taken by D Boyle). Murray, *Memories of the Old College of Glasgow* (n 6) 222 does not appear to describe Glasgow University Library MS Murray 332 (Jurisprudence) and Glasgow University Library, MS Murray 93–95 (on the *Pandects*, possibly a copy of notes taken by D Boyle). He may have acquired them later.

who gave a short summer course on Criminal law and procedure which became the foundation of his great work on Criminal Law.[43]

This raises two issues. First: did Millar give a "fuller treatment" of criminal law and procedure than earlier Scots professors? Second: what is the relationship between the work of Millar and that of his pupil? In the course of this paper I hope to answer both these questions. (Dr Paton, here followed by Professor Walker, suggested that Millar gave a special summer course on criminal law. This is based on an obvious misreading of Murray, whom both cite.[44] There is no evidence for such a summer course on criminal law.)[45]

The next part of this paper will set out Millar's legal philosophy in order to explain his approach to Scots law generally, and especially to its criminal law. The succeeding section will discuss Millar's classification of the crimes found in Scots law in relation to those of his predecessors. This will be followed by a section in which it will be argued that Millar's account of Scottish criminal law is based on his classification of it according to his theory of punishment. The paper will conclude with a general assessment of Millar's lectures on Scottish criminal law, and with an epilogue discussing their influence on Hume.

43 Murray, *Memories of the Old College of Glasgow* (n 6) 223–224. He is also drawing on the preface to Hume, *Commentaries* vol i, xxxviii–lxii [*Commentaries* (1986) vol i, 1–2] where Hume justifies his work.

44 See G C H Paton (ed), *Baron David Hume's Lectures, 1786–1822,* 6 vols, Stair Society vols 5, 13, 15, 17, 18 and 19 (1939, 1950, 1952, 1955, 1957 and 1958) (henceforth Hume, *Lectures*) vol vi, "A Biography of Baron Hume" 327, 333 (henceforth Paton, "Biography of Baron Hume"); Walker, *Scottish Jurists* (n 17) 316 and 329. Both cite Murray, *Memories of the Old College of Glasgow* (n 6) 223; but Walker's statement in his chapter on Hume derives from Paton's mistake, since at *Scottish Jurists* (n 17) 252, drawing heavily on Murray, he writes of Millar: "There appears to have been rather fuller treatment of criminal law and procedure than was given by his predecessors. Mackenzie's *Matters Criminal* was by this time largely outdated and Erskine's treatment of that branch of the law in his *Principles,* and even in his *Institutes* (published only in 1773), was only a sketch and did not deal with procedure. There were, moreover, no reports of criminal cases. Hume later adopted a similar practice in Edinburgh, giving a short course on criminal law in the summer." (Cf quotation from Murray in text at n 43 above.) It may be noted that in the chapter on Millar in *Scottish Jurists* (n 17) Walker does not mention Millar giving a summer course, even citing Professor Davidson (at 252) as stating that Millar "did not lecture on criminal law at all". Walker has recently repeated the erroneous opinion derived from Paton that Millar gave a summer course on criminal law in his unpaginated introduction to Hume, *Commentaries* (1986).

45 It is not mentioned by Craig, *Life and Writings of John Millar* (n 22) xi–xxiii in his account of Millar's teaching; see also J Sinclair (ed), *The Statistical Account of Scotland* (1799) vol 21, appendix, "Statistical Account of the Universities of Scotland" 40. No MS lecture notes mention such a course and see further below.

C. MILLAR'S LEGAL PHILOSOPHY AND SCOTS CRIMINAL LAW

From Craig's description of the lectures on jurisprudence (the second course on the *Institutes*)[46] and from the surviving lecture notes taken in that course,[47] it is possible to set out sufficiently Millar's general philosophy of law to explain his treatment of criminal law.[48] For Millar, law was a branch of ethics, but the two had nonetheless to be kept separate, "if we would establish any system of rules for the conduct of individuals which society has a title to enforce".[49] If law and ethics were not strictly separated, jurisprudence would resemble moral precepts. Millar conceived of law as based on "the various rights acknowledged and protected by society".[50] These rights derived from our moral sentiments:

> The infringement of the rules of Justice . . . never fails to excite resentment in the breast of the person injured, and indignation in that of the spectators; – an indignation, sometimes satisfied with the redress of the wrong, sometimes demanding the infliction of farther pain or mortification on the delinquent. At the same time, he who has thus subjected himself to merited punishment, can never complain of a sentence, which his own conscience must approve, or pretend that he was not aware of the natural consequences of his crimes.[51]

46 Craig, *Life and Writings of John Millar* (n 22) xxiii–xli.

47 NLS Adv MS 28.6.8 (1777–1778, first and second course on the *Institutes*); NLS Adv MS 20.4.7–8 (1778, second course on the *Institutes*, not recognised in catalogue as a set of notes from Millar's lectures); NLS MS 3930 (1779–1780, first and second course on the *Institutes*); GUL MS Murray 78–82 (1788–1789, first and second course on the *Institutes*); GUL MS Murray 96–98 (1789–1790, first and second course on the *Institutes*); GUL MS Gen 812–4 (1789, first and second course on the *Institutes*); GUL MS Murray 332 (1793, second course on the *Institutes:* incomplete, lectures 19–26 only); Edinburgh University Library (henceforth EUL), MS Dc 2.45–46 (1794, second course on the *Institutes*); GUL MS Hamilton 117 (1798, second course on the *Institutes*). NLS MS 2743 (incomplete) and GUL MS Murray 77 contain only the first course, in which Millar expounds J G Heineccius, *Elementa juris civilis secundum ordinem Institutionum* (1725 and many later editions). I have discussed Millar's place in Roman law teaching in Scotland in an unpublished paper delivered to the Seventh British Legal History Conference, Canterbury, 1985, entitled "Scottish University Education in Law in the Eighteenth Century: The Vocation of the Age for Roman Law". I hope ultimately to present the results in a more permanent form.

48 I am heavily indebted here to Haakonssen's important paper, "John Millar and the science of a legislator" (n 16).

49 Craig, *Life and Writings of John Millar* (n 22) xxv.

50 Ibid xxxii.

51 Ibid xxxiii.

In short, the "rules of justice . . . are satisfied, when a man abstains from injuring others . . .".[52] This is derived from Adam Smith.[53] Millar concluded that "it is on the virtue of Justice, and on that virtue alone, that Laws, the object of which is to maintain rights and repress injuries, must be altogether founded".[54]

In his lectures on jurisprudence, Millar explained the origin of law in the resolution of disputes between individuals in accordance with the moral sentiments and self-interest of the spectators: he thought they would assist those with whom they sympathised, not only disinterestedly, but also because they would be aware that they themselves might come into a similar predicament.[55] From this foundation, the modern legal systems evolved, different because of the varying political histories, climates, and economies of different states.[56]

Millar thus had a comprehensive understanding of the laws of any system as the sum of the rules asserting and protecting the *rights* of men and women, deriving from the original enforcement of rights according to the moral sentiments of spectators, and elaborated through the course of the histories of different peoples. Criminal law was one aspect of this system of rights.[57]

The printed *Heads of the Lectures on the Law of Scotland* stated (in part):

> Order to be observed in the following Lectures. They will be divided into two parts. The 1st concerning *rights;* the 2d concerning *actions.*
>
> Rights arise, either from the state of *persons*, or of *things.*[58]

The schematic type of lecture notes say no more than this: "The objects of Law relate 1. To Rights. 2. To Actions".[59] After this brief division, they have a table setting out the different rights. The fuller type of notes contain a more detailed account and explanation of rights and actions and their various divisions. Millar is reported as having told his students:

52 Ibid xxxii (following Haakonssen, "John Millar and the science of a legislator" (n 16) at 46 in amending "virtue" to "justice" in accordance with the printed errata).

53 See, above all, Haakonssen, *Science of a Legislator* (n 16) 45–98, 114–123; see also P Stein, "Adam Smith's jurisprudence – between morality and economics" (1979) 64 CornellLRev 621.

54 Craig, *Life and Writings of John Millar* (n 22) xxxiii–iv.

55 Ibid xxiv.

56 Ibid xxiv–xli.

57 For further discussion of Millar's jurisprudence, see now, above all, Haakonssen, "John Millar and the science of a legislator" (n 16).

58 [Millar,] *Heads of the Lectures on the Law of Scotland* 3.

59 GUL MS Gen 1078 fo 4r.

> The Law of any Country comprehends that a Set of Rules which the Inhabitants are bound to obey and wherever there is a Rule for performing an obligation there must be a corresponding right to inforce the performance – To every Rule therefore there is a corresponding Right – The enumeration of these Rights will be the same thing as the enumeration of the Rules – To enumerate the Rights then is the first object of Law.
>
> But as it is necessary that every Rule of conduct be promulgated to the people that they may know how to observe them, So it is necessary that some provision be made for enforcing these Rules and compelling the people to observe them – For this purpose Courts of Justice are established – The knowledge of different Courts – The Causes to which they are competent – and the legal methods of obtaining redress of grievances before these Courts, constitute the second great object of Law.[60]

He next pointed out that the topics of the different courts and the jurisdictions of judges would best be dealt with in the lectures on government,[61] and stated:

> The Lectures therefore proposed to be given on the Law of Scotland naturally divide themselves into the consideration of
>
> 1st. Rights and 2d Actions.
>
> Rights may be divided into two Grand divisions, vizt. such as arise from the distinctions of persons and their Ranks in society – and such as are independent of this distinction which is understood to comprehend every other Right – These Rights are therefore distinguished into
>
> 1st. Rights of Persons
> 2d. Rights of Things.[62]

He next explained that persons could be distinguished as members of a particular state (and the rules to which they were subject under this classification fell under public law) or as members of a family, "and the Rules respecting them in this character as well as in the character of members of a small Community, come under the denomination of Private law, and the first character affect them" in the relationships of husband and wife, parent and child, master and servant, and guardian and ward.[63] The "Rights of Things" were divided by Millar into real and personal, and "Real

60 GUL MS Gen 178 2.

61 Ibid: in lectures 44–46 and 48 of the course on Government. See, e.g., [Millar,] *A Course of Lectures on Government; Given Annually in the University* (1778) bound in at the front of NLS MS 3931. The same, dated 1787, is bound in at the front of the first volume of GUL MS Gen 180(1–3). Another copy, dated 1783, is in the pamphlets collection of Glasgow University Library.

62 GUL MS Gen 178 2–3.

63 Ibid 3.

Rights respect inanimate things or irrational Creatures" and were divided into four classes: property, servitude, pledge and exclusive privilege. On the other hand:

> Personal Rights respect Rational creatures only and take place by their intervention[.] Such rights are of three kinds vizt.
>
> 1st. Rights arising from Contract or Agreement
>
> 2nd. Those which arise from the Commission of Crimes, for when a person commits a Crime he violates the Right of another, who has of consequence a Right to be indemnified.
>
> 3d. Those Rights which arise from Equity or Utility without the intervention of any Contract or Crime.[64]

Though these lecture notes do not make it explicit, the class of rights arising from crime, as they put it, also included delictual liability. The printed *Heads of Lectures on the Law of Scotland*, for example, described the class as "Rights and obligations proceeding from a crime, or delinquency".[65]

Though Millar had claimed the structure of his lectures to be substantially taken from that of the *Institutes*, and there is indeed some resemblance, his general scheme of treatment of rights is very closely derived from Adam Smith's lectures on jurisprudence.[66] That Millar has not dealt with criminal law where the category of public crimes and their prosecution is dealt with at the end of the fourth book of the *Institutes* demonstrates the importance he placed on a proper analytical structure for his discussion of Scots law. Though Millar is copying Smith, and the treatment of criminal law with delictual liability had earlier precedents, and would be reinforced by the consideration that Roman law classed as delicts wrongs now classed as public crimes,[67] he was fully committed to a philosophical approach which led to

64 Ibid 4.

65 [Millar,] *Heads of the Lectures on the Law of Scotland* 13 and 15. At ibid 17 is the following description of delinquencies:

> – View of particular delinquencies.
> – Against the person.
> – Against property.
>
> 1 Spuilie [sic]. 2. Ejection and intrusion. 3. Molestation. 4. Extortion. 5. Circumvention. 6. Collusion—Collusive deeds executed by bankrupts to the prejudice of creditors. 7. Falsehood.
>
> – Delinquencies against character and reputation.

66 A Smith, *Lectures on Jurisprudence*, ed R L Meek, D D Raphael and P G Stein (1978) (henceforth Smith, *Lectures on Jurisprudence*) 7–13, 399–401.

67 I suspect that the relationship between Roman delicts with their penal character, Roman *publica indicia* and early modern classifications of criminal law is one of considerable historical complexity; but the above suffices for our purposes.

this particular siting of criminal law in his lecturing scheme. Millar thus used an identical structure for his lectures on English law,[68] on Jurisprudence (the second course on the *Institutes*),[69] and, most significantly, on Justinian's *Digest*.[70]

Millar's lectures on criminal law confirm the significance of his general analysis for his account of particular topics. A crime or delinquency was defined as "a wilfull violation of any Rules of Justice".[71] Crimes deserved punishment, which had two foundations: "The Injured party is from the Common feelings of mankind entitled to a Compensation for the Injury"; and second, punishments restrained crimes. The injury could be either pecuniary loss or "some Indignity, disturbance or additional uneasiness of some kind or other". In the former case, "it appears Just that the Criminal should make a Pecuniary reparation", while in the latter case, "he should also make some amends by Submitting to a Penalty as a Solatium to the Sufferer". Millar added that "Corresponding to this feeling of Justice there is a degree of Resentment in the Sufferer and Indignation and Sympathy in the impartial Spectator".[72] As one set of notes puts it:

68 GUL MS Gen 243, "Notes from Profr: Millar's Lectures upon the Law of England, Glasgow College. Session 1800/1801".

69 See references in n 47 above.

70 GUL MS Murray 91–92, and GUL MS Murray 93–95. From these it is obvious that Millar used as his textbook J G Heineccius, *Elementa juris civilis secundum ordinem Pandectarum* (1727 and many later editions). Millar dealt with the *Digest* in the following order over 116 lectures: D 1.5; 40.5,6 and 10; 1.6; 23.1,2; 23.2,3; 23.4,5 and 24.1; 24.2; 24.3; 25.1,2; 25.3,4,7; 26.1; 26.6,7,8; 26.10 and 27.1,2; 27.7,8,9; 27.10; 1.8 and 6.1; 6,1; 6.2; 41.2; 41.3; 41.3,4,5; 7.1; 7.2,3,4,5,6,7,8,9; 8.1.2; 20.1; 20.1; 20.1; 20.4; 20.5; 28.1,2; 28.3,4,5; 28.6; 29.3,5,7; 30 and 31 and 32; 33.1; 33.5,6; 34.5,7; 36.1; 38.16; 37.6; 38.2,6; 5.2,3,4,5; 44.7 and 2.14; 2.14; 2.14,15; 12.1 and 13.5; 13.6 and 16.3; 17.1; 18.1.2; 18.4,5; 18.6; 19.2; 21.1; 21.2; 39.5; 45.1 and 46.1; 46.2,3; 46.7 and 3.5 and 4.1; 4.2; 4.3; 4.3,4; 4.5,6; 4.7,9; 10.1,2; 10.3,4; 12.2; 12.2,3; 12.4; 12.6; 13.2,3; 13.4; 14.2; 14.3; 15.1; 14.2; 22.1; 22.1,2; 39.1; 39.3 and 42.3; 42.4,5,6; 42.7,8; 43.1; 44.1,2,3; 44.4,5; 13.1; 3.6 and 9.1; 9.2; 9.3,4 and 11.3; 11.5,6,7,8; 39.4 and 47.11 to end; 48.1,2; 48.4; 48.8; 48.17,18,19,20,21,22,23,24; 1.9; 1.9,10,11,12,13,14,15; 1.16,17–22; 2.1; 2.2,3; 2.4,5; 2.6,7,8,9,10,11,12; 2.13; 3.1,2; 3.2; 3.3; 3.4 and 4.8; 5.1; 5.1; 11.1 and 22.3 and 42.2; 22.4,5; 42.1; 49.1. The titles between semi-colons are what was dealt with in one lecture: they do not add up to 116, because it was not possible to separate out all the lectures, especially at the start, thus, only from lecture 6 on D 23.2,3 can the lectures be distinguished, and no lecture 34 or 61 is noted, the numbering jumping from 33 to 35 and 60 to 62 respectively. Craig, *Life and Writings of John Millar* (n 22) xx, stated that, in his lectures on the *Pandects,* Millar "follow[ed] very nearly the order of the Institutes", because "the ordinary arrangement is confused, and almost unintelligible". Craig also stated, ibid, that Millar published a syllabus for these lectures. This presumably resembled the small pamphlets which survive for the lectures on Scots law and Government (see nn 27 and 61 above). A copy has not been discovered.

71 GUL MS Murray 85 fo 93r.

72 Ibid fos 93r–94r.

> When a person's rights are infringed without any just cause, the offended person naturally feels resentment and demands that the offender should suffer – These feelings naturally pass to persons not immediately concerned from the supposition of their being in the predicament of the injured person and conclude that the offender ought to suffer punishment tho it were only for the good of the public, without regard to these feelings of resentment.[73]

The second principle underlying punishment, namely the discouragement of crime, Millar thought, "though . . . *Secondary* in the order of time is the most Considerable in importance", because the "private Interests of Individuals must in all cases yield to the General Interests of Society".[74] These arguments explained the joint foundation of criminal and delictual liability; but the two had nonetheless to be distinguished:

> Distinction between *Public* and *private* offences – The former prosecuted at the Instance of the Public (tho without Excluding the private party) The latter at the Instance of the private party only. –
>
> The former may in a Strict Sense be Called *Crimes*. The Latter Delinquencies.[75]

This analysis of criminal law derived from Adam Smith's jurisprudence amounts to a rejection of the views of Millar's other mentor, Lord Kames. Kames argued that certain actions were perceived as *wrong*, the actor *guilty*, and as deserving punishment for his guilt. Those who acted wrongly feared the resentment of the injured person, while corresponding to dread of punishment was indignation at gross crimes, an indignation felt even by those who did not suffer from them. Though Kames argued there could be degrees of resentment, and that heinous crimes aroused the indignation of all, his theory lacks the sophistication of the impartial spectator as the control of the measure of punishment: revenge for a wrong done was merely a privilege according to natural law. Kames saw the progress of punishment, which he traced through various stages, in the gradual increase of public control over private revenge, until public interest prevailed over private interest, so that punishment served to deter as well as to assuage private resentment. Kames did not attempt a classification of crimes, noting that they were punished for the immorality of the action and their tendency to disrupt the public peace.[76]

73 GUL MS Gen 178, 280.
74 GUL MS Murray 85 fo 94r.
75 Ibid fo 96r.
76 Kames, *Historical Law-Tracts* (n 40) 1–65.

D. SCHEMES OF CLASSIFICATION OF SCOTS CRIMINAL LAW

The order in which Millar dealt with specific crimes is based on a division of crimes into: those against the religious establishment (blasphemy, atheism, heresy, witchcraft, adultery, fornication, bigamy, incest, sodomy); those against the civil government (treason, sedition, smuggling, usury); and those against individuals, first in their persons (homicide, rape, mutilation and demembration), second in their property (theft, robbery, fraud, falsehood), and third, tending to hurt individuals in their character.[77] To explain this classification it is first necessary to place it in the historical context of other classifications of Scottish criminal law.

The first detailed account of Scots criminal law was published in 1678, under the title, *The Laws and Customes of Scotland, In Matters Criminal. Wherein is to be seen how the Civil Law, and the Laws and Customs of other Nations do agree with, and supply ours*, by Sir George Mackenzie of Rosehaugh, then Lord Advocate, and the outstanding legal scholar of seventeenth-century Scotland.[78] It is a distinguished and erudite work.

77 In all the MSS, criminal law and criminal procedure are dealt with in the same place: GUL MS Gen 347, lectures 32–37, 274–331 and lectures 50–51, 445–467; GUL MS Gen 178, lectures 29–34, 279–314 and lecture 50, 453–456; GUL MS Murray 83–87, lectures 29–34, vol iii (MS Murray 85) fos 93r–136r and vol iv (MS Murray 86) fos lr–25r, and lectures 48–49, vol v (MS Murray 87) fos 53r–62r; GUL MS Gen 181(1–3), lectures 29–34, vol iii MS Gen 181(3) 451–537 (lectures 39–50 are missing: there was originally a fourth volume); GUL MS Gen 1078, lectures 29–34, fos 101r–126r, and lectures 49–50, fos 173–176. See [Millar,] *Heads of the Lectures on the Law of Scotland* 15–16 and 22.

78 G Mackenzie, *The Laws and Customes of Scotland, In Matters Criminal. Wherein is to be seen how the Civil Law, and the Laws and Customs of other Nations do agree with, and supply ours*, 1st edn (1678); 2nd edn with (as appendix) *A Treatise of Mutilation and Demembration and their Punishments, by Sir Alexander Seton of Pitmedden Knight Baronet; Also a Second Edition of the Observations upon the 18 Act. Parl. 23. K. James Sixth. Against Dispositions Made in defraud of Creditors, &c. Corrected, and in several Paragraphs much Enlarged by the Author, the same Sir George Mackenzie himself before his Death* (1699). I have used the text in *The Works of that Eminent and Learned Lawyer, Sir George Mackenzie of Rosehaugh, Advocate to King Charles II and James VII*, 2 vols (1716, 1722) (henceforth Mackenzie, *Works*) vol ii, 49–275. On Mackenzie and criminal law, see A J MacLean, "Sir George Mackenzie and Scots criminal law", unpublished paper read on 13 October 1984 to the Scottish Legal History Group, abstract in (1986) 7 JLH 88. I have also benefited from two other unpublished papers by Mr MacLean on a similar theme in the history of Scots criminal law, one delivered to the Edinburgh Law Faculty's Legal History Discussion Group, the other to a joint colloquium of the Scottish Legal History Group, the Scottish Jurisprudence Discussion Group, and the Edinburgh Centre for Criminology and the Social and Philosophical Study of Law.

Mackenzie generally defined crimes as "these Injuries done to the Commonwealth, which are so immediate and hainous, as that they are punished by express Law". In more detail, he wrote:

> The true Nature then of a Crime may be comprehended under these general Conclusions. 1. That is a Crime, which is declared such by an express Statute . . .; and it were to be wished, that nothing were a Crime which is not declared to be so by a Statute. . . . 2. The transgressing any municipal Law, which prohibits that which either the Law of God, or the civil Law punishes criminally by corporal Punishment, or a pecuniary Mulct, is a Crime. . . . 3. That is a Crime whereby the publick Peace is immediately disquieted, or whereby the Law of Nature is violated. . . . 4. That is a Crime, which long Custom hath punished by corporal Punishment, or by a pecuniary Mulct, in the Justice Court. . . .[79]

Mackenzie set out a number of possible "divisions" of crimes. The first division was, by the Civil Law, into public and private crimes; but though this was a Roman or civilian division, he mentioned that there were vestiges of it in Scotland in suits by the Lord Advocate without the concurrence of the person injured. He next pointed out that the Civil Law divided crimes into ordinary and extraordinary. The third division he stated to be into capital and not capital crimes, noting the distinction between what is meant by "capital" in Civil and Scots law. Crimes were also divided into occult and manifest: the division being significant either as to modes of proof or prescription. Mackenzie next divided crimes into those atrocious and those not – the distinction was based on moral culpability. Finally he stated: "In *Scotland* Crimes are divided in statutory, and such as are not punished by an express Statute", concluding his remarks with his familiar plea: "From all which it appears, that the Essence of a Crime consists in its being forbidden, and not in having its Punishment stated by an express Statute, though I wish it were otherwise." In Mackenzie's account of the possible divisions of criminal law, he only briefly alluded to the very important jurisdictional distinction in Scotland between the pleas of the Crown and other crimes.[80]

Mackenzie did not state, however, how he would organise his account of particular crimes, nor did he explain how it related to any division of an analytical nature between them. It is, however, difficult to accept that Mackenzie's order of discussion of individual crimes was random. Examination of the sequence of topics suggests that it is arranged, to

79 Mackenzie, *Works* (n 78) vol ii, 53.
80 Ibid vol ii, 60–61.

some extent, according to punishment, but with certain crimes, punished differently, inserted beside others of a similar character. What is more, those crimes of similar punishment are grouped together according to their character. For example, after a group of capital crimes concerned with homicide (murder, duels, self-murder, parricide) comes a group of capital crimes of a sexual nature (incest, sodomy, bestiality, rape, adultery – though one may note of the last that only notour adultery was capital). Added to these is bigamy, which was not a capital offence. After bigamy, the sequence of titles returns, with theft and theftbote, to capital offences. We can discern a rough structure: crimes against religion; treason, crimes of the nature of treason, and crimes punished as treason; crimes involving homicide; sexual crimes; crimes against property; miscellaneous; crimes against the enforcement of justice; crimes involving deceit; miscellaneous.[81] The division between statutory and non-statutory crimes is not reflected in this. Given Mackenzie's general definition of crime, it is possible that the order of topics also reflects the seriousness of the "Injuries done to the Commonwealth". It is important to note, however, that, though one can discern an attempt at classification according to punishment, and nature and seriousness of offence, it is not explicit and is somewhat muddled.

In 1684 Mackenzie published *Institutions of the Law of Scotland*,[82] which was to be the standard textbook for learning Scots law until the 1750s.[83] Mackenzie deliberately adopted the Gaian division of law in Justinian's *Institutes*,[84] and concluded his account of actions with a title "Of Crimes".[85] The treatment is reminiscent in its brevity of the final title of the *Institutes*. Mackenzie distinguished private crimes (or delicts) from public crimes, where the injury was "committed immediately against the *Common-wealth*". After noting that private crimes or delicts gave rise to an obligation of reparation, he wrote that "*Crimes* are in *Scotland* either

81 Ibid vol ii, 61–179.

82 G Mackenzie, *The Institutions of the Law of Scotland*, 1st edn (1684); 2nd edn (1688). All references here will be to the 2nd edition (henceforth Mackenzie, *Institutions*).

83 See J W Cairns, "Mackenzie's *Institutions* and Law Teaching in Eighteenth Century Scotland", unpublished paper read to the Scottish Legal History Group, 13 October 1984, abstract in (1986) 7 JLH 86.

84 Mackenzie, *Institutions* (n 82) 9–10: "Having resolved to follow *Justinians* method, (to the end there may be as little difference found betwixt the Civil Law and ours, as is possible: And that the Reader may not be distracted by different methods) I do resolve first, to lay down what concerns the Persons of whom the Law treats: *Secundo*, what concerns the things themselves treated of, such as *Rights, Obligations, &c. Tertio*, The *Actions whereby these Righftjs are pursued*, which answers to the *Civilians, objecta juris, viz. Personae, res, & Actiones*."

85 Ibid 392.

punished Capitally, by death; or Pecunially, by a certain fine; or Arbitrarly at the discretion of the judge".[86] Mackenzie listed crimes according to these divisions, and added that there were a number of "other *Crimes*, whereof the punishment is not reduceable to any of these kinds",[87] which he then set out. The detailed list follows a different sequence from that in the treatise on criminal law.[88]

In 1702 John Spottiswoode started to teach Scots law privately, using Mackenzie's *Institutions* as his textbook.[89] From a set of surviving student notes, he appears to have said little on criminal law, though adopting a variation of Mackenzie's scheme of classification:

> Crimes with us have a 4 fold punishment Namely Capitall, which is the loss of life and fortune; Corporeall which is a Corporeall punishment, inflicted upon the Committer; Pecuniall by a certain mulct or fine; or arbitrary at the Discretione of the Judge, and the persone capitally punished loses all his moveables *quia mobilia sequuntur personam.*[90]

Much more interesting is the approach of the first Professor of Scots Law in the University of Edinburgh, Alexander Bayne, in his lectures on Mackenzie's *Institutions.* When Bayne came to Mackenzie's title on crime, he commented:

86 Ibid; cf Inst 4.18.2.

87 Mackenzie, *Institutions* (n 82) 400.

88 Ibid 393–402: Mackenzie listed as capital crimes: treason (which included, in the pre-Union treason laws, theft in landed men, murder under trust, the murder of a pupil by a tutor, the firing of coal heughs, assassination, pursuing another for treason without proving it, the taking of bonds by Jesuits, seminary priests and "traffecking Papists", and the purchasing of benefices at Rome); blasphemy; manslaughter or homicide; theft (unless small theft); notour adultery; incest; buggery; duels; "the invading of any of his Majesties Officers, for doing His Majesties Service"; forgery; witchcraft and also consulting witches; sorning; wilful hearing of Mass and concealing of the same; mutilation; sedition; striking a judge sitting in judgement; mixing of wine; and hamesucken. Crimes to be "pecunially punished" were: slaying red fish; killing deer; destroying beehives, fruit trees or green-wood; muirburn, except in March; keeping green lint in running water or lochs; abominable oaths; and fornication. Crimes to be punished at the discretion of the judge were: negligence in judges and king's officers; murmuring against the same; breaking the king's protection; importing "erroneous" books; troubling clergymen; the wrongful refusal by craftsmen to fulfil work taken in hand; simple adultery, and verbal injuries and scandals against private parties. Mackenzie noted that mutilation was, in practice, punished arbitrarily. The crimes which did not come into these three classes were: perjury; bigamy; deforcement of messengers; breaking arrestment; forestalling markets; usury; stellionate; keeping victuals to dearth; bribing judges; and barratry.

89 See NLS MS 2934 fo 129r.

90 NLS MS 3412 474; cf NLS MS 3413 383 for an identical passage in a MS made up from both Spottiswoode's and John Cuninghame's lectures. I hope to discuss both Spottiswoode and Cuninghame elsewhere in detail.

> Our Author having now finished his Institutes of the private Law Gives in the Conclusion one title of publick Law and of that part of it which we are most concerned to know, namely of Crimes. But that Subject Our Author Treats here very Superficially and gives us hardly any more than a short Definition of the Crimes. . . . Our Author's title of Crimes will not so much as Serve me for a Text So that I have Chused to prepare some few discourses to you on the Subject of Crimes without being tyed down to the method and order of a Text which can give us no assistance. . . .[91]

Bayne was thus free to develop his own classification. He pointed out that crimes could be distinguished in a variety of ways, for example, into public or private offences, or according to the public interest, or according to their object, or according to their punishment.[92] He added:

> But the most naturall & Justest Light wherein to consider them is to find out in them some mark and Character which is Common to them all by which they are accounted Crimes and offences and to remark in them what each Crime has peculiar and Singular in it's nature which makes it to participate of this common Character.[93]

Bayne identified this common character as the disturbance of "the peace and order of the Society of Mankind" which was the reason they deserved punishment.[94] He argued that it was possible to "distinguish Six different parts which are the foundations of [the order of Society]", so that crimes could accordingly be divided into six kinds, as they offended against any of those six parts. The six parts were: the dependence of the order of society "upon the Supreme Being who formed it"; second, the authority derived from the supreme being to the temporal powers for government of the society; third, the general policy of the state; fourth, the bonds arising from the "engagements" of marriage, birth, and family; fifth, all other "Engagements" which united men together in labour and industry; and the sixth related "to every Individuall person considering him as a member of the Society and with Respect to what he ows [sic] in his person to the Society . . . by avoiding to prostitute it in a manner unworthy of that Character". Bayne concluded:

> [T]he Character which is common to all Crimes consists in this, That they Disturb that order And therefore it is naturall to distinguish them by the relation they

91 NLS Adv MS 22.7.34 fo 109r.
92 Ibid fo 110r–110v.
93 Ibid fo 110v.
94 Ibid fos 110v and 111r–111v.

have to some one of these Six parts which makes Six different kinds of Crimes and offences which Comprehends them all.

Examples of the first type of crime were: blasphemy, atheism and sacrilege; of the second type: treason; of the third type: species of treason such as counterfeiting the coin; of the fourth type: rape, adultery, bigamy, incest and parricide; of the fifth type: murder, robbery, theft, forgery, and other unnamed injuries; and of the sixth type: "the bade use some make of their persons by Lewdness of all kinds & prodigality & By Crimes of that kind of prostitution which decency forbids me to name".[95] Bayne treated specific crimes in accordance with this scheme.[96]

In 1730, Bayne published his textbook on criminal law.[97] In it he merged the earlier second and third class of crimes, and ignored the sixth:

> Of the first Class is the Crime of *Blasphemy*; of the second, *High Treason, Sedition, Deforcement*, and *breaking of Prison*; of the third, *Bigamy, Adultery, Rape* and *Incest*; of the fourth, *wilful Fire-raising, Murder, Parricide, Duels, Poison, Theft, Reset of Theft, Robbery, Falshood, Stellionate, Perjury, Usury* and *Injuries*.[98]

95 Ibid fos 111v–112v.

96 Thus: class 1: blasphemy, heresy, simony, barratry; classes 2 and 3: high treason; class 4: parricide, incest, rape, adultery, bigamy; class 5: murder, theft, robbery, perjury, falsehood, hamesucken, usury, stellionate and injuries of "diverse kind"; class 6: those decency prevented him discussing. See NLS Adv MS 22.7.34 fos 113r–141v. Other MSS of Bayne's lectures which contain this account of crimes are: NLS Adv MS 25.6.18; EUL MS La III 391/1–2; EUL MS Dc 6.17; EUL MS Gen 67D; GUL MS Murray 613; and Royal Faculty of Procurators of Glasgow, MS dated 1725. The last two MSS contain the text of Mackenzie's *Institutions* bound with folio sheets which have the MS notes. MSS which lack the account of crimes are: NLS MS 14497 at fos 148–241 (not identified in catalogue as Bayne on Mackenzie); EUL MS Gen 794D; EUL MS Gen 2183D; GUL MS Murray 74 (not identified in catalogue as Bayne on Mackenzie); and NLS Adv MS 81.5.9 (which ends in the middle of the second book). As with all such material these notes contain puzzles. The second last above, for example, clearly dates from the late eighteenth century. It, and some of the others, may be copies of Bayne's published *Notes, for the Use of the Students of Municipal Law in the University of Edinburgh: Being a Supplement to Sir George Mackenzie's Institutions* (1731). A number of those MSS with notes on criminal law can be dated to before 1730.

97 A Bayne, *Institutions of the Criminal Law of Scotland* (1730) (henceforth Bain *Institutions*).

98 Ibid 9; at ibid 7–8 he wrote:

> The most capital *common Character* of all Crimes consists in the Disturbance they create to the Peace and Order of the *Society* . . . Of which Order, we reckon four chief Parts which are the Foundations of it. The *First* consists in the Dependence which the Society, and every thing thereto relating, has upon the *supreme Being*. The *Second*, in that Authority which is derived to the *temporal Rowers*, for the Government of Society. The *Third*, in the Preservation of the Ties of *Marriage* and of *Birth*, which are the chief Bonds of the Society. And the *Fourth*, in maintaining the Use of those *Engagements* which contribute to unite Men together by a Communication of their Labour and Industry.

This fourfold classification is also found in a manuscript which contains the lectures given in a special summer course on criminal law which Bayne appears to have initiated in 1729, presumably to give greater scope for a proper discussion of the topic.[99] This lecture course probably explains why his account of criminal law was published separately from his notes on Mackenzie's *Institutions*.[100]

Bayne's conceptual organisation of his account of criminal law according to what he saw to be its essential purpose is more sophisticated than the classifications of Mackenzie and Spottiswoode; but like those, it sees the only aim of criminal law as the maintenance of order in society, and thus it is fundamentally different from Millar's account, which it otherwise resembles to some extent in the grouping together of various crimes of a similar nature.

Contemporary with Bayne was William Forbes, first incumbent of the chair of Civil Law in Glasgow. In the same year as Bayne published his text for students on criminal law, Forbes published the second volume of his *Institutes*. This was also devoted to criminal law,[101] and had presumably been developed out of his lectures.[102] Like Bayne he perhaps had found it desirable in teaching to cover criminal law apart from private law, if not necessarily in a separate course. Forbes described crimes in Scotland as including "not only those which have a direct Tendency to the Detriment of the Common-wealth, but also such as more immediately hurt private Persons".[103] He accordingly stated:

99 NLS Adv MS 25.3.12 (2 vols) vol i, fos 12r–13r. It is catalogued as Bayne's own, and it may indeed be, though that is unimportant for our purposes. It certainly is of his lectures. I suggest the date 1729 for the innovation, because at ibid vol 1, fo lr, Bayne stated: "I projected four years ago an Examinatory College for the Summer Session", while in a broadsheet dated 12 April 1725, and addressed by Bayne "To the Gentlemen who have attended his College of PRELECTIONS", he stated that: "The last Time he had the Pleasure to see you in his College, he communicated to you his Purpose to commence an Examinatory College on the first of *June* ensuing". That the special summer course started in 1729 suggests that all those MSS containing the brief lectures on crimes referred to above should be dated earlier than this: and all those that do have dates are in fact dated earlier than 1729. It should be noted that those MSS *lacking* the account of crimes cannot confidently be dated to *after* 1729.

100 See nn 96 and 97 above.

101 W Forbes, *The Institutes of the Law of Scotland. Volume Second. Comprehending the Criminal Law. In Two Parts* (1730) (henceforth Forbes, *The Institutes*). The first volume, on private law, was published in 1722: see n 21 above.

102 Forbes, *Institutes* (n 101) i, ii–v.

103 Ibid vol ii, 2. He must stress this to make the point that, in contrast to the Civil Law, Scots law did not distinguish between private and public "crimes": cf ibid vol ii, 27.

> Crimes and Offences may, under divers Views, be variously distinguished, and placed in different Orders, but I shall range them in what I conceive to be the most simple and natural Way, by dividing them, 1. With respect to the Objects they may have Relation to, or the Parties injured, into those more immediately levelled against God, and such as Man is more directly offended by. 2. Many Crimes may be more particularly distinguished into those relating to Offices, Law-suits, and the Execution of Law and Justice. Mean Time it is necessary to observe, that there are some Crimes and Offences of a complex Nature, which consist of double Characters, and have Relation to more than one Kind: These shall be ranked according to what I think to be their most natural Situation.[104]

Forbes ends up with four classes of crime which, to some extent, correspond to those of Bayne, and which, like those of Bayne, show the influence of the order of treatment in Mackenzie's work on criminal law. The first class is of crimes against God: atheism, blasphemy, heresy, apostasy, witchcraft, perjury, and "other open Immoralities and Profaneness".[105] The second class consists of crimes relating to royal authority, government, the peace and welfare of the kingdom: high treason, misprision of high treason, recognising the authority of the Pope or any foreign power and disowning that of the monarch or Parliament, leasing-making, recusancy, nonconformity, vagrancy, wearing unlawful weapons, breaches of the public peace, and common nuisances.[106] The third class of crimes is those "that directly touch private Persons, and are committed either against their Bodies, or against their Fame and Honour, or against their Estates and Possessions". Within this class, those crimes committed against the body were divided into three types: (i) those resulting in the taking of life or its exposure to danger (homicide in its various types, duelling, and giving or accepting challenges to fight); (ii) those "whereby the Body is abused to lustful Purposes" (sodomy or buggery, incest, bigamy, adultery, fornication, bawdry and rape); and (iii) those whereby the body is maimed (mutilation or mayhem and demembration). The crimes against a person's fame and reputation were verbal, real or written injuries, and hamesucken, all of which could be aggravated as to place or person. Crimes against the property of a private person were committed either by deceit or fraud (theft, fire-raising, falsehood, fraudulent bankruptcy, and stellionate) or by force (robbery, piracy, oppression and extortion – oppression and extortion including false arrest and imprisonment, spuilzie, forestalling, regrating and ingrossing, monopolies,

104 Ibid vol ii, 28.
105 Ibid vol ii, vii and 28.
106 Ilbid vol ii, vii–viii and 50.

black-mail, usury, and private imprisonment).[107] The fourth class of crimes was divided into: (i) those relating to offices (simony, barratry, bribery, partiality, negligence, breach of trust, and extortion); (ii) those relating to law-suits (maintenance, champerty, buying of pleas, and battery); and (iii) those relating to the execution of justice (breach of arrestment, deforcement, resisting and maltreating officers of the customs or excise, and prison-breaking).[108] Like Bayne, Forbes sought a natural order for exposition of the penal laws which by their "Terror" protected "Good Order and Government, Life, Property, Possession, and other sublunary Enjoyments".[109] The order of treatment by Forbes resembles to some extent Millar's division of crimes into those against religion, those against government, and those against persons; but the conceptual basis is quite different. For Forbes, crimes against private individuals were merely to be punished in the public interest in good government and security of property.[110]

In 1737 John Erskine succeeded Bayne in the chair of Scots Law in Edinburgh. Four sets of notes from Erskine's lectures in the session 1740–1741 survive.[111] Three of these contain remarks on criminal law; but though the reports are too skimpy to be particularly helpful, two of them show that Erskine dealt with crimes in the following order: dole; treason; blasphemy; murder; parricide; theft; adultery; "sundry crimes" including incest, demembration, mutilation, and sedition; hamesucken; seditious speeches and verbal injuries; duels; rape; witchcraft; sorning; invading his Majesty's subjects; falsehood and forgery; deforcement; usury; and stellionate.[112] This reflects the fact that he was commenting on Mackenzie's *Institutions*.[113] Erskine elaborated and altered his lectures during his tenure of the chair,[114] and a set of notes, dated 1753, contains a somewhat fuller treatment of crimes, essentially in the same sequence, explicitly following

107 Ibid vol ii, viii–ix, 96, 130–131 and 147.
108 Ibid vol ii, x and 198.
109 Ibid vol ii, 2.
110 See, e.g., ibid vol ii, 2 and 27.
111 Signet Library (henceforth SigL), MS 106:38; NLS Adv MS 25.3.7 (incorrectly identified in the *Summary Catalogue of the Advocates' Manuscripts* (1971) 72 no 900); GUL MS Murray 76; NLS MS 3862. These four MSS are puzzling. Why is Erskine always referred to in the third person? Two of them are described by D B S[mith], "Mr Erskine's lectures" 1962 SLT (News) 74 (henceforth Smith, "Mr Erskine's lectures").
112 SigL MS 106: 38, 264–281; GUL MS Murray 76, 213–223. NLS Adv MS 25.3.7 contains only a very few notes on crimes at fos 189v–90v. Though National Library of Scotland, MS 3862 has no discussion of crimes, there are indications at 278 that one was possibly intended to be included.
113 See n 88 above.
114 See S[mith], "Mr Erskine's lectures" (n 111).

the order of Mackenzie's *Institutions*[115] Erskine displays dissatisfaction with Mackenzie's structure, commenting that the method chosen of explaining crimes according to the differing degrees of punishment caused Mackenzie to treat separately some crimes of the same class.[116] Despite this, for as long as Erskine based his lectures on Mackenzie's *Institutions*, he followed the order of Mackenzie's treatment of crimes.[117]

In 1754 Erskine published the first edition of his *Principles of the Law of Scotland*[118] as a student textbook, and, though no lecture notes taken in his class based on this book have yet been discovered, it is fair to assume that from the later 1750s he used it as his text.[119] In both this, and the second edition of 1757, Erskine basically preserved the sequence of discussion of specific crimes found in his earlier lectures on Mackenzie's *Institutions*.[120] Given Erskine's stated dissatisfaction with Mackenzie's lack of an appropriate classification, it is scarcely surprising that, in the third edition of the *Principles* in 1764, he developed a new, tripartite analysis of crimes.[121] He wrote that "[c]ertain crimes are committed more immediately against God himself; others, against the State; and a third kind, against particular

115 SigL MS 7 (Law) "A Commentary on Sir Geor McKenzie's Institutions of the Scots Law in [Two] Volumes. 1753". Probably because of the title, this MS has not hitherto been recognised as a set of notes from Erskine's lectures. The notes on crimes are at ibid vol ii, 313–364.

116 Ibid vol ii, 344; see also vol ii, 349.

117 EUL MS Dc 8.131 dates from 1755–1756. Erskine was still lecturing on Mackenzie. Though notes of what he said exist only as far as the eleventh title of the second book, the notes proper are preceded by sheets paginated 1–97 containing references additional to those given by Mackenzie: those on criminal law at 95–97 suggest he still followed Mackenzie's order.

118 [J Erskine,] *The Principles of the Law of Scotland: In the Order of Sir George Mackenzie's Institutions of that Law*, 2 vols (1754) (henceforth [Erskine,] *Principles* (1754)).

119 If EUL MS Dc 8.131 is correctly dated to 1755–1756, Erskine continued to give lectures on Mackenzie's *Institutions* at least for a short period after publication of his own *Principles*.

120 See [Erskine,] *Principles* (1754) (n 118) and [J Erskine,] *The Principles of the Law of Scotland: In the Order of Sir George Mackenzie's Institutions of that Law*, 2nd edn, 2 vols (1757) both at 4.4.7–46. The order of discussion is as follows: treason; misprision of treason; blasphemy; murder; self-murder; parricide; concealment of pregnancy; theft and pickery; robbery and stouthreif; blackmail, sorning and gypsies; reset of theft; theftbote; adultery, both notour and simple; incest; rape; duelling; falsehood; forgery; perjury; bigamy; witchcraft; hamesucken; sedition and leasing making; deforcement of messengers; breach of arrestment; usury; buying of pleas; real and verbal injuries; stellionate and fraudulent bankruptcy; battery *pendente lite*, and, finally, wrongous imprisonment.

121 [J Erskine,] *The Principles of the Law of Scotland: In the Order of Sir George Mackenzie's Institutions of that Law*, 3rd edn (1764) (henceforth [Erskine,] *Principles* (1764)). In the "Advertisement" in ibid at [iii] was written: "in the last title of the book, the several crimes, which were before explained without any order, have been reduced to something, that has at least the appearance of a regular arrangement".

persons".[122] This classification continued in the posthumous fourth edition of 1769,[123] and in his posthumously published major work, *An Institute of the Law of Scotland.*[124] The following discussion is based on the more developed treatment in the *Institute.* Crimes against God were blasphemy, cursing God and denying his existence, and witchcraft and sorcery.[125] Of the second type of crime Erskine stated that "some are levelled immediately against the supreme power, and strike at the constitution itself, while others merely discover such a contempt and disregard to the law, as may contribute to baffle its authority, or slacken the reins of government".[126] In this category he included: treason, misprision of treason, sedition and leasing-making, corruption of judges, barratry, theft-bote, wrongous imprisonment, beating and affronting of judges and disobedience to their authority, deforcement of messengers, breach of arrestment, battery *pendente lite,* and also "[o]ffences against the laws enacted for the police or good government of a country" because they were "truly crimes against the state",[127] such as forestalling and regrating, being a sturdy beggar and vagabond, spoiling timber, and the like.[128] Erskine described his third class of crimes, those against particular persons, as being "directed, either against life, limb, chastity, goods, or character".[129] Those crimes directed against a man's life were murder, assassination, suicide, parricide, presumptive or statutory murder, and duelling.[130] "The crimes directed against a man's limbs, or the other members of his body, without any intention of killing, [were]",

122 Ibid 4.4.7.

123 [J Erskine,] *The Principles of the Law of Scotland: In the Order of Sir George Mackenzie's Institutions of that Law. The 4th ed., with the last corrections of the author* (1769) 4.4.7 (not seen, but study of the 5th edn of 1777 shows that Erskine retained the discussion of crimes found in the 3rd edn).

124 J Erskine, *An Institute of the Law of Scotland. In Four Books. In the Order of Sir George Mackenzie's Institutions of that Law*, 2 vols (1773) (henceforth Erskine, *Institute*) at 4.4.16: "Certain crimes are committed more immediately against God himself, others against the state, or public peace, and a third sort against particular persons."

125 Erskine, *Institute* (n 124) 4.4.16–18; *Principles* (1764) (n 121) 4.4.7–8.

126 Erskine, *Institute* (n 124) 4.4.19; see also *Principles* (1764) (n 121) 4.4.9 for a near identical statement.

127 Erskine, *Institute* (n 124) 4.4.38; note that, in *Principles* (1764) (n 121) 4.4.24, battery *pendente lite* is classed in the *third* type of crime.

128 See Erskine, *Institute* (n 124) 4.4.19–39. *Principles* (1764) (n 121) 4.4.9–18 lists: treason, sedition, riot, corruption in judges, theftbote, buying of claims, deforcement, breach of arrestment, forestalling of markets, and offences against game, planting, and the like.

129 Erskine, *Institute* (n 124) 4.4.40. Cf [Erskine,] *Principles* (1764) (n 121) 4.4.19: "Crimes against particular persons, may be directed, either against life, limb, liberty, chastity, goods, or reputation." In the *Institute*, the crime against the liberty of a person, wrongous imprisonment, has been reclassified as one of the second category of crimes.

130 Erskine, *Institute* (n 124) 4.4.40–49.

wrote Erskine, "chiefly mutilation, demembration, and haimesucken".[131] He stated that there were "chiefly" four crimes directed at "our neighbour's chastity": adultery, bigamy, rape and incest.[132] He also included sodomy and bestiality.[133] Erskine pointed out that, while there were many crimes against the property of another, the "most noted" were theft, falsehood, stellionate, usury, and fraudulent bankruptcy.[134] In this class he discussed theft, reset of theft, robbery as a species of theft (which included black-mail, reif or stouthreif, sorning, and piracy), falsehood (which included forgery, perjury, and using false weights and measures), usury, and stellionate (which included fraudulent bankruptcy).[135] The category of crimes against a person ends with "crimes . . . aimed against one's good name and character".[136] This included verbal and real "injuries".[137]

Millar's threefold division of crimes obviously derived from Erskine's account. This is unsurprising, as in one set of student notes Millar is reported as stating: "We intend to Follow the method of Justinian, which is much the same with Mr Erskine's method."[138] In discussing, in the same lecture, various works on Scots law, Millar said:

> As to the commentaries on the Law of Scotland, Erskines small Compend is the most distinct book on this Subject, and as his method is much the same with that we intend to Follow. I shall take notice of the Book and title of that treatise which relates to the different parts of these Lectures. There was published a larger Institute of the Law of Scotland by the same Author; and these two books I would cheifly Recommend to the Students of Scots-Law.[139]

E. MILLAR'S THEORY OF PUNISHMENT AND HIS CLASSIFICATION OF SCOTS CRIMINAL LAW

Though Millar has adopted a classification derived from Erskine's work, he has amended it in accordance with his theory of the origin of the right

131 Ibid 4.4.50 and 51.
132 Ibid 4.4.52 and discussed 52–56.
133 Ibid 4.4.57.
134 Ibid 4.4.58.
135 Ibid 4.4.58–79.
136 Ibid 4.4.80.
137 Ibid. The *Principles* (1764) (n 121) 4.4.19–45 have essentially the same list of crimes against particular persons with the variations pointed out in nn 127 and 129 above, and with mutilation and demembration discussed between homicide and self-murder.
138 GUL MS Gen 347 1.
139 Ibid 6–7.

of punishment. For Millar, punishment was based on the resentment felt by the injured party, supported by the indignation and sympathy of the impartial spectator, and reinforced by the consideration that the public good required the suppression of crime by means of punishment. In the lecture notes on Scots law, Millar is reported as having stressed that the public interest in suppressing crime was the more important, though secondary in the order of time.[140] In lectures on jurisprudence, he explained that "Every Crime may be considered as an invasion of the peace of society – which must be maintained by punishing Crimes",[141] so that "We not only are disposed to punish crimes from our immediate feeling for the sufferer, but also from considerations of utility".[142] But he nonetheless said:

> Those punishments . . . appear most expedient and proper which are neither increased nor diminished, from considerations of utility, above or below what is calculated to afford a reasonable gratification to the private sufferer, or corresponds to the natural indignation of an impartial spectator.[143]

This view derives from Smith.[144] Millar's argument for the basis of the punishment of crime may be contrasted with that of Erskine who wrote that "crimes are those breaches of the law which have a more direct tendency to subvert the government or constitution, or loosen the bonds of society; and therefore call for the public justice . . . that the transgressers may be punished . . . for the terror of others . . .".[145] Similar explanations of the punishment of crimes for "utility" – to use Smith's and Millar's term – are made by Mackenzie, Bayne and Forbes.[146]

While Erskine argued that crimes should be punished because they

140 See, e.g., GUL MS Murray 85 fo 94r; GUL MS Gen 181(3), 453; GUL MS Gen 1078 fo 102r.

141 GUL MS Murray 98 fo 99v.

142 Ibid fo 100r.

143 Ibid fo 100v.

144 Smith, *Lectures on Jurisprudence* (n 66) 475: "It is to be observed that our first approbation of punishment is not founded upon the regard to public utility which is commonly taken to be the foundation of it. It is our sympathy with the resentment of the sufferer which is the real principle." See Haakonssen, *Science of a Legislator* (n 16) 114–23.

145 Erskine, *Institute* (n 124) 4.4.2.

146 Bayne, *Institutions* (n 97) 6: "The Object of [that Part of our Law which treats of Crimes] is the *Peace* and *Order* of the Community, chiefly to be accomplished by the condign Punishment of Crimes . . .". Forbes, *Institutes* ii, 2: "Good Order and Government, Life, Property, Possession, and other sublunary Enjoyments, are fenced and secured by the Terror of penal Laws, made against such as presume to destroy, hurt, invade, or disturb the Same by Crimes and Offences. . . ." He later points out, ibid vol 2, 27, that offences against individuals are prosecuted as "public", "it being the publick Interest that none should pass unpunished". On Mackenzie, see text above at nn 78–79.

threatened the fabric of society, Millar approached punishment in the first instance from the perspective of a wrong done to an *individual.* Though expediency and utility also required the punishment of crimes, and were ultimately more important, they were secondary. Leaving aside, for the moment, Millar's categories of crimes against the religious establishment and crimes against the civil government, and focusing on that of crimes against individuals, it is possible to find a provisional explanation for the differences between him and Erskine.

Millar removed from Erskine's class of crimes against "particular persons": first, adultery, incest, bigamy and sodomy; and second, usury. Erskine grouped the first few crimes, with rape, as crimes "against our neighbour's chastity".[147] Millar classed rape with mutilation, demembration and assault to form the category of crimes against the person of an individual. The others from Erskine's group could not be classified this way, as there was no wronged person physically injured. One cannot immediately conclude, however, that Millar excluded these four crimes from his category of wrongs against individuals because there was no injured individual to feel resentment, and with whom an impartial spectator might feel sympathy, because, while this would apply probably to incest and certainly to sodomy, it would not necessarily apply to adultery and bigamy. On the other hand, adultery and bigamy did not fit comfortably into Millar's threefold division of crimes against individuals, as neither were obviously an injury to the body, the property, or the reputation of the person wronged. This may have been sufficient to endorse an alternative classification as more suitable. Erskine classed usury as a crime against a person's property. This is not a particularly compelling classification. One can readily appreciate that the unconvincing nature of Erskine's categorisation would reinforce any view that usury should not be dealt with as a crime against an individual, because there was no individual who felt resentment. The crime demanded a different classification.

By returning to Millar's two other categories of crimes, and examining where he dealt with adultery, incest, bigamy, sodomy and usury, it becomes possible to understand why he excluded them from the category of crimes against individuals. He told his students that:

> Crimes may be divided into two kinds. The 1st. Such as tend directly to hurt individuals, and the society in consequence of the harm done to individuals. The 2nd. Such as affect Society more directly – and individuals only as members of

147 Erskine, *Institute* (n 124) 4.4.52 and 57.

> Society – of the latter kind, are all offences which lead to overturn, or to disturb the Government either in Church or State.[148]

One set of notes described the latter category as "Public Crimes, or those directed against Society".[149] Under the heading of "Crimes against the religious establishment – or the rules of morality which have been taken under the Cognizance of the Church",[150] Millar explained that, among the inhabitants of the same country, uniformity of "circumstances" would tend to produce "a degree of uniformity in religious opinion", and that the government would accordingly protect certain types of worship, and that a clergy to direct worship and instruct would be "established by the public", and that such establishment would prevent the neglect of religion. He next commented: "Upon the same view of expediency, which justifies the establishment of a natural religion, it is lawful to punish every attempt to overturn that system, or to disturb the modes of worship it prescribes."[151] Crimes against religion have to be punished on the principle of expediency alone, because there is no injured person to feel resentment. This principle explained the punishment of blasphemy, atheism, heresy, witchcraft, cursing, swearing, profanation of Sunday and the like.[152] One set of notes explains that: "As Religion is calculated to promote the happiness and welfare of mankind, so every action that tends to destroy that system, ought to be punished according to its demerit."[153] Of the offences of adultery, fornication, drunkenness, bigamy, incest and sodomy, Millar next remarked that their punishment was "directed by particular religious considerations, more than by regard to the rules of justice" and that their punishment seemed "to constitute a part of *ecclesiastical police*".[154] In other words, these acts were punished as crimes because of the objections to them of established religion, rather than because of the demands of justice, in the sense of resentment felt by an injured person, as judged by the indignation and sympathy of an impartial spectator. Millar has here drawn on Smith's distinction between "laws of justice" and "laws of police".[155]

148 GUL MS Gen 1078 fo 106r.
149 GUL MS Gen 178 289.
150 Glasgow University Library, MS Gen 1078 fo 106r.
151 Ibid fo 107r.
152 Ibid fos 107r–108r.
153 GUL MS Gen 178 289.
154 GUL MS Gen 1078 fo 108r. Cf GUL MS Gen 178 290: "There are some crimes tho not altogether of a religious nature, yet as falling under the cognizance of church Courts may be here taken notice of."
155 See Haakonssen, *Science of a Legislator* (n 16) 93–98; and "John Millar and the science of a legislator" (n 16) at 52.

Turning to crimes against the civil government, Millar stated:

> The necessity, or expediency of having an established civil government is yet more obvious and certain than of having an established ecclesiastical government.
>
> Hence it is indisputable that the Community have a right to defend their government by penal sanctions.[156]

The most serious offence in this class was treason, but there were "Inferior offences against government", such as sedition, "or against the regulations respecting the *police* of the country'"[157] which included usury, and Millar added that "Various other offences . . . might be brought under the head of violating the regulations of Police – such as Forestalling and Regratting – offences against game laws – Begging with out Badges".[158] Usury was thus excluded from the category of offences against the property of individuals because it did not contravene the rules of justice, but instead was regulated, for utility, as a police matter.

F. CONCLUSION

Millar's classification of Scots criminal law can thus be seen to result from the interaction of the categories of crimes he found in Erskine's *Institute* and *Principles* with the natural jurisprudence he adopted from Smith to provide a foundation for Scots law.[159] The extent to which his analysis of types of crime was linked with Smithian jurisprudence may be glimpsed from his comment that: "violations of property do not commonly excite the same degree of indignation, and resentment, with those offences which tend to destroy our personal safety".[160] He also noted that attitudes to crime could vary in different historical periods.[161] His philosophy of law similarly brought him to discuss crimes in relation to delicts as an integral part of the rights which it was the purpose of the law to protect, rather than as

156 GUL MS Gen 1078 fo 110r.

157 [Millar,] *Heads of the Lectures on the Law of Scotland* 16; see also GUL MS Gen 1078 fo 114r.

158 GUL MS Gen 1078 fo 115r.

159 It is worth noting that Smith does *not* deal in his lectures on jurisprudence with crimes against religion and against government, and also that Smith's classification of crimes against the individual differs to some extent from that of Millar: Haakonssen, *Science of a Legislator* (n 16) 114–23. Millar's scheme is not a slavish copy.

160 GUL MS Gen 1078 fo 122r.

161 See ibid fo 122r and GUL MS Gen 181(3) 523 on the differences between attitudes to property in "the infancy of Society" and when "men become opulent and civilized". Cf GUL MS Gen 181(3) 517 on rape.

an epilogue to actions in the manner of Justinian's *Institutes*, Mackenzie's *Institutions*, and Erskine's works, much less than as a separate summer course in the fashion of Bayne. It may be noted in this connection that Millar, contrary to the statement of Murray, did not devote more attention to criminal law and procedure than his predecessors; if anything, the evidence of Bayne's summer course, Forbes' *Institutes*, and Erskine's lectures and statement that "the Doctrine of Crimes, if properly explained, would take up a whole Course of Lectures by itself",[162] shows that the opposite is the case. For Millar, criminal law was merely an integral part of his Smithian conception of Scots law.

Millar's stress on the primacy of wrongs done to individuals as the basis of criminal justice, with considerations of utility and expediency as secondary, though ultimately of greater importance, distinguishes him from earlier Scots professors of law. It is particularly successful. Not only did his approach enable him to classify Scots criminal law and provide a philosophical and historical basis for why certain types of behaviour were criminal, it also made possible the development of a critique. First, appeal to the standard of utility would allow assessment of laws which made criminal certain acts solely on the grounds of utility (some of which would be victimless crimes in modern terms). Second, the basis of punishment in resentment and spectatorial sympathy allowed criticism of existing laws on the grounds that the punishment exceeded what this principle required. It should nonetheless be pointed out that, in his lectures on Scots law as reported, he did not use the opportunity to develop a critique of the criminal law: the lectures tend to be explanatory and technical. In all this, Millar is very much the heir of Smith. Since the focus of this paper does not permit direct confrontation with the various interpretations of Millar's thinking, assessment of them will be eschewed; but it is fair to point out that the view of Millar's theory of justice and law here put forward is generally supportive of Haakonssen's argument that Millar was the "sceptical Whig" inheritor of Smith's science of law and politics.[163]

G. EPILOGUE: MILLAR AND HUME

It is impossible to conclude a discussion of Millar's account of Scots criminal law without considering his influence on his pupil, David Hume, and through

162 SigL MS 7 (law), vol ii, 313. See above, text at nn 43–45 and 77–136.
163 Haakonssen, "John Millar and the science of a legislator" (n 16).

Hume, potentially on modern Scots criminal law. Murray, Paton and Walker have all suggested that Hume's discussion of criminal law was influenced by Millar's teaching.[164]

Hume taught criminal law in a summer course separate from the rest of his lectures on Scots law.[165] This in itself suggests that he was not particularly influenced by Millar, whose view of the origins of rights and justice would have made such a proceeding intellectually difficult to justify. The difference of outlook from that of Millar is readily confirmed.

At the start of his course on Scots private law Hume told his class that one of the advantages to a student of attending lectures on law was that of preventing "his contracting too great a fondness for speculative notions". If a student had "no preceptor to guide him at his outset" he might come to prefer "too much those arguments which bear the appearance of deducing a conclusion logically from general principles", so that the student would run "a great risk of becoming ingenious rather than sound as a lawyer". Hume continued this attack on rationalist natural law by informing his class that, "[t]he law, under which this or any other nation lives, was not contrived by metaphysicians". Accordingly, "it were vain to imagine that we can chain it down, in rules as simple and constant, as those in which Sir Isaac Newton has bound the phenomena of the heavenly motions".[166] Hume carefully distinguished his own approach from that of Millar. He told his class:

> We may find in the laws of different nations many points of analogy, which may be collected into a treatise of universal jurisprudence, a noble department of science, and fit to employ an ingenious mind, but which it is not the proper business of this class to teach. You are here to be made acquainted with the special laws of your own country, as they actually stand; and must not expect to find everywhere, the beauty and harmony of a Philosophical System.[167]

He nonetheless adopted Millar's Smithian system of law:

> [The lawyer] is . . . employed in considering the connections formed by mankind with the things around them, and the rights, the claims and obligations which

164 Murray, *Memories of the Old College of Glasgow* (n 6) 223–224; Paton, "Biography of Baron Hume" (n 44), 333; Walker, *Scottish Jurists* (n 17) 316, 329. See n 44 above.

165 See GUL MS Murray 135–139 covering, though with some gaps, the first 14 lectures delivered 12–27 May 1795; and SigL MS 105:a:21, summer 1793 (not seen: this set has been mislaid).

166 Hume, *Lectures* (n 44) vol i, 4–6.

167 Ibid vol i, 6–7.

> arise among the several orders or classes of persons. The correct division of objects of law is, therefore into Rights and Actions . . .[168]

His lectures on Scots law follow the structure of those of Millar, except in the exclusion of a detailed treatment of criminal law in the discussion of personal rights, and the reversal of Millar's treatment of real and personal rights over things, with some other, more minor, rearrangements of the material. There is, however, no indication of interest in the philosophy underpinning this structure, which seems to have been used merely as a convenient order of exegesis.

Hume's definition of a crime further demonstrates his departure from Millar's approach. He wrote in the *Commentaries*:

> In determining the extent of that part of the law which has relation to CRIMES, I shall be guided by the ordinary acceptation of that term, and shall consider every act as a crime, for which the law of Scotland has appointed the offender to make satisfaction to the public, beside repairing, where that can be done, the injury which the individual hath sustained. It is obvious, (and I do not think it necessary to say more concerning the nature of crimes, as contradistinguished to civil wrongs), that in exacting any such atonement of him, the Legislature always proceed on the opinion of an infringement on his part of that social regard, which, as a citizen, he owes to the community; whether it be that he has violated their security, or their tranquillity, or has trespassed with respect to some of those other articles of wholesome government and regulation, which affect the public polity and general welfare of the realm.[169]

Hume then stated he would not discuss the source of the right of inflicting punishment, "an inquiry which would only be proper . . . in the very beginnings of society and legislation", nor "trace the natural history of crimes" (for which he referred to Kames' essay). He then added:

> [S]till less shall I think it any part of my duty, to enlarge at this time in observations on the due measure, proportion, or application of punishments, or on the style, the objects, and proper qualities, of penal laws, which are rather the business of the political philosopher, than of the lawyer, and on which subjects, let me say, much hath been rashly written, in a loose and general way, by authors but moderately skilled in the business of life, and very unequal to the arduous task to improving the science of legislation.[170]

168 Ibid vol i, 9–10.

169 Hume, *Commentaries* (n 41) vol i, 1–2.

170 Ibid vol i, 2–3; in the 2nd edn, these three pages were reduced to one paragraph (*Commentaries* (1819) vol i, 21):

> In determining the extent of that part of the Law of Scotland, which has relation to CRIMES, I shall take that term in its ordinary acceptation; and shall consider every act as a

This is a complete rejection of Millar's treatment of Scots criminal law. There is no trace of Millar's use of natural justice and utility to understand Scots law. For Hume, a crime was simply an act for which Scots law exacted a penalty, because some wrong had been done to the public. The origin of punishment, its justification, and its due extent in differing crimes were topics he specifically refused to discuss in a general fashion. In line with this, in the summer lectures which were the basis for the *Commentaries*,[171] in dramatic contrast to the lectures on private law, Hume completely departed from the structure of Millar's account. He wrote:

> I mean to open up to the young lawyer the Elements of our Criminal Practice; and to lay before him such authorities and materials, as may serve to guide him in his future researches . . . I have no intention of bringing forward a Philosophical treatise of Criminal Jurisprudence, in which the history of the human species, with respect to this branch of the science of law, is to be traced; and an attempt made to ascertain, on abstract and universal principles, the nature of the several offences, and the application and proportion of punishments.[172]

These words were published when Millar still occupied the Glasgow chair: Hume must have intended them to be read as distinguishing his work from that of his teacher, or even as a veiled criticism.[173] Though elements of Millar's philosophy may have continued in an attenuated way to influence Hume,[174] in contrast to Millar's classification of crimes and order

> crime, for which our Practice has appointed the offender to make some satisfaction to the public, besides repairing, where that is possible, the injury sustained by the individual. It is obvious, that in exacting any such atonement, the law always supposes that the delinquent has infringed, in some respect, those duties which he owes to the community: He has set a dangerous example of violence, dishonesty, falsehood, indecency, irreligion; or he has trespassed with respect to some of those other articles of wholesome discipline, or wise oeconomy, which affect the public welfare, and are matters of general concernment.

The further remarks on punishment and the science of legislation are entirely deleted.

171 See GUL MS Murray 135–139, which, though incomplete, show that the structure of the *Commentaries* is that of the lectures.

172 Hume, *Commentaries* (n 41) vol i, lv.

173 These same remarks were probably made to his class, and thus go back beyond 1797 to when Millar was at the height of his vigour and fame, and at GUL MS Murray 135 fo 4r he is reported as stating: "Do not here mean to enter into a philosophical discussion on the nature of crimes."

174 GUL MS Murray 135, fo lr states: "The Law respecting Crimes is more simple in its nature, than that with regard to civil Rights. The former is drawn [from] the natural feelings of humanity, and general views of Expediency common to all Mankind." In *Commentaries* (n 41) vol i, 326, Hume wrote: "In like manner, as a man may kill in resistance of an attempt on his life, a woman also hath a right to kill in resistance of that injury to her honour, which cannot be repaired if it be committed, and of which she is entitled to feel the highest resentment. By parity of reason, the husband or the father of a woman thus invaded, has right to feel the like resentment, and to defend her from this extreme and cruel injury, at the hazard of the invader."

of discussion derived from philosophical theories of justice, he stated that in explaining criminal law the order of treatment is less important than in Civil Law, and "that it is often an almost arbitrary matter, to what subject the student shall first direct his attention". He commented that he has chosen to treat "the several crimes in the order rather of their frequency and practical importance, than of their rank in other respects". He explained:

> Thus I begin with those offences which are committed against individuals, and among these with the offences against property; after which follow the several modes of injuring an individual in his person or his fame. Having exhausted these, I proceed to such offences as more immediately concern the public; which, after the example of Judge Blackstone, I have distributed into several classes: as they are hostile to the course of public justice; to the public peace; to the police and public oeconomy of the kingdom; or to its interest in point of trade. The next division includes the high crimes of treason, sedition, and some others which are levelled directly against the Sovereign and the State. And the last consists of those transgressions which related to God and to religion.[175]

Within the class of crimes against the property of individuals, Hume included: theft and stouthreif; reset of theft; wilful fire-raising and malicious mischief; falsehood and fraud; within that of injuring individuals in their person and reputation: homicide; rape; hamesucken; real injuries; offences against reputation. This resembles Millar's classification of crimes against individuals, and probably derives from it, though Hume has placed it at the very beginning of his account. It is worth noting that Blackstone has a similar grouping of "crimes and misdemeanors against private subjects", which he described as "against their *persons*, their *habitations*, and their *property*";[176] but its differences from that of Hume suggest that it did not influence him in his class of crimes against persons.[177]

Hume acknowledged that his classes of crimes affecting the polity derived from Blackstone's *Commentaries*. His classification is not quite identical with Blackstone's, because he omits the latter's grouping of crimes against public

It is difficult to know what emphasis to put on these statements; there is no sign of sustained influence from Millar's theory of justice, and indeed these very remarks lack mention of spectatorial sympathy.

175 Hume, *Commentaries* (n 41) vol i, lxiii.

176 W Blackstone, *Commentaries on the Laws of England*, 1st edn, 4 vols (1765–1769) vol iv, 177. These classifications remain in subsequent editions.

177 Offences against the *persons* of private subjects, according to Blackstone, were: homicide; mayhem; forcible abduction and marriage; rape; buggery; assaults; batteries; wounding; false imprisonment; kidnapping. Offences against their *habitations* were: arson; burglary. Offences against their *property* were: larceny; malicious mischief; forgery.

health,[178] and the details within the classes are not the same.[179] Furthermore, contrary to Blackstone, Hume in the body of his text contradicts the classification set out in the introduction quoted above, and groups offences against the state and against religion with Blackstone's offences against the commonwealth. For example, Hume wrote:

> I have now spoken of the principal offences, which are to the injury of individuals in person, fame, or property . . . I shall now be led to inquire concerning such transgressions as are chiefly vindicated on account of their pernicious tendency with respect to the public polity, and general welfare of the realm. These may be distributed into several classes, – as they are injurious to the administration of Justice; to the conservation of peace; to public order, police, and economy; to the interests of trade; to the rights of the King and his government; or to the reverence of God and of religion.[180]

This classification in fact resembles Millar's division of crimes into those against individuals and those against society,[181] so that Hume's treatment could be seen as Millar's discussed in reverse order, though strongly influenced by Blackstone.

There is nothing surprising in this, nor is it particularly important whether this possible influence from Millar was conscious or unconscious. It would rather be a matter for remark if Hume had not been affected by a professor as compelling as Millar by all accounts was, with whom he had boarded, and notes from whose lectures he still possessed, bound in calf, at his death.[182] On the other hand, it is notable how slight the influence from Millar was: there is no overt trace of the type of philosophical discussion and approach which obviously mattered to Millar. In stark contrast to Millar's teaching of criminal law, Hume's treatment lacks any consideration of the basis and purpose of punishment as an aid to understanding. He preferred to specialise – and to do so in detail – in an account of the actual law. Contrary to the suggestions of Murray, Paton and Walker, there is no evidence that

178 Ibid vol iv, 161–162: offences relating to the plague, to quarantine, and to selling unwholesome provisions.

179 Cf ibid vol iv, chs 10–13 with Hume, *Commentaries* (n 41) vol ii, chs 11–25.

180 Hume, *Commentaries* (n 41) vol ii, 126; cf ibid, vol ii, 406.

181 See text at n 148 above.

182 NLS MS 348 is a bookseller's catalogue of Hume's Library. At fo 135r we can recognise his MS notes of Millar's lectures on Jurisprudence (second course on the *Institutes*), on the Pandects, and on Government. There are other notes which may be of Millar's lectures on Scots law. The lectures on Jurisprudence and the Pandects were dated 1779 which suggests Hume made copies of them in that year, perhaps preparatory to his trials for admission as an advocate, as Paton, "Biography of Baron Hume" (n 44) 333–334 has shown that he boarded with Millar in 1775–1776 and 1776–1777.

Millar's teaching stimulated Hume's interest in criminal law more than in any other particular legal topic.

The essentially Enlightenment synthesis of Scots criminal law with moral philosophy achieved by Millar was thus sundered by his pupil, who explicitly distinguished the provinces of the lawyer and the philosopher. It was Hume's approach which was to influence the development of Scots criminal law through the nineteenth century. This is not to denigrate Hume's *Commentaries*, which are an outstanding achievement of legal scholarship, and worthy of study in their own right; but the spirit which informs them is not that of Millar's science of legislation.

11 Hamesucken and the Major Premiss in the Libel, 1672–1770: Criminal Law in the Age of Enlightenment

Stallard v HM Advocate was one of the last criminal appeals over which Lord Emslie presided as Lord Justice-General of Scotland.[1] The case raised the controversial, if apparently simple, issue of whether or not a husband could be guilty of the rape of his wife, other than art and part, while they were still cohabiting. *HM Advocate v D*[2] and *HM Advocate v Paxton*[3] had already determined that, where spouses were living apart, a husband could be guilty of raping his wife. The authority for the traditional view on marital rape is a passage dealing with art and part guilt in the chapter on rape in Hume's *Commentaries*: "This is true without exception even of the husband of the woman; who, though he cannot himself commit a rape on his own wife, who has surrendered her person to him in that sort, may however be accessory to that crime . . . committed on her by another."[4] The court suggested in *Stallard* that Hume had adopted this view from Sir Matthew Hale's *Historia placitorum coronae*, where Hale had written: "But the husband cannot be guilty of a rape committed by himself upon his lawful wife, for by their mutual matrimonial consent and contract the wife hath given up herself in this kind unto her husband, which she cannot retract."[5] The court did not consider it necessary to decide in *Stallard* whether or not

1 1989 SCCR 248.

2 1982 SCCR 182.

3 1985 SLT 96.

4 D Hume, *Commentaries on the Law of Scotland, Respecting* Crimes, 2 vols; 4th edn (1844) vol i, 306 (henceforth Hume, *Commentaries*, 4th edn (1844)); see also D Hume, *Commentaries on the Law of Scotland, Respecting the Description and Punishment of Crimes*, 2 vols (1797) vol ii, 10 which has trivial differences in wording. All quotations below will be from the first edition of 1797, unless otherwise noted (henceforth Hume, *Commentaries*).

5 M Hale, *Historia placitorum coronae. The History of the Pleas of the Crown*, 2 vols (1736) (henceforth Hale, *Pleas of the Crown*) vol i, 629.

Hume had correctly stated the law of his own day, accepting that, even if Hume's statement ever had been good law in Scotland, it no longer was.[6] The English Court of Appeal, Criminal Division, has recently followed this lead, and rejected the marital rape exemption found in Hale.[7]

Hume acknowledged that he drew on English law in writing his *Commentaries*:

> Let me add, that while I thus disclaim that superstitious admiration of the English Law, which prevails among some persons, and especially, like other superstitions, among the ignorant; and which would set up that system as a standard of perfection, after the likeness whereof we are to reform and new-model our own; yet on a proper occasion, and for a proper purpose, I have been ready to avail myself of the important assistance which its doctrines may often afford me. I have already said, that as a great body of written and practical reason, and recommended by the example of a free and an enlightened people, it has every where, and certainly in our country more than elsewhere, (because the form of our Government, and the general spirit of our jurisprudence are the same with that of England), a strong claim to deference and regard. In matters, therefore, which depend on the common feelings of equity and right, and are not determined otherwise by our municipal custom, nor are anywise involved in it, I have made liberal use of the sentiments, and sometimes even of the words of the English writers on law: An obligation, which, as their works cannot properly be quoted as authorities in a book of Scots Law, I beg leave in this place, once for all, to acknowledge.[8]

It is therefore unsurprising that he may have adopted the doctrine on marital rape found in Hale in the absence of any Scottish authority on the issue. Yet Gane and Stoddart, writing before the decision in *Stallard*, put an obvious and attractive argument on Hume's view of rape in marriage:

> [I]t is not at all clear that the "marital rape exemption" is really a rule of Scots law at all. There is no sign of it prior to Hume, and the other authorities which refer to it merely repeat Hume. Hume himself does not refer to any Scottish authority in support of his view, and it is likely that the rule was adopted by Hume from Hale's *Pleas of the Crown* . . . [9]

6 1989 SCCR 248 at 253–254.

7 *R* v *R* [1991] 1 All ER 747; [1991] 2 All ER 257. The husband and wife were no longer living together; but the court pronounced a general principle that husbands could be convicted of the rape of their wives, although pointing out that, had it been decided otherwise, they would have ruled that where a wife had withdrawn from cohabitation, as in this case, so that the marriage was effectively at an end as far as she was concerned, the husband's immunity was lost. At the time of writing the Court of Appeal had given leave to appeal to the House of Lords certifying the point of law as of general public importance. See now [1991] 4 All ER 481.

8 Hume, *Commentaries* (n 4) vol i, liv; cf *Commentaries*, 4th edn (1844) (n 4) vol i, 13, in which edition "common feelings of equity and right" reads "common feelings of equity and reason". There are other trivial changes.

9 C H W Gane and C N Stoddard, *A Casebook on Scottish Criminal* Law, 2nd edn (1988) 671.

They thus bluntly attack the authority of Hume on the grounds that his statement is one of English law rather than Scots law. Gane and Stoddart were the first to suggest that Hume may have drawn this doctrine from Hale. Certainly it is not found in earlier published treatises on Scots criminal law, and only in Hale of the English authors whom Hume stated he consulted.[10] The suggestion is plausible, because, though the words used by Hume and Hale are not very close, after the passage quoted above, Hale also went on to discuss when a husband could be indicted for the rape of his wife by assisting another as the actor.[11]

Gane and Stoddart's challenge to the authority of Hume's proposition undoubtedly reflects a traditional view that, since there is no appeal to the House of Lords from the High Court of Justiciary,[12] and since Scots criminal law is primarily common law rather than statutory in basis, it is somehow more "Scottish" and has been less open to English influence than Scots private law.[13] Indeed, Sheriff Gordon has remarked that "Scots criminal law has grown up more or less independently of Anglo-American law, and Anglo-American concepts and cases must therefore be treated with care when considering Scots law".[14] Hume's adoption of a doctrine of English law could thus be stigmatised as somehow illegitimate.

It is undoubtedly correct that to some extent Scots criminal law has developed independently of that of England, and I do not wish here to challenge Sheriff Gordon's view. Instead, I wish to explore the issue raised by Gane and Stoddart (and perhaps implicitly by the court in *Stallard*) of whether demonstration that Hume adopted a doctrine of English law in the absence of Scots authority necessarily impugns the validity of that doctrine as Scots law. I shall do this by examining the law on hamesucken between 1672 and 1770. These two dates are not arbitrary. The first is the year of the creation of the new Court of Justiciary; the second provides a terminus since the previous year had seen the last trial for hamesucken before the High Court of Justiciary until the nineteenth century, when, as I hope to

10 Hume, *Commentaries* (n 4) vol i, [lxiv] states that, as well as Hale, he consulted W Hawkins, *A Treatise of the Pleas of the Crown: Or, A System of the Principal Matters relating to that Subject, digested under their Proper Heads*, 2 vols, 3rd edn (1739); and W Blackstone, *Commentaries on the Laws of England*, 4 vols, 1st edn (1765–1769).

11 Hale, *Pleas of the Crown* (n 5) vol i, 629.

12 On which, however, see A J MacLean, "The House of Lords and Appeals from the High Court of Justiciary, 1707–1887" (1985) *Juridical Review* 192.

13 Cf T B Smith, "English Influences on the Law of Scotland", in *Studies Critical and Comparative* (1962) 116 at 130–131.

14 G H Gordon, *The Criminal Law of* Scotland, 2nd edn (1978) (henceforth Gordon, *Criminal Law*) 3.

argue elsewhere, the crime of hamesucken gained a new lease of life after the publication of Hume's *Commentaries*. Discussion of hamesucken will allow me to place Hume's account of the marital rape exemption in the more general context of Scots criminal law and practice; furthermore, in one important case on hamesucken, the question of marital rape was considered.

The first section of the paper will be devoted to an account of procedure in criminal trials between these dates, the second will discuss the law of hamesucken as found in treatises and the practice of the Justiciary Court, while the third and fourth will examine one crucial trial in 1752. The final section will return to marital rape, and will offer some tentative conclusions, suggesting that if Hume adopted the marital rape exemption from Hale, he was following the practice, well established in Scottish criminal law, of drawing on the criminal laws of other countries to explain and develop Scots law. This practice was necessary because the manner of conducting trials and the records of the court tended to leave the law imprecise and without an authoritative judicial statement. It remained vague and inchoate to some extent. Furthermore, criminal law was not viewed as narrowly Scottish: it was legitimate to borrow from the laws of other countries. Scottish criminal law was common law in the sense both of being located in the custom of the courts and in being part of the *ius commune*. Hume's *Commentaries* perhaps marked or continued a turning away from the *ius commune*, and a favouring (if limited in scope) of English law as a source of borrowing; they also continued to some extent an existing traditional approach in these matters.

A. PROCEDURE IN CRIMINAL TRIALS, 1672–1770

The High Court of Justiciary was established by the Courts Act 1672, c 40. Under this Act, the judges were the Lord Justice-General, Lord Justice-Clerk and five Lords Commissioners of Justiciary appointed from the Lords of Session. As well as sitting in Edinburgh, the judges went on circuit in twos, once a year under the Act of 1672 and twice a year after 1746.[15] Prosecution was based on a libel which took the form either of an indictment or of criminal letters. The main distinction between the two was that the former could only be used by the Lord Advocate, while the latter could be used by others, such as private individuals.[16] Whether the prosecution was by way

15 W Croft Dickinson, "The High Court of Justiciary", in G C H Paton (ed), *An Introduction to Scottish Legal* History, Stair Society vol 20 (1958) 408 at 411.

16 See, e.g., D Hume, *Commentaries on the Law of Scotland Respecting Trial for Crimes*, 2 vols (1800) (henceforth Hume, *Trial for Crimes*) vol i, 244–247.

of indictment or criminal letters, the libel was in the form of a syllogism, with a major premiss or proposition setting out the crime charged, usually by a *nomen juris*, or if there were none, by a general description, while the minor premiss or proposition named and designed the accused and set out allegations of fact which, if proven, would demonstrate the pannel's guilt of the crime specified in the major premiss. After this came the conclusion, stating that the pannel on conviction should be punished as provided by the law for the crime.[17] It is unnecessary to go through the steps of a criminal prosecution in detail. With lists of witnesses and assizers, the libel was served on the accused who was cited to compear at a stated time at either the High Court or a Circuit Court. When the accused compeared at the trial diet, the libel was read to him or her and he or she was required to plead guilty or not guilty. On the pannel's pleading not guilty, there normally was a debate on the relevancy of the libel. In the later seventeenth century, the procurators for the pannel and the prosecutor normally dictated their objections, replies, duplies, triplies, quadruplies and so on to the clerk who entered them in the record. The Act of 1695, c 6 required that relevancy be debated *viva voce*, to be followed by the giving in of written informations that were entered, recorded, and publicly read to the court, and that could then, if necessary, be debated *viva voce*. This Act was repealed by the Heritable Jurisdictions (Scotland) Act 1746 (c 43) s 41, which substituted the provision (s 42) that, after the oral debate on the relevancy, informations could be given in to the court by the procurators for the pursuer and the pannel. On the basis of this debate, the judges pronounced an interlocutor on the relevancy, which could set out in detail which matters were to be proved and which defences considered. After this, the pannel would be put to the cognisance of an assize, that, on the basis of the interlocutor and evidence presented, would either determine the guilt or innocence of the pannel or give a special verdict.[18]

The debate on the relevancy of the libel focused attention on the definition of the crime set out in the major premiss and on whether or not the averments in the minor premiss, if proved, would constitute that crime.

17 Ibid vol i, 247; see also Hume, *Commentaries*, 4th edn (1844) (n 4) vol ii, 155.

18 J Irvine Smith, "Criminal Procedure" in [Paton (ed)], *Introduction to Scottish Legal History* 426 at 439–443; for a good contemporary account of procedure and the steps in a prosecution, see J Louthian, *The Form of Process before the Court of Justiciary in Scotland* (1732) (henceforth Louthian, *Form of Process*); and *The Form of Process, before the Court of Justiciary in Scotland In Two Books*, 2nd edn (1752) which updates it. Louthian concentrates on the formal steps and styles of documents and records.

The law on the construction of the major premiss or proposition is set out by Hume in some detail, and it is unnecessary to consider it here.[19] But since much of what follows will revolve around the way in which the major premiss of the libel was phrased, some remarks are appropriate. Alison described it thus:

> The major proposition sets out with the words, "That albeit by the laws of this and of every other well governed realm, theft, especially when accomplished by means of housebreaking, is a crime of an heinous nature, and severely punishable." In cases of murder, it is usual to add the words, "albeit by die laws of God and of this and every other well governed realm, murder is a crime," . . . [20]

The exact wording or style of the formula of the major premiss varied historically, as Hume explained, glossing the phrase "and all other well-governed realms":

> For it had long ago grown into a fashion, not to be content with referring in this respect to our own laws alone, but to confirm their decision with an appeal to all other high authorities, such as the law of God and nature, or the law and practice of other civilized states, as concurring in the same notions of the offence in question. In times when the authority of the civil and the canon law was higher than it is now, it was not uncommon to call in the aid also of those systems; describing them as "the *common law*, baith civil and cannon," in contradistinction to the peculiar and municipal practice of Scotland. Nay, I find, that, in some few instances, the prosecutor had gone the length of setting forth in this part of his libel, the particular texts and authorities of the civil or canon law on which he grounded his proposition, or which might be quoted in support of his conclusion.[21]

Hume's suggestion that the appeal to the laws of God, of nature, and the common law was a matter of changing fashion in drafting may be presumed to be to some extent correct. Nonetheless, he did relate the reference to common law, that is to the Civil and Canon Laws viewed as *ius commune*, to the authority it had once enjoyed in Scotland, thus further suggesting that such allusions to laws other than Scots did have a function in the libel, and were not merely decorative.

19 Hume, *Trial for Crimes* (n 16) vol i, 263–300; Hume, *Commentaries*, 4th edn (1844) (n 4) vol ii, 164–181; see also A Alison, *Principles of the Criminal Law of Scotland*, 2 vols (1832) (henceforth Alison, *Criminal Law*) vol ii, 228–245.

20 Alison, *Criminal Law* (n 19) vol ii, 228.

21 Hume, *Trial for Crimes* (n 16) vol i, 264; Hume, *Commentaries*, 4th edn (1844) (n 4) vol ii, 164 is substantially similar.

B. HAMESUCKEN IN TREATISES AND THE PRACTICE OF THE JUSTICIARY COURT

Sheriff Gordon has written that until 1887 "to assault a man in his own house after having invaded the house for that purpose constituted the capital crime of hamesucken".[22] The Criminal Procedure (Scotland) Act of that year (c 35) basically limited the imposition of capital sentences to cases of conviction for murder.[23] As the same Act also abolished the need to specify a *nomen juris* in a criminal libel,[24] the crime of hamesucken could reasonably have been expected to vanish, facts which would formerly have been described as amounting to the crime becoming treated as a species of aggravated assault.[25] The recent cases of *HM Advocate v Brown*[26] and *McAdam v Ingram*[27] indicate, however, that judges are still willing to use the term "hamesucken" to describe a particular offence.

Gordon's definition of hamesucken seems clear enough, and certainly encapsulates the essential core of the crime. Yet, down to the publication of Hume's *Commentaries*, there were uncertainties about the nature and punishment of it. Indeed, one of Dirleton's doubts (first published in 1698) had been: "If Hamesucken . . . be Capital, though no Person be killed?" Sir James Steuart may have answered in 1715 that "Hame-sucken is thought *capital* though no Person be killed, but in that Case it should be both violent and evident;"[28] it could still be argued, however, in *Macgregor* in 1752[29] and in *Morton Craigieknow* in 1763[30] that the crime was not (or no longer) capital, while the drafter of one libel in 1703 could be sufficiently uncertain that he wrote in the major premiss:

> Where By the Laws of this and all other well governed realms, The Invading of Her Majesties, peaceable subjects and Leidges violently . . . Speciallie when

22 Gordon, *Criminal Law* (n 14) 818.

23 Section 56.

24 Section 5.

25 Gordon, *Criminal Law* (n 14) 818.

26 1989 GWD 35-1604.

27 1990 GWD 22-1226. See also "Hamesucken charge", *The Scotsman*, 14 July 1978, a reference for which I am indebted to David Sellar.

28 J Steuart, *Dirleton's Doubts and Questions in the Law of Scotland, Resolved and* Answered, 2nd edn (1762) 112.

29 Books of Adjournal, S[cottish] R[ecord] O[ffice] JC 3/28 529 at 562, 569–570 and 618–620 (apart from the case cited in n 30 below, all cases not cited from a published work are cited from the Books of Adjournal and this will not hereafter be noted; not all the volumes are paginated). In quoting from these MS records I have retained the original spelling, use of capitals and punctuation, but have expanded common contractions.

30 Minute Book of Southern Circuit, SRO JC 12/11 (16 September 1763).

> committed by way of Hamesucken upon any man within his own dwelling house precinct thereof, or entry thereto, are Crimes punishable with the pains of death. Particularly by Caput 9 and 10th Lib: 4th of the Majestie, Which makes the Crime of Hamesucken punishable as that of Ravishment. . . . At least the saids Crimes are severly punishable by the highest degree and pitch of Arbitrary punishment.[31]

The main difficulty in prosecuting and defending charges of hamesucken arose from the lack of a clear definition of the crime, and the above premiss seems uncertain as to whether the hamesucken should be libelled as an aggravation or as the principal crime, the former only resulting in an "arbitrary" punishment, that is, one, other than death, in the discretion of the court.

As procurator for the pannel, Sir Robert Colt argued in *Crawford* in 1690 that "the ffoundations of Hamesucken as to the quality of the cryme Has its very ryse from the Reg[iam] Majest[atem]".[32] This was a common view through much of the eighteenth century, and it was based on the following passages:

> (4.9) Gif ane man will challenge ane other of Haimsuckin, it is necessare, that he alledge, that his proper house quhere he dwelles, lyes and ryses; daylie and nichtlie, is assailzied.
>
> 2. And swa he sall make ane lawfull soyt, because na man may challenge ane other of the crime of haimsuckin, bot in his proper and certaine dwelling house.
>
> 3. And mairover, he sall follow and persew his crime in the forme, as is vsed, anent the Revising of wemen.
>
> (4.10) It is to wit, that na man sal be heard to accuse ane other of Reif, Revissing of wemen, or of Haimsuckin, except he make any lawfull soyt, in maner foresaid.
>
> 2. And gif he delayes be the space of ane nicht, to the effect, he may haue the connsell of his friends; and swa makes not fresh and recent persute; and that be proven against him, the defender sall be quite, and the accuser sail be in the Kings mercie.[33]

In the case of *Balfour*, Sir James Steuart as Lord Advocate triplied that "as for the words of the Regiam Majestatem They doe not at all defyne the cryme but only tell whatt Hame is".[34] This is certainly correct. Though *Regiam* only stated what a person's home was (where he lay and rose, nightly and daily), and how hamesucken should be prosecuted, it was nonetheless relatively common in the late seventeenth and early eighteenth century to mention

31 *Drummond*, SRO JC 3/1 545 (29 November 1703).

32 SRO JC 2/17 (10 March 1690).

33 J Skene, *Regiam Majestatem. The Auld Lawes and Constitutions of Scotland. . . . Quheruneto are adjoined, Twa Treatises, The ane, anent the Order of proces observed before the Lords of Counsell, and Session: The other of Crimes, and Judges in criminall causes* (1609) fo 68v.

34 SRO JC 2/19 (4 June 1694) 341 at 355.

these passages specifically in the major premiss of the libel, as in that of 1703 already quoted;[35] they were of limited assistance, however, in explaining the nature of the crime, which it was accordingly necessary to establish from the practice of the courts. To do so, however, presented a number of problems. First, no reports of the decisions of the Justiciary or Circuit Courts were to be systematically published until the 1820s, though Maclaurin and Arnot did publish some selected cases in the later eighteenth century, and the *Scots Magazine* and newspapers such as the *Caledonian Mercury* could carry extensive reports of notable trials.[36] Secondly, though the original records were readily accessible to those advocates who acted as procurators in the Justiciary Court, the form of the official record was limited. It recorded the libel, the debates on the relevancy, and the interlocutor on the relevancy; but it did not include the reasoning of the judges on the procurators' arguments. Thus, there was no recorded judicial ruling on what exactly was the nature of any particular crime. It was necessary to infer it from the libel, the debates, and the interlocutor. This made for a further measure of uncertainty: arguments on past cases tended to focus on whether or not particular earlier libels had been found relevant. Thirdly, procurators in their arguments on the relevancy of the libel necessarily put forward definitions of crimes: these were inevitably geared towards their aims in the debate, and, while plausible definitions, could scarcely be conclusive. The precise nature of individual crimes could thus remain somewhat indeterminate.

In these circumstances, accounts of crimes in legal treatises assumed importance. Thus, in the case of *Macgregor* in 1752, to demonstrate that hamesucken was not obsolete as a capital crime, the Lord Advocate, William Grant of Prestongrange, cited Mackenzie's treatise on criminal law and the short works of Alexander Bayne and William Forbes.[37] The earliest attempt

35 See, e.g., *Wylie*, SRO JC 2/17 (11 July 1687); *Balfour*, SRO JC 2/19 41 (4 June 1694), *Margaret Johnstoun*, SRO JC 3/1 598 (12 June 1708). Louthian, *Form of Process* (1732) (n 18) 11 founds hamesucken as a capital crime on these passages of *Regiam*.

36 J Maclaurin, *Arguments, and Decisions, in Remarkable Cases, Before the High Court of Justiciary, and other Supreme Courts, in Scotland* (1774) (henceforth Maclaurin, *Remarkable Cases*); H Arnot, *A Collection and Abridgement of Celebrated Criminal Trials in Scotland from AD 1536, to 1784. With historical and critical Remarks* (1785).

37 *Macgregor*, SRO JC 3/28 529 at 570; he is citing G Mackenzie, *The Laws and Customs of Scotland in Matters Criminal: Wherein is to be seen how the Civil Law, and the Laws and Customs of other Nations do agree with, and supply ours* in *The Works of that Eminent and Learned Lawyer, Sir George Mackenzie of Rosehaugh, Advocate to King Charles II. and King James VII. With Many learned Treatises of his, never before* printed, 2 vols (1716, 1722) vol ii, 49–275 at 136–138 (henceforth Mackenzie, *Matters Criminal* from this edition); A Bayne, *Institutions of the Criminal Law of Scotland* (1730) (henceforth Bayne, *Criminal Law*)

at a doctrinal account of Scots criminal law was by Skene, who wrote that "Haymesukin, is quhen ane man searches, and seeks ane other man at his house; or assailzies his house, to slay him, or to doe him any injurie, quhilk crime is punished be death, and confiscation of his moveable gudes, *lib.* 4.*c*.9."[38] He wrote essentially the same in his treatise *De verborum significatione*, where he described hamesucken as "[a]ne Dutch word", adding that "*Haim* signifies an house or habitation", while "*Suchen*" in German meant "to seike, or search, persew, or follow", defining the crime thus:

> [H]ame-suchen, or hame-sucken, is quhen onie person violentlie, without licence, and contrair the Kinges peace, enters within an mans hous, or seiks him at the same, or assailzies his hous (as is written in the best buikes) quhilk crime is punished, as ravishing of wemen . . . quhilk is esteemed an greate crime contrair the common weill, quietnes, and peace of the cuntrie . . . [39]

Sir George Mackenzie argued that for certainty and the security of the people criminal law ought to be based on statutes.[40] Whether or not *Regiam majestatem* was a statute was hotly debated, but Mackenzie argued that it was "authentick" *in criminalibus*.[41] He accordingly purported to base his account of hamesucken on *Regiam*, developing the very basic account given by Skene by reference to the practice of the courts. He also pointed out that the prescriptive period for prosecution given in *Regiam* was now obsolete, and that when it was libelled as an aggravation of another crime the punishment was arbitrary *eo casu*.[42] By the second half of the eighteenth century, Erskine could give the following as a standard brief account of the crime:

> Haimesucken, from *haime*, home, and *soecken*, to pursue, is the crime of beating or assaulting a person within his own house. A man's house is considered as his sanctuary; and for that reason the violence that is committed there, is deemed an aggravation of the crime, both by Jewish law, . . . and by the Romans . . . On this

182–186; and W Forbes, *The Institutes of the Law of Scotland. Volume Second. Comprehending the Criminal Law. In Two Parts* (1730) 139–141 (henceforth Forbes, *Institutes*).

38 J Skene, *Of Crimes, and Judges in Criminall Causes, Conforme to the Lawes of this Realme*, in *Regiam Majestatem* (henceforth Skene, *Of Crimes*) fo 134r (second sequence of foliation). This treatise is almost certainly by Skene.

39 J Skene, *De verborum significatione, The Exposition of the Termes and Difficill Wordes, Conteined in the Foure Buikes of Regiam Majestatem* (1681) (henceforth Skene, *De verborum significatione*) sv "Haimsuken" (first published 1597). On the etymology, see further R V Colman, "Hamsocn: its meaning and significance in early English law" (1981) 25 *American Journal of Legal History* 95. Knud Haakonssen has informed me that the Danish and German words "hjemsøge" and "heimsuchen" as well as the literal meaning have the connotation of "hounding", "persecuting", "plaguing" and "pestering".

40 Mackenzie, *Matters Criminal* (n 37) 53 and 60–61.

41 Ibid 55.

42 Ibid 136–138.

> ground, the punishment of haimesucken is, by the books of the Majesty, declared to be the same as that of a rape . . .; and the pains of death have been by our constant practice inflicted on the committers of it. . . . The bare aiming a blow, or offering to strike, though no blow be actually given, has been found sufficient to infer this crime.[43]

In fact, it was exceptional in the eighteenth century for anyone to suffer the death penalty for hamesucken. Furthermore, it is evident that there was considerable scope for argument over the various elements of the crime: What was a house? What type of assault or injury was necessary? What if someone was lured out of his house to be assaulted elsewhere? What if a brawl developed elsewhere and was then continued in a person's house? What if an individual was invited into someone's house and then a fight subsequently ensued in which the householder was assaulted? All of these points arose and had to be argued before the courts.[44] Furthermore, Erskine might have confidently written that no blow need actually be given, but this was not so certain. Prosecutors were willing to concede that the injury needed to be atrocious, and there was obviously authority for this.[45] And, as we have seen, Sir James Steuart thought hamesucken, to be capital, needed to be "violent" and "evident". Craig, for example, had written that "Hamesuckin *dicimus de eo, qui quempiam occidendum in domo sua quaerit*".[46] Even if the intention was not necessarily to pursue someone to compass his or her death, the *de minimis* principle arguably applied. Moreover, although such points frequently arose in debates over the relevancy of the libel, prosecutors commonly restricted the libel for an arbitrary penalty, so the judges did not need specifically to rule in their interlocutor whether the averments in the

43 J Erskine, *An Institute of the Law of Scotland. In Four Books. In the Order of Sir George Mackenzie's Institutions of that Law*, 2 vols (1773) IV.iv.51.

44 For some examples, see *Leith*, SRO JC 2/17 (15 November 1686) (what is a dwelling-house?); *Crawford*, SRO JC 2/17 (10 March 1690) (what is included in a dwelling-house?); *Master of Tarbat*, SRO JC 2/18 (18 August 1691) (is it hamesucken to assault soldiers where quartered?); *Balfour*, SRO JC 2/19 341 (4 June 1694) (*inter alia*, pannel invited in); *Irvine*, SRO JC 3/2 776 and JC 3/3 26 (20 February and 2 March 1710) (invasion arose out of earlier tumult); *Phillip*, SRO JC 3/9 273 (9 November 1719) (pannel entered peaceably; accidental quarrel subsequently arose); *Thomson and Inglis*, SRO JC 3/9 290 (16 November 1719) (quarrel started elsewhere; victim forced subsequently from house); *Home*, SRO JC 3/11 630 and JC 3/12 1 (9 and 16 October 1723) (not master of house who was assaulted); *Falconer and Arbuthnott*, SRO JC 3/15 264 (22 January 1728) (lured out of house); *Macgregor*, SRO JC 3/28 529 and JC 3/29 1 (13 July 1752) (woman carried out of house in order to be married forcibly).

45 *Haldane*, SRO JC 3/8 543 (28 July 1718) at 620 (5 August 1718) (interlocutor rules that attack not sufficiently atrocious to infer hamesucken).

46 T Craig, *Jus feudale* (1732) II.viii.12 (henceforth Craig, *Jus feudale*) (first published 1655): "We call it hamesucken when anyone seeks someone in his home with a view to killing him."

minor premiss if proven would have amounted to hamesucken.[47] Indeed, in some cases it appears that individuals sought criminal letters libelling hamesucken to secure, not the capital punishment of the pannel, but rather damages as amercement or assythment.[48]

C. THE CASE OF MACGREGOR

James Macgregor was indicted in 1752 at the instance of the Lord Advocate, William Grant of Prestongrange, in a libel, the major premiss of which read (in part) as follows:

> Whereas by the Laws of God, and of this and all other well Governed Realms, Hamesucken, or the violent Entering into any person's house without Licence, or Contrary to the King's peace, or seeking or assaulting him or her there; where he or she was dwelling at the time, and lying and rising nightly and Dailly, Especially when that was done against a woman, or minor, a widow, lately become such, and an Heiress, with Intent to do her a most heinous and attrocious Injury . . . [and various other crimes libelled] are all and Each of them Crimes of the most attrocious, shocking and detestable nature, and most severely punishable.

Also libelled were forcible abduction, forced marriage, and rape. The libel alleged that Macgregor, along with two of his brothers, Ronald and Robert, and other persons, including Duncan Macgregor, had invaded the house of Edinbelly (in the parish of Balfron) on 8 December 1750, where lived ("lying and rising nightly and daily" in the words of *Regiam*) Jean Key, a young, widowed heiress, carried her off forcibly, and compelled her to go through a ceremony of marriage with Robert, who had then raped her. Robert was already outlawed for failing to stand trial for murder in 1736.[49] James, Ronald and Robert were sons of Rob Roy, and Robert and Duncan Macgregor were also subsequently to be separately tried for hamesucken

47 See, e.g., *Morton*, SRO JC 3/1 292 (16 April 1701), at 294; *Drummond*, SRO JC 3/1 545 (29 November 1703) at 547; *Irvine* SRO JC 3/2 776 and JC 3/3 26; *Trotter of Mortonhall*, SRO JC 3/5 541 (8 November 1714) at 542; *Phillip*, SRO JC 3/9 273 (9 November 1719) at 294; *Thomson and Inglis*, SRO JC 3/9 290 (16 November 1719) at 324–325; *Johnston*, SRO JC 3/10 556 (30 August 1721) at 558; *Johnston*, SRO JC 3/30 129 (9 December 1754) at 151 (16 December 1754); *Morton Craigieknow*, SRO JC 12/11 (16 September 1763); *Liddel and Jeeves*, SRO JC 3/36 (19 June 1769) (no debate on relevancy as libel restricted to an arbitrary punishment).

48 *Wood*, SRO JC 3/2 574 (25 July 1709), esp at 583; *Trotter of Mortonhall*, SRO JC 3/5 541–542 (8 November 1714); *Phillip*, SRO JC 3/9 273–275 (9 November 1719) (concluding for damages and assythment in the libel) (see comment at 285, information for the pannel); and *Liddel and Jeeves*, SRO JC 3/36 (19 June 1769) (assythment).

49 SRO JC 3/28 530–537 (13 July 1752).

arising out of these events, the latter being acquitted and the former convicted and executed (probably the only person executed for hamesucken on a sentence of the Court of Justiciary in the eighteenth century). With these subsequent trials we shall not be concerned.[50]

The libel against Macgregor was read and debated *viva voce* on 13 July, and the court ordered informations to be given in. As was the practice, the first given in and entered in the record was that of the Lord Advocate.[51] I shall concentrate here on the discussion of hamesucken. The procurators for the pannel had argued in the debate "Impugning the Relevancy of the Lybell, in so far as it Charged the Crime of Hamesucken, and alledging, that, at this Day, that is no longer a distinct Capital Crime by the Law of Scotland; however in former times, it was held or accounted as such."[52] Grant's argument on hamesucken in his information was intended to counter this claim. He referred to the English law on burglary, citing and quoting from Coke's *Reports*, and pointing out that this crime was a felony punished capitally without benefit of clergy.[53] While this species of crime was "unknown in the law of Scotland" it was intended "for the Security of mankind within their own Dwelling Houses during the night season". Grant argued:

> In like manner the Law of Scotland, and with yet greater Reason for the Security of mens persons within their own Dwelling Houses, where they are lying and Rising nightly and Daily for the Safety and Repose of Mankind at home, and to render it true by peculiar Sanctions which the Civil Law well defines Domus tutissimum cuique refugium ac receptaculum est (L.18.ff. de in jus vocando) hath in ancient times received and established a particular name for the Crime that is Committed by the violation of this asylum, calling it Hamesucken, and making it punishable capitally, even as ravishing of women 4th. Book of the Majesty C.9. where it is not first introduced or enacted, but spoke of as a known thing.[54]

The analogy may have been suggested by Hale's *Pleas of the Crown*, though it is not mentioned by Grant, as the work would have been familiar to him, having been cited for the pannel in connection with the charge of rape.[55] Hale

50 SRO JC 3/29 151 (15 January 1753); JC 3/29 250 and 290 (6 August and 24 December 1753). See also (1753) 15 *Scots Magazine* 49 and 626–627, (1754) 16 *Scots Magazine* 49–50, and *Caledonian Mercury*, 16 January 1753 and 7 February 1754.

51 SRO JC 3/28 540–594.

52 Ibid 562.

53 *Vaux v Brooke* IV Co Rep 39b. The quotation is not exact from the English version of Coke's *Reports*, and may be a free translation of the text in law French. It is very similar to the definition of burglary in E Coke, *The Third Part of the Institutes of the Law of England*, 4th edn (1670) 63; JC 3/28 564.

54 SRO JC 3/28 564. The citation is to D 2.4.18, the Latin meaning: "His home is to each man his most complete refuge and asylum."

55 See, e.g., SRO JC 3/28 597 and 631, citing Hale, *Pleas of the Crown* (n 5) vol i, 635.

had written: "The common genus of offenses, that comes under the name of *Hamsecken*, is that which is usually called house-breaking, which sometimes comes under the common appellation of *burglary*, whether committed in the day or night to the intent to commit felony . . .".[56] Grant next quoted Skene's definition of hamesucken from his treatise on crimes,[57] and commented that:

> [I]t is observable that the Definition of the Crime Corresponds with that [of] Burglary, and the Essence of it Consists, not in the actual Completion of the farther Crime intended, let it be murder, or other lesser Injury; but, in assaulting his House, or seeking him there with Intent to do him such Injury . . .[58]

Grant next quoted Skene's remarks in his treatise *De verborum significatione*, before writing that "[n]either was this Constitution peculiar to Scotland: The like Law we find Established in other Neighbouring Nations, with whose customs our own, in other Respects, have great affinity".[59] For these other laws, Grant cited Antonius Matthaeus' treatise *De criminibus*, which he described as an "approved work", and which indeed was much cited in the Court of Justiciary in this period.[60] He quoted Matthaeus' views on various types of violent intrusion into a person's home, their *tutissimum refugium atque receptaculum*, meriting capital punishment,[61] before adding:

> The same Author proceeds to Confirm his opinion from Authoritys, which at the same time prove that the like Law takes Places [sic] in divers other Countrys and States on the Continent, for the Author immediately proceeds as follows, the whole passage being materiall to the present argument, and serving to explain the Nature of this Crime or Species of *vis publica*, to which the Law of Scotland, in Antient Times, gave the particular Name of Hamesucken, which is still retained in our Law Books and Records. . . . [62]

Grant accordingly quoted a lengthy passage from Matthaeus' work in which the author instanced and discussed a few statutory provisions on capital crimes analogous to the Scots law on hamesucken, and commented:

> These passages serve, not only to show, that the like Law, and upon the same Reason, is established in other Countrys, but to Explain the sense and meaning of the Law it self, and what kind of Assault, or Injury to the owner of the House,

56 Hale, *Pleas of the Crown* (n 5) vol i, 547–548.
57 Skene, *Of Crimes* (n 38) fo 134r.
58 SRO JC 3/28 565.
59 Skene, *De verborum significatione* (n 39) sv "Haimsuken"; SRO JC 3/28 565.
60 SRO JC 3/28, 565; A Matthaeus, *De criminibus ad lib. XLVII. et XLVIII. dig. commentarius*, 4th edn (1679) (henceforth. Matthaeus, *De criminibus*) This was the most recent edition and the one likely used by Grant.
61 Matthaeus, *De criminibus* (n 60) 465 and 467 (*ad leg Iul. de vi publica, & privata* (D 48.4) cap 4, *de usu et jure municipali*, ss 2, 3, and 6).
62 SRO JC 3/28 566.

> or any of his Family, being Committed by persons who forcibly Entered the House, with Intent to Committ such Injury falls within this Law and subjects the Committer to the punishment thereof; and these are described by the following Expressions, si aliquem ex inhabitantibus male multaverit, which is a Phrase used by Terence and Cicero, and signifies to abuse, to handle, or use one ill vel si eundem expuelerit, verberaverit, capital erit, vim quamcunque personae vel corpori eius illatum, all which exactly corresponds to Sir John Skene's Definition above recited of the Crime of Hamesucken, being to seek another at his house, to slay him or to do him any Injury. And such being the nature of this Crime, can there be any possible Doubt that the particular Injurys, with Intent to Committ which Jean Key was assaulted in her own house, were of a nature sufficiently heinous and Atrocious to come up to the Crime of Hamesucken. . . . [63]

Grant argued that if Macgregor and his accomplices had boxed Jean Key's ears in her home or beat her in any way short of murder it would have been hamesucken, but all of these would have been lesser injuries than what this hamesucken was committed for, "which was to rob her, not indeed of Life, but of every thing that is valuable in it, her Liberty, her Chastity, her peace and Content of Mind, her Estimation and Character in the World, and her whole ffortune or Estate". He argued that even if all the other acts had not occurred, to carry her off "was a Crime independent of all that followed . . . that would have highly merited the severest Censure of the Law, for the atrocious Hamesucken alone".[64]

Grant next turned to the argument that hamesucken either was obsolete or the capital punishment of it was. He argued:

> It may be true, that of latter Times Examples have more rarely occurred of putting the same in Execution, and that hath been plainly owing to the advances of Civility and good manners in this Country; but it ill becomes those, who, in these happier Times in which we Live, take upon them to disgrace and shock the present age by Committing such Barbarities as were more frequent in Times, past, to alledge that the Law is obsolete that was introduced for restraining of such Enormities, as they themselves, by now Committing, demonstrate the necessity that such law should be still in fforce for the Common Safety of Mankind, and in reality the Law is still in Force, although this, like all other penal Laws, lys asleep till the occasion offerrs for exerting its Terrors.[65]

As already noted, he argued this by citing the works of Mackenzie, Bayne and Forbes.[66] He also referred to the case of *Haldane* in 1718, where a libel alleging hamesucken resulted in an interlocutor that the facts libelled

63 Matthaeus, *De criminibus* (n 600 467 (the second quotation by Grant is not exact; I have corrected part of it silently); SRO JC 3/28 567–568.

64 SRO JC 3/28 568–569.

65 Ibid 569.

66 Ibid 570.

were not sufficiently atrocious as to infer hamesucken,[67] and argued that this meant "the Law of Hamesucken stands yet in full force".[68] He next referred to the curious case of *Campbell and MacKinnon* who were indicted before the Sheriff of Inverness for hamesucken. The indictment was found relevant, they were convicted by a jury, and sentenced to death by the sheriff-depute. The questions then arose, first, of whether the sheriff-depute had jurisdiction to try hamesucken capitally, and secondly, of whether the libel was relevant, as those who had been injured were servants, not the person whom Campbell and MacKinnon intended to injure who had been absent. A bill of suspension was presented to three Lords of Justiciary who did not pass the bill, but sisted execution to 16 July 1725 when the sentence was to have been executed if there had been no further action. The aim obviously was that the full Justiciary Court would hear the case.

There was, however, no further application by the suspender, and the Lords decided on 8 June 1725 to act no further. Campbell and MacKinnon were accordingly executed.[69] Grant argued that the Court of Justiciary would not have acted in this way if it had been of the view that hamesucken was no longer capital in Scotland.[70] He ended his discussion of hamesucken thus: "Upon this head, therefore, the pursuer Concluded that the Lybell was Relevantly laid upon this article of Hamesucken, to Inferr the pains of Law for that Crime, and which pains are Capitall."[71]

As procurator for Macgregor, Alexander Lockhart gave in an information which addressed the same points.[72] He argued:

> [T]hat however in antient Times, some Instances might have occurred where the Crime of Hamesucken, may have been Capitally punished, yet as this was not Established by any positive Statute to be the Law of Scotland, and as the practice of later years had justly receded from such erroneous precedents, these could not now be resorted to for Establishing a point so directly inconsistent with the first principles of Law and Justice.

67 *Haldane*, SRO JC 3/8 543 (28 July 1718), at 619–620 (5 August 1718).

68 SRO JC 3/28 571–575.

69 I have been unable to trace any details of this case: the proceedings noted by Grant are not entered into the relevant volume of the Books of Adjournal, SRO JC 3/12, nor into the relevant Minute Book, SRO JC 7/12. I have also been unable to locate any relevant records of the Sheriff Court of Inverness. A similar bill of suspension was presented in 1741 against a death sentence for hamesucken passed by the Sheriff Depute of Ross-shire: see *Caledonian Mercury*, 6 July 1741. The diet in connection with it can be traced being twice continued (on 3 November 1741 and 11 January 1742) but it is not mentioned on the date (13 January 1742) to which it was continued, and it thereafter cannot be traced: SRO JC 3/23 680 and Minute Book, JC 7/23.

70 SRO JC 3/28 575–576.

71 Ibid 576–577.

72 Ibid 594–634.

He admitted that since a person's house was his or her asylum, an offence committed against a person in his or her home was highly aggravated, and justly more severely punished, "but that this speciality Should so Inflame the Reckoning, as to Convert that Injury into a Capital Crime, was humbly Contested". He argued that though the Romans venerated the home "no Instance could be given where any Injury or offence, otherways punishable *poena extraordinaria*, was by that Law subjected to the *ultimum Supplicium*" by virtue of having taken place in a person's home. He continued:

> That there is no Statute making this a Capital Crime by the Law of Scotland, was acknowledged; and as no authority could be produced, either from the positive Law of God, or from the Civil Law, which must needs be admitted . . . to be the Fountains and Sources of the Criminall Law of Scotland, so far as not departed from by Municipall positive Constitutions or Invariable Practice; whereby Injurys of this kind should be capitally punished, it remained to be Enquired upon what other Foundation this principle is assumed.[73]

Lockhart next turned to Grant's arguments from English law and Matthaeus. He argued:

> For as to the positive constitutions of other countrys, where something similar to this may possibly have been Enacted, and to which the prosecutor was pleased to resort . . . the Pannel is advised, that though the Laws of Nations in Generall may, with Reason, be Resorted to in cases of Difficulty, where our own Law is defective, it would be of a Dangerous precedent to adopt every peculiar Conceit of other Nations to be the Law of Scotland, especially in regulating the Degree of Punishment, unless these could be supported upon the generall Principles of Equity, and that this must the rather hold, for that the prosecutor, after all the Research into all the Laws of all other Countries, has been able to condescend upon very few, where a Capital Punishment is inflicted for any offence of this kind, not on account of the nature of the Injury it self, but from its being committed against a Person within his own House.[74]

Lockhart claimed that Grant's admission that the wrong needed to be atrocious underlined the absurdity of his argument, as he could point to no law authorising that distinction.[75] Lockhart next argued that it did not follow from the words of *Regiam* and Skene's annotation on it[76] that hamesucken was to be punished as was rape, but rather was merely to be prosecuted in

73 Ibid 618–619.
74 Ibid 619.
75 Ibid 619–620.
76 See *Regiam majestatem Scotiae veteres leges et constitutiones, ex archivis publicis, et antiquis libris manuscriptis collectae, recognitae, et notis juris civilis, canonici, Nortmannici auctoritate confirmatis, illustratae, opera & studio Joannis Skenaei, Regiae Majestati a conciliis & archivis publicis* (1609) fo 97r. The annotation to the Latin edition of *Regiam* is similar to the discussion in Skene's treatise *De verborum significatione*.

the same manner, especially since "these Crimes, [were] of their nature so very different, the one Infinitely more Grievous than the other". Rape "by the Laws of all Nations and by the first principles of Justice, is a Crime of so enourmous a nature as well merits the punishment of Death", but this should not extend to crimes of an inferior nature merely because they were committed in a dwelling-house. Furthermore, if this were to have been the case, even the most trivial of injuries if committed in a dwelling-house would have merited death.[77] Lockhart next dealt with the records of the Court of Justiciary arguing that "for many years past" hamesucken had been prosecuted either as an aggravation of another wrong or only to infer an arbitrary punishment, and claimed that this showed that the crime was in desuetude. He argued that the case of *Haldane* could not be viewed as a judgment of the Court deciding hamesucken to be capital, while that of *Campbell and MacKinnon* was extraordinary and iniquitous, and could not be viewed "as a precedent of the Court of Justiciary", since the court stayed execution of the sheriff's sentence, but was unable to pronounce on the matter by reason of the failure of anyone to apply to it. Lockhart argued that no other case could be found in Books of Adjournal where the libel in hamesucken had not been restricted to infer an arbitrary punishment. He wrote:

> [A]nd as the Principles of Justice thus coincide with the later Practice, it would be highly unreasonable to resort to those more ancient Precedents, supported by no positive Law, to revive a practice which probably had taken rise from these ffeuds and animositys, which this Nation in former Times was unhappily engaged in, when every private ffamily was in a State of war, which made it the more necessary to make man's house his Sanctuary; but as these Times are now long ago happily at an End, and as in Consequence thereof the practice has conformed itself to the Rules and Principles of Justice, it would be highly inexpedient now to revive that antiquated and obsolete Practice, of making every Injury offered to a person within his house a Capital Crime.[78]

Lockhart's final argument on hamesucken was that the *species facti* charged in the indictment did not amount to hamesucken. He argued that the essence of hamesucken was assault in a person's house *animus injuriandi*, while here the alleged criminal act "did not proceed from any purpose and Intention to assault and Injure the person, *sed libidinis causa*". He drew an analogy with the Roman law of theft which required *animus lucri faciendi*, so that, if anyone seized a slave girl, not for gain, but for libidinous purposes, it was not theft. This applied to Macgregor's case, where

77 SRO JC 3/28 620–621.
78 Ibid 621–625.

the forcible entry and abduction were not from a premeditated purpose to injure or assault but to accomplish the intended marriage. He could not therefore be guilty of hamesucken as a separate crime, but at the most as an aggravation of another.[79]

The Lords pronounced an interlocutor on 31 July 1752 to the effect that: "They found the Crimes charged against the said panel in the foresaid Indictment jointly and separately Relevant to infer the pains of Law But allowed the pannel to prove all ffacts and Circumstances that may tend either to his Exculpation or Alleviation of his Guilt". The diet against Macgregor was continued until 3 August 1752.[80] There was then a lengthy proof lasting two days and two nights.[81] The assize delivered a special verdict on 5 August, unanimously finding it proven that Macgregor with accomplices had entered Jean Key's house and attacked her in order to carry her away. By a majority it was found not proven that she had consented in advance to this abduction. The jury unanimously also found it proven that she had been carried to various places; but, again unanimously, found it proven that she afterwards acquiesced in her condition "for Alleviation of the pannel's Guilt in the premises". Finally, the forcible marriage and rape were unanimously found not proven.[82] The next day counsel argued *viva voce* on the import of this verdict, and the procurators for the defence asked the court for the opportunity to inform upon the debate. This was granted, and the diet was continued to 20 November.[83] The same day as the *viva voce* debate, however, twelve of the jurors attempted to intervene, tendering to the court a declaration that they had believed what they had found proved to alleviate Macgregor's guilt, namely Jean Key's later acquiescence, would have exempted him from capital punishment. Another of the assizers appeared in court, stating that he had refused to sign the declaration, but declaring that he also wished only an arbitrary punishment to be inflicted. The court refused to receive the declaration, and it was not entered into the record of the court.[84]

It is particularly interesting that the assize should have delivered a special verdict. The interlocutor on the relevancy was phrased in such a way

79 Ibid 625–626. He cited the following text: D47.2.39.

80 SRO JC 3/29 1–2.

81 Ibid 2–84; for the length of the trial, see *Caledonian Mercury*, 3, 4 and 6 August 1752. There is a lengthy account of the case in (1752) 14 *Scots Magazine* 345, and in Maclaurin, *Remarkable Cases* (n 36) 137–152.

82 SRO JC 3/29 84–86.

83 Ibid 88–89 (6 August 1752).

84 See ibid 98–99 (information for Macgregor) and 122–124 (information for Lord Advocate); for the text of the letter, see (1752) 14 *Scots Magazine* 351.

that a general verdict of guilty or not guilty would have been possible, and Lockhart and Grant apparently considered it to have been open to the assize simply to acquit.[85] The reason for delivering a special verdict in part seems likely to have been the difficulties faced by the jury and the court in knowing exactly in what the crime of hamesucken consisted. The jury evidently were sympathetic to Macgregor and did not want him to suffer the death penalty for hamesucken, but were nonetheless conscious that he was culpable in some way.

The informations on the import of the special verdict do not need to be considered here in detail.[86] Lockhart accepted that the court viewed hamesucken as a capital crime (which shows that the judges must have so ruled) and that this could not now be contested. He added:

> [T]hat as the punishment is noways adequate to the offence and as for many years past no one Instance has occurred where an offence of this kind has been capitally punished or sustained relevant to inferr the punishment of Death, but on the Contrary even where the Injuries offered to the person within his own house were extremely attrocious the Indictments have been restricted so as to import only an Arbitrary punishment every alleviating Circumstance should operate to reduce the punishment within reasonable Bounds and to commensurate the same to the Offence.

Furthermore, the punishment was established by ancient usage rather than statute, while "neither Law nor practice has determined from what particular ffacts this Crime shall be inferred, so that in every Case it becomes an arbitrary Question from what particular ffacts the Crime of Hamesucken shall be established".[87] Lockhart accordingly argued that the findings in the special verdict did not amount to hamesucken, or that the punishment should be restricted, on the grounds that: the injury was not atrocious; the house was not entered *animo injuriandi*; the jury had not found that the house was where Jean Key lay and rose nightly and daily; she had later acquiesced and such injuries could be remitted; the time passed before prosecution had prescribed the crime; and finally, the jury were justified in finding the acquiescence enough to alleviate the guilt and had not intended to convict of a crime meriting the *ultimum supplicium*.[88]

85 SRO JC 3/29, 114–115 and 141–142.
86 Ibid 91–116, 117–143.
87 Ibid 103.
88 Ibid 104–116.

Grant argued that the verdict showed a clear case of hamesucken. Criticism of the wording of the verdict was not to the point. The jury's finding that she later acquiesced did not alleviate the guilt proven in the first part of the verdict, as by acquiescing one could not mitigate a public wrong. He stated that: "In support of this answer there seem to be apposite Authorities in the practice of England where Trialls by Jury and Doctrine of Verdicts are more practised and perhaps better understood than with us." He accordingly cited the English work, *The Complete Juryman*, which was published in the year of the trial, from which he quoted the following passages:

> If the first Part of a Verdict be full to the Issue, either expresly, or by Implication, and the latter Part any Ways contradicts the first Part; the first Part shall be good, and the latter Part void. *Per Dodderidge* J. *James* versus *Harris*, 2 *Bulst*. 56. 2 *Rol. Abr.* 718, *p*. 11, 13, 14. *Cro. Car.* 75 . . . If the Jury in a special Verdict find the Issue, all which they find afterwards to the contrary, is Surplusage. 2 *Ld. Raym.* 860, 865.[89]

On this authority, Grant argued that the jury's finding alleviating Macgregor's guilt was surplusage to be ignored. He finally rejected Lockhart's arguments of acquiescence and prescription.[90]

When on 6 August the diet had been continued to 20 November 1752, Macgregor had been committed to the Edinburgh Tolbooth. He did not compear on the required date. It was moved that the magistrates of Edinburgh and the keeper of the Tolbooth should be called. The keeper of the Tolbooth and George Drummond, lately Lord Provost, were present and were interrogated about Macgregor. It was explained that, on a warrant from the Lord Justice-Clerk, Macgregor had been conducted to the Castle because of fears of an attempt to escape; he had nonetheless escaped from there.[91] The case against Macgregor was continued for some time,[92] but he was not apprehended, and the Lords of Justiciary never pronounced judgment on whether or not Macgregor was guilty of hamesucken, nor passed sentence on him.

89 *The Complete Juryman; Or, A Compendium of the Laws Relating to Jurors* (1752), 258–259; SRO JC 3/29, 132–133.

90 SRO JC 3/29, 126–143.

91 Ibid 145–146; for an account of his escape, see "Edinburgh" (1752) 14 *Scots Magazine* 555 at 556–557, and *Caledonian Mercury*, 20 November 1752.

92 The last mention I have noted was on 17 June 1754, SRO JC 3/29, 566 where the case was continued to 12 August; on that date it is not mentioned. I have not searched beyond this.

D. THE IMPORTANCE OF MACGREGOR

The prosecution of Macgregor for hamesucken is of great interest in a variety of ways. It is noteworthy how both Grant and Lockhart appropriated the language of civility and manners, so crucial in eighteenth-century Scotland, to argue their respective case: either that there had been so few prosecutions because of the advances in civility, but that when such modern manners were threatened, the old law still existed to preserve them; or that such advances had rendered the law obsolete, as it had been intended for a society given over to feuding, In this respect, it is telling that Grant commented as follows in the information on the special verdict lodged with the court:

> The Trial of this pannel was in reallity and has justly been treated by the Court as a Case of great Importance. It was brought to indicated in the due Course of publick Justice one of the most attrocious and scandalous violations of publick peace accompanied with the most grievous wrong to the private party injured, that the present age has seen, or that the most barbarous of the tribe of Macgregors to which the pannel belongs, noted as they are by the Laws, have in any age committed.

The threat posed by the Macgregors was located in the wilderness of the Highlands:

> The most frequent Enormities committed by the unruly parts of that Tribe have been to prey upon the property of their fellow Subjects that by their Situation have been exposed to their Thefts or Depredations of their Cattle and by the Residence of these people amongst the Rocks Lochs and Woods in the highest parts of the Shires of Stirling and Perth where upon the East hand they were in the Neighbourhood of the Low Country from which to take their Spoils and on the Northward had access through desart uninhabited Countries to the remotest parts of the Highlands to dispose of it.[93]

The trials of the Macgregors offered an opportunity to be rid of a lawless element in the Highlands, and Grant evidently viewed the prosecutions as an important part of the government's policy of "civilising" and pacifying the area in the aftermath of the '45. The threat that the Macgregors posed to polite, lowland Scotland of the Enlightenment required to be extinguished using laws that, deriving from more barbarous times, were well adapted to dealing with those who were themselves barbarous. Lockhart was undoubtedly correct in his claims that libels or interlocutors had restricted hamesucken to an arbitrary punishment: it cannot but be significant that Grant pursued the Macgregors for the death penalty when the forcible marriage and rape

93 SRO JC 3/29, 118.

had been found not proven, so that all that remained was the crime of seizing Jean Key in her home and abducting her. Political and social considerations undoubtedly promoted the seeking of the death penalty. It is likewise surely significant that Archibald, Duke of Argyll, presided over the court as Lord Justice-General on 20 November 1752, when it investigated the circumstances in which Macgregor had been able to escape from Edinburgh Castle.[94] Enlightened Scotland with its focus on politeness and modern manners allowed no place for what were seen as relics of more barbarous times.

The arguments of counsel also clearly demonstrated the difficulties with the law on hamesucken in the eighteenth century. What weight was to be given to *Regiam majestatem* as a source of Scots law? What was to be concluded from the records of past cases preserved in the Books of Adjournal? Was the common understanding that hamesucken was capital enough to outweigh the contrary practice in prosecution (and vice versa)? Lockhart attempted to answer these questions by appeal to equity and principles of justice: in the face of a lack of clear statutory definition of the crime and provision for its punishment, justice required that hamesucken should be considered as an aggravation of another crime and its punishment be appropriate to that crime as aggravated, especially when there was no invariable practice to the contrary. It might have been possible to cite similar provisions in the laws of other countries, but they were too few to be of significance, he argued, hardly demonstrating that the law of nations punished hamesucken capitally, and could not be used to introduce into Scots law pernicious principles contrary to justice. Society had developed since the time of *Regiam majestatem*, the books of "which for certain, contain a variety of particulars repugnant to the first Principles of the Law of Scotland".[95]

Grant's answer to the uncertainty and indeterminacy of the law on hamesucken was apparently different. The major premiss in the indictment against Macgregor was phrased in terms of "the Laws of God, and of this and all other well Governed Realms". While in some libels for hamesucken the major premiss referred only to the municipal law,[96] the vast majority of

94 SRO JC 3/29 145; Argyll was in Edinburgh for the election of a representative peer: *Caledonian Mercury*, 20 November 1752.

95 SRO JC 3/28 620.

96 See, e.g., *Wylie*, SRO JC 2/17 (11 July 1687): "Notwithstanding be the lawes and acts of parliament off the Kingdome and Constant practique thereof particularlie be the lawes of Reg[iam] Majestat[atem] the Cryme off Hamesucken and the searching and seeking for any [person] or persons in or about their dwelling house to doe them hurt or prejudice is punishable with the panes of death"; *Trotter of Mortonhal*, SRO JC 3/5 541 (8 November 1714): "That where, By

them used the standard formula (or a close variation of it) that "whereas by the laws of this, and all other well governed realms the crime of hamesucken etc.".[97] As in Macgregor's indictment, there were occasionally more elaborate allusions to the laws of God, the laws of nature and nations, and the common law (in the sense of Civil and Canon Law) – sometimes all together.[98] Such references in the major premiss to laws other than that of Scotland legitimated drawing on them to explain Scots law. Grant quoted Craig's view that when there were no statutes or customs in Scotland recourse was to be had to the laws of neighbouring nations,[99] and argued:

> This last principle does more specially hold and take place in the Criminal Law of Scotland, where by the long received and accustomed Form of the Libells, the major proposition Contains an averment, as the said Lybell against the Pannel did, that the Crimes Charged were such, and, punishable by the Laws of God, and the Laws of this, and other well Governed Realms. And from the Records of the Court of Justiciary, called the Books of Adjournal, it appeared that such hath been the Constant Practice, not only in the Lybels, but in the Arguments of the Council on the Relevancy either of the Lybell or Defence, that frequent appeals are made to Texts of the Holy Scripture, or the opinions of foreign Lawiers, or the Decisions of fforeign Courts in similar Cases; and the Reasonableness of such usage and appeal consists in this, that Crimes are offences against Common Humanity, and are equally such in all Civilized Nations, and depend not upon peculiar Constitutions, in such manner as the Laws Concerning private Right and publick Government may do, and which are therefore more various in different Countrys . . . [100]

Lockhart commented that "the prosecutor was pleased to resort [to foreign laws], by reason that criminal lybels do for ordinary referr to the Laws of all other well governed Realms".[101] Grant thus argued that the statements

the Municiple Law of this Kingdome, The Committers of the Crime of Hamesucken . . . As Also, Robbery, Stouthreiff and Oppression . . . are all Crimes of a high nature and severely punishable by death, Confiscation of moveables or otherwise"; *Home*, SRO JC 3/11 630 (9 October 1723): "By the Laws of this Realm, The Crimes of Murder, Hamesucken and violent Invasion of his Majesties Leiges . . . are all Crimes of a high nature and Severly punishable".

97 See, e.g., *Drummond*, SRO JC 3/1 545 (29 November 1703); *Forbes*, SRO JC 3/1 687 (18 December 1704); *Muirhead*, SRO JC 3/2 385 (14 April 1708); *Wood*, SRO JC 3/2 574 (25 July 1709); *Irvine*, SRO JC 3/2 776 (20 February 1710); *Seton and Porteous,* SRO JC 3/7 340 (16 July 1716); *Thomson and Inglis*, SRO JC 3/9 290 (16 November 1719); *Anstruther*, SRO JC 3/9 428 (25 March 1720); *Johnston*, SRO JC 3/10 556 (30 August 1721); *Torrance and Baillie*, SRO JC 3/13, 340–341 (8 March 1726); *Arbuthnott and Falconer*, SRO JC 3/15 265 (22 January 1728).

98 *Master of Tarbat*, SRO JC 2/18 (18 August 1691); *Keith*, SRO JC 2/18 (11 January 1692); *Balfour*, SRO JC 2/19 341 (4 June 1694); *Munro*, SRO JC 3/ 1 155 (9 December 1700); *Morton*, SRO JC 3/1 292 (16 April 1701); *Haldane*, SRO JC 3/8 543 (28 July 1718); *Johnston*, SRO JC 3/30 128 (9 December 1754); *Liddel and Jeeves*, SRO JC 3/36 (19 June 1769).

99 Craig, *Jus feudale* (n 46) I.viii. 15.

100 SRO JC 3/28 582–583; see also 585.

101 Ibid 619.

of Matthaeus could be used, not only to show that other countries had similar provisions, but also to explain Scots law. This was not an exceptional argument. In the information for the pannels in *Thomson and Inglis*, for example, it had been claimed on etymological grounds, presumably relying on Skene, that the Scots laws on hamesucken had flowed from those of Germany, and one of the passages of Matthaeus used by Grant was drawn on to explain the law.[102] Though used for "German" law, Matthaeus was still a Civilian writer, and the passages cited by the Scots lawyers on hamesucken, occurred, after all, in a commentary on D 48.4; and Lockhart, for example, argued, as was not unusual, that the positive law of God and Roman law were the sources of Scots law except where varied by statute or practice. Grant, however, went beyond this, citing English law to argue that hamesucken was capital, and later using an English work and case law to explain special verdicts. Underlying his argument from English law was a view that the basis of Scots criminal law was ultimately moral, founded on the laws of God and of nature and nations, so that English law could accordingly be used to support an argument that hamesucken was a capital crime, since, if it had similar provisions in similar situations, the view of Scots law being argued for could be seen to be, at the very least, not contrary to the law of nations.

Grant did not use the language of the law of nature and nations; Lockhart did to some extent with his allusions to principles of justice and equity and the laws of nations. Nonetheless, though in many ways very different, both their arguments at some level rely on it. This, of course, is scarcely surprising in eighteenth-century Scotland where moral philosophy had come to be defined in terms of the natural law of Grotius and Pufendorf (especially of the latter).[103] And there were examples of reliance on natural law in Scotland going back at least to the time of Craig. We have already noted that the major premiss of the libel sometimes referred to the law of nature and nations to found the crime, and it is possible to find Pufendorf cited by procurators in their informations, while the style given by Louthian in

102 SRO JC 3/9 290 (16 November 1719) at 313; Matthaeus, *De criminibus* 467–468 (cap 4 s 6 on D 48.4).

103 See now, above all, K Haakonssen, "Natural Law and Moral Realism: The Scottish Synthesis", in M A Stewart (ed), *Studies in the Philosophy of the Scottish Enlightenment* (1990) 61. See also Haakonssen, "Natural law and the Scottish Enlightenment" (1985) 4 *Man and Nature* 47; Haakonssen, "Hugo Grotius and the history of political thought" (1985) 13 *Political Theory* 239; and J Moore and M Silverthorne, "Natural Sociability and Natural Rights in the Moral Philosophy of Gerschom Carmichael", in V Hope (ed), *Philosophers of the Scottish Enlightenment* (1984) 1; "Gershom Carmichael and the Natural Jurisprudence Tradition in Eighteenth-Century Scotland", in I Hont and M Ignatieff (eds), *Wealth and Virtue: The Shaping of Political Economy in the Scottish Enlightenment* (1983) 73.

1732 for an information for the pannel included argument from the laws of nature, of God, and of other nations.[104] Thus, while of primary significance were Scottish statutes and practice, the law of nature and nations was regarded as underpinning Scots criminal law, legitimating reference to the laws of other countries to explain obscurities and supply deficiencies. Further study would be required, however, to know whether this was a tendency reinforced after natural law became such a popular study in the later seventeenth and early eighteenth centuries, and how it related to arguments on the development of the law made with reference to the historical source (or alleged historical source) of the law, typically taken to be in that of Rome. It does show, however, that the subtitle given by Mackenzie to his work on criminal law – "Wherein is to be seen how the Civil Law, and the Laws and Customs of other Nations do agree with, and supply ours" – is of some importance, and not a mere scholarly puff.[105]

E. MARITAL RAPE

Lockhart argued that neither law nor practice had determined from what facts hamesucken would be inferred, so that in each case it became an arbitrary question; if perhaps exaggerated, this claim was certainly not unfounded.[106] There were a number of causes of this indeterminacy of the law. *Regiam majestatem* was an unsatisfactory and suspect source from which to derive the crime: it really only dealt with the nature of "home" and the mode of prosecution. It was not always easy to infer practice from the Books of Adjournal because of their nature as a record: there were no authoritative judicial definitions of the law; judicial views had to be deduced from interlocutors on the relevancy of libels which had commonly been restricted by prosecutors so that judges did not have to rule on the question of whether or not the *species facti* averred amounted to capital hamesucken.

An argument on one area of Scots criminal law focusing on one case is not a sufficient basis from which to extrapolate to the law as a whole; it does provide enough evidence, however, to suggest that Scots criminal law may have suffered more generally from problems of uncertainty, and at least one

104 *Trotter of Mortonhall*, SRO JC 3/5 541 (8 November 1714) at 549, citing S Pufendorf, *De jure naturae et gentium libri octo* (1672, and many subsequent edns) II.v.4 and 16 (the passages concern self-defence and defence of property: I consulted the edition, Amsterdam, 1688, at 186–187 and 198–199); Louthian, *Form of Process* (n 18) 139–184.

105 See n 37 above.

106 SRO JC 3/29 103.

well-informed contemporary commentator was of this view, while it is also possible to find arguments to this effect in other cases.[107] Turning to the area of law at issue in *Stallard*, William Forbes, for instance, felt able to define the crime of rape as including that of a man by a woman. He explained: "for that as there are weak faint harted and effeminate men, and stout harted masculine women: nothing hinders a woman to force a man to ly with her by the same power that she carries him away".[108] One can see here some influence of the Roman Crime of *raptus*, though Forbes stressed that "there is no Rape without carnal Commerce".[109] In the face of such conflicts over definitions and scope of crimes, the solution adopted by procurators for the pannel and the prosecution was to argue from analogous laws in other countries and from natural law: a solution suggested by the form of the major premiss of the libel and validated by the natural-law thinking of Scots lawyers in this period. The reference to the laws of other well-governed realms was therefore not an empty formula devoid of significance. In so far as Scots criminal law was vague and inchoate, secreted in the practice of the courts, it could be elaborated from the laws and doctrinal writings of other states considered as the law of nations.

It was perhaps this indeterminacy of Scots criminal law which ensured the outstanding success of Hume's treatise. For the first time lawyers had access to a comprehensive and fully argued account of crimes, defining them, explaining their nature, and discussing them on the basis of the records of the Justiciary Court. Hume himself eschewed overt philosophising about the basis of Scots law, and he had little sympathy for natural law of the speculative and rationalist type.[110] Yet, he regarded English law "as a great body of written and practical reason", on which, in "matters . . . which depend on the common feelings of equity and right", he considered himself able to draw to expound Scots law where "not determined otherwise by our municipal custom".[111] In doing so, Hume was following the well-established practice of Scots advocates when they acted as procurators in the Court of Justictary.

107 H Arnot, *The History of Edinburgh* (1779) (henceforth Arnot, *History of Edinburgh*) 486; *HM Advocate v Gray et al* conveniently reported in (1751) 13 *Scots Magazine* 353 (I am grateful to Roger Emerson for bringing the latter to my attention).

108 G[lasgow] U[niversity] L[ibrary], MS Gen 1249, 414–415 (this is part of his unpublished "Great Body", GUL MSS Gen 1246–1252); Forbes, *Institutes* ii, 125.

109 Forbes, *Institutes* (note 37) ii, 125.

110 See the remarks in J W Cairns, "John Millar's Lectures on Scots Criminal Law" (1988) 8 *OJLS*, 364 at 395–400.

111 Hume, *Commentaries* (n 4) vol i, liv.

If Hume adopted from Hale the doctrine that husbands could not be guilty of the rape of their wives other than art and part, he had done nothing unusual: indeed, eighteenth-century Scots criminal law presupposed and upheld such borrowing. Furthermore, he was probably only making articulate a doctrine on rape already accepted in the common understanding of the legal profession in Scotland. Thus, between 1736 and 1745, Forbes added the following passage to his manuscript treatise on Scots law: "A Husband cannot be guilty of a Rape committed by him upon his Lawful wife, for by their mutual matrimonial consent the wife hath given up herself in this kind to her Husband". He went on to discuss the situation of a husband aiding and abetting another to rape his wife. His authority for this was Hale's *Historia placitorum coronae*, and the passages are virtual quotations from Hale.[112] Though Forbes did draw comparisons with English law, he nonetheless appears from the context to have accepted this as Scots law. It is therefore unsurprising to find Lockhart arguing in the debate *viva voce* on the relevancy in *Macgregor* (where one of the offences libelled was rape), "that no man can be guilty of a Rape on the Body of his own wife".[113] Grant conceded:

> It may be true that the Husband, who is Lawfully such with the Consent of [the] wife, cannot committ a Rape upon her Body, because he is intitled to the Enjoyment of it, and seldom would have to Employ fforce to be allowed the exercise of his Right; but if that should happen it would be no Crime in him . . .[114]

It is possible that Hale suggested this to Lockhart and Grant, since the former cited him on rape (but not on this point which he did not argue in his information);[115] it seems obvious, however, that neither man doubted the correctness of the proposition. Though these statements were not authoritative, they would have been known to Hume who had read *Macgregor*, and would have indicated to him that Hale (if he was following him in this respect) either expressed what was already Scots law or, at least, established a principle at one with Scots law. It would in any case be difficult to accept that this doctrine was contrary to the mores of Hume's day.

Yet, it may be that Hume's *Commentaries* in one respect marked a change or confirmed one that had already taken place. Writing in 1730, Alexander Bayne had contrasted the private with the criminal law of Scotland. Though

112 GUL MS Gen 1249, 415; Hale, *Pleas of the Crown* (n 5) vol i, 629.

113 SRO JC. 3/28, 562 (the quotation is from Grant's information where he is recapitulating Lockhart's *viva voce* arguments).

114 Ibid 578.

115 See, e.g., Arnot, *History of Edinburgh* (n 107) 597 and 631, citing Hale, *Pleas of the Crown* (n 5) vol i, 635. He did not need to argue the point on marital rape because Grant conceded it.

based on the Civil (Roman) and feudal laws the former had developed – he argued – and become "accommodated to the particular Genius and Manners of our Country". Criminal Law was different. It was concerned with "the *Peace* and *Order* of the Community", but fewer rules were needed than in private law, and it was less necessary "to accommodate them to our particular Constitution, since the Nature of Man remaining the same in all Times and Places, Crimes affect all States and Kingdoms almost in the same manner". Roman criminal law accordingly had needed "small Alteration to make it ours", and "being thus fit for our Use, as it stood in the Body of the *Roman* Laws, superseded the Necessity of reducing it into a peculiar System of our own".[116] Grant had likewise argued in *Macgregor* that, in contrast to matters of private right, "Crimes [were] offences against Common Humanity, and [were] equally such in ail Civilized Nations, and depend[ed] not upon peculiar Constitutions", so that:

> [W]hen the Neighbouring Customs are thus settled by the Statutes or Edicts formed on generall Principles, which are for the Common Interest and Utility of Mankind, it would altogether defeat Craig's Rule, for having Recourse to the Laws of other well Governed Nations, *quoties jure proprio et consuetudine destituimur*, if every foreign Law was to be rejected, merely because they were so much wiser than we, as to Enact it by positive authority.[117]

Such views of criminal law supported the use, for example, of Matthaeus' commentary on the *libri terribiles* to understand and interpret Scots law. In contrast, Hume wrote in 1797:

> If I have . . . paid but little regard to the compilations of Justinian; still less have I thought it material to detain the reader on every occasion, with a scrutiny into the sentiments of the numerous modern commentators on them in modern times. Not that I mean to speak of their works as useless or nugatory in themselves; but that it were absurd to look into any of them for an exhibition of the practice of Scotland, which the foreign authors could know nothing about.[118]

The years since the publication of Bayne's work had seen a revolution in thought about law in Scotland, carried out, not least, by Hume's teacher John Millar, in which the historical development of law and its relationship to different types of society and forms of government had come to be ever more stressed.[119] The passage from Hume's *Commentaries* quoted at the

116 Bayne, *Criminal Law* (n 37) 5–7.

117 SRO JC 3/28 582–583, 585.

118 Hume, *Commentaries* (n 4) vol i, lx.

119 Cairns, "John Millar's lectures on Scots criminal law" (1988) 8 OJLS 364; and "Rhetoric, language, and Roman law: legal education and improvement in eighteenth-century Scotland" (1991) 9 *Law and History Review* 31.

beginning of this essay emphasised that English criminal law was eminently suitable for transplanting – to use Alan Watson's term[120] – "because the form of our Government, and the general spirit of our jurisprudence are the same with that of England".[121] Influenced by Enlightenment thought on law in Scotland, Hume thus perceived the works of English lawyers to be the best to which to resort "for confirmation of what equity and reason dictate";[122] English criminal law was that "of a free and enlightened people".[123] The natural-law thinking of men such as Grant and Lockhart had become the more historical, perhaps sociological, natural jurisprudence associated with Adam Smith and John Millar. No longer could someone such as Bayne argue as easily that humanity was everywhere the same as regards crimes. The result of this greater sensitivity was that England was now the "well governed realm" (in the terms of the major premiss of the libel), the law of which was the appropriate source to which to turn to develop and elucidate indeterminate Scottish criminal law. A tendency to look to England would only have been reinforced by the now generally accepted view that English and Scots law had had a common mediaeval origin; while this recognition can be traced back to Craig,[124] it had been made popular by the writings of eighteenth-century scholars such as Kames.[125] It could no longer be simply assumed that Scots criminal law could be much the same as Roman law.

HM Advocate v D[126] and *HM Advocate v Paxton*[127] showed that "the general spirit of our jurisprudence" – in Hume's phrase redolent of Montesquieu – was no longer in favour of the marital rape exemption. Even if it had been appropriate for Scots law in 1797, it no longer was in the 1980s. In *Stallard*,[128] the Lord Justice-General and the Lords Commissioners of Justiciary laid it to rest.[129]

120 A Watson, *Legal Transplants: An Approach to Comparative Law* (1974).

121 Hume, *Commentaries* (n 4) vol i, liv.

122 Ibid vol i, lxi.

123 Ibid vol i, liv.

124 See, e.g., B P Levack, *The Formation of the British State: England, Scotland, and the Union 1603–1707* (1987) 77–78; J W Cairns, T D Fergus and H L MacQueen, "Legal Humanism in Renaissance Scotland" (1990) 11 *Journal of Legal History* 40 at 56–57.

125 See, e.g., H Home, Lord Kames, *Historical Law-Tracts*, 2nd edn (1761) xiv.

126 1982 SCCR 182.

127 1985 SLT 96.

128 1989 SCCR 248.

129 I am grateful to Beverley Brown, Roger Emerson, Hector MacQueen, David Sellar and Alan Watson for comments on earlier drafts

12 Ethics and the Science of Legislation: Legislators, Philosophers, and Courts in Eighteenth-Century Scotland

A. LEGISLATION AND COURTS IN SCOTLAND

In 1686, Sir George Mackenzie of Rosehaugh, the able apologist for Stewart absolutism, wrote that "our Statutes . . . be the chief Pillars of our Law".[1] While seventeenth-century attitudes to the sources of Scots law are complex and ambiguous and most certainly do not quadrate with our own, an emphasis on the centrality of statutes, going beyond a simple view of them as having primacy in a hierarchy of sources, was common. In part, this was because some members of the bench were regarded as corrupt and ignorant. Moreover, believers in absolutism, such as Mackenzie, could claim that the statutes were made by the king alone, Parliament only consenting, so that focusing on statutes emphasised the direct link between the monarchy and the law. This approach also had the benefit of avoiding any awkward potential claims arising from the traditional argument that custom was valid through the tacit consent of the people.[2]

1 G Mackenzie, *Observations on the Acts of Parliament, Made by King James the First, King James the Second, King James the Third, King James the Fourth, King James the Fifth, Queen Mary, King James the Sixth, King Charles the First, King Charles the Second. Wherein 1. It is Observ'd, if they be in Desuetude, Abrogated, Limited, or Enlarged. 2. The Decisions relating to these Acts are mention'd. 3. Some new Doubts not yet decided, are hinted at. 4. Parallel Citations from the Civil, Canon, Feudal and Municipal Laws, and the Laws of other Nations, are adduc'd for clearing these Statutes* (1686) sig A4r. On Mackenzie's thinking in general political and intellectual context, see now, above all, J C L Jackson, "Royalist Politics, Religion and Ideas in Restoration Scotland, 1660–1689", unpublished PhD thesis, University of Cambridge, 1998, passim.

2 The most sophisticated contemporary account of the sources of Scots law is that by Mackenzie in his MS treatise "Discourse on the 4 First Chapters of the Digest", British Library, Add MS

One aspect of such a focus on statutes undoubtedly derived from a general Scottish view that the "native" sources of law were unsatisfactory. From the fifteenth century onwards, as well as promoting a reception of Roman law partly because of the perceived advantages of its written nature, this attitude had led to variety of attempts to reduce aspects or all of Scots law to statutory form.[3] Thus, in September 1681, a commission was granted in Parliament "for revising the Laws". The preamble noted "the many prejudices which arise from the great number of useles indistinct and undigested Laws" and the advantages that would accrue from having laws "not only just in themselves, but consonant to one another, purg'd from what is superfluous or intricat, and reduced into a free and plaine method, therby to establish constant and clear Rules". Having studied all printed and unprinted statutes and all other sources such as customs and court decisions, the commissioners were "To collect and digest the Laws and Acts of Parliament, Customs, decisions, and formes of Process, into such order and methods as shall seem most fit and expedient to them". They were "also to determine the true Sense meaning and Interpretation of all such Laws Acts and practicks, as are unclear or doubtfull in themselves, Or have or may receive divers senses or interpretations". They were finally to digest and reduce the collections they made "into such convenient order As they shall judge fitt" and, omitting all obsolete or abrogated acts, deliver the still valid acts to be enacted in the form of laws.[4]

The 1681 Commission produced no results;[5] continuing interest, however, led, in 1695, to the granting of another Parliamentary commission, the preamble of which stressed the "Concern of all his Majesties Liedges for the Security both of their lives and ffortunes that the written Lawes and Acts of Parliament as also the Decisions and Practiques of the Lords of Session

18,236. The argument in the work (first published 1681; 2nd edn 1693) of James Dalrymple, Viscount Stair, *The Institutions of the Law of Scotland: Deduced from its Originals, and Collated with the Civil, Canon and Feudal Laws, and with the Customs of Neighbouring Nations*, D M Walker (ed) (1981) 73–94 (1.i.1–23) in favour of the superiority of custom as a source of law is therefore against the normal run of Scottish thinking of the period.

3 J W Cairns, "The Civil Law Tradition in Scottish Legal Thought", in D L Carey Miller and R Zimmermann (eds), *The Civilian Tradition and Scots Law* (1997) 191 (henceforth Cairns, "Civil Law Tradition") at 201–203; J W Cairns, T D Fergus and H L MacQueen, "Legal Humanism and the History of Scots Law: John Skene and Thomas Craig", in J MacQueen (ed), *Humanism in Renaissance Scotland* (1990) 48 at 50–52.

4 Act 1681, c 94, in *Acts of the Parliaments of Scotland* ed T Thomson and C Innes (1814–1875) (henceforth *APS*) vol viii, 356.

5 Sir John Lauder of Fountainhall, *Historical Notices of Scottish Affairs Selected from the Manuscripts of Sir John Lauder of Fountainhall, Bart, One of the Senators of the College of Justice* (1848) vol i, 322.

be cleared and ascertained as much as possible". The commissioners were instructed to examine "the whole written Lawes and Acts of Parliament . . . and to take notice and remark what Lawes and Acts are gone in desuetude in haill or in part". Moreover, they were to note "what seeming inconsistencies or defects they may find in them . . . and how the same may be best helped or supplied". The need "to define the pains of all Crimes not already defined by Acts of Parliament" was emphasised. The commissioners were "to take notice and remark what Acts of Sederunt are in use and what Decisions should be held for Practiques to be still adverted to in Judgement, and what not". Moreover, they were to take note of contradictory Acts of Sederunt and decisions and "give their opinion which of them shall for hereafter be observed And generally to do all and sundry other things that may best clear ascertain and establish the Practique or course of Decisions to be hereafter observed by the Lords of Session in judgement".[6]

The second of these two proposals for codification specifically mentioned the principle of *nulla poena sine lege*. In *The Laws and Customes of Scotland, In Matters Criminal* (1678), Mackenzie also expressed the regret that some crimes were not defined in statutes, as to do so would favour the liberty of the subject.[7] This seems obvious enough. Yet, at the end of the eighteenth century, the noted authoritative writer on Scots criminal law, David Hume, Professor of Scots Law at Edinburgh, and nephew of the philosopher, rejected this stress on a statutory basis for criminal law. Rather, he emphasised the decisions of the High Court of Justiciary, the major Scottish criminal court, as the appropriate source from which to draw Scots criminal law. It was necessary to carry out "accurate and extensive research into the records and decisions of Court, which are the only key to the peculiar practice of Scotland respecting crimes". He pointed out that Mackenzie's work was basically obsolete. This was because of "the great change which has happened . . . in the manners, and temper, and way of thinking of the nation". There was a "natural correspondence between the state of the Criminal Law, and the condition of the people as to its manners and ways of feeling". At the time of the publication of Mackenzie's work "this

6 Act 1695, c 57, in *APS* (n 4) vol ix, 455. Acts of Sederunt are rules issued, under a delegated legislative power, by the Court of Session, the Supreme Scottish civil court, to govern practice and procedure.

7 G Mackenzie, *The Laws and Customes of Scotland, In Matters Criminal: Wherein is to be seen how the Civil Law, and the Laws and Customs of other Nations do agree with, and supply ours*, in *The Works of that Eminent and Learned Lawyer, Sir George Mackenzie of Rosehaugh, Advocate to King Charles II. and King James VII. With Many Learned Treatises of His, Never before Printed* (1716–1722) vol ii, 53, 60–61.

country had advanced but little in any sort of improvement; and indeed, whether we consider it with respect to the administration of its Government, its internal discipline and oeconomy, or the opinions, temper, and habits of the people, it was at that time utterly remote from what Scotland has since become". Arguing for a close relationship between morals and criminal law, Hume saw the need for its "general spirit . . . always, in some measure, [to] be bent and accommodated to the temper and exigencies of the times".[8] An account of Scots criminal law had therefore to be constructed from the practice of the courts. This same emphasis on the importance of the decisions of the courts on the law and the need to reflect changing manners is found in Archibald Alison's work printed in 1832. He noted that "besides embodying every decision in Hume and Burnett on the subjects on which it treats of practical application at this time, this Volume contains above a thousand unreported cases".[9]

A similar focus on the importance of the courts in developing the private law in Scotland can be found at the end of the eighteenth century. Hume's magisterial account of Scots private law is founded very much on a brilliant synthesis of the decisions of the Court of Session, the civil court.[10] He also stressed that "the greater part of our Law" was formed by custom in contrast to statute.[11] Such custom, "our Common Law", was to be found in reports of the decisions of the courts and in the writings of authors.[12]

In a hundred years, therefore, Scots lawyers changed their general attitude to the sources and nature of their law. From emphasising the significance of statute and setting up projects for reduction of all law to statutory form, the focus had become the decisions of the courts. To some extent, of course, this must have been a pragmatic response to the reality of the situation in which Scots lawyers found themselves. After the Union with England in 1707, the Parliament of Great Britain rarely legislated on Scots law, the most notable

8 D Hume, *Commentaries on the Law of Scotland, Respecting the Description and Punishment of Crimes* (1797) vol i, xxxviii–xli. There is some relevant discussion of Hume, from a different perspective, in L Farmer, *Criminal Law, Tradition and Legal Order: Crime and the Genius of Scots Law, 1747 to the Present* (1997) 21–56.

9 A Alison, *Principles of the Criminal Law of Scotland* (1832) vol i, vi. The treatise referred to with that of Hume is J Burnett, *A Treatise on the Various Branches of the Criminal Law of Scotland* (1811). There is a good modern biography of Alison: M Michie, *An Enlightenment Tory in Victorian Scotland: The Career of Archibald Alison* (1997).

10 G C H Paton (ed), *Baron David Hume's Lectures 1786–1822*, 6 vols Stair Society vols 5, 13, 15, 17–19 (1939–1958).

11 Ibid vol i, 12.

12 Ibid 14.

items of legislation all being the product of a political crisis.[13] But there is more than this to the re-orientation away from statute as the preferred form of law; indeed, in the early nineteenth century, some Scots were now to argue strongly against codification.[14]

The explanation lies in part in the development of moral theory in eighteenth-century Scotland. In this paper, I shall revisit some of my earlier work, particularly on Adam Smith, in which I located aspects of the thinking on law of the Scots *philosophes* against some of the debates on legal education and on the courts in eighteenth-century Scotland.[15] This will allow the development of an argument that, in the context of legislative quiescence, ethical theory provided Scots lawyers with a strong endorsement of law-making through the courts. This, however, brought its own particular concerns. Reliance on the courts for law reform required the judges and advocates to be equipped for this legislative role. Furthermore, the operation of the court had to be such as to facilitate rather than hinder its law-making function.

Given that the argument for this paper to some extent runs contrary to a generally received vision of law in the Enlightenment, the next section will be devoted to a discussion of the idea of the "legislator", exploring some of the attitudes taken to it and the ambiguities of the term. The third section will examine the development of ethical theory in eighteenth-century Scotland, as the necessary background to the discussion of Smith's legal philosophy in the fourth. The fifth section will consider Smith's science of legislation, while the sixth and final will assess its implications in the context of Scottish legal history.

13 N T Phillipson, "Public Opinion and the Union in the Age of the Association", in N T Phillipson and R Mitchison (eds), *Scotland in the Age of Improvement* (1970) 125 at 140–142.

14 See J W Cairns, "The influence of the German Historical School in early nineteenth century Edinburgh" (1994) 20 *Syracuse Journal of International Law and Commerce* 191 at 199–201.

15 J W Cairns, "The Influence of Smith's Jurisprudence on Legal Education in Scotland", in P Jones and A S Skinner (eds), *Adam Smith Reviewed* (1992) 168; J W Cairns, "Adam Smith's Lectures on Jurisprudence: Their Influence on Legal Education", in H Mizuta and C Sugiyama (eds), *Adam Smith: International Perspectives* (1993) 63; J W Cairns, "Adam Smith and the Role of the Courts in Securing Justice and Liberty", in R P Malloy and J Evensky (eds), *Adam Smith and the Philosophy of Law and Economics* (1994) 31 (henceforth Cairns, "Adam Smith and the Role of the Courts").

B. THE ENLIGHTENED LEGISLATOR

However one may wish to define that troubling and elusive term "Enlightenment", an evident feature of the thinking of the period we use this term to describe is concern with legislation to improve the lot of humankind. What one is inclined to think of in this connection are the endless legislative projects of the tireless Englishman Jeremy Bentham, who left no Enlightened ruler undisturbed in his quest to promote codification around the world.[16] One also thinks of the *Codex Theresianus juris civilis*, of the legislative projects of Joseph II, of the work of Franz von Zeiler.[17] A reading of a standard work such as Franz Wieacker's *Privatrechtsgeschichte der Neuzeit* gives the impression that, in law, the Enlightenment is marked by the translation of the modern "law of reason" into the codification projects of the Enlightened absolutists of Prussia and Austria. The work of the legal philosopher Christian Wolff is represented as providing the theoretical underpinning for such legislative projects of codification.[18] More recently, Peter Stein has written in *Roman Law in European History:* "The rationalist natural law philosophy proclaimed that a complete set of laws could be stated simply and rationally, with existing complexities eliminated, and all that was needed to enact it was the will of the prince."[19] The Legislator is seen as the key figure who could maximise the happiness of human beings through careful provision for their welfare.

There is not the opportunity here to trace the history of the idea of the role of the Legislator in promoting human happiness. It is obviously rooted in the classical tradition. The legends of Moses, Lycurgus and Solon are crucial. Aristotle himself remarked that "Legislators make citizens good by forming their habits. That is what all legislators wish to do . . ."[20] In the eighteenth century, the new science had emphasised that legislative wisdom need no longer be derived from divine revelation or metaphysics, but could

16 For sensitive appreciations of Bentham's thinking, see G J Postema, *Bentham and the Common Law Tradition* (1986); D Lieberman, *The Province of Legislation Determined: Legal Theory in Eighteenth-Century Britain* (1989) 219–290.

17 See, e.g., H E Strakosch, *State Absolutism and the Rule of Law: The Struggle for the Codification of Civil Law in Austria, 1753–1811* (1967).

18 See F Wieacker, *A History of Private Law in Europe*, trans T Weir (1995) 251–255, 257–269.

19 P Stein, *Roman Law in European History* (1999) 110 (translated as *Römisches Recht und Europa: Die Geschichte einer Rechtskultur* (1997) 181).

20 Aristotle, *Ethics*, II.i.5:1103 b 2; see generally, J H Burns, "The Fabric of Felicity: The Legislator and the Human Condition", in P King (ed), *The Study of Politics: A Collection of Inaugural Lectures* (1977) 207 (the quotation from Aristotle is at 212); D A Wisner, *The Cult of the Legislator in France 1750–1830: A Study in the Political Theology of the French Enlightenment* (= *Studies on Voltaire and the Eighteenth Century* 352) (1997) 14–32.

be acquired from empirical observation. This, of course, is the significance of Montesquieu's *L'esprit des loix* of 1748, a work of profound importance in eighteenth-century Scotland.[21] Montesquieu's work purported to provide a means to identify the needs of particular societies so that their laws might be adjusted by a system of fine-tuning to maximise the happiness of that society.

Modern social science, however, has tended to question the possibility of such an approach. It has stressed the complexity of social life. Individuals as legislators have been denied such significance. The idea of a "Legislator" has been viewed as an anachronism necessarily discarded on the path to a modern social science. Durkheim in particular emphasised this. In what I suspect is itself a somewhat anachronistic reading, certain Scots of the Enlightenment, taken as forerunners of modern social science, have been credited with destroying the myth of the Legislator. The names normally mentioned in such an argument would include those of Adam Smith, John Millar, and Adam Ferguson.[22] The last wrote that "nations stumble upon establishments, which are indeed the result of human action, but not the execution of any human design".[23] A certain reading of Smith's *laissez-faire* economics would also suggest the futility of the work of a Legislator. And the social and historical analysis of Smith, Millar, and Ferguson does indeed suggest that the idea of a Legislator who could create the good society is false.[24]

Here, of course, the progress of such an argument is confronted with the fact that in the *Wealth of Nations* Adam Smith described "Political oeconomy . . . as a branch of the science of a statesman or legislator".[25] Smith's contemporaries also so described the work. Thus, in the *Memoir* of Smith, Dugald Stewart described the *Wealth of Nations* as "the most comprehensive and most perfect work that has yet appeared, on the general principles of any branch of legislation".[26] A certain amount of modern

21 See, e.g., P Stein, "Law and Society in Eighteenth-Century Scottish Thought", in N T Phillipson and R Mitchison (eds), *Scotland in the Age of Improvement* (1970) 148 at 156–159.

22 See D Forbes, "Introduction", in A Ferguson, *An Essay on the History of Civil Society* (1966) xxiv.

23 Ibid 122.

24 For a recent interesting and important rehabilitation of the significance of legislation in political theory, see J Waldron, *The Dignity of Legislation* (1999).

25 A Smith, *An Inquiry into the Nature and Causes of the Wealth of Nations*, ed R H Campbell, A S Skinner and W B Todd, Glasgow Edition of the Works and Correspondence of Adam Smith II (1976, repr 1979) (henceforth WN) IV.introd.1.

26 D Stewart, "Account of the Life and Writings of Adam Smith, LLD", in W P D Wightman and J C Bryce (eds), *Adam Smith, Essays on Philosophical Subjects*, Glasgow Edition of the Works and Correspondence of Adam Smith III (1980) IV.7.

scholarship (notably the work of Donald Winch and Knud Haakonssen) has been devoted to exploring the implications of this.[27] I think that Winch sums up Smith's attitude rather well:

> [T]he strategy of persuasion . . . lies behind the *Wealth of Nations*, and it provides the basis of Smith's case for bringing science to bear on the conduct of legislators. . . . [I]t is necessary to distinguish this vision from its Utopian or technocratic alternative. Smith's ideal legislator may be wiser and more public-spirited than the mere politician, but he is not an omnipotent or benevolent despot equipped by personality or science with powers of rational foresight that go beyond those of ordinary mortals. True wisdom often consisted in respecting the superior knowledge that actors in the social drama have of their own affairs, and in recognising the limits or constraints on legislative action posed by entrenched habits and privileges, including those that arose out of ignorance and prejudice.[28]

It is therefore evident that the idea of a legislator and of the possibility of legislation is a complex one, not to be too readily identified with swingeing projects of social and legal reform.

C. THE SCOTTISH REJECTION OF ETHICAL RATIONALISM

While it is necessary to touch on the history of the teaching of ethics and moral philosophy in the Scottish universities in the eighteenth century, the ground has been so much traversed that I do not feel the need to cover it fully yet again. A seminal figure was Gershom Carmichael who taught at Glasgow from 1694 to 1729. Carmichael used Pufendorf's textbook *De officio hominis et civis* as a teaching text for moral philosophy, and produced an edition with an extensive commentary in 1718. Carmichael was not an uncritical admirer of Pufendorf. For example, he criticised Pufendorf's theory of property, preferring that of John Locke. What he saw of importance in Pufendorf was the identification of moral philosophy with natural jurisprudence. For us, Carmichael's importance lies in his firm establishment of the natural jurisprudence tradition in the Scottish universities.[29]

27 See, e.g., K Haakonssen, *The Science of a Legislator: The Natural Jurisprudence of David Hume and Adam Smith* (1981) (henceforth Haakonssen, *Science of a Legislator*); and *Natural Law and Moral Philosophy: From Grotius to the Scottish Enlightenment* (1996) 154–181, 226–293; D Winch, *Adam Smith's Politics: An Essay in Historiographic Revision* (1978) and "Science and the legislator: Adam Smith and after" (1983) 93 *Economic Journal* 501 (henceforth Winch, "Science and the legislator").

28 Winch, "Science and the legislator" (n 27) 503.

29 On Carmichael, see J Moore and M Silverthorne, "Gershom Carmichael and the Natural Jurisprudence Tradition in Eighteenth-Century Scotland", in I Hont and M Ignatieff (eds), *Wealth and Virtue: The Shaping of Political Economy in the Scottish Enlightenment* (1983) 73–87.

Carmichael was succeeded in the moral philosophy chair by Francis Hutcheson. Hutcheson was a follower of the philosophy of Lord Shaftesbury. He attempted to ground ethics in observation and study of the thinking and behaviour of human beings. To put it simply, he argued that humanity is able to judge of the lightness or wrongness of an action by virtue of a moral sense as moral actions are motivated by benevolence. In other words, the foundation of moral judgement was not in the reason, but in the senses, as morally beautiful actions give pleasure. He also taught natural jurisprudence using Pufendorf. Some debate has accordingly arisen over whether or not there is an inconsistency here, so that his philosophical contributions to moral sense theory are in conflict with his use of Pufendorf.[30] We need not consider this here.

After Hutcheson's death in 1746, Thomas Craigie briefly held the chair until he died in November 1751. In April 1752, Smith, who had already been elected Professor of Logic in Glasgow, was translated to the Moral Philosophy chair. Smith followed the basic outline of the curriculum for moral philosophy as developed by Hutcheson. It was divided into four parts: natural theology, ethics, justice, and political regulations founded on expediency. Of Smith's account of natural theology we know nothing. His ethics was published as *The Theory of Moral Sentiments* in 1759. The fourth part of the course was published in 1776 as *The Wealth of Nations*. Student lecture notes survive from the third and fourth part of the lectures. They have been published as his lectures on jurisprudence.[31]

Other Scots followed Hutcheson's rejection of ethical rationalism and espousal of a moral sense as the best explanation of how moral judgement was possible. Among lawyers, the most noted of these was Lord Kames, a judge and prolific author. He refined Hutcheson's views by suggesting that justice was derived not from the benevolence of the moral sense but rather from its sense of duty: many moral actions were right but could not be compelled, while just actions could be.[32] The most famous exponent of

30 See J Moore, "The Two Systems of Francis Hutcheson: On the Origins of the Scottish Enlightenment", in M A Stewart (ed), *Studies in the Philosophy of the Scottish Enlightenment*, Oxford Studies in the History of Philosophy vol 1 (1990) 37; Haakonssen, *Science of a Legislator* (n 27) 63–85 and "Natural Law and Moral Realism: The Scottish Synthesis", in M A Stewart (ed), *Studies in the Philosophy of the Scottish Enlightenment*, Oxford Studies in the History of Philosophy vol 1 (1990) 61.

31 On Smith at Glasgow, see I S Ross, *The Life of Adam Smith* (1995) 109–156.

32 Kames first set out his moral theory in Henry Home, Lord Kames, *Essays on the Principles of Morality and Natural Religion* (1751). He further developed it in *Principles of Equity*, 2nd edn (1767) and *Sketches of the History of Man* (1774). See generally I S Ross, *Lord Kames and the Scotland of his Day* (1972).

a version of moral sense theory was David Hume. In his *Treatise of Human Nature* (1739), he mounted a devastating attack on ethical rationalism and natural law. When it came to justice, however, he rejected the approach of Hutcheson or Kames. Justice was not derived from the moral sense. Justice was an "artificial" virtue. That is, it originated in social convention. By this he did not mean anything approaching the natural lawyers' idea of a social contract. Instead, what he meant was that rules for the allocation of the scarce resources necessary for life developed out of customary practices on the basis of expediency and necessity. In his later *Enquiry Concerning the Principles of Morals* (1751), he stressed emphatically that the sole origin of justice was utility.[33] I think it may be necessary to consider once again and reassess the relationship between Hutcheson, Kames and Hume; this important topic is, however, outwith the scope of this paper.

D. SMITH'S LEGAL PHILOSOPHY

Smith likewise accepted the Hutchesonian and Humean critique of ethical rationalism. Moral judgements were not the product simply of reason. They were founded in another faculty. He firmly rejected, however, a utilitarian origin for justice. Here we need to turn to his *Theory of Moral Sentiments*, much of which deals with the issue of how moral judgement is possible. As is well known, Smith built up his theory of moral judgement using his ideas of sympathy and the impartial spectator. He thus argued that, as human beings, we have the capacity to enter sympathetically into the feelings of others and could appreciate, though at a lesser level than they did, their pains and their pleasures by an act of the imagination. He also pointed out that we took pleasure in the agreement of our sentiments or feelings with those of others and judged the appropriateness of another's sentiments by their correspondence with our own. When we felt some passion, we wished spectators to do the same, which required us to reduce the pitch of our passion to correspond with that of the spectators.[34]

33 From a huge literature, see, e.g., Haakonssen, *Science of a Legislator* (n 27) 4–44; 12 *Jahrbuch für Recht und Ethik*, 8(2000).

34 A Smith, *The Theory of Moral Sentiments*, ed D D Raphael and A L Macfie, Glasgow Edition of the Works and Correspondence of Adam Smith I (1976) (henceforth TMS) I.i.l–4. The literature on the idea of the spectator is enormous. See, e.g., D D Raphael, "The Impartial Spectator", in A S Skinner and T Wilson (eds), *Essays on Adam Smith* (1975) 83; V M Hope, *Virtue by Consensus: The Moral Philosophy of Hutcheson, Hume, and Adam Smith* (1989) 83–117; and T D Campbell, *Adam Smith's Science of Morals* (1971) 87–126. The discussion of Smith that follows derives very closely from the discussion in Cairns, "Adam Smith and the Role of the

We were thus able to form judgements about the behaviour of others in two ways. First, we could judge the propriety of their behaviour; secondly, we could judge its merit or demerit. Our sense of the propriety of behaviour was socially created through the mechanism of mutual sympathy:

> Upon these two different efforts, upon that of the spectator to enter into the sentiments of the person principally concerned, and upon that of the person principally concerned to bring down his emotions to what the spectator can go along with, are founded two different sets of virtues. The soft, the gentle, the amiable virtues, the virtues of candid condescension and indulgent humanity, are founded upon the one: the great, the awful and respectable, the virtues of self-denial, of self-government, of that command of the passions which subjects all the movements of our nature to what our own dignity and honour, and the propriety of our own conduct require, take their origin from the other.[35]

Judgement of merit or demerit arose from observations of the sentiments that gave rise to an action. Approval of that sentiment meant that the action was meritorious or deserving reward. Disapproval meant it was demeritorious or deserving punishment.[36] Smith explained:

> The sentiment which most immediately and directly prompts us to reward, is gratitude; that which most immediately and directly prompts us to punish, is resentment.
>
> To us, therefore, that action must appear to deserve reward, which appears to be the proper and approved object of gratitude; as, on the other hand, that action must appear to deserve punishment, which appears to be the proper and approved object of resentment.[37]

Smith argued that we entered into the feelings of gratitude of a person whom we had seen benefited and into those of resentment of one whom we had seen wronged. We only did so, however, where we approved of the conduct of the person conferring the benefit and disapproved of the conduct of the person committing the wrong.[38] For Smith, the "sense of merit" was "a compounded sentiment" made up of two emotions: "a direct sympathy with sentiments of the agent, and an indirect sympathy with the gratitude of those who receive the benefit of his actions". Demerit was also

Courts" (n 15) at 36–40. It will be evident to all who know Haakonssen's work that my approach is strongly indebted to his work on Smith.

35 Smith, TMS (n 34) I.i.5.1.

36 Ibid II.i.introd.2.

37 Ibid II.i.1.2 and 3.

38 Ibid II.i.2.4 and 5; II.i.3.2 and 3.

"a compounded sentiment": "a direct antipathy to the sentiments of the agent, and an indirect sympathy with the resentment of the sufferer".[39]

Justice here enters Smith's argument. Beneficent actions might deserve reward; but such reward, if not forthcoming, could not be extorted by force. Refusal by a person to reward his or her benefactor might cause disapprobation, and "[t]he heart of every impartial spectator rejects all fellow-feeling with the selfishness of his motives". Such an ungrateful person was not the object of resentment as "mere want of beneficence tends to do no real positive evil".[40] It was otherwise with hurtful actions. Smith had earlier commented: "The natural gratification of this passion [of resentment] tends, of its own accord, to produce all the political ends of punishment; the correction of the criminal, and the example to the public."[41] In comparing the virtues of justice and beneficence Smith wrote: "Resentment seems to have been given to us by nature for a defence, and for defence only. It is the safeguard of justice and the security of innocence." Further, "the violation of justice is injury: it does real and positive hurt to some particular persons, from motives which are naturally disapproved of. It is, therefore, the proper object of resentment, and of punishment, which is the natural consequence of resentment."[42] In contrast with other virtues, we felt a particular need to observe justice; even the person who committed an act of injustice recognised the propriety of the use of force to obstruct or punish him. Indeed, we felt greater sympathy with a person's pain than with his joy, as it was a keener, more universal sentiment.[43] The foundation of punishment in the sentiments of the wronged individual and the sympathy of the spectator was "natural":

> Among equals each individual is naturally, and antecedent to the institution of civil government, regarded as having a right both to defend himself from injuries, and to exact a certain degree of punishment for those which have been done him. Every generous spectator not only approves of his conduct when he does this, but enters so far into his sentiments as often to be willing to assist him.[44]

Smith's discussion has tended to shift between spectators considered as real individuals acting sympathetically to assist wronged individuals and impartial spectators.

The latter, much more abstract concept, he was ultimately to conceive of

39 Ibid II.i.5.2 and 5.
40 Ibid II.ii.1.3.
41 Ibid II.i.1.6.
42 Ibid II.ii.1.4 and 5.
43 Ibid I.ii.2; II.ii.1.5; II.ii.2.3. See further Haakonssen, *Science of a Legislator* (n 27) 83–87.
44 Smith, TMS (n 34) II.ii.1.7.

as conscience. He called on it to explain our sense of justice and remorse and our consciousness of merit. The only proper motive for hurting another individual was "just indignation for evil which that other has done to us". While individuals preferred their own happiness to that of others, to injure others to promote our own happiness was "what no impartial spectator can go along with". We had to view our actions not in the light in which they appeared to ourselves, but in the light in which they appeared to others. An individual might naturally prefer himself to all others "yet he dares not look mankind in the face, and avow he acts according to that principle". The mechanism of mutual sympathy operated:

> If he would act so as that the impartial spectator may enter into the principles of his conduct, which is what of all things he has the greatest desire to do, he must, upon this, as upon all other occasions, humble the arrogance of his self love, and bring it down to something which other men can go along with.[45]

The spectator also provided the test of just punishment:

> The most sacred laws of justice, therefore, those whose violation seems to call loudest for vengeance and punishment, are the laws which guard the life and person of our neighbour; the next are those which guard his property and possessions; and last of all come those which guard what are called his personal rights, or what is due him from the promises of others.[46]

The laws of justice supported "the immense fabric of human society". Without them human society would be impossible. Yet, we upheld justice, not for its evident utility, but because as human beings we abhorred injustice.[47]

Rights derived from the spectatorial test: initially these were rights to defend oneself against injury and to punish someone who had caused one injury. These rights arose out of concrete instances and experiences of injury. Smith wrote of the rules of morality:

> They are ultimately founded upon experience of what, in particular instances, our moral faculties, our natural sense of merit and propriety, approve, or disapprove of. We do not originally approve or condemn particular actions; because, upon examination, they appear to be agreeable or inconsistent with a certain general rule. The general rule, on the contrary, is formed, by finding from experience, that all actions of a certain kind, or circumstanced in a certain manner, are approved or disapproved of.

He gave as an instance the man who saw the first murder:

45 Ibid II.ii.2.1.
46 Ibid II.ii.2.2.
47 Ibid II.ii.3.4, 6 and 9–11.

> His detestation of this crime, it is evident, would arise instantaneously and antecedent to his having formed to himself any general rule. The general rule, on the contrary, which he might afterwards form, would be founded upon the detestation which he felt necessarily arise in his own breast, at the thought of this, and every other particular action of the same kind.[48]

Such general rules arising in this fashion would then serve as guidelines to others for future conduct.[49]

The purpose of natural jurisprudence was to elaborate and explain the rules of justice arising from the moral sentiments. It thus provided "a theory of the general principles which ought to run through and be the foundation of the laws of all nations".[50] In this sense, natural jurisprudence was a practical discipline. Smith commented in an addition to the 1790 edition of the *Theory of Moral Sentiments:*

> The wisdom of every state or commonwealth endeavours, as well as it can, to employ the force of the society to restrain those who are subject to its authority, from hurting or disturbing the happiness of one another. The rules which it establishes for this purpose, constitute the civil and criminal law of each particular state or country. The principles upon which those rules either are, or ought to be founded, are the subject of a particular science . . . that of natural jurisprudence.[51]

Natural jurisprudence was to give guidance as to what the laws ought to be.

E. SMITH'S SCIENCE OF LEGISLATION

At first sight, these remarks might seem to suggest that Smith saw a major role for a Legislator in turning natural jurisprudence into law. After all, he did at one stage define "what are properly called laws" as "those general rules which the sovereign lays down to guide the conduct of his subjects".[52] In fact, however, Smith was far from believing that a Legislator in this sense should determine the laws. In additions to the sixth edition of the *Theory of Moral Sentiments* published in 1790, Smith remarked that "[t]he man of system . . . is apt to be very wise in his own conceit; and is often so enamoured with the supposed beauty of his own ideal plan of government, that he cannot suffer the smallest deviation from any part of it". On the basis of these general remarks, he added:

48 Ibid III.4.8 (this passage is differently located in editions earlier than the sixth).
49 Ibid III.4.11 (this passage is differently located in editions earlier than the sixth).
50 Ibid VII.iv.37.
51 Ibid VI.ii.introd.2.
52 Ibid III.5.6.

> Some general, and even systematical, idea of the perfection of policy and law, may no doubt be necessary for directing the views of the statesman. But to insist upon establishing, and upon establishing all at once, and in spite of all opposition, every thing which that idea may seem to require, must often be the highest degree of arrogance. It is to erect his own judgment into the supreme standard of right and wrong. It is to fancy himself the only wise and worthy man in the commonwealth, and that his fellow-citizens should accommodate themselves to him and not he to them. It is upon this account, that of all political speculators, sovereign princes are by far the most dangerous.[53]

This seems to me to allow little scope for a Joseph II or a Frederick the Great.

Smith remarked that "Justice is violated whenever one is deprived of what he had a right to and could justly demand from others, or rather, when we do him any injury or hurt without a cause".[54] There is no need here to explore further his analytic jurisprudence. What should be noted is his view that certain rights were "natural", in the sense they existed in any society, and would always be recognised by the spectatorial test: these were injuries to a man's body or reputation. Other rights were "adventitious" (*iura adventicia*): they only arose at particular stages in social development.[55] Smith analysed the development of rights through the device of four stages in society: that of hunting and fishing; that of pastoralism; that of agriculture; and that of commerce. I shall only say here that in my opinion Smith does not have a simple mechanical and deterministic view of progress from one stage to another. Moreover, the stages are an *analytic* device.[56]

It is easy to explain simply the kind of thinking lying behind Smith's view of the development of rights. In a society of hunters, property (*Eigentum*) would be limited to possession (*Besitz*) acquired through occupation and spectators would protect that possession.[57] In the age of shepherds, propriety (*Anstand*) would require the recognition of acquisition of property

53 Ibid VI.ii.2.17 and 18.

54 A Smith, *Lectures on Jurisprudence*, ed R L Meek, D D Raphael and P G Stein, Glasgow Edition of the Works and Correspondence of Adam Smith V (1978) (henceforth cited as LJ(A) by volume and page of original MS (report of 1762–1763) and LJ(B) by page of original MS (report of 1766)) LJ(A) i.9.

55 See, e.g., Smith, LJ(A) (n 54) i.12–i.23; Smith, LJ(B) (n 54) 7–11. For a further discussion of my views on this, see Cairns, "Adam Smith and the Role of the Courts" (n 15) at 40–42.

56 Again there is an extensive literature: see, e.g., R L Meek, *Social Science and the Ignoble Savage* (1976) 68–202; P Stein, *Legal Evolution: The Story of an Idea* (1979) 23–50; P Stein, "The Four Stage Theory and the Development of Societies", in *The Character and Influence of the Civil Law: Historical Essays* (1988) 395.

57 Smith, LJ(A) (n 54) i.36–37; i.42–44.

by *accession* as well as by *occupation*.[58] Agriculture would multiply the opportunities for acquisition by *accession*.[59] Spectators would eventually recognise the acquisition of property by prescription and succession.[60] Ultimately the impartial spectator would recognise rights arising out of contracts.[61]

This development does not explain how the rights recognised by the spectators became laws. A preliminary remark must be made. Smith only loosely mapped the development of government onto his device of the four stages. No doubt this was because he did not have a crudely determinist theory of social change. It means, however, that he never directly addressed the development of certain institutions of government in a detailed or precise way. This certainly applies to his account of the growth of legislative and judicial powers. Even so, it is obvious that, for Smith, the development of private property in the age of shepherds was the key: property required government as property meant inequality, so that it was necessary to protect the possessions of the rich.[62] Smith accordingly saw that "Settled laws therefore, or agreements concerning property, will soon be made after the commencement of the age of shepherds".[63] These remarks are placed in the context of a view that courts developed before legislatures. What Smith seems to have envisioned was that assemblies started to arbitrate and progressively moved from compromising between individuals to laying down rules of law. But the early law "would be but very short and have few distinctions in it, so that every man would understand it without any written or regular law".[64] This must mean that he saw the laws as being created through court-type institutions – in other words a type of primitive common law (in the sense of *Präzedenzfälle*).

Legislation for Smith followed the creation of judges:

> The thing which has given occasion to the establishment of laws has always been the generall or partiall institution of judges. When any nation has retaind [sic] its liberty, and property has been established amongst them, judges must soon be appointed to determine the many disputes which must occurr concerning it. A judge to such an early nation will appear very terrible.[65]

58 Ibid i.64–65; Smith, LJ(B) (n 54) 152.
59 Smith, LJ(A) (n 54) i.65–66.
60 Ibid i.77, i.93; i.150–152.
61 Ibid ii.43.
62 Ibid iv.7; Smith, LJ(B) (n 54) 20.
63 Smith, LJ(A) (n 54) iv.23.
64 Ibid iv.35.
65 Ibid v.108.

He later continued:

> What shall be done in this case? The only way is to establish laws and rules which may ascertain his conduct; . . . for when it is known in what manner he is to proceed the terror will be in a great measure removed. Laws are in this manner posterior to the establishment of judges. At the first establishment of judges there are no laws; every one trusts to the naturall feeling of justice he has in his own breast and expects to find in others. Were laws to be established in the beginnings of society prior to judges, they would then be a restraint upon liberty, but when established after them they extend and secure it, as they do not ascertain or restrain the actions of private persons so much as the power and conduct of the judge over the people.[66]

It would be wrong to assume that here Smith is necessarily thinking of laws as the product of a Legislator.

What Smith said in his Lectures on Jurisprudence is amplified and explained in his contemporary Lectures on Rhetoric and Belles Lettres. There he said that once government is established, the first judges are eminent men such as kings and chieftains or the consuls at Rome. Such men would have found this judicial office burdensome. "They therefore were very bold in passing sentence. They would pay very little regard to the conduct of their predecessors, as this was the least important part of their office."[67] To ease their burdens, the judicial functions of these great men were given to specialist judicial magistrates, who "would be at pains even to strengthen their conduct by the authority of their predecessors. . . . Whatever therefore had been practised by other judges would obtain authority with them and be received in time as Law".[68] In other words, judges started to follow precedent and precedent made law. Moreover:

> This is the case in England. The sentences of former Cases are greatly regarded and form what is called the common law, which is found to be much more equitable than that which is founded on Statute only, for the same reason as what is founded on practise and experience must be better adapted to particular cases than that which is derived from theory only.[69]

Common law allowed the spectatorial mechanism to operate to recognise and enforce rights as they arose historically, rather than theoretically through legislation.

Smith accordingly has created a science of legislation without a Legislator.

66 Ibid v.110–111 (reading "extent" as "extend" as suggested in n 69).

67 A Smith, *Lectures on Rhetoric and Belles Lettres*, ed J G Bryce, Glasgow Edition of the Works and Correspondence of Adam Smith IV (1983) ii.199–200.

68 Ibid ii.200.

69 Ibid ii.200.

A system of precedent, as in England, created the best law, as judges and juries operated according to the mechanism of sympathy to create just laws that recognised new rights as they arose. Smith commented thus on the English common law:

> The English law was . . . formed into a system before the discovery of Justinians Pandects; and its courts established, and their method of proceedings pretty much fixed, before the other courts in Europe were instituted, or the civil and cannon law came to be of any great weight. It is for this reason that it borrows less from those laws than the law of any other nation in Europe; and is for that reason more deserving of the attention of a speculative man than any other, as being more formed on the naturall sentiments of mankind.[70]

What this meant was that to ensure the best kind of law – that is, the most just – what was important was the structure of the courts and their modes of operation. From Smith's published works and the student notes of his lectures one can infer what he thought was necessary to have good courts to create good law: competition between courts or among judges; courts consisting of small numbers of judges, so that each has a sense of responsibility; historical continuity (new courts did not have precedents to follow).[71]

In general Smith saw new laws as "great evills" because "[i]t takes time and repeated practise to ascertain the precise meaning of a law".[72] In the United Kingdom, as in most countries, legislation tended to be in the hands of "that insidious and crafty animal, vulgarly called a statesman or politician" rather than in those "of a legislator, whose deliberations ought to be governed by general principles".[73] Smith's political realism caused him to see that "the length of the Parliaments, and the great extent of the Civil List" might "obtain the passing of bad laws".[74] He was not, however, entirely opposed to legislation; but the legislation he favoured was of a piecemeal type to respond to specific problems. He pointed out that the fact that English law was "more formed on the naturall sentiments of mankind" meant that it was "[o]n this account . . . very imperfect with regard to contracts"[75]. There are many instances in the Lectures on Jurisprudence where Smith called for legislative reform. For example, he noted of the laws on primogeniture: "Laws frequently continue in force long after the circumstances, which first

70 Smith, LJ(A) (n 54) ii.74–75.
71 See Cairns, "Adam Smith and the Role of the Courts" (n 15) at 46–53.
72 Smith, LJ(A) (n 54) v.43.
73 Smith, WN (n 25) IV.ii.39.
74 Smith, LJ(A) (n 54) v.12.
75 Ibid ii.75.

gave occasion to them, and which alone could render them reasonable, are no more."[76] Legislation, however, had to be pursued sensitively and carefully, as when a sovereign decided to turn a duty of beneficence into law:

> Of all the duties of a law-giver, however, this, perhaps, is that which it requires the greatest delicacy and reserve to execute with propriety and judgement. To neglect it altogether exposes the commonwealth to many gross disorders and shocking enormities, and to push it too far is destructive of all liberty, security, and justice.[77]

Swingeing Benthamite projects of codification were to be avoided as likely to produce uncertainty in the law and arbitrariness in its execution. Both continuity and innovation were necessary, but existed in a delicate tension, requiring reform sometimes to be left to the judiciary and sometimes to the legislature.

F. LEGISLATION IN ENLIGHTENED SCOTLAND

So far the argument has focused exclusively on Adam Smith; it is important to realise that he was not the only Scot to argue for law reform primarily through the mechanism of common law. Lord Kames also stressed the importance of courts in developing the law. He described this function as their equitable jurisdiction, whereby the judges developed the law on the bases of justice and utility. His argument was, to put it somewhat simply, that historical development constantly turned duties of beneficence into duties of justice. The courts had to recognise this and develop the law accordingly.[78]

Kames saw that this meant that lawyers and judges had to be properly educated. The science of legislation required that there be suitable training. Kames stressed that "[l]aw in particular only becomes a rational study when it is traced historically, from its first rudiments among savages, through successive changes, to its highest improvements in a civilized society".[79] This allowed the law student to appreciate the development of law and its close and intimate links with social changes. He later argued that what students needed to learn was *historical* reasoning about law, concluding that:

76 Smith, WN (n 25) III.ii.4.

77 Smith, TMS (n 34) II.ii.1.8.

78 See generally, Henry Home, Lord Kames, *Principles of Equity* (1760) (henceforth Kames, *Principles of Equity*).

79 Henry Home, Lord Kames, *Historical Law Tracts*, 4th edn (1792) [iii] (1st edn 1758).

> Were law taught as a rational science, its principles unfolded, and its connection with manners and politics, it would prove an enticing study to every person who has an appetite for knowledge. We might hope to see our lawyers soaring above their predecessors; and giving splendor to their country, by purifying and improving its laws.[80]

The science of legislation required well-educated lawyers: not an Enlightened despot or philosopher king, but the philosopher lawyer.

The most renowned law teacher in late eighteenth-century Scotland was Smith's pupil, John Millar, who had also enjoyed the patronage of Lord Kames.[81] He put the type of principles set out by Kames and Smith into practice in his classes. Thus, he turned the traditional second course on Justinian's *Institutes* into a general class on Smithian jurisprudence.[82] His biographer described it as a class "in which [Millar] treated of such general principles of Law as pervade the codes of all nations, and have their origin in those sentiments of justice which are imprinted on the human heart".[83] Millar's jurisprudence directed "the enlightened Legislator . . . in the noble, but arduous, attempt, to purify and improve the laws of his country". The historical aspect of Millar's legal theory prevented "inconsiderate innovation, and indiscriminate reform", since it demonstrated that "no institutions, however just in themselves, can be either expedient or permanent, if inconsistent with established ranks, manners, and opinions".[84] Millar also applied his critical jurisprudence in his account of Scots law.[85]

Millar was not alone in such an approach. From 1779, Allan Maconochie held the chair of Public Law and the Law of Nature and Nations in Edinburgh. In 1780, his class was described thus:

> He traces the rise of political institutions from the natural characters and situation of the human species; follows their progress through the rude periods of society; and treats of their history and merits, as exhibited in the principal nations of ancient and modern times, which he examines separately, classing them according to those general causes to which he attributes the principal varieties in the forms, genius, and revolutions of governments. In this manner

80 Henry Home, Lord Kames, *Elucidations Respecting the Common and Statute Law of Scotland* (1777) vii–xiii.

81 See, e.g., J W Cairns, "'Famous as a School for Law as Edinburgh … for Medicine': Legal Education in Glasgow, 1761–1801", in A Hook and R B Sher (eds), *The Glasgow Enlightenment* (1994) 133.

82 Ibid at 140–141.

83 J Craig, "Account of the Life and Writings of John Millar, Esq", prefixed to John Millar, *The Origin of the Distinction of Ranks: Or, an Inquiry into the Circumstances which give rise to Influence and Authority, in the Different Members of Society*, 4th edn (1806) xx.

84 Ibid xl–xli.

85 J W Cairns, "John Millar's lectures on Scots criminal law" (1988) 8 OJLS 364.

> he endeavours to construct the science of the spirit of the laws on a connected view of what might be called the natural history of man as a political agent; and he accordingly concludes his course with treating of the general principles of municipal law, political oeconomy and the law of nations.[86]

Like Millar's classes, this course was evidently intended to promote the education of Enlightened lawyers.

Enlightened lawyers also needed an appropriate forum for their talents. Smith's account of what made courts successful can be read as a criticism of the contemporary Court of Session. The Scottish court had a collegiate structure with a multiplicity of judges; there was no competition or emulation to encourage judges to improve the law; it was a new court, so that historical continuity had been broken, thereby allowing a reception of the Civil Law.[87] Moreover, procedure in the Court of Session did not facilitate the making of clear decisions on competing issues presented to the court. As counsel in *Millar v Robertson* in 1712, David Dalrymple commented:

> *In Cumulo* one of your Lordships is moved by one Reason, and another by another, which Reasons, if they were examined or determined separately, would be repelled by the Plurality, which also is the Case why in most Sovereign Courts, especially in England, the Judges do resolve particular Points, which renders the Reason of the Decisions clear, and makes the Precedent of greater Use in other Cases.[88]

Procedure had developed into a largely written process in which advocates were not compelled to isolate the issues in the case for decisions in a simple and clear fashion. There were no civil juries. The judges who made the final decision relied on evidence reduced to writing.[89] The system was not one in which the Smithian mechanism of sympathy would easily work.

From the later eighteenth century, there was increasing pressure to reform the court. The motives underlying the proposals for reform were complex: to reduce costs; to speed business; to discourage appeals to the House of Lords. Whiggish views of English liberty also encouraged the

86 H Arnot, *The History of Edinburgh*, 2nd edn (1788) 398.

87 Cairns, "Adam Smith and the Role of the Courts" (n 15) at 46–53.

88 Found quoted in J A Inglis, "Eighteenth-century pleading" (1907–1908) 19 *Juridical Review* 42 at 52.

89 See N Phillipson, *The Scottish Whigs and the Reform of the Court of Session, 1785–1830*, Stair Society vol 37 (1990) (henceforth Phillipson, *Scottish Whigs*) 42–61; J W Cairns, "Scottish Law, Scottish Lawyers and the Status of the Union", in J Robertson (ed), *A Union for Empire: Political Thought and the British Union of 1707* (1995) 243 at 259–267.

introduction of the civil jury.[90] Yet, a desire to create a court from which clear precedents emerged in response to pleading from well-educated advocates was evidently one of the products hoped for from reform. For example, Lord Kames, given his particular view of the role of equity, debated the question of whether it was better that there should be separate equity and common law jurisdictions.[91] Even Sir Walter Scott, no radical reformer, talked of a need for reform in language reminiscent of that of Smith.[92]

After some earlier proposals, the Court of Session was split into two divisions in 1808, in the hope of doubling the business got through.[93] In 1810, a more clearly hierarchical structure was created, with a permanent division of the functions of the judges.[94] In 1815, civil juries were introduced to try specific issues.[95] The reforming trend continued, with, in 1825, the introduction of a new mode of pleading, with the open and closed record designed to focus the issues at stake more clearly, and procedures to compel more precise and specific argument on law and greater oral argument.[96] The Act itself alluded to the important role of the judges when it provided for causes to be heard by the whole court "in order to preserve the uniformity of the decisions of the court, and to settle doubtful questions of law which may arise".[97] At the same time, there was a concerted movement to change the nature of reports of the proceedings of the Scottish courts in order to provide a form of report more responsive to the new orientation in the law, with its overwhelming emphasis on judicial decisions.[98] This need was reinforced by the ending of the older jurisprudence based on interpretation

90 For a general account of this, see Phillipson, *Scottish Whigs* (n 89) 62–110.

91 Kames, *Principles of Equity* (n 78) xiii–xiv.

92 W Scott, "View of the Changes Proposed and Adopted in the Administration of Justice in Scotland", in *Edinburgh Annual Register for 1808* vol 1 part 2, 342–372, reprinted in K Curry (ed), *Sir Walter Scott's Annual Register* (1977) 170–211, the relevant comments being at 174.

93 Court of Session Act 1808 (48 Geo III, c 151).

94 Court of Session Act 1810 (50 Geo III, c 112); see also the Act 53 Geo III, c 64. See also the Acts of Sederunt, 20 October and 11 November 1808 and 7 February 1810, in *The Acts of Sederunt of the Lords of Council and Session, From the 11th July 1800, to the 7th March 1810* (1815) 34–35, 35–36, 49–50.

95 Jury Trials (Scotland) Act 1815 (55 Geo III, c 42). See also the Court of Session Act 1830 (11 Geo IV and 1 Will IV, c 69).

96 Court of Session Act 1825 (6 Geo IV, c 120). On issuing the related Act of Sederunt on 12 November 1825, Lord President Hope made a speech that covers many of the features of the reform most interestingly: *The Acts of Sederunt of the Lords of Council and Session from the 19th June 1821 to the 8th July 1831* (1831) 97–103.

97 Court of Session Act 1825 s 23.

98 See, e.g., R Hannay, *Letter to the Dean of the Faculty of Advocates, Relative to a Plan which has been proposed for Reporting the Decisions of the Court of Session. By a Member of the Faculty* (1823).

and debate of the texts of the *Corpus iuris civilis*. Where once the texts of Roman law had given a measure of certainty, now the only building blocks of Scots law were the decisions of the courts.[99]

The development of ethics in eighteenth-century Scotland through ideas of a moral sense and its focus on the significance of individual judgement rather than systematic *a priori* thought in elaborating rights promoted a culture that favoured, not systematic codification of law, but piecemeal, incremental reform through operation of common law. Among a number of other factors (which I should not be thought as depreciating) it did lead, however, to one massive legislative reform – that of the structure of the civil court and its procedures. The result is indeed somewhat Smithian: the best law was to be allowed to emerge from competitive litigation as individuals sought resolution of a myriad of individual disputes. The task of the Enlightened Legislator was therefore to establish conditions in which the courts could operate to recognise new requirements of justice as new circumstances were presented to the judges for decision in the course of litigation between private parties.

99 Cairns, "Civil Law Tradition" (n 3) at 220–221; see also J W Cairns, "Rhetoric, language and Roman law: legal education and improvement in eighteenth-century Scotland" (1991) 9 *Law and History Review* 31.

13 Stoicism, Slavery, and Law: Grotian Jurisprudence and its Reception*

A. INTRODUCTION: THE PROBLEM OF SLAVERY

The late Sir Moses Finley, in his well-known work, *Ancient Slavery and Modern Ideology*, asserted that:

> The one sphere in which the ancients could, and did, provide assistance [i.e. to early modern defenders of slavery] was the practical one of law. Roman law offered unbroken continuity, first through the Germanic codes, then through the revival of Roman law in the later Middle Ages. The basic texts survived in more than sufficient quantity and there were learned commentaries. Hence the Europeans who peopled the New World with imported African slaves had a ready-made legal system at their disposal, which they adopted almost *in toto*, modifying it slowly to meet certain conditions, for example, in the eventual restriction of manumission to a minimum.[1]

The extent to which the colonisers of the New World did in fact import Roman rules on slavery is an interesting one that will not be dealt with here, other than to remark that it was not really the straightforward adoption Finley implies.[2] Finley in fact comments that "the defenders of slavery" had difficulty in finding acceptable evidence or argument from the ancient world with which to support the institution:

> Aristotle offered no more than learned embroidery to the main argument, which rested on Scripture. To justify the enslavement of God's creatures, the support of God was needed, not of history or of pagan philosophy, which knew neither sin nor baptism.[3]

* The author gratefully acknowledges the permission of Mr Angus Stewart, QC, Keeper of the Advocates Library, of the Librarians of the Signet Library and Edinburgh University Library and of the Keeper of the Records of Scotland to use and cite manuscript and other material under their care.

1 M I Finley, *Ancient Slavery and Modern Ideology* (1980) (henceforth Finley, *Ancient Slavery and Modern* Ideology) 18–19.

2 See generally A Watson, *Slave Law in the Americas* (1989).

3 Finley, *Ancient Slavery and Modern Ideology* (n 1) 18.

Finley is much concerned to explore the attitude of thinkers of the Enlightenment (whom he sees as varied and somewhat ambiguous) and nineteenth-century and more modern historians to the phenomenon of ancient slavery. The one important group of writers whom he ignores are the secular natural lawyers of the seventeenth century, whose works strongly influenced the *philosophes* whose attitudes he finds so intriguing. In this paper, I shall argue that the advocates of slavery in the eighteenth and nineteenth centuries could find in their works an apology for slavery and arguments in its favour that legitimated it in the New World and elsewhere.[4]

Here the work of Hugo Grotius (1583–1645), specifically his *De iure belli ac pacis libri tres* of 1625, is of particular importance.[5] Since his own era, Grotius has been seen as the founder of the new school of modern secular natural law. While both the originality of his doctrines and the reality of this history of the school of natural law can be and have been extensively and rightly questioned, that does not matter here.[6] What is important is the resounding power of Grotius' thought through the seventeenth and eighteenth centuries. Grotius is now considered of great importance in the history of a development of a theory of subjective rights. Here he is seen as having drawn much from the Spanish scholastics and their revival of a Thomist natural law ultimately derived from Aristotle. So much is incontrovertible. This is indeed the general understanding of the background to Grotius' thinking.[7] On the other hand, Gerhard Oestreich has challenged this traditional view by tantalisingly asserting that "[t]he ideological foundations of natural law, which dominated the jurisprudence of the seventeenth and eighteenth centuries – even where Grotius is concerned – are to be sought not so much in Scholasticism as in

4 It is worth noting that these arguments were not explicitly racist, unlike the racist version of natural law deployed, for example, in T R R Cobb, *An Inquiry into the Law of Negro Slavery in the United States of America* (1858; repr 1999) (henceforth Cobb, *Inquiry into the Law of Negro Slavery*).

5 I here have used H Grotius, *De iure belli ac pacis libri tres*, B J A de Kantervan Hettinga Tromp (ed), with new notes added by R Feenstra and C E Persenaire with the assistance of E Arps-De Wilde (1993) (henceforth Grotius, *De iure belli ac pacis*). For an English text of Grotius, though adapting freely where I thought appropriate, I have drawn for convenience on H Grotius, *De jure belli ac pacis libri tres*, trans F W Kelsey (1925). (This in fact appeared in 1927 and 1928: see the introduction by Feenstra in the 1993 edition at 929.) I have ignored any issues arising from the development of the text through editions.

6 See the remarks in K Haakonssen, "Hugo Grotius and the history of political thought" (1985) 13 *Political Theory* 239 (henceforth Haakonssen, "Hugo Grotius") at 239.

7 See, e.g., Q Skinner, *The Foundations of Modern Political Thought*, 2 vols (1978) vol ii, 135–173; B Tierney, *The Idea of Natural Rights. Studies on Natural Rights, Natural Law and Church Law, 1150–1625* (1997).

the Stoa".[8] In fact, at least since the historical writings of Wilhelm Dilthey in the nineteenth century, what has often been described as "Neostoicism" has been considered by some as central in a transition to modernity.[9] In such an analysis, Justus Lipsius (1547–1606), professor successively at Lutheran Jena, at the newly founded Calvinist University of Leiden, and later at Catholic Leuven, and Hugo Grotius have generally been considered seminal and indeed as most significant.[10]

This raises a number of interesting challenges for scholarship. The most cursory glance at citations in the *De jure belli ac pacis libri tres* – the work of Grotius at issue here – indicates plentiful reference to authors generally regarded as Stoic. This does not in itself necessarily demonstrate significant Stoic influence on Grotius. It can be expected that any author of his era would show knowledge of such writers. An interesting point to note, however, is that Grotius increased the references to Stoicism in subsequent editions of the *De iure belli ac pacis.* Thus, by the edition of 1642, the *Prolegomena* at least had a more Stoic appearance than it did in 1625.[11] Such identification of the Stoic aspects of Grotius' thinking in such a rich and complex work as *De iure belli ac pacis* and an assessment of their impact on subsequent jurisprudence would be an enormous task and far outwith the scope of this study.

In a paper such as this, a more fruitful approach to Grotius' thinking on Stoicism and law and its impact on later jurisprudence is instead to take a particular legal institution and examine it in some depth. The obvious institution to examine is slavery. From the Stoic point of view, slavery was a problem. Stoics considered each man to be an aspect of the divine *logos*; this meant that all men were necessarily created equal. The Stoics accordingly regarded slavery as contrary to the law of nature. If they did not call for its abolition – and they generally did not – they none the less considered that masters had a duty to recognise the moral worth of slaves and to treat them

8 G Oestreich, *Neostoicism and the Early Modern State* (1982) (henceforth Oestreich, *Neostoicism and the Early Modern State*) 38.

9 See, e.g., L Frohman, "Neo-Stoicism and the transition to modernity in Wilhelm Dilthey's Philosophy of History" (1995) 56 *Journal of the History of Ideas* 263.

10 J L Saunders, *Justus Lipsius: the Philosophy of Renaissance Stoicism* (1955) 3–58 (henceforth Saunders, *Justus Lipsius*) gives a straightforward account of his life, as does C S Edwards, *Hugo Grotius, the Miracle of Holland: a Study of Legal and Political Thought* (1981) 1–8 for the lawyer.

11 This is made clear by L Winkel, "Les origines antiques de *l'appetitus societatis* de Grotius" (2000) 68 *Tijdschrift voor Rechtsgeschiedenis* 393 (henceforth Winkel, "Les origines antiques") at 394–395. I will not here explore systematically this issue.

appropriately.[12] In contrast, of course, Aristotle considered some men as slaves by nature,[13] a view that was later picked up by Thomists.[14] On the other hand, a theory of subjective rights has also to work hard to justify slavery. This makes Grotius' discussion of slavery in *De iure belli ac pacis* of particular interest.

One of the most obvious features of the *De iure bellis ac pacis* is its relatively extensive discussion of the law of slavery. While I cannot claim to have made a comprehensive search through all the literature on Grotius – far from it – this does not seem to have excited any particular attention among modern scholars. Yet, slavery seems to loom relatively large in his work and it became a standard topic in works on natural law. The discussion below to some extent will reveal why this was so, when Grotius obviously realised that Europeans no longer routinely enslaved captured soldiers or hostile citizens. Of course, as a lawyer, Grotius was familiar with the discussions of slavery in the *Corpus iuris civilis*, as well as in other ancient texts. Given he was setting out to write a treatise on war and peace, these mentions were quite significant and should be briefly referred to here. Thus, the Roman jurist Florentinus, in a passage that also appears in Justinian's *Institutes*, stated that: "Slavery is an institution of the *ius gentium* by which one person is subjected to the ownership of another contrary to nature."[15] It was contrary to nature because of the universal equality that Roman discussion of natural law presupposed.[16] The Roman jurists stressed that slavery was part of the *ius gentium*, however, because it originated in war: the term *servi* (slaves) being somewhat imaginatively derived from *servare* (to save). In this view, slaves originally were captives who had generously been saved from the death that victors in war were entitled to inflict.[17] Of course, Roman law recognised other means by which an individual properly became a slave: birth to a slave mother, another rule of the *ius gentium*;[18] punishment;[19] and, in late law, sale of young children under pressure of poverty, though with a right later to redeem the child.[20] Although there is no time to explore

12 M C Colish, *The Stoic Tradition from Antiquity to the Early Middle Ages*, 2 vols (1985) (henceforth Colish, *Stoic Tradition*) vol i, 36–37.

13 Aristotle, *Politics* 1, 2.

14 See, e.g., J M Kelly, *A Short History of Western Legal Theory* (1992) (henceforth Kelly, *Short History of Western Legal Theory*) 148–149.

15 D 1.5.4.1; Inst 1.3.2; D 12.6.64.

16 See W W Buckland, *The Roman Law of Slavery* (1908) 1.

17 D 1.5.4; 50.16.139.1.

18 Inst 1.3.4; D 50.2.9pr; C 7.14.9.

19 D 48.19.2pr.

20 C 4.43.2.

the topic, such texts were glossed and discussed in the Middle Ages, while Canonist texts, like the Civilian, accepted that slavery was not founded in natural law, but originated in sin.[21]

When Grotius wrote the *De iure belli ac pacts*, Spain and Portugal had been trading in slaves for a century and a half; France, the country in which Grotius wrote his *chef d'oeuvre*, had been doing so for some eighty years. The other major maritime powers, England and the United Provinces of the Netherlands, were set to become major traffickers in slaves.[22] It seems unlikely that Grotius had any particular concern with this trade when he composed his treatise (although I have not researched the point), though presumably, given his work for the Dutch East India Company, he must have been perfectly aware of it.[23]

Slave trading and the colonial slave presence were to present a variety of legal problems for all the major colonial powers. For example, what was the status of slaves taken from the colonies to the homeland? Did they become free? Did they remain slaves? How was this affected if they were baptised as Christians? What if they were runaways? Could such individuals be bought and sold in the homeland? If they were, could the courts enforce the contracts?[24] What Grotius had provided in his *De iure belli ac pacis* was an ideological support for the institution of slavery that was becoming important to the economies of the maritime colonial powers. It was a support, however, that was not entirely unequivocal because of the influence of Stoic moralising in his account.

To present the argument here, it will first be necessary to discuss Stoicism and Neostoicism, and emphasise some features that affect the topic under discussion, while also taking into consideration Grotius' theory of natural law. This will be followed by a detailed consideration of Grotius' discussion of slavery. Some examples of the reception of Grotius' account of slavery will

21 Kelly, *Short History of Western Legal Theory* (n 14) 148.

22 For a general introduction to the spread of the slave trade, see H Thomas, *The Slave Trade: the History of the Atlantic Slave Trade 1440–1870* (1977) (henceforth Thomas, *The Slave Trade*) 153–231.

23 See J Fox, "'For Good and Sufficient Reasons': an Examination of Early Dutch East India Company Ordinances on Slaves and Slavery", in A Reid, *Slavery, Bondage and Dependency in South East Asia* (1983) 246; J M Postma, *The Dutch in the Atlantic Slave Trade, 1600–1815* (1990).

24 For such problems in the Dutch Republic, see A H Huussen, "The Dutch Constitution of 1798 and the problem of slavery" (1999) 67 *Tijdschrift voor Rechtsgeschiedenis* 99 at 104. On Scotland, see J W Cairns, "The Scottish law of slavery" (forthcoming) (henceforth Cairns, "The Scottish law of slavery").

be considered, before exploration of actual Scottish litigation over slaves will show the influence of Grotius in specific cases.

B. STOICISM AND NEOSTOICISM

Ancient Stoicism was hardly a strictly uniform body of thought, consisting, as it did, of a set of doctrines that developed and changed through the centuries.[25] The Stoicism most at issue here, however, is that of Ancient Rome, associated, above all, with Seneca (4 BC–AD 65), Epictetus (c AD 50–130), and the Emperor Marcus Aurelius (AD 121–180), although its thinking influenced others such as, most notably, Cicero, who extensively commented on, criticised, and expounded Stoic ethics. Seneca and Cicero were to exercise particular influence in the Stoic revival because of the accessibility of their works written in Latin.[26]

Whereas the philosophers of the early and middle Stoa were concerned with logic, physics and ethics, those of the Roman Stoa were almost exclusively concerned with the last, focusing on practical and political aspects of the philosophy.[27] Yet, their thinking remained dependent on Stoic physics. Stoics saw the universe as an outward, living expression of the divine *logos* (God) and necessarily rational, that is, governed by laws of cause and effect. Individual human beings were thus also part of and governed by the divine *logos*. A virtuous life was one that was lived in accordance with the divine *logos* of which humanity was part. This participation of all human beings in the divine *logos* entailed that all humans were equal. Common possession of reason meant that all humans had moral obligations to one another. The law of nature required that individuals participate in society. Since nature was by definition good, all evil in the world flowed from human vice. Human vice was the product of the passions uncontrolled by reason, while some passions are rational passions consistent with duties imposed by the *logos:* such as friendship, benevolence, mercy, and sympathy. Human beings ought to use their free will to control the passions and live a virtuous life. All that was morally relevant was what humans could

25 I have found illuminating G Verbeke, "Ethics and Logic in Stoicism", in M J Osier (ed), *Atoms, Pneuma, and Tranquility: Epicurean and Stoic Themes in European Thought* (1991) 11; and "Le stoïcisme, une philosophie sans frontiers", in H Temporini (ed), *Aufstieg und Niedergang der Römischen Welt: Geschichte und Kultur Roms im Spiegel der Neuren Forschung* (1973) vol I-4, 3–42, Colish, *Stoic Tradition* (n 13); E Zeller, *The Stoics, Epicureans and Sceptics*, trans O J Reichel (1870).

26 See Colish, *Stoic Tradition* (n 12) vol i, 7–152.

27 Ibid vol i, 12–21.

control through the exercise of their reason. Everything else was morally neutral or irrelevant: *adiaphora*.[28]

Stoics also emphasised the importance of cosmopolitanism. Individuals were citizens of the world. The citizenship of any individual state was not significant. The rational equality of all human beings in a universal moral community necessitated this. Stoicism, however, did not emphasise participation in actual public life as necessarily significant. A virtuous man might well participate in public life; but it was not such participation that made him virtuous – a life of private contemplation could also be virtuous. In fact, Stoicism did not develop any political theory as such; a failure of any actual society to approximate to the Stoic ideal did not justify rebellion of revolt. The wise Stoic would still serve an imperfect society as best he could.[29] The Stoic slave would endure.[30]

This makes Lipsius' contribution to the Stoic revival particularly interesting. His major Stoic works are the early *De constantia libri duo* (1584) and his later studies, *Manuductio ad stoicam philosophiam* (1604) and *Physiologia stoicorum* (1604).[31] A noted textual scholar, as indeed his interests required him to be, he also edited Seneca, publishing his edition in 1605.[32] One of Lipsius' earlier works had been his magisterial edition of Tacitus (1574), raising the interesting issue of the impact of the thought of this historian on the revival of Stoicism with which Lipsius is associated. Tacitus' works were a major source of information on prominent Stoics, most notably, Seneca, whom he depicts as a hypocrite. The Roman historian's relationship to Stoicism is at best ambiguous.[33] This makes particularly crucial Lipsius' collection of information about the government of the ancient world in *Politicorum sive civile doctrinae libri sex* (1589). This humanistic work was a collection drawn from the writings primarily of ancient historians, in which were woven together quotations with Lipsius' commentary. In the compilation of this work, Tacitus and Tacitean *prudentia* featured strongly.[34]

28 This account is derived from ibid vol i, 22–60.

29 Ibid vol i, 38–41. The attempt in A Erskine, *The Hellenistic Stoa: Political Thought and Action* (1990) to discuss the politics of the Middle Stoa has been subject to a stringent critique: P Green, "Philosophers, kings and democracy, or, how political was the Stoa" (1994) 14 *Ancient Philosophy* 147–156.

30 Colish, *Stoic Tradition* (n 12) vol i, 36–37.

31 Saunders, *Justus Lipsius* (n 10) 54–56.

32 Ibid.

33 M Morford, *Stoics and Neostoics: Rubens and the circle of Lipsius* (1991) 139–180; on Tacitus and Stoicism, see Colish, *Stoic Tradition* (n 12) vol i, 304–313.

34 See M Morford, "Tacitean *prudentia* and the Doctrines of Justus Lipsius", in T J Luce and A J Woodman (eds), *Tacitus and the Tacitean Tradition* (1993) 129 (henceforth Morford,

A work manifestly conceived to serve modern political ends, it allowed Lipsius to articulate how a *vita civilis* for a society of men, requiring a Stoic subjugation of the passions, should best be achieved in practice through the exercise of prudent and virtuous princely government.[35] Scholars, such as Gerhard Oestreich, have thus seen Lipsius as the apologist or propagandist for the Europe of absolutist princes.[36] But what one may note here is the extent to which it is possible for the Neostoicism associated with Lipsius to be permeated with the influence of Tacitus.

Oestreich has also argued that Grotius was strongly influenced by Lipsius.[37] What he is concerned with is Grotius' view of sovereignty and government. Grotius had a strong and legalistic view of sovereignty, which he argued could be exercised by a variety of different types of government. The crucial point was the extent to which individuals gave up their individual rights in certain respects to a sovereign.[38] This, as we shall see, is crucial in Grotius' account of slavery.

C. GROTIUS AND NATURAL LAW

Central to Grotius' account of natural law is human beings' capacity for society. In the *De iure belli ac pacis*, he is concerned to stress in the *Prolegomena* § 6 (to use the conventional numbering) that human beings possess an *appetitus societatis*. As Laurens Winkel has demonstrated, Grotius, in later editions of the work, emphasised a Stoic source for this idea, in the concept of οἰκείωσις (*oikeiosis*), while also adding in further relevant references to Stoic authors.[39] It is worth noting, however, that Grotius increasingly wished to stress the foundation of this fundamental idea of his natural law in the Stoic cosmopolis.[40] Humans had the capacity to know and to act according to

"Tacitean *prudentia*"); on the *Politica*, see Oestreich, *Neostoicism and the Early Modern State* (n 8) 39–75.

35 See, e.g., M van Gelderen, "The Machiavellian Moment and the Dutch Revolt: the Rise of Neostoicism and Dutch Republicanism", in G Bock, Q Skinner and M Viroli (eds), *Machiavelli and Republicanism* (1990) 205 at 206–210; Morford, "Tacitean *prudentia*" (n 34); G Oestreich, "Die Antike Literatur als Vorbild der praktischen Wissenschaften im 16. und 17. Jahrhundert", in R R Bolgar (ed), *Classical Influences on European Culture A.D. 1500–1700: Proceedings of an International Conference Held at King's College Cambridge April 1974* (1976) 315.

36 Oestreich, *Neostoicism and the Early Modern State* (n 8) passim.

37 Ibid 36–37, 51, 58.

38 See Haakonssen, "Hugo Grotius" (n 6) at 240–247.

39 Winkel, "Les origines antiques" (n 11) at 394–395.

40 See also Grotius, *De iure belli ac pacis* (n 5) 1.1.3.

general rules in order to secure society; the protection of which in conformity with human intellect was the source of law.[41] Humankind had thus to use their will to govern their passions in order to live in the society they craved. The "mother of natural law" was thus human nature, which impelled us to seek out mutual society; the "mother of civil law" was that obligation created by consent, which derived its obligatory force from natural law. Nonetheless, expediency (*utilitas*) reinforced the natural law, as the *Auctor naturae* had decreed that human weakness and need for many things to live properly (*ad vitam recte ducendam*) would make us promote society. Expediency (*utilitas*) also gave occasion for Civil Law: this was because that which we have called *consociatio* or *subiectio* began to be instituted by reason of such expediency (*utilitas*).[42]

Natural law (*ius naturale*) was the "dictate of right reason", that is, an act was either morally necessary or morally wicked according to whether or not it was in conformity (*convenientia*) with rational nature itself.[43] Likewise, that was unjust (*iniustum*) that was contrary to the nature of a society of those who used reason.[44] Reinforcing the emphasis on rational nature and sociability was Grotius' argument that a priori proof of the law of nature required proof of the necessary conformity (*convenientia*) or otherwise of something with "rational and social nature" (*a posteriori* proof required demonstration that something was thought to be the law of nature by all nations).[45] All of this indeed suggests the influence of Stoicism – and of Cicero – rather than of Aristotelian scholasticism. Nonetheless, Grotius has clearly also conceded rather a lot to expediency as the source of social obligations.

Grotius also stressed that *ius* was what was just (*iustum*) and that this was best described negatively, so that a *ius* was what was not unjust (*iniustum*), which was that which was contrary to the nature of a rational society. There could be a *societas* that was equal, such as those between brothers, citizens, friends and allies; there could also be an unequal *societas*, such as those between father and children, master and slave, king and subjects, and God and men. The equal *societas* gave rise to *ius Aequatorium*, the unequal to *ius Rectorium*.[46] He also pointed out that *ius* could also refer to a body of

41 Ibid Prolegomena, §§ 7–8.
42 Ibid Prolegomena, § 16.
43 Ibid 1.1.10.
44 Ibid 1.1.3.
45 Ibid 1.1.12.
46 Ibid 1.1.3.

rights that an individual possesses. These could either be perfect (*facultas*) or imperfect (*aptitudo*).[47] Grotius conceived *of facultas* or *ius proprium* using Roman legal categories: he included under the term authority over oneself, which was freedom, over others, which was either paternal authority or ownership (that is of slaves), full ownership or lesser rights of ownership and contractual rights.[48] The term *facultas* covered both the private rights of individuals and public rights.[49] Grotius further argued that *ius* had the third meaning of *Lex*, in the sense of a rule commanding us to do what is morally right. This could be either the *ius naturale* or the *ius voluntarium.*[50] We have already seen how Grotius defined the *ius naturale*; *ius voluntarium* was either human or divine. Human voluntary law was either: *ius civile* (the law of a state); wider than the *ius civile*, such as the *ius gentium*, the law of all, or many nations; or narrower than the *ius civile*, such as the commands of a father or master (*praecepta patria, dominica*).[51]

(1) Grotius and slavery

Grotius' main discussions of slavery come in three chapters of the *De iure belli ac pacis*: in Book 2, cap 5, *De acquisitione originaria iuris in personas: ubi de iure parentum; de matrimoniis: de collegiis: de iure in subditos: servos*; in Book 3, cap 7, *De iure in captivos*; and in Book 3, cap 14, *Temperamentum circa captos*. The first of these loosely reflects categories of Roman law, while the other two deal with one of the main explanations for how slavery arises. Grotius' texts on slavery are thus divided into two groupings. The first of these (in the first and second books) generally concerns how slavery can arise *naturaliter*, or at least in a fashion that is not *iniustum*, according to the *ius naturale*; the second grouping principally deals with slavery under the *ius gentium*. There are other incidental mentions of slavery in other parts of the work. Indeed, his mentions of *dominica potestas* as a *facultas*, a *ius proprium*, while *praecepta dominica* were a form of *ius voluntarium humanum* have already been noted. The rest of this section will be devoted to a close and detailed examination of Grotius' texts on slavery.[52]

47 Ibid 1.1.4.
48 Ibid 1.1.5.
49 ibid 1.1.6.
50 Ibid 1.1.9.
51 Ibid 1.1.13–14.
52 Most of this will consist of a paraphrase and commentary. As will be obvious, in making the paraphrase I have availed myself freely of the Kelsey translation (n 5).

The first significant mention of slavery in *De iure belli ac pacis* comes in Grotius' discussion of sovereignty (*summa potestas*). After arguing that sovereign power is that whose actions cannot be subject to the legal control of another, he is anxious to argue that sovereignty does not everywhere reside in the people. He argues that anyone is permitted to assign himself in private servitude to whomsoever he should choose as appears by both Roman and Jewish law. In the same way a people can submit itself irrevocably to one person or several persons.[53] This theme continues in the chapter *De acquisitione originaria juris in personas*. Having explained that such rights are acquired by generation, consent and delict (*crime*), he states that subjection to another arising from consent is either public or private. There are many forms of private voluntary subjection of which the noblest type is *arrogatio*.[54] The basest type of voluntary subjection is that by which a man gives himself into complete slavery (*in servitutem perfectam*). After discussing examples of this practice, Grotius explains this institution of voluntary slavery as being "without excessive harshness if kept within natural limits" (*in terminis naturalibus*). *Servitus perfecta* was the perpetual giving of labour (*perpetuae operae*) in return for aliment and the other necessities of life. Indeed, he comments that it has the benefit of certainty of aliment, which those who are day labourers lack. A benefit he supports by a reference to the histories of Posidonius Stoicus.[55] He adds that masters do not have the *ius vitae ac necis* over slaves (*de plena et interna iustitia*), "for no man is entitled to kill another man except for commission of a capital offence". The laws of some peoples (*quorundam populorum legibus*), however, provided that a master, who has killed his slave, for whatever reason, is left unpunished, just as is the case everywhere for kings who have the most unrestricted power. He justifies this analogy by reference to Seneca, before pointing out that the fact that, while his master may injure the slave with impunity, that does not mean that the master has a right (*ius*) to injure the slave, as Seneca also affirms.[56]

Grotius therefore is clear that individuals, having the natural right of liberty, can use that liberty to place themselves in slavery or perpetual servitude. He does not ground this on a Stoic position, although he is willing to use Stoic authors for supporting historical evidence. He also considers

53 Grotius, *De iure belli ac pacis* (n 5) 1.3.8.
54 Ibid 2.5.26.
55 Ibid 2.5.27.
56 Ibid 2.5.28

that ownership of others was a *ius proprium*,[57] creating an unequal *societas*, where the master had a *ius Rectorium*.[58] These rights of masters over slaves are analogous to those of a sovereign over subjects. Thus, just as individuals can subject themselves to a sovereign, thereby departing from a state of nature or universal society, so an individual can subject himself to another individual as a slave. Sovereignty and slavery give the sovereign and the master a similar *facultas moralis*.[59] What this seems to suggest is that while, by the law of nature, no one is a slave, the law of nature gives one the capacity to enter freely into servitude.

Grotius next turns in this chapter to the difficult question of the status of the children of slaves. He points out that, by Roman law and the law of nations concerning captives (*Romano iure & iure gentium circa captivos*), just as with animals, the offspring of human beings in a servile state follow the status of the mother. He argues that this was not according to the law of nature in cases where the father can also be known and concludes that children are not less likely to follow the status of the father than the mother, if the *lex civilis* is silent on the point.[60] This leaves the point somewhat unclear, but he later states that the children of parents, one of whom is free, the other a slave, *naturaliter* seem to be in a state of *imperfecta servitus*, the type of status in which are individuals such as *nexi, ascriptitii glebae, statuliberi*, and *liberti*. Such individuals are in slavery temporarily, or under a condition, or for certain purposes.[61]

He then goes on to deal with the issue of children born to parents both of whom are slaves. Would such children *naturaliter* be of that status? He argues that, if there is no other way for the children to be brought up, then parents have the power to surrender their future children to that status, especially since in such circumstances parents are allowed to sell their children into slavery. This right (*ius*) has arisen *naturaliter* from necessity; otherwise parents are not allowed to sell their children into slavery. The right of the master over slave progeny derives from his provision of food and other necessities of life to them; this means that, since the children of slaves will not provide a return for such provisions for a long time, they are not permitted to flee from their status of slavery until they have returned to the master enough for the aliment received. On the other hand, the slaves of

57 Ibid 1.1.5.
58 Ibid 1.1.3.
59 On this see Haakonssen, "Hugo Grotius" (n 6) at 244.
60 Grotius, *De iure belli ac pacis* (n 5) 2.5.29; see also 2.8.18.
61 Ibid 2.5.30.

a grossly cruel master are entitled to run away from him, even if they have given themselves into slavery voluntarily. He explains that the prohibitions made by the Apostles against slaves fleeing their masters do not apply here, as those prohibitions were directed against those who mistakenly argued that all subjection, whether private or public, was contrary to Christian liberty.[62]

The children of a slave parent and free parent are thus in some way temporary slaves, while children sold into slavery because of necessity or born to slave parents are naturally (*naturaliter*) slaves in return for the aliment and support they receive. Presumably the temporary slavery is justified on a similar ground. Again, it is obvious that, for Grotius, what is also a significant issue here is sovereignty. Once more he stresses that *publica subiectio*, as distinct from *subiectio privata* (slavery) is the condition arising when a people surrenders itself to one man or even another people.

What Grotius has been discussing so far is slavery (and the linked topic of sovereignty) under the rubric of the original acquisition of a *ius* over other individuals. It is obvious that the state of slavery could not have existed for Grotius in the original simple and primitive position of humanity: when all property was in common, neither could individuals have the need to sell themselves or their children for support, nor could such a state of individual ownership of another human being exist. While by an act of will, individuals could subject themselves to slavery, slave children seem to have been in that status *naturaliter* from necessity. Grotius generally allowed necessity to override other rights, especially property rights.[63] He here seems to have considered that the same principle, that of survival, allowed the enslavement of children. It is important to note, however, that though slave children acquired that status *naturaliter*, it was not a status enjoined by the *ius naturae*.

Thus, while Grotius does allude to Aristotle's view that some men were slaves by nature,[64] he also implicitly attacks this view in a passage that argues that an unjust cause of war would be the desire to rule others against their will on the claim that it would be for their own benefit. This was because it would be to subdue such individuals "as if they deserved to be enslaved, and were slaves by nature (*naturaliter*) as the philosophers call them". Further, "[t]hose who have the use of reason ought to have the free choice of the *utile* and the *inutile*, unless some type of right over them has been acquired by

62 Ibid 2.5.29.
63 Ibid 2.2.6–8.
64 Ibid 1.3.8.

someone else". The slavery of children could be justified when it was in their interest, as they were not able to exercise free choice.[65]

Grotius, however, also argues that slaves should be contented with their lot. Again the context is an analogy with war by a people who have lost their freedom. The search for liberty (*libertas*) – αὐτονομία – was not a just cause for war by either individuals or peoples, "as if it was fitted by nature (*naturaliter*) and always for everyone whomsoever they might be". Thus the liberty that is said to be belong to men and peoples has to be understood as the liberty of the *ius naturae* that precedes all human deeds (*de jure naturae praecedente factum omne humanum*). A human deed or action such as consent or crime could give rise to a state of slavery. This liberty is a liberty that meant that by nature (*natura*) no one is a slave, not that one does not have the right (*ius*) to enter into slavery, since in this sense no one is free. Grotius supports this view with a saying from Albutius drawn from Seneca: "No one is born free, no one a slave; fortune afterwards imposes these names on individuals." From Aristotle is quoted the view that whether or not one was a slave was a matter of law (*lex*). Finally, the Apostle Paul is quoted to bolster the view that those who have come into slavery through a *legitima causa* should be content with their lot: "Hast thou been called a slave? Be not concerned thereat."[66]

By the *ius naturae*, therefore, everyone is free. Such freedom, however, includes the freedom to sell oneself into slavery. Moreover, children acquire the status of slave *naturaliter*, either through birth to slave parents, or through sale by their parents in case of necessity. There is no trace here of the Aristotelian idea that some are slaves by nature; a measure of Stoicism comes through in some of the justifications given by Grotius and his stress that the slave ought to be contented with his lot. Nonetheless, for Grotius these rules are not at all contrary to natural law; in fact they are perfectly consonant with his ideas of natural justice. Slavery was perfectly consonant with a rational society. It was not *iniustum*.[67] Nor was it a product of voluntary law, although the orders between a master and his slave were a minor form of *ius voluntarium humanum*, which the slave did not need to obey if contrary to the laws of God or criminal in nature.[68]

It is obvious that much of Grotius' discussion of the slavery of individuals is necessitated by his seeing sovereignty over a people and mastery over an

65 Ibid 2.22.12.
66 Ibid 2.22.11.
67 Ibid 3.7.1.
68 Ibid 2.26.3 (the sources for this are St Paul and Seneca).

individual as deriving from a similar *facultas moralis*. In a sense his approach to sovereignty required him to have such an attitude to slavery, especially when his idea of natural law was so minimal.

In 3.7, *De iure in captivos*, Grotius turns to the law of slavery according to the *ius gentium*, that is according to the *ius voluntarium*, rather than the *ius naturale*. Stressing again the limited sense in which slavery was *contra naturam*, he points out that it is compatible with *iustitia naturalis* that slavery should originate in a human act, that is by agreement or crime (*pactione aut delicto*). He now argues that, by the law of nations (*ius gentium*), slavery has a wider scope, both as regards persons and effects. Thus, as well as those who give themselves or promise themselves as slaves, all those captured in war are enslaved. This proposition is backed with a number of historical examples.[69] Furthermore, not only prisoners of war, but also their descendants in perpetuity become slaves. Here the children follow the status of the mother, a view supported by the *Digest* and Tacitus.[70] Moreover, according to the *ius gentium*, the authority of masters over their slaves is unlimited: they can inflict any cruelty on them; the only limitations on such brutality are those, if any, set by the *lex civilis*. Moreover, anything captured with the slave is acquired by the master.[71]

Grotius gives the traditional explanation that the *ius gentium* encouraged the enslavement of prisoners of war in place of killing them, quoting the Roman jurist Pomponius for the derivation of slaves (*servi*) from the verb to save (*servare*). The enslavement takes place, not because of any pact between captor and captive, but by the *ius gentium* to encourage mercy. For the same reason, this right (*ius*) can be transferred to others, just like the ownership of things. It has also been agreed, Grotius reports, that ownership (*dominium*) extends to any children born, as their very birth takes place only because the captors did not use their full right to kill. The nations also accept that the status of children here follows that of the mother, as slave unions are neither regulated by law nor monitored sufficiently carefully for certainty as to the father. While Ulpian had described this rule as according to the law of nature, Grotius explains that this law is rather a general custom that has developed from natural reason (*ratio naturalis*). Precise ownership of individual captives is determined by the law of nations on booty.[72]

The issue of captives who flee next occupies Grotius. Those who flee to

69 Grotius, *De iure belli ac pacis* (n 5) 3.7.1. See also ibid 3.10.1–2.
70 Ibid 3.7.2; D 1.5.5.1; Tacitus, *Annales* 1.59.
71 Grotius, *De iure belli ac pacis* (n 5) 3.7.3–4.
72 Ibid 3.7.5.

their own nation while the war in which they have been captured is still being waged regain their freedom on the principle of *postliminium*; if, however, they do so after peace has been concluded, or run away to another nation, then they should be returned to their master should he reclaim them. This form of slavery is only binding externally on the slave, not on his conscience. There are many forms of ownership and this type is only binding in the *iudicium humanum*. Moreover, since this is a law, not arising from *aequitas naturalis*, but to avoid a greater evil, an interpretation should be favoured that does not render sinful an action otherwise permitted. Those canons which forbid anyone from persuading a slave to desert his master are correct if the slave is a voluntary slave or a slave being justly punished; if, however, the slaves are captured in an unjust war or born to captives, Christianity shows that they should be patient, rather than engage in acts, which, though permitted, might offend those whose spirits are foreign to Christianity or are otherwise weak. The advice of the Apostles to slaves is to be obedient, which is in line with *naturalis aequitas*, since the provision of aliment and that of services are mutual.[73] This leads Grotius into the argument that it is unjust for slaves to resist a master who is exercising this type of external right (*ius illud externum*). This is because the external right not only means the master has impunity but that the courts will protect his right. If it is permissible to resist a master, then it is permissible to resist the magistrate, even when, according to the *ius gentium*, the magistrate has a duty to protect the master in his ownership. Thus, just as it is not legally or morally permissible to resist the magistrate, so it is likewise with the slave-owner: a point reinforced by a quotation from Augustine.[74]

Grotius next points out that the law of nations on captives has not always been received, although the Romans described it as universal. Moreover, he also points out that this practice is not observed among ourselves, so that those captured in war do not become slaves and subject to sale, to labour, and to suffer all else that slaves endure. The Muslims also do not follow this practice among themselves.[75]

In his chapter *De postliminio*, Grotius discusses the rights that are recovered by *postliminium*, that is by the return of individuals or by the recovery of property after capture in war. Among such recovered rights of property are listed those over male and female slaves, even after they have

73 Ibid 3.7.6.
74 Ibid 3.7.7.
75 Ibid 3.7.8–9.

been alienated several times or manumitted. For recovery of the right of ownership of a slave, it is probably necessary that the master actually gain physical possession of the slave. For the further elaboration of these rules, Grotius refers to the writers on the Roman law.[76]

In the chapter *Temperamentum circa captos*, Grotius further develops the theme of how slaves ought to be treated. He first argues that in those parts where capture and slavery of men are customary (*in more*), their acquisition, on the model of that of *res*, ought to be limited, according to *interna iustitia*, to the amount of an original or successive debt. The only exception being when the individual has committed a particular crime (*peculiare delictum*) that justly (*aequitas*) deserves loss of liberty. This is the limit of the right (*ius*) that arises over those captured in a just war; a right that may be validly transferred to others.[77] Thus, morally, an enslaved captive is not necessarily justly made a slave for life.[78]

The rest of this chapter goes on to consider how such slaves should be treated. The *ius* that arose in this way over captives was not so extensive as that over those who were enslaved as a punishment. Grotius argues that the general right over captives in a just war is no greater than the right masters have over those who, because of poverty, sell themselves into slavery. This means that the basis for this slavery is perpetual obligation to perform services in return for a perpetual obligation to provide aliment. Here comes a distinction between the *ius gentium* (*ius voluntarium humanum*) and *naturalis ratio:* the former permits much more to be done to a slave with impunity than the latter. On this point, Grotius cites a number of passages from Seneca, St Paul, and early Christian authors. Thus, he is concerned to emphasise that masters should restrain their actions against their slaves. Even if the *ius gentium* provides no sanction against such actions, masters should be guided by the *iudicia interna* and control what they do.[79]

This means that the *ius vitae necisque* that masters hold over slaves is held as a domestic jurisdiction and should only be exercised with the same scrupulousness in which a public jurisdiction would be exercised. In other words, Grotius is emphasising that masters ought not to understand this *ius* as giving them unfettered authority over their slaves: again quoting passages from Seneca he is concerned to argue that they have to consider not what

76 Ibid 3.9.11.

77 Ibid 3.14.1; on the comparison with captured property, see ibid 3.13.1–4.

78 Grotius also emphasises, as earlier in discussing killing in war (ibid 3.11), the duty to exercise equity and goodness and discriminate among captives.

79 Ibid 3.14.2.

they can do to a slave with impunity, but rather what the nature of equity and goodness permits (*aequi bonique natura*).[80] In even minor punishments, such as beating, it is necessary to be aware of equity and mercy (*aequitas . . . et clementia*): again Seneca (along with the Bible and Philo) is cited.[81] Grotius also stresses that the work exacted from slaves and their health should be humanely considered. He points out that the Jewish Sabbath was intended to secure this to give a rest to slaves, while citing a great many classical authors (again including Seneca) to the effect that slaves should be well-treated.[82]

Grotius returns to the point that there is a certain reciprocity in slavery: slaves give their services in return for aliment. The master's duty in this respect is set out by quotations from Cicero, Seneca, Cato, Aristotle and the jurist Marcian. Grotius draws further on Seneca to argue that in certain issues a slave is free. This occurs when the slave confers a benefit on his master by voluntarily – rather than by command – carrying out some action that exceeds his duty as a slave: the slave has crossed the boundary from service to friendship. This idea is in harmony with the notion that if a slave has saved something in his leisure hours, it is his own. Such a *peculium* is a "natural patrimony", just as a servile *contubernium* is a "natural marriage". In other words, it seems that the slave has a natural right to it, even if the master can take it away at will, since if he does so without reason (*sine causa*), he does so without justice (*aequitas*). Such removal of the *peculium* would presumably be contrary to *iustitia interna*. A cause would include not only punishment of the slave, however, but also the master's necessity, since the *utilitas* of the slave is subordinate to that of the master, just as that of the citizen is to the state: all this is again illustrated by an apposite quotation from Seneca. Grotius next discusses some of the consequence of this approach, dealing with the natural obligations of slaves. He points out that some peoples have allowed slaves greater rights of acquisition. The laws (*leges*) of some nations have even reduced the external *ius* of masters to the level of the *interna iustitia*, which is the object of the present discussion. Beneficence and humanity have often led to the emancipation of slaves for long service and emancipation followed the *ius gentium*'s recognition of slavery. Finally, Grotius points to Plutarch's criticism of Cato the Elder for selling slaves exhausted through old age: "forgetful of that common nature that there is between humans".[83]

80 Ibid 3.14.3.
81 Ibid 3.14.4.
82 Ibid 3.14.5.
83 Ibid 3.14.6.

He next points out that those who have been captured in a just war are not entitled to escape; this is because they, by the common agreement of nations (*ex conventione gentium communi*), owe these services in the name of their *civitas*.[84] Grotius also returns to the vexed question of the children born to those enslaved this way and whether they are bound to the master by the *internum ius*. He stresses that, if the parents were enslaved for crimes deserving death, then their future children would be bound to a life of slavery, as otherwise they would not have been born. Moreover, as already stated, parents can sell their children into slavery. For future children born to enslaved parents, their slavery can only be due to two causes: either the express consent of their parents along with the necessity of supporting such children, in which case the state of slavery may be perpetual; or the mere provision of aliment by the master, in which case the slavery ought only to last until the costs have been repaid by services. Any rights beyond these given to masters derived from the *lex civilis*, rather than from equity (*ex lege civili . . . plus aequo*).[85]

This has been a lengthy and somewhat complicated discussion. I shall draw out a few themes here. While, for Grotius, individuals are not slaves according to the *ius naturae*, slavery is not contrary to the law of nature, in so far as individuals, being free, could enslave themselves by contract or be enslaved as an appropriate punishment. Moreover, children could be sold into slavery through necessity, while the children of slaves are enslaved in return for the aliment they necessarily receive. Slavery does not exist because some individuals were slavish by nature. By the *ius voluntarium*, captives in war become slaves. While, by the *internum iudicium* and *interna iustitia*, there might be restrictions on how masters treat these slaves, their status is governed by the *ius gentium* and by the *ius civile* of individual states. The restrictions on the rights of masters and duties of slaves enjoined by *interna iustitia* are binding in conscience: masters were reminded that they should always be aware of the fact that the slave is a fellow human being.

Slavery in fact seems generally to be justified by Grotius on the grounds of debts owed. The individual who contracts to become a slave owes labour in return for aliment; slave children have to work to pay off the cost of their upkeep; enslaved prisoners of war are working to pay off the debt of their people to the other party in the war. This reciprocity entails restrictions on the

84 Ibid 3.14.7.

85 Ibid 3.14.8. Grotius concludes this chapter with the practice among nations who do not enslave their captives: ibid 3.14.9.

rights of masters; but these restrictions are binding only in conscience. Stoic influence can be detected in Grotius' stress that masters should remember that they share a common humanity with their slaves. In a sense, masters should remember to use their reason to control their passions. Moreover, Stoic moralising drawn from Seneca supports much of Grotius' account of the restrictions on slavery through the *interna iusticia*. While the *iudicium publicum* and the *ius gentium* or *leges civiles* might give unfettered power to masters (such as the *ius vitae necisque*), masters should control their actions by reference to the *iudicium internum*. In a similar fashion, while slaves might be bound only in conscience by the *interna iusticia*, they should respect the *ius gentium* or the *ius humanum voluntarium* and remember that, rather than flee, they should exercise a Stoic self command and endure their lot and serve as best as they could. Again this is supported by Stoic moralising and by quotations from St Paul and other Christian authors.

(2) Slaves, Scots law, and the reception of Grotius

It is important to set out some of the background to the Scottish cases that considered these issues. In 1713, by the Treaty of Utrecht, Great Britain acquired the contract – the *asiento* – to import slaves into the Spanish Indies. The government sold this potential bonanza to the South Sea Company for £7,500,000. We need not consider the vagaries of this and the Company's famous collapse thereafter.[86] It is one simple indication of the extent to which Britain as a country and the British as a people were deeply involved in the transatlantic slave trade in the eighteenth century. And this was indeed a British concern. After the Union with England in 1707, Scottish participation in the trade with the North American and Caribbean colonies and with India was vigorous. This trade, Scottish investment in the colonies, and Scottish service in the armies led to the bringing to Scotland of individuals who had been held as slaves in the colonies. In general, such men and women seem to have continued to be held as slaves in Scotland. Thus, I have so far found eleven individuals (including a mother with her baby) being offered for sale by advertisements in the Scottish newspapers. I have also traced over thirty advertisements for runaways, some of which make it perfectly clear that the individual involved was held as a slave. These individuals were generally all, of course, black (except for one native American youth, a persistent runaway from his master in Glasgow).

86 See, e.g., Thomas, *The Slave Trade* (n 22) 235.

I have also found references to quite a considerable number of other black individuals in Scotland, whose status is generally unclear, although one of them appears to have been given his freedom. They were not all of African origin, however; a number of these slaves came from India. Many were obviously house servants chosen for their exotic looks and were frequently dressed in elaborate liveries (especially when featured in exotic dress in portraits with their owners, in which their wearing of slave collars was usually obvious). Others exercised menial tasks or had been sent temporarily to Scotland to learn a trade, such as carpentry, that would enhance their value in the colonies.[87]

Scots law in itself had little to say on the status of such individuals. Scots lawyers were, of course, familiar with the writings of Grotius, Pufendorf and others of the natural law school. It was typical for Scots in the era when they commonly studied law in the Netherlands to take a *collegium Grotianum* from one of the professors whose classes they attended. For example, many took such a class with Ph R Vitriarius, for long the teacher they favoured most at Leiden.[88] I have found some later studying with Barbeyrac.[89] The first chair in law founded in the modern era in Scotland was that of *Public Law and the Law of Nature and Nations* in the University of Edinburgh in 1707.[90] While its first occupier had difficulty in gaining a class, subsequent occupiers of the chair were more successful, and, by the 1760s, the Faculty of Advocates was encouraging its intrants to attend the classes given by Professor Bruce, the current holder.[91] Bruce taught from a compend of Grotius' *De iure belli ac pacis*, specially published in Edinburgh.[92]

If Scots law said little on slavery, there was material in it arguably compatible with slavery. First, colliers and salters lived a quasi-servile life, frequently described as equivalent to being *ascriptitii glebae*. Statute forbade

87 See generally Cairns, "Scottish law of slavery" (n 24).

88 K van Strien and M Ahsmann, "Scottish law students at Leiden at the end of the seventeenth century: the correspondence of John Clerk, 1694–97" (1992) 19 *Lias* 271 at 290–293, 297.

89 See, e.g., T Dundas to C Mackie, 10 January 1728 in Edinburgh University Library, MS La II.91.

90 J W Cairns, "Importing our Lawyers from Holland: Netherlands' Influences on Scots Law and Lawyers in the Eighteenth Century", in G G Simpson (ed), *Scotland and the Low Countries, 1124–1994* (1996) 136 at 148–149.

91 See A Stewart (ed), *The Minute Book of the Faculty of Advocates. Volume 3, 1751–1783*, Stair Society vol 46 (1999) 94, 112 and 119. For a discussion, see J W Cairns, "The Influence of Smith's Jurisprudence on Legal Education in Scotland", in P Jones and A S Skinner (eds), *Adam Smith Reviewed* (1992) 168.

92 *Hugonis Grotii de jure belli ac pacis librorum III. compendium, in usum studiosae juventutis Academiae Edinensis* (1760). I intend to discuss this compend elsewhere.

them to quit their employment. They could not be bought and sold and their children were not *ascriptitii* until they opted for the parental profession; but, when the colliery or salt pans were sold, they passed to the new master.[93] The first act ameliorating their condition came in 1775.[94] Secondly, what very much opened Scots law to the influence of the discussions of slavery by the authors on the law of nature and nations was the tendency of Scots lawyers to argue seriously from the *ius naturale* and *ius gentium* in the written pleadings that were the major way of developing legal argument in eighteenth-century Scottish procedure.[95]

This emphasis on the *ius naturale* and the conscious location of Scots law within a framework derived from the law of nature and nations had a long tradition, going back at least to the *Jus feudale* of Thomas Craig written around 1600.[96] For Craig, it largely served to justify reliance on Roman and Canonist sources in Scots law because of their *aequitas*. By 1700, the development of the modern school of natural law had transformed the possibilities that arose from such arguments. Here one can glance at Lord Stair, author *of Institutions of the Law of Scotland*, first printed in 1681, but substantially written by the early 1660s. He provides an account of law that is closely derived from that of Grotius, although Stair preserved a greater role for the divine will in natural law than did the Dutch author, and was also strongly influenced by Scottish Presbyterian thought.[97] Stair starts his account with the very Grotian (and Stoic?) remark:

> Law is the dictate of reason, determining very rational being to that which is congruous and convenient for the nature and condition thereof; and this will extend to the determination of the indifferency of all rational beings. Even God Almighty, though he be accountable to, and controllable by none, and so hath the absolute freedom of his choice, yet doth he unchangeably determine himself

93 C A Whatley, "The Dark Side of the Enlightenment? Sorting out Serfdom", in T M Devine and J R Young (eds), *Eighteenth-century Scotland: New Perspectives* (1999) 259. An older and highly sensationalised attitude to the position of colliers and salters can be found in Anon, "Slavery in modern Scotland" (1899) 189 *Edinburgh Review* 119.

94 15 Geo III, c 28. The legislation was instigated by coalmasters such as the Earl of Abercorn on economic grounds.

95 See J W Cairns, "Historical Introduction", in K G C L Reid and R Zimmermann (eds), *A History of Private Law in Scotland: Volume 1: Introduction and Property* (2000) 14 at 120–122, 137–138.

96 See J W Cairns, "The Civil Law Tradition in Scottish Legal Thought", in D L Carey Miller and R Zimmermann (eds), *The Civilian Tradition and Scots Law: Aberdeen Quincentenary Essays* (1997) 191 at 200–203.

97 See J D Ford, "Stair's Title 'Of Liberty and Servitude'", in A D E Lewis and D J Ibbetson (eds), *The Roman Law Tradition* (1994) 135–158; P G Stein, "Legal thought in eighteenth-century Scotland" (1957) *Juridical Review* 1 at 4–5.

> by his goodness, righteousness, and truth; which therefore make the absolute sovereign divine law.[98]

Moreover, there was "an inclination in the will to observe and follow those dictates, which is justice".[99] Private rights of men were constituted by either divine or human laws.[100] Divine law was that "which is written in man's heart . . . This is the law of nature, known naturally, either immediately, like unto those instincts which are in the other creatures." This meant that the first principles of natural law were "known to men without reasoning or experience . . . and so are known to men everywhere in the world".[101] As well as these principles God gave men reason, "that thence they might deduce by consequence his law in more particular cases".[102] This law was also called "Conscience" and "Equity", "from that equality it keeps amongst all persons". Equity, however, was "also taken for the law of rational nature, whereby nothing is to be done, which is not congruous to human nature".[103] Stair also argued:

> And there is no doubt but there is more of the law of nature founded in the rational nature of man, as he is a rational and sociable creature, so that even that, which appeareth to be in the sensitive nature, is truly founded in the rational nature; and therefore is not properly communicable unto the beasts, who have no law but their natural instincts.[104]

God had also set out the law of nature in Scripture, since man's nature was corrupted by "sin and evil custom".[105] God had also given men voluntary and positive laws.[106] Furthermore:

> Human law is that which, for utility's sake, is introduced by men: which is either by tacit consent, by consuetude or custom, or by express will or command of these in authority, having the legislative power.[107]

These laws were "either common to many nations, or proper to one nation, or peculiar to some places or incorporations in the same nation".[108]

98 J Dalrymple, Viscount Stair, *Institutions of the law of Scotland*, ed D M Walker (1981) 1.1.1.
99 Ibid 1.1.2.
100 Ibid.
101 Ibid 1.1.3.
102 Ibid 1.1.4.
103 Ibid 1.1.5–6.
104 Ibid 1.1.7.
105 Ibid.
106 Ibid 1.1.8–9.
107 Ibid 1.1.10.
108 Ibid.

That common to many nations was "that which is commonly called the law of nations, which stands in the customs owned and acknowledged by all, or at least the most civil nations". This was generally just "the law of nature and reason", but there were also positive laws "introduced by the common consent of nations". These included the "laws of captivity and bondage, of these taken in war". Moreover, "for the same reason [i.e. common utility's sake], though slavery be against the natural law of liberty, yet it is received for conveniency by the nations, being more willing to lose liberty than life".[109] The law of each nation "under the same sovereign authority" is called the Civil Law.[110] Stair then raised the issues of why have human law and what its authority was. The latter he answered by writing:

> [A]s by the law of nature man is a free creature, yet so he may engage himself, and being engaged, by the same law of nature he must perform: so men's laws are nothing else but the public sponsions of princes and people, which therefore even by the law of nature they must perform.

He then enumerated the reasons for having human laws.[111] He also argued that law is a "rational discipline", citing Grotius and Duarenus.[112] He also sets out the three first principles of "equity" or "right" as "obedience, freedom, and engagement". That is: man must obey God; so far as he is not bound to obey God, he is free; his freedom is under his own power, but he can engage himself, and so far as he has engaged himself he is bound. There were also "three prime principles of the positive law", which aimed at "the profit and utility of man". While the natural law was *in aequo*, these were *in bono* or *utili.* These principles were: "society, property, and commerce".[113] Stressing again that "it being our voluntary obliging of ourselves, where by nature we are free",[114] he further stated that the objects of law are "the rights of men". Such rights consisted in a power or faculty. There were three types of rights: personal liberty; dominion; and obligation.[115] Without further analysis, I think it is clear just how much Stair has taken from Grotius.

This emphasis on these three types of rights leads Stair to start with an account "Of Liberty and Servitude", before going on to deal with obligations. Thus, while Stair considered that human beings had a natural liberty, he also

109 Ibid 1.1.11.
110 Ibid 1.1.12.
111 Ibid 1.1.15.
112 Ibid 1.1.17.
113 Ibid 1.1.18.
114 Ibid 1.1.21.
115 Ibid 1.1.22.

pointed out that that liberty was "not absolute, but limited". The fifth way by which liberty might be limited for Stair – in fact "wholly taken away" – was "by bondage, slavery or servitude". He stated that "[b]ondage was introduced by the law of nations, and it is amongst the positive laws of nations settled by common consuetude". Thus, "it took first place in those who were taken by war, who being under the power of their enemies' sword, did lose their liberty in lieu of their life". Moreover, the status of servile offspring "by the custom of nations, and the Roman law, . . . followed the mother and not the father"; 'in some cases . . . free parents might sell and give their children in bondage". He finally remarked:

> Bondage, though contrary to the nature of liberty, yet it is lawful, liberty being a right alienable, and in our disposal, so that the natural law constitutes us free, but puts no necessity on us to continue. And therefore servitude is approven both in the Old Testament and in the New . . . [116]

Stair's remarks on this clearly follow Grotius. We are free; but we can transfer ourselves into slavery. Moreover, we have already seen that he accepted that by the *ius gentium* captives could be enslaved. He also added, however, that:

> Christian lenity and mercy hath almost taken away bondage, except amongst the Spaniards, Portugals, and other Christian nations bordering upon the Turks; where, because the Turks extremely exercise slavery, especially upon Christians, their neighbours do the like, that they may have slaves to exchange with slaves. But little of slavery remains elsewhere among Christians, except the *adscriptitii:* who are not absolutely slaves . . .; but in Scotland there is no such thing.[117]

And later, in his account of probation, he stated:

> The chief general presumptions approved by our customs are these; I. Liberty is presumed in opposition to slavery. Of this presumption we have but little use, slavery being abolished; yet there remains some vestiges of it in colliers and salters, who are astricted to these services by law . . .[118]

Stair thus demonstrates a reception by Scots lawyers of Grotius' thinking on natural law and slavery. His account of Scots law, while stressing that there are no slaves in Scotland nonetheless provided, from Grotius, an account of liberty and servitude that provided an argument for the validity of slavery both under the law of nations and under the principle that individuals, being free, can by contract give themselves into a state of servitude.

116 Ibid 1.2.5–11.
117 Ibid 1.2.11.
118 Ibid 1.2.17.

It thereby had the potential to open up arguments in Scots law to the rules of the law of nature and nations on slavery, or perhaps to demonstrate their compatibility.[119]

D. THE SCOTTISH SLAVERY CASES

There were four civil cases concerning slavery in eighteenth-century Scotland: *Sheddan v Montgomery* (1757); *Spence v Dalrymple* (1770); *Stewart Nicholson v Stewart Nicholson* (1770); *Knight v Wedderburn* (1778). There was also one criminal case, where the Court of Justiciary apparently recognised the panel as a slave: *HMA v Bell alias Belinda* (1771). *Spence v Dalrymple* does not have surviving detailed arguments and will not be discussed here; nor will *Stewart Nicholson*, which dealt with slavery only incidentally (could a black and a slave be a valid witness?). The following discussion will therefore only deal with *Sheddan v Montgomery* and *Knight v Wedderburn*. It will demonstrate how Grotius' account of slavery influenced the arguments of the lawyers and some of the opinions of the judges.[120]

James Montgomery was a black slave, born in Virginia, who was sent to Scotland by his master, Robert Sheddan, to be trained as a carpenter. There he had been baptised by John Witherspoon, minister at Beith. In 1756, Sheddan, after trying to persuade Montgomery to return to Virginia, allegedly kidnapped him and took him forcibly to Port Glasgow to be put aboard a ship for Virginia. Montgomery escaped and fled to Edinburgh where he was arrested and imprisoned under the jurisdiction of the Bailies of the Burgh Court.[121]

On 19 May 1756, Sheddan petitioned the Bailies for the delivery to him of Montgomery. His Petition stressed that, while a modern Scots legal author might say that slavery was abolished, in fact that only applied to the excesses of Roman slavery with the *ius vitae necisque*. Christianity disallowed this. Rather, it argued, "in all Other respects Slavery has been allowed where the publick Utility requires it such is the Case is with our American Collonies". The Petition cited a passage of Grotius for the Stoic view (supported by St Paul) that "those who from a lawful cause have come into personal or

119 There were of course contrary arguments, with which I shall not deal here. It is worth mentioning, however, W Sypher, "Hutcheson and the 'classical' theory of slavery" (1939) 24 *Journal of Negro History* 263.

120 For a further discussion with a different focus, see Cairns, "The Scottish law of slavery" (n 24).

121 See ibid for details. Brief details of the case are found in *Sheddan v A Negro* Mor 14545 (1757).

political slavery ought to be satisfied with their lot".[122] On 19 May 1756, Answers to the Petition were provided on behalf of Montgomery. These stressed that, though the laws of Virginia made him a slave and property, this was not the case in Scotland. The quotations from St Paul and Grotius were dismissed as mere exhortations, having "no Earthly Concern with respect to the Civil or Municipal Laws as to Slavery", while references to "Spiritual freedom" were mere "trifling". Instead, Montgomery's answers stressed Scottish cases and writers.[123] The Bailies found for Sheddan.[124] Montgomery sought advocation of the cause to the Court of Session, where his Bill followed a similar line of reasoning; Sheddan's Answers to the Bill reprised his earlier claims, even to the reliance on Holy Scripture and the same passage of Grotius to prove that slavery was not inconsistent with Christianity.[125]

The Bill of Advocation was reported to the Inner House of the Court of Session by the Lord Ordinary (Lord Bankton) and, in advance of the Court's advising, printed Memorials were produced setting out the legal argument.[126] Sheddan's Memorial stressed that slavery originated both in the practice of sparing captives in war and in the need for the poor sometimes to sell themselves to gain aliment. It argued that an institution "calculated to correct Barbarity to Enemies, and want of attention to our own citizens" could not be argued to be "contrary to Nature".[127] It noted that "we find Slavery by the greater Philosophers adopted". Grotius was cited to support the claim that "the best Writers upon the Law of Nature and Nations hold the Institution of Slavery to be exceeding consistent with both" Christianity and a free government.[128] Scriptural texts were relied on to demonstrate that slavery was not inconsistent with revealed religion, as were texts of Canon law, glossed with Grotius' remark that "the prohibition by which the Apostles and the early canons forbid slaves to leave their masters is a general prohibition, which is opposed to the error of those that denied all subjection, either private or public, as inconsistent with Christian

122 See the Petition of Sheddan in National Archives of Scotland (henceforth NAS), unextracted processes of the Court of Session, CS 234/S/3/12. The passage of Grotius quoted is *De iure belli ac pacis* (n 5) 2.22.11. I have quoted from the Kelsey translation.

123 Answers for James Montgomery, NAS CS 234/S/3/12.

124 See the interlocutor written on the Petition of Sheddan in NAS CS 234/S/3/12.

125 See the Bill of Advocation and the Answers in NAS CS 234/S/3/12.

126 These Memorials dated 9 July 1756 and 23 July 1756 are found in the Advocates Library, Session Papers, Campbell's Collection vol 5, and also in the Signet Library's Collection of Session Papers.

127 Memorial for Robert Sheddan 3–5.

128 Ibid 6; Grotius, De *iure belli ac pacis* (n 5) 2.5. Also cited were Pufendorf and Bodin.

liberty".[129] The Memorial for Montgomery argued that slavery was contrary to the law of nature, but had been introduced by the law of nations, whereby the enslavement of captives in war had been permitted; this was no longer the case among Christians, as Grotius himself pointed out.[130] It quoted a great many Biblical texts to argue against the support of the Bible for slavery, in an attempt to argue that slavery was contrary to the laws of nature and nations.[131] A series of European authors were surveyed along with the laws of a number of European countries to show that slavery was not recognised and that there were instances of slaves from colonies being judged to be free when they landed. The laws of Scotland and England were also explored to produce similar arguments. The practice of slavery in Virginia was roundly condemned, citing Montesquieu's famous criticism of black colonial slavery.[132] Before the litigation was concluded, Montgomery died; there was therefore no final decision, although there is some evidence to suggest that the Court was inclined to uphold the claims of Sheddan.[133]

Joseph Knight had been brought from Africa to Jamaica as a child by a Captain Knight, where he had been sold to John Wedderburn of Ballendean, a Jacobite sitting out an awkward period secure on his family's Jamaican estate. Around 1769, Wedderburn felt safe to return to Scotland and took with him Knight as a servant. From the papers in the case one gets the impression that Knight was very much a favourite of Wedderburn. In Scotland, Knight struck up a relationship with a servant girl of Wedderburn's and a child was conceived. Wedderburn helped with the expense of lying in but dismissed the girl (the child did not survive). Knight married her, and wanted Wedderburn to either take her back or give him a house on the estate in which he could live with her. Wedderburn refused. Knight decided to leave Wedderburn's service in order to gain a job such that he could support a wife, as, of course, he received no wages. Wedderburn had him seized by the Justices of the Peace of Perthshire, who determined he should be returned to Wedderburn as a "perpetual servant". (Knight claimed that "perpetual service" was simply slavery and that he could not

129 Memorial for Robert Sheddan 6–8; Grotius, *De iure belli ac pacis* (n 5) 2.5.29 (I have quoted the Kelsey translation). There was considerable further legal argument about the practice of other countries with which I shall not deal here.

130 Memorial for James Montgomery-Sheddan 5–6; Grotius, *De iure belli ac pacis* (n 5) 3.7.9.

131 Memorial for James Montgomery-Sheddan 6–9.

132 Ibid 9–24; C de Montesquieu, *The Spirit of the Laws*, trans T Nugent, 2nd edn, 2 vols (1752) vol ii, 341–342; see also the modern translation and edition by A Cohler, B Miller and H Stone (1989) 250.

133 See the MS note on the Memorial for Robert Sheddan 1 in the Signet Library.

be compelled to comply, nor could Wedderburn forcibly send him abroad.) Knight succeeded in having the case brought before the Sheriff Substitute of Perthshire, who eventually took it to avizandum before the Sheriff Depute, John Swinton of Swinton.[134]

Knight's case was argued before the Sheriff Substitute and Sheriff Depute basically on the ground of natural liberty, or that, even if he had been a slave in Jamaica, in setting foot in Scotland he became free. Wedderburn's lawyer argued that, although slavery might be "repugnant to natural Liberty", it was "countenanced by the Laws even of these that were most civilized", which was shown by Grotius and Pufendorf and "Indeed every Author of any Credit that has wrote upon the Law of Nations". More particularly, Grotius had laid down the principle "that a person taken captive in a just war and reduced to a State of Slavery, ought not to desert his master".[135] Moreover, it was argued that Wedderburn had purchased Knight when he was very young, and had clothed him and maintained him ever since, and it was only recently that he started to make a return for all this expense. This meant that "independent of his undoubted Right to the said Service, he has a just claim thereto upon the Footing of Natural Equity".[136] This was in obvious reliance on Grotius' arguments about entitlement to the service of slaves in return for the money paid out on their support.[137] On 20 May 1774, Swinton issued the following interlocutor:

> [T]he said Sheriff Depute having advised the process recalled the Interlocutor of the fifth of January last and found That the State of Slavery is not recognised by the Laws of this Kingdom and is inconsistent with the principles thereof and Found that the Regulations in Jamaica concerning Slaves do not extend to this Kingdom and repelled the Defender's Claim to perpetual Service and In respect the pursuer does not alledge wages were agreed to be paid him repelled his claim thereto and decerned.[138]

Wedderburn sought advocation of the cause to the Court of Session in May 1774. On 7 February 1775, counsel for Knight and Wedderburn argued the cause before the Lord Ordinary on the Bills, Robert Bruce of Kennet.

134 For the details see (MS) Extract Process [from the Sheriff Court] Joseph Knight against Sir John Wedderburn of Ballendean, Bart 1774, in NAS CS 235/K/2/2. A brief account is found in *Knight v Wedderburn* Mor 14545 (1778).

135 (MS) Extract Process Knight against Wedderburn 20–21; the reference is probably to Grotius, *De iure belli ac pacis* (n 5) 2.7.6.

136 (MS) Extract Process Knight against Wedderburn 21.

137 See, e.g., Grotius, *De iure belli ac pacis* (n 5) 2.5.29; 3.7.6; 3.14.8; and the discussion above.

138 See (MS) Extract Process Knight against Wedderburn 27–28; see also Diet Book, Sheriff Court of Perthshire, 20 May 1774, NAS SC 49/1/64.

Knight's advocates went so far as to argue that Wedderburn "had no Title to the Property of the Pursuer as a Slave even in the West Indies". This was a short hearing and Lord Kennet, before answer, ordered the parties to give in written memorials by 16 February.[139] Lengthy Memorials were prepared.

Knight's counsel admitted in his Memorial that slavery was known in Africa for captives in war, criminals and descendants of slaves; but he argued that the introduction of articles of luxury from Europe had greatly encouraged the enslavement of individuals for the most petty of reasons in order to gain money from the sale of slaves. Moreover, perpetual petty wars were now carried on purely in order to gain captives to sell as slaves. Princes of the area, when they did not have enough captives or criminals to sell, did not hesitate to sell their own people. All of this was supported by reference to travel literature (and the personal reminiscence of the black servant of Knight's counsel).[140] The importance of this argument was to attack the legitimacy of the enslavement of individuals in Africa: their enslavement did not follow the models set out in Grotius' work and other writings of the modern school of natural law. The Memorial also pointed out that colonial laws did not require the slave trader to prove that he came by the slaves properly and generally assumed that all black men were validly slaves.[141] It was argued that these colonial regulations and the state of slavery itself were not compatible with the "genius" of the law of Scotland.[142] The whole contained a highly rhetorical attack on slavery and colonial slavery in particular, drawing on the ideal of the noble African savage contrasted with the brutality of the slave regime.[143] Any claim to perpetual service as an alternative to slavery was also dismissed on the rounds that it would be a pactum illicitum and contrary to statute.144 Montesquieu was also cited to the effect that a free man cannot sell himself. Finally it attacked the expediency of slavery in the West Indies – the traditional justification for slavery under the *ius gentium* – dealing with it by quoting Montesquieu once again.[145]

Wedderburn's counsel argued in his Memorial that it was unfair to use the term "slavery" against him, as what he sought was his right to the

139 Advocation, issued 30 May 1774; Interlocutor, 7 February 1775; (MS) Memorial for John Wedderburn, Esqr of Bandean Defender 10 (henceforth (MS) Memorial for Wedderburn); and (MS) Memorial for Joseph Knight late Servant to Sir John Wedderburn of Ballandean Bart 5 (henceforth (MS) Memorial for Knight), all in NAS CS 235/K/2/2.

140 (MS) Memorial for Knight (n 139) 7–15.

141 Ibid 16–17.

142 Ibid 18–28.

143 Ibid 34–35.

144 Ibid 38–39.

145 Ibid 39–40.

services of his servant, whom he had always treated well and justly. This right was personal service during life in return for clothes and necessaries: although he does not cite Grotius here, this is clearly the type of service Grotius thought was permissible under the *ius naturae.*[146] Nonetheless, he argued that he was entitled to hold Knight as a slave under the law of Jamaica and even to take him back there should he choose. First, the law of nature allowed the enslavement of prisoners in place of their extermination; secondly, poor men were allowed to bind themselves perpetually to richer ones in return for maintenance. These two causes of slavery were authorised by Roman law. Moreover, slavery was permissible by the law of nations, "the best Commentary on the Law of nature". History showed that slavery had been near universal around the world. It was found among the Greeks and Romans, the ancient Germans, and the ancestors of the Scots, and was currently practised in Europe by the Spaniards, Italians, and Russians, while being universal in all European colonies in America or the Indies. In a passage borrowed from the Memorial for Sheddan, the names of Plato, Thomas More, Cicero, and Andrew Fletcher of Saltoun were brought forward in favour of slavery "as a proper ingredient in a perfect Government". Grotius and Pufendorf were adduced as inclining "to the same opinion".[147] Slavery was necessary in the West Indies on economic grounds; moreover, it has to be black slavery, as Europeans could not labour in the conditions there:

> If there had therefore never Existed a Slave in the other parts of the World That Institution must have been Introduced upon Absolute Necessity in the West Indies, and it must there be considered as the Law of Nature, and of every Nation which chooses to make use of those Countrys.[148]

The Memorial next, reasonably enough, pointed to the extensive support for the slave trade in the royal charters for companies and the legislation of England and, after 1707, Great Britain; moreover, in international treaties, the slave trade was often enough supported. This meant that British laws supported slavery at least in the plantations.[149]

Wedderburn's Memorial next dealt with the foundation of his personal right over Knight. It argued that, since the laws of Africa allow parents to sell their children, masters their slaves, and conquerors their prisoners of

146 (MS) Memorial for Wedderburn (n 139) 9–10.
147 Ibid 10–15, citing Grotius, *De iure belli ac pacis* (n 5) 2.5.
148 (MS) Memorial for Wedderburn (n 139) 15–17.
149 Ibid 17–23.

war, and that since Wedderburn had purchased Knight fairly, he had a clear right to him and he did not need to produce a written contract. Baptism did not alter the status of black slaves. All the Bible taught about slaves was "to make them contented with their Lott and to act their parts with propriety and Chearfulness in that Situation where Providence had placed them". Grotius in particular was now relied on for the view that Christianity taught that slaves should be content.[150] There was then an argument that, since by the laws of Jamaica Knight was Wedderburn's property, the laws of Scotland should recognise this. Wedderburn was accordingly entitled to carry Knight back to Jamaica should he choose. It was necessary for it to be possible to send black slaves to Europe to train in arts they could practise in the colonies.[151]

Finally, Wedderburn's Memorial argued that "in point of equity" he was entitled to Knight's service. He paid a considerable price for him; he had clothed him and fed him; he had benefited him by taking him from the rigorous conditions of Jamaica to the easy ones of Britain. Now Knight was in a position to make a return for these benefits; it would be unjust if he did not. Scots law was compatible with such service.[152] Again this alludes to Grotius' foundation of continuing servitude in a duty to make a return for the aliment and support given.

On 7 March 1775, Lord Kennet considered the Memorials and decided to take the cause on avizandum to the whole Lords. The parties were ordered to produce printed Informations.[153] After some delays, they did so, and the cause entered in the Inner House Rolls. Apart from some minor rewriting to take into account the arguments of the other side, each printed Information closely followed the earlier Memorials discussed above.[154] The cause was argued *in praesentia* over several days in February 1776. After hearing the arguments in *praesentia*:

> The Lords . . . agreed, that as this was a new and most important question, it deserved to be determined with the utmost deliberation and solemnity; and, as it was a very different cause in the pleadings from what it was in the papers already given in, it would be proper to have the arguments on both sides distinctly stated in writing. Their Lordships therefore ordered memorials to be put in their boxes on the 20th of April next that judgment may be pronounced next summer session.[155]

150 Ibid 24–27; Grotius, *De iure belli ac pacis* (n 5) 2.5.29.

151 (MS) Memorial for Wedderburn (n 139) 29–43.

152 Ibid 43–45.

153 See the interlocutor written on ibid 60.

154 Copies are found in the sets of Session Papers in the Advocates Library.

155 *Caledonian Mercury*, 21 February 1776. See also the various interlocutors written on (MS) Memorial for John Wedderburn (n 139) 60–61.

After a number of delays, the cause resumed in January 1778.[156]

Knight's *Additional Information* continued to devote considerable attention to showing the evils of the slave trade and the bad condition of slaves in the colonies.[157] Moreover, it argued that some of the problems with working in the colonies could be solved by the use of technology rather than slaves: there was no necessity to have slave labour.[158] It also argued that Knight's status could not be settled by the law of Jamaica as he was not born there; he did not go there of his own free will; and he received no protection or benefit from it. Moreover, the injustice of the Jamaican laws meant that a Scottish court ought not to enforce them.[159] The claim to perpetual service was also rejected.[160]

Wedderburn's *Additional Information* introduced some new points. It gave an historical explanation of the introduction and growth of slavery, but one still compatible with Grotius' view of the *ius naturae*. The universality of slavery in the ancient world was then argued. The continuation of slavery after the fall of the Roman Empire was next discussed, but its progressive disappearance was then admitted. The main intention was evidently to argue that slavery did not disappear because anyone argued or legislated against it, but simply because of historical and economic development.[161] Villeinage in Scotland and its disappearance were also discussed, and it was claimed that the status of colliers and salters was a historical survival of the system of villeinage. They had continued in this status because their masters had not found it profitable to release them from such bondage. The whole argument was designed to stress that there was tremendous historical variation in levels of servitude and that it was "expediency alone" that had determined the changes. The cultivation of the colonies was dependent on slave labour from Africa, as all European nations had realised. Expediency now therefore required the historic recognition of the validity of black slavery in the

156 *Caledonian Mercury*, 17 January 1778.

157 *Additional Information for Joseph Knight, a negro of Africa, pursuer; against John Wedderburn of Ballandean, esq; defender*, Session Papers, Advocates Library 5–11.

158 Ibid 11–12. This was probably influenced by the recent publication by John Millar of *Observations Concerning the Distinction of Ranks in Society* (1771) (henceforth Millar, *Distinction of Ranks*). At 200–202, 237–242 he condemned the economic inefficiency of slavery, using examples from the West Indies. This was repeated in the second edition of 1773.

159 Ibid 13–30.

160 Ibid 34.

161 *Additional Information for John Wedderburn of Ballandean, esq; defender; against Joseph Knight, a negro of Africa, pursuer*, Session Papers, Advocates Library 12–23. Much of this information was clearly derived from Millar's *Distinction of Ranks* (n 158).

Indies.[162] There was then a lengthy argument from private international law to demonstrate that since Wedderburn owned Knight by the law of Jamaica, the law of Scotland ought to recognise that right and that he was also entitled to take him out of the country against his will. The argument was rounded off with a few points including that servitude in America allowed slaves to live a useful and safe life way from the miseries of Africa and make a useful contribution by providing necessary commodities.[163]

The Lords delivered their opinions on 15 January 1778.[164] Sir David Dalrymple, Lord Hailes, a noted antiquarian, preserved an account of his opinion and those of his brother judges. Twelve Lords sat. There is no need to go into their separate opinions in details. Suffice it to say that the decision was ultimately in Knight's favour, but it was relatively narrowly so. Thus, Lord Covington claimed that it was blasphemy to state that slavery was against the law of morality and accordingly stated that Wedderburn could force Knight's return to Jamaica. Lord Monboddo stated that "unless it can be proved that slavery is contrary to the *jus gentium*, there can never be turpitude in it". If they were not for full slavery, quite a number of the Lords thought that in Scotland there could be servitude for life, in return for aliment.[165]

Despite these varied views, the Lords issued the following interlocutor: "having advised the Memorials and Additional Informations They Remitt the Cause Simpliciter in Common form".[166] The import of this was to affirm the terms of John Swinton's interlocutor against slavery, which seems significantly further than the judges collectively can be taken to have intended.

E. CONCLUSION

In *De iure belli ac pacis*, Grotius had provided a justification for slavery under the *ius naturae* and the *ius gentium*. By arguing that an individual could exercise his liberty to sell himself into slavery and could sell his children in case of necessity, while justifying slavery under the law of nations as resulting from capture in war, he unintentionally provided a strong support for black slavery in the American colonies of the European powers. If the black men and women purchased in Africa had been captured in war or had properly

162 Ibid 23–45.

163 Ibid 45–78.

164 *Caledonian Mercury*, 17 January 1778.

165 *Knight v Wedderburn in Decisions of the Lords of Council and Session, from 1/66 to 1791, collected by Sir David Dalrymple of Hailes*, Bart, 2 vols (1826) vol ii, 776–780.

166 See the interlocutor, dated 16 January 1778 on (MS) Memorial for Wedderburn (n 139) 62.

sold themselves into slavery, the law of nature and nations justified their continued enslavement and the enslavement of any children born to them, at least until they had worked off the cost of their keep. Their purchasers had acquired a good title to them.

There is therefore no surprise that, when the status of individuals held as slaves in Scotland came to be litigated, Grotius provided arguments for those in favour of slavery. His basic arguments were not only familiar, but had been adopted by Stair to explain Scots law. Moreover, the strain of Stoic moralising found in his work, along with the long humanistic string of quotations from the Bible and classical sources, all served to stress that individuals who were enslaved ought to bear their position with fortitude. Moreover, his version of an Aristotelian natural law, while rejecting any idea that individuals might be slaves by nature, allowed men to renounce their natural liberty for servitude.

In *Sheddan v Montgomery*, Grotius provided much useful ammunition for the upholders of Montgomery's slave status. The Court seemed inclined to hold that Montgomery's only remedy was a Stoic or Pauline resignation to his lot. By the time of *Knight v Wedderburn*, however, the lawyers arguing the case were finding the views of Grotius unhelpful or irrelevant. Much more so than in the case of *Sheddan*, there was a move away from the natural law tradition associated with Grotius. The justifications for slavery found in more traditional writings on natural law no longer worked so easily to persuade. The Neostoic and Christian arguments that suggested that slavery must simply be endured no longer were acceptable; nor were the arguments that natural law did not oppose slavery and the law of nations permitted it. Slavery was an historical phenomenon (as Wedderburn admitted); moreover, as Knight's counsel stressed, it was simply unjust and not permitted by Scots law. Also, for Knight's slavery to be "valid", the title had to be good. Here the recognition of the evils of the slave trade were used by his counsel to show that the claim that his slavery was justified by the law of nature and of nations was unjustified. His counsel's emphasis that his own black servant remembered being kidnapped as a boy served to underline the point.[167] Contemporary evidence and historical discussion had undermined the utility of Grotius as an apologist for slavery. To support it as an institution, more explicitly racist justifications had to emerge.[168]

167 (MS) Memorial for Knight 13.

168 Such as that in Cobb, *Inquiry into the Law of Negro Slavery* (n 4).

CRITIQUES: LITERATURE AND LEGAL HISTORY

14 The Noose Hidden Under Flowers: Marriage and Law in *Saint Ronan's Well**

A. INTRODUCTION

It is particularly appropriate in an issue of this Journal honouring its founding editor to offer a paper on law and literature – a theme close to the heart of Albert Kiralfy.[1] It is worth remembering that into the mouth of one of his more attractive lawyers, Paulus Pleydell, Sir Walter Scott put the claim that the best editions of the best authors were his "tools of trade. A lawyer without history or literature is a mechanic, a mere working mason; if he possesses some knowledge of these, he may venture to call himself an architect" (*Guy Mannering* ch 37). If this harkens back to the ideals of the Legal Humanism of the Renaissance, rather than being the earliest known manifesto for the now-emerging discipline of law and literature, it nonetheless indicates a belief that law was not the autonomous discipline claimed by the positivism of the later nineteenth century.

Belles-lettristic essays by lawyers on legal themes in certain classic works of literature, almost in the spirit of light-hearted relief from more serious toils, are a moderately popular form; in recent years, however, there have been increasing attempts to map out a discipline of law and literature as a subject of scholarly and academic study.[2] The increasing intensity of such endeavours can largely be dated from James Boyd White's work, *The Legal Imagination*, published over twenty years ago.[3] There has been no agreement

* The first version of this paper was read to the Legal History Discussion Group of the Faculty of Law, University of Edinburgh, on 30 June 1992 under the title "Union, Marriage, Madness, and Scot(t')s Law". I am grateful to the participants for their comments. I have benefited considerably from the generous criticism of Beverley Brown, Peter Garside and Mark Weinstein.

1 See A Kiralfy, "Underworld Cant and the Names of Characters in *The Pickwick Papers* and *Oliver Twist*; Jekyll and Hyde: The Case of Two English Judges", in *Studi in memoria di Gino Gorla* (1994) vol i, 765–773 (henceforth Kiralfy, "Underworld Cant").

2 See, e.g., R A Posner, *Law and Literature: A Misunderstood Relation* (1988).

3 J Boyd White, *The Legal Imagination: Studies in the Nature of Legal Thought and Expression* (1973).

as to how this discipline is to be constituted. It is unnecessary here to engage with these debates, though there will be a few remarks below about literature and legal history.[4]

Sir Walter Scott is one author who has understandably attracted attention for the use he has made of legal material in constructing the Waverley novels, especially the "Scottish" ones. He had a busy professional life as a member of the Faculty of Advocates, holding the offices of Sheriff-Depute of Selkirkshire from 1799 and Clerk of Session from 1806.[5] David Marshall accordingly has fairly commented that "[a] lawyer writing of Scottish history and Scottish manners in or shortly before his own time must almost inevitably draw on his professional knowledge and experience for material for his literary products". He then demonstrated how Scott drew on legal material in the construction of some of his early novels.[6]

It is perhaps tempting to read Scott's accounts of Scots law and Scots lawyers as celebrations or justifications of his native legal system – a reading promoted by considering them alongside comments such as the following from his biographer Lockhart:

> It is not to be denied, that the Scottish lawyers have done more than any other class of their fellow-citizens, to keep alive the sorely threatened spirit of national independence in the thoughts and in the feelings of their countrymen. . . . It is a right and proper thing, then, that Scotland should be proud of her Bar . . .[7]

In his *Life of Scott*, he wrote of Scott's "deep jealousy of the national honour of Scotland, his fear lest the course of innovation . . . should end in a total assimilation of her Jurisprudence to the system of the more powerful sister country".[8] Scott himself wrote in his *Journal* on 9 June 1826 of his fears that eventually

> the Scottish Supreme court will be in effect situated in London. Then down fall – as national objects of respect and veneration – the Scottish bench – the Scottish

4 For two recent British contributions, see I Ward, "The educative ambition of law and literature" (1993) 13 *Legal Studies* 323; M Aristodemou, "Studies in law and literature: directions and concerns" (1993) 22 *Anglo-American Law Review* 157.

5 J Chisholm, *Sir Walter Scott as a Judge* (1918); J Aikman Smith, "Sir Walter Scott as a lawyer" (1972–1973) 12 *Journal of the Society of Public Teachers of Law* (NS) 30; A G Stevenson, "Walter Scott at the Bar" (1993) *Juridical Review* 74.

6 D Marshall, *Sir Walter Scott and Scots Law* (1932) 5; and "Sir Walter Scott and Scots law" (1934) 50 *Scottish Law Review* 263 (henceforth Marshall, "Scott and Scots law"). See also W G M Dobie, "Law and lawyers in the Waverley Novels" (1920) 32 *Juridical Review* 244, 317.

7 J Gibson Lockhart, *Peter's Letters to his Kinsfolk*, ed W Ruddick (1977) 66.

8 [J G Lockhart,] *Memoirs of the Life of Sir Walter Scott, Bart*, 2nd edn, 10 vols (1839) (henceforth Lockhart, *Memoirs of Sir Walter Scott*) vol iii, 305.

> Bar – the Scottish Law herself– And – And there is an end of an auld Sang. Were I as I have been I would fight knee deep in blood ere it came to that.[9]

One might see Scott of the letters of Malachi Malagrowther turning his pen in the Waverley novels to the defence of Scots law.[10] When reflecting on the recent reforms in Scots law, he indeed recorded that he would "always be proud of *Malachi* as having headed back the Southron or help[e]d to do so in one instance at least".[11] Moreover, reading the novels this way would also seem to be consistent with a relatively popular interpretation of the novels as literary resolutions of the conflicts in Scottish life. One could view the Scottish legal profession and legal system as one way in which the old Scotland continued in the new.

If some of Scott's well-known objections to reform of Scots law in a manner which he (arguably) viewed as Anglicisation could be called on for support of such an interpretation,[12] it is also fair to say that the account of Scots law and lawyers can also be pervasively critical. In *Redgauntlet*, for example, Peter Peebles is commonly regarded as a comic figure, and in some respects so he is; yet he is also fundamentally tragic, a victim of the law whom years of protracted and confused litigation have deprived of fortune and sanity.[13] Ridiculous as Peebles has become, the reader never forgets that it is the law that has driven him mad. He may glory in his magnificent lawsuit, but he does remark of his great cause that when it is called it brings "a' the best lawyers in the house fleeing like eagles to the prey" (*RG* ch 23, 387). He seems unaware that it is he who has already been devoured. Peebles, however, is not too sympathetic a figure, having himself earlier used the law to hound others to the workhouse, to their death, and to the streets (*RG* ch 20, 354–356). The sympathy that is nonetheless felt for Peebles indicates that what is under attack is the possibility of abusive use of process: the novel indicts the law's proverbial delays, confusions, and potential harshness towards debtors. Scott would have been well aware

9 W E K Anderson *The Journal of Sir Walter Scott* (1972) (henceforth *Sir Walter Scott's Journal*) 156–157.

10 See Sir Walter Scott, "Thoughts on the Proposed Change of the Currency", in D Simpson and A Wood (eds), *Thoughts on the Proposed Change of Currency and Two Letters on Scottish Affairs* (1972).

11 *Sir Walter Scott's Journal* (n 9) 157.

12 Consider the well-known anecdote of his weeping on the Mound after the vote in the Faculty of Advocates on the introduction of civil jury trial: see Lockhart, *Memoirs of Sir Walter Scott* (n 8) vol ii, 328.

13 Sir Walter Scott, *Redgauntlet*, ed K Sutherland, The World's Classics (1985). All references henceforth to this novel will be in the text and abbreviated to *RG*.

of such problems, having served as Secretary to the Royal Commission appointed in 1808 to investigate the form of process before the Court of Session.[14] It is also perhaps telling that at the time *Redgauntlet* was written further reforms to streamline litigation in the Court of Session were in an advanced stage of preparation.[15] *The Heart of Midlothian*, to take another novel where legal themes are to the fore, is scarcely a celebration of Scottish criminal law. Furthermore, the lawyers who frequent the pages of the Waverley novels are not uniformly noble characters. Paulus Pleydell in *Guy Mannering* may be a noble and learned representative of the Faculty: his name is, after all, that of one of the greatest of Roman lawyers, while his surname is surely a pun to indicate his skill in litigation – he was one who would plead well. The Fairfords, father and son, in their different ways, are also as exemplary and just as their name might suggest. But Glossin in *Guy Mannering*, Micklewhame in *Saint Ronan's Well*, and Greenhorn and Grinderson in *The Antiquary* range from being simply dishonest to, at best, venal, disreputable, and foolish, and, in short, as dubious as their names would suggest.[16] Scott's attitude to Scots law and lawyers is ultimately ambiguous.

As literature exists within and is the product of specific social contexts, exploring Scott's novels will help to explain aspects of Scottish legal history. The novels can therefore be looked upon as in some circumstances offering a commentary on Scots law and society analogous to that found in, say, the *Edinburgh Review*. Legal themes that emerge from them can indicate more general contemporary legal concerns. This general point has been very well demonstrated in Bruce Beiderwell's argument that the Waverley novels made an important contribution to general discourse about crime and punishment at a crucial period in the development of new penal strategies and of reform in the criminal law.[17]

14 Marshall, "Scott and Scots law" (n 6) 2; N Phillipson, *The Scottish Whigs and the Reform of the Court of Session 1785–1830*, Stair Society vol 37 (1990) 117–126.

15 *Report into the Forms of Process and Course of Appeals in Scotland* (1824); Court of Session Act 1825. See generally *The Laws of Scotland: Stair Memorial Encyclopaedia*, 25 vols (1987–) vol vi, 414–416. For a different approach, see I Campbell, "Justice in Scott's *Redgauntlet*" (1985) 9 *Scotia* 17.

16 Is "Glossin" an allusion to the medieval Roman lawyers who wrote "glosses" on the text of Justinian's *Corpus juris civilis*? From the sixteenth century onwards their work was much disparaged as a disfigurement of the pure Roman law: is there here a contrast with the more classical Paulus?

17 B Beiderwell, *Power and Punishment in Scott's Novels* (1992). For similar themes relating to narrative in novels and the development of the law of evidence, see A Welsh, *Strong Representations: Narrative and Circumstantial Evidence in England* (1992).

Modern critics have recognised the extent to which much of the power of the Waverley novels comes from the manner in which they transgress the boundaries of literary genres – especially those of history and fiction.[18] It is no surprise that from the time certain novels were published this particular transgression caused considerable controversy.[19] Here we will discuss another such transgression in the novels – that of the boundaries of fiction and legal discourse. This in many ways ought to be a much less troubling transgression for legal historians than that of fiction and history has proved to be. Legal historians are used to the use of texts other than those produced by the formally constituted structures of courts, legislatures, and legal authors. To take just one instance, since the Renaissance the study of Roman law has required the study of epigraphy and works of literature alongside that of legal texts narrowly defined. A legal history that restricts itself to study of doctrines found in court reports and legislation is a legal history seriously diminished. Moreover, legal historians ought to be keenly aware of the historical linkage of texts that literary scholars refer to somewhat loosely as intertextuality and that is exposed through the techniques of form criticism.[20] One can expect the novels of Scott to have legal discussion embedded in them.

The novel that will be the object of investigation is *Saint Ronan's Well*, first published on 27 December 1823, with a title page dated 1824.[21] There has been little critical attention devoted to *SRW*. It is true that this partly results from the general eclipse of Scott's novels that had taken place by the early years of this century.[22] Yet, the revival of scholarly interest in Scott has also largely ignored *SRW*, and it is important to understand why. To explore this it is necessary to have a brief investigation of the history of Scott criticism.

If the Waverley Novels were initially much admired, the publication of Lockhart's *Life* encouraged Thomas Carlyle to sound the attack on Scott in

18 See, e.g., J Kerr, *Fiction against History: Scott as Storyteller* (1989); I Ferris, *The Achievement of Literary Authority: Gender, History, and the Waverley Novels* (1991) (henceforth Ferris, *Literary Authority*).

19 Ferris, *Literary Authority* (n 18) 137–160.

20 See, e.g., D Daube, *Forms of Roman Legislation* (1956); A Watson, *Jesus and the Jews: The Pharisaic Tradition in John* (1995) 4–10.

21 W Scott, *Saint Ronan's Well*, ed M Weinstein, Edinburgh Edition of the Waverley Novels, ed D Hewitt vol 16 (1985) 380 (henceforth cited in text as *SRW* by chapter and page). Where necessary, I shall cite Sir Walter Scott, Bart, *St Ronan's Well,* Waverley Novels, Centenary Edition vol 7 (1871). The Centenary Edition follows the "Magnus Opus" edition: see J Millgate, *Scott's Last Edition: A Study in Publishing* History (1987); *Scott's Interleaved Waverley Novels (The "Magnum Opus": National Library of Scotland MSS. 23001–41): An Introduction and Commentary*, ed I Gordon Brown (1987) 119.

22 See, e.g., R Waswo, "Scott and the Really Great Tradition", in J H Alexander and D Hewitt (eds), *Scott and his Influence: The Papers of the Aberdeen Scott Conference*, 1982 (1983) 1.

an essay of 1838. As condemnation of Scott's worldliness and condemnation by faint praise gave way in the essay to a wonderful crescendo of vituperation, Carlyle wrote "We might say in a short word, which means a long matter, that your Shakespeare fashions his characters from the heart outwards; your Scott fashions them from the skin inwards, never getting near the heart of them." Ultimately, "Scott's career of writing impromptu novels to buy farms with, was not of a kind to terminate voluntarily, but to accelerate itself more and more; and one sees not to what wise goal it could, in any case, have led him".[23] The ultimate products of such thinking were the strictures, for example, of F R Leavis in 1948 ("Out of Scott a bad tradition came") reflecting and reinforcing contemporary disparagement of the works of the author of *Waverley*.[24]

The recent, serious confrontation with Scott may be not unfairly dated from the publication in 1951 of David Daiches' seminal essay "Scott's Achievement as a Novelist". Daiches presented a reading of the Waverley novels that saw Scott as attempting to reconcile at a literary level the old Scotland of religious and political conflict with the new Scotland of peace and commercial prosperity by mapping out the changes that had brought the new Scotland into being. The Waverley novels told a story of resolution or potential resolution: the story was essentially tragic, however, as in progress much of value had been lost.[25] This powerful and persuasive reading of Scott inevitably privileged a few novels, the "Scottish" novels – *Waverley, Guy Mannering, The Antiquary, The Black Dwarf, Old Mortality, Rob Roy, The Heart of Midlothian, The Bride of Lammermoor, A Legend of Montrose*, and *Redgauntlet* – as embodying what was important in Scott's *oeuvre*. *SRW* was not included in this group, and was perceived as something rather different from a literary resolution of the old and the new. Jane Millgate, for example, in pointing out that the Scottish novels gain most attention (while rightly criticising aspects of this approach) does not include *SRW* as one of those novels generally considered a "Scottish" novel, even though it is set very specifically in Scotland.[26]

23 T Carlyle, *Critical and Miscellaneous Essays*, 5 vols (1899) vol iv, 22–87 at 75, 83.

24 F R Leavis, *The Great Tradition* (1962, reissued 1983) 14. See also E M Forster, *Aspects of the Novel* (1962) 38.

25 D Daiches, "Scott's Achievement as a Novelist", in *Literary Essays* (1956) 88–121. This is not to deny the impact of G Lukács, *The Historical Novel*, trans H and S Mitchell (1962); but it is a question as to how influential Lukács' views were until his work was translated into English.

26 J Millgate, *Walter Scott: The Making of the Novelist* (1984) (henceforth Millgate, *Making of the Novelist*) viii–ix. Millgate does not mention *SRW* in this study, because of the time-period she covers; but she is obviously not to be read as endorsing or ignoring this reading of *SRW*.

While still influential, Daiches' approach has lost ground.[27] For example, Graham McMaster has recently argued against Daiches' interpretation of Scott's *oeuvre* as a whole. Instead he has maintained that only *Waverley* really conforms to the pattern claimed by Daiches. Through a careful, comparative reading of *Waverley* and *Redgauntlet*, McMaster convincingly suggests that, although apparently similar, the two novels are fundamentally different. He aimed "to show that the novels are in fact dominated not by figures and situations that are rationally calculated to make certain historical (to Scott) trends palpable, but by patterns, metaphors and symbols, and by a very restricted range of them".[28] This recaptures the remainder of the novels, and denies total significance to the "Scottish" ones.[29] This fruitful approach emphasises reading the novels together, as do those recent critics who have explored Scott's complex playing with the notion of authorship – with concealment and revelation – with genres, and with the narrative act, and who have pointed to his deconstruction of his own novels.[30] Indeed, modern theories of literary criticism have reclaimed the Waverley novels as objects of serious analysis, pointing out that "[a]ll of Scott's novels embody [Mikhail] Bakhtin's theory of narrative art",[31] and the Russian writer's theories of fictional discourse have in fact proved compelling in recent analysis of Scott's *oeuvre*.[32]

SRW remains largely ignored because it has always been considered a failure. One of the few recent discussions of it describes it as "flawed".[33] On publication it met savage criticism: "The production before us must be regarded as a failure," commented the *Monthly Review*, explaining that

27 For a useful survey of trends in recent criticism of Scott, see J Rubenstein, "Scott Scholarship and Criticism: Where are we now? Where are we going?", in J H Alexander and D Hewitt (eds), *Scott in Carnival* (1983) (henceforth Alexander and Hewitt, *Scott in Carnival*) 594.

28 G McMaster, *Scott and Society* (1981) 4.

29 In ibid 215–220, McMaster therefore discusses *SRW*.

30 See, e.g., S Cooney, "Scott's anonymity – its motives and consequences" (1973) 10 *Studies in Scottish Literature* 207; T R Dale, "One word more on Scott's anonymity" (1979) 14 *Studies in Scottish Literature* 137; F Jordan, "Chrystal Croftangry, Scott's last and best mask" (1980) 7 *Scottish Literary Journal* 185; R Waswo, "Story as historiography in the Waverley Novels" (1980) 47 *English Literary History* 304; S F Kiepetar, "Levels of narration in *Old Mortality*" (1982) 13 *The Wordsworth Circle* 38; see also Millgate, *Making of the* Novelist (n 26) passim but esp at 128.

31 J Diedrick, "Dialogical History in *Ivanhoe*", in Alexander and Hewitt, *Scott in Carnival* (n 27) 280 at 280.

32 See, e.g., preface in Alexander and Hewitt, *Scott in Carnival* (n 27) vii. The most influential of M M Bakhtin's works in this respect is *The Dialogic Imagination: Four Essays*, ed M Holquist, trans C Emerson and M Holquist (1981).

33 J S Elbers, "A contrast of fictional worlds: *Redgauntlet* and *St Ronan's Well*" (1980) 7 *Scottish Literary Journal* 155 (henceforth Elbers, "A contrast of fictional worlds") at 158.

Scott had been foolish to depart from his usual themes of history to tackle the domestic novel, especially when others – D'Arblay, Edgeworth, Austen – were excellent exponents of this type of work.[34] Scott promoted such a reading of the novel in his own later introduction to *SRW*:

> It is intended, in a word – *celebrare domestica facta* – to give an imitation of the shifting manners of our own time, and paint scenes, the originals of which are daily passing round us, so that a minute's observation may compare the copies with the originals. It must be confessed that this style of composition was adopted by the Author rather from the tempting circumstance of its offering some novelty in his compositions, and avoiding worn-out characters and positions, than from the hope of rivalling the many formidable competitors who have already won deserved honours in this department. The ladies, in particular, gifted by nature with keen powers of observation and light satire, have been so distinguished by these works of talent, that, reckoning from the authoress of Evelina [Miss Burney] to her of Marriage [Miss Ferrier], a catalogue might be made, including the brilliant and talented names of Edgeworth, Austin [sic], Charlotte Smith, and others, whose success seems to have appropriated this province of the novel as exclusively their own. It was therefore with a sense of temerity that the Author intruded upon a species of composition which had been of late practised with such distinguished success.[35]

Scott, who clearly had the notice from the *Monthly Review* in front of him when he wrote the above, thus invited readers to read *SRW* as a contemporary domestic novel, comparable to, say, Jane Austen's *Persuasion*, also substantially set in a spa town. And readers have been seduced into so regarding it. It has thus continued to be viewed as a novel apart. A O J Cockshut, for example, comments that "*St. Ronan's Well* [may be singled out] for its honest attempt to achieve something alien to the author's temperament, the comedy of Jane Austen".[36] If read in this way, *SRW* seems to add nothing to Daiches' interpretation of Scott's *oeuvre*; moreover, as a comedy of domestic satire it is indeed an evident failure. But to read it as one seems perverse.

SRW is a powerful and compelling novel, dark in tone. Aspects of it may conform to an Austenish comedy, but the treatment of the characters at the Well is savage rather than satirical; it is notable that they are indeed regularly compared to animals (for example, *SRW* ch 7, 62, 67, 68; ch 15, 137; ch 39, 372). Furthermore, even if the genre of satirical comedy of

34 Review of *St Ronan's Well* (1824) 103 *Monthly Review, or Literary Journal* 61 at 61.

35 *SRW*, Centenary Edition (n 21), Introduction, 1–2.

36 A O J Cockshut, *The Achievement of Walter Scott* (1969) 13. See also J Buchan, *Sir Walter Scott* (1932) 26–64. J Sutherland, *The Life of Walter Scott: A Critical Biography* (1995) 264–267 seems to flirt with this interpretation of the novel, while recognising the significance of the seedy world it portrays, and that there seem to be patriotic tensions in it.

manners is drawn on, it is appropriated to another purpose and subverted. Lady Penelope Penfeather, a leading "Weller", describes Clara Mowbray as looking "so like something from another world, that she makes me always think of Mat Lewis' Spectre Lady" (*SRW* ch 6, 54). This Gothic allusion indicates that Clara is indeed from another world – that of tragedy – and Lady Penelope's remark prepares us for Clara's later appearance to others just shortly before her death as if she were indeed a spectre lady (*SRW* ch 38, 365–366). Lady Penelope's comment, intended as the sarcasm of an old maid at the expense of a younger, more beautiful woman, indicates to the readers that we should not easily accept the novel as one of manners: the remarks of Sir Walter Scott on the writings of the author of *Waverley* need always to be treated with caution. In fact, *SRW* is yet another novel where Scott plays with genres: in this case comedy of manners and the Gothic novel.[37] It is the conjunction and confrontation of the two that make the novel so strong and tragic. If much of the criticism of the novel has been based on a failure to appreciate the importance of this transgression of the Gothic and the domestic, such critiques and Scott's later preface also indicate the extent to which the novel was and has been condemned on the grounds of transgression of gender as well as genre. Scott himself and the critic of the *Monthly Review* emphasised how in *SRW* he had inappropriately wandered into women's territory.[38]

The opening paragraph of *Saint Ronan's Well* evokes the problematic legacy of the Scottish Enlightenment:

> Although few, if any, of the countries of Europe, have increased so rapidly in wealth and cultivation as Scotland during the last half century, Sultan Mahmoud's owls might nevertheless have found in Caledonia, at any term within that flourishing period, their dowry of ruined villages. Accident or local advantages have, in many instances, transferred the inhabitants of ancient hamlets, from the situations which their predecessors chose, with more respect to security than convenience, to those in which their increasing industry and commerce could more easily expand itself; and hence places which stand distinguished in Scottish History, and which figure in David Macpherson's excellent historical map, can now only be discerned from the wild moor by the verdure which clothes their

37 On Gothic in the Waverley Novels, see, now, F Robertson, *Legitimate Histories: Scott, Gothic, and the Authorities of Fiction* (1994) (henceforth Robertson, *Legitimate Histories*). In a powerful essay, Marilyn Orr explores the Gothic themes in *SRW*: "Repetition, reversal, and the Gothic: *The Pirate* and *St Ronan's Well*" (1990) 16 *English Studies in Canada* 187 (henceforth Orr, "Repetition, reversal, and the Gothic"). There are also elements of mediaeval romances: see J Mitchell, *Scott, Chaucer, and Medieval Romance: A Study in Sir Walter Scott's Indebtedness to the Literature of the Middle Ages* (1987) 165–168. Mitchell remarks that "Scott must have enjoyed pretending that his story was 'entirely modern'".

38 Ferris, *Literary Authority* (n 18) 1–15, 253–255.

site, or, at best, by a few scattered ruins, resembling pinfolds, which mark the spot of their former existence (*SRW*, ch 1, 1).

It is notable that the first sentence talks of a "dowry of ruined villages". The phrase no doubt at one level simply conveys the sense that Scotland is endowed with such villages; it also, however, necessarily reminds the reader that dowry is a legal institution normally associated with a marriage, and Scott's reference to it here – taken from "The Fable of the Two Owls" in Henry Weber's collection, *Tales of the East* – is to that specific context. Two owls were reported to Sultan Mahmoud by his vizier Khasayas as wishing a prosperous long life to the Sultan as in his reign "we shall never want destroyed villages". This was important to the owls, as one was to give his daughter a dowry of ruined villages on her marriage to the son of the other.[39]

In this paper I wish to argue that the theme of marriage is central to *SRW* and I hope thus to show that the appearance here of the word "dowry" is scarcely chance. In doing so, it should become apparent that *SRW* offers a severe critique of aspects of the Scots law on the constitution of marriage and, at another level, of that other union, the political one of Scotland with England.

B. SCOTS LAW SUBVERTS GOOD ORDER

If there has scarcely been the attention devoted to *SRW* that has been devoted to, say, *Redgauntlet*, modern critics generally concur in a view of the novel as bleak or pessimistic.[40] It has been compared to *The Wasteland*.[41] Like all of the Waverley Novels, rich in imagery, allusion and metaphor, *SRW* is distinctive for images of illness and health and of gambling.[42] The regular references to these build up an atmosphere suggesting a sick society given over to chance, but where Fortuna's wheel has taken a distinctly downward spin.

Pretence and artifice are also pervasive in the novel's imagery. The middle chapter of the novel is devoted to the acting out of certain scenes

39 *SRW* (n 21) 447.

40 Elbers, "A contrast of fictional worlds" (n 33) passim; K M Sroka, "Wealth and illth in *St Ronan's Well*" (1980) 7 *Scottish Literary Journal* 167 (henceforth Sroka, "Wealth"); B A Pike, "Scott as pessimist: A view of 'St Ronan's Well'" (July 1966) 7 *Review of English Literature* 29.

41 J MacQueen, *The Rise of the Historical Novel*, vol ii of *The Enlightenment and Scottish* Literature (1989) 56–58 (henceforth MacQueen, *Rise of the Historical Novel*); Elbers, "A contrast of fictional worlds" (n 33) at 165.

42 Elbers, "A contrast of fictional worlds" (n 33) at 159–160; Sroka, "Wealth" (n 40) passim.

of *A Midsummer Night's Dream* as a masque or dumbshow (*SRW* (n 21) ch 20). In one sense, this both points up the general "masquing" in the novel and reflects the frequent inability of the characters to communicate with one another: Francis Tyrrel and Valentine Bulmer originally represent themselves as cousins, but in fact they are brothers; Bulmer later assumes the title of Earl of Etherington to which Tyrrel rather than he is entitled; Scrogie has adopted the name Touchwood in preference to that of Mowbray; in a crucial scene setting the tragedy in train Lady Penelope Penfeather pretends to be Clara Mowbray; earlier Bulmer has impersonated Tyrrel to marry Clara Mowbray; MacTurk is the "Man of Peace", though he promotes violence; and Micklewhame is the "Man of Law", but he subverts legal order. Allusions to masking and metaphors of masking are commonplace throughout the novel: for example, at one point Jekyl writes to Bulmer of "the masquerade of your marriage" (*SRW* (n 21) ch 27, 250). But the use of *A Midsummer Night's Dream*, and allusions to Greek myth – especially to the Roman poet Statius' *Thebaid* underlying and related to Shakespeare's play – point up some of the focuses of the novel on fraternal rivalry and jealousy. The masque and dumbshow unify and structure the work, linking the superficiality of life at Saint Ronan's Well with the deeper, darker, more Gothic themes of the novel.[43]

A Midsummer Night's Dream is a play concerned with marriages: that of Theseus to Hippolyta, of Hermia to Lysander, of Helena to Demetrius, and, at a different level, with the existing state of that of Titania to Oberon. The play moves from Athens to the woods and back to Athens. The woods effect changes, sorting out problems with the love affairs of Hermia and Lysander and Helena and Demetrius – no longer are Lysander and Demetrius rivals for Helena; back in Athens Theseus overrules the demands of Egeus, father of Hermia, in order to allow her to marry Lysander. There is no need to demonstrate that marriage is the central theme of *A Midsummer Night's Dream*: it is sufficient to point out that it has often been argued that the play was written to be performed at the marriage of a noble couple.[44] Whether or not this was so, Peter Hollindale is correct in stressing that "the main emphasis falls on the thematic prominence of marriage in the play: it is an integral, organic and continuous subject in this drama to an extent unparalleled in any other Shakespeare comedy".[45]

43 MacQueen, *Rise of the Historical Novel* (n 41) 66–78.

44 For a recent (though qualified) support of this view, see P Hollindale, *William Shakespeare: A Midsummer Night's Dream* (1992) 17–19.

45 Ibid 19.

The performance in the central chapter of *SRW* of a dumbshow of parts of this play about marriage serves to underline the theme of marriage in the novel: Lady Binks has trapped Sir Bingo Binks into marriage; Augusta Bidmore married with unfortunate consequences for Josiah Cargill; Valentine Bulmer has gone through a private ceremony of marriage with Clara Mowbray; the old Earl of Etherington married privately in France and then publicly and bigamously in England; Hannah Irwin married "a wretch, who maltreated [her] – plundered [her] – sold [her]" (*SRW* (n 21) ch 38, 364); Mrs Blower marries Dr Quackleben. Normally marriage is seen as an institution supporting and upholding society: it creates a new family and the family was viewed as the historical foundation of society in eighteenth-century conjectural accounts of social development.[46] The family continued to be viewed as the central institution of society and marriage is, after all, one of the most common resolutions of the nineteenth-century novel. In an essay published in 1824 shortly after *SRW*, Scott described marriage as "at once the institution of civil society most favourable to religion and good order, and that which, in its consequences, forms the most marked distinction between man and the lower animals".[47] But, apart perhaps from the last, all these marriages in *SRW* were subversive of society, and even that of Quackleben and Mrs Blower was entered into by the doctor for largely mercenary reasons. It is perhaps therefore especially significant that the Wellers are frequently compared to lower animals. In obvious contrast, the marriages in *A Midsummer Night's Dream* offer resolution and happiness and affirm society and its continuity. It is thus significant that the single status of Meg Dods is stressed through the discussions of her rejection of her numerous suitors (*SRW* (n 21) ch 1, 6). Despite the irascibility suggested by her name, she is the warmest, most life-enhancing character in the novel.

In *A Midsummer Night's Dream* the woods have a transformative effect: the lovers' night in the woods resolves their conflicts. The woods around Shaws-Castle feature prominently in *SRW*, but they take on a nightmarish, Gothic, threatening quality, especially in John Mowbray's dash through them, drunk and desperate – a ride that results in his near-murder of his sister – and even more so in Clara's last journey through them in her despair and madness (reconstructed from circumstantial evidence almost in the style of a police report). It is in the woods, for example, that Lady Binks acted to entrap Sir

46 For a discussion of, e.g., Adam Smith's views on this, see P Stein, *Legal Evolution: The Story of an Idea* (1980) 34.

47 Found quoted in Orr, "Repetition, reversal, and the Gothic" (n 37) at 194.

Bingo into marriage, that Tyrrel courted Clara and they eventually had illicit sexual intercourse, that Bulmer and Tyrrel came close to fratricide, and that Mowbray killed Bulmer. The imagery of the woods is clearly vital to an understanding of the novel – Shaws-Castle is so named because of the woods (*SRW* (n 21) ch 24, 223) – and evidently linked to the predominant themes of marriage and fraternal rivalry. Again there is another Shakespearean reference to point this up. In *As You Like It*, visits to the woods resolve the murderous conflicts between two sets of brothers – Oliver and Orlando, Duke Senior and Duke Frederick. The time in the woods allows the four marriages that end the play to take place. *SRW* points to *As You Like It* through characters twice calling Touchwood "Touchstone", the fool and professional jester in the play (*SRW* (n 21) ch 17, 158; ch 30, 282). But in *SRW*, we are as far from Shakespeare's gentle mockery and upholding of Elizabethan pastoral convention as we are from an eighteenth-century sentimental reading of the woods as linked with the natural and the innocent: here the woods are associated with murder, madness, and disastrous marriage. Far from resolving fraternal conflict, they permit its acting out and exacerbation. In this context, the descriptions of Clara as a "wild kitten" who may "take [to] the woods, one day, and become as savage as the Princess Caraboo" (*SRW* (n 21) ch 11, 99), or "as wild and beautiful a woodland nymph as the imagination can fancy" (*SRW* (n 21) ch 25, 235) take on a dark, ironical aspect. Moreover, Mowbray, referring to Tyrrel's courtship and seduction of her, upbraids her thus: "You roamed the woods a little too much in my father's time, if all stories be true" (*SRW* (n 21) ch 23, 219). Driven mad by the pressure to marry Bulmer and her guilt over her physical intimacy with Tyrrel, Clara does indeed take to the woods in a frenzy in her final flight from Shaws-Castle to the Aulton.

Bulmer reported thus his father's speech to him on the prospect of his first visit to Scotland: "[H]e enlarged on the folly and iniquity of private marriages, warned me that in the country I was going to, the matrimonial noose often lies hid under flowers, and that folks find it twitched round their neck when they least expect such a cravat . . ." (*SRW* (n 21) ch 25, 234). With this sexual allusion, Scott brings forward openly the theme of the Scots law on the constitution of marriage, and its contrast with the English law. The marriages of Sir Bingo to Lady Binks, of Bulmer to Clara, and of Mrs Blower to Quackleben could not have taken place in England in the way that they did. The first mention of Sir Bingo's marriage comes from Meg Dods in conversation with Tyrrel:

> Every Jack will find a Jill, gang the world as it may – And, at the warst o't, better hae some fashery in finding a partner for the night, than get yoked with ane that you may not be able to shake off the morn. . . . Was it not the last season . . . that

> young Sir Bingo Binks . . . gat cleekit with Miss Rachael Bonnyrig, the auld Lady Loupengirth's lang-legged daughter – and they danced sae lang thegither, that there was mair said than suld hae been said about it – and the lad would fain have louped back, but the auld leddy held him to his tackle, and the Commissary Court and somebody else made her Leddy Binks in spite of Sir Bingo's heart . . . (*SRW* (n 21) ch 2, 22–23).

This marriage was due to "the assistance of the Scottish Themis, so propitiously indulgent to the foibles of the fair": after some persuasion by Lady Binks' brother and his friend, Sir Bingo had acknowledged a marriage to her (*SRW* (n 2) ch 6, 51). What has to be deduced is that Sir Bingo and Lady Binks entered into an irregular marriage either by declaration *de praesenti* or *per verba de futuro subsequente copula*. That is, they were married either by exchanging words (or other indications) of present consent to a marriage, or by promising future marriage, on the basis of which sexual intercourse took place. The act of sexual intercourse was regarded as completing the marriage.[48] The second of these seems most likely given Lady Binks' brother's intervention and Mowbray's waspish comment to her, when she mentions the danger of women riding without an attendant, that "accidents happen as frequently when ladies *have* attendants as when they want them". Scott pursues the obvious sexual reference by commenting that she "in her maiden state, had cantered a good deal about these woods under Sir Bingo's escort" (*SRW* (n 21) ch 8, 79). For Sir Bingo the noose had indeed been hidden under the flowers, and Themis – the personification of justice – had drawn it tight around his neck through operation of the Commissary Court, the court that had jurisdiction to deal with issues of the validity of marriage. These two modes of proving or constituting marriage originated in the mediaeval canon law of the Catholic Church;[49] they had not been possible in England since Lord Hardwicke's Act of 1753 restricted the solemnisation of marriages (except for those of Jews and Quakers) to public ceremonies, preceded by the calling of banns, performed by clergymen of the Church of England, with persons under the age of twenty-one, not being widowed,

48 It is unclear whether the sexual intercourse between Clara and Tyrrel took place consequent to a promise of marriage: if so, it would have completed the marriage, which means that the marriage to Bulmer would have been both bigamous and incestuous.

49 See W D H Sellar, "Marriage by Cohabitation with Habit and Repute: Review and Requiem?", in D L Carey Miller and D W Meyers (eds), *Comparative and Historical Essays in Scots Law: A Tribute to Professor Sir Thomas Smith*, QC (1992) 117 at 120–126. For accounts of the Scots law contemporary with Scott, see J Erskine, *An Institute of the Law of Scotland in the Order of Sir George Mackenzie's Institutions of that* Law (1773) I.vi.2–6; *Baron David Hume's Lectures 1786–1822 Volume I*, G Campbell H Paton (ed), Stair Society vol 5 (1939) 21–69 (henceforth *Hume's Lectures Volume 1*).

requiring the consent of parents or guardians.[50] Thus, had Sir Bingo Binks and Miss Rachael Bonnyrig met in England, they would have remained in their separate, unmarried states.

By contrast, Bulmer's marriage to Clara was probably in theory void in Scots law on the grounds of error as to person, as indeed is admitted in the text (*SRW* (n 21) ch 26, 241; ch 37, 352). But there would have had to be litigation to determine this: Jekyl suggested to Bulmer that Clara might be willing to go through a more formal marriage to avoid a lawsuit (*SRW* (n 21) ch 27, 250–251), and raised with Tyrrel the issue of whether or not, because of delay, Clara might be personally barred from raising the issue of error to avoid the marriage (*SRW* (n 21) ch 29, 272–273). The fact that she had allowed so many years to go by without taking any formal steps to repudiate the marriage might indeed have suggested to a court that she had acquiesced in a marriage perfectly proper on the record, which was why it was so important to her to have the evidence of Hannah Irwin who could testify to the deception (*SRW* (n 21) ch 38, 363–361). It is also worth noting that, probably under the prompting of the lectures on Scots law he attended at the University of Edinburgh, Scott carefully constructed one of the few plausible situations where error as to person could exist in a contract of marriage.[51] One further significant point is the age of the characters, all of whom were minors: at the time Clara went through a ceremony of marriage with Bulmer, both were around sixteen years of age (*SRW* (n 21) ch 25, 235; ch 26, 240). Francis Tyrrel was eighteen (*SRW* (n 21) ch 26, 238).[52] English law would have prevented the occurrence of this emotional and legal mess, first, by requiring parental consent, and secondly, by prohibiting clandestine marriages such as here took place.[53]

The Scots law on the constitution of marriage could thus be seen as undesirable and subversive of good social order: it is therefore undoubtedly

50 Statute 26 Geo II, c 33. See L Stone, *Road to Divorce: England 1530–1987* (1990) 121–134 (henceforth Stone, *Road to Divorce*); R B Outhwaite, *Clandestine Marriage in England, 1500–1850* (1995) (henceforth Outhwaite, *Clandestine* Marriage) 75–144.

51 *Hume's Lectures Volume I* (n 49) 24. See also James, Viscount Stair, *The Institutions of the Law of Scotland*, ed D M Walker (1981) I.iv.6; I.ix.9; IV.xl.24.

52 In the first edition and MS, Tyrrel is eighteen. Subsequent editions give his age as nineteen (see *SRW*, Centenary Edition (n 21) ch 26, 281). Nothing hinges on this. See the editorial discussion of the development of the text in *SRW* (n 21) 395.

53 Another private marriage was that of Quackleben to Mrs Blower by Chatterley, a minister of the Church of England (*SRW* (n 21) ch 39, 371). The same disastrous consequences as flowed from the two other marriages do not seem likely to have resulted from it; but it is worth noting that such a private marriage would not have been possible in England where the calling of banns and public celebration would have been required.

significant that the "good" representative of Scots law in the novel is named Bindloose. Lady Binks had deliberately used Scots law to entrap a rich English husband, but, as a result, "she was miserable" and hated her husband, although she had expected to be able to reconcile herself to him after the marriage (*SRW* (n 21) ch 6, 50–51). It had resulted in the perplexities of Tyrrel, Bulmer and Clara. Such difficult consequences would have been familiar and currently controversial to Scott's readers in 1824. Gretna Green was notorious as the resort of eloping English couples evading that country's laws of marriage.[54] But what would have come especially to many readers' minds must have been the recent litigation between Johanna Gordon and John William Henry Dalrymple, and it seems very likely that it influenced Scott in writing the novel. This notorious case, first litigated in the Consistory Court in London, arose out of Johanna Gordon's claim to have been married clandestinely by an irregular form to Dalrymple, a guards officer, in Edinburgh in 1804. At the time of the alleged marriage, he was nineteen years of age and she over twenty-one. Dalrymple, though of Scots descent, was domiciled in England. Dalrymple later went through a public ceremony of marriage with Miss Laura Manners in London in 1808. Sir William Scott, the judge in the Consistory Court, decided in 1811 that Dalrymple had been married to Johanna Gordon in 1804 either by declaration *de praesenti* or *per verba de futuro subsequente copula*. The purported marriage of Dalrymple to Laura Manners was therefore void and bigamous.[55] Sir William Scott's decree was appealed to the Court of the Arches and eventually to the High Court of Delegates in 1814 where it was upheld.[56] Laura Manners raised an action against Dalrymple and Johanna Gordon in the Commissary Court in Edinburgh in 1812; Dalrymple himself also sued Johanna Gordon. These actions, aiming to assert the invalidity of the marriage of 1804, failed. Dalrymple next tried to sue Johanna Gordon for divorce on the ground of adultery, but failed, while she tried to sue him for separation and aliment.[57] She eventually divorced him in Scotland in 1820 on the

54 See, e.g., Stone, *Road to Divorce* (n 50) 133–134; S Parker, *Informal Marriage, Cohabitation and the Law, 1750–1989* (1990) 63–64.

55 J Dodson, *A Report of the Judgement, Delivered in the Consistorial Court of London, on the Sixteenth Day of July, 1811, by the Right Honourable Sir William Scott, Chancellor of the Diocese, in the Cause of Dalrymple the Wife, against Dalrymple the Husband* (1811); *Dalrymple v Dalrymple* 2 Hag Con 54.

56 2 Hag Con 137 n *; J Fergusson, *A Treatise on the Present State of the Consistorial Law in Scotland. With Reports of Decided* Cases (1829) (henceforth Fergusson, *Consistorial Law*) 22–23.

57 Fergusson, *Consistorial Law* (n 56) 21–23; *Reports of Decided Cases* (same volume) 1–7.

ground of his adultery.[58] These twelve years of litigation involved persons of high society: Dalrymple was the son of General Dalrymple, the Governor of Chelsea Hospital, and in 1821 he was to succeed his cousin as Earl of Stair; Johanna Gordon was from a prominent and wealthy family of landowners much involved in the legal profession in Edinburgh; Laura Manners was the sister of a duchess whose mother was to become a countess in her own right. The significance of this case can hardly have escaped the attention of many of Scott's readers: aspects of it resembled the position of the old Earl of Etherington in *SRW* (who contracted a private marriage in France and then a bigamous, public one in England) and that of Sir Bingo and Lady Binks. Moreover the liaisons of Johanna Gordon and Dalrymple were supposed to have taken place in the woods around the Hermitage of Braid, one of her family's places of residence.[59]

C. MANNERS AND MONEY

One of the primary oppositions in *SRW* is between the Aulton of Saint Ronan's and the new spa town of Saint Ronan's Well. The latter is the centre of gossip, intrigue and malevolence. The former, unimproved and decaying, is where, as John MacQueen has pointed out, "everyone, whose character has any kind of life-enhancing quality, chooses to make his or her abode, or make contact with the society of the neighbourhood".[60] It is the real source of human warmth and support, and it is there that Clara and Hannah Irwin find succour and eventual rest in death supported by Cargill the Minister and Meg Dods. It is significant that Micklewhame, the crooked lawyer, should describe the Well as "the greatest improvement that has been made in this country since the year forty-five" (*SRW* (n 21) ch 8, 73). This reminds the reader that the action in *SRW* is set in the period roughly some "sixty years since" the setting of *Waverley*.[61] Bindloose, the honest lawyer with a very ambiguous name, also sees great improvement in the country in the period since the forty-five Rebellion (*SRW* (n 21) ch 15, 135): Touchwood, however, disagrees, and focuses on the Well as "the very fountain-head of folly

58 Fergusson, *Consistorial Law* (n 56) 24; *Hume's Lectures Volume I* (n 49) 168.

59 For a full discussion, see J W Cairns, "A note on the *Bride of Lammermoor:* why Scott did not mention the Dalrymple legend until 1830" (1993) 20 *Scottish Literary Journal* 19. See also "Historical Note" in *SRW* (n 21) 443–445.

60 MacQueen, *Rise of the Historical Novel* (n 41) 65.

61 The precise date at which the novel is set is impossible to determine. There are a number of contradictory pointers. Mark Weinstein has convincingly suggested that it is sometime in the period 1809–1812: *SRW* (n 21) 442–443.

and coxcombry – a Babel for noise and a Vanity-fair for nonsense" (*SRW* (n 21) ch 15, 137).[62] It is very obvious that in *SRW* the hope for the future of Scotland that is hinted at in, for example, *Redgauntlet* (although there not unambiguously) is found to have been unfulfilled and disappointed. In so far as the Spa stands for modern Scotland, it is a world that has turned to farce and tragedy. The legacy of the Scottish Enlightenment – with its emphasis on improvement – has been found both wanting and deeply flawed. Joan Elbers has rightly remarked that "[t]he nineteenth-century world of *St. Ronan's Well* bears little resemblance to the world we would expect to have come into being fifty years after the close of *Redgauntlet*".[63]

In discussing the Well and the Wellers, Touchwood at one point stated a longing "for the days of the Spectator" (*SRW* (n 21) ch 15, 137). Touchwood is here not simply acting his part as a praiser of past times, he is alluding directly to one of the works that exerted most influence on eighteenth-century Scotland, as Scots, after the Union, cultivated models of Addisonian politeness and "modern" manners, the values of which were notably propagated by Scottish periodicals such as *The Mirror* and *The Lounger*.[64] But the cultivation of manners has now become the artificiality of the Well, where the esentially rootless characters generally affect "knapping English" rather than Scots, referring, for example, to Mowbray of Saint Ronans as "The Squire" (*SRW* (n 21) ch 2, 14; ch 3, 27).

It is an alienated society given over to the love of money, where even close and affectionate family links are affected by greed: thus Mowbray defrauded his sister of her small inheritance. While it is to be expected that Micklewhame "thinks of nothing else but his filthy self" (*SRW* (n 21) ch 6, 56), even Bindloose, the good lawyer, finds it difficult to interpret Meg Dods' concern for Tyrrel in other than economic terms (*SRW* (n 21) ch 14, 126–129). The rational improvements effected by Touchwood in the Aulton were also dependent on the use of money (*SRW* (n 21) ch 28, 255–259). Medical attention could only be secured by money: health and wealth were inextricably linked (*SRW* (n 21) ch 7, 60–63; ch 32, 306; ch 38, 361).[65] And while the society of the Well and elsewhere was given over to the pursuit of money, with consequent

62 In the *Magnum Opus*, Scott here added "no well in your swamps tenanted by such a conceited colony of clamorous frogs", *SRW*, Centenary Edition (n 21) ch 15, 163. See on the text here, *SRW* (n 21) 400.

63 Elbers, A contrast of fictional worlds" (n 33) at 163.

64 N Phillipson, "Politics, Politeness and the Anglicisation of early Eighteenth-Century Scottish Culture", in R A Mason (ed), *Scotland and England 1286–1815* (1987) 226.

65 See further on this connection, Sroka, "Wealth" (n 40) passim.

corruption of manners, much of the wealth was illusory – bubble wealth or air wealth, such as credit raised on accommodation bills (*SRW* (n 21) ch 15, 136). Even the curative properties of the Well are illusory, based on the supposed cure of Lady Penelope Penfeather (whose house at Windywa has notably been renamed Air-castle (*SRW* (n 21) ch 2, 20). All is founded on falsity.

This selfish pursuit of money has affected the institution of marriage, central to social life. So greed has corrupted the very heart of society. Lady Binks married Sir Bingo for money and status even though she despised him. Dr Quackleben married the forthright and down-to-earth widow, Mrs Blower, for her money. Bulmer impersonated Tyrrel to marry Clara in order to secure an estate and tried to assert this marriage for the same reason. If marriage has brought Lady Binks only unhappiness, for Clara it has brought madness.

D. UNION AND MARRIAGE

It is noteworthy that the bridegrooms of Clara and Lady Binks were Englishmen. Sir Bingo – whose name is an overt reference to the dog that jumped over the stile in the folk-song with the spelling chorus (*SRW* (n 21) 459) – is represented as a stupid, brutish lout, a very caricature of bluff John Bull, and he is once explicitly compared to "a butcher's bull-dog" (*SRW* (n 21) ch 13, 115).[66] Lady Binks commented on some criticism of the mode by which she achieved her marriage: "Not being conscious of any high elevation, . . . I do not know any arts I have been under the necessity of practising to attain it. I suppose a Scots lady of an ancient family may become the wife of an English baronet, and no very extraordinary great cause to wonder at it" (*SRW* (n 21) ch 7, 69). But nonetheless, she is the archetypal tocherless lass with a long pedigree, who has rescued her financial and social situation at the cost of great personal unhappiness by trapping an Englishman into marriage. Clara's "marriage" to an Englishman was achieved on his part by strategem and deception: he is plausible, perfidious and utterly unscrupulous about achieving his end of marriage with her.

That these loveless and disastrous marriages were between Scotswomen and Englishmen suggests that it is important to ask if there is a further political allusion here and whether the Union of England and Scotland is somehow symbolised in them. If so, then the novel may be arguing at one level that the artificiality of modern life at the Well is somehow a product of

66 His fellow Wellers also compare him to a dog (*SRW* (n 21) ch 7, 62).

the Union. And contrasts between the manners of England and Scotland are certainly drawn in the novel (*SRW* (n 21) ch 19, 179–180).

Peter Garside has convincingly argued that a close exploration of the changes in dating in *The Bride of Lammermoor* between the first and *Magnum Opus* editions demonstrates that this novel about marriage is also dealing at a metaphoric level with the Union of 1707.[67] There is much to suggest that we should have *The Bride of Lammermoor* in mind in reading *SRW*. Both novels are dominated by the theme of marriage. The heroines of both novels – Lucy Ashton and Clara Mowbray – are driven mad by marriage; both also are susceptible because of the excessive reading of old romances and novels in their youth which has perverted their sensibilities and understandings (*SRW* (n 21) ch 7, 66; ch 32, 309–310).[68] And the madness of both is clearly not the *furor uterinus* of early-nineteenth-century psychology.[69] Moreover, both novels involve ill-omened springs: the fountain to which the Master of Ravenswood carries Lucy in *BL* ((n 68) ch 5, 57–59), and the very Well itself in *SRW* (the reviewer in the *British Critic* was alive to this possible link, but saw it as underlining the contrast between the novels).[70] That *SRW* is to be related to *BL* is demonstrated by a further sign – an inn sign. Meg Dods had employed "the celebrated Dick Tinto to re-paint her father's sign" (*SRW* (n 21) ch 1, 9); she also advised Tyrrel to follow Tinto's practice of painting portraits for money, as people preferred portraits of themselves to sketches of landscapes (*SRW* (n 21) ch 3, 25). This is the Dick Tinto to whose life the opening chapter of *BL* is largely devoted, and from whose sketches and brief account of the life of the bride the narrator Peter Pattieson supposedly elaborated the story of *BL* ((n 68) ch 1, 13–25).

If the allusions to *BL* in *SRW* support a reading of the marriages as offering a criticism of the Union of 1707, then the "dowry of ruined villages" resulting from improvement is the marriage portion of the Union. The Union brought apparent prosperity and peace; but it upset old ways and broke the bonds of society. For example, the lairds of Saint Ronans, now called squires, no longer

67 P D Garside, "Union and *The Bride of Lammermoor*" (1984) 19 *Studies in Scottish Literature* 72.

68 Sir Walter Scott, *The Bride of Lammermoor*, ed F Robertson, The World's Classics (1991) 40 (henceforth cited as *BL* in text). The influence on women's minds of the reading of romances is of course a cliche of the period, as satirised, for instance, by Jane Austen, in *Northanger Abbey*. It is therefore interesting to note that Bulmer claims to Jekyl that his "ideas of marriage were much founded on plays and novels": *SRW* (n 21) ch 26, 241. Further on the theme of madness in *The Bride of Lammermoor*, see E Showalter, *The Female Malady: Women, Madness, and English Culture, 1830–1980* (1987) 14–17; P W Martin, *Mad Women in Romantic Writing* (1987) 99–109.

69 On this, see the different views expressed in Showalter and Martin (n 68).

70 Review of *St Ronan's Well*, (1824) 21 *British Critic*, NS 16 at 16.

live surrounded by the village, in the Scottish society of the Aulton, but have retreated to a castle enclosed in dangerous woods. The current laird's only social contacts are with the idlers of the Well. He was also educated in England: a miseducation textually linked with that of his sister (*SRW* (n 21) ch 7, 66). When the suggestion is put to him that he should have joined other lairds as a member of the Faculty of Advocates, thus following the traditional means adopted by Scottish gentry of slender means to augment and uphold their fortunes, he rejects it in favour of gambling with money tricked from his sister (*SRW* (n 21) ch 10, 93–94). What he wished to do was emulate the mode of life of the loutish English baronet, Sir Bingo Binks. The virtuous and honest Scottish peasantry have now turned hostile and mercenary (*SRW* (n 21) ch 15, 135–136). In this brave new world, the "most unpardonable offence in modern morality" was "a solecism in the code of honour" (*SRW* (n 21) ch 12, 105). Lives were to be destroyed over trivialities, while real wrongs could be committed unpunished and indeed be applauded,[71] in a society in which women "have given up their virtue to preserve their character, which is, after all, only the shadow of it" (*SRW* (n 21) ch 27, 251). The Addisonian politeness emulated in the Scottish Enlightenment has degenerated into unreality and artifice, just as the desire for commercial improvement has become lust for money. *SRW* offers no resolution of this conflict between the old, traditional, essentially Scottish values represented by the Aulton and its guardian spirit Meg Dods, "the sole assertor of its ancient dignities" (*SRW* (n 21) ch 12, 106), and the values of the new, "improved", post-Union Scotland represented by the Well and the Wellers. This suggests the need to reformulate Daiches' interpretation of the Waverley novels, as many features of *SRW* are typical of his class of "Scottish" novels – an English hero in Scotland, for example, whose birthright is uncertain. The political and social reconciliation that a marriage of Clara and Tyrrel might have made possible cannot now take place: she is dead and he, perhaps in a Moravian mission, has vanished abroad. Touchwood, who appeared able to avert tragedy but in fact helped, through his vanity, to precipitate it, continues "forming plans which have no object, and accumulating a fortune, for which he has apparently no heir". The prodigal Mowbray has fled abroad, joined the army, and become a miser. All that is left is Meg Dods running her inn in the Aulton: it is not obvious that she will find a successor (*SRW* (n 21) ch 39, 371–372). Josiah Cargill, that other luminary of the Aulton, presumably continues lost in the past,

71 See V G Kiernan, *The Duel in European History: Honour and the Reign of Aristocracy* (1988) 223–237 for a discussion of duelling in *SRW*.

pursuing obscure antiquarian researches, without result. No future appears possible: the only solution is destruction, and Mowbray buys back the feus of the buildings of the Well and orders their demolition (*SRW* (n 21) ch 39, 372). Union, love and community have become impossible in a shoddy, third-rate world. The lines of verse (probably by Scott) given as a motto to the final chapter are particularly telling, in a novel that in many ways reads like a critique of the 1980s and 1990s as much as of the 1810s and 1820s:

> Here come we to our close – for that which follows
> Is but the tale of dull, unvaried misery.
> Steep crags and headlong linns may court the pencil,
> Like sudden haps, dark plots, and strange adventures;
> But who would paint the dull and fog-wrapt moor,
> In its long track of sterile desolation?

E. CONCLUSION

Dramatic effect would suggest that we should leave the discussion there. It is, however, impossible to do so. At the very end of the novel, we find a mock advertisement, which the critic of the *Monthly Review* seems to have taken seriously (perhaps correctly).[72] This is for *An Account of the Seige of Ptolemais* by Josiah Cargill (*SRW* (n 21) 373). With its contemporary setting, *SRW* lacks the framing narrative that most of the other Waverley novels possess. These narratives tend to subvert the novels they prefaced and concluded. The sudden appearance of this advertisement has a similar effect on the reader who has already been told that Cargill was "deeply engaged with the siege of Ptolemais" when Hanah Irwin's desire to confess was communicated to him (*SRW* (n 21) ch 38, 361). What are we to make of this? It alerts us to the multiplicity of possible readings of a Scott novel. Earlier, it was pointed out that the world of Scotland of the Well was not what one would have expected from *Redgauntlet*. Yet, in the conclusion to *Redgauntlet*, we find that Alan Fairford acquired the territorial designation of "Clinkdollar" (*RG* (n 13) 400). Perhaps, the future was not to be looked upon as so full of bright potential.[73] Turning to *SRW*, is it also possible to offer an alternative or inversion of the reading given here? Meg Dods may be single and life-enhancing, but we cannot interpret Lady Penelope Penfeather's single status in quite the

72 *Monthly Review* (1824) 75. In fact, Scott's later *Tales of the Crusaders* do develop from this: see, e.g., Robertson, *Legitimate Histories* (n 37) 135–136.

73 On the issues posed by Scott's endings in general, see F R Hart, "Scott's endings: the fictions of authority" (1978) 33 *Nineteenth-Century Fiction* 48.

same way. Were the bitter machinations of this Scotswoman due to her lack of union? The Scots law of marriage may be the object of criticism, but the most evil marriage surely was that of Lord Etherington to Anne Bulmer, conducted under regular English forms: it was this union that made the tragedy possible. What can we make of that? One can see how another reading might be possible.

This said, it cannot be denied that themes in *SRW* were clearly related to current anxieties about the Scots law of marriage. We are justified in reading the novel as connected with these concerns. James Beattie, the popular poet and moral philosopher, had earlier remarked about the contrast between the English and the Scots laws that "[i]f the law of England be too rigid in this particular, as some think it is, that of Scotland is undoubtedly too little so". He pointed out that the English law was very easily evaded by a visit to Scotland.[74] At the same time, conflicts over the differences between the Scots and English laws on divorce and the difficulties thereby arising were being debated.[75] There had been considerable parliamentary controversy over the law on marriage in England from 1820 onwards, and the crucial provisions of Lord Hardwicke's Act had been affirmed by a subsequent Act near-contemporary with the writing of *SRW*.[76] Scott's novel reflects and contributes to these anxieties. There definitely was an anxious discourse concerning the Scots marriage laws in the first half of the nineteenth century, focusing on young English noblemen being trapped into marriage by older Scotswomen of ill repute.[77] Moreover, that the novel expresses anxieties about both the Enlightenment and the Union is clear. Of course, Scott is as ever enigmatic and ambiguous, but as Albert Kiralfy has rightly pointed out, "[g]reat authors seem to like to tease their readers".[78] Scott simply provided complex allusive texts capable of many readings.

74 J Beattie, *Elements of Moral Science*, 2nd edn, 2 vols (1793) vol ii, 282.

75 J Fergusson, *Reports of Some Recent Decisions by the Consistorial Court of Scotland, in Actions of Divorce, Concluding for Dissolution of Marriages Celebrated Under the English Law* (1817).

76 Statute 4 Geo IV, c 76 (1823); Outhwaite, *Clandestine Marriage* (n 50) 152–159.

77 See W D H Sellar, "Marriage, Divorce and the Forbidden Degrees: Canon Law and Scots Law", in W N Osborough (ed), *Explorations in Law and History: Irish Legal History Society Discourses, 1988–1994* (1995) 59 at 63–65.

78 Kiralfy, "Underworld Cant" (n 1) 773.

15 A Note on *The Bride of Lammermoor*: Why Scott did not Mention the Dalrymple Legend until 1830

A. INTRODUCTION

The opening sentence that Scott provided for the introduction to the *Magnum Opus* edition of *The Bride of Lammermoor* is familiar: "The Author, on a former occasion, declined giving the real source from which he drew the tragic subject of this history, because, though occurring at a distant period, it might possibly be unpleasant to the feelings of the descendants of the parties."[1] The former occasion to which Scott alluded was probably the writing of the introduction to *Chronicles of the Canongate* in 1827.[2] This means that, as first published in 1819, the novel opened with Peter Pattieson's entertaining account of the life of Dick Tinto, the obscure painter, and of the latter's discussions with Pattieson on the respective merits of narrative in the novel and in the pictorial arts. Tinto had made sketches of an ancient castle, but from legends that he had learned concerning the castle, he had become tempted, instead of drawing the ruins in the landscape, to represent the most interesting legend in a historical painting. This legend was, of course, that of *The Bride of Lammermoor* which Pattieson proceeded to tell (*Bride* (n 1) 23–25). Neither Tinto nor Pattieson – nor, for that matter, Jedediah Cleishbotham as editor – referred to the story of the unfortunate Janet Dalrymple, which Scott identified in the *Magnum* edition in 1830 as the source of his "ower true tale" (*Bride* (n 1) 340), and the historical and legendary material on which Scott drew has been the subject of scholarly investigation, confirming how Scott used various versions of the story of Janet Dalrymple to form his own tale.[3]

1 Sir Walter Scott, *The Bride of Lammermoor*, F Robertson (ed) (1991) 1. (Henceforth page references in the text will be to this edition as *Bride*).

2 Editor's note: *Bride* 363.

3 C O Parsons, "The Dalrymple legend in *The Bride of Lammermoor*" (1945) 19 *Review of English*

Recent scholarship has shown the extensive nature of the revisions Scott made for the *Magnum Opus* edition of *The Bride of Lammermoor*. The most important of these changes were those redating the period of the action of the novel to after the Union of 1707;[4] they do not appear, however, to have a bearing on why Scott felt reticent about alluding to the Dalrymple legend until 1830. Indeed, the explanation Scott gave in 1830 seems undoubtedly to have been the motive for his omitting any mention of Janet Dalrymple. The reasons for doing so in 1819 and shortly thereafter were, however, much more compelling than has hitherto been noticed in the critical literature on *The Bride of Lammermoor*. A story of marital problems and irregularities in the family of Dalrymple of Stair had a very powerful and painful contemporary resonance in 1819, affecting highly placed members of Edinburgh and London society, such that to mention it in a work as widely disseminated as one of the Waverley novels would have been in distinctly bad taste and potentially interfering with matters *sub judice*.

This paper will accordingly suggest that what restrained Scott in 1819 from allowing Peter Pattieson to refer to Janet Dalrymple were the severe and well-publicised marital problems of John William Henry Dalrymple, who was to succeed in 1821 as seventh Earl of Stair.[5] These problems had resulted in twelve years of litigation in England and Scotland. The year *The Bride of Lammermoor* was published was the year that saw the commencement in Edinburgh of the sixth and final court action arising out of Dalrymple's matrimonial misadventures. By 1830, however, the immediate scandal must have settled, and the source of *The Bride* had become a relatively open secret: Scott would have considered himself free to reveal and discuss the relationship of the novel to the legends about Janet Dalrymple.

Finally, it is worth pointing out that Dalrymple's affairs did not influence the plot of *The Bride of Lammermoor*. It is likely, however, that Scott's awareness of the twelve years of law suits fed into aspects of the plot of *Saint Ronan's Well*. This paper will close with some brief remarks on this.

Studies 51 (henceforth Parsons, "Dalrymple legend"); C Lamont, "Scott as story-teller: *The Bride of Lammermoor*" (May, 1980) 7,1 *Scottish Literary Journal* 113; W S Crockett, *The Scott Originals: An Account of Notables and Worthies the Originals of Characters in the Waverley Novels*, 3rd edn (1932) (henceforth Crockett, *Scott Originals*) 249–268.

4 J Millgate, "Text and context: dating the events of *The Bride of L·ammermoor*" (1979) 9 *The Bibliotheck* 200; P D Garside, "Union and *The Bride of Lammermoor*" (1984) 19 *Studies in Scottish Literature* 72 (henceforth Garside, "Union and *The Bride of Lammermoor*").

5 Sir James Balfour Paul (ed), *The Scots Peerage*, 9 vols (1904–1914) (henceforth *Scots Peerage*) vol viii, 157–158.

B. MATRIMONIAL MISADVENTURES AND LITIGATIONS

John William Henry Dalrymple was a domiciled Englishman (and he passed virtually all of his life south of the border and latterly in France). His father was General Dalrymple, who had been Governor of Chelsea Hospital, and was brother to the fifth Earl of Stair. Dalrymple came to Scotland in March or April 1804, aged nineteen, as a young officer in the fifth Dragoon Guards, and there struck up an intimate acquaintance with Miss Johanna Gordon, daughter of Charles Gordon of Cluny. She was over twenty-one years of age. The pair had a number of secret assignations and, on at least one occasion, passed the night together. They also exchanged a number of promises of marriage in the future or of present consent to marriage. Some of these were recorded in writing. Their connection was kept secret on his insistence as knowledge of it would have incurred his father's disapproval. As it happened, General Dalrymple became aware that some type of connection had been formed, and removed his son to England on 21 July 1804. Secret correspondence continued between Miss Gordon and Dalrymple. He sailed for Malta in 1805, and set up a channel for further correspondence. He stayed abroad until 1808. His affections apparently altered in 1806. General Dalrymple died in Spring 1807, whereupon Miss Gordon started to try to assert her rights as Dalrymple's alleged wife. Dalrymple returned to England in May 1808. He was advised by a family friend to hold to his connection with Miss Gordon; a few days later, however, he went through a regular and formal ceremony of marriage in England with Miss Laura Manners, a sister of the Duchess of St Albans, on 2 June 1808.[6] When Miss Gordon heard of this (perhaps from the *Caledonian Mercury* of 14 June 1808), she raised an action in the Consistory Court of London to assert her rights as his wife. This first came before the Court in the Michaelmas Term of 1808.[7] The litigation was protracted. Witnesses were examined in

6 These details are drawn from J Dodson, *A Report of the Judgment, Delivered in the Consistorial Court of London, On the Sixteenth Day of July, 1811, By the Right Honourable Sir William Scott, Chancellor of the Diocese, in the Cause of Dalrymple the Wife, against Dalrymple the Husband. With An Appendix, Containing the Depositions of the Witnesses the Letters of the Parties, and Other Papers Exhibited in the Cause* (1811) (henceforth Dodson, *Report*); and *Dalrymple v Dalrymple* 2 Hag Con 54.

7 See the printed proceedings relating to this litigation found in the process in *Manners or Dalrymple v Dalrymple and Gordon or Dalrymple*, S[cottish] R[ecord] O[ffice], Commissary of Edinburgh, Consistorial Processes, CC 8/6/96. The printed proceedings were part of no 11 in the process, an inventory of writs and the writs themselves; they are currently located at the end of the bundle of the process. Reference to cases in the Commissary records will be given in full only when first cited; thereafter they will be cited by name and archival number alone.

Edinburgh, London and Glasgow over 1809 and 1810.[8] Sir William Scott, Chancellor of the Diocese of London, delivered his judgement on 16 July 1811. He found on the evidence that Miss Gordon and Dalrymple had been married in 1804 according to the law of Scotland by a *de praesenti* declaration of consent, or, alternatively, *per verba de futuro subsequente copula*, and that Miss Gordon was not barred from asserting her rights by reason of delay. The purported marriage of Dalrymple to Miss Manners was accordingly void and bigamous.[9]

It is important to point out that this type of irregular marriage had been impossible in England since Lord Hardwicke's Act of 1753 had come into force. The same Act would have prevented Dalrymple, as a minor, from marrying in England without parental consent.[10]

Sir William Scott's judgement did not end the litigation, as Dalrymple appealed it to the Court of the Arches. There Laura Manners appeared for her interest on 4 November 1811, and was admitted as a party by way of interpleader. Her proxy was presented to the Court on 9 November 1811. The Court rejected her prayer for more time on 4 December 1811 and subsequently affirmed the sentence of the Consistorial Court. Laura Manners next petitioned Lord Chancellor Eldon for the appointment of a High Court of Delegates, and on 7 February 1812 Eldon granted a Commission appointing Delegates to consider Laura Manners' case.[11] Dalrymple meanwhile moved north to Edinburgh to reside for a sufficient period to become subject to the jurisdiction of the Commissaries of Edinburgh; and in June 1812 Laura Manners raised before that court against Dalrymple and Johanna Gordon an action of declarator of marriage and of putting to silence.[12] Johanna Gordon claimed in her defences of 30 July 1812 that she had raised an action against Dalrymple to establish her marriage in the Consistorial Court in London as the appropriate forum, that Sir William Scott had found in her favour, that

8 Dodson, *Report* (n 6) Appendix.

9 Ibid 1–96; 2 Hag Con 54.

10 Statute 26 Geo II, c 33.

11 Details of this action are drawn from the petition of Laura Manners given in to the Commissary Court in Edinburgh on 18 February 1820 in *Dalrymple v Dalrymple*, SRO Commissary of Edinburgh, Consistorial Decreets, CC 8/5/38 (this volume is unpaginated) and from the defences, replies, duplies, memories and writs found in the process in *Manners or Dalrymple v Dalrymple and Gordon or Dalrymple*, SRO CC 8/6/96.

12 *Manners or Dalrymple v Dalrymple and Gordon or Dalrymple*, SRO CC 8/6/96. The summons against Johanna Gordon is missing from the process; for the date of 19 June 1812 for the raising of the action, see the petition of Laura Manners given in on 18 February 1820, in *Dalrymple v Dalrymple*, SRO CC 8/5/38. Her mandate to Hay Donaldson is dated Malvern, 21 June 1812 and is no 2 of the process in CC 8/6/96.

an appeal was pending, that the present action was collusive between Laura Manners and Dalrymple, and accordingly argued that the action ought to be disapproved of on the grounds of *lis alibi pendens* (that is, it was already being pursued in a different and appropriate court) and because it was unprecedented and irregular for a pursuer such as Laura Manners to raise an action of putting to silence against one such as her. Moreover the merits could not be discussed because the relevant documents were in London. To vouch for her claims she produced various documents relating to the litigation in London. Dalrymple entered defences on 7 August 1812, denying he was the pretended husband of Johanna Gordon.[13] The same day, Dalrymple also raised a summons against Johanna Gordon for declarator of freedom, scandal, and putting to silence.[14] He produced it with his defences to Laura Manners' action. Laura Manners gave in answers dated 14 August 1812 to both defences. These argued that she had been astonished to find out about the action in the Consistorial Court in London, that an appeal was pending in London, that the litigation concerned a question of Scots law, but expert witnesses had disagreed, so that it seemed appropriate to sue in Scotland to get an authoritative determination on the Scots law. After a long discussion of *lis alibi pendens*, claiming it did not apply, the Commissaries were asked to repel the preliminary defences and ask for defences on the merits. The Commissaries issued an interlocutor on 28 August 1812 requiring the giving in of replies and duplies. Johanna Gordon's replies of 18 September reasserted the appropriateness of London as the forum for the action, while Laura Manners' duplies restated her case. A protestation against Dalrymple for not complying with the interlocutor of 28 August was admitted on 9 October. In a minute of 18 December Johanna Gordon noted that the Court of Delegates had given leave on 4 December to Laura Manners to bring in an allegation, and she produced a copy of the decree and once more pleaded *lis alibi pendens*, to which Laura Manners responded with answers on 19 December. After avizandum, the Commissaries issued an interlocutor on 29 January 1813 requiring the giving in, interchanging and printing of memorials. Memorials were given in, resulting in an interlocutor of 2 April 1813 repelling Johanna Gordon's preliminary defences, and sustaining the action as competent and relevant, but sisting further procedure since there was an

13 Nos 3–5 of process in *Manners or Dalrymple v Dalrymple and Gordon or Dalrymple*, SRO CC 8/6/96.

14 No 1 of process in *Dalrymple v Gordon*, SRO Commissary of Edinburgh, Consistorial processes, CC 8/6/100.

action depending in England.[15] At the same time, Dalrymple's summons against Johanna Gordon had been executed on 8 August 1812. She gave in defences dated 18 September, suggesting Dalrymple had raised this action because she had pleaded that it was not competent for Laura Manners, with whom he was in collusion, to sue her for putting to silence, and arguing that Dalrymple was barred from insisting in the action because the defender had sued him in England, and the action was now depending in England before the Court of Delegates. Once more she pleaded *lis alibi pendens*. Dalrymple's answers of 25 January 1813 argued that it was competent for him to sue Johanna Gordon, and that the plea of *lis alibi pendens* did not apply because the London courts were foreign courts. The Commissaries issued an interlocutor – also on 29 January 1813 – again appointing the giving in of memorials. The memorials of February 1813 reasserted the same arguments, and by an interlocutor of 2 April 1813 the Commissaries noted that an action depended in England which was the proper forum of the pursuer at the time that action was raised, and superseded giving any deliverance on the competency of the action until the issue of the earlier action in England.[16]

In England meanwhile, the Court of Delegates had rejected Laura Manners' first allegation on 17 February 1813, and shortly thereafter rejected her second, ruling to this effect on 24 February. She had argued, *inter alia*, in the first allegation for a stay of proceedings until a decision had been given in the court in Scotland as providing the best evidence of the Scots law on marriage. The second allegation had been on the rules of proof. Formal judgement, however, had not yet been entered.[17] She accordingly petitioned the Commissaries in Edinburgh on 22 April asking for a review of the interlocutor sisting the process of declarator of marriage on the grounds that, in the action in England, Scottish rules of evidence had been ignored, so that evidence to prove marriage in Scotland had been admitted that would not have been admitted by the Scots courts. She further claimed that

15 Nos 7–14 of process in *Manners or Dalrymple v Dalrymple and Gordon or Dalrymple*, SRO CC 8/6/96. The interlocutor of 29 January 1813 is written on p 50 of Laura Manners' duplies and that of 2 April on no 13. Dalrymple's summons against Johanna Gordon (no 6 of process) is missing from the bundle.

16 Nos 1–5 of process in *Dalrymple v Gordon*, SRO CC 8/6/100. The two interlocutors are written on nos 3 and 4 of process.

17 See the inventory of writs, no 15 of process, and writs themselves, esp 1st allegation and certified copy of judgment of 24 February 1813 in *Manners or Dalrymple v Dalrymple and Gordon or Dalrymple*, SRO CC 8/6/96; see also petition of Laura Manners, 18 February 1820, in *Dalrymple v Dalrymple*, SRO CC 8/5/38.

the Delegates has refused to try her case on the merits, and argued that if the Commissaries intended to disregard the decision of the Delegates there was no reason why they should wait for formal judgement; if they did not, it was unfair, because, the English court having refused to hear her, if the Commissaries also refused, there was no court that would give her justice. Johanna Gordon gave in answers on 3 June 1813, accusing Laura Manners of misrepresenting the English court proceedings, and referring to the record of them already entered in the process, and asking the Commissaries to adhere to their interlocutor as judgement was expected soon in the English action. By their interlocutor of 25 June 1813, the Commissaries adhered to the interlocutor of 2 April reclaimed against.[18]

The High Court of Delegates entered a judgement on 19 January 1814 affirming Sir William Scott's decision.[19] Dalrymple accordingly on 22 April 1814 entered a minute moving the Commissaries to resume consideration of his case against Johanna Gordon, as it had now been affirmatively decided in England that they were married, and requesting that they should dismiss the present action. Johanna Gordon's answers of 20 May agreed. And the Commissaries accordingly assoilzied her on 27 May 1814.[20] Laura Manners' action was allowed to sleep. This first phase of the litigation accordingly came to an end.

If one phase of litigation had concluded, another was beginning. From 24 February 1813, it had been obvious that the validity of the marriage of Dalrymple to Johanna Gordon would be upheld in the English courts. This must have decided Dalrymple to try to divorce her. It was certainly rumoured in 1813 that he would attempt to do so.[21] In contrast with England, judicial divorce had been possible in Scotland since the sixteenth century. The competent court was again that of the Commissaries of Edinburgh.[22] Accordingly, a libelled summons of the Commissaries was issued on 4 April 1814 and Johanna Gordon was cited the same day to compear.[23] The litigation

18 Nos 16 and 17 of process in *Manners or Dalrymple v Dalrymple and Gordon or Dalrymple*, SRO CC 8/6/96; the interlocutor is endorsed on p 19 of no 16.

19 For date, see summons (no 1 of process) p 2, in *Gordon or Dalrymple v Dalrymple* SRO Commissary of Edinburgh, Consistorial Processes, CC 8/6/99.

20 Nos 6 and 7 of process in *Dalrymple v Gordon*, SRO CC 8/6/100. The interlocutor is written on no 6.

21 See the deposition of Major Dalzel in *Dalrymple v Gordon or Dalrymple*, SRO Commissary of Edinburgh, Consistorial Decreets, CC 8/5/34 93–246 at 206.

22 C J [Lord] Guthire, "The History of Divorce in Scotland" (1911) 8 *Scottish Historical Review* 39; R H Helmholz, *Roman Canon Law in Reformation England* (1990) 73–74; L Stone, *Road to Divorce: England 1530–1887* (1990) 301–308.

23 *Dalrymple v Gordon or Dalrymple*, SRO CC 8/5/34 93–100.

was protracted as the Commissaries, on the plea of the defender, compelled the pursuer to provide ever-more specific condescendences averring details of the alleged adultery. The defender also alleged, one suspects with justice, that Dalrymple was basically engaged on a fishing expedition, trying to use the court process to dredge up information damaging to her; and in her pleadings she made great play of the fact that Dalrymple seemed reluctant to take the oath of calumny and wanted a witness examined on deposition before he did so: indeed he did not take the oath until 28 June 1814.[24] There was much fencing over the examination of this witness, Major Dalzel, with whom Dalrymple alleged Johanna Gordon had committed adultery. The problem was his likely call for service abroad before the action reached the stage of proof. Eventually on 25 August the Commissaries issued an interlocutor allowing Major Dalzel to be examined; Dalzel meanwhile arrived in Edinburgh and the Commissaries issued on 2 September a new interlocutor for his examination on 7 September on the most recent condescendence of the pursuer. The deposition was thereafter sealed to await the further progress of the action.[25] The most material allegations in the condescendence were that Dalzel had rented a room in a house in Rose Street devoted to illicit assignations where Johanna Gordon had visited him, and further that a servant of the family had seen her have sexual intercourse with Dalzel in the open air in the grounds of her father's house at Braid, and had commented: "Ah Jacky Jacky, will ye no gie oer your auld tricks yet."[26]

Johanna Gordon had meanwhile in her turn raised an action of separation and aliment against Dalrymple, claiming not only that he had deserted her but also "maltreated her in a manner the most afflicting, and severe to a woman of Honor and Character and more especially to a person of the pursuers situation and rank in life". The grounds of separation were his causeless accusation of adultery making her an object of calumny and obloquy, and his abandonment and failure to support her. As well as separation *a mensa et thoro*, she sought aliment of £1,000 per annum. Dalrymple was cited at the Market Cross of Edinburgh and foreshore at Leith to compear before the Commissaries on 29 July and 19 August, the first and second diets of the cause.[27] Dalrymple gave in defences dated 2 September noting the pending action of divorce, and calling for details of the pursuer's funds if interim aliment was sought, but suggesting the pursuer was amply provided for and

24 Ibid 106–121; see also 164–182.
25 Ibid 158–163.
26 Ibid 136–143.
27 *Gordon or Dalrymple v Dalrymple*, SRO CC 8/6/99, nos 1 and 2 of process.

that the matter should rest until the cause of divorce had been determined.[28] The action rested there until after the divorce.

In Dalrymple's action against Johanna Gordon, the Commissaries issued an interlocutor on 30 September 1814, on the basis of her answers to his condescendence, finding the condescendence too vague and irrelevant to be admitted to proof; they ordained Dalrymple to give in an additional and more specific condescendence that articulately stated time and place as to each of the facts alleged.[29] This he did on 14 October 1814. There were now twenty-three paragraphs in the condescendence, and Dalrymple tried to specify less vaguely and more precisely the allegations of adultery at the house in Rose Street, in the woods in Braid and in her father's houses in St Andrews Square and at Braid.[30] An interlocutor of 21 October 1814 appointed answers to be given in by the defender; this was done on 25 November 1814. The answers noted the changes of the dates of the allegations through the four condescendences, attacked the probability of some of the allegations and the fact that the evidence was to be proved by persons "of the lowest description". Furthermore, the averments were again challenged for vagueness, generality, and irrelevance. The most interesting answer was the suggestion that Dalrymple was trying to confuse matters and dates and thereby use witnesses' hazy memories of the meetings of Johanna Gordon with himself in 1804 as evidence of Dalzel's alleged meetings with her. The answers concluded with a request for a much more articulate condescendence that also condescended on the witnesses by whom it was intended to prove the averments.[31] The Commissaries ordained the pursuer by an interlocutor of 9 December 1814 to give in a list of witnesses indicating those articles of the condescendence that they were intended to prove. The pursuer's procurator, however, on 16 December gave in a minute abandoning the process, requesting the opening of Dalzell's deposition, and calling for a decree of absolvitor. An interlocutor of 23 December allowed the defender to see the minute and answer it should she wish.[32] The defender's answers given in on 30 December were to the effect that she was as ignorant of why the pursuer had started the action as of why he now abandoned it. She did not want absolvitor as a favour, but requested that the Commissaries open the deposition of Dalzel held *in retentis*, the

28 No 3 of process in ibid.
29 *Dalrymple v Gordon or Dalrymple*, SRO CC 8/5.34 182.
30 Ibid 183–190.
31 Ibid 190–201.
32 Ibid 201–202.

only evidence brought, and issue a judgement thereon. An interlocutor to this effect was issued on 20 January 1815, and the Commissaries went to avizandum on the whole process.[33] Dalzel's deposition offered no support to Dalrymple's allegations.[34] The Commissaries accordingly issued an interlocutor on 20 January 1815 stating there was no evidence and the pursuer ought not to have instigated the action, and assoilzied the defender from the conclusions of the libel and decerned as requested.[35] After a dispute over costs and their taxation, the final sentence and decreet was issued on 21 April 1815.[36]

After gaining this decree of absolvitor, Johanna Gordon gave in answers, dated 8 June 1815, to Dalrymple's defences to her libel in the action for separation and aliment. These provided details of Dalrymple's supposed income, based on his father's will, estimating it at £3,000 to £4,000 per annum, and discussing her own fortune of £10,000 from which his *jus mariti* was expressly excluded.[37] There was a protestation against the defender for not replying to the answers, but on 25 August 1815 the Commissaries issued an interlocutor requiring Johanna Gordon as pursuer to give in a condescendence stating the grounds in fact and in law on which she maintained her action, in which would also be pointed out the authorities or cases on similar facts where no physical violence or maltreatment of the pursuer had been libelled.[38] Johanna Gordon thereafter appears to have let the action fall asleep, thus ending this stage of the protracted litigation.

The next formal step, initiating the final phase of these lawsuits arising out of the marital affairs of Dalrymple, took place when a libelled summons dated 22 June 1819 was served the next day on Dalrymple in the New Town of Edinburgh, citing him to compear in an action of divorce against him on the grounds of his adultery in London and in the City and suburbs of Edinburgh.[39] The action was first called on 13 August 1819: Dalrymple made no appearance and did not do so after an interlocutor of 20 August appointing Johanna Gordon to take the oath of calumny, which she did on 7 September 1819. By an interlocutor of 10 September she was required to give in a special and articulate condescendence of facts

33 Ibid 202–203.
34 Ibid 203–207.
35 Ibid 207–208
36 Ibid 245–246.
37 *Gordon or Dalrymple v Dalrymple*, SRO CC 8/6/99, no 4 of process.
38 Written on no 1 of process in ibid.
39 *Dalrymple v Dalrymple*, SRO CC 8/5/38 (I shall give no further specific references to this volume since it is unpaginated).

averred that she offered to prove with a list of witnesses. This she did on 13 September 1819. She averred their marriage, and Dalrymple's adultery in London and elsewhere with Laura or Louisa Manners from 1809 to 1815, further adultery with several women in Edinburgh and its suburbs five or six years before, and in various months in late 1818 and early 1819. Proof was allowed by an interlocutor of 21 September granting a commission to take evidence in London on deposition. This related to Dalrymple's cohabitation with Laura Manners. Evidence was given in Edinburgh by a number of women who lodged in the house of a Mrs Milligan first in James Street and then in Hanover Street. One suspects that Mrs Milligan maintained an establishment well suited to providing evidence of adultery for actions of divorce. The marriage was proved by an extract of Scott's decree of 1811 and by reference to the defender's admission in the process of divorce at his instance in 1814. Witnesses in London proved cohabitation with Laura Manners. An extract of the parish register of St Mary le bone in London proved the ceremony of marriage with Laura Manners in 1808. An interlocutor of 26 November 1819 found facts relevant to infer adultery and a decree of divorce was pronounced. Johanna Gordon next petitioned the Court on 4 December 1819, noting that the name of Laura Manners, "one of the adulteresses", was not mentioned in the sentence of divorce and asked that this be reviewed, given the regulation forbidding an adulterer from marrying a paramour, and given that Laura or Louisa Manners, "sister of late Duchess of St Albans", was one of the women with whom the defender was proved to have committed adultery over the years 1808 to 1814. The petitioner concluded that she was entitled to insist that Laura Manners' name be inserted in the decree; she did not insist in the insertion of the names of the other women. The Commissaries, by an interlocutor of 10 December 1819, now found adultery specifically proved with Laura Manners and two other women, and so decerned. An Act of Parliament of 1600 forbade adulterers or adulteresses from marrying their paramours, and to prevent this it had become the practice to insert their names in the decreet.[40] The cause was called once more on 24 December 1819, and a procurator entered appearance for Dalrymple and asked for the interlocutor to be recalled to allow the defender to prepare defences. An interlocutor of 31 December 1819 allowed the defender to see the process for fourteen days but refused the rest of the petition. The same procurator

40 *Acts of the Parliaments of Scotland*, ed T Thomson and C Innes, 12 vols (1814–1875) vol iv, 233 c 29.

on 7 January 1820 appeared in the cause acting for Laura Manners, asking for the interlocutor to be reviewed insofar as her name was mentioned in it and asking to be heard against it. An interlocutor of 14 January 1820 allowed her to be heard against the interlocutor before answering. A petition was given in on the same date for Dalrymple asking for Laura Manners' name to be expunged from the decreet. On 21 January Laura Manners' procurator gave in a petition to the same effect. The Commissaries refused the petition on 28 January 1820. Dalrymple and Laura Manners now threatened Johanna Gordon with years of litigation in the Court of Session and House of Lords in order to pressure her to petition the Commissaries to remove Laura Manners' name from their decreet.[41] She did so on 4 February 1820. Laura Manners' procurator gave in another petition on her behalf on 18 February 1820, arguing that she had been in good faith in continuing to live with Dalrymple pending the conclusion of the appeals in England and the actions in Scotland, that adultery in the relevant period had not been proved, and that, in any case, she had given up sexual relations with Dalrymple at the relevant period. She claimed that it was unjust to stigmatise her as an adulteress, and on such flimsy proof. After *avizandum*, on 18 February 1820 the Commissaries refused the desires of the petitions and adhered to their interlocutor of 10 December 1819, noting that adultery was adequately proved between the date of the High Court of Delegates' decision and the relevant time in 1814 and that their duty was to give effect to the Act of 1600, despite the wishes of the parties, to avoid evasion of the statute. By Bill of Advocation, Laura Manners and Johanna Gordon removed the action from the Commissary Court to the Court of Session. It was considered by Lord Meadowbank, who consulted the First Division, where Scott was one of the Clerks, and who then remitted the case back to the Commissaries with instructions to alter their interlocutor to omit the name of Laura Manners. This they did by an interlocutor of 30 June. After the usual argument about costs and their taxation, the final sentence and decreet of divorce was issued on 17 November 1820.

C. REVELATION OF THE SOURCE

The third series of *Tales of My Landlord*, which contained *The Bride of Lammermoor*, was published in Edinburgh on 10 June 1819. Jane Millgate has commented that the novel perhaps was begun as early as May 1818,

41 This is stated in the dispute over expenses concluding the action.

that it was certainly being written by early autumn 1818, and that it was not finished and sent off to Ballantyne until 2 May 1819.[42] This means that the novel was written as Johanna Gordon's action of divorce against Dalrymple was being prepared: indeed the novel was published in the same month as the summons was issued. Given Scott's professional position, it is difficult to believe he could have been unaware of this impending action. Even if this was not enough in itself to explain why Scott remained shy of mentioning the legend of Janet Dalrymple in Peter Pattieson's introduction, he must have been aware of the earlier litigation: indeed, these actions must have been notorious. Sir William Scott's decision in 1811 was recounted in *The Times* on 17 July, and merited no less than three reports in Edinburgh in *The Caledonian Mercury* on 18, 20 and 25 July (this last was very full). For lawyers, the judgement was taken as settling and clarifying the Scots law on irregular marriages, and a galaxy of distinguished advocates had given expert advice on Scots law.[43] Dodson's report of the case was published for, among others, the well-known publishers and sellers of law books in Edinburgh, Bell and Bradfute. And although the subsequent actions were not noticed in the newspapers, they would not have escaped Scott's attention or, for that matter, general gossip. The parties were prominent. The sixth Earl of Stair was aged seventy in 1819 and unmarried. He had had a prominent military, diplomatic and parliamentary career. It was obvious that John William Henry Dalrymple, his cousin, would soon succeed to the earldom and estates.[44] Laura Manners' father was John Manners of Grantham Grange, Lincolnshire, an illegitimate son of Lord William Manners, a son of the second Duke of Rutland, and her mother was born Lady Louisa Tollemache, from the English family that held the Scottish earldom of Dysart, and she was to succeed as Countess of Dysart in her own right in 1821. As was regularly noted through the litigation, Laura Manners' sister was Duchess of St Albans.[45] Though not quite so dazzling, Johanna Gordon's background was also thoroughly respectable and such as to make her prominent in Edinburgh. Her father was the second son of John Gordon of Cluny in Aberdeenshire, and had become a Writer to the Signet

42 J Millgate, *Walter Scott: The Making of the Novelist* (1984) 169–170. For the date of publication, see J G Lockhart, *Memoirs of the Life of Sir Walter Scott*, 5 vols (1902) vol iii, 356.

43 See Dodson, *Report* (n 6) Appendix, pp iii–iv.

44 *Scots Peerage* (n 5) vol viii, 157.

45 G E C[okayne], *The Complete Peerage*, revised edn (various editors), 14 vols (1910–1959) vol iv, 565–566; *Scots Peerage* (n 5) vol iii, 412–14; *Complete Peerage* vol xi, 291.

in Edinburgh.[46] Her mother was Joanna Trotter, daugher of Thomas Trotter of Mortonhall.[47] Her uncle, Cosmo Gordon of Cluny, who died in 1800, had been an advocate, MP for Nairnshire, and a Baron of the Exchequer in Scotland. He was a wealthy man, able to purchase an estate in Nairnshire for £4,200 in 1763. He was also well connected. He was a good friend of the Campbells of Calder, who controlled the seat in Nairnshire, of the Duke of Gordon, and of Henry Dundas. His seat on the Scottish Exchequer bench was his reward from Lord North for supporting the latter's North American policy. He was a member of the Poker Club and was closely associated with such luminaries of the Scottish Enlightenment as James Beattie, Hugh Blair, Lord Monboddo and Adam Smith. On his death without issue in November 1800, his brother succeeded to the estate of Cluny.[48] Johanna Gordon's other uncle, Alexander, who died in 1810, was a wealthy merchant and estate owner in Tobago.[49] Her sister, Charlotte Gordon, married a baronet, Sir John Lowther Johnstone, who was a considerable landowner and who was one of the claimants to the vacant title of Marquess of Annandale.[50] The Duke of Gordon gave evidence in 1809 that "he hath been on terms of great intimacy with the family of . . . Johanna Gordon . . . for many years, and hath known and been acquainted with . . . Johanna Gordon from her childhood, and hath frequently received visits from her, with her father and others of her family, at his . . . seat, called Gordon Castle . . . and hath also been on visits to her father, and hath there been in company with her".[51] Her grandfather, John Gordon, a merchant in Edinburgh whose origins are obscure, was factor to Cosmo George, the third Duke of Gordon, and tacksman of the salmon fishings on the Spey which had made him a wealthy man, allowing him to purchase the estate and castle of Cluny: the family

46 *Register of the Society of Writers to Her Majesty's Signet* (1983) (henceforth *WS Register*) 122; J M Bulloch, *The Gordons of Cluny from the Early Years of the Eighteenth Century down to the Present Time* (1911) (henceforth Bulloch, *Gordons of Cluny*) 19–32.

47 *WS Register* (n 46) 122; Bulloch, *Gordons of Cluny* (n 46) 20; Sir Robert Douglas of Glenbervie, *The Baronage of Scotland* (1798) 204–208 recounts the Trotters of Mortonhall, but at 208 does not note Joanna's marriage to Charles Gordon – it seems to have been accidentally omitted because in the index, under the entry "Gordon of Braid" (601) there is a reference to 208 i.

48 F J Grant (ed), *The Faculty of Advocates in Scotland 1532–1914 with Genealogical Notes* (1944) 83; Sir L Namier and J Brooke, *The House of Commons 1754–1790* 3 vols (1964) (henceforth Namier and Brooke, *House of Commons*) vol i, 490; vol ii, 512–513; Bulloch, *Gordons of Cluny* (n 46) 9–18.

49 Bulloch, *Gordons of Cluny* (n 46) 4, 8.

50 Dodson, *Report* (n 6) Appendix, i; G E C[okayne], *The Complete Baronetage*, 5 vols (1900–1906) vol ii, 395. On the final settlement of the Annandale Peerage claim, see *Earldom of Annandale and Hartfell* [1986] 1 AC 319.

51 Dodson, *Report* (n 6) Appendix, xviii–xix.

obviously remained very intimate with that of the Dukes of Gordon, and her uncle was evidently named after the third Duke, while John Gordon had been one of the tutors to the fourth Duke.[52] Furthermore, the Duke of Gordon successfully solicited from Henry Dundas the position of Clerk of Session for Johanna Gordon's father in 1788.[53] She thus came from a typical Scottish family of minor, but very prosperous landowners (even if the land was relatively recently acquired), who supplemented their earnings from their rents by professional work; no doubt had her father been the elder son he would have been the advocate. But the family were relatively wealthy as the house in St Andrew Square and estate of Braid would suggest, and both her father and brother qualified as electors in the County of Edinburgh in 1812.[54] Indeed, her brother, Colonel John Gordon, notorious for clearances on his lands in the Hebrides, ultimately possessed enormous estates.[55] The death of her father in May 1814, just as Dalrymple started his action of divorce, left her a wealthy woman.[56] Dalrymple indeed tried to argue against having to pay money in advance towards her defence on the ground that her father had left her one of the largest fortunes in Scotland by providing £10,000 in her favour under his settlement, excluding Dalrymple's *jus mariti*.[57] Given the social prominence of the Gordons of Cluny in Edinburgh and more generally of the Dalrymples of Stair and of Laura Manners' family, it is impossible to doubt but that the scandal was considerable. This can be confirmed from the correspondence of Charles Kirkpatrick Sharpe, who was to become a close friend of Walter Scott, over 1809 to 1811.[58] Sharpe wrote thus to Thomas Stapleton in 1811:

> Did you laugh when you saw in the newspapers Miss Laura Manners's degradation from the altar of Hymen? Unfortunate Laura, I fear that she will now be reduced to divert herself like her sister, the Duchess; but Miss Jacky Gordon is certainly a heroine – she carries everything with flame and fury. In fact, a woman of her temper, after she hath been debauched swells forth a demon; the spear of Ithuriel is applied, and the toad starteth up a devil.[59]

52 Namier and Brooke, *House of Commons* (n 48) vol ii, 512–513; Bulloch, *Gordons of Cluny* (n 46) 5–18.
53 Bulloch, *Gordons of Cluny* (n 46) 19.
54 See the report of the election in *Caledonian Mercury*, 29 October 1812.
55 Bulloch, *Gordons of Cluny* (n 46) 33–40.
56 *WS Register* (n 46) 122; Bulloch, *Gordons of Cluny* (n 46) 20.
57 SRO CC 8/5/34 105–106.
58 A Allardyce (ed), *Letters from and to Charles Kirkpatrick Sharpe, Esq*, 2 vols (1888) (henceforth *Letters from and to Charles Kirkpatrick Sharpe*) vol i, 367–369, 470–473,489–493.
59 Charles Kirkpatrick Sharpe to Thomas Stapleton, 19 October 1811, in ibid vol i 473.

He wrote similarly to Lady Charlotte Campbell: "And so Miss Jacky Gordon is really clothed with a husband at last, and Miss Laura Manners left without a mate! She and Lord Stair should marry and have children in mere revenge."[60] Sharpe and his friends cannot be the only persons who followed these events with relish and waspish glee. They must have been well known to Scott, especially given his office as Clerk of Session (the office Charles Gordon of Cluny had also held).

This current scandal involving the marriage of a Dalrymple thus seems likely to explain why Scott made no allusion to the legend of Janet Dalrymple in 1819 beyond the tantalising comment that

> By many readers this may be deemed overstrained, romantic, and composed by the wild imagination of an author, desirous of gratifying the popular appetite for the horrible; but those who are read in the private family history of Scotland during the period in which the scene is laid, will readily discover, through the disguise of borrowed names and added incidents, the leading particulars of an ower true tale.[61]

It is less easy to explain why he continued this policy in *Chronicles of the Canongate* in 1827, where, in his first published acknowledgment of authorship of the Waverley novels he took the opportunity to comment on aspects of the origins and sources of some of them. He there wrote:

> I may mention, for example's sake, that the terrible catastrophe of the Bride of Lammermoor, actually occurred in a Scottish family of rank. The female relative, by whom the melancholy tale was communicated to me many years since, was a near connexion of the family in which the event happened, and always told it with an appearance of melancholy mystery, which enhanced the interest. She had known, in her youth, the brother who rode before the unhappy victim to the fatal altar, who, though then a mere boy, and occupied almost entirely with the gallantry of his own apearance in the bridal procession, could not but remark that the hand of his sister was moist, and cold as that of a statue. It is unnecessary further to withdraw the veil from this scene of family distress, nor, though it occurred more than a hundred years since, might it be altogether agreeable to the representatives of the families concerned in the narrative.[62]

It seems fair to assume that Scott considered it still too close to the twelve years of litigation over the marriage of Johanna Gordon and John William Henry Dalrymple, now seventh Earl of Stair. But shortly after the publication of *Chronicles of the Canongate*, Scott must have decided to

60 Charles Kirkpatrick Sharpe to Lady Charlotte Campbell, 1811, in ibid vol i 491.

61 *Tales of My Landlord, Third Series. Collected and arranged by Jedediah Cleish-botham, Schoolmaster and Parish-Clerk of Gandercleuch*, 4 vols (1819) vol iii, 111–112.

62 *Chronicles of the Canongate; by the Author of "Waverley," &c.*, 2 vols (1827) vol i, x–xi.

reveal in the new *Magnum Opus* edition the historical and legendary source material on which he had drawn. Thus, his letter of 11 December 1827 to Charles Kirkpatrick Sharpe requested information about Lord Rutherford and Dunbar of Baldoon.[63] This suggests he was considering the material to include in the new Introduction, and may have already decided to reveal the sources. A year later he was considering publication of "an old black-guard Scotch Lampoon . . . It has reference to the tragical events from which I took the Story of the Bride of Lammermoor."[64] This proposal was forestalled by the inclusion of a version of it in Maidment's *Scotish Pasquils*, but Scott could inform a correspondent in December 1828 that he was now intending to refer to the Dalrymple legend in the forthcoming *Magnum Opus* edition.[65] He cited and quoted from his version of the lampoon on Stair in the Introduction of 1830 (*Bride* (n 1) 5–6). It was at this time, late December 1828, that he was revising the text of *The Bride*, with some further work on it in 1829,[66] In any case, by this time many must have known of the origins of Scott's story. In the Introduction in the *Magnum Opus* edition, Scott referred to two works that had discussed the story of Janet Dalrymple (*Bride* (n 1) 1). The first of these was the edition of Law's *Memorialls* edited by Scott's friend, Charles Kirkpatrick Sharpe, published in 1818. Law had written: "The president had a daughter before this time, being married, the night she was bride in, she was taken out from her bridegroom and harled through the house, and afterward died."[67] In a lengthy footnote Sharpe had recounted two versions of the legend of Janet Dalrymple.[68] The other work was the edition by Thomas Maitland in 1823 of Symson's *Large Description of Galloway*. At the end of the work, some of Symson's poems were included, one of which was "On the unexpected Death of the Vertuous Lady, Mrs. Janet Dalrymple, Lady Baldone, Younger". The editor noted: "This unfortunate lady was daughter to President Dalrymple.

63 H J C Grierson et al (eds), *The Letters of Sir Walter Scott*, 12 vols (1932–1937) (henceforth *Letters*) vol x, 329.

64 Scott to J H Markland, 20 November 1828: *Letters* (n 63) vol xi, 46.

65 Scott to Markland, 19 December 1828: *Letters* (n 63) vol xi, 69; *A Book of Scotish Pasquils &c.* ed [J Maidment] (1827) 43–55. Maidment had also hesitated about publishing "the virulent and unprincipled attack upon the Stair family" (xiii).

66 Garside, "Union and *The Bride of Lammermoor*" (n 4) 86–87; J Millgate, *Scott's Last Edition: A Study in Publishing History* (1987) 22.

67 R Law, *Memorialls; or, the Memorable Things that fell out within this Island of Brittain from 1638 to 1684*, ed C Kirkpatrick Sharpe (1818) 225–226 (copies with the title page dated 1819 appear to be a re-issue: certainly there is no variation in the section with which we are here concerned).

68 Ibid 226–227n.

She was seized with madness on her marriage-night, and nearly murdered her Husband. It has been supposed, that her disastrous fate suggested the idea of that beautiful romance, *The Bride of Lammermoor*." Maitland then referred to Sharpe's note on Law's *Memorialls*.[69] This was not, of course, definite identification of Lucy Ashton with Janet Dalrymple; but those who followed up Maitland's reference to Sharpe's note could have been in little doubt as to the source of inspiration for the plot of *The Bride*. These two scholarly, historical editions of seventeenth-century works were not likely, however, to reach an audience even approaching that as wide for the Waverley novels. Nor were excerpts from them likely to appear in, for example, *The Caledonian Mercury*. In private Scott seems to have been open about his use of the Dalrymple legend;[70] and in 1823, two great-great-grandchildren of Lord President Stair could regret that he had not been aware of a further version of the story still current in the family.[71] Maidment included "Upon the long wished for and tymely Death of the Right honble The Lady Stair" in his third collection of pasquils in 1828. In an introductory note he described her as "this remarkable female, the Lady Ashton, of the 'Bride of Lammermoor'".[72] Again, however, this note in a privately printed work of very restricted distribution was scarcely general publication of the source of the novel to the world. But by 1829 Scott must have been completely reassured that some members of the family of Dalrymple were happy to see in print an account of the story of Janet Dalrymple relating it to that of Lucy Ashton, as Sir Robert Home Dalrymple Elphinstone was anxious to ensure that Scott knew yet another version of the legend which exonerated Janet Dalrymple from stabbing her husband.[73] Scott may also have consulted Sir John Dalrymple – who was ultimately to succeed Johanna Gordon's bridegroom as eighth Earl of Stair – with whom he was on familiar terms and could visit at his home at Oxenfoord.[74] Moreover, by 1830, Sir John Dalrymple would have been the effective head of the

69 A Symson, Minister of Kirkinner, *A Large Description of Galloway . . . M.DC.LXXX.IV. With an Appendix, Containing Original Papers, From the Sibbald and Macfarlane MSS* (1823) 192 n 1.

70 See, e.g., Scott to James Ballantyne, 10 September 1818: *Letters* (n 63) vol v, 186.

71 Sir Robert Dalrymple Horn Elphinstone to Sir James Stewart of Coltness, 5 September 1823, National Library of Scotland, MS 683 fos 45–47; found quoted in Parsons, "Dalrymple legend" (n 3) 52–53. See also Crockett, *Scott Originals* (n 3) 256–257n.

72 *A Third Book of Scotish Pasquils, &c* [J Maidment (ed)] (1828) 75.

73 W Clerk to Scott, 1 September 1829, in *The Journal of Sir Walter Scott from the Original Manuscript at Abbotsford*, 2 vols (1890) vol ii, 300n.

74 W E K Anderson (ed), *The Journal of Sir Walter Scott* (1972) 307 (19 May 1827), 392 (8 December 1827), 521 (18 February 1829). On the eighth Earl, see *Scots Peerage* (n 5) vol iii, 158–159.

Dalrymples of Stair and must have seemed likely to succeed, as the seventh Earl suffered some kind of cataclysmic stroke or apoplexy in 1829, as his obituary in 1840 noted that he had "been for the last eleven years confined to his bed speechless, and almost unconscious".[75] Sir John's view would have carried considerable weight with Scott.

All this must have meant that by the time Scott came to pen the Introduction to *The Bride* for the *Magnum Opus*, it would have seemed pointless and artificial to make no mention of the legend of the marriage of Janet Dalrymple. Furthermore, enough time had passed from the end of the litigation that such revelation would not be immediately associated in the public mind with the marital problems of Johanna Gordon, Laura Manners and John Dalrymple, which by 1830 must have become somewhat stale scandal and gossip. Moreover, and more importantly, the nature of the *Magnum Opus* required Scott to refer to this source material. After the earlier games of concealment of authorship, the prefaces and notes were in part autobiographical and in part explanatory of the sources used to construct the novels: to ignore the tragic legend of Janet Dalrymple and the use made of it would have now been impossible, despite the seventh Earl's problems.

There can be little doubt that these events and law suits deeply affected – indeed blighted – the lives of the persons concerned. The scandal had been considerable. The society of the day would have seen the reputations – and hence marriage-prospects – of the two women in particular as ruined. Dalrymple was not shown in a particularly agreeable light, and Kirkpatrick Sharpe's following pointed comment has some merit: "As to Miss Gordon, she's a Venus well suited to such a Vulcan, whom nothing but money and a title could have rendered tolerable, even to a kitchen-wench."[76] It is telling that none of the three ever married again. Laura Manners died first, in 1834, but she changed her surname to Tollemache by royal licence in 1821 when her mother succeeded as Countess of Dysart. Thereafter she was known as Lady Laura Tollemache.[77] Dalrymple was the next to die, in 1840; but as noted, he seems to have suffered an incapacitating stroke in 1829.[78] Johanna

75 *Gentleman's Magazine*, new series, 14 (1840) 333; see also *Scots Peerage* (n 5) vol viii, 158.

76 Charles Kirkpatrick Sharpe to Lady Charlotte Campbell, 1811, in *Letters from and to Charles Kirkpatrick Sharpe* (n 58) vol i, 491. The remarks in the letter of A Robertson to Charles Kirkpatrick Sharpe of 2 March 1809, in ibid vol i, 369 are suggestive of Johanna Gordon's determined character.

77 *Gentleman's Magazine*, new series, 2 (1834) 219; *Scots Peerage* (n 5) vol iii, 412–414.

78 *Gentleman's Magazine*, new series, 14 (1840) 333; *Scots Peerage* (n 5) vol viii, 158.

Gordon lived until 1847; despite the divorce of 1820, she assumed the title of Countess of Stair, and her death-notice described her as "the Right Hon. Johanna Countess dowager of Stair".[79]

It is not obvious that the current scandal involving the heir to the Earldom of Stair coloured the way in which Scott wrote *The Bride of Lammermoor*, except in giving him a good reason to conceal the source material in 1819. The issues of marriage dealt with in the novel have no relationship to the troubles of Johanna Gordon, Laura Manners and Dalrymple, beyond the obvious general theme of the disasters that follow unfortunate marriage. It is worth noting here, however, that the position of the Earl of Etherington, the father of Francis Tyrrel and Valentine Bulmer, in *Saint Ronan's Well* (1824) rather resembles that of Dalrymple: a secret marriage outwith England and then a public marriage in that country without the first marriage being dissolved. Furthermore, in the same novel the marriage of Sir Bingo with Lady Binks rather resembles that of Dalrymple and Johanna Gordon, though Lady Binks had only to go to the Commissary Court in Edinburgh, not to the Consistory Court in London, to prove her marriage. It may be that the scandal of the seventh Earl of Stair's marital adventures suggested aspects of the later novel to Scott. When he made Bulmer write that his father "enlarged on the folly and iniquity of private marriages, warned me that in the country I was going to the matrimonial noose often lies hid under flowers, and that folks find it twitched around their neck when they least expect such a cravat" (ch 25), he may have had in mind the sad affair of Johanna Gordon and John William Henry Dalrymple. Moreover, Captain Jekyl commented to Bulmer in the same novel that "All women are necessarily the slaves of their reputation. . . . I therefore would not conceive it difficult for Clara Mowbray to persuade herself to become a Countess, rather than be a topic of conversation for all Britain, while a lawsuit betwixt you is in dependence; and that maybe for the greater part of both your lives" (ch 27). Here we may also see Scott's further reflections on the effects and the length of twelve years of litigation between Johanna Gordon and Dalrymple.[80] Supporting the suggestion that Scott had this scandal in his mind when writing *Saint Ronan's Well* is the fact that several times in the manuscript he rather strangely wrote "Laura" rather than "Clara" for Clara Mowbray: like Laura Manners, Clara Mowbray was also a

79 *Gentleman's Magazine*, new series, 27 (1847) 454; *Scots Peerage* (n 5) vol viii, 158.

80 See further J W Cairns, "Union, Marriage, Madness, and Scot(t')s Law" (forthcoming).

party to an ambiguous marriage of doubtful validity.[81] But however this may be, it seems fair to conclude that the marital problems of the contemporary heir to the Dalrymples of Stair made it seem prudent, and, at the very least, tactful and in good taste, to omit in 1819 any mention of the legends surrounding Janet Dalrymple.

81 I am indebted for this point to Professor Mark A Weinstein, the editor of the forthcoming new edition of *Saint Ronan's Well*; see Sir Walter Scott, *St Ronan's Well*, autograph manuscript, the Pierpont Morgan Library, New York, MA 449.1 am indebted to the Pierpont Morgan Library for permission to quote from this manuscript.

Index

EU Authorised Representative:
Easy Access System Europe Mustamäe tee 50, 10621 Tallinn, Estonia
gpsr.requests@easproject.com

Printed and bound by CPI Group (UK) Ltd, Croydon, CR0 4YY
14/09/2026
02216781-0013